P9-DFI-979

WILLIAM M. KUNSTLER

Other Books by David J. Langum

From Maverick to Mainstream: Cumberland School of Law, 1847–1997
(with Howard P. Walthall)

Crossing Over the Line: Legislating Morality and the Mann Act

Thomas O. Larkin: A Life of Profit and Patriotism in Old California
(with Harlan Hague)

*Law and Community on the Mexican California Frontier: Anglo-American
Expatriates and the Clash of Legal Traditions, 1821–1846*

Law in the West (editor)

DAVID J. LANGUM, 1940 –
III

WILLIAM M. KUNSTLER,

The Most Hated Lawyer in America

New York University Press • *New York and London*

NEW YORK UNIVERSITY PRESS
New York and London

© 1999 by New York University
All rights reserved

Library of Congress Cataloging-in-Publication Data
Langum, David J., 1940–
The most hated lawyer in America / David J. Langum.
p.   cm.
Includes bibliographical references and index.
ISBN 0-8147-5150-4 (cloth : acid-free paper)
1. Kunstler, William Moses, 1919– 2. Lawyers—United
States—Biography. 3. Radicals—United States—Biography.   I. Title.
KF373.K8 L36 1999
340'092—dc21   99-6393
[B]   CIP

New York University Press books are printed on acid-free paper,
and their binding materials are chosen for strength and durability.

Manufactured in the United States of America

10 9 8 7 6 5 4 3 2 1

For Frances, for so many reasons . . .

Contents

All illustrations appear as a group following p. 132.

Preface

William Moses Kunstler was such a controversial figure that no biographer can hope to please everyone. The balance will never be quite right. For some, any biography will seem too sympathetic, for others, too critical. The cases that are discussed can also become an issue. Why did you not discuss such-and-such case that shows Kunstler in his worst light, some critics might ask, while fans could protest that I should have discussed so-and-so case that was a brilliant Kunstler victory.

I analyzed a case in detail if enough public material was available to make a meaningful discussion possible, and if I judged the case to be important enough. The importance could be the public notoriety of a case, its impact on Kunstler's career, or whether it illuminated some aspect of his practice or character. As for the tone of the book, it might help if I explained why I wrote it.

I became interested in Kunstler because of my strong libertarian beliefs. Many libertarians are alarmed by the truly draconian anticrime measures pushed by politicians onto a frightened public when FBI figures show that criminal activity has actually decreased. At the same time, the federal judiciary, which ought to be a bulwark against government intrusion, in recent years has approved such things as a steady erosion of search and seizure protections, the sentencing of convicted defendants for charges on which they were acquitted, anonymous juries, and the trial in federal courts of defendants acquitted in state courts, Double Jeopardy notwithstanding.

From this perspective, it does not matter that Kunstler was a political radical while I am not. I can admire Kunstler for his willingness to do battle against the government, to throw a monkey wrench into its well-oiled machinery of oppression, and it makes no difference whether Kunstler is a candidate for sainthood or perpetual damnation. We need thousands of Kunstlers to fight the government and try to preserve our beloved country as a land of liberty.

I started the biography with this viewpoint. As I went further along in my research and understanding of Kunstler, my perspective changed slightly. I learned that Kunstler was far more complex as a man than certainly his critics ever saw and probably his fans ever knew. Those nuances made Kunstler a more interesting figure. In this biography, I want to bring those points to life, give texture to the man, and save him from becoming merely a figurehead of either admiration or scorn. Of course, I also want to chronicle his career and professional techniques.

In the end, I came to a point not too far from where I began. I still admire Kunstler primarily for his willingness to take on the government, though not necessarily sharing his affinity for all the clients for whom he conducted those struggles. I have reinforced my earlier suspicion that Kunstler is no candidate for sainthood, on either a personal or professional level. However, I have also found Kunstler to be a far more interesting individual, combining many talents and faults in strange configurations, than I realized before I began this project. I hope my readers can suspend the judgments of Kunstler that most people have, appreciate the skill with which he approached his cases, regardless of the side he took, and ponder the fallibilities and strengths of this complex man.

I have many thanks to give. My own institution, Cumberland School of Law of Samford University, was generous with travel funds, as usual. Dean Barry A. Currier and Provost James S. Netherton kindly permitted me to take a sabbatical one year early so that I could complete this biography in a timely manner. Laurel R. Clapp, director of the Beeson Law Library, assigned a large conference room with book shelves for my exclusive use. For eighteen months this was my command post. There, student research assistants sorted and I read the many thousands of newspaper articles, hundreds of journal pieces, and dozens of books that concern Kunstler. Those very helpful research assistants were Donna K. Vandever, Lloyd C. Peeples, and Alison M. Etheredge. My daughter, Virginia E. Langum, also helped greatly. Edward L. Craig, Jr., once again assisted with interlibrary loans. My secretary, Natasha S. Worthy, helped in many and varied ways.

When the writing began, William G. Ross, colleague, fellow legal historian, and good friend, read every chapter and helped considerably with editorial suggestions and insights. He claims to enjoy editing; since he is a former newspaperman, perhaps he really does. I know only that I am truly benefitted by his fine feel for words and his extensive knowledge of American history. All I can do to repay is offer my thanks, my friendship, and my limited help with his own manuscripts.

Prior to his death in February 1998, my father, John K. Langum, read the portions of the manuscript that were then written, and also gave me several helpful suggestions. This was only the last of so many favors, advantages, and kindnesses he gave me, for all of which I will always be grateful. Ucross Foundation provided me with a month's residency in its serene location in Clearmont, Wyoming, and provided for all my material needs. That gave me time for extensive writing with absolutely no distractions.

I interviewed dozens of people who knew Kunstler in many contexts. I talked with people who knew Kunstler from his younger years, Milton Berner, William Hurst, Fred Marks, Graham Marks; with his family, Lotte Kunstler, his first wife, Margie Ratner, his widow, all of his children, Karin, Jane, Sarah (although briefly), and Emily, and with his sister, Mary Kunstler Horn. Karin's husband, Neal Goldman, and Mary's husband, Manny Horn, also helped. I spoke with two former clients, David Dellinger and the Reverend Fred Shuttlesworth; three judges before whom he appeared, Jack Weinstein, Constance Baker Motley, and Sol Wachtler; two prosecutors with whom he tangled, Steven Phillips and David S. Gould; former colleagues, Steven Hyman, Arthur Kinoy, and Michael Ratner; close personal friends, Bruce and Diane Jackson and Brice Marden; and partner at this death, Ronald L. Kuby. I am sure I have forgotten someone, and I apologize. All were kind and helpful. I gathered the views toward Kunstler of twice that number of other judges and prosecutors through published interviews. Then too, dozens of persons responded to my author's query. They are credited in the endnotes.

Many libraries assisted me by sharing their treasures. The most helpful were the Birmingham Public Library, Manuscripts and Archives Department; the King Center, Atlanta; and the State Historical Society of Wisconsin, Madison.

Above all, I must thank my wife, Frances. I began this project only a few months before we were married. For her to tolerate cheerfully the disruptions and time pressures of a major research project at the very outset of a marriage shows a commendable faith in the future. Not only did she overlook my lack of attentiveness toward her, she herself undertook some of the computer-based research needed at the beginning of the work. Toward the end, I labored diligently to complete the first draft of the manuscript before the arrival of our son, David John, Jr. We succeeded, but only by one week.

David J. Langum
Birmingham, Alabama

1

Introductory Images

MOST AMERICANS DISLIKE lawyers, but we generally either hold our tongues or express our disdain quietly. In particular, we tend to speak only good of the dead, even of dead lawyers.

This was not to be the fate of William Moses Kunstler. When Kunstler died on September 4, 1995, controversy followed him to the grave. His many obituaries spoke of hatred as much as praise. One journal entitled its obituary "The Pariah's Farewell," and a second reminded its readers that *Vanity Fair* had branded Kunstler "the most hated lawyer in America." Another obituary recalled that the *New York Times* had labeled Kunstler both the "most hated and most loved lawyer in America." These same conclusions arrived from overseas. For the London *Times*, Kunstler was "the most celebrated and detested lawyer in America," and the *Economist* observed that Kunstler's "critics came in all colours of the political rainbow . . . and he missed no chance to infuriate them with glib throw-away lines honed for maximum offense."

Controversy followed Kunstler even after the obituaries. Kunstler was not conventionally religious, and there was no funeral service. However, friends held two memorial celebrations, one in Chicago and another in New York. The Cathedral of St. John the Divine hosted the New York celebration on November 19, 1995. Over three thousand clients, colleagues, friends, family, and well-wishers attended. Members of the Jewish Defense Organization also showed up to protest behind police barricades. Their leader shouted, "William Kunstler is where he belongs!" The group argued that Kunstler had betrayed his Jewish roots by representing Arabs, such as Sheikh Omar Abdel-Rahman and others charged with bombing the World Trade Center, and El Sayyid Nosair, the Arabic youth charged with murdering Rabbi Meir Kahane.

Kunstler's delight in representing society's outcasts and pariahs, in seeking out criminal defendants most loathed by mainstream, conventional America, generated this controversy. If he agreed with their politics, Kunstler embraced these individuals, usually representing them free of charge and sometimes achieving acquittals in hopeless cases. For his often penniless clients, Kunstler represented a lifeline of hope for the possibility of a life other than execution or lifetime incarceration. His harshest critics saw him simply as a publicity seeker, forever hogging the limelight. To his more thoughtful detractors, such as Alan Dershowitz, a civil rights lawyer and Harvard law professor, "Bill was a radical revolutionary lawyer. He stretched the line for where lawyer ends and revolutionary begins. . . . his support of free speech was because it was a tactic of the left . . . his views were cause oriented." Immediately following Kunstler's death, Dershowitz said, "I have great compassion for God now, because I think Bill is going to start filing lawsuits as soon as he gets to heaven." For his friends on the Left, Kunstler "identified with those struggling against racism and capitalism." He was a "friend of the people . . . and a consummate people's lawyer, who both knew the legal system and treated it with the contempt it richly deserves."

After his death, both friends and foes agreed on one thing: Kunstler had been a happy man who enjoyed every minute of his life exuberantly and fully. He loved his work and "plunged" (a word used repeatedly by colleagues, secretaries, and friends) into each of his cases with enthusiasm. He fought doggedly once he had entered a case. If he lost at trial, he looked forward to the appeal. If he lost the appeal, then he looked forward to habeas petitions or other post-appellate remedies.

With his long, unruly hair, glasses pushed back onto his forehead, rumpled suit, and deep, resonant voice extravagantly condemning authority and system, yet exuding personal charm, Kunstler seemed like an actor playing a part. Even in private, he acted as though he were on stage, flamboyantly instructing or entertaining, sometimes dissembling. In public, through thousands of interviews and "bites" for radio and television, Kunstler's own persona largely formed our collective image of the role of radical lawyer, what one looked and sounded like. Indeed, toward the end of his life Kunstler embarked on a minor acting career. In some of his roles he simply played himself, as he did in an October 1994 episode of the NBC police show *Law & Order*.

Nevertheless, the picture of Kunstler as hardworking, enthusiastic, radical gadfly is far from complete. Many of his cases were not merely matters involving political opponents of American society and government, nor were they simply important cases. Instead, and especially in the 1960s and 1970s, many of Kunstler's cases defined and encapsulated the turmoil through which America was passing. Then too, William Kunstler as a man was more nuanced and complicated than the term "radical lawyer" suggests. To listen merely to his oratorical pronouncements would suggest that Kunstler had a Manichaean view of the world, that the people, the movement, and racial minorities were clearly identifiable as "good" on one hand, and the racists, capitalists, and authoritarians as "bad" on the other. But that is far too simplistic a view of a man who wrote twelve books of prose and poetry, most having little to do with politics, and was himself profoundly torn between the values and lifestyle he inherited from the middle-class professional family into which he was born and the youthful radicals he often represented.

Kunstler was hated because of the clients he represented and the relish with which he sought out pariahs and outcasts. He knew he was "disliked, even despised, by those who hate my clients," whom he characterized as "outcasts, individuals who are hated for their skin color or religion or political beliefs, people who fight the government. These are exactly the kind of clients I want . . . the damned, those whom society wants to destroy."

Kunstler did not begin his legal career with this attitude. After he had practiced conventional civil law for a dozen or so years, in 1961 the American Civil Liberties Union asked Kunstler to act as an observer in Mississippi, to protect the rights of several hundred Freedom Riders. His experience in the South began his transformation. After he witnessed the beatings inflicted on blacks by white southerners and the encouragement of this oppression of blacks by the southern legal system, he joined the civil rights struggle. "No longer satisfied practicing conventional law and talking liberal politics," as he later wrote, Kunstler began traveling hectically throughout the South, playing a major role in enlisting the federal judicial system to support the civil rights movement. In the early to mid-1960s he served as a private attorney to Martin Luther King, and also to such Black Power advocates as H. Rap Brown, who startled white observers by his declaration that violence "is as American as cherry pie," and Stokely Carmichael, who advised black audiences in 1966 and 1967 that "the only way these honkies and honky lovers can understand is when they're met by resistance. . . . If their armed aggression continues, we will resist by any means necessary."

In the late 1960s and early 1970s, Kunstler's attention shifted to the struggle against the Vietnam War. He represented Fathers Daniel and Philip Berrigan, the Roman Catholic priests who sprayed napalm on draft files in Catonsville, Maryland, and set them afire to protest the American use of napalm against the Vietnamese people. He represented the surviving Kent State students, charged with riot by the state of Ohio, which at the same time refused to prosecute the National Guardsmen who shot and killed their fellow students. Kunstler's single most important case arose out of the antiwar movement when he represented the Chicago Seven before the cantankerous federal judge Julius Hoffman. The Nixon administration prosecuted these defendants for rioting at the 1968 Democratic National Convention, precipitating a trial that many Americans, of varying political persuasions, believed was politically motivated. The obdurate obstinacy of Judge Hoffman, the theatrical temperaments of the defendants Abbie Hoffman and Jerry Rubin, and the spectacle of Bobby Seale, the only black defendant, bound and gagged in open court because of his insistence on being represented by Charles Garry, his personal attorney, led to a breakdown of all decorum in the courtroom. The five-month trial became a judicial circus, with constant, acerbic bickering between Kunstler, who was the defendants' lead counsel, and the judge. This 1969 trial thrust Kunstler into national attention.

The average American today only vaguely recalls these names, Rap Brown, Stokely Carmichael, the Berrigan brothers, and of the Chicago Seven: David Dellinger, Tom Hayden, Abbie Hoffman, and Jerry Rubin. However, the late 1960s and early 1970s experienced the heat of the sit-ins and race riots, Vietnam demonstrations, patriotic exhortations, and returning body bags, the fear in some quarters, and hope in others, of actual insurrection. These individuals were then household words. Among Main Street Americans, a man who would eagerly and enthusiastically represent such persons himself became a pariah. And in the minds of many, Kunstler stayed just that throughout the rest of his life.

Few of those patriotic Americans who hated Kunstler because he represented anti–Vietnam War protesters knew that he was a decorated hero of World War II. In 1941, when he graduated from Yale University after majoring in French, Kunstler underwent extensive dental work. The purpose of the painful procedure was to enable him to enlist in the navy, although ultimately the navy rejected his application twice. He successfully enlisted in the army, volunteered for cryptographic school, served in the Signal Corps under fire in the Pacific, and left the service with the rank of major and a Bronze Star. Few of his detractors would have known that while in the Pacific, Kunstler saved a man's life (or so the GI remembered it) and once, after a buddy died, searched Japan to find a rabbi to bury him.

If his experiences in the civil rights era began Kunstler's transformation, the trial of the Chicago Seven in 1969 completed it. In that trial he learned of the FBI's cynical practice of talking privately with judges to frighten them into requesting additional protection. A courtroom bristling with armed guards would implant the notion in the jury's mind that here were truly dangerous defendants and thereby create bias before a trial began. In his civil rights work in the South, the federal courts had been friends and allies in the struggle against segregation. Kunstler had believed that there was "essential justice" in the federal courts and that eventually wrongs would be righted. But the Chicago Seven trial was a "dramatic eye-opener that put a tragic twist" on those beliefs. He claimed it was a personal Rubicon.

> In Chicago, in the same type of federal court I had relied on for years, I was suddenly confronted by a tyrannical judge, malicious prosecutors, and lying witnesses. It was the shock of my life. . . . It taught me the hardest lesson of my life: The judicial system in this country is often unjust and will punish those whom it hates or fears.

However, because of the government's use of perjured testimony, its writing of threatening letters to frighten jurors, and its eavesdropping on attorney-client conferences, Kunstler learned valuable lessons. He learned to use the media and publicity for his clients' purposes, and to use his body, voice, and humor in trial. He learned to follow the political line of his clients, rather than his own, to risk contempt charges in order to fight back against what he perceived was oppression, to become "a battler rather than a barrister," and to "see the legal system as an enemy."

As the years progressed, Kunstler's clients became even more closely associated with violence, but violence in the cause of matters Kunstler and his clients deemed political. Kunstler represented the Attica prisoners during their uprising in 1971 and in the prosecutions that followed. He represented Dennis Banks, Russell Means, and the American Indian Movement (1973–74) and Native Americans Darelle Dean

Butler, Robert Robideau, and Leonard Peltier, charged with murdering an FBI agent (1975). Kunstler represented Larry Davis, accused and acquitted of the wounding and attempted murder of six New York policemen (1986); El Sayyid Nosair, accused and acquitted of the murder of the fanatical Rabbi Meir Kahane (1990); and Yusef Salaam, one of the principal defendants in the shocking Central Park jogger rape case (1990).

Kunstler was lead counsel in or participated in many other high-profile cases that earned him considerable enmity. In the 1960s he successfully appealed the conviction of Jack Ruby, the killer of John F. Kennedy's assassin, Lee Harvey Oswald; in the 1980s he persuaded marine sergeant Clayton Lonetree that he was being prosecuted, for espionage in allowing the KGB to penetrate the security of the American embassy in Moscow, because he was an American Indian, and served as Lonetree's trial lawyer at his court-martial; in the 1990s he represented Sheikh Omar Abdel-Rahman, the blind Muslim cleric accused of being the inspiration behind the New York World Trade Center bombing conspiracy; and, until fired by his deranged client, he represented Colin Ferguson, the mass murderer on the Long Island Railroad, and proposed the infamous "black rage" defense.

These are among the more publicly notorious of Kunstler's cases. The clients themselves would alienate many Americans. Moreover, Kunstler also had the infuriating (to many) habit of ascribing a racial motivation to prosecutions of blacks and other racial minorities. He believed that "our society is always racist," and that young black men do "not stand a chance of obtaining a fair trial because of the racism inherent in the criminal justice system." He tried to take on those cases that were "the most difficult, where there is the least chance of an acquittal." In Kunstler's view, as the years moved along, Native Americans and then Arabs joined blacks among the most despised groups.

Kunstler's critique of American racism was combined with a fundamental attack on the legal system. By 1974 he regarded "law in the United States as a charade and a buttress to a system. I happen to think it's unfair and unfairly applied, that it's just a terroristic device, in many ways, to keep control of the system." In the 1960s and early 1970s Kunstler could count on many sympathetic ears, but in more conservative 1982 he drew hisses from Harvard law students when he told them that "law is a control mechanism of the state." As the New Left movement collapsed in the 1970s, Kunstler never wavered or bent with the wind:

he held on to his convictions in the face of mass opposition. In 1994 he addressed a meeting of the New York State Association of Criminal Defense Lawyers, and repeated that law "is nothing other than a method of control created by a socioeconomic system determined, at all costs, to perpetuate itself by all and any means necessary, for as long as possible." The United States Supreme Court was "an enemy, a predominately white court representing the power structure."

Although Kunstler said all these things, he did not always act on these beliefs. He never became a revolutionary himself. He went to court day after day and argued and cross-examined, he wrote appellate briefs, he acted in every way as though he believed that judges could be convinced, and that, at some level, the system might work. To his dying days he continued to work enthusiastically on legal arguments. Ronald Kuby, his colleague since 1982, believes that Kunstler had "an abiding faith that people were fundamentally good," even federal judges. He may have believed that the legal system was the enemy, but there were many other enemies too, and to some degree the legal system could function fairly. At the level of rhetoric, however, Kunstler was always unrepentant of his 1960s and 1970s radicalism, even unto his old age.

Kunstler knew that he was despised by many people. The cases he took sometimes caused friction among his colleagues at the Center for Constitutional Rights. Some generated criticism among the Jewish community, especially vehement at times because Kunstler was Jewish by birth. Some even caused contention within his family. He ignored the criticism and put it aside. Nor did threats of judicial contempt or censure from the various bar associations deter him. Neither judicial anger nor public anger bothered him, and he believed that "lawyers must take chances with their liberty, and with their licenses, to advance their client's political views." He acknowledged, "I pay a steep price for what I do, some might think a ridiculously steep price, but it's my life, and I'm willing to pay it. Sometimes I lose friends; sometimes I bring down the wrath of my family on my head. But I always do what I believe is correct."

A central paradox of Kunstler's life was that he was a man who desperately wanted people to love and admire him. At the same time, he did things and made statements that he knew fully well would cause much of the public to despise him. Kunstler was a man who craved love and harvested hatred.

Few of Kunstler's many detractors would have known of his sense of humor. When a man called him and asked, "Are you *the* William Kunstler? All the other Kunstlers I've been calling have been hanging up on me," he answered in his bass voice, "*I'm* the one who won't hang up on you!" His humor even played on the intense public hatred. He delighted in responding to verbal assaults. If someone recognized him on the street and angrily shouted, "That's William Kunstler," Kunstler would turn around and say, "Where? Where? I hate that son of a bitch! Where is he?" His personal charm had a disarming effect on his critics. One quieted critic recalled that he spotted Kunstler across a quiet street in the West Forties: "I yelled, 'William Kunstler, you're a jerk!' Quickly turning his head, he stared and yelled in reply, 'So are you!' Then, without missing a beat, he waved. I waved back, astonished at what I was doing. Whatever personal feelings people may have about his practice of the law, everyone must agree that he had style." Ronald Kuby recalls that "Bill lived his life with a tremendous amount of joy, as pure a joy as I've ever seen in anybody. He viewed most things with a tremendous amount of amusement, as serious as he was, including himself. He saw the humor in his own conduct as well as that of others."

Kunstler's critics would not have known of his gusto for life. Kunstler loved opera, classical music, and Cole Porter. In his younger years he went to the Metropolitan Opera in New York; later he listened to opera at home. He was always trying to convert his colleagues to his passion for serious music. In the 1960s he dragged his partner, Arthur Kinoy, to classical music concerts, but apparently did not make a convert of him. In the 1980s Kunstler tried to interest Kuby in the pleasures of opera, with somewhat more success. Kunstler enjoyed hamming it up singing Puccini duets with Mario, the produce man at Balducci's, a grocery around the corner from his home. A favorite opera was *Tosca*, appropriately enough, since its plot follows the fate of a nineteenth-century revolutionary.

Those who hated him would also have missed Kunstler's warmth and compassion. He walked around on the streets and would see people he knew or wanted to meet, and often invited them into his home for coffee. He talked with his neighbors, with the street people, with reporters, with clients, and he kibitzed with the waiters at the Waverly Restaurant, a nearby coffee shop. He helped neighborhood panhandlers settle disputes over choice corners. A neighbor recalls,

I so loved the chance sightings on the street! I would often see him coming down the sidewalk with his head down, walking briskly. I'd muster up my courage to say "Hello, Mr. Kunstler!" as he passed. Sometimes he seemed to be totally wrapped up in thought and not respond. Then inevitably he'd pass, and a moment later I'd hear a voice call out, "Well, hellooooo!"

Kunstler called Greenwich Village home for the last twenty years of his life, and in particular that part of the Village centered around Sixth Avenue. He lived and practiced law in a small brownstone located at 13 Gay Street, a short distance west of Sixth Avenue. Upstairs was home; the law offices were the basement, enough for Kunstler, his partner, a student intern, and a secretary or two. Kunstler's office, "an impenetrable warren of books, papers, sprung couches, and bric-a-brac," was to the front, toward the street. Without his booming voice and animating spirit, the quarters might seem gloomy, perhaps dingy.

Typically, Kunstler got up early in the morning, made coffee for himself and Margie, his wife, and went down to his office to begin work by 7:00.* He did paperwork until 8:30, together with Ronald Kuby, his partner, who came in at 8:00. About 8:30 they began gathering their papers together for court, where they often spent the day trying a case, grabbing junk food for lunch, rare hamburgers or bacon sandwiches, washed down with white-and-black sodas. At the end of a trial day, Kunstler often held a press conference, then dashed back to his office for a few more hours of work, signing letters, interviewing witnesses, and returning phone calls from clients, investigators, and reporters.

Kuby recalls that Kunstler in his seventies had the stamina of two lawyers half his age. "After a day with Bill, I would be tired, just dog tired." Because he was so driven, so productive and hardworking, Kunstler wanted everything at his fingertips immediately. When it was not, he sometimes flew into fits. Papers that were misfiled or mislaid drove him nuts. Sometimes the staff had misfiled something, but often he himself was to blame. In fact, his partner made it an office policy that if Kunstler were missing something, the first order of search would be an

*No familiarity is intended by the use of "Margie." Just as everyone who knew Kunstler called him "Bill," so everyone who knows Margaret Ratner calls her "Margie." Although "Bill" can be referred to as "Kunstler," it would be ludicrously stilted to refer to his wife consistently as "Mrs. Kunstler," and incorrect to refer to her as "Margaret."

archaeological excavation of the numerous layers of papers on Kunstler's own desk.

Larger matters of practice concerned him very little. If he assigned the preparation of a motion or the drafting of a brief to an associate, he would, as likely as not, simply glance at the documents and say, "Hey, it's great! Where do I sign?" However, he expected things to be accomplished immediately. A clerk joked that if you handed him a letter, Kunstler would sign it and put it back in your hand, asking, "is it mailed yet?" Any little thing that went wrong could cause serious distress and sometimes anger. The little things drove him crazy. His office handled hundreds of clients and thousands of pieces of paper, and it was difficult to keep track of it all. Time pressures were enormous. However, if Kunstler was a one-man pressure cooker, he never became abusive. Two secretaries, who had worked for him for many years, never felt abused. Both were enthusiastic about him; neither thought of him as a "boss." In fact, he insisted that everyone, his clients, colleagues, student interns, and secretaries, call him simply "Bill." Rosa Maria de la Torre, who was with Kunstler for the last nine and a half years of his life, never minded "doing more" for him because he was himself so busy and active.

Indeed, Kunstler did "do more." By 1991 he had conducted 230 jury trials. He had little by way of hobbies with which to relax, but he did enjoy the company of his children. He married Lotte Rosenberger, his first wife, in 1943, and his first two daughters, Karin and Jane, were born in late 1943 and 1949. Kunstler divorced and was remarried, to Margaret (Margie) Ratner, in the mid-1970s. With Margie he had two more daughters, Sarah and Emily, who were still youthful, in college and high school respectively, at the time of his death.

Kunstler drank very little. However, he enjoyed parties and all forms of socializing, where he could dominate conversations with his deep resonant voice and display his personal charm. Occasionally he went out to dinner with his wife and friends (Gus' Place in the Village was his favorite restaurant). He listened to opera at home, read, and watched the Mets play baseball on television. He relaxed at night by smoking a joint.

Probably Kunstler's greatest pleasure, aside from work, was his delight in people. He frequently embraced men and kissed women. He made superficial but enduring friendships with many colleagues and clients. An example is Stew Albert, a lawyer and junior member of the

Chicago Seven defense team. They became friends, smoked pot together, and called each other "dumbfuck" as a nickname. Although always very busy, Kunstler served as the master of ceremonies at Albert's wedding, in which role, Albert says, he was "hilarious." Kunstler formed an even deeper friendship with H. Rap Brown, a client from the Black Power days of the 1960s. Brown's wedding took place at Kunstler's home (then in Westchester), and whenever Kunstler was in Atlanta he went to Brown's grocery store to visit and eat pickles. He esteemed both the pickles and the friendship: "best kosher dills I have ever tasted . . . there is probably no one I love more among men than H. Rap Brown; with him, I broke my old childhood pattern of remaining a bit of a loner and not forming intimate friendships."

What fueled William Kunstler's immense drive, his rambunctious energy? We will be asking this question throughout the book. For now, however, we can rule out one motivation, and consider another that, at least on a superficial level, was clearly present. Kunstler definitely did not work for money. His attitude on wealth was that he wanted "just . . . enough to live on. Animals that overeat die." Kunstler's worldly accumulations were modest. One statistic is revealing. In the 1980s and 1990s half of his legal work, measured by time expended, was uncompensated. The remainder of time was employed for fees that were low compared to value. Economics was not the source of his energy.

On the other hand, one motivation for Kunstler's drive was his great need for intellectual stimulation. Most of his cases were very difficult matters, into which the police and prosecutors poured considerable resources. The uneven nature of the fights only fired his enthusiasm. Kunstler's need for intellectual stimulation was of long standing and continued throughout his career. While he was in law school and early in his practice, Kunstler wrote book reviews for a dozen newspapers and magazines. He wrote so many reviews for the *Herald Tribune* that the newspaper assigned him a pseudonym, so that readers would not notice the duplication. At the same time, he was a reader for Paramount film company's story department.

In the late 1940s and early 1950s he was the announcer, and then host, of several radio programs. In 1941, just out of Yale, Kunstler published his first book, a collection of poetry coauthored with a classmate. He returned to books in the 1950s and 1960s, starting with tedious books on legal topics for laymen and followed by much more interesting popularizations of famous trials and courageous lawyers. He enjoyed a best-seller in 1964 with *The Minister and the Choir Singer* and in 1966 wrote a memoir of his civil rights work in the South, with forewords by James Forman and Martin Luther King. These were solid books with very reputable publishers. In addition, Kunstler wrote several academically oriented law review articles and served as an adjunct law professor for most of his career.

Kunstler continued to write poetry, more specifically sonnets. He worked on his poetry as opportunity presented, in courthouse hallways, cabs, and airport waiting lounges. He originally published these mostly political sonnets in the *Amsterdam News* and then followed with two book compilations. Late in his career Kunstler appeared in several movies and television shows, and coauthored his autobiography. In addition to this, he frequently spoke to audiences of all sizes, ranging from large student demonstrations of thousands to small neighborhood meetings of a dozen people.

Visual images had great impact on Kunstler. Three images, in particular, do much to explain the man, his motives, and his methods. The first is a photograph by Margaret Bourke-White of the victims of the 1937 floods in Louisville, Kentucky. Kunstler kept a print in his office. The photograph is a study in ironic juxtaposition. It captures a line of poor blacks with pails and bags waiting in a bread line. Above the line of black men, women, and children is a billboard with an advertisement for an automobile. A white family smiles from within the car. The billboard bears the legend "There's no way like the American Way." Kunstler explained the personal significance of the photograph:

> It made such an impression on me that I bought a print as soon as I could find one. . . . Whenever I have been tempted to put out of my mind, even for a moment, the enormous gulf that exists between the races in this country, I look at Bourke-White's picture, and I am immediately at one again with the stark reality of my own environment.

Race was always the cutting edge in Kunstler's practice. He thought of racism as the great cancer in American society. According to Kuby, Kunstler had "an instinctive understanding and a hatred of racism the way that few white people do, in a way that all black people recognized and in a way that won him a tremendous appreciation in the black community." Kunstler thought that racism was so entrenched in the American legal system that blacks could not obtain fair trials, and that when a black was charged with assaulting a white, certainly a white policeman, the proceedings would be tainted by racism. For these reasons, defending blacks accused of murdering white policemen had a political element to Kunstler that most Americans simply did not see.

Gradually Kunstler extended his feelings about blacks to other racial minorities, such as Native Americans and Arabs. But blacks always held a special claim on his emotions. Racism sometimes created internal conflict for Kunstler. In the 1980s he defended Pang Ching Lam, a diminutive Chinese immigrant accused of murdering a black panhandler who had caused a disturbance at Lam's mother's restaurant. The decedent's race caused real angst:

> It was the first time I had ever represented someone who killed a black person. Pang was Third World, the decedent was a hopeless psychotic with drug problems. He was twice the size of the defendant. It was clearly self-defense. And even then I had misgivings. It's been such a lifetime of representing black people abused by white people. I'm not sure, if Pang had been white, I would have taken it.

Kunstler's memory of a lithograph once owned by his grandfather, a doctor, is a second visual image important in understanding the man. He recalled that

> a white-coated doctor, with a stethoscope hanging out of his pocket, is holding a naked young woman in his arms. A skeleton, representing Death, I assume, stands behind them, trying to grab the woman out of the doctor's arms. I could never stop looking at this picture. Of course, as a young boy, I was very interested in the naked woman, but it was the savior image that most drew me—and still does. I loved the notion of being a deliverer, of saving people. Today I often feel, somewhat grandiosely, that my work is the only thing that stands between a victim and the destructive forces of oppression, punishment, or public retribution.

This image of savior focuses our attention on the clients Kunstler represented and his need for the limelight, the public's attention on his work as savior. In the halcyon days of the 1960s, Kunstler identified almost totally with the radical political goals of his clients. It was in that spirit that he made his celebrated remark, for which he was attacked by the American Bar Association, that "I only defend those whose goals I share. I'm not a lawyer for hire. I only defend those I love." As the movement faded in the 1970s and 1980s, obviously political cases became hard to find. Kunstler began representing, at least on occasion, accused rapists, mobsters, and others with little discernible political motive for their actions. By 1987 he acknowledged that he was accepting some clients "even though I don't share much politics with them." That even included a few policemen picked on, Kunstler thought, by their superiors. But even while he tried to rationalize the political dimensions of rather ordinary criminal cases, by 1993 Kunstler admitted the difficulty in doing so. He recalled the movement cases of the 1960s and 1970s and acknowledged, "those were people that you could really say, 'I love them.' Now it's harder to do that. I'm dealing with people who are much different than me."

Kunstler could always fall back on a political rationale of struggling against an oppressive government. By 1994 his attitude was considerably reformulated. "Today, I would say I only defend those who are being oppressed by society and whose beliefs are not anathema to me. That means I don't have to love them but I certainly can't hate them." Of his newer clientele, he often remarked that at least they gave him a chance to attack the government.

Kunstler was skillful at using the media, perhaps subconsciously drawing the public's attention to his savior self-image. He held frequent press conferences, gave many interviews, often talked with reporters on the telephone, and was ready with provocative, highly quotable copy. Grandstander, limelight hogger, and publicity seeker were almost constant criticisms. "To some extent, that has the ring of truth," he once admitted. "I enjoy the spotlight, as most humans do, but it's not my whole raison d'etre."

Clearly, Kunstler had a personal taste for publicity far more massive than most lawyers. One theory of that, advanced by both Margie Ratner and Sheila Isenberg, the coauthor of his autobiography, was that he wanted everyone to love him, and if that were not possible, then to like him, and if even that were not possible, at least to notice him and give him respect. A craving for admiration and approval is undoubtedly the greatest single reason for his seeking attention and publicity. At some level, Kunstler also had insecurities, unacknowledged and probably not consciously understood, that created a need for reassurance and admiration.

Kunstler had many reasons beyond ego to seek publicity. Through media coverage he sought to advance and promote the political lines of those clients who were self-consciously political. Publicity also helped Kunstler's general defense practice. His nearly constant charges of racism brought him popularity in the minority communities from which many jurors came, and this popularity helped him at trial. His provocative statements about particular cases also created themes for quick jury identification of the issues. Every good defense strategist knows that a criminal defense has to have a theme, and Kunstler was a master strategist. Inside and outside court, he asked the question, "Why am I doing this? What does it have to do with the case's theme?" Comments to the press reflected that theme, as did speeches to rallies organized by defense committees.

For example, in the Larry Davis case Kunstler's theme was a "case of a black man defending himself against white crooked killer cops." Given enough publicity, the jury pool might remember this theme. They might not recall the details, but hopefully they would think, "Oh yeah, Larry Davis. He's the one who was defending himself against a bunch of killer cops." The development of such a theme would create an initial climate of opinion in the jury favorable to the defense.

There was still another purpose for Kunstler's play for media attention. With an appropriate case, media attention gives a radical lawyer an opportunity to "demystify" the law, to explain to the public the oppressiveness of the establishment and the political system. It was incumbent on Kunstler as a radical lawyer to constantly educate and agitate, to explain to the public, the media, the jurors, and if necessary the clients, that the legal system does not practice what it preaches. The dissatisfaction thereby induced, radical lawyers hope, will ultimately aid profound structural change by armed or peaceful revolution. In addition to practical lawyering, Kunstler held this ideological motivation.

A third visual image that helps to explain Kunstler is Michelangelo's statue of David. With young attorney colleagues, he used the analogy of David as a probing for a single weakness in cases everyone thought unwinnable. But Michelangelo's *David* held a deeper significance for his own psyche. Margie gave him a replica, which he kept in his office. He often looked at it to draw strength from the image.

David is standing there, thinking, . . . Do I dare? Do I dare? He has the rock in his right hand, the sling over his left shoulder, and he's watching this giant Philistine. . . . He is thinking, If I throw the rock and miss, I am one dead Israelite. If I just wound him, I'm in the same position. But if I hit him and kill him, I've done a great deed for my people and maybe for myself as well.

David is portrayed in that exact moment of hesitation that comes to everyone, the moment when the idea crosses your mind that you might stand up and say something, do something, prevent the library from banning the book, stop the injustice, or whatever it happens to be. But as long as it's a thought in your head, no one knows about it; if you don't act, no one will be the wiser.

> That's the key to the *David*. David won't be ostracized if he doesn't release the rock in his sling. . . . Since there's no personal urgency, he's in that finite moment when he must make a fateful decision, one that no one will be aware of until it's made, one that no one will criticize him for not making.
>
> It is a moment that occurs often in my life. Every time I decide to take on a Larry Davis or a Yusef Salaam, I make a choice. While I'm hardly comparing myself to David, my choice is whether to take on the giant or to let it slide. No one will know. When I choose, I choose what I believe is the right thing, despite the odds against it. Over the years, my David moments have come more frequently. Do I dare? Do I dare? I usually do when I can take on the system or when I believe that a certain defendant won't get a fair trial.

Kunstler garnered strength and courage from the *David* statue. Kunstler's physical courage ranged from his civil rights days, when he was menaced by angry southern whites, to his later days, when death threats were often made against him and his family. He was often physically intimidated, and on one occasion New York City policemen beat him so severely as to cause permanent injury. But his courage, his fearlessness went beyond the physical. As a lawyer he was unflappable under government pressure and intimidation. He did not hesitate to resist law enforcement oppression by countersuit or subpoena, or to risk judicial contempt or disbarment, in the face of a gag order, if disclosures would aid his clients.

Like David, William Kunstler was a man of action. He seldom looked back after trial, to analyze what went wrong, or what went right.

Instead, he looked forward to the next step of a case, the appeal or petition. In his career as a whole, he acted in the same manner. He had an instinctive feeling about injustice and about racism, and he acted on those feelings by taking on clients whom he felt had been treated unjustly. The words "instinctive" and "action" are used by almost everyone who knew Kunstler, but almost never the word "analytical." He engaged in very little self-reflection.

Even though he was a master strategist, critics sometimes charged that Kunstler failed to prepare adequately for trial. His workdays were so crowded that at times he did rush into trial. However, his great capacity to size up situations and personalities and to master complex arguments quickly usually saw him through any rough spots. However, even colleagues acknowledged that Kunstler would sometimes "wing it" during cross-examination.

Although the avoidance of minute, microscopic preparation for trial suited Kunstler's flamboyant personality, it was hardly just a matter of style. It was definitely not a question of laziness. Rather, it was his own enthusiastic overextension of himself, his abundant energy, that sometimes left him with insufficient time for preparation. If anything, his own instinctual drive to play the savior and his Davidian fearlessness caused the time pressures of overcommitment.

A savior self-image is one thing, and fearlessness is another. Very few men have acted on these feelings with the zeal shown by Kunstler. What caused this zeal, this drive? What caused the insecurities and lack of self-esteem for which this drive may have been an overcompensation? We will never know for certain, yet there are suggestive clues in Kunstler's childhood and memories.

2

Family and Early Years

WILLIAM KUNSTLER CAME into the world on July 7, 1919, the oldest child of what he later described accurately as a "solid, middle-class Jewish family" of German-Jewish descent. The family surname means "artist" in German. *Künstler* can also denote performer, virtuoso, and, in certain contexts, even wizard. Yiddish has two related words, rendered in German as *kunst* (art) and *kunts* (trick or stunt), spelled differently but pronounced nearly identically.

Because of the nature of his legal practice, Kunstler had an interesting and appropriate name, with its complicated overtones of performer, virtuoso, and even wizard and trickster. He was fickle about his name, sometimes pronouncing Kunstler in the German style with an umlaut over the *u*, similar to "rule," but usually without, as in "run." Never pushing the point, Kunstler was aware of the ambiguities of his name. In July 1969, while explaining to a reporter how he would like to be a black man, he remarked, "but I'm no magician. I have to be Kunstler."

William Kunstler was the son of Monroe Bradford Kunstler, a physician of general practice, later a proctologist, and Frances Mandelbaum Kunstler, herself the stepdaughter of a physician. Three years after Bill was born, Michael arrived, and three years after that, Mary completed the three-sibling family. The Kunstlers changed apartments a few times, but, because of the father's neighborhood practice, they lived within a tightly defined area of the Upper West Side of Manhattan, between Central Park West and Broadway and between Eighty-ninth Street and Ninety-first Street. For his primary education, Billy (he did not become Bill until he left for college) attended P.S. 93 and P.S. 166.

As a youngster Billy misbehaved continuously. For example, one day when his class took a test, Billy gathered up the test papers and threw them out the window. Hardly a week went by without his father being called to the school to hear a complaint. In these early years, Kunstler was very physical and beat up on other school kids. As a result, he was not popular. A friend of those years recalls that the hitting was not so much bullying as simply a means that Billy then used to express anger or attract attention. Later in the elementary grades, as his verbal skills improved, Kunstler turned to language to show irritation or displeasure.

When he was thirteen the family moved to Central Park West, where he joined an interracial gang of blacks and Hispanics. Because he was the only Jew, the gang members nicknamed Kunstler "Yiddle," and he reciprocated by calling the group (at least later) a "gang of goyim." This was the first showing of a pattern in Kunstler's life—the desire to join groups in which he did not quite belong. The gang members raided gum machines, shot pellets through windows, roughed up other kids, and busted into warehouses. They swam in the Hudson River, snickering at the condoms that floated by, calling them "Harlem whitefish." Policemen, who were often Monroe Kunstler's patients, frequently visited the family apartment to warn that their son Billy was destined for the penitentiary.

Some of the pranks were truly dangerous. One day Billy led his six-year-old brother and three-year-old sister for a walk along the third rail of the Long Island Railroad. Another time, he scampered over the roof of Temple Israel, the family's synagogue, and crashed through the skylight, only to be saved from a considerable fall by the grillwork underneath. His mother was very strict and had a lot of household rules (which Billy ignored), but his father was more lenient. One morning during a school vacation, Billy and Michael wanted to enjoy a fresh snowfall by sledding down Dead Man's Gulch off Riverside Drive. The ride was more than five hundred yards from a hill almost to the railroad tracks by the Hudson River. His mother was opposed, but his father argued that on vacation they ought to be allowed to have a good time. Kunstler managed to steer the sled into a tree, and the sled runner sliced his kidney, keeping him out of school for a month. Mary still remembers the commotion when Billy was carried home bleeding, with her mother screaming while her father tried to patch him up.

Kunstler had childhood heroes, of course. Among them were Charles Lindbergh and the New York Yankees. When the Yankees were playing home games, he and his friends would closely watch the Concourse Plaza Hotel in the Bronx, trying to spot the players and ask for autographs. That is Kunstler's recollection. His sister recalls her father, Michael, and Billy sitting around the radio listening to the New York

Giants. "That was their team. They didn't like any of the other New York teams, but the Giants. Oh, my God. They were avid fans, the three of them." The financial exigencies of the Depression prevented them from going to many games, but they listened to them on the radio. Kunstler may have cheered either the Yankees or the Giants during his youth, but he clearly transferred his allegiance to the New York Mets as an adult. In his later years Kunstler enjoyed watching the Mets on television and occasionally went out to the park.

As badly as Billy behaved, so Michael acted the opposite. During these pre–high school years, Michael always behaved himself and seldom got into trouble. Where Billy was rambunctious, Michael was calm; where Billy was talkative, Michael was quiet. If a question was asked in the family circle, Billy was always the one to answer. In fact, this loquaciousness persisted: throughout Kunstler's life, his mouth was almost constantly in motion. Some people who knew the adult Kunstler personally and had no argument with his politics or lawyering disliked talking with him simply because he monopolized the conversation.

Some other character traits began in Kunstler's early years. One was a great desire to help others, particularly those weaker or in a less fortunate position. This was combined with an almost total disregard for money. When Kunstler was a youth, a man one day injured himself by a fall on the sidewalk in front of their apartment building on Central Park West. Bystanders brought him to Monroe Kunstler's office and Billy went in to help. Dr. Kunstler did whatever was required and then said to his patient, "That will be two dollars." Billy was outraged. He turned to his father and remonstrated: "You're not going to charge this man! It was an accident!" His father simply asked his son whether he wanted to go to college and collected his fee. Years later, in his law practice in the 1980s and 1990s, about half of Kunstler's professional time was spent on cases for which he charged no fee or minimal fee because the client had no money. His personal friends Bruce and Diane Jackson recall that "Bill just couldn't care less about money. . . . He'd take cases either for nothing or where there was almost no money or if there was money, he'd give it to the client. We've seen him just take the check . . . and say, 'They need it more.' And just give it to the client."

Another characteristic that developed in Kunstler's early years was a physical problem with debilitating migraines. His physician daughter says that this is a familial trait. Kunstler tried hard to never let these headaches incapacitate him at trial or in appellate argument. "It was a personal rule of mine," he wrote, "that if a migraine hit me during court, I would not ask for a recess and would wait for the break." Occasionally, however, he had to ask permission to make an argument sitting down. When he was sixty the headaches suddenly vanished.

Kunstler's closest childhood friends were books. He had very few intimate friendships with males, a pattern that persisted throughout his life, notwithstanding a superficial gregariousness. He borrowed a different book each week from the Eighty-third Street and Amsterdam Avenue branch of the library, often beginning the new book on his walk home. Robert Louis Stevenson was his favorite, but he also devoured the adventures of Tom Swift, the Hardy Boys, and the Rover Boys. Billy snapped up pulp magazines from the newsstands, especially "Doc Savage," who led a gang that battled mightily for justice and good. Lying in bed at night on Central Park West, he would imagine he could "go anywhere, be anyone," perhaps even Doc Savage. Then he could "stomp through the park, through the streets of Manhattan, arms folded, prowling for thieves in the bricked alleys, golden-skinned, beholden to no one." It is easy to see this little boy still at work in Kunstler years later, in his delight in tweaking the noses of authority and disarming the dignity of judges.

Two aspects of Kunstler's early life offer significant clues to his later development. First is the development of a deep feeling of guilt over the treatment of black people, and the second is his very ambivalent relationship with his father, especially as contrasted with Pa Moe, his maternal grandfather.

Kunstler had a heavy dose of white guilt, and he himself attributed it to childhood experiences. His mother did no housework nor cooking (excepting her chocolate cake). Black maids (plus one Irish girl) did all the work, cooking and cleaning the nine-room apartment. Kunstler wrote later that his mother "was snobbish and treated the maids and governesses as if they were her inferiors. Like many Jews then—and today, unfortunately—my parents and their friends referred to blacks as *shvartzes* [blackies, niggers], not viciously, perhaps, but thoughtlessly." His father once "called out to another driver who had cut him off: 'Nigger!'" Kunstler took his parents to task about these racist attitudes but to no avail. In fact, he was attracted to black people who were not middle-class, or so he later claimed, the very sort most disapproved by his parents.

An incident when Kunstler was ten or eleven crystallized his feelings. He had heard about a black boxer named Sam Langford who had been injured somehow. Kunstler wrote him a letter of encouragement, and told the boxer that he would like to meet him. Langford wrote back that Kunstler could indeed meet him, indicating a time and place in Harlem.

> But then I told my father about it and he told me, "*Harlem!* You can't go up there, they'll cut you up with razors." When I wouldn't listen he brought in this police detective he knew who tried to scare me with all these stories of dangerous criminal black people who'd rob me and kill me. . . . I bought this bill of goods, I didn't go. I didn't go. I always regretted it.

This story held remarkable staying power. He repeated this story to interviewers in 1969 and 1992. He mentioned it in his 1994 autobiography. His first wife, Lotte, recalls Kunstler mentioning this incident as one of the causes of his antiracist zeal. The reporter to whom he told the story in 1992 thought he had discovered the linchpin, the Rosebud, to understanding Kunstler:

> You can hear it in his voice as he tells it: he still has a mortifying vision of the injured black boxer sitting in a lonely room somewhere up in Harlem sorrowfully waiting for the white boy who never showed up. . . . magnified by the distorting lens of adolescent emotion and guilt, the wounded black athlete is *still* there waiting, an eternal reproach to the boy who let him down. And a constant metaphorical admonition embedded in the psyche: Never let a black man down again, never fail to come to his rescue, never give in to that white middle-class caution ever again. What that means in practice is crucial: that Kunstler is virtually unable to criticize, or even advise moderation to, any black radical for fear that the impulse to restraint comes from the same infirmity—white middle-class inhibitions—that held him back from visiting that boxer.

Kunstler is too complex a man to have such a simple key to his character and life. This would not explain his role in the anti-Vietnam movement, his representation of the American Indian Movement, Arabs, Puerto Ricans, or white radicals. Doubtless, white guilt played an enormous role. "All white men, including me, look on black people with fear," he said in 1969. "It's a feeling of guilt. You can destroy or atone." Kunstler spent most of his professional life defending blacks, believing that American racism would otherwise deprive them of a fair trial. However, there was more to his practice and more to his motivation.

Kunstler's lifelong guilt over racism, derived from childhood, resulted in a profound sense of identification with blacks. He wanted to be black. In 1969 he told one reporter that "I would like to be black and have the education and profession that I have, because black people have been involved in almost everything proud that has happened to me." And again in 1970, he lamented,

> Oh, yes, I belong to the white world. And it's not only on the basis of skin color but also on the basis of my background. It's impossible for any white man to comprehend fully what it's like to live every day as a black man in this country . . . Black men may think of some whites as friends but not as black men. I guess I want desperately to be part of that black world for many reasons—some of which are probably deeply psychological. I will continue inceasingly to resist, personally and as an attorney, much of what the white world represents and what it does—but as a white man.

Kunstler's desire to be a part of the black world is similar to his desire to be a part of that "goyim gang": he cannot quite do it. He desperately wanted something that was unattainable. Not only could Kunstler not change his skin color, he realized that his family background controlled him still. Although he had liaisons with many black women (and white gentiles, too), for both of his wives he chose Jews. In 1970 a *Playboy* interviewer asked him why he did not sell his possessions and give them to the Black Panthers. His answer was candid, although it must be remembered that he cared for money and material possessions far less than most.

> I guess I haven't got the nerve or the guts to do that at this time. Maybe that's what I ought to do—sell everything I have and give it to the movement. Maybe I just talk a good game. Maybe I'm too middle class, too much the product of this society, to do that. On the one hand, I complain that I have these goodies because of an unjust system; but on the other hand, I keep them.

Kunstler's very ambivalent relationship with his father offers a second clue to his later life. In his autobiography he wrote that his father was a "plodding, sloppy man" with "wrinkled collars and nicotine-stained fingers." At least while a child, Kunstler thought that his father's specialty, proctology, was undignified. He implies that his father had a girlfriend even prior to his mother's death, on whom he lavished attention and the excitement of museums and theaters that he denied his mother. When Monroe Kunstler died in 1967, Kunstler rushed to the hospital, ran into his father's room, grabbed the corpse, and yelled, "You son of a bitch, wake up! You can't leave us now!" Years later, Ronald Kuby, Kunstler's close law associate for the thirteen years prior to his death, speculated that the zealous drive for public recognition derived from a desire to make up for the perceived failings of his father.

That explanation, much like the story of the foregone visit to the boxer, seems too simplistic, however much it may add to a total understanding. However, there is no question that Kunstler's affection for his maternal grandfather, Pa Moe, overshadowed his regard for his father. Moses Joseph Mandelbaum was not Kunstler's biological grandfather, since he married his widowed grandmother when William's mother was two years old. However, their relationship was that of grandfather/grandson, and Kunstler greatly admired and esteemed Pa Moe. He spends far more space in his autobiography discussing Pa Moe than he does his own father.

Pa Moe was an eccentric, a bon vivant, and a ladies' man. He was urbane and always nattily dressed in bow ties and tweed suits. People noticed him, and waiters, bartenders, and maître d's remembered him. Pa Moe had made a fortune (mostly lost in the 1929 stock crash) from his ear, nose, and throat practice, and was a world traveler. He was a raconteur and could spellbind an audience with his stories of old New York.

Pa Moe was also an inventor. Some of his inventions were crazy and gave his grandson a stock of stories. He invented a stencil for women to color their eyebrows with indelible ink. He tried it out on Kunstler's grandmother, got the alignment wrong, and Ma, as she was called, was angry for the many months it took the clearly visible double set of eyebrows to disappear from her forehead. Pa Moe invented an automatic mattress turner, of which he was able to make exactly one sale: to a brothel. He invented a collapsible bed that could be mounted on top of a car. Pa Moe, his butler, and Michael took the contraption across the country, until one morning they forgot to put it down and sheared it off under a bridge.

Kunstler made good use of these stories at cocktail parties and elsewhere. As he always did with stories, Kunstler embellished them, altered them to suit his audiences' reactions, and, being a good lawyer, usually came to believe in the improved versions. By the time he wrote his autobiography, Kunstler fairly extolled his grandfather: Pa Moe had treated every mayor of New York from John Hylan to William O'Dwyer, he was a founder of Mt. Sinai Hospital and the physician for the New York Giants. He "collaborated" with a well-known physician, Chevalier Jackson, in the discovery of the bronchoscope. The truth is that Mandelbaum *was* important enough to rate a full obituary in the *New York Times*. Mandelbaum, unfortunately, *was not* important enough to have done all the things his grandson claimed. He "studied under" Dr. Jackson before establishing his own practice; he helped found the less important New York Diagnostic Hospital, not Mt. Sinai; and there was no mention of his having served as physician to the mayors or the New York Giants. Nor was there mention of a claim his grandson made to a reporter in 1994 that his grandfather had been the official greeter of the city of New York.

Notwithstanding the inaccuracies of recollection, Pa Moe's influence as a role model is undoubted. When Kunstler was a child he "always wanted to be just like him." Although he never became an inventor, nor did he become a doctor, in other ways Kunstler *did* become just like him. While no one could accuse Kunstler in his badly rumpled suits of being nattily dressed, he was a great conversationalist, witty, eccentric, and a ladies' man. Kunstler's sister recalls that Pa Moe "liked the limelight . . . [and] I think he influenced Bill tremendously. . . . Bill liked that, the notoriety that Pa Moe had. And he was always looked up to and that probably did influence him."

Kunstler attended DeWitt Clinton High School at its annex on West End Avenue. Once there, he underwent a complete transformation. He no longer misbehaved. Instead, he became a straight A student, joined the honor society, and graduated at the head of his class. He developed a love of swimming and qualified for the school swimming team. Kunstler was not quite good enough to earn the team letter, and was so envious of the swimmers who had, that he stole a letter and had it sewn on his sweater. "I so wanted the recognition that I wore the sweater everywhere—except to school—always worried that I would be found out." This may itself be an embellishment, since a classmate recalls that Kunstler was one of the leaders of the swimming team.

Perhaps as a result of his changed behavior, Kunstler became the clear favorite of his parents, and Michael became his follower. Michael later followed his brother into DeWitt Clinton, then into Yale, then into the Signal Corps. In only one thing did Michael lead: he entered Columbia Law School first, leaving William to follow. The pride of Kunstler's parents in his high school success led to a pattern of constant approval followed by his seeking that approval. He wrote in 1994, "my parents . . . gave me constant reinforcement and approval. Throughout my life, well into adulthood . . . I always sought their approval."

William Kunstler was not the only one who recalled his parents' praise. Mary recalls that "my parents thought that . . . no one could be better than the three of us. And whatever Bill did was the greatest. And they always told all of us that. . . . I think that's why Bill did what he did. Because even after they died, he would have known they would have thought it was great. They were very encouraging parents." His oldest daughter, Karin, recalls that her grandparents gave her father constant reinforcement. Kunstler's first wife, Lotte, notes that her husband both needed his parents' approval and received it. They bragged about him to their friends in his presence.

Kunstler's need for parental approval continued for years. He explains, "throughout my career, I always told my parents about any big case I was working on, and even though I was middle-aged by the early sixties, I still needed their approval." After his parents died in 1966 (mother) and 1967 (father), that was no longer possible. Kunstler's widow, Margie Ratner, recalls that even late in his life, when something good happened to him, he would remark, "It's too bad my parents aren't around to see this." It was Kunstler's own theory that it was then that he developed a powerful need for public approval:

> When my mother and father were alive, it was acceptable for me to be the center of the world, to boast about my exploits. I may have transformed my need for approval from them to the world at large, for there is within me a powerful drive to make everyone like me—even love me, the way my parents did.

This drive for general approval and admiration was a constant throughout Kunstler's life, but it started long before his parents died. Lotte remembers it from the 1950s. We will see this strong need for approval still earlier, in his undergraduate years at Yale. Karin thinks he needed the approval not just of his parents, but of a lot of people, that her father had a compulsion for approval. Mary believes that "he liked approval all along wherever it came from. . . . He always loved getting that feedback that he was doing the right thing. He probably needed it. . . . He liked people saying, 'Bill, you're doing the right thing. You're great.' Even up to the moment he died." His partner recalls that "his need to be recognized, to have his achievements recognized in public was very powerful. . . . no public was too small and no public was too big. He needed that kind of public recognition."

But whence this craving for recognition, admiration, and a sense of belonging? Kunstler's own theory that it resulted from a transfer of the approval he had received from his parents does not ring true because he curried approval and admiration long before his parents died. Lotte believes that for some unexplained reason, Kunstler had a low sense of self-esteem, that he needed to be pumped up by praise and words of admiration, and that it was a bad day if he received none. That would make his craving for the limelight overcompensation for insecurity, at least in part. At least one close friend concurs, although adding that the insecurity was buried deeply, "far away from anything you could sense." Karin never saw insecurity in her father, but she believes some people who were close to him sensed it.

Kunstler also had an enormous need for love. His second wife, Margie, thinks that was the reason he craved the limelight, that he substituted attention for love. That is not a sufficient explanation, because Kunstler's search for public attention also served utilitarian purposes: fund-raising for his clients, favorable jury regard, name recognition, and even political education of the public. Beyond these practical matters, however, Kunstler's need for love, admiration, and belonging was deeper and more private. Probably it resulted from low self-esteem and insecurity, although we may never know exactly what caused those. Throughout his life we will find evidence of insecurity and low self-esteem, and the most we can do is to identify it as it appears. The underlying causes of the condition will remain buried, probably forever.

Even though Kunstler may have thought his parents were "too conservative, too ordinary," he was also observing patterns of behavior in them that he would adopt for himself. Monroe Kunstler brought his wife breakfast in bed each morning. His son William did likewise with both his wives. Margie generally did not eat breakfast, but Kunstler brought her coffee. Until nearly the end of his years, Kunstler rose early, and around 7:00 went down to his office in the basement of his Greenwich Village townhouse. He then made coffee, but before beginning work he took a cup upstairs to his wife.

Frances (or Fanny), Kunstler's mother, was eccentric in the area of religion. The family honored the major Jewish holidays, and Fanny enjoyed the Jewish services. She also attended Catholic masses, lit candles in her neighborhood church of St. Gregory the Great, and even prayed to her own patron saint, St. Anthony. She pinned medals of saints to the underwire of her corset. During World War II she stuffed St. Christopher medals into the uniform pockets of Manny Horn, her son-in-law.

In his later years, Kunstler no longer considered himself a Jew, although he did continue to attend seders every year. "We've doctored up the Haggadah [liturgy of the Passover seders] to eliminate sexism," he reported. However, he went to other religious ceremonies as well. He told a reporter in 1993 that he attended "Catholic churches and Sikh temples and native American ceremonies. I go to mosques." He did not re-embrace his Jewish roots at the end of his life. His partner recalls,

> Bill found all religious orthodoxies oppressive and rigid. However, he loved the pomp and ritual of religious celebration. He was given the Native American name Wambli Wicasa [Soaring Eagle Who Watches over Us], and the Muslim name Musa Mohammed. He wore a steel Sikh bracelet. In the last summer of his life, a young Hasidic student interviewed him, then bound him with tefillin and led him in prayer. With his arm wrapped in leather straps, Bill prayed, showing the same enthusiasm with which he would sing "Abide with Me" in a storefront church.

Without doubt, Kunstler's own life experiences led him to reject orthodox religion and to substitute a love of the rituals of many religions. However, it is not hard to see the influence of his mother at work in his religious evolution. In one striking parallel, at least in the late 1960s Kunstler wore a St. Jude medallion (patron saint of lost causes) given him by the fiancée of a client.

In his autobiography Kunstler spends considerable time discussing his early, unconsummated sexual experiences. They were mainly necking and petting sessions. During Kunstler's high school years, the family spent their summers in Westbrook, Connecticut. In a Westbrook cemetery when he was fifteen, Kunstler had his first sexual experience. As he explains, "it wasn't really intercourse, because I lost all control and ejaculated beforehand." Nonetheless, he rushed home to wash himself, "frightened that I would contract an awful disease."

He had a steady girlfriend in New York during the next school year, with whom he "enjoyed many necking sessions." That summer at sixteen, Kunstler had an emergency appendectomy. When he returned home from the hospital, his girlfriend became his first visitor. He persuaded her to have sex with him, assuring her that his entire family was out. But Monroe Kunstler returned home unexpectedly, when the couple had just started to kiss and snuggle. He played his role of doctor and lectured the girlfriend on postoperative treatment and the danger of bursting the stitches. Nothing was said about the morality involved, and Kunstler's girlfriend quietly left. That was the end of that opportunity and that relationship. Kunstler did not experience a consummated sexual experience until his college years. He spent summers working as a camp counselor, and while working at Camp Chicopee in Pennsylvania, he visited a prostitute in Scranton. "She was blond and tall," he recalled, and "afterward, I felt so grown up."

Kunstler traveled to Europe in the summer of 1936, between his junior and senior years in high school. Pa Moe promised him a trip to Europe on condition he kept a diary for a year beforehand. Kunstler did not keep the diary, but he really wanted to go to Europe. Just weeks before the end of the year, he wrote out a year's worth of diary recollections, and his grandfather sent him off to France. Once in France, he borrowed an English touring car from a medical school classmate of his father under a promise to deliver it to a hospital in the Alps.

Kunstler had read with excitement about the outbreak of the Spanish Civil War, and the need for ambulance drivers. Together with two young men he had met on the ship going over, he drove to Barcelona. The automobile was immediately stripped and converted to an ambulance. The boys did not go out on calls, but spent their time making love to Spanish girls. As Kunstler explains, however, at that time he "really didn't know what I was doing." Eventually he made contact with his family. His mother dramatically threatened to jump off the Empire State Building if her son did not return home immediately. He did. Later, his father compensated his classmate for the damage to his car.

During the 1930s many Jews fled Nazi Germany with the help of American relations. Pa Moe sponsored a family named Rosenberger because they were distant relatives of his wife. After the Rosenbergers had arrived in New York, Monroe and Frances invited them over for tea. The Rosenbergers' eleven-year-old daughter, Lotte, came along. William Kunstler was then seventeen (Lotte remembers the ages as sixteen and ten). He recalled in 1969 that "she was a beautiful little girl with long pigtails down her back. I was entranced by her." Since Lotte was still a girl and Kunstler almost a man, he suppressed his feelings for the time.

Kunstler graduated from high school in 1937. Yale University had accepted him, but it bothered him that Columbia, his father's college, had not. How Kunstler worked this out in his mind reflects this growing desire to belong, to fit in, to be admired. He persuaded himself that the admissions officials at both universities had met and decided that Yale was really better for him than Columbia. That thought allowed him to conclude that Columbia had not really rejected him. Kunstler enrolled at Yale, an institution that by 1980 he had come to regard as "a spawning ground for capitalist society."

Kunstler signed on as a premed major to please his father and grandfather. His grades in science courses showed that his heart was not in that direction. His adviser suggested that Kunstler invite his father to meet with him. The adviser, a history professor, pointed out to Monroe that his son had received a D in organic chemistry, while he had an A in every humanities subject. He suggested that Monroe allow his son to choose another major, and to Kunstler's delight, his father reluctantly agreed. After he was past the science courses, Kunstler earned straight A's, and was invited to join Phi Beta Kappa, the honorary scholastic fraternity, in his senior year.

It was well that Kunstler's father was so reasonable. Kunstler's second daughter, Jane, herself a physician, recalls that her father was very squeamish. Not only could he not stand blood, he lacked the temperament of a scientist. When Jane was sixteen she stepped on an embroidery needle that became embedded in her foot. Kunstler took his daughter to the emergency room, where she was laid out on a table. Her father stood by her head to "comfort" her. Every time the doctor dug into her foot, her father slammed her head down onto the table and cried out, "Oh, no!" Years later, he visited her while she was in medical school in Buffalo. She took him to her anatomy lab, where he turned blue.

Kunstler developed a great love of literature at Yale. His appreciation for the Bible, which he often quoted to juries, came from a favorite course, "The Bible as Living Literature." He read deeply into the English romantic poets: Byron, Coleridge, Keats, Shelley, and Wordsworth. He loved Dylan Thomas's poetry and began a correspondence. Kunstler had the temerity to add stanzas to the poems, and sent on his improved endings to the Welsh writer, until Thomas wrote back saying that he would appreciate it if Kunstler would allow him to finish his poems himself.

Kunstler published pieces in the *Yale Literary Magazine* and the *Yale News,* and began a habit of composing Elizabethan-form sonnets, virtually every day, a practice that he continued throughout his busy years as a lawyer. With his high level of intellectual activity, it is not surprising that he became friends with many of the Yale faculty. One of them suggested a collaboration on a book of poetry with William Vincent Stone, another student who wrote verse. As a result of the collaboration, Kunstler published the first of his twelve books, a slim collection of youthful and flowery poetry, *Our Pleasant Vices,* which appeared in 1941. He read some of his sonnets at a poetry contest held at Mount Holyoke College in April 1941. Kunstler wanted to participate if only, he acknowledged at the time with prefigurative insight, "for the thrill of having an audience." A romantic pose of love and lost love fuels the majority of this early Kunstler poetry, but there are also religious themes and even a few topical references to the destruction then raging in Europe. It is not particularly good writing:

> *I come to you with open mind and heart,*
> *The lover sans the outward marks of love;*
> *I speak, and yet the words are words apart*
> *From me, as if the very lips that move*
> *Are lips and nothing more; and then you turn*
> *Towards me and smile, and I forget the line*
> *Of what I say and do not care to learn*
> *The bookish sense of things save you are mine.*

Kunstler majored in French at Yale, and naturally he acquired an appreciation of French authors, especially Anatole France, Pierre Loti, and Molière. Kunstler found very little use for French in his later life, but he was proud of his French major. Throughout his professional career, he listed French as a language in which he could practice in his biographical sketch in *Martindale Hubbell*, the major lawyer reference book. In the 1980s, shortly after the Goetz subway shooting, a Montreal radio station called Kunstler's office to ask for an interview. Ronald Kuby took the call and assured the caller that not only would Kunstler be pleased to give them an interview, but he would do it in French. At first Kunstler panicked, but he practiced a bit with a secretary in the office who was a native French speaker, and Kuby recalls that he did just fine. "Certainly what he lacked in precision he more than made up in the enthusiasm that he showed."

The Kunstler family was not particularly musical, although they listened to the popular music of the day on their radio. William enjoyed Cole Porter songs; "Begin the Beguine" was his favorite. At Yale, Kunstler began a lifelong love of opera. Puccini's *Tosca*, a fervent story of a young revolutionary, quite appropriately became one of his favorites. Also while at Yale, he made the school's swimming team, did some boxing, and attempted to play football for Berkeley, his residential college. He broke his finger after a few minutes of scrimmage and decided he would stick with swimming.

In the 1930s Yale was rife with anti-Semitism. Nazi flags festooned numerous student rooms, and Jews were excluded from many clubs and societies. "I heard so much anti-Semitism," Kunstler much later confided, "that I felt that maybe it was bad to be a Jew, and so I began to surround myself with goyische friends." And indeed, Kunstler's best friend at Yale, Shepard Krech, was a gentile. The reflection on this phase of life in his autobiography is very revealing:

> The message given by anti-Semitic Yalies was that it was not okay to be different. I ended up feeling uncomfortable and sometimes ashamed of being Jewish. At that age, I wanted acceptance more than anything, so while I don't recall ever attending synagogue, I sat through many church services in the company of my poetry collaborator, Bill Stone, a very religious Catholic.

Kunstler himself acknowledged that several of his sonnets in *Our Pleasant Vices* had Christian themes. Some are quite obvious:

> *If I forget thee, Bethlehem, then let*
> *My hand and arm be cut away from me!*

They walk and they will walk your path, and see
What you have seen, and meet whom you have met:
Perchance they dream your hopes, but they forget
The shrouded times they glimpse Gethsemane.

Kunstler roomed by himself his first three years at Yale. He was clearly shy, and wanted to be accepted, to belong, to fit in. Paradoxically, he chose groups with which to identify where he would never easily and comfortably belong. With needs that strong, Kunstler doomed himself to frustration. It was just as it had been years earlier, when as Yiddle, the only Jew, he ran with a gang of blacks and Hispanics on the Upper West Side. It was just as it would be years later, when Kunstler, a white man, would desperately want to be a black man and a part of the black world.

Several other traits that originated in this period were to last throughout Kunstler's lifetime. During his high school days he always hugged his parents, but in the Yale years he started a lifelong practice of greeting people generally with a hug or kiss. He developed a sense of the dramatic and with that a tendency to embellish stories. Publicity and attention began to allure Kunstler. With his brother and sister, however, he remained simply brother Bill, and could not get away with embellishment and attention seeking. An interest in left-wing politics also surfaced at Yale when Kunstler became a leader in the Student Labor Party.

The flamboyance and immodesty that characterized his later years also began at Yale. Mary recalls an incident in the late 1930s. She and brother Bill were invited to a prom at Mary's high school. Their parents wanted to take a picture of the two of them. Out wandered Kunstler, dressed with his tuxedo jacket and shirt but from the waist down stark naked. He stood behind Mary for the picture. "He was never a modest man," she recalls. "He could walk out stark naked anywhere. It never bothered him."

Her husband, Manny, remembers a similar incident from that time:

We had a group of fellows over to the house one time. And he walked out with a pair of glasses over his [exposed] penis and said, "Meet Mr. Jones." And I looked at the faces of these other fellows. They didn't know what the hell to make of him. He was a fun lover and a fun seeker. He had a marvelous sense of humor. He would do things that

. . . would be something out of the ordinary. He was always pulling some kind of a gag. We had a lot of fun.

"Self-centered" is a word that many critics applied to Kunstler. That trait also began during his Yale years. When Mary graduated from high school, she planned on attending the very well respected Katherine Gibbs secretary school. She told her brother Bill about this, and he replied, "That's awful. I'm so shocked. What will I tell my friends if you're not going to a regular college." In fact, she ended up at Barnard. Mary recalls that he said this in all seriousness:

> He was, I guess, a little bit of a snob at the time. He didn't want to tell his friends that his sister was going to go to a secretarial school. Like that was terrible. He wanted to tell them that I was going to go to a regular college. . . . He was at Yale and I guess they were all sort of snobby up there. He wanted to be able to tell his friends that his family went to college.

Although Mary attributes this bizarre conversation to snobbery, self-centeredness rings out more clearly. Kunstler's problem with Katherine Gibbs had nothing to do with education; he was concerned over how it would look to his friends. Would it help him fit in, to belong? That is a terribly self-centered issue to raise concerning his sister's education.

Self-centeredness remained a problem for Kunstler his entire life, as he acknowledged.

> [After my parents died], I no longer had anyone to whom I could say, "Look how well I'm doing." Today I have my wife, Margie, and my two youngest daughters, but I have to be careful not to overdo it. They help by reminding me. "All we hear about is Bill, Bill, Bill. We have our own lives to lead," they tell me. . . . One of my family's most serious criticisms is that I see events and people mainly in terms of my own relationship to them.

Not all of Kunstler's self-centeredness involved impositions on others, as had his dismay with his sister. Not all was heavy-handedness or braggadocio. Kunstler learned to apply it with a light touch, and could even poke fun at his own sense of importance. In 1989 he and Margie went to Bermuda for a vacation with their friends Bruce and Diane Jackson. Kunstler had a terrible time remembering which side of the road vehicles drove on in Bermuda. One day the four of them were out walking along a back road to a cove to go snorkeling. A moped came suddenly around a corner, and just about hit him. As soon as he had recovered his dignity, Kunstler cried out to his friends and wife in his deep bass voice, "It comes to this—death by a moped in Bermuda! It's not seemly! It's not seemly! It won't look good in my obit!"

In the year before he graduated from college, Kunstler applied to Yale Law School. He did not want to become a lawyer, and went through the formality of applying mainly to please his mother and father, who now expected him, after he left the premed program, to become an attorney. However, Yale Law School accepted him, and Kunstler reluctantly bought some law books and rented a room in New Haven. He felt that the law school application, book purchases, and apartment hunt were pieces of a charade: with the clouds of war hanging over the United States in the fall of 1941, his academic work could not continue. This belief proved correct.

3

Getting Started in the Law

WHEN KUNSTLER GRADUATED from Yale in 1941, he had not yet been called by the military draft, reestablished just the year before. However, the prospects for American involvement in the war raging around the world were clear, and he applied for a commission in the Naval Officers Program, on the theory that service on a ship would be safer than on the ground. The navy advised he would be rejected unless he had his tooth fillings replaced. Kunstler went through the painful procedure of having all his gold and silver fillings removed and replaced with amalgam. But the navy still rejected him for undisclosed reasons.

In college Kunstler had taken an army correspondence course in cryptography. He had enjoyed it and decided that if he could not be on a ship, cryptography would be the next best thing. In September 1941 he enlisted in the army to attend a cryptographic school at the Signal Corps post in Fort Monmouth, New Jersey. When his mother drove him down to the post, she saw young recruits picking up debris on the grounds and naively asked her son, "Can they make a Yale man do that?"

Kunstler assured his mother that as a Yale man he would not be asked to do that. In fact, he did draw a different duty: the care of a thirty-six-hole latrine. But worse was the lack of uniforms in his size and the need for him to work in his civilian clothes. That annoyed him, and only hours after his enlistment he went AWOL, and holed up in a nearby town for a few days until a new shipment of uniforms was due to arrive. Then he returned, confessed his absence, but was not charged.

What caused his disappointment was not the latrine duty, but that he had to work without a proper uniform. His comment on this episode in his autobiography reveals yet another instance of Kunstler's desire to belong, to fit in: "once in uniform, I lost the feeling of being an outsider and from that point on became a gung-ho soldier." It may seem paradoxical in light of Kunstler's general sentiments about the federal government and his antimilitary stance in the Vietnam and Gulf conflicts, but the evidence from his family is that he enjoyed his service in the army.

After basic training, Kunstler went to cryptographic school. The work was not enough to occupy his time, and he tried out for and won a part in a military production of a comedy, *Whistling in the Dark.* Kunstler invited his entire family to come down from New York to see him perform. It opened on December 7, 1941, and because of Pearl Harbor all leaves were canceled. "We had a full house," he recalled, "because nobody could leave the post." A New York critic attended, and Kunstler was thrilled by his first notice in the *New York Times*: "Everyone in the cast is enormously educated. William Kunstler, a Phi Beta Kappa from Yale, plays the part of a thug."

Kunstler discovered that he loved theatrics and that he had a genuine flair for the dramatic. He never forgot these early lessons. Kunstler said many times in later life that trials were essentially theatre. Aside from trial juries, he always enjoyed being in front of any audience, no matter how large or small. Even in private conversation he was often theatrical. It was precisely this flair for the dramatic that caused the embellishment of so many of his stories. While others might call it lying, Kunstler simply sought to make his stories more interesting. If he told a story in a better way, and received a better reaction, he adapted the story to the new version. Over time, he himself believed in the new version. His daughter Jane sums it up: "He was an actor. Things didn't sound just ordinary when he said them."

Kunstler realized that war meant he would be in the army for more than his two-year enlistment. In light of that, he enrolled in the officer candidate program, and graduated in June 1942 as a second lieutenant in the Signal Corps. After an initial army-style foulup, in which he was sent to Jacksonville, Florida, to supervise syphilitics unloading dirty laundry, the military rerouted him to his correct post, the Second Army Headquarters in Memphis, Tennessee.

Kunstler's job was to keep the equipment current, supply other units with coding machines, and encode or decode messages. He worked in a locked room in a partitioned old building on the fairgrounds. When a coded message came in, a teletype operator took it to the locked room, knocked on the door, and handed it to Kunstler or another officer. Occasionally, he would emerge to hand a message in code for transmission. Bill Hurst, then a young private, recalls Kunstler as friendly but businesslike, frequently saying, "Good morning" or "How are you?" on his way to work, but little else.

Kunstler also experienced his first contact with segregation. He noticed the segregated public facilities, the "colored only" and "white only" signs on drinking fountains and rest room doors. He recalled an incident when he was ordered to take Brigadier General Benjamin Davis from the railroad station to his hotel, only to be refused service because this was Tennessee and that brigadier general was black. He remembered fruitless arguments with Pa and Ma Frain, his kindly but bigoted landlords, owners of his boarding house. "It's good to have the Nigras in their world and us in our world," Pa Frain claimed.

Kunstler remembered Lotte Rosenberger from their first meeting back in his high school days. After enlisting in the army he corresponded with her regularly. Kunstler proposed by mail, Lotte accepted, and they were married when he was home on leave, January 14, 1943. He was twenty-three, and she was seventeen. In the summer of 1943 Kunstler was transferred to Lebanon, Tennessee, for the massive Second Army maneuvers. Lotte, then six months pregnant, moved from Memphis with him. The couple rented an apartment from the owner of the Lebanon mortuary, who had converted a former hearse garage into four apartments. Their place had a kitchen and bathroom and a living room that was seven by nine feet. The bedroom was about the same size, with a bed that consumed six feet, leaving three feet in which to walk. There was also room for a trunk in the bedroom. That was it.

As Lotte's due date approached, Kunstler looked through the Yale graduate catalogue and eventually found a doctor practicing in Nashville. When Lotte's water broke, Kunstler commandeered a military car and driver (in his autobiography it became a truck; Lotte comments, "Well, truck makes a better story. It was a sedan"), and they started out:

> It was thirty miles and we had gone halfway when a convoy came the other way. At the intersection, we had to wait for a convoy, and it was not very comfortable for me. And when we got to Nashville, we didn't know where the hospital was. So they both got out to see if they could get information. And the car started to roll backwards. The driver and Bill both jumped in. And I don't know whether they ever asked anybody or how we found the hospital. But I was really in labor.

And [at] the hospital, it looked like to me the Supreme Court steps. I had to go up all that way.

It all ended well. Bill and Lotte Kunstler's first daughter, Karin Fernanda Kunstler, was born October 15, 1943. After the mandatory ten-day hospital stay of those years, Lotte returned to Lebanon by ambulance, another requirement of the times. She rode in their landlord's combination hearse-ambulance, lying behind red plush curtains and enjoying a "gorgeous ride. [With] the leaves turning, it was just beautiful." The apartment had no room for a crib, but Karin's little bassinet was placed on top of the trunk. Characteristically, Kunstler's recollection improved the story and had Karin's first bed a footlocker perched on top of a chicken crate. Karin received her first piece of mail shortly after she was born. One of her father's professors at Yale sent her a postcard with the message, "Take good care of your father. He is going to do great things." Kunstler saved the card all his life and gave it to Karin shortly before he died.

In the spring of 1944 the military ordered Kunstler overseas, to serve in the new Eighth Army. Lotte and Karin drove to New York, along with another officer's wife, and then lived with Kunstler's parents on Central Park West for the duration of the war. Kunstler traveled by train to San Francisco and then on the USS *John Pope* to Hollandia, New Guinea. That was a safe location, but in October 1944 Kunstler's unit joined in the invasion of Leyte, as a part of the recapture of the Philippines. Their ship was constantly attacked by Japanese planes. Kunstler had to stay below along with the rest of the headquarters personnel, while the sailors and marines staved off the planes. "From my berth in the belly of the ship, I could do nothing but look out through the portholes. I found having no control, with my life in the hands of others, terribly disturbing."

Kunstler received a Bronze Star (given for "heroic or meritorious achievement or service in connection with military operations against an armed enemy") and (perhaps) also a Purple Heart (given to "anyone wounded in action while serving with the U.S. armed forces") for his service while in the Philippines. It is hard to figure out what really happened. His daughter Karin remembers that "he used to talk to us a lot about his experiences during the war and his acts of heroism. Some of them we know aren't true, and some of them may be exaggerated." Curiously, Kunstler's résumés, interviews, and autobiography all include the Bronze Star but fail to mention the Purple Heart. Yet his friends and family all recall that he also mentioned a Purple Heart. His service record confirms the Bronze Star but fails to mention the Purple Heart.

One story involved a jeep. Lotte recalls that her husband said "he got the Purple Heart for a little cut on his nose when he fell out of a jeep which was turning over." In his autobiography Kunstler recalled merely that he was once strafed by a Japanese plane when he was sent to an airstrip in a jeep to pick up some code machines. "I leaped under the jeep; from there I could see the little dust puffs, each of which marked a bullet hitting the ground. I closed my eyes and hoped hard that no bullets would hit the jeep's gas tank, and none did."

Another frequently told story concerned a collapsing tent. The full version has a rumor that the Japanese had infiltrated their camp while Kunstler was living in an eight-man tent. Panic set in, an American officer fired his gun, the support pole fell, and the tent crashed down on Kunstler and his mates. Ultimately, the men "crawled out, feeling a little ashamed that we had been so frightened. We later learned that the whole thing had been a false alarm." Another version his daughter recalls him telling is that he was in a tent while there was some shooting and some blood from somebody else dripped on him. Diane Jackson recalls the story as the tent pole falling down and hitting Kunstler.

Neal Goldman, Kunstler's son-in-law, remembers a story where Kunstler's unit chased some Japanese, who holed up in a baseball stadium. The Japanese set up machine guns in the dugouts and Kunstler "said he knew exactly how high a pitcher's mound was because he was hiding behind it to evade the crossfire." In his autobiography Kunstler describes an incident when he was sent on a mission by himself and stumbled onto a firefight. He joined in with a rifle company and fired away. "Then it ended. I ran out of ammo, I was grimy, and I'd had enough of shooting. I walked slowly [away]."

Taken as a whole, Kunstler's war stories have an "aw shucks" quality to them, an insinuation that nothing much really happened. Look how silly the military is, they seem to say, when for this nothingness I ended up with a Bronze Star and Purple Heart. They are quite unlike most Kunstler stories. The war stories are almost put-downs; they are certainly not the more typical self-aggrandizements. In the circles with which Kunstler identified, to which he "belonged" with his strong need for belonging, service in the American military was a problematic matter. The Vietnam War resisters, the New Left radicals, the Gulf War objectors—these people did not much care for the army. Casting his own wartime record in a light of phony heroics, Kunstler was able to present it in a manner palatable to his colleagues without denying the reality and value of his own past.

Occasionally in later life, Kunstler became entirely carried away from reality with his war stories. For example, in 1992 he wrote an article supporting conscientious objectors during the Gulf War. In that piece he claimed that during World War II he had been bayoneted and that a conscientious objector had prevented the military doctors from cutting off his arm. In fact, his son-in-law clearly recalls, "he said that the only time he ever came close to being wounded" was the tent collapse episode, when, in the version he heard, Kunstler found "some blood and he had no idea whether it was his or the guy's above him."

After the surrender, Kunstler went to Japan and headed a program in which classified documents were carried by officers serving as couriers and routed all over the Far East. Shortly before he was due to be shipped home, he planned a trip where he himself would be the courier, and selected a route through all the places in the East that he personally wanted to visit. The trip was all set; Kunstler was packed and the plane was set to leave in the morning. But Leo Penn, a fellow officer, begged Kunstler to let him take the trip in his place. Penn was scheduled to return home in days, this trip would be his only chance to see these exotic places, and so forth. Kunstler refused, but Penn wore him down, and ultimately he relented.

Then fate took a cruel twist. The plane on which Kunstler was scheduled to ride, and in which his ambitious substitute, Leo Penn, was riding instead, crashed into a mountain. Everyone aboard was killed. Kunstler undertook the difficult task of finding a rabbi to conduct the funeral service. He searched all over Japan and eventually found one. Kunstler was racked by guilt, "not only because I had allowed him to go in my place but also because I couldn't escape feeling happy that it wasn't I." He wrote to Penn's widow and "poured out my heart to her, describing all my feelings of guilt in great detail." Although she comforted him with assurances that her husband's death was not Kunstler's fault, his family believes that he suffered guilt over this for years. The story gives insight into Kunstler's later capacity to feel guilt over racial matters. White guilt was more than an empty phrase to a man who could feel deep guilt over the Leo Penn affair, for which he was quite blameless.

Kunstler shipped back to the States on the *Takanis Bay* a short time before the end of 1945. He caught a troop train from San Francisco to New York, sitting up four days on a hard seat. When he arrived at Penn Station, he had a beard, wore a helmet and a pistol, carried a Samurai sword, and "felt like a Bill Maulden cartoon of GI Joe." Lotte met him and they took a taxi to his parents' apartment on Central Park West. When he had last seen Karin she was only nine months old; now she was more than two. Lotte had shown her pictures of her father while he was gone, and had asked her to kiss her father's photographs good-night. When the elevator reached their floor, "Karin was standing there waiting for me. She yelled, 'Daddy!' ran, and threw herself in my arms. The elevator operator, Kimball, who had taught me to play chess when I was much younger, cried like a baby as Karin and I hugged. . . . I put my arms around him and cried also." Kunstler was discharged in March 1946, although he remained in the reserves for a few years longer. He ultimately rose to the rank of major in the army.

When Kunstler left the army, he aspired to become a writer and "not go to law school." Parental expectations for a legal career had lessened, and his sister felt that "he was going to be a writer, because he loved writing." In fact, while Kunstler was in the army he had published some pieces about his army experiences in the *Patterson Evening News*. He wrote to Lotte about his hopes and his plan to attend Columbia School of Journalism, and she encouraged him by mailing a copy of the catalogue. He pored over the course catalogue in the Philippines, and decided that he would become a journalist and a writer. Kunstler resolved to apply to Columbia as soon as he got home.

But when he returned he discovered that his younger brother, Michael, was in law school. The army had discharged Michael earlier; Michael had returned to Yale, completed his degree, and entered Columbia Law School. Angry that his baby brother had gotten ahead of him, Kunstler dropped journalism and decided on law school—"for no other reason than that Michael was going." At least that was how he remembered it for his autobiography. His sister remembers a less dramatic but more likely version: Michael simply encouraged his brother to attend Columbia and even at the outset the brothers had the expectation that they would go into practice together. In another rendition of his motive, Kunstler himself later said that he attended Columbia Law School "for all the wrong reasons: because it offered status, prestige and the promise of a reasonably high income." For whatever motive, he applied to Columbia Law School and entered in February 1946; the GI Bill paid Kunstler for his books and tuition and gave him a ninety-dollar monthly stipend.

Columbia in the postwar years ran a sharply accelerated program for the benefit of returning veterans who had already lost many years of their potential careers. It compressed a three-year program into two years, and the pace was brisk. Kunstler found the going difficult in his first semester. Partly, it was a problem of readjustment to being a student, and it was also a matter of resentment that his professors had not served in the army and that they treated him—he who had so recently been an officer with power—as though he were a child. Then too, Kunstler was not a terribly serious student, although his sister recalls Bill and Michael with a law school study group working around the dining room table at their parents' apartment in the spring of 1946.

Initially, he received barely passing law school grades. He even applied for a job as a writer for a motorist touring magazine. *Esso Road News* offered him a job, and that forced Kunstler to think carefully about what he wanted from life. If he quit law school, his brother would have a degree and he would not. He decided to make a go of it and work harder, although he continued to spend a lot of time playing bridge in the student lounge. His grades improved by the time he graduated.

Kunstler had some interesting classmates during his years at Columbia Law School. Jack B. Weinstein and Constance Baker Motley, later prominent federal judges, studied with him, as did Roy Cohn, later notorious as the mean-spirited lawyer for Senator Joseph McCarthy. Arthur Kinoy, later a politically conscious "people's lawyer," involved with Kunstler in many civil rights cases, and ultimately a law professor, was also a classmate.

While he was a law student, Arthur Kinoy and four friends organized Columbia's first student chapter of the National Lawyers Guild. The National Lawyers Guild was and is a distinctly left-wing association of lawyers. In the context of the Cold War, it opposed loyalty oaths, resisted congressional investigators, and attacked prosecutions of communists. By 1950 the House Committee on Un-American Activities labeled the National Lawyers Guild the "legal bulwark of the Communist Party." Kunstler joined the student chapter while at Columbia, although he was not one of its organizers. Arthur Kinoy characterized him as "a joiner, not an active member" of the chapter, but like his leadership of the left-wing political party at Yale, it demonstrates Kunstler's growing interest in leftist attitudes and ideologies.

After graduation, Kunstler took a job at Macy's to support his family while he studied for the bar. He entered its executive training program, but disliked it. Although he studied bar review texts during his lunch hours, he did not pass the bar exam on his first try. Michael, still single and with few expenses, took a bar review course and did pass the first time. Kunstler's love of writing had not abated at all during his law school days. He confessed this love of writing to a Macy's executive, and obtained the job of revising a Macy's training manual as his only employment duty. That improved his closing days at Macy's.

Kunstler passed the bar on his second try, and the character committee then approved him. At age twenty-nine, on December 15, 1948, Kunstler was admitted to the New York state bar. The entire family celebrated. Both brothers were now lawyers, and sister Mary had married an attorney in Baltimore. Within a matter of weeks, William and Michael had entered into the partnership of Kunstler and Kunstler. The brothers had an uptown office on Fifth Avenue, but a rather ordinary practice. Their first case was a negligence suit against a taxicab company, settled for $1,500, from which the two brothers earned $500. The cab company's name was Paradise Taxi Company, and their client's surname was Christ. Other than the case caption of *Christ v. Paradise*, it was pure routine.

For the most part during the 1950s, William Kunstler handled divorces and annulments and did trust and estate work. "I was bored out of my skull," he later remembered. He did have a few unusual clients. His daughter recalls his discussion of a woman who would bring him cigar bands to put into a safety deposit box. Kunstler himself vividly recalled Mrs. Mae Wightman, a nearly blind woman for whom he drafted a will, believing she probably had no assets. After her decomposing body was discovered by the police in her cramped apartment, the Kunstler brothers discovered that the woman had land, mineral deposits, furniture, and other assets scattered over the United States and Canada. The will had created a trust for a mentally retarded niece. After the Kunstlers traced all the assets and liquidated them, they continued as trustees, investing the estate and making payments to their former client's niece. After Michael died in 1984, Bill Kunstler continued as the sole trustee. All through his career as a radical lawyer, throughout his defense of the Black Power advocates in the 1960s, the Chicago Seven, the revolutionaries of the 1970s, and the terrorists of the 1980s and 1990s, Kunstler continued with this last remnant of his former practice. Until 1994, when he finally asked for the appointment of a successor trustee, he faithfully invested Mrs. Wightman's assets and remitted funds to her niece.

Kunstler had two other unusual clients during the 1950s. One was Dylan Thomas, the poet he so much admired. Smith College refused to pay Thomas's speaking fee because the poet had sexually harassed a student. Kunstler arranged a settlement that Thomas used to travel back to Wales. At another point in the 1950s, incredibly enough for a radical lawyer, Kunstler drafted a will for the arch red-baiter, Senator Joseph McCarthy. It was at a time before McCarthy had reached the heights of his paranoia. Roy Cohn, ally in McCarthy's crusade, a classmate of Kunstler at Columbia Law School, and a colleague as adjunct professor at New York Law School, recommended Kunstler to Mc-Carthy.

He tried a few minor cases in his early practice. Lotte recalls that while he was never intimidated by judges, he held his flair in check in those days. He did not display the zeal and drive he would later. Even so, she thought he was satisfied with his early work. However, he told his friend Fred Marks at the time that he was "profoundly bored." Kunstler always had tremendous energy and need for intellectual stimulation. He assuaged his boredom throughout his years of tedious practice, before the civil rights movement, by teaching, writing, and broadcasting.

Even while in law school, Kunstler began teaching as a lecturer in English at Columbia University, teaching writing in its School of General Studies; he continued in that capacity from 1946 to 1950. He also taught as an associate professor of law at Pace College's Business School from 1951 to 1960. Kunstler often took his daughter Karin along to his classes, held on Saturday mornings, and had lunch with her on the way home. Kunstler was also a law professor at New York Law School from 1949 to 1961. He taught common law pleading, creditors' rights, conflicts, and trusts and estates, first as instructor, then assistant professor, and finally associate professor. His law students thought highly of him as a teacher. What surprised them after Kunstler became famous as a radical lawyer was that he had never talked about politics in class. Kunstler must have shown his theatrical tendencies to his colleagues, however, as a friend on the full-time faculty used to call him "Broadway Bill" with affection.

Roy Cohn taught at New York Law School as a colleague with Kunstler, just as he had been earlier a classmate at Columbia. When Cohn began his red-baiting hysteria with Senator McCarthy, Kunstler began to hate him. In fact, Kunstler regarded Roy Cohn as so vile and despicable that "when I heard he died of AIDS, for a moment I felt that perhaps there was a God." While teaching at New York Law School, Kunstler punished Cohn in a most creative manner. As in most evening division programs, the law school broke the night classes into two segments. Apparently there was just one men's room in the school's older quarters. According to Lotte, "Bill would go in there [the men's room] and lock the door until recess was over so that Cohn couldn't get in before he had to go back to class. I don't know if this is true. This is what he told me. Stories of that type were half, three-quarters made up."

Kunstler loved teaching. Lotte recalls a time when he took his entire class to visit Litchfield Law School in Litchfield, Connecticut. America's oldest law school, Litchfield began in the 1770s and its log cabin dates from 1784. The administrators of the historical monument allowed Kunstler to address his class inside the cabin. After he was fully engaged in the civil rights movement, very busy and traveling throughout the country, and even later, he returned to the classroom to teach. Kunstler taught as a lecturer in law at the New School for Social Research in the years 1965–66, 1970–71, and 1989. He served as a lecturer at Cooper Union in 1986–87. As late as the fall of 1992 he returned to New York Law School, and as a visiting professor of law taught a seminar in constitutional litigation with Arthur Kinoy.

Kunstler also wrote to relieve boredom. Before entering law school, he had wanted to become a writer, and even during law school Kunstler engaged in many literary projects. Primarily, he wrote book reviews. He turned out so many reviews for the *New York Herald Tribune* that the newspaper assigned him a pseudonym, David Tilden, so that it would not appear that one person was contributing so frequently. Paramount Films hired him to read books and articles, at twenty dollars apiece, and report on their suitability for films. Finally, he and his brother jointly published summaries of law courses to sell to fellow students. Kunstler undertook these activities partly to earn extra money, but also to satisfy the itch he still felt to write. While he was in law school, this extra income enabled Kunstler to move his family into their first home, an inexpensive apartment on Twenty-third Street in Queens.

He continued this work after law school and reviewed books for journals such as *Life*, the *Saturday Review*, and *Atlantic Monthly*. Kunstler's reviews appeared in newspapers as well, including the *New York Times*, *Chicago Tribune*, *Boston Herald*, *New York Sun*, *Omaha World Herald*, and *San Francisco Chronicle*. Writing reviews gave him free books, a few dollars of compensation, and publicity during a time, the 1950s, when lawyers could not advertise. He was very proud of these reviews and always told his friends when they were about to be published.

Kunstler continued to review books for years, but in the late 1950s he turned primarily to writing books. Kunstler's first books, excepting his earlier book of poetry at Yale, were short texts on legal topics, written in nontechnical language and designed for lay audiences. In that vein he wrote *The Law of Accidents* (1954), published by Oceana Publications, and *Corporate Tax Summary* (1954).

He published *First Degree*, a study of eighteen murder cases, in 1960, also with Oceana. This was a much longer book, better written and designed for a broader audience. In 1961 William Morrow and Company brought out Kunstler's next book, *Beyond a Reasonable Doubt? The Original Trial of Caryl Chessman*. Kunstler hit a broad span of the reading public through clear writing and the choice of a popular and controversial case. It sold well enough to be reprinted by Greenwood Press in 1973 and 1977. In 1961, Kunstler was in Los Angeles on a publisher's publicity tour for this book when he received the telephone call that he said would change his life forever.

That is a little ahead of our timeline. Before he received that call, he wrote still another book that was published in 1962, also by Morrow. This next book, *The Case for Courage*, was the last to be written before Kunstler's involvement in the civil rights movement. In some ways the book was a sort of legal takeoff on John Kennedy's *Profiles in Courage*. The publisher described its contents on the cover as "the stories of ten famous American attorneys who risked their careers in the cause of justice." It also was reprinted several times.

Years later, in the late 1980s, Kunstler had lunch one day with a friend in a West Village restaurant called Anglers & Writers. By then he was a famous radical lawyer, had published several books, even a bestseller in 1964, and had raised the general public's hackles and leftists' joys with many celebrated and controversial cases. People coming up to him in public places was by then a familiar occurrence. Kunstler was not surprised that day in the 1980s, while eating lunch with Brice Marden, when a man came up to him and told him that he had wanted to meet him for years. It seemed the man greatly admired one of Kunstler's early works, it had helped him greatly, and he wanted to thank him for it. Kunstler relished the adulation and absorbed it with ease. He inquired as to which of his early books the man so highly regarded. Could it be, he asked, *Our Pleasant Vices*—a work Kunstler always held dear? No, the man replied, it was his *Corporate Tax Summary.* It was one of the few times in his life that Kunstler was stumped. All he managed to say was "Oh, geez."

A law practice, teaching at three schools (even if part-time), writing a great number of book reviews in addition to four books, all in the period 1948–61, would be more than enough to fill up or absolutely exhaust the intellectual capacities of most men. All this activity was not enough to occupy Kunstler. During the late 1950s he also wrote radio scripts and broadcast several of his own shows.

Kunstler had begun to dabble in radio even earlier, while in law school. He was the host of a program begun in 1946, *World Security Workshop: World Issues on Trial.* The ABC station WJZ, later WABC, ran this weekly half-hour program as a courtroom debate, featuring a judge and counsel on either side of an international issue. Kunstler had very little of a role in this show, and used his resonant bass voice simply to introduce the "trial judge" and to sign off at the end, announcing the next week's program.

One of his earliest shows was *The Law on Trial,* in which Kunstler gave short descriptions of celebrated trials for the YMCA's radio station, WMCA. Later the station changed the name and format to *Pro and Con,* and in this show Kunstler interviewed various important people with differing viewpoints on controversial issues. These shows aired overseas through the Voice of America, as well as locally. Kunstler interviewed such people as Eleanor Roosevelt and Alger Hiss, and on March 3, 1960, he moderated and posed questions in a debate between William E. James, the noted Harlem minister, and Malcolm X. This was Malcolm X's first public debate. Still later, WMCA produced another show called *Justice,* in which hired actors dramatized famous trials, such as those of Jesus, John Brown, Sam Sheppard, and Sacco and Vanzetti. The station hired Kunstler to write the scripts and paid him $200 per trial.

In the late 1950s WNEW carried *Counterpoint*, a Sunday evening show in which Kunstler also interviewed people about controversial legal matters. In June 1958, for example, he interviewed Roy Cohn, one of the former prosecutors, and the law professor Malcolm P. Sharp concerning the Rosenberg-Sobell trial. WEVD, a left-of-center station named for Eugene Victor Debs, hired Kunstler in 1959 to produce one-man stories of famous trials, broadcast Friday evenings in prime time, 8:30–8:45. He narrated the trials of left-wing figures such as Alger Hiss and Julius and Ethel Rosenberg, but also nonpolitical defendants— Lizzie Borden, Leopold and Loeb, and even an early colonial woman, Anne Hutchinson, tried on trumped-up charges of sedition because of her religious views. Although it was a short program, Kunstler's skill and the favorable broadcast time brought the show much attention.

The *New York Times* favorably reviewed the *Famous Trials* show of WEVD in July 1959. The reviewer wrote that Kunstler "tells a lucid, straightforward narrative geared to the understanding of the layman; the inherent drama creates its own suspense. . . . Treated in an essentially uncolored way by Mr. Kunstler within the framework of his narrative, [the defendants] nonetheless emerge with definite personalities." The reviewer turned reporter and asked Kunstler what relation there was between his practice of law and the radio programs. Kunstler's answer in July 1959, long before he had acquired fame as a defense lawyer and developed a talent for media manipulation and theatricality, was prophetic: "Many lawyers are theatrical by the very nature of their profession. I feel that this quality can be effectively transmitted to radio."

Beginning in 1961, Kunstler's involvement in the civil rights movement absorbed so much of his time as to essentially close his broadcasting career, excepting the thousands of radio and television interviews and panels on which he was a participant. Kunstler made a brief return to the other side of the desk, as interviewer. He stood in for Barry Gray on his popular late-evening interview program for eight evenings in late September and early October 1962. He appealed to Martin Luther King, Jr. to participate in one segment, and he brought in Malcolm X for another.

According to Lotte, Kunstler enjoyed his radio shows immensely. "It was talking. It was an audience, anything with an audience." Also, he met very interesting people. Jayne Mansfield, the movie actress, amused him by primping before a radio interview as though she would be seen. Lotte accompanied him to the late-evening shows when he substituted for Barry Gray. She was amused by his commercials for Roquefort cheese because "he tried to do it so well. And I knew that the very thought of Roquefort cheese made him gag."

How did Kunstler do it? How did he find time for this hectic pro-fusion of books, multiple radio shows, and scripts—all in the midst of a law practice? Kunstler radiated nervous energy, and he had a great ca-pacity for work. He wrote, reviewed notes, or listened to tapes while in a cab, driving his car, or riding the commuter train. During the civil rights period and later, he worked on planes and in airport waiting rooms. He worked at all available moments, and even took papers to the bathtub for reading or editing. Much later Kunstler recalled with nostalgia that in the late 1950s out in the suburbs "every night I'd hang out in my attic and bang out these [radio] scripts." Lotte confirms this but adds that this meant "there wasn't that much family time."

In 1950 Kunstler moved his family, just increased the previous year by the birth of his second daughter, Jane. They settled in Port Chester (now Rye Beach) in Westchester County, taking advantage of his veteran's benefits for the financing. Kunstler lived here until 1965. His brother, Michael, and his family bought a house across the street, and the two brothers commuted together to their one-room office in New York. They garnered many clients from their neighborhood. There were over two hundred houses built in their suburb, and William Kunstler did the closings on most of them. In some respects, Kunstler was a typical suburban husband of the 1950s. He came back from New York at dinnertime, Lotte met him at the train station, and he went home.

Kunstler spent a great deal of time in the evenings working on his writing projects. However, he also mowed the lawn, listened to baseball games, and read. He read Dylan Thomas aloud to both his daughters, and Shakespeare, American history, and European history to himself. He helped Karin and Jane with their homework. On Saturdays he gen-erally listened to the Texaco Metropolitan Opera broadcasts, and occa-sionally to other opera through records. *Tosca, La Bohème,* and *La Travi-ata* were his favorites. Lotte adds that although Kunstler truly enjoyed listening to opera, and was often "transported" by his favorites, he was never as knowledgeable about music as he was about literature. Some men feel a freedom to express their emotions through opera in a way that our culture generally denies them. Kunstler was one of those. His friend Fred Marks recalls that Kunstler sometimes cried at the beauty of a favorite aria.

Bill and Lotte made good friends with several sets of their neighbors, including the Berners, Milton and Joan, the Gorens, Bernard and Doris, and the Martins, Mark and his wife, and participated in many social activities together. In the period before civil rights fame, the Kunstlers vacationed once in Europe with the Gorens and in Mexico once with the Berners. Kunstler persuaded Milton Berner to attend law school, and arranged for his acceptance to New York Law School. Milton studied around the calendar for two years, during which, especially when Milton studied for exams, Kunstler looked out for Milton's three boys and acted like a father to them. The couples all had young children, and their regular weekend activities included early-morning Saturday picnics at the reservoir or some other uncrowded public park. Kunstler was often in charge of cooking hamburgers or chicken, and almost always there was a baseball game. He was still fond of the New York Yankees, and he spoofed with the many kids involved in the gatherings that he, Kunstler, was Joe Pepitone, a then-famous Yankee ball player. Kunstler loved to play baseball in those years, and, with his fine persuasive abilities, he had the children half believing that he really was Pepitone. The festivities broke up in time for him to get home and listen to the Texaco broadcasts of the Metropolitan Opera.

He stayed very close to his sister, Mary, even though she lived in Baltimore after 1946, and for the rest of his life they talked on the telephone once a week, usually on Sundays. During the late 1940s and early 1950s Mary and her husband, Manny, drove to New York to spend a weekend with the Kunstlers every month and found time to be together over the holidays.

Occasionally he took his daughters to his office on the weekend. Karin recalls helping him collate papers. He played tennis and loved swimming. In warm weather Kunstler took the girls to Rye Beach, and in colder weather they went sleigh riding. He was already flamboyant and showed his flair for the dramatic even with his daughters. It sometimes embarrassed them.

Karin remembers an embarrassing incident when she was a freshman or sophomore in high school. She had been reading *Will Success Spoil Rock Hunter?* and the edition featured a large-breasted woman on the cover. Her teacher took it away from her, and the principal summoned her father to a conference with Karin present. Kunstler told the principal, "Right, I think this is a terrible book for a kid to read. I would rather have her reading *The Iliad* or something. But if this is what she picked, she can read it. If it's written on paper, let her read it. Give it back to her!"

He had a great love for animals. He surrounded himself with pets throughout his adult life. In the 1950s the family had cats, but Kunstler had always wanted a dog. One day, Jane recalls, a cabbie gave Kunstler a dog. The dog made a mess of their house and chewed on shoes and the kitchen tile. Lotte was the only one taking care of it, and eventually she revolted: the dog had to go. Kunstler gave it away, but then telephoned the new owner every week to ask how the dog was doing. Eventually the fellow tired of it and told Kunstler that he had called enough.

The Kunstlers also entertained frequently and attended others' parties. Lotte recalls that "Bill was a great guy to have at parties." He was "bright and knowledgeable, and full of bullshit." He could speak with authority about poetry and cultural matters as well as liberal politics. Some of his friends' recollections were darker. Fred Marks remembers that Kunstler "would be buoyant, noisy, apt to take off his clothes. He was constantly ripping off his shirt, showing off his physical attractions. So very often at a party, we'd see Bill in the buff." Everyone was supposed to admire his physique. Milton Berner, another friend, agrees that Kunstler was the life of the party and that he "would go into some sort of a dance or start to strip," but all in fun.

Berner recalls him in the late 1950s at parties, poised to enter a room, looking around to see who was there to make sure he was noticed. Already, glasses perched up on his forehead were Kunstler's calling card and trademark. In time, these glasses became a symbol of Kunstler, but actually they were purchased over the counter and were quite inexpensive. Kunstler bought them in multiple pairs. He often lost his glasses, then found them again on top of his head. Sometimes, inadvertently he wore two pairs on top of his forehead. But in the 1950s he used the glasses as a way of making sure everybody knew when he walked into a room.

Just as later in his life, so in the 1950s: Kunstler talked incessantly. He was very entertaining and funny at parties, and told stories (including his stock of Pa Moe stories) with a sense of drama. He captured attention quickly and always acted as though he were on stage with the spotlight turned on him. Many friends liked to be with him for the en-

tertainment, but some disliked his self-centered habit of always bringing the conversation around to what he was doing. He was always performing, and he changed his stories and his approach to them depending on the feedback he received from his audiences. Milton Berner felt
that Kunstler's craving for attention was fueled by "a need to be accepted and approved by the people that knew him."

Lotte recalls that while they did have a family life in the 1950s, her
husband "did not put aside something that really interested him for
family life." In other words, his self-centeredness continued. They both
loved entertaining, but Kunstler never helped with the work. A telling
incident occurred when Karin was six years old and wanted to visit her
aunt Mary in Baltimore. Lotte took her down for a weekend and Kunstler agreed to stay home and care for Jane, then three months old. Lotte
remembers,

> When I came back, Jane was . . . unwashed and practically unchanged.
> [Her] diaper was sopping wet and I said to Bill . . . if I ever wanted to
> go away again, I would really hesitate. . . . I said, "You could do bet-
> ter." He said, "Well, I could. But if I did, you would ask me to do it
> again." He made no bones about it. He didn't want to be stuck for
> forty-eight hours with a baby.

In the late 1950s Lotte started going to college, an experience she
had missed by marrying young. Transportation in the suburbs drove
Lotte to despair. Only after she had driven her husband to the train station and then taken their two daughters to school could she take a train
to New York to attend Hunter College. Then she had to dash back to
Port Chester and repeat the two transportation legs. She asked if he
could take a taxi to the station or join a carpool, so she might squeeze a
couple more hours into her day. Kunstler responded that he could not
be held to the hours of a carpool, could not afford a taxi, and could not
take a taxi at night because "it was so lonely" not being picked up by his
wife. Lotte was able to attend college only one semester and had to wait
until their separation to complete her education.

Bill and Lotte were active in progressive causes and interested in
the politics of civil rights long before 1961, although neither could be
considered an activist. They joined the NAACP and the Urban League,
wrote letters to the editor, organized meetings, and tried to steer local
politics in a liberal direction. Kunstler was associated also with the

Committee on Social Action of the American Jewish Congress. In the late 1950s the Kunstlers gave summer space to a black youth from Harlem.

In the mid-1950s Paul Redd, the head of the local NAACP, found himself unable to rent an apartment in Port Chester and alleged discrimination. His lawyer asked Bill and Lotte Kunstler to obtain evidence by shilling: inquiring of landlords whether an apartment was available and then sending in black applicants. If the landlord indicated availability to the whites and unavailability to the blacks, then there was prima facie evidence of discrimination. Kunstler helped win that case and then began to organize groups of people to demonstrate against discrimination and to serve as shills.

This excited him. At home, he talked about this work and his growing enthusiasm for it, more than his practice. At the same time, he began acquiring a local reputation for "radicalism" in the working-class, conservative town of Port Chester. As early as 1956, a friend and then president of the local chamber of commerce had difficulty persuading his colleagues that Kunstler would be an appropriate person to talk to their meeting. Karin was red-baited in her school, and there were racial slurs as well. Once her science teacher inquired if she were going to an upcoming high school dance. When she replied that she was, the teacher asked whether she had a date. When Karin told him that she did, he replied that it was probably "with a nigger." Karin recalls that sort of incident happening a lot, because of her father's local reputation, even before 1961, when he began his work for the civil rights movement in the South.

In 1956 Rowland Watts, the legal director of the American Civil Liberties Union, referred a case to him of constitutional dimensions. William Worthy, a black journalist from Baltimore, had traveled to China in violation of the restrictions then printed by the State Department on American passports. The federal government confiscated Worthy's passport upon his return to the "land of the free," and refused to issue him another.

Kunstler sued for the return of Worthy's passport in the district court of the District of Columbia. His efforts brought him into contact with Leonard Boudin, then one of the leading lights of progressive lawyers, who taught Kunstler a great deal about the techniques of constitutional litigation against federal agencies. Although the lawsuit led nowhere and Kunstler lost, it permitted him to experience, as he later put it, a first "taste for a certain kind of law where you are dealing with national issues, constitutions and the rights of individuals."

A few years later Worthy needed to do research on Cuba, another country the federal government prohibited Americans from visiting. As he did not have a passport, Worthy used an affidavit of identity to enter Cuba. When he tried to return home, the federal government arrested him and charged him under an archaic statute criminalizing a return to the United States without a valid passport. Kunstler represented him on the criminal trial, lost, and then argued the appeal in 1961. The court of appeals struck down the statute, holding it unconstitutional for the government to create a crime out of an American citizen's return without a passport. Although the appeal was argued and the opinion came down after Kunstler's entry into civil rights work, the work energized him and confirmed his direction:

> This was my first experience arguing an issue about which I felt passionate. . . . This was the first time I had ever invalidated a statute. . . . Let the other lawyers draft wills and do real estate closings. I had *changed* the law! I had made a contribution! I felt an enormous thrill and a desire for more of the same.

William Worthy's trial as well as his work with the NAACP in Port Chester primed Kunstler and rendered him receptive to another telephone call from Rowland Watts. This time the experience transformed Kunstler's life.

4

The Shock of the South

THE CALL REACHED Kunstler in Los Angeles early on the morning of June 15, 1961. Rowland Watts, the legal director of the American Civil Liberties Union, telephoned to ask if Kunstler could fly to Jackson, Mississippi, on his way home from Los Angeles to New York. Freedom Riders were being arrested by the hundreds, and only one overworked lawyer was available to help them. "You don't have to do anything," Watts assured Kunstler. "Just introduce yourself to [Jack] Young and tell him that the American Civil Liberties Union is ready to help him in any way it can." Kunstler agreed.

The Freedom Riders started their journey in the spring of 1961. Sponsored by the Congress of Racial Equality (CORE), a northern civil rights organization, small, integrated groups of mostly young people started out on bus journeys to the South. Their purpose was to test and challenge the segregation of waiting and eating facilities in bus and train stations. Since 1955, the Interstate Commerce Commission had banned segregation by interstate carriers. However, segregation continued in waiting rooms and eating facilities in the stations. The viability of continued segregation in the bus and train stations had been thrown into doubt by a December 1960 ruling of the United States Supreme Court that reversed a Virginia conviction under a trespass statute. A black man who was in interstate travel had refused to leave the white section of a restaurant in the Richmond Trailways bus terminal. The Court reasoned that the defendant had a federal right to remain in the white portion of the restaurant since he was there as an interstate passenger and the federal statute mandated equal treatment. The Freedom Riders set about to test the actual effect in the South of this December 1960 ruling.

The southern authorities permitted white mobs to brutally attack the Riders in South Carolina and especially in Alabama, where their bus was firebombed and destroyed. The Riders then proceeded to Jackson,

Mississippi, where they experienced not violence but a different tactic. The police arrested them all, black and white, when they refused to leave the terminal or white areas of its restaurants and washrooms. The Mississippi authorities cleverly did not arrest the Riders for trespassing, the traditional southern technique that the Supreme Court had just struck down in its December 1960 ruling. Instead, Mississippi had recently enacted a new statute criminalizing the congregating of persons "under circumstances such that a breach of the peace may be occasioned thereby." The Riders' protest was entirely peaceable and quiet. But under this statute, since ruffians arguably were likely to attack the Riders, Mississippi could arrest the protesters for disturbing the peace. In other words, instead of being protected, the victims were punished for upsetting local rednecks.

James Farmer, the head of CORE, was arrested after riding the second bus to arrive in Jackson. From his cell he issued a call, and hundreds of young people flooded into Mississippi to defy the segregation of the Illinois Central train station, the airport, and the two bus terminals. Their experience was the same as the first waves of Freedom Riders. Unlike in Alabama, there was no violence. Instead, racially mixed groups were all efficiently arrested for disturbing the peace. In the midst of these mass arrests, Watts asked Kunstler to carry the ACLU's message of support to the sole attorney handling Riders' cases.

When Kunstler found a frantic Jack Young in his office and extended the regards of the ACLU, Young made it clear he did not want regards. He needed other lawyers to help. "Fuck the ACLU," he said. "I need bodies here. I'm going crazy." He suggested that Kunstler go over to the Greyhound station, where there would be fresh arrests as soon as the next bus came in, and then come back to talk.

There were good reasons for Young to feel so frantic. Southern lawyers willing to represent civil rights defendants on federal constitutional grounds were threatened with disbarment, beatings, bombing of their homes, arrest and harassment for specious charges, and the ruin of their practices. Charles Morgan, Jr., of Alabama and William L. Higgs of Mississippi, two white lawyers who represented civil rights advocates, eventually were forced to flee. As a result, few southern lawyers were willing to represent civil rights clients. Southern demagogues frequently charged that racial strife was fomented by "outside agitators." If they had northern lawyers in mind, they were in a sense correct. Northern lawyers did carry the brunt of civil rights litigation along with the few black lawyers in the South, but primarily because the gentle-men of the southern bar abandoned their ethical duty to defend the powerless without regard to personal considerations or popularity. In the event, in 1961 there were only four lawyers in Mississippi, three black and one white, willing to take on civil rights cases, and the bulk of the work fell on Young.

Kunstler went over to the bus station and observed five young Rid-ers arrested for their failure to leave a lunch counter when they sat down at empty stools. The incident angered him, and he returned to Young's office willing to enter the fray. They tried various techniques, including federal habeas corpus petitions to test the legality of the Rid-ers' arrests, alleging that the "breach of peace" statute was simply a pre-text for continued illegal discrimination. Their pleas were rejected. Fed-eral judges told them that they could not raise these issues until they had been convicted and appealed in the state courts.

Later in the civil rights struggle, the federal courts evolved a doc-trine through which they could stop state prosecutions in advance if the purpose of the criminal prosecution was unconstitutional; Kunstler was a cocounsel in *Dombrowski v. Pfister,* the 1965 case that established this. But as things stood in 1961, a Mississippi defendant charged with breach of the peace was initially tried in a municipal court, and upon conviction had to file an appeal bond to obtain a new trial in the county court. Upon reconviction, appeal was to the circuit court and then to the Mississippi Supreme Court. Only then, in 1961, could the federal courts become involved.

In the process of making and losing his arguments, Kunstler expe-rienced the full force of southern bigotry and ignorance. In his June 21, 1961, argument before the federal district court on the habeas corpus writ, the first time Kunstler had argued a case outside of New York state, he mentioned a cross-burning incident that had occurred in Rye, New York, not in the South at all. Kunstler contended that "it is an in-decency that the symbol of Christianity should be used to sanctify seg-regation and discrimination." That remark, touching on both race and religion, the twin sources of southern bigotry, moved a gentleman in the rear of the room to rise and bellow at Kunstler, "Why don't you shut your goddamned mouth and stay the hell out of Mississippi!"

The next day Kunstler called upon the Mississippi governor, Ross Barnett, concerning a Rider who had gone on a hunger strike while in-carcerated in the state penitentiary (the Riders were not held in jails for their misdemeanors but in the state prison). After he had stated his business and had turned to leave, the governor stopped him and asked, "Just why are you mixed up with these trouble makers?" Kunstler responded with vague generalities about brotherhood and human dignity.

> He looked at me quizzically. "Mr. Kunstler," he asked, "do you have any children?" I nodded. "Two girls," I replied.
>
> His tone hardened. "Mr. Kunstler," he snapped, "what would you think if your daughter married a dirty, kinky-headed, fieldhand nigger?"
>
> It was my turn to raise my voice. "I think that such a step would be her own responsibility. She has a right to select her own husband."
>
> The governor looked stricken. "Mr. Kunstler," he roared, "that sounds like some of the Eleanor Roosevelt junk. If it were my daughter, I'd disown her."
>
> I tried to point out to him that I didn't think that marrying white women was the goal of Negroes involved in the integration movement, but he would have none of this. "That's all the niggers want," he retorted.

Kunstler wrote in his 1966 civil rights memoir that it was this conversation that finally convinced him. A few days earlier Charles Oldham, a St. Louis attorney and another of CORE's leaders, had asked him if he would like to work regularly with Jack Young to defend the four hundred or so Riders who were in various stages of Mississippi's criminal law system. Kunstler had asked for time to think. But following his conversation with Ross Barnett, he went to Young's office, called Oldham, and told him, "if you still want me, I'm available." An example of Kunstler's personal friendliness with his opponents came two years after this conversation. Kunstler was in Jackson and passing by the governor's mansion when a colleague pointed out that the governor's son, about thirty years old, had just walked out of the mansion. Kunstler vigorously waved at him, and a somewhat confused Barnett walked over. Kunstler introduced himself when suddenly the young man remembered who Kunstler was, "gulped, backed away, and, walking fast, escaped to the other side of the street."

Kunstler tried other extraordinary remedies in defense of the Riders, including state habeas corpus writs and an appeal to the federal circuit court of the denial by the federal district court, all to no avail. Then he tried another somewhat quirky weapon, the federal removal statute. This statute was passed by the Reconstruction Congress in 1866 and provided that if a criminal defendant alleged that he could not get a fair trial in a state court, he could file a petition to that effect with a federal district court and serve it upon the state court. Doing this *required* the federal court to take jurisdiction, at least temporarily, and *required* the federal court to set bail. To be sure, state prosecutors could then file motions in the federal courts asking the federal judge to remand or send a case back to the state court. Some state prosecutors were not aware of the remand procedure, and even if they were, the removal gave the protesters a temporary victory and respite from the authorities' steady oppression, and permitted their release on reasonable bail so that they could resume their protests or go back home.

One of Kunstler's true claims to fame in the civil rights movement is his refinement of the removal procedure into a standard technique of the movement. It is not quite true that this removal procedure "lay practically dormant until 1961, when it was disinterred, singlehandedly, by William Kunstler," as an article in the *Village Voice* claimed in 1964. Kunstler always told interviewers and wrote in his memoir and autobiography that William L. Higgs pointed the statute out to him. But apparently Kunstler was the first attorney in the modern period to actually use the procedure.

At first Kunstler found little success with removal. In the Riders' cases, the federal trial judge to whom the case was assigned granted the state's motion to send the cases back to the state courts. Judge William Harold Cox, a blatant racist appointed by John F. Kennedy, dismissed Kunstler's argument and abundant evidence that the legislature's purpose for the new breach of peace statute was to continue segregation by indirect means. Cox found that the Riders, many of whom after Farmer's call were clergymen and professors, were "counterfeit citizens from other states deliberately asking to cause trouble" and not entitled to federal protection. He called them "publicity clients" and sent their cases back to the state court. One of Kunstler's embellishments grew out of this incident. In later years he claimed to have won this round. In 1992 he was quoted as saying, "But Cox, who was a bastard but at least read the law, he granted the motion." The temporary removal was automatic upon Kunstler's filing; the only motion Cox granted was the state's to send the cases back to the state courts.

Meanwhile in the state justice system, Mississippi was throwing every roadblock it could to hinder the Riders. The state was systematically unreasonable in setting bail, grouping cases for trial, and refusing to permit more than four out-of-state lawyers from representing the Riders. The idea was to bleed the movement by requiring the Riders to come back and forth from all over the country for various phases of their judicial process. Ultimately, a complete record was made of the first case to come up for jury trial. A team of lawyers represented the state and a team of lawyers represented the defendant. Kunstler handled the preliminary motion to dismiss because of the systematic exclusion of blacks from jury service. After an extended trial, probably the longest misdemeanor trial in Mississippi history, it took an all-white, all-male, all-Mississippi jury only forty minutes to convict the defendant of breaching the peace for the heinous acts of riding quietly into town on a bus and sitting down at a lunch counter.

This first case established an ample record for appellate review, and thereafter CORE began to advise defendants to plead no contest. Ultimately, in 1965, the U.S. Supreme Court reversed the Rider conviction, on the same theory it had used to reverse the trespass conviction of the interstate passenger in Virginia five years earlier, that the equality of interstate commerce extends to the station facilities. Even before that happened, the Interstate Commerce Commission tightened its regulations and clearly forbade segregation in terminal facilities. The agitation of the Riders had forced the reluctant Kennedy administration to move forward on the issue.

Back in New York and almost a week after the Rider trial ended, Kunstler received another significant telephone call. Wyatt Walker, the executive director of the Southern Christian Leadership Conference (SCLC), Martin Luther King, Jr.'s organization, called Kunstler to ask if he could join him in Monroe, North Carolina. Some Riders returning to their homes from Mississippi had stopped to participate in demonstrations in Monroe. Ultimately there were fights with white mobs, and the returning Riders were arrested for picketing charges and inciting to riot. Kunstler represented the defendants in their trial, along with Len Holt, a very competent and articulate black lawyer active in Virginia. The judge acquitted the defendants of the picketing charges, convicted them of inciting to riot, but suspended their sentences.

Robert F. Williams, a local civil rights leader, had been responsible for inviting the Riders to Monroe. Williams was a prototype of the later

Black Power advocate. He believed in armed self-defense for blacks, drilled his followers in tactics and marksmanship, and was an avowed admirer of Fidel Castro. In summarizing the results of the Monroe trial, Kunstler wrote to Walker that "it was a grievous error for the Riders to associate themselves with Williams, but I feel that we did the best we could with a difficult situation." In later years, Kunstler's views on black empowerment through arms reflected his growing radicalization. Kunstler eventually accepted the right of the ghetto to arm for self-defense. In the summer of 1969 he told a Black Panther rally in Oakland, California, that "the right to self-defense legally is tied up intimately with the right of self-protection of the black ghetto. Without that self-protection, the black ghetto is at the mercy of whatever power structure happens to sit in the city halls throughout this country."

Immediately after the Monroe trials, Kunstler dashed to Washington, D.C., and attended the CORE convention. Clearly, he was becoming hooked on his growing civil rights practice. Wyatt Walker called him again within days after he had returned to New York. Walker had two requests. First, there was more trouble in Monroe. During one of the melees, a white husband and wife, not involved in the disturbances, claimed they were forced into Williams's house by several Riders. Four Riders allegedly had been involved, and the SCLC wanted Kunstler to represent John Lowry, a white Rider facing these kidnapping charges. Second, there was a query from Martin Luther King, who wanted to know whether Kunstler would speak briefly on legal aspects of the Freedom Rides at the forthcoming annual convention of the SCLC in Nashville in late September.

Kunstler quickly agreed to both requests and took Lotte with him to Nashville on September 27, 1961. When they arrived at the dining room of the conference motel, Walker met them and suggested he meet Martin Luther King. He conducted them to King's table, where they dined with Martin and Coretta. It was their first direct meeting. Kunstler felt comfortable with King and was very favorably impressed. Apparently King was equally impressed with him. Kunstler would write in 1994 that it was at this meeting that King asked him to serve as his special counsel on matters unsuited for his regular attorneys, the Legal Defense and Educational Fund Inc. (more commonly, the "Inc Fund") of the NAACP. The dramatic story told in 1994 of this "purpose behind this casually arranged meeting" may be one of Kunstler's embellishments, as a more contemporary writing in 1966 states that "I don't remember what we discussed that night," although he realized that King was a most unusual man.

Whether the offer was made then or at a later time, or is merely implicit from a series of representations that Kunstler later made for King is really immaterial. It is clear that both Lotte and Bill Kunstler were nearly mesmerized by the speech King gave the following evening and that Kunstler did thereafter undertake specifically commissioned assignments from the SCLC and King, representing specific clients in specific situations. This relationship has been often confused. Some reporters have written that Kunstler was King's personal attorney, which is untrue, or that he was King's special trial counsel, which is also untrue. On the other hand, some Inc Fund lawyers have denied that Kunstler ever did any work on behalf of King, and that is equally untrue.

Kunstler himself best described the relationship in a correction letter to a reporter dated November 30, 1964:

> I am not counsel to Dr. Martin Luther King, Jr. In the past, I have served as trial counsel to the Southern Christian Leadership Conference in various parts of the south but I have never been Dr. King's personal attorney. There are many lawyers who do legal work for him in the civil rights field and, while I am proud to be among them, I am only one of many who so act.

Much later Kunstler somewhat ruefully acknowledged that "over the years I received many special assignments from Martin and remained loyal to him, although I never joined his inner circle." He clearly would have liked to. Kunstler claimed that King had congratulated him on several occasions, and objective evidence supports this. When Fred Shuttlesworth was languishing in a Birmingham jail and both the federal and state courts refused to aid him, King sent out a circular letter to black clergy asking for donations. He wrote, "We had to secure additional counsel to . . . free him. William Kunstler, Esq., of New York City is now in our employ on this matter. . . . SCLC is responsible for all these expenses." In an unusual procedure, Kunstler filed a writ of habeas corpus directly with the Supreme Court that induced that body to act quickly and order Shuttlesworth's release. When Kunstler wrote King to report on the complete victory, King responded in a personal letter on December 30, 1963: "Thank you for sending me a copy of the decision. . . . I, too, am happy to know that it resulted in a complete victory. You certainly did a magnificent job on this case, as you have done in so many others. We are eternally indebted to you for your great legal work."

Kunstler made it amply clear in letters to Wyatt Walker and Martin Luther King that he felt privileged to be a part of the civil rights movement, that he was inspired by it, and that his services were available. Not only did King commission Kunstler's legal work but he had social contact with him as well. King entertained Kunstler on occasion while he was in the South, and Martin and Coretta extended their hospitality to both Kunstlers on several occasions when Bill brought Lotte along with him. Wyatt Walker, King's executive director, also entertained the Kunstlers, was entertained by them, and hired Kunstler to represent him personally in a civil rights trial.

There were good reasons why King and Walker would need occasional help from specially commissioned lawyers. The different civil rights organizations generated considerable squabbling among themselves. The grandfather organization, the NAACP, had thousands of black members in the South. By the 1950s and 1960s it had become quite conservative, financed by northern middle-class money, and was interested in establishing legal precedent through appeals to the U.S. Supreme Court, primarily in the area of school desegregation. The NAACP had little interest in mass picketing, protests, or demonstrations. Although nominally independent, its legal arm, the Inc Fund, shared the conservative bent of the parent group.

CORE was primarily a northern group, whereas King's SCLC was primarily southern. The Student Nonviolent Coordinating Committee (SNCC) was a very activist group of young people, interested in confrontations, sit-ins, demonstrations, and the like. Several individual lawyers and lawyers' organizations represented these groups. These lawyers' groups all squabbled as well, but the greatest friction was between the Inc Fund and National Lawyers Guild (NLG) lawyers. Kunstler was a member of the National Lawyers Guild.

In general, Kunstler and other NLG attorneys were more daring and imaginative, more supportive of demonstrations and sit-ins, less legalistic, and less interested in whether they antagonized the local power structure. Generally, they had a strong personal commitment to the activists' goals. The Inc Fund lawyers demanded control over the trials and tactics of local affiliates, whereas the NLG attorneys deferred to the desires of the activists they represented. In addition to major differences in tactics, the NAACP was very concerned about the image of the National Lawyers Guild as a communist organization. The NAACP worried that it would be red-baited and that any association with the NLG would support the segregationists' equation of integration with communism. In some cases these antagonisms became very personal. For example, Jack Greenberg, the head of the Inc Fund, quit a civil rights bar's coordinating committee when Kunstler became a member. His second in command, Constance Baker Motley, now a federal judge, insisted as late as 1996 that she was sure Martin Luther King never asked Kunstler to do anything for him as a lawyer.

King's primary legal representation and that of the SCLC was through the Inc Fund. However, there were civil rights cases in which he or his organization became interested that did not fit the pattern the Inc Fund desired, and that required more dash or more obstreperousness. Amidst all this antipathy, King occasionally used an outside attorney. It was in this context that he called upon Kunstler from time to time.

Kunstler jumped into the civil rights movement. It more than just excited him. As Fred Marks, a personal friend, put it, he "started living. This is what his whole life was directed towards. The civil rights movement provided an outlet for energy and for interests that were just made for him." In the North, Kunstler wrote letters on civil rights matters to the *New York Times* and his local newspaper, published articles in the *Nation*, and sponsored and participated in numerous fund-raisers. In the late fall of 1962 Lotte organized a major fund-raising event for King in Westchester County. The Kunstlers' older daughter, Karin, spent a term of her college years at Tougaloo, a historically black college outside Jackson. Kunstler also organized local protests over housing for minorities in the Westchester community where he lived, and testified before congressional committees.

His major efforts were in the South. Kunstler was everywhere. In the years 1962–65 Kunstler practically lived on airplanes, dashing about the South, then back and forth from New York. Kunstler thought of himself as an itinerant lawyer in the American colonial tradition. Borrowing from *Have Gun—Will Travel*, a popular television western of the day, he chose as a motto "Have Writ, Will Travel." We can discuss only a few of the thousands of matters Kunstler handled during these years.

Martin Luther King often organized his work along campaigns for the desegregation of specific cities, modeled somewhat after Billy

Graham's religious crusades. Kunstler participated in the campaigns in Albany, Georgia (1962–63), Danville, Virginia (1963), Birmingham, Alabama (1963), and St. Augustine, Florida (1964). In these locales, Kunstler represented the protesters, tried to remove state or city prosecutions to federal court, arranged for bail, and often brought innovative lawsuits, such as federal cases seeking to halt the actions of local sheriffs and judges. In short, Kunstler developed a much more aggressive response than merely defending the matters in which the protesters were accused. In Birmingham he became a demonstrator himself. At King's request, Kunstler also represented Thomas Wansley, a black man facing a trumped-up capital conviction in Lynchburg, Virginia; John Lowry for kidnapping; the pray-in movement in Jackson; and Fred Shuttlesworth's conviction and jailing in Birmingham for a bus protest incident going back to 1958.

Kunstler was an important participant in *Dombrowski v. Pfister* (1965), a monumental case in which the U.S. Supreme Court held that a federal court could halt racially motivated state criminal prosecutions without waiting for the state procedure to run its course, and *Hobson v. Hanson* (1967), which halted the District of Columbia's school tracking and placement system based on racially biased intelligence tests. This gave blacks much greater educational opportunities, and Kunstler told reporters many times that *Hobson* was the single most gratifying case of his career. In 1964 Kunstler actively participated in Freedom Summer, when dozens of northern lawyers went to Mississippi to protect the college students who attempted to register black voters.

After the Mississippi Freedom Democratic Party lost its challenge to the Mississippi delegation at the 1964 Democratic Convention, it fired its more conservative lawyers and chose Kunstler and Kinoy as its lead attorneys to oppose the seating of the congressional representatives from Mississippi in January 1965. Kunstler, Arthur Kinoy, and Morton Stavis took over ten thousand pages of depositions that clearly established that Mississippians dismissed blacks from their jobs, beat them, and sometimes even killed them, for attempting to vote. Although the challenge itself failed, the documentary evidence Kunstler and those helping him obtained and the publicity surrounding the effort were of crucial importance in the passage of the Voting Rights Act in 1965.

These are just samples of Kunstler's work. It is difficult to appraise the exact contribution of any one participant to the legal phase of the civil rights struggle because most cases were handled by teams of attorneys. Kunstler rarely acted alone. Especially after 1963, he often teamed with Arthur Kinoy, who was briefly an actual partner in Kunstler, Kunstler and Kinoy. Lotte accompanied him on some of his trips to the South. She was present at the SCLC convention, many court hearings, and several meetings with King, and she participated as a demonstrator in the Albany campaign.

As he dashed around the South, Kunstler's very arrival improved the morale of protesters locked in a southern jail. He inspired confidence. Fred Shuttlesworth, an active black leader in Birmingham, recalls that Kunstler "was a very jovial type person. If you were with him, you [would be] titillated at his humor, his sense of humor and his ability to carry on a conversation. You never doubted that he was real in what he did. I never had that thought. I didn't think that he was down here posturing." Kunstler was brave as well; more than once southern ruffians threatened him with bodily harm.

As a result of his personality, bravery, innovative tactics (primarily turning the tables on the power structure by suing it), and constant presence, Kunstler acquired a considerable reputation in the civil rights community. Len Holt, himself an almost legendary civil rights lawyer, wrote in 1965 that Kunstler was "among the best known American lawyers because of his extensive and creative work in civil rights litigation." Howard Zinn, an activist with SNCC, said in 1965 that Kunstler was "one of the legal mainstays of the movement" and called him a "brilliant and seasoned lawyer."

While engaged in his civil rights work, Kunstler continued and extended some of the personality traits we have already seen. The civil rights movement gave him an abundance of opportunities for myth making and embellishment on the truth. It also allowed him to indulge in his penchant for grabbing the spotlight in dramatic moments. As for embellishments, the best example is the myth he developed that his civil rights work was all pro bono, that is, without fee. A 1968 interview quoted Kunstler directly as saying, "I have never taken fees on any civil rights case that I can recall." A reporter in 1980, quoting him indirectly, wrote that "from the time Kunstler started taking civil rights cases, he insisted that he would not, on principle, accept any fees." He repeated this in his 1994 autobiography.

In fact, during the summer of 1961 while defending the Freedom Riders, Kunstler was on a monthly retainer from CORE, the sponsoring organization. Thereafter, the different civil rights organizations often split Kunstler's traveling expenses, although it appears from the correspondence that the ACLU paid the lion's share of travel money. Kunstler apparently charged the SCLC a $500 fee for representing the Riders in Monroe, North Carolina. The value of money in 1961 was approximately five times that of now, so that fees quoted here are in 2000 about five times their stated values. Snippets from the correspondence between Kunstler and Walker undeniably show the economic nature of Kunstler's Monroe representation. Walker to Kunstler (October 25, 1961): "I am enclosing a check in the amount of $250.00 as a partial payment of the $500.00 due you. We will forward the balance at a later date." Kunstler to Walker (October 26, 1961): "Your check came in a few moments ago, and I am most appreciative. If all my clients were as prompt as SCLC, my economic life would be considerably rosier." Kunstler to Walker (January 23, 1962): "If you can shake our $250.00 loose from your coffers, I'd appreciate it." Walker to Kunstler (January 26, 1962): "Just as soon as we get through this 'desert period,' we will take care of the balance on your fee."

On the Fred Shuttlesworth matter, Kunstler sent the SCLC a bill dated March 30, 1962, for the "balance of Shuttlesworth retainer" in the amount of $250, which was paid under cover of a letter from Walker on May 31, 1962. On the Thomas Wansley case, the SCLC's general counsel sent Kunstler a check for $1,000 (again, about $5,000 today) on October 23, 1963, "for services rendered jointly by you, Messrs. Arthur Kinoy and Len Holt, pursuant to a request for assistance from the Society made by Rev. Wyatt Tee Walker." On the John Lowry kidnapping matter, Kunstler quoted a $1,000 retainer in 1961 and after a nine-day trial asked the SCLC for an additional fee of $100 per day and indicated that he would attempt to get an additional sum from a defense committee.

These may not be huge fees. Compared to his previous house closings and divorces, however, they are not inconsiderable. Kunstler unquestionably did some civil rights work without fee, and on other occasions he waived a fee already billed. Nevertheless, his claim that he did his civil rights work without fee is just not true.

The dramatic moments came most readily for Kunstler in the various victory celebrations. During the 1964 St. Augustine campaign, the sheriff issued an order banning further demonstrations. Kunstler promptly sued the sheriff in federal court for a judgment forbidding such high-handed orders. The hearings brought out that the sheriff had hired Klansmen as deputies, and Kunstler won an indication from the judge that an injunction against the sheriff would soon be issued. A local black church held a celebration service the night the hearings concluded. The preacher drew great applause as he told of the discomforting of the local sheriff during the day's hearing. Just then, Kunstler entered the church. As a witness described it, Kunstler

> came forward with arms outstretched, grinning, and Reverend Vivian moved down from the pulpit to meet him, and these two men, white and black, northern and southern, embraced each other there in front of a church full of people who had seldom seen this sort of thing before, and in the silence of seeing it, a sweet soprano voice rose, and others joined it, and they sang to it—this sight that said so much, still, of the meaning and truth and simple hope of the movement—sang "Amazing Grace/How sweet the sound . . ."

Of course, this was a genuinely dramatic moment, but Kunstler fully exploited its potential. Another high drama came during the 1963 "pray-ins" in Jackson, Mississippi. An integrated group of mostly Tougaloo students was arrested when it tried quietly to enter the Capitol Street Methodist Church for worship. Kunstler and Arthur Kinoy were summoned and immediately filed removal papers to transfer the cases to federal court. After a day's hearing, Judge Cox, the racist judge we have met before, refused to sign writs to place the defendants in federal custody. Kunstler and Kinoy went to Atlanta and obtained an order from the Fifth Circuit Court of Appeals directing Cox to issue the writ; a bail hearing was thereafter held in Jackson, and the students were released.

A rally ensued in the Tougaloo chapel. Lotte had joined Kunstler in Atlanta for the hearing before the Fifth Circuit.

> When Lotte and I tried to find empty seats in the rear of the room, a group of students seized my arms and rushed me up to the platform. . . . As each of the students finished describing his or her experiences in jail, the entire audience broke into a freedom song. By the time it was my turn to say a few words, I had become so caught up in the emotion of the evening that it was difficult to speak.

"I can't tell you how much meaning you have given to my life," I blurted out. "Without you as my clients and my friends, I would never have known how deeply I could feel about people and ideals. It makes much more sense for me to thank you than for you to thank me."

Since he was active in the Birmingham campaign, Kunstler learned of King's "Letter from the Birmingham Jail" before most people and instantly recognized it for the classic it would become. Kunstler volunteered himself for a book to be jointly written by himself and King, but his offer was set aside as opportunistic. Eventually, however, King did write a foreword to Kunstler's civil rights memoir and Kunstler wrote one for an early edition of King's *Why We Can't Wait*.

The Thomas Wansley capital rape case and the Danville campaign brought Kunstler into an important association with Arthur Kinoy. Following two trials, in the spring of 1963 Virginia sentenced Thomas Wansley, a seventeen-year-old black youth of limited intelligence, to death for the rape of two white women. The trial court refused to permit the making of a transcript, notwithstanding the defendant's request for a continuance to arrange for a reporter at his own expense. In the second trial, the trial judge advised the jury, pursuant to its inquiry, that a life sentence would not necessarily imprison Wansley for life. Needless to say, there had been an extensive amount of adverse pretrial publicity. In contrast to Wansley's death sentence, a white defendant, convicted the same week for rape in the same city, received probation. Just a few weeks before the execution date, Wansley's lawyer died. At that point, the SCLC asked Kunstler to look at the case.

Kunstler, desperately busy with other civil rights work, called on Arthur Kinoy, a classmate from Columbia, to carry the laboring oar on the appeal. Kinoy performed brilliantly and induced the Virginia Supreme Court to reverse the convictions. Thereafter, Kunstler took a dominant role at the retrial, along with Arthur Kinoy and several other lawyers—the typical team approach. A retrial on one of the rape charges resulted in a hung jury and a mistrial. Kunstler began a flurry of activity. Before the third trial, he made bail application and upon denial pursued a writ in the federal courts. He moved for removal of the case to the federal courts, and when that was denied, appealed to the federal court of appeal. He moved for a change of venue and appealed that denial. Kunstler defended Wansley at still another trial in 1967, in which Wansley was convicted of one rape (the other alleged victim had left the area), but the jury did not sentence Wansley to death.

Wansley was no longer a celebrated death penalty case, and Kunstler could have quietly folded his tents and left the case. If, as some critics have charged, all Kunstler wanted was publicity, there was no further publicity to be had. However, Kunstler did not abandon his client. He appealed the new conviction to the Virginia Supreme Court and thereafter pursued a writ to the U.S. Supreme Court. He pursued further writs in the federal courts. Kunstler appeared for Wansley in a total of ten separate legal actions, in addition to two trials. At every occasion Kunstler entered Lynchburg for some stage of the proceeding, the newspapers red-baited him. Every article mentioned that Kunstler had been linked with Communist-front organizations and often recited his southern civil rights activities on behalf of blacks.

Wansley is the perfect case to answer those critics who charged that Kunstler dropped his interest in a client after the publicity value had declined. After the final conviction and sentencing, Kunstler and Wansley began a long-term correspondence. As late as 1969 Kunstler told a reporter, "we're going to have that kid back on the street. He's completely innocent." Actually, the Virginia Parole Board released Wansley in the mid-1980s, after he had served almost twenty years in prison. By that time, Kunstler's fame had escalated far beyond what it was when he tried the Wansley case, with Chicago, Attica, and Wounded Knee behind him. However, he was still in touch with Wansley. A reporter who had followed the story called Kunstler much later and discovered that

> he managed to keep up with his humble client as late as 1990, telling me in a phone conversation that year exactly what Wansley was doing, where he was living, and even how many children he had. His [Kunstler's] account of how Thomas Wansley was now an honest and productive member of society exuded the pride that one might expect of a father whose son had just made the dean's list.

Arthur Kinoy continued to associate with Kunstler, first in the campaign in Danville, Virginia, near Lynchburg, and thereafter in many locales throughout the South. Danville was a particularly rough campaign. It featured a local judge who wore a gun, and a police department that was especially brutal in its clubbing of demonstrators. Authorities charged most demonstrators with violating an injunction, and a few leaders with serious felonies, including violating the "John Brown statute" that made it a crime to "incite the colored population of the State to acts of violence and war against the white population."

Once Kunstler was involved in Danville, he urged using the removal statute, by now so well associated with William Kunstler that Len Holt referred to it as the "Kunstler statute." Although the NAACP lawyers were opposed to using the removal procedure, calling it a waste of time and "playing with the courts," Kunstler's urgings prevailed. Although the removal statute had given the movement some very temporary respites in various campaigns, the remands by federal judges to the state courts had generally been prompt. The common wisdom held that defendants could not appeal a federal district court's order to send their cases back to a state court. However, in the Danville campaign Kunstler persuaded the federal circuit court of appeals to consider an appeal from the federal trial court's remand order. Such appeals kept these cases in the federal courts, where reasonable bail would be set, throughout the appeals process. These appeals extended considerably the amount of time the demonstrators could be relieved from the state prosecutions. Ultimately, Kunstler testified before Congress about the removal procedure and was one of those responsible for a provision in the 1964 Civil Rights Act expressly providing for such an appeal.

Following their work together in Lynchburg and Danville, Kunstler and Arthur Kinoy became closely associated in civil rights cases. In August 1963 Kinoy became a partner in his firm, along with Michael Kunstler. Kinoy explains,

> We were constantly receiving calls for immediate help from all over the South. . . . Despite enormous differences between us, both Kunstler and I realized that we had the ability to work well together. The strengths of one, compensating for the weaknesses of the other, produced a powerful combination. On the one hand, Bill Kunstler had a drive and self-confidence that led him unhesitatingly into the center of the fray, sometimes without a thought-out plan or strategy. On the other hand, I often overplanned and hesitated too long, in a desire to think through all the consequences before moving ahead.

The two men worked together almost constantly in 1963 and 1964. In the fall of 1964 Kinoy left the firm to become a law professor at Rutgers.

Even thereafter, they were associated in many civil rights lawsuits. Kinoy recalls, "when Bill and I were together, we were working around the clock, day and night." At least a few amusing things also happened as they rushed around the South, passionately trying anything and everything to beat back segregation. One thing was an amusing play on their firm name of Kunstler, Kunstler, and Kinoy. Kinoy recalls,

> Bill always used to love this. When he would get up in the courtroom in the deep South, the judge would stare at us and say, "Now who are you?" And he would say, "We're the new KKK!" Our folks sitting in the back of the room, because in those days black people were allowed to sit only in the last two rows of the courtrooms in the South, they would jump up and say, "We're for the new KKK!"

There must have been some good-natured tussles between the two of them as they traveled over the South. Kinoy did not fancy classical music, but recalls that Kunstler "would always try to drag me into a place where they were playing classical music. . . . he liked old music."

Kinoy was "the brains and strategist," recalls Michael Standard, an attorney who worked with the two of them in the South, and "Bill was the able implementor. . . . But Bill was a very brave, very ballsy litigator. I can't emphasize enough how brave the man was." Steven Hyman, an associate in their firm, later a partner, recalls that "they worked very well together. They were really a very good team. But Arthur was clearly the master of the mind, Bill was the master of the theater." Kinoy himself gives much credit to Kunstler, but hardly denies that he was himself the strategist.

> There was a difference in our way of working. When we were together on an intense case, I would do the main work of planning out the strategy we would have to follow the next morning in the courtroom or in arranging the papers. But then I would throw these ideas at Bill and he would come back with very important and strong ideas and concepts. Then we would merge them together. So I was the one who would always start the work on strategy, on theoretical approaches. He would be helpful, though.

There is no question that Kunstler's work was of great importance to the civil rights movement. True, there were many litigators in the

South, and he was merely one important player among others. Still, Kunstler's extensive use and popularization of the removal statute, the "Kunstler statute," was significant to the struggle. However, there is little question that the civil rights movement was of more importance to Kunstler than the other way around. The importance of his work in the South was both personal and professional.

A big part of the personal significance, which he freely acknowledged, was that it gave him a purpose and a niche: "I wanted to practice meaningful law, and although I didn't realize it at the time, my civil rights work began as a selfish gesture. It gave me a way out of the mundane and petty work of a regular law practice as well as an opportunity to live a more stimulating life." The civil rights movement also impacted on Kunstler's insecurities. At one level the enormous responsibilities thrust on him increased his anxiety. In his 1966 civil rights memoir he came close to acknowledging this when he wrote of a group of black supporters looking on him with trust as he prepared to argue their case. "Such open trust made me feel as if I was an imposter who had come into town under false colors." But in the main, the civil rights movement gave Kunstler's ego a tremendous boost by giving him massive doses of the adulation and approval that he always craved.

The experience in the South shaped all the remaining years of Kunstler's career. Although he would represent clients of many colors and embrace many causes, all who knew him—associates, family, and foes—agree on the dominant strain of Kunstler's thought for the remainder of his life. His heart and soul were to be rooted forever in fighting antiblack racism; race would always be the cutting edge to his work. This evolved far beyond civil rights, and by the end of his life he would feel that

> minorities, and blacks in particular, get almost nothing from civil rights legislation. At best it's a sop; at worst it's hypocrisy. The only way they will get anything is by going into the streets. I was once convinced that everything could be done by legislation, litigation and perhaps a little education. But as time has passed I've come to see that the civil rights laws have not ended white racism, and that's the central problem.

Kunstler learned a great deal from Arthur Kinoy. Kinoy came out of the labor movement, dedicated his practice to radical political causes, and styled himself a people's lawyer. Kinoy felt that the appropriate strategy for progressive change was through direct action, demonstrations, protests, and marches, of a mass-based people's movement. From this understanding, legal tactics should not be based on the likelihood of success in court but on the effect of the legal tactic on the activists, their motives, their interests, and their morale. For example, if the filing of a particular lawsuit—a counterattack on government or an economic oppressor—might boost the movement's morale, then it was appropriate even if it stood little or no chances of success. It was especially useful to do more than defend, and to fight back affirmatively with lawsuits designed to vex and harass an opponent.

Kunstler admired Kinoy, and their association helped to radicalize him and especially to shape Kunstler's thinking about the structure of movement practice. The traditional view of lawyers has been that they should remain independent from their clients and not be too closely identified with them. The standard reason offered for this is that the lawyer's objectivity will enable the attorney to better represent the client. Kinoy rejected that, and influenced Kunstler to do so as well.

For the radical lawyer, there is nothing sacrosanct or inviolate, nothing especially praiseworthy, about the law or the legal system. It is merely a tool to gain the political objectives of clients. Kunstler learned this from the civil rights struggle.

> The [first Freedom Rider's case] was the beginning of my involvement in what was called "movement law," the practice of law which considers the political objectives of defendants—the integration goals of the Freedom Riders, for example—most important. In the past, lawyers, myself included, viewed the law as sacred and inviolate. But movement law considered the legal system as something to be used or changed, in order to gain the political objectives of the clients in a particular case. Movement law was created and refined in the South by lawyers like me, and dozens of others, as we rushed from one civil rights crisis to another, inventing legal remedies as we went, with the goal of desegregation before us at all times.

It was not just the *law* that was to be subordinated to the political objectives; the *lawyer* had to bend the knee and subordinate himself to the movement. "Lawyers should be guided by their clients' politics, not by their own legal agenda. . . . during the sixties I learned that I had to listen to movement people and tailor my actions to their needs." Even more, Kunstler learned that the movement lawyer had to identify personally with the political goals of his clients and realize that he was only another laborer working for their common goal. In the 1960s he wrote,

> a lawyer is just another worker with special skills. . . . to be a surrogate to the movement, one has to be a member of it in every sense of the word. [The lawyer] possesses a skill which must be put to use in pursuit of the mutual goal. He is activated, not by the promise of fame and fortune, but by the sharing of a common cause with those he represents. I no longer know where the movement ends and the law begins. In fact, for me now there is no significant dividing line. The movement has given my life heightened meaning and purpose. In return, I have put at its disposal all the energies I possess. I hope that the exchange is not too greatly in my favor.

If these be some of the notions of a radical lawyer, then these ideas came from the civil rights movement, long before the Chicago Seven trial, which Kunstler would later claim had radicalized him. To a significant but undefinable extent, they came from Kunstler's association with Arthur Kinoy rather than the work in the South. However, racism as the dominant motif of Kunstler's career came from the civil rights movement itself. As that movement transformed itself from civil rights in the first half of the 1960s to Black Power in the second half, Kunstler's concern with antiblack racism remained central to his practice.

5

Black Power Advocate

FROM 1965 TO 1968 black insurgency spread rapidly throughout the United States. Desegregation, by then achieved, led to a feeling of futility. Of what use to the young black man was the right to sit at the lunch counter, if he had no money to buy anything once he was there? Blacks now wanted jobs and clout, economic and political power.

The black movements changed considerably over the course of the sixties. For one thing, in the late sixties blacks wanted to make their own headway without dependence on the largesse of white liberals. For another, the movement had already vanquished the easily identified targets of protest in the civil rights days, the southern bigots and their segregation statutes. The causes of despair became much more amorphous. Whom does one picket to protest poverty in the black ghetto? Which companies are to blame for a lack of employment? What demonstration can be launched to challenge white flight to the suburbs, leaving blacks behind in the decaying inner city? Under these conditions, economically radical and even violent solutions attracted the new generation of black youth.

Young black leaders, dedicated to black self-empowerment, seized control of the more militant of the civil rights groups, such as the Student Nonviolent Coordinating Committee (SNCC). Urban riots and fires, originating in black ghettos, inaugurated a series of long, hot summers beginning with the Watts Riot in 1965 and then spreading in 1967 to Newark, Detroit, and over a hundred other cities. Black paramilitary groups advocated the arming of black ghettos and violent resistance to the white man's police. The most prominent of these groups, the Black Panthers, organized in Oakland, California, in October 1966. It soon startled mainstream America when thirty Panthers appeared in their characteristic black berets and black leather jackets at the California state capitol, brandishing weapons.

The black nationalist groups called for armed resistance, separation from white America, even revolution. At times during the late 1960s the possibility of revolution did not seem remote. Ironically, white fears peaked even as black militant groups began a steep decline, especially from 1968 to 1970. Many factors contributed to this collapse. White liberals were satisfied with the blacks' attainment of de jure equality through the Civil Rights Act of 1964 and the Voting Rights Act of 1965, and were unwilling to follow into the thickets of radical polemic that attacked the American political, cultural, and economic system. White youth especially, and some older liberals, found other issues to involve them: the plight of the California farmworkers, and then, increasingly, the war in Vietnam.

Government repression was the major cause of the collapse of black militancy in the late 1960s. Although the federal government dominated the repression, it came from all levels and it took many forms. Some was extralegal, for example, the FBI's wiretaps of Martin Luther King, Jr., to dig up dirt on his sexual peccadillos and imagined ties to communists. At least through wiretaps the FBI searched for real dirt. With the COINTELPRO program, the FBI manufactured dirt and cynically splintered and disrupted Indian, black, and other radical groups. Insofar as black groups were concerned, the FBI manufactured false letters and other documents that stated or implied that certain black leaders were FBI informants, that certain black leaders were conducting affairs with other leaders' wives, that King was a sex pervert, that various black leaders had uttered anti-Semitic statements, that various Jewish leaders had uttered antiblack statements, and so forth. These documents were then delivered to the persons in whose hands the most disruption and distrust could be generated. Ultimately, investigative reporters unearthed COINTELPRO, a Senate committee headed by Senator Frank Church investigated and denounced it, and various federal courts declared its activities unconstitutional and awarded damages to its victims. Meanwhile, COINTELPRO, approved at the highest levels of the federal government, had caused divorces and even suicides.

Of course, local police were not as sophisticated as the FBI, especially the Chicago police, whose conduct during the Democratic Convention in 1968 was characterized by the Walker Commission as a "police riot." On December 4, 1969, the Chicago police contributed their bit toward the repression of the Black Panthers by raiding the home of Fred

Hampton, the charismatic leader of the Illinois Panthers, and murdering him in his bed. Forensic evidence exposed the Chicago authorities' flimsy attempt to disguise the circumstances of Hampton's shooting, and ultimately the city of Chicago paid a substantial damage claim to his family. This was only the most spectacular and notorious of the numerous police beatings and killings of black militants during the late 1960s.

Not surprisingly, however, the authorities' chief tactic in the struggle against black militants was a monopoly on legitimate coercion represented by the legal system. The FBI and local police constantly harassed SNCC leaders, Panthers, and other black militants. Police stopped their cars on any pretext, raided their houses and made arrests on the flimsiest of excuses. Prosecutors demanded bail as high as could be obtained. Convictions were not the object. Indeed, an abnormally large number of black militant trials resulted in acquittals. The idea was to wear the militants down, divert their time and attention from pursuing their cause to raising bail money and defending themselves. This wholesale abuse of criminal process has been noted by quite neutral observers. Professor Anthony Oberschall commented in 1978 that "the government's strategy appeared to be to tie down leaders in costly and time consuming legal battles which would impede their activities and put a tremendous drain on financial resources regardless of whether the government would be successful in court."

The plan succeeded beautifully. Black Panthers and other militant groups bled to death. Raising bail money and defending the very existence of their organization dominated black militants' thoughts, at the expense of expanding their activities within the community. The Black Power wing of the movement was fatally wounded. However, by no means was that apparent as the struggle was unfolding in the late 1960s. The fact that this struggle was fought out in the criminal courtroom only expanded the role of those radical lawyers, such as Kunstler, who had followed the civil rights struggle out of its southern phase and into the period of Black Power advocacy.

We cannot follow Kunstler's every case but will concentrate on his representation of his most important black militant clients, first the East Coast Black Panthers and then H. Rap Brown, the militant chairman of SNCC. A brief examination of some of Kunstler's other Black Power cases of the late 1960s and of his role in this type of representation will conclude the chapter.

Armed with a strong element of legalism, even constitutionalism, along with their guns, the Black Panthers stood for opposition to perceived police oppression and illegality. Among other things, it was a political party, it offered meal programs to disadvantaged youth, and it had educational programs along vaguely Marxist lines. It also armed its members. Armed patrols, dressed in black berets and jackets, patrolled the police, following squad cars and reading loudly from law books at the scenes of arrests. The party popularized the term "pigs" for police, and on the rhetorical level promoted armed resistance to the police. Panther rallies often chanted "Off the pigs!" and "The Revolution has co-ome, it's time to pick up the gu-un."

Huey Newton and Bobby Seale founded the Black Panther Party in October 1966 in Oakland, California. The party's center of gravity would always be in California, and its primary attorney, Charles Garry, was a California lawyer. The party did spread to the rest of the country, however, and appointed Kunstler as attorney for the East Coast Panthers. As such he did some miscellaneous work for the party and its members, such as representing Panthers before the New York Civilian Complaint Review Board after several off-duty, out-of-uniform patrolmen attacked them in a courthouse corridor, or in aiding local counsel outside New York defending Black Panthers in preparation of pretrial motions.

Much of Kunstler's work on behalf of the Black Panthers was in getting bail reduced. Kunstler and the militant Left saw high bail as a tactic used by the authorities to prevent the Panthers from effectively organizing, by keeping leaders in jail and diverting the energies of their followers from party work to raising bail money. The levels of bail set for Panthers, the later revelations of the COINTELPRO program, and, indeed, some of the contemporary prosecutorial arguments support this motivation. Instead of bail being used as an assurance that the defendant would appear in court for trial, the legitimate function of bail, prosecutors and courts used bail as a tool to harass and cripple the Black Panther Party, a thoroughly illegitimate purpose.

As one example, in January 1969 two New York City blacks, members of the Black Panther Party, were accused of carrying loaded pistols onto an airplane. The federal commissioner set bail at $50,000 each, around $175,000 in 2000 dollars. The possibility of two black men, aged eighteen and nineteen, raising that kind of money was just about zero.

Kunstler characterized the bail as "arbitrary, malicious and outrageous" and immediately filed motions for reduction.

Another example is from August 1968. Police arrested three Black Panthers after the defendants allegedly had thrown rocks and bottles at firemen battling a rubbish fire in the ghetto. The prosecutor charged the three with felonious assault on a policeman, resisting arrest, and possession of stolen property. The Brooklyn Criminal Court set bail at $50,000 for two defendants, and $11,500 for the third, in a hearing where twenty off-duty policemen stood along a wall, "their badges hanging out of the breast pockets of their sports shirts and jackets," as a reporter put it. Outside on the street, white demonstrators picketed with placards reading "Hands Off Black Panthers" and "Stop Cop Harassment of the Black Panther Party."

Following the hearing, Kunstler immediately denounced the level of bail as "discriminatory and highly unconstitutional," and promised an immediate motion to reduce. He also made one of his earliest criticisms of massive police presence in court, charging that their loitering about was designed to create "an atmosphere of fear" and persuade the judge that "he was dealing with caged animals." Kunstler noted that all over the country "large numbers of police invariably turn up when a black militant is on trial."

Within days Kunstler went before a different judge, seeking a bail reduction. He charged that the $50,000 bail was "unconstitutionally excessive" and simply a part of the "police vendetta against the Black Panthers in New York." The prosecutor seemed to support Kunstler's charge by dwelling on these defendants' political views as a primary ground for not reducing bail. Originally arrested for throwing rocks and bottles, the young men seem much more sinister in official rhetoric. "These three young men," the prosecutor argued, "are being used as tools by people intent on political movements bordering on anarchy. I think they can be rehabilitated in prison rather than released on the streets where they will be used again." This came close to arguing that keeping these men locked up for the purpose of indoctrination was an appropriate purpose of bail. This second judge lowered bail, to $26,500 and $15,500 from the original $50,000, and in the case of the defendant whose bail had been set at $11,500, to $5,000. Although victorious, Kunstler was unsatisfied. He called the reductions "meaningless," and promptly filed motions seeking further reductions.

These two bail cases are examples of defendants who just happened to be Black Panthers. Their activities were not in any meaningful sense actions of the party itself. Kunstler also defended Black Panthers for activities alleged to be more official. In 1971–72 he represented Arthur F. Turco, Jr., a white lawyer, alleged to have ordered the killing of a suspected police informer after two days of confinement and torture by the Black Panthers. Kunstler tried the case in Baltimore before a jury of eight blacks and four whites. As a lawyer Turco had himself represented several black militants, including Black Panthers. He was also an officer of a white militant organization. Kunstler took the rhetorical offensive immediately, and in his opening statement noted that the prosecution's evidence would consist of "the most dangerous kind of testimony," that of accomplices who had cut a deal for immunity. However, the major issue, one of "overwhelming social importance," Kunstler told the black-dominated jury, was "whether the Government can use its resources to crush a movement of black men and women."

Whenever Kunstler tried a case in Baltimore, he stayed with his sister. He used his brother-in-law's office for conferences until late at night, then went to their home for a few hours of sleep before returning to court. Strangely enough, when his sister did see him during a trial, he seemed relaxed. Mary remembers her brother as "just plain old Bill," although he made quite a mess and she could barely get into his room to clean.

The jury deadlocked, and Turco was freed on bail after a seven-month confinement. Ultimately the prosecutor reduced the charge from torture-murder to simple assault, Turco pled guilty, and the court ordered straight probation with no jail other than that already served waiting for the murder trial. The wholesale reduction from torture-murder to simple assault, together with the sentence of mere probation, strongly suggests that this was not such a serious case as to justify confinement without bail. This lends credence to Kunstler's accusation that the primary purpose of the original charge was indeed to crush Turco's political activities, confine him, and thereby stop his representation of Black Panthers.

On April 3, 1969, the *New York Times* carried on page 1, column 1, district attorney Frank S. Hogan's announcement of a twelve-count indictment, charging twenty-one Black Panthers with a most fantastic conspiracy. They were planning, the district attorney alleged, to plant bombs in midtown Manhattan stores, including Macy's, Bloomingdale's, and Abercrombie and Fitch among others, timed to explode at the height of the Easter season shopping. Allegedly, the conspirators also plotted to dynamite railroad tracks and police stations.

Twelve of the purported conspirators were arrested immediately. At the bail hearing Gerald Lefcourt, associated with Kunstler on the case, argued to the judge (and implicitly to the black community from which jurors would be chosen) the standard militant position that "it is the feeling of the Black Panther party that this indictment was an attack on the Black Panthers directed from Washington. The desire of the Government to wipe out the Black Panther party was obvious."

The judge was unimpressed and set bail at $100,000 for each defendant. Kunstler became the Panthers' chief counsel, although Gerald Lefcourt nominally represented some defendants. This became a pattern often adopted by Kunstler and other radical lawyers. Two defense counsel, each representing different defendants, permitted two separate sets of cross-examination. They denounced the bail as unconstitutionally high, and sought reduction through a long series of motions and appeals, which ultimately reached the U.S. Supreme Court. As late as March 1970, thirteen of the Black Panthers were still held in jail in lieu of bail, and bail had been reduced for only four of these defendants. Eventually most of the defendants made bail, and two of them fled after being freed on bond.

Tension pervaded many of the pretrial hearings, for bail reduction, suppression of evidence, dismissal, and the like. On June 11, 1969, Kunstler won a minor victory. The police had scattered the defendants in six or seven jails, probably to make it difficult to coordinate a defense, and the judge ordered that Kunstler be permitted to confer with all the defendants "all together, in one place, at the same time." A *New York Times* reporter estimated that four hundred pro-Panther sympathizers picketed on the sidewalk outside the Criminal Courts Building, chanting, "All power to the people" and carrying signs reading "Free all political prisoners." Hundreds of policemen ringed the courthouse. Two hundred more sympathizers crowded inside the building, trying to enter the hearing room. The spectators inside the courtroom were largely pro-Panther, although a row of police stood behind the defendants during the hearing. At the close of the hearing, a defendant raised a clenched fist in the Black Power salute and shouted, "All power to the people," after which the spectators chanted the slogan in response.

The district attorney's original account of the conspiracy indictment and initial arrests was quite specific as to which stores and which
police stations were to be bombed, and offered lurid details on the Black
Panthers and the prior arrests and malefactions of the principal defendants. Understandably, this account garnered considerable publicity,
especially in New York City. Kunstler regarded publicity as one of defense counsel's primary weapons. He was always anxious and eager to
counteract the head start advantage of the prosecutors in their widely
publicized announcements of sensational indictments. He never held
back his comments and targeted his remarks to the public generally, but
with hopes of reaching his minority constituency and special hopes of
reaching potential jurors.

In the case of the Panther 21, he reached a national audience. On
July 25, 1969, *Life* magazine ran a feature article on Kunstler, giving him
one of his first pieces of widely distributed national press, and quoted
him extensively. His remarks, though they may be substantially true, fit
the pattern set by the Left:

> Since their beginning as a political party in 1967, the Panthers have
> been accused of increasingly serious crimes. Now they are faced with
> mass arrests on conspiracy charges. Along with the arrests came a
> whole series of false accusations against the Panthers which began to
> poison the air. . . . These accusations were deliberately planted by fed-
> eral and state authorities to prejudice the public against the Black Pan-
> ther Party. I am afraid that a fair trial is virtually impossible.
>
> And this isn't the only form of harassment. Bail is so high that no
> bondsman would handle them. Their conditions in jail are horren-
> dous—lights are kept on 24 hours, there are no exercise privileges, no
> reading material, and in some cases they are even denied the legal pa-
> pers that we send to them.
>
> The favorite tactic of the power structure in the U.S. is to turn black
> people against their more vociferous spokesmen. . . . The idea is to cre-
> ate the impression that militant blacks are wild animals who have
> nothing whatsoever in common with human beings. They have been
> turned into outlaws, and no attempts have been made to understand
> either their point of view or the reasons for their militancy.

In the late summer of 1969, both the Panther 21 and the Chicago
Eight (there were eight defendants before Bobby Seale's case was sev-

ered) appeared headed for immediate trial. Obviously, Kunstler could not try them both. According to Kunstler's recollection, he and Gerald Lefcourt tossed a coin. Kunstler won Chicago and went on to national fame. Lefcourt did not do badly. He tried the Panther 21 (reduced to thirteen defendants for trial) in the longest criminal trial (eight months) in New York history. The jury almost immediately acquitted all defendants, even those who had jumped bail, of all charges. This sounds like a victory for the Black Panthers, and the newspapers were filled with letters to the editor swelled with proudful, liberal assertions that the legal system had vindicated itself. But did the Panthers really win? The prosecutors and judges had succeeded in locking up the defendants for over a year with a bail they could not possibly raise; then, after bond release, they had kept the Panthers preoccupied with their trial for almost another year. They had thoroughly disrupted the New York Black Panthers, and left them no time for their political work. If that had been the prosecutorial and judicial objective all along, the authorities truly won.

No man more epitomized the Black Power movement in the late 1960s than H. Rap Brown. He was a fiery speaker, and from 1967 to 1970 his frequent calls to burn America down struck terror in white America, especially in the context of the hundreds of black riots that *did* produce major conflagrations. Because of his rhetoric and the fear it produced in white America, Brown was "deluged with state and federal charges," Kunstler charged, "in a no-holds-barred attempt by the government to stop him." As with the Black Panthers, the strategy may have worked. Kunstler claimed that Brown, like other militants, "had no time or energy to do any organizing; it all went into fighting his legal cases."

The reader may decide for himself whether Kunstler's conclusion is correct. Without question, however, Brown entered into a vortex of criminal litigation extending over ten years, in which Kunstler was his primary attorney. Kunstler appealed every denied motion or denied writ among the hundreds made in the course of nearly a half dozen prosecutions, often as far as the U.S. Supreme Court. The following account describes through neutral sources only the main channels of a complicated story.

Brown became a militant during his Baton Rouge high school years in the late 1950s. He attended Southern University from 1960 to 1963 and then followed his brother to Howard University in Washington,

D.C., in 1963. His political activism increased in Washington, and he participated in marches and as a member of various militant organizations until 1966, when he began to devote all his energies to SNCC. Brown rose dramatically in that organization, and won election as chairman in 1967.

Brown already had a reputation for talk. His formal name was Hubert Geroid Brown, and two versions compete for the origin of his nickname Rap. One attributes it to the ability he developed during his political apprenticeship in the mid-1960s for a grassroots ability to "rap" with poor black people. The other version holds that his brother Eli gave him that nickname because of his facility at playing the "dozens," a black street game in which a man tries to humiliate his opponent by quick verbal jousting.

For a time after his election as SNCC chairman, Brown tried to tone down his rhetoric, but with his temperament, abilities, and beliefs, that became an impossible task. He quickly reverted to form and uttered many oft-quoted phrases such as, "if America chooses to play Nazis, black folks ain't going to play Jews" and his best-known aphorism, "Violence is as american [sic] as cherry pie." His speeches and writings were explicitly revolutionary. Some examples from his 1969 autobiography illustrate this, although he made these sorts of remarks long before that year:

> We stand on the eve of a Black revolution. These rebellions are but a dress rehearsal for real revolution. . . . Racism stems from an attitude and it can't be destroyed under the capitalist system. . . . Fuck attitudes. Fuck a muthafucka who hates me, because if I ever get him on the wrong end of my gun he's in trouble. . . . Violence is a necessary part of revolutionary struggle. . . . The very fact that white folks fear guns shows the value in being armed. Power, indeed, must come from the barrel of a gun. . . . This country has delivered an ultimatum to Black people; america says to Blacks: you either fight to live or you will live to die. I say to america, Fuck It! Freedom or Death. Power to the People!

Brown's pronouncements were not merely idle talk. After he became chairman of SNCC, Brown traveled all over the country addressing black crowds. He was at his most inflammatory when in the midst of mass gatherings with riotous potential. Shortly after a riot in Atlanta,

Brown arrived with other SNCC militants and proclaimed "we came here to blow Atlanta up." Brown told a crowd in Dayton, Ohio, according to a United States attorney, "we intend to wage revolution by any means possible. We intend to burn this place down." A riot ensued. Although he briefly faced criminal charges for the Dayton remarks, Brown's real legal entanglement began as a result of remarks he made in Cambridge, Maryland, on July 24, 1967, at the height of the nationwide 1967 race riots.

Against a backdrop of black rioting throughout the country, and in the immediate context of black guerrilla warfare in Detroit, Brown urged racial pride and assertiveness to a crowd of several hundred black Cambridge residents. He further declaimed that "if America don't come around, we going burn it down, brother. We are going to burn it down if we don't get our share of it." Brown urged blacks to take over white-owned stores. "You got to own some of them stores. I don't care if you have to burn him down and run him out." According to prosecutors, there was also talk of burning down the dilapidated Pine Street Elementary School.

Within an hour or so of Brown's address, a riot began, during which several white-owned stores were looted and torched, as was the Pine Street Elementary School. Seventeen buildings were damaged or destroyed in total. Police and black residents exchanged gunshots, and whether by deliberate police firing or simply being caught in the crossfire, Brown received a minor injury for which he received medical treatment. He then left the area. There was no evidence whatsoever that Brown personally participated in the riot or the burning of any building, and the authorities never contended this. In the following year, the National Advisory Commission on Civil Disorder determined that Cambridge city officials and police "overreaction" had been responsible for the riot.

Maryland charged Brown with riot, inciting to riot, and arson, and asked the FBI to pick him up on a federal fugitive warrant. Brown contacted Kunstler, the SNCC's New York attorney, who advised him to surrender. Kunstler and Brown thought they had an arrangement whereby Brown would fly back to New York from Washington, D.C., to surrender, but the FBI arrested him at the Washington airport en route. The federal government delivered Brown to the Virginia authorities to await extradition to Maryland. Brown resisted extradition and was released on $10,000 bail.

The Maryland indictment was formally returned by the grand jury on August 14, 1967. Brown was in Los Angeles and that day traveled back to New York, where he visited with friends and with Kunstler, his attorney. The major news media, radio, television, and newspapers, prominently carried the news of Brown's indictment. On August 16 Brown flew to New Orleans to visit with his family in Baton Rouge. He took a rifle in a carrying case with him on the plane, which he reported to the airline crew. In 1967, the carrying of a disclosed rifle onto an airplane was legal except for those persons who had been convicted of a felony or *were under indictment* for a felony.

After a few days spent visiting his family, Brown returned with the rifle to New York. The FBI arrested him within days under the somewhat obscure law prohibiting persons under indictment for a felony from traveling in interstate commerce with a gun, with a warrant issued out of New Orleans. Bail in New Orleans was set at $25,000, which Kunstler immediately attacked as excessive and a political maneuver designed to prevent Brown from speaking at his numerous engagements around the country. Kunstler filed lawsuits to enjoin the enforcement of the firearm statute as unconstitutional and motions to attack the constitutionality of the grand jury that indicted him in New Orleans based on underrepresentation of blacks. Kunstler lost both motions. But he did succeed in reducing Brown's bond to $15,000, which his supporters posted, and on September 8 Brown was released, with restrictions that he could not travel outside the Eastern District of Louisiana and the cities of New York and Atlanta without court approval.

Meanwhile in Virginia, the governor's extradition warrant had been issued, preparing the way for immediate removal to Maryland, but Brown still resisted extradition and sought bail from the governor's warrant while it was attacked by motion. The federal district court in Virginia released Brown into Kunstler's custody, without bond, on condition that he remain in New York City except for court appearances or travel necessary to prepare his defense. Brown thereafter sought permission to travel for speaking engagements, which was denied. Kunstler attacked those travel restrictions on First Amendment grounds but lost.

On February 17–18, 1968, Brown traveled to California, in part to consult there with his peripatetic attorney, Kunstler, but once in California he also spoke at a couple of meetings. When he returned to New York the FBI arrested Brown for bail violation and took him back to

New Orleans. In a hearing on bail revocation, a black FBI agent testified that he had heard Brown speaking at one of the California meetings. Brown recalled that in a recess, he told the black FBI agent, "I hope your children don't grow up to be a Tom like you are." When the recess was over, the FBI agent retook the stand and testified that Brown had just threatened his life. Brown was immediately arrested for threatening a federal officer. The Louisiana federal judge, Lansing Mitchell, about whom controversy would later center, revoked the $15,000 bond, increased the firearms bail to $50,000 and set an additional $50,000 bail for a threat on a federal officer, for a total of $100,000.

Thereafter the Virginia district court also revoked Brown's release to Kunstler's custody, based on the California trip, and ordered his appearance once released from New Orleans. That meant that the New Orleans federal prosecution would go first. Kunstler's effort in the spring of 1968 to block the extradition to Maryland on the basis that Brown's life would be in danger there was rejected. The federal appellate court noted that Maryland law permitted the trial court itself to move Brown's trial to another part of the state, and suggested it might do so if the potential for disorder or danger to Brown appeared to be as represented. This turned out to be a hint that Maryland later accepted with a vengeance.

In New Orleans the appellate court reduced Brown's bond back to $15,000 but continued the travel restrictions. On May 22, 1968, a New Orleans federal jury convicted Brown of transportion of the firearm on his return trip from New Orleans to New York but acquitted him for the trip from New York to New Orleans. Perhaps the jury thought that Brown could not have had knowledge of the indictment only two days after it was filed but thought he did by the time of his return trip. After the verdict, Judge Lansing Mitchell sentenced Brown to five years imprisonment and a $2,000 fine, continued his bail pending appeal, and sent him to Virginia, where he was promptly removed to Maryland for trial on the rioting and arson charges.

Once back in Maryland, the state requested a change in venue for trial from Cambridge, in Dorchester County, to Bel Air, in Harford County. An application to change the place of trial is often made by defendants for fear of hostility toward a defendant at the location of an alleged crime, but it is almost never made by the prosecution. The prosecution alleged that a trial in Cambridge would create a danger of violence, but there is every reason to believe that the real prosecution

motive was that it would be easier to obtain a conviction in conservative Harford County, with its 5 to 10 percent black population, than in
Dorchester County, with a 35 to 40 percent black population. Kunstler
vigorously attacked the change in location of trial in proceedings before
both state and federal courts, arguing that the Sixth Amendment of the
Constitution, properly interpreted, guaranteed Brown a trial "in the vic-
inage" of the alleged crime. He based this on an all but forgotten ex-
planatory letter written by Alexander Hamilton. Kunstler also argued
that the white jurors in Bel Air could not give the proper interpretation
of the black slang Brown had used in his speech.

On the eve of the riot and arson trial, on the evening of March 10,
1970, an explosion demolished an automobile in Bel Air, killing two
black men, one a friend of Rap Brown and fellow militant, and another
man whose identity could not be immediately determined. For hours
rumors abounded that it was Rap Brown himself, but it was soon determined that it was not. Authorities said that the blast resulted from an
attempt to transport explosives, and blacks attributed the blast to the
Klan or other extremist whites. At nearly the same time, authorities
sought a white woman seen leaving the Cambridge County Courthouse, the original site of the trial, after a bomb blew a thirty-foot hole
in a brick wall of the courthouse. Kunstler demanded that the proceedings be postponed, arguing that a fair trial was impossible because of
the fear of violence.

Meanwhile Rap Brown had disappeared. No one, neither Kunstler
nor Brown's wife, knew where he was. Kunstler said he suspected foul
play and argued for an indefinite postponement. The trial was delayed
for a week and reset at a third location. Kunstler resisted the new location in both state and federal courts on the basis that the third county
had only 5 percent blacks and Brown still would be tried by an all-white
jury. He also attacked the indictment on the grounds that Brown had
been singled out for prosecution when the actual rioters had not been
charged. But he lost those efforts and the riot and arson trial was ready
to proceed by late April 1970. However, Rap Brown was still missing
and had not been heard from since March 7. Kunstler stated that he did
not know where Brown was, but feared the worst. In fact, Rap Brown
did not surface until October 16, 1971, nineteen months after his disappearance.

During these extensive pretrial developments, Kunstler also kept
busy on the public relations front. Through the media and in speeches

Kunstler presented his clients' positions to the public. He saw this as counteracting the prosecutors' headstart propaganda when an indictment was handed down, and as an effort to assure a less hostile jury pool. On October 19, 1967, shortly after Brown's initial troubles began, Kunstler spoke before a special public forum on civil disobedience sponsored by the New York County Bar Association. He compared Rap Brown to Patrick Henry, who, he claimed, had certainly incited violence when he proclaimed from a pulpit, "our brethren are already in the field, why stand we here idle?" Kunstler pointed out that Rap Brown "says much the same thing. If he had the majority with him, he'd be a Patrick Henry but he represents a bare minority at this moment."

In another example, Kunstler spoke before the national convention of Unitarians on June 24, 1968. He spoke extensively about Rap Brown, starting out with the pleasing observation that Brown had just recently been married by a Unitarian minister. Kunstler again compared Brown with Patrick Henry and stated that their appeals to violence were the same and that people have a right to make this sort of appeal. "The people have the right to alter the system in any way they see fit and by whatever means they see fit." He charged that the black community's only political weapon was the white community's fear of violence. Free speech had come to mean that "you may speak in a dissenting way only if people do not think you might succeed."

Through these speeches and articles Kunstler sought to soften Brown's image in the public's eye and present a justification for his conduct. Kunstler did this for most of his controversial defendants, but did it more extensively for Brown, if only because Brown's legal saga continued so long. In the early 1970s Kunstler and Brown coauthored an article about Brown's legal troubles. The publication of this piece in the *University Review* ultimately played a major role in his struggles because it was read by just the right person in the right circumstances. The publicity campaign was always worth the effort, in this case spectacularly so.

Even during the nineteen months of Brown's disappearance, Kunstler remained busy fighting Brown's court battles. In New Orleans Kunstler appealed Brown's firearms conviction. The appellate court vacated the trial court's judgment and sent the case back for a hearing on wiretapping conducted on Brown's telephone conversations in the jail where Brown was confined awaiting his trial. The government disclosed the snooping before the May 1968 trial, but the trial judge, Lansing Mitchell, had refused an open hearing and determined on his own, without disclosing the contents of the calls to the defense, that the telephone calls had no relevance. After the appellate court sent the case back to Mitchell, he determined that although ten of Brown's telephone conversations were monitored, all but one of the eavesdroppings had been conducted in the interest of national security involving foreign powers and that the wiretapping had not been directed against Brown. However, in at least one instance, the jail authorities wiretapped conversations between Brown and Kunstler, thus showing governmental disdain for attorney-client relationships. Mitchell found this conversation irrelevant, of no use to the prosecution, and rejected the contention that it tainted the trial process. Mitchell set September 9, 1970, for resentencing, and when Brown did not show up, this being within the time of his nineteen-month disappearance, Mitchell resentenced him in absentia to the same five years plus $2,000. Kunstler appealed that, and the federal circuit court of appeals again reversed. It held that the defendant must be present for sentencing, and the trial court would have to issue a warrant and await Brown's reappearance.

Developments ensued in the Maryland case, even in the absence of Rap Brown or a trial. In January 1971 a Maryland prosecutor revealed that the lead prosecutor in the Brown case had told him that the arson charge had been "fabricated" in order to involve the FBI. The FBI enters the search for state fugitives only if the crimes are felonies. The riot and incitement charges were mere misdemeanors, but arson is a felony. The revealing prosecutor called it a "phony indictment" and a "perversion of justice" and said that his boss had admitted he charged Brown with arson solely "to get the FBI into the case." His bosses, the chief prosecutors, promptly hauled the whistle blower into the Maryland courts, where the judges obliged the prosecutors and fined their colleague for contempt.

However, Kunstler seized on the information. If there was no valid felony charge in Maryland, his client should not be on the FBI's ten-most-wanted list. Nor would his client's transportation of a rifle on an airplane have been a felony. Kunstler concluded from the whistle blower's revelation that it was "obvious that Rap Brown has been framed." After various maneuverings, Kunstler won a full court hearing with the taking of evidence on the issue of whether the arson charge was fabricated, but on May 8, 1971, after two days of testimony, the

Maryland trial judge found that the evidence was not sufficient to sustain the allegation of fabrication.

On October 16, 1971, Rap Brown burst spectacularly from his hiding, shot in a gun battle with police following an armed robbery of a West Side New York bar. A group of four men with guns forced the predominantly black clientele of the Red Carpet Bar on West Eighty-fifth Street to lie on the floor and hand over their money and jewelry. As the police closed in, the robbers escaped and engaged in a running gun battle. Rap Brown and a policeman blazed away in a shootout on the roof of an adjacent building.

At first Brown denied his identity, but that quickly fell apart; this was in fact the man who had been on the FBI's ten-most-wanted list for over a year. Kunstler scrambled to keep Brown in New York, presumably so that any sentence from the armed robbery could be served at the same time as a sentence from the New Orleans federal court. However, the federal government secretly flew Brown to New Orleans, where Judge Mitchell resentenced him to five years, the maximum term, and $2,000. Kunstler asked Mitchell to excuse himself from sentencing because of "ill feeling toward the defendant," but Mitchell refused. Flown back to New York, Brown then faced the robbery charges.

Kunstler attempted to remove the New York charges of robbery, assault with a deadly weapon, and attempted murder of the policemen to a federal court, but predictably lost that appeal. His trial theory was that Brown was not involved in the robbery, but had taken to the roof merely to evade the police since he knew he was a fugitive. He attacked the identification of Brown as a shooter on the basis that the evening was foggy. In particular, Kunstler attacked the motive of a former deputy police commissioner who published an article, "The Man Who Shot Rap Brown," in *New York* magazine the day before jury selection was scheduled to begin. The purpose, he charged, was to prejudice Brown in the eyes of the jurors. The article contained vivid details and featured drawings of Brown in a shooter's position and using a gun that was not involved. "Everything about the article smacks of a calculated attempt to deprive [Brown] of fair play," Kunstler contended. "Never has there been a more blatant and deliberate attempt to poison the atmosphere against a person accused of crime than that represented by this article."

Kunstler successfully moved to exclude testimony of the statements made by Brown's alleged confederates, because the robbers had not been warned of their right to silence. In the course of the hearing on the motion to exclude, the prosecutors called police detectives as witnesses, to repeat the statements thereafter excluded. Kunstler charged that the prosecution was using the exclusion hearings themselves to poison the jury pool. "I think a fraud is being perpetrated in this court," Kunstler alleged. "What's being done here is that excludable testimony is getting pumped out to the public through the press."

Kunstler did win a few procedural matters, aside from the exclusion of the robbers' statements. Brown had become a Black Muslim during his wanderings, and the trial was recessed on Fridays, days that are holy to Muslims. On Kunstler's motion, the court also permitted Brown to act as cocounsel to the extent of making an opening statement to the jury, an important advantage to a defendant who might thereafter choose not to testify on the stand. Kunstler moved for a mistrial, contending that the prosecution systematically used its challenges to exclude black jurors, lost the motion, and ultimately obtained a jury with only two blacks.

The trial was essentially nonpolitical, and the judge very liberal in accommodating Kunstler's requests for subpoenas to *New York* magazine, about the allegedly prejudicial article, and to the police department, about allegedly excessively friendly relations between policemen and the Red Carpet Bar that might make the patrons biased as witnesses. When a reporter asked Kunstler why a civil libertarian such as himself would attempt to invade the sanctity of a publication, Kunstler bristled: "I'm not a civil libertarian and never have been. These constitutional niceties don't mean a damned thing to me when my client's life is at stake."

Kunstler did his best, but he had very little to work with. The jury convicted Brown and his confederates of robbery and assault, but deadlocked on the attempted murder charges, which were thereafter dropped. On May 9, 1973, the trial judge sentenced Brown to a five- to fifteen-year term, less than the maximum of twenty-five years, "taking into account," as the judge told Brown, "that you have done much to help your people. You have devoted much of your life to helping your fellow man."

Brown still faced trial in Maryland on the riot and arson charges, and the five-year federal sentence to be served when he was finished with the New York time. The eve of trial in Maryland in the fall of 1973 produced a very favorable plea bargain. Brown pled guilty to a new charge of failure to appear for his trial in 1970; Maryland dropped the riot and arson charges that were the beginning of this entire saga; and the judge ordered a one-year sentence on the failure to appear charge to run at the same time as the New York sentence. This meant that Brown would not receive any additional prison time. The federal charge in New Orleans of threatening the FBI officer had somehow disappeared, but the conviction for transporting the rifle, for which Brown received a yet unserved five-year sentence, was affirmed in August 1973. The U.S. Supreme Court denied to review the conviction, Justice William Douglas dissenting.

Meanwhile, the FBI's COINTELPRO activities were exposed, and in July 1974 Kunstler again attacked the New Orleans federal sentence on the basis that Brown had been specially targeted and entrapped, using the harassment technique the government had developed of piling on charge after charge to exhaust the defendant's resources for bail money. He again asked Judge Mitchell to excuse himself because he had showed his bias by levying excessive bail and the maximum sentence. This time, however, Kunstler had specific information that Mitchell was biased. Mitchell did excuse himself, and the motion was heard by Judge Fred Cassibry.

Almost three years earlier, when Kunstler and Brown published an article on Brown's legal entanglements in *University Review,* an obscure journal circulated primarily among college students, they could hardly have imagined its consequences. James B. Lake, Jr., a New Orleans patent attorney, read the article and was moved to send Kunstler a card, describing an incident about which he later testified to in Cassibry's courtroom. Prior to Brown's firearms trial in 1968, Lake met Judge Lansing Mitchell at a meeting of the Louisiana State Bar Association. While he, Judge Mitchell, and some other lawyers were sitting around a pool, someone inquired as to Mitchell's health, as he had been unwell recently. Judge Mitchell responded that "he was taking very good care of it [i.e., his health] because he had heard that he had been drawn as the Judge on the trial of Rap Brown . . . and . . . he was going to be very sure that he didn't get sick because he was going to get that . . . nigger."

Judge Mitchell denied that he would have made such a statement but did not recall what was said. At the conclusion of the hearing, Judge Cassibry stated from the bench that "I think Mr. Lake's version of what happened, happened. . . . Mr. Lake's recollection was clear and I think his version of what was said was probably said. That, taken with all of the other remarks that the Judge [i.e., Lansing Mitchell] made in some of his rulings, his sentences, his rulings, the bond[,] cast a serious shadow on this case as far as the appearance of justice is concerned." In his formal order of September 15, 1975, Cassibry found that the trial had been nonetheless fair, and refused to set aside the sentence. On appeal, however, the Fifth Circuit Court of Appeals reversed the conviction and sentence. It ordered a new trial on the basis that the judge's statement made an appearance of injustice and the record alone could not show whether Brown received a fair trial. The written record could not reveal Mitchell's facial expressions or unspoken attitudes and mannerisms, all of which may have influenced the jury. The appellate court went on to strongly suggest that on retrial, the trial judge allow defense counsel to themselves examine the COINTELPRO documents concerning Brown and not rely on a representation that they held no relevant information.

On September 24, 1976, the New York State Board of Parole announced that Brown would be released on parole in October, presumably, as they thought, to begin serving his federal sentence. However, on that same day, the Circuit Court of Appeals announced its reversal. On October 21, 1976, New York released Brown from prison on parole, and the federal prosecutors in New Orleans announced that they would not retry him and had dismissed the gun transportation charge. Brown was free at last.

While in prison, Brown became an even more devout Muslim and took the name of Jamil Abdullah Al-Amin. Later he became an imam, or spiritual leader, of Muslims in the rough part of Atlanta known as the West End. He also runs a grocery store there, where he has, according to Kunstler, excellent kosher dill pickles. The authorities still enjoy harassing him, however. In August 1995 the Atlanta police claimed that a victim of a shooting incident had identified Brown as his assailant. The policeman who made the subsequent routine arrest of Brown, invited agents of the FBI and ATF federal agencies to help him make the arrest. The invited federal agents were merely "friends" of the Atlanta officer, according to the official FBI spokesman, and did not participate in the arrest officially. Presumably they were invited to help share the joy of arresting the former H. Rap Brown. The victim later insisted he did not know who had shot him and that Brown's name came up only through police suggestion and pressure, and the case was dropped.

During this long legal saga, Brown and Kunstler became good friends. Brown married his wife, Lynne, now Karima, in a ceremony at the Kunstler house in Mamaroneck in May 1968. Brown included Kunstler among the persons to whom his 1969 autobiography was dedicated. Later, Kunstler watched Brown play on the prison football team. In his own autobiography, Kunstler wrote that Rap was his closest friend from the 1960s. Lotte Kunstler agreed. They each led busy lives, but took the time to call each other when passing through their cities. Rap came to Kunstler's seventy-fifth birthday celebration and sat at his table.

Throughout the last of the 1960s and early 1970s, Kunstler defended other militant blacks accused of serious crimes. The Harlem Five case, where black youths were accused in 1966 of plotting to steal arms and blow up various New York City bridges, became one of the best known of these. The major charges were dropped and Kunstler argued that "the entire case was part of a plan to arouse the public so that it would be willing to tolerate police brutality during the racial rebellions expected that summer." The Harlem Six/Four faced murder charges for the 1964 killing of a Jewish shopkeeper in Harlem. They were convicted in their first trial, but Kunstler helped secure a reversal. In the second trial, the judge refused to appoint Kunstler as trial counsel, but the jury hung. Kunstler was among the team that tried the third trial to another hung jury. Prior to the fourth trial, the chief prosecution witness recanted, then repudiated his recantation. The remaining defendants pled guilty to manslaughter charges, against Kunstler's advice, in return for suspended sentences. Kunstler commented, "The fact they had to plead guilty to crimes they didn't commit is a tragic reminder justice is truly blind."

Kunstler assisted militant blacks in other ways. He defended Daniel T. Taylor in disbarment hearings before the Kentucky State Bar Association. Taylor, like Kunstler, was a white lawyer who flamboyantly defended black militants. Kunstler was also among the team that convinced the U.S. Supreme Court that Congress had unconstitutionally denied the black politician Adam Clayton Powell the seat in the House of Representatives that he had won. Kunstler also defended Bobby Lee Williams, accused of assaulting a patrolman, John Gleason, with intent to kill during July 1967 riots in Plainfield, New Jersey. According to the prosecutor's theory, Williams "lured" Gleason into a black neighborhood. Williams threatened Gleason with a hammer, Gleason shot Williams in the stomach, and an angry black mob then followed Gleason and stomped him to death. It was in connection with this case that Kunstler made one of his most "outrageous" statements or, at least one on which he was continually questioned throughout his career. In connection with the Williams/Gleason, case he told a summer 1969 Black Panther rally in Oakland, California,

> In my opinion he [Officer Gleason] deserved that death. . . . The crowd justifiably, without the necessity of a trial and in the most dramatic way possible, stomped him to death. The reason was one that comes from 400 years, from the pillaging and marauding of black communities throughout the United States and the world by white power structures that have preyed upon the ghetto the way vultures prey on meat.

Kunstler became one of the few whites significantly involved with the earlier civil rights movement who successfully accommodated to the black empowerment movement of the late 1960s. Perhaps the reason for that was Kunstler's understanding of white racism. He believed that all white Americans, always including himself, were fundamentally racist, in the sense that whites grew up with an unconscious feeling of racial superiority. Blacks had a corresponding and unconscious feeling of racial inferiority. Therefore, black leadership, be it through SNCC, the Black Panthers, or something so benign as a black caucus in Congress or a church organization, was an essential part of blacks becoming truly equal. Black haircuts, black styles of clothing, beads, and the like also symbolized the strong urge of blacks to psychologically separate from white America. To Kunstler, it was a matter of blacks fighting for the right to look upon themselves as men, to be defined on their own terms. He repeated this theme in most of his talks during these years, be they before church conventions, as in his 1968 talk before the national Unitarian convention, or bar association groups, as in a talk of October 18, 1967, before a group of New York lawyers:

> It is an unprovable truism that all white people in the United States, from one end to the other, feel, consciously or subconsciously, depending on the locality they come from, that the black man is inferior to the white. . . . Generation upon generation of black men and women have grown to maturity with this built-in inferiority psychosis while white people have absorbed a correlative feeling of racial superiority.
>
>   This black-white schism can't even begin to be bridged by brotherhood dinners, by inter-racial marriages or by any other type of social

contact. It can only be altered, I believe, by centuries of time and generations of human beings. Today, when a black man in Newark is incensed by the fact that a policeman does this or that, the nature of the incident is essentially immaterial. If the springs of manhood are dammed by a situation intolerable to him, all of this history with its inherent hatred, all of this pent-up desire to have your destiny for one shining moment in your own hands pulsates to the surface. . . . He must have that moment. . . . Whether you call it black power, or self-determination, he must eventually control his own destiny.

We have already seen that Kunstler had a powerful need for approval and acceptance. In particular, he needed a sense of belonging to groups in which he could never quite fit, such as the Hispanic and black gang of his youth or the Christian groups of his college years. In the Black Power groups Kunstler sought not only approval but also a sense of belonging that was impossible. The inherent tension of trying to belong to a group in which it was impossible to have full membership must have given Kunstler many emotional highs and lows.

A reporter for an article appearing in *Life* in July 1969 asked George Fleming, an eighteen-year-old black militant, why he had a white man, Kunstler, as his lawyer. The youth answered, "He's the blackest white man I ever saw. He can be trusted." That would have been an emotional high for Kunstler. In contrast, two years later in New Orleans, a newly appointed black federal judge, Israel Myer Augustine, Jr., was about to preside over the prosecution of a Black Panther group. Kunstler attacked the trial as a "legal lynching," and specifically denounced the new judge as "very much a part of the white system." Judge Augustine replied to a reporter, "Bill Kunstler doesn't know me very well. However I might feel, I'm a hell of a lot blacker than he will ever be."

Representation of controversial black militants brought Kunstler a considerable amount of publicity. For readers of the *New York Times* his name and stance would be quite familiar by 1969. However, by the end of 1969 Kunstler's name would become a household word across all of America. Black Power brought Kunstler attention, but the Chicago Eight/Seven trial would bring him fame.

6

Circus in Chicago

ON SEPTEMBER 24, 1969, at the beginning of the almost five-month Chicago Seven trial (eight original defendants, later reduced to seven), an official of the American Civil Liberties Union predicted that the trial would be "probably the most important political trial in the history of the United States." Twenty-six years later, another writer could still comfortably refer to it as "one of the most political and publicized trials in American history." Few trials have exhibited such blatant bias on the part of an American judge, who ordered the gagging and hog-tieing of a defendant who merely wished to represent himself; few trials have prompted defendants to interrupt and jeer at the judge and prosecutor, wear casual clothes, stomp on judicial robes, refuse to rise, talk back to the judge, call him a racist and fascist, and encourage cheering sections to shout "right on"; and few trials have prompted national demonstrations of young people protesting the trial itself. Commentators call many trials "circus," although few trials deserve that sobriquet. However, the Chicago Seven trial is well entitled to the description.

It was the theatrics of the defendants and their supporters and the sharpness of the repartee between Kunstler and the judge that attracted the bulk of the wide publicity given the trial, not the seriousness of the issues involved. The national press and a considerable sector of the international press covered the trial. Some newspapers, such as the *New York Times,* assigned a writer the exclusive job of that trial's coverage for its duration. The federal courts did not permit cameras, but the frequent courtroom interruptions lent themselves well to cartoon representation on national television, which frequently carried reportage of the trial. It was this exposure that gave Kunstler national media attention and fame.

Abbie Hoffman, one of the principal defendants, estimated that as of 1980, some twenty books already had been written about the trial. Journalists assigned to the story wrote contemporary books, several of the defendants and attorneys included lengthy discussions of the trial in their memoirs, and scholarly accounts followed. BBC-TV staged the trial as a television drama as early as 1969, and it became one of the most popular English shows of the year. An HBO version, *Conspiracy: The Trial of the Chicago Eight,* appeared in May 1987. A&E's series *American Justice,* aired a documentary, *Riot: The Chicago Conspiracy Trial,* [i.e., Chicago Seven], in November 1994 that was rebroadcast in August 1996. Radio also adapted the Chicago trial to play form, most recently in 1993 but on earlier occasions as well. Finally, the theatre itself utilized the Chicago Seven trial. A successful stage play, *The Chicago Conspiracy Trial,* first appeared in 1979 and was revived in 1994.

The trial constituted the culmination of the 1960s, emotionally as well as chronologically. Its immediate causes began with the government's reaction to the many, and very different, political and cultural groups that held demonstrations to coincide with the Democratic National Convention in Chicago in late August 1968. Most of these groups protested against the Vietnam War, despised President Johnson, and then, after he stepped aside, denounced the refusal of Hubert H. Humphrey, his heir apparent, to disavow Johnson's Vietnam policies. Various other left-wing and revolutionary groups voiced their protests, as did the youth of the counterculture, in revolt against the mainstream values and mores of traditional America.

Five men constituted the principal movers and shakers of the protesters. David Dellinger, the oldest of the Chicago defendants at age fifty-four, was a Christian socialist and an old-line pacifist. He organized the National Mobilization Committee to End the War in Viet Nam, or MOBE, a loose coalition of over one hundred anti-Vietnam groups. Two younger defendants, Tom Hayden and Rennie Davis, founders of the left-of-center student group Students for a Democratic Society, or SDS, were more revolutionary in their thought than Dellinger, but together the three planned protests and demonstrations in Chicago during the Democratic Convention under the auspices of MOBE. Abbie Hoffman and Jerry Rubin were two young men of a quite different persuasion than the other defendants. Although equally opposed to Vietnam, Hoffman and Rubin were counterculturalists in orientation, opposed to what they deplored as the bourgeois standards and mores of mainstream America. They had formed an extremely loosely organized group, Youth International Party, or Yippies. It planned a youth festival, the "Festival of Life" (as opposed, in their minds, to the Convention of

Death), for August 1968, which would feature rock concerts, "be-ins," and political education. Although there were vast differences between these men, in both tactics and goals, they worked together in a loose way to plan demonstrations in Chicago in the months preceding the convention. They applied for various march permits from the city, whose administrators chose to play a game of evasion and ultimately, at the last moment, turned them down.

During the week of the convention, these five men made many speeches to a large, youthful crowd of several thousand. The speeches were fiery in nature, intemperate by conventional standards, and incitements to riot by police standards. There was loose talk of "taking the streets," "offing the pigs," and other expressions of violence. Bobby Seale, the chairman of the Black Panther Party, made two of these fiery speeches. He replaced another speaker at the last minute, stayed in Chicago only briefly, and prior to his indictment for conspiracy with the other defendants had never met them, except for a brief encounter with Jerry Rubin. Two other defendants, John Froines and Lee Weiner, were marshals during the demonstrations, and attempted to bring order to the parades and marches. Seven of the eight defendants were between the ages of twenty-nine and thirty-one.

The police blocked most of the parades. That led to pushing and shoving, taunts by the demonstrators, and some minor acts of violence. In response, the police went berserk. Many took off their badges and waded into the crowd, indiscriminately clubbing demonstrators and any bystanders in the way. Walter Cronkite, the television newsman, captured the events for national television and called the Chicago policemen "thugs." The Chicago police slugged Dan Rather, the CBS reporter. After the riots, in which hundreds were seriously injured by the police, a commission investigated the disturbances. Daniel Walker, a prominent local attorney and the head of the Chicago Crime Commission, conducted a very comprehensive investigation, and had access to 3,437 eyewitness accounts, together with the FBI and police records. The official conclusion of the Walker Commission is notable:

> During the week of the Democratic National Convention, the Chicago police were targets of mounting provocation by both word and act. . . . The nature of the response was unrestrained and indiscriminate police violence on many occasions, particularly at night. That violence was made all the more shocking by the fact that it was often inflicted

upon persons who had broken no law, disobeyed no order, made no threat. . . . To read dispassionately the hundreds of statements describing at firsthand the events . . . is to become convinced of the presence of what can only be called a police riot.

The report made Chicago mayor Richard J. Daley livid with anger. He demanded vindication for Chicago, a purification of the city's name through the prosecution of the protests' leaders. He had longtime friends and political cronies in the persons of Chief Judge William J. Campbell of the federal district court in Chicago, the man in charge of the federal grand juries, which indict criminal defendants, and Thomas A. Foran, the United States attorney in Chicago. These men investigated the Chicago riots with an eye toward prosecuting the men who led the demonstrations.

In the spring that preceded the Chicago police riot, Congress had passed what was popularly called the "Rap Brown law," since it was designed to criminalize the movement of black militants, especially H. Rap Brown and Stokely Carmichael, from place to place throughout the country, igniting black rebellions in the ghettos. The statute is complex and is contained in Section 2101 of Title 18 of the United States Code. As applied to the Chicago situation, the law made it a felony to travel in interstate commerce with the intent to incite, organize, promote, and encourage a riot and thereafter, after having crossed a state line, do an act, such as making a fiery speech, with the purpose of inciting, organizing, promoting, and encouraging a riot.

During the remaining tenure of the Johnson administration, Attorney General Ramsey Clark refused to prosecute the demonstrators, believing that the violence was primarily a police riot. The new Nixon administration, elected in part to "restore law and order," did not hesitate to indict Dellinger, Hayden, and Davis (the MOBE group) along with Hoffman and Rubin (the Yippies) under this statute. Although the Black Panthers were not really allied with these two groups, and Bobby Seale had no planning role in the demonstrations whatsoever, he was also included because of his alleged incendiary remarks in the parks of Chicago prior to the skirmishes with the police. The government charged Froines and Weiner with teaching the use of an incendiary device, a bomb. All eight defendants were charged with a conspiracy with each other to violate these statutes. The statute carried a five-year punishment and the conspiracy count added five additional years.

It was a most peculiar conspiracy, since each of the defendants pursued his own agenda, and the goals of the Yippies were far different from the more dedicated revolutionary aims of the SDS contingent. The aims of Seale and his Black Panthers were still different. Abbie Hoffman's quip, that it was a hell of a conspiracy since the defendants could not even agree on lunch, was on the mark. However, the defendants and their lawyers saw a very different purpose behind their inclusion together as joint defendants in the conspiracy charge. It was, they claimed, an ideological prosecution against dissent itself, since each defendant represented a different part of the spectrum of American protest.

Dellinger represented old-line pacifism; Hoffman and Rubin, the counterculture; Hayden and Davis, the student radicals. The prosecution threw Seale in to include the black militants. Even Froines and Weiner, minor figures as they were, counted as representatives of academic protest, since one was a professor and the other a graduate student. The defendants' attorneys charged that the prosecution represented the government's coordinated effort "to jail in one prosecution prominent individuals representing almost every shade of opinion along the spectrum of contemporary political and social dissent." Contemporary scholars and journalists observed much the same government purpose. Even were a prosecution unsuccessful, it would tie the defendants down and prevent them, so government officials reasoned, from doing much political and protest work during the course of the trial. Much later, documents obtained under the Freedom of Information Act indicated that the FBI director J. Edgar Hoover had informed his key lieutenants as early as October 1968 that "approximately twenty principal leaders and activists of various New Left organizations" would be charged under the federal antiriot law for their Chicago activities. Such prosecution, Hoover argued, "should seriously disrupt and curtail the activities of the New Left."

Although from many different radical traditions and backgrounds, the Chicago Eight united around the belief that theirs should be a political defense. They had followed the earlier case of the Boston Five, involving the conspiracy prosecution of Dr. Benjamin Spock and his codefendants for their Vietnam protests. The Boston Five had submitted meekly to a trial judge's rulings that evidence of American atrocities in Vietnam was irrelevant, had dressed "properly" for court, had curtailed their own speaking engagements, had permitted their attorneys to conduct a narrow, legal defense, and in the end had been duly convicted. The Chicago Eight wanted none of that. As Tom Hayden explained in a newsletter, *The Movement*, in May 1969, four months before the beginning of the trial,

> We want to make sure we win our case in Chicago not by narrow technical maneuvers in the courtroom. . . . We want to use our case to go over once again what the basic issues raised in Chicago were. We want to win our case on the basis of widespread popular support. . . . In order to do this, we'll have to define the issues quite differently from the way they'll be defined by the judge. . . . We're going to have to bring into the courtroom the fact that the real conspiracy in Chicago was planned by an element of the ruling class, including President Johnson and others associated with him, as a direct attempt to intimidate the anti-war movement and the revolutionary movement in this country.

Dave Dellinger wrote much the same thing later:

> At the beginning the commitment to conduct a political trial meant conducting a collective defense and having the defendants control the lawyers rather than allowing them to control the line of defense on technical, legal grounds. . . . we wanted to bring our politics into the courtroom, not in the form of arbitrary outbursts . . . but by dressing in our natural style, by acting as naturally as possible instead of like robots or Uncle Toms . . . , and in the presentation and handling of the evidence. We wanted not only to affirm what we had done and why but to make it clear to any honest observer that the guilty parties were the government and the system. We wanted to do this not only through the evidence and in news conferences and speeches but also by continuing as active members of the movement.

Hoffman and Rubin wanted Kunstler as a part of the defense team, as Kunstler had earlier represented them before the House Un-American Activities Committee. Dellinger's top choices were unavailable, but one of them, Arthur Kinoy, recommended his former partner Bill Kunstler. According to Dellinger, Hayden objected to Kunstler, arguing that he "was a liberal whose conventional approach to law and the courts would interfere with the kind of trial we had in mind." Hayden's personal choice was Leonard Weinglass, who Hayden judged to have the sensitivity and courtroom skills to win any jury, although Hoffman and Rubin (who wanted Kunstler) worried that Weinglass was too "straight" and inexperienced.

The fate of Bobby Seale overrode these concerns. Seale faced capital murder charges in Connecticut, and the result of the Chicago trial might be monumental for him. Seale did not know or feel comfortable with the attorneys advanced by the other defendants and insisted that only Charles R. Garry, his personal attorney and general counsel to the Black Panther Party, could represent him. The other defendants acceded to his wishes out of deference to blacks in the movement, because of their shock that Seale had been included in the indictment for his minor involvement in the Chicago demonstrations, and in view of the serious other charges he was facing.

Nevertheless, the other defendants did not truly want Seale's California lawyer. At their first joint meeting, Garry handed the seven defendants a bill for $375,000 and informed them he would enter the case only if he could be chief counsel and make all the final decisions. Garry warned them against any outbursts or disrespectful behavior during trial. The $375,000 bill was apparently not pursued, and the defendants did reach some agreement with Garry whereby they would continue their antiwar activities. That left the second chair attorneys to be selected. Dellinger argued for Kunstler, agreeing with Hayden that while Kunstler was no radical, his background in civil rights cases indicated good instincts that meant "there's something inside him that we can build on."

The defendants selected a team of Garry as chief counsel, assisted by Bill Kunstler, Leonard Weinglass, and Gerald Lefcourt. Lefcourt quickly withdrew because of the Panther 21 trial in New York, but, as Abbie Hoffman put it, "Bill Kunstler swallowed his big ego long enough to agree to play second fiddle at what would have been Garry's wedding." As of the summer of 1969, with a trial date set for September 24, Charles R. Garry was the lead attorney, albeit a somewhat reluctant choice by seven of the eight defendants.

The judge chosen to try the case, by a process probably not as random as the court clerk claimed, was Julius J. Hoffman (no relation to Abbie), a 1953 Eisenhower appointee. Hoffman was a short man of seventy-four, with a balding head and sometimes comical manner; the defendants thought of him as Mr. Magoo, the cartoon character. Chicago attorneys interviewed by journalists reported that Judge Hoffman always identified with the government and saw "the defense in any criminal case as the enemy and . . . his duty to help put them away." He was vain, pompous, formal, a stickler for dignified decorum—a perfect martinet. When a reporter telephoned him for press credentials in September, on the eve of trial, Hoffman asked him, "Tell me something. Do you think this is going to be the trial of the century?" Kunstler quickly sized him up as a man who could be baited. Drawing Hoffman as the trial judge became, as Kunstler many years later acknowledged, the first major break for the defendants.

The defense filed motions. It asked that Hoffman excuse himself for bias. Denied. It asked that the trial date be postponed because of prejudicial publicity in Chicago concerning the defendants. Denied.The most important pretrial motion that Hoffman denied was for a six-week continuance. The defendants' chief counsel had been advised by his doctors that his life was in danger unless he had a gall bladder operation. Garry made those representations in person and with medical affidavits. The prosecutor termed the motion a "ploy" Hoffman denied the motion, and the trial proceeded without Garry and with Kunstler as chief counsel.

The absence of Garry had profound ramifications. Garry was the only attorney with the ability and will to control the theatrics of certain of the defendants. When Hoffman denied Garry's motion, Garry advised him that Seale would be unrepresented at trial, and it was Hoffman's subsequent refusal to allow Seale to represent himself that was the cause of most of the later commotion at trial. Interestingly enough, on February 17, 1970, while waiting for the jury's verdict, Hoffman heard another motion for a six-week delay in a criminal case. In that case, the defense counsel sought a continuance, not to address a life-threatening condition, as had Garry, but to take a six-week Caribbean vacation. Hoffman readily granted that motion. The different treatment reflected Hoffman's bias toward the government and against these defendants; the second defense attorney who wanted the continuance to take a vacation had formerly been an assistant United States attorney.

Judge Hoffman found a few more ways to display his prejudice against the defendants even before the trial began. When the jury selection began, the defense submitted forty-four questions, most touching on lifestyle attitudes, that it requested the judge to ask prospective jurors, such as "Do you have any hostile feelings toward persons whose

lifestyles differ from your own?" "Would you let your son or daughter
marry a Yippie?" "Do you believe that Martin Luther King, Jr., should
have come to Chicago in 1967 to lead demonstrators?" The judge rejected all but one of the defendants' questions and conducted only a
perfunctory examination of prospective jurors. Hoffman also displayed
anger toward the defense when he ordered the arrest of all the attorneys
who had appeared for pretrial motions but had sent in their notices of
withdrawal by wire instead of appearing before him personally.

The details of the trial are not as important as *how* it was conducted,
and the reaction of the defendants and their attorneys, especially Kunstler, to the conduct of the judge and prosecutor. After the trial ended,
the trial judge imposed massive contempt sentences on all defendants
and all defense attorneys. It was a most unruly trial. The most neutral
source that summarized the trial was the reviewing appellate court, the
United States Court of Appeals for the Seventh Circuit. That court in its
1972 opinion observed that

> Trial decorum often fell victim to dramatic and emotionally inflam-
> matory episodes. . . . There were numerous disorders and outbursts
> among spectators . . . On occasion, trial procedure seems to have dis-
> integrated into uproar. The record indicates that at times there were as
> many as 19 marshalls in the courtroom. It also shows provocative,
> sometimes insulting, language and activity by several defendants. . . .
>
> The district judge's [i.e., Julius J. Hoffman's] deprecatory and often
> antagonistic attitude toward the defense is evident in the record from
> the very beginning. It appears in remarks and actions both in the pres-
> ence and absence of the jury. . . . the judge was more likely to exercise
> his discretion against the defense than against the government. . . . [He
> made] remarks in the presence of the jury, deprecatory of defense
> counsel and their case. These comments were often touched with sar-
> casm, implying rather than saying outright that defense counsel was
> inept, bumptious, or untrustworthy, or that his case lacked merit.
> Sometimes the comment was not associated with any ruling in ordi-
> nary course; sometimes gratuitously added to an otherwise proper
> ruling; nearly always unnecessary. . . . cumulatively, they must have
> telegraphed to the jury the judge's contempt for the defense.

The appellate court also criticized the prosecutors for remarks before the jury that were not justified by the defense conduct and "fell

below the standards applicable to a representative of the United States."
It was, however, primarily the judge's misconduct that determined the
response of the defense and Kunstler. It gave the defendants ample opportunity to engage in theatrics far beyond those originally planned
and for Kunstler to engage in acerbic repartee with the trial judge. In
doing so, they appealed to a public beyond the jury, to the alienated
young men and women of the nation as a whole, to make their case
against the war in Vietnam and for the legitimacy of their lifestyles and
revolutionary ideas.

In fact, Kunstler later claimed that being assigned Judge Hoffman
was "our first big break. He was the perfect judge for this case." He explained in 1970, months after the trial and before the appeal had been
decided,

> I think the trial might have taken a very different turn if there had been
> another kind of judge. But from the point of view of the political edu-
> cation that we intended as a vital part of the trial, Hoffman was the
> best judge we could have had. His total lack of sensibility, his total lack
> of a sense of public relations, his total commitment to the conviction of
> the defendants all made him commit not only legal errors but also er-
> rors in the area of public opinion. And it was these errors which helped
> gain the defendants so much public support, particularly among the
> young. . . . a much fairer judge—would perhaps not have enabled the
> defendants to present as dramatic and convincing a case as they did to
> the general public.

At the beginning of the trial, the defendants had put much hope for
an eventual hung jury on a single juror, Kristi King, a twenty-three-
year-old housewife, who had been carrying a book written by the black
writer James Baldwin when she was called to the jury box. Very early in
the trial, during the first witness's testimony, it was reported that King
and an older juror had received notes saying "You are being watched.
The Black Panthers." Hoffman held a hearing as to what should be
done. The older juror, Ruth Petersen, testified she would not be affected
by the note and remained on the jury. King had not actually read her
note since her family had turned it over to the FBI. Even though she had
not actually seen it, Hoffman made her read the note aloud, and then
asked her whether she could continue to be fair and impartial. According to journalists' reports, she stared at Bobby Seale, appeared to be on

the verge of tears, and said she could not. Judge Hoffman excused her and appointed an alternate.

When Kunstler informed Bobby Seale about the two notes, he responded, "We're not going to send any stupid notes like that, man. Somebody's railroading us." The defendants held a press conference and charged that the notes were FBI forgeries. As Seale put it, the notes constituted "a plot by the FBI and other lackey pig agents to tamper with the jury and then try to blame it on the Black Panther Party." When Hoffman heard of this press conference he ordered the trial jury held in a hotel and sequestered for the remaining four months of trial. This also worked to the disadvantage of the defense. Juries held in custody tend to blame the defendants for their plight rather than the judge who orders, or the prosecution that requests, what is in effect a high-class jailing.

There is a high probability that the "Black Panther" notes were forged by the FBI. This was a high point in the COINTELPRO program, and forged notes with this type of disinformation fit its profile. Kunstler later charged a much broader interference by the FBI: "Prior to and during the trial, judge, prosecutors, and FBI agents had colluded and conspired. They conferred daily, infiltrated the defense by taping some of our key legal meetings, and had secret communications with some of the jurors." These were not just ravings. In the late 1970s Kunstler obtained FBI documents under the Freedom of Information Act that corroborated this.

Ten years after the trial, after he had received the documents, Kunstler brought a court motion to expunge the few remaining contempt citations on the basis of the FBI's illegal actions. The federal courts denied this on the basis that the FBI's "dirty tricks" did not contribute to the contempt of counsel or defendants. However, the federal appellate court summarized the FBI documents, and this revealed the illegal interference by the FBI with the earlier trial. One FBI memorandum, the appellate panel found in 1981, "suggests that Judge Hoffman had *ex parte* conversations with Foran [the chief prosecutor] concerning both the defendants' possible claim of adverse publicity and the possible contempt citations against the defendants." In other words, the judge and prosecutor were talking the trial over in the absence of defense counsel, or as Kunstler put it, they colluded—a matter of gross impropriety.

The government secretly and illegally spied on legal strategy meetings between the Chicago defendants and their lawyers. The federal appellate panel in 1981 wrote that three of the FBI documents indicated that "the Chicago Police and possibly the FBI had surreptitiously attended and/or surveilled several meetings of the defendants and their counsel. It appears that information obtained in this manner (including trial strategies and potential arguments on appeal) was forwarded to Assistant United States Attorney Richard Schultz, one of the prosecutors." Even at the time of the trial in 1969, defense counsel complained that police agents were spying on their meetings with the defendants. At the time the FBI records showed he was currently receiving the surveillance reports, the same U.S. Attorney, Richard Schultz, denied it, saying, "we know what's illegal. We don't do illegal acts." The later evidence clearly showed that not only do United States attorneys do illegal acts, they also lie to cover them up.

As for the "Black Panther" notes, the FBI records indicated that Hoffman promised an investigation but later secretly halted it. Without informing defense counsel, Hoffman and the chief prosecutor ordered that "no investigation should be undertaken" without the consent of the United States attorney. In other words, the inference is that the notes were phony, the prosecutor and Hoffman knew that, and they prevented any investigation that might reveal that truth. The federal appellate panel that reviewed this evidence of judicial and prosecutorial corruption, even though it refused to disturb the contempt citations, was plainly disturbed by these revelations: "We have little doubt that the wrongdoing suggested by the FBI documents would have required reversal of any convictions obtained in the 1969 conspiracy trial [they had already been reversed for other reasons]. The government's alleged acquiescence in the surveillance of private meetings of the defendants and their counsel appears particularly egregious."

As we have seen, before the beginning of the trial Hoffman denied a motion for a continuance because of the chief attorney's gall bladder operation. When the selection of the jury began on September 24, 1969, Kunstler signed an appearance for four of the defendants and Weinglass appeared for the four others, although the attorneys made it clear on the record that the defendants were not fully represented because of Garry's absence. Two days later and before the first witness had testified, Seale discharged Kunstler and filed a motion that he be permitted to represent himself if Garry could not do so for him. Hoffman denied the motion and ignored Seale's firing of Kunstler.

From September 26 until November 5, the courtroom became the scene of rising tensions and hostilities between Seale and Hoffman. Seale insistently and with rising forcefulness demanded that he be allowed to represent himself and to cross-examine witnesses who referred to him. The judge repeatedly refused him that right, stating that Kunstler was his lawyer. Kunstler thereupon always insisted that he was not, that he had been discharged, and that the other defendants supported Seale's right to represent himself.

In the early stages of this rising tension, Seale rarely spoke except at moments when it would have been appropriate for an attorney representing him to speak, as for example a time for cross-examination. As October wore on, and the judge showed no sign of relenting, Seale increasingly began stating to the jury his perception of the judge's unfairness in not allowing him the right to represent himself. He began berating the judge. When the judge threatened Seale with contempt, Seale responded by calling Hoffman "racist," "fascist," and other taunts. Ultimately, Hoffman ordered the marshals to bind and gag Seale and chain him to his chair.

This procedure caused its own problems. At times the gag and binding were so tight that they caused Seale obvious physical distress, apparent to everyone in the courtroom. The other defendants issued loud and profane protestations. At other times the gag was so loose that Seale could speak his demand to represent himself audibly from beneath the gag. On another occasion Seale broke loose from his bindings. Marshals then lunged at Seale, toppled over several reporters, and caused vigorous protest from other defendants and cries of indignation from spectators. Sometimes the jury was present for these proceedings, and other times it was hustled out. At one altercation between the marshals and Seale, Kunstler called the proceedings "medieval torture."

> MR. KUNSTLER: Your Honor, are we going to stop this medieval torture that is going on in this courtroom? I think this is a disgrace.
>
> MR. RUBIN: This guy is putting his elbow in Bobby's [Seale] mouth and it wasn't necessary at all.
>
> MR. KUNSTLER: This is no longer a court of order, your Honor;

this is a medieval torture chamber. It is a disgrace. They are attacking the other defendants also.

MR. RUBIN: Don't hit me in my balls, motherfucker.

MR. SEALE: This motherfucker is tight and it is stopping my blood.

MR. KUNSTLER: Your Honor, this is an unholy disgrace to the law that is going on in this courtroom and I as an American lawyer feel a disgrace.

MR. FORAN [CHIEF PROSECUTOR]: Created by Mr. Kunstler.

MR. KUNSTLER: Created by nothing else than what you have done to this man.

MR. ABBIE HOFFMAN: You come down here and watch it, Judge.

MR. SEALE: You fascist dogs, you rotten, low-life, son-of-a-bitch.

A short time later, when the jury had returned, Rennie Davis stood up and addressed the jury. He told them, "He [Seale] was being tortured while you were out of this room by these marshals. They come and torture him while you are out of the room. It is terrible what is happening. It is terrible what is happening." The judge immediately ordered the jury to leave again, and as they left the defendants chimed in again:

MR. HAYDEN: Now they are going to beat him, they are going to beat him.

ABBIE HOFFMAN: You may as well kill him if you are going to gag him. It seems that way, doesn't it?

THE COURT: You are not permitted to address the Court, Mr. Hoffman. You have a lawyer.

ABBIE HOFFMAN: This isn't a court. This is a neon oven.

MR. FORAN: That was the defendant Hoffman who spoke.

MR. SCHULTZ: Prior to that it was Mr. Hayden who was addressing the jury while they were walking out of here.

MR. HAYDEN: I was not addressing the jury. I was trying to protect Mr. Seale. A man is supposed to be silent when he sees another man's nose being smashed?

ABBIE HOFFMAN: The disruption started when these guys got into overkill. It is the same thing as last year in Chicago, the same exact thing.

THE COURT: Mr. Hoffman, you are directed to refrain from speaking. You are ordered to refrain from speaking.

Once Seale had been gagged, all the defendants refused to rise when the judge entered or left. These uproars continued until November 5, 1969, when Seale was severed from the rest of the defendants for separate trial and sentenced to four years imprisonment for contempt. The Chicago Eight became the Chicago Seven.

As the trial became more obstreperous and the defendants became increasingly convinced they would not be treated fairly in Julius Hoffman's courtroom, the defendants, especially the Yippies, increased their guerrilla-theatre tactics of taunts and pranks. These were designed to discredit the judge, the prosecutors, and the political nature of the prosecution itself. They aimed their tactics at the greater public; certainly they had no thought that the jury or judge could ever view them humorously.

One day the defendants brought in a Vietcong flag and displayed it on the defendants' table, resulting in a tug-of-war with the marshals, who removed it; another day, the defendants entered the courtroom wearing judicial robes covered by Stars of David, and while Judge Hoffman watched removed the robes, threw them on the floor, and wiped their feet on them. They taunted the judge verbally. Abbie Hoffman insulted him in Yiddish (Judge Hoffman seemed very sensitive about his Jewishness), and asked him, "How is your war stock, Julie?" Jerry Rubin told him, "You're the laughing stock of the world. Every kid in the world hates you because they know what you represent. You are synonymous with Adolf Hitler." The defendants sat at their table, often reading, writing speeches, munching jelly beans, making faces, or laughing. Sometimes they slept. Litter piled up on their table and the carpet underneath it.

Both Kunstler and Abbie Hoffman insisted later that these outbursts were not spontaneous or impulsive, but a deliberate part of the defense strategy. Kunstler saw them as part of their strategy of putting the government on trial. "The defendants taught us how to show up the government's weaknesses and follies by satirizing and mocking its pompousness. . . . all of these actions [defendants' flamboyant outbursts], no matter how wacky and spontaneous they appeared, contributed to the defense strategy of putting the government on trial." The media cooperated wonderfully, giving great publicity to the trial. A song about the gagging of Bobby Seale rose to the Top 40 chart.

Abbie Hoffman agreed with Kunstler's description of their strategy:

[Some of the defendants] went the nonlinear route of communicating through symbols, gestures, and other means to a television audience. We didn't exactly stage the trial for television, but one could not be unaware of its lurking presence. Millions of viewers saw us, not as we actually were but as cartoon figures sketched by day [literally, as live television was not allowed] and flashed every evening into the nation's living rooms. . . . Cartoons are graphic, exaggerated, and action-oriented. Yippie politics could scarcely conceive of a better means of expressing ideas.

We wanted to reach young people. We wanted to "show" we were different from those prosecuting us. We wanted to present a synopsis of the issues dividing the nation, thereby elevating our cause to equal footing with the government. We could never hope to accomplish this power struggle with arms; we could only begin to manage it with imagery. An imagery designed to force those in between to choose sides. Once involved in the trial, most people quickly allied themselves with either the defendants or the prosecutors. . . . [I]n general we divided the population to a far greater extent than had any trial in U.S. history. It brought us one step shy of armed civil war and proved a fitting summary for a decade of confrontation.

On Kunstler's part, he and Len Weinglass decided to

put the government on trial. Len and I attacked, fought like dogs, ripping the government's witnesses apart, often with wit and ridicule. . . . I learned how to handle Judge Hoffman. I began to fight fire with fire, sarcasm with sarcasm. . . . Once, protesting obviously perjured testimony, I said, "It doesn't smell like Chanel Number 5 to me." "Is that the perfume you use, Mr. Kunstler?" asked the homophobic judge. "No, I'm a Brut man myself," I responded. The jury laughed, and this time the joke was on Hoffman. Whenever I could, I would take his barbs and digs and turn them against him using every bit of wit I possessed to offset his hostility.

On another occasion Kunstler protested the prosecutors' reference to defense counsel being "phony and two-faced."

MR. KUNSTLER: You know it is not right. To call a man "phony" and "two-faced" in oral argument is not right. We both know

that. You don't say anything and you are countenancing the
remark.

THE COURT: For your information, maybe you don't know it,
the word "phony" is in the dictionary.

MR. KUNSTLER: So is the word "pig," Your Honor.

One of Kunstler's wittiest responses came during one of many discussions about whether this was a political trial. Kunstler insisted that
it was indeed a political case.

JUDGE HOFFMAN: It is a criminal case. There is an indictment
here. I can't go into politics here in this court.

KUNSTLER: Your Honor, Jesus was accused criminally, too, and
we understand really that was not truly a criminal case in the
sense that it is just an ordinary—

JUDGE HOFFMAN: I didn't live at that time. I don't know. Some
people think I go back that far, but I really didn't.

KUNSTLER: Well, I was assuming Your Honor had read of the
incident.

The classic was Kunstler's marijuana motion. The Chicago defendants received a great deal of mail every day, addressed to them in care
of Judge Hoffman. The marshals delivered it twice a day. Once an en-
velope of marijuana arrived with the mail. Kunstler covered it up with
a newspaper and worried about it all day. He proposed leaving it for the
cleaning woman to find. His clients vetoed that idea, protesting that
perfectly good marijuana ought not be wasted.

So I made my first and only marijuana motion. "Your Honor, there was
delivered to us, courtesy of your courtroom deputy, a supply of
cannabis, a controlled substance under the federal code. I would like
your instructions on what to do about it."

"Mr. Kunstler, you're a resolute attorney. I'm sure you'll know how
to dispose of it," replied the judge. "Your Honor," I promised, "it will
be burned tonight."

In a 1994 interview Kunstler told a reporter that it was promptly divided up in the washroom. He assured the reporter that "it was burnt
that night."

It may be helpful to once again turn to a neutral source to appraise the cause and impact of the alleged disturbances that plagued the Chicago Conspiracy Trial. Ultimately the contempt matters were retried before a different judge. As to the disturbances that surrounded the gagging of Bobby Seale, the second judge noted that "the principal cause of this disintegration was the appalling spectacle of a bound and gagged defendant and the marshals' efforts to subdue him. The evidence does not establish beyond a reasonable doubt that the conduct charged to these defendants in these specifications was the cause of the breakdown of the proceedings." As to the remainder of the trial, the reviewing judge noted that "almost every session was punctuated by spectator disorder and outbursts and by recriminatory exchanges between the judge and prosecutors, on the one hand, and the defendants and their counsel on the other. . . . On a number of occasions, the trial so completely disintegrated that it could not be said that a judicial proceeding was in progress." The reviewing judge also noted the appellate court's finding of judicial and prosecutorial misconduct and found that most of the questionable conduct of the defendants and their lawyers "cannot be considered apart from the conduct of the trial judge and prosecutors. Each reacted to provocation by the other."

This contrasts with the later assertions of both Kunstler and Abbie Hoffman that the courtroom theatrics were planned, in an effort to put the government on trial and promote the defendants' political objectives. Kunstler made those assertions in his 1994 autobiography; Hoffman, in his 1980 book. While the contempt matters were still pending, Kunstler took the position that the reviewing judge later did in 1973. For example, in his October 1970 interview in *Playboy*, Kunstler argued that the defendants' courtroom outbursts were merely spontaneous reactions to provocations by the judge. Either the notion of purposeful planning made for a better story later on, or it was too dangerous to admit it while the contempt matters were pending.

In the midst of the theatrics and the outbursts, a trial was still in progress, and there were witnesses called to the stand, questions asked, objections made, answers given, the same as in any trial. The prosecution evidence consisted of undercover agents who had infiltrated the demonstrators' ranks, witnesses to inflammatory speeches, witnesses to the marches, and so forth—all tending to show that the Chicago activities of the defendants promoted riot. The defense objected on the theory that the defendants' speeches in Chicago were protected by the

First Amendment. The prosecution countered that the essence of the violation was the crossing of a state line with the wrong intent, a little like the Mann Act, and that the later speeches might well be protected by the First Amendment but they did show the intent in the defendants' minds.

The defense presented a large number of witnesses. Some testimony attempted to prove that the defendants had come to Chicago with intentions of peaceful protest and the violence had been caused by the police. Other testimony tried to show the jury (and the nation beyond) the nature of the defendants' lifestyles and their hopes and aspirations for the future. The defense witnesses ranged widely, from the Reverend Jesse Jackson, civil rights activist, to Timothy Leary, drug guru of the youth. Ramsey Clark, former United States attorney general, and Ralph Abernathy, Martin Luther King's successor, were in court to testify for the defense, although Judge Hoffman denied them permission to do so.

The comedian Dick Gregory testified for the defense, as did the Pulitzer Prize–winning author William Styron. Judge Hoffman stopped the singers Judy Collins, Phil Ochs, and Arlo Guthrie from singing, but did permit them to read the lyrics of various songs of protest. Objection from the prosecution halted Allen Ginsberg after his second chanted "om," but Ginsberg renewed the chant on his own to calm Kunstler and the judge after they got into a confrontation. Dozens of less-celebrated witnesses who had simply been witnesses to (or victims of) the police brutalities paraded to the stand. Hugh Hefner was a notable victim of the police assault who did *not* testify. The defense subpoenaed him, but, according to Kunstler, he bought his way out of the subpoena by a $10,000 contribution to the defense fund, a sum so high it could not be refused.

Kunstler even called Mayor Daley to the stand, although he made little headway as Hoffman refused to permit Kunstler to cross-examine him as an adverse witness. Throughout the testimony, Judge Hoffman seemed to impose a double standard in his evidentiary rulings. He was much more stringent on the defense, and his refusal to permit the jury to hear or see certain evidence offered by the defense became a separate ground for the ultimate reversal of the conviction.

After the jury was instructed and sent out to deliberate, Judge Hoffman found the defendants guilty of 159 contempts and sentenced them to jail for terms ranging from as short as two months and eight days (Weiner) to as long as four years and thirteen days (Kunstler). Case law limited judges to sentences of no more than six months without a jury trial, but Hoffman attempted to circumvent that. He limited the sentence per incident to the maximum or less, but then ran them consecutively, resulting in a high total.

Many of the defendants made powerful remarks when they were sentenced for contempt. Kunstler's was among the most notable:

> I have tried with all of my heart faithfully to represent my clients in the face of what I consider repressive and unjust conduct toward them. If I have to pay with my liberty for such repression, then that is the price of my beliefs and sensibilities.
>
> I can only hope that my fate does not deter other lawyers throughout the country, who, in the difficult days that lie ahead, will be asked to defend clients against a steadily increasing governmental encroachment upon their most fundamental liberties. If they are so deterred, then my punishment will have effects of such terrifying consequences that I dread to contemplate the future domestic and foreign course of this country.
>
> But to those other lawyers who may, in learning of what may happen to me, waver, I can only say this, stand firm, remain true to those ideals of the law which even if openly violated here and in other places, are true and glorious goals, and, above all, never desert those principles of equality, justice, and freedom without which life has little if any meaning.

Meanwhile, the jury deliberated as to the main charges. Twice it sent notes to the court indicating that it was deadlocked, and Judge Hoffman's suppression of these communications was yet another of the many grounds for reversal. Ultimately it reached a compromise verdict. It acquitted all defendants of conspiracy and Froines and Weiner of all other charges, and convicted the remaining defendants of violating the Rap Brown statute of interstate movement with the intent of causing riot. Judge Hoffman imposed the maximum sentences of five years and $5,000.

Hoffman also refused bail, for either the contempt sentences or the sentences on the jury's conviction. Within hours for the attorneys and two weeks for the defendants, appellate courts permitted bail on appeal. The circuit court of appeals reversed the contempt sentences, including Seale's, on the theory that because the aggregated time was more than six months, the defendants were entitled to a jury trial. It reversed all the contempts, dismissed some, and gave extensive directions for a retrial. The prosecution elected to retry some of the contempts before a well-respected judge, from the distant state of Maine. The government reduced the contempt charges to fifty-two and stipulated to punishment below six months so that it could avoid a jury. Kunstler promptly charged that since the prosecutors "cannot control the American jury system, they are going into another forum without a jury. The Government can no longer trust the American people."

Judge Edward Gignoux tried the contempt charges in a new trial in December 1973. Curiously, Kunstler brought in another federal judge as a character witness. Gignoux found the defendants and attorneys not guilty of all alleged contempts but thirteen, two of which involved Kunstler. However, he thought punishment would serve no purpose and imposed no fine or jail sentence. It was this finding of contempt that was unsuccessfully challenged in 1981 upon the discovery of the prosecutorial misconduct and spying.

The criminal convictions of the defendants, as distinct from the contempts, were reversed in November 1972. The appellate court cited numerous errors: inadequate questioning of potential jurors concerning pretrial publicity and attitudes toward the youth culture, rulings on evidence, and suppression of communications from the jury were among them. However, Hoffman's antagonistic attitude toward defense counsel and the prosecutors' remarks constituted the appellate court's chief concerns. It concluded that "the demeanor of the judge and prosecutors would require reversal if other errors did not." Even before the appellate opinion was published, Hoffman had become the target of significant criticism. In May 1972 the *New York Times* editorialized that the trial had been an inglorious chapter: "Dubious charges opened the way for puerile radicals to use the courtroom for their propaganda purposes; Judge Hoffman aided them by providing a caricature of judicial authority."

After the reversal but before he had read the opinion, Kunstler, always quotable, told a reporter, "I don't think the Government will have the indecency to retry these defendants." He was correct. By January 1973 the government announced that it would not retry the defendants on the original charges, but would push for a retrial of the contempt matters, with the results we have seen. Seale *could not* be retried since he was indicted only for conspiracy, and as to that charge all the other defendants had been acquitted. It was legally impossible for Seale to conspire with himself.

The Chicago Conspiracy Trial became a defining experience for its participants, one that branded them for life. At first, the defendants thought they might form a political unit, under the name "Conspiracy," but that plan soon fell apart under the weight of their different agendas. However, they did meet for reunions. Kunstler threw the first reunion at his Mamaroneck home on October 16, 1971, to help celebrate Bobby Seale's birthday. Lotte Kunstler recalls Bobby saying that it was the first time anyone had ever given him a birthday cake. Years later, five participants, Dellinger, Hoffman, Kunstler, Rubin, and Seale, gathered with the cast of the 1987 HBO movie of the trial. Hayden and Froines attended the opening screening. Subsequent reunions in Chicago (1988) and New York (1993 and 1994) drew many of the former defendants and their lawyers. During the August 1996 Democratic Convention in Chicago, activists organized a program, "Return to Chicago, 1968–1996," at a local theatre. Although Hoffman, Kunstler, and Rubin were dead by then, Hayden (now an actual Democratic delegate), Froines, Seale, Davis, and Dellinger once more stood together. This reunion was particularly well publicized.

A separate reunion remembered Abbie Hoffman, who committed suicide in 1989. Every year thereafter, Abbie's friends gathered for a party on his birthday in December, usually held at the Wetlands, an environmentally correct New York club. Jerry Rubin died in late 1994, just two days before the annual party. Kunstler decreed that "there should be a party. If I know Jerry, he would have said, 'Go on with the party.' They were two partners in life and now they are two partners in death." Thereafter, it became a celebration honoring both men. Kunstler participated in most of these reunions, with fiery nostalgia, as in 1994, when he said, "The entire government was corrupt and evil, and I was going to fuck them any way I could." By December 1995 Kunstler was dead, but his widow recited a Kunstler poem about Hoffman that he had read the previous year.

Over the years numerous feature stories appeared about the trial. When something newsworthy occurred about the trial's participants, a news column often mentioned their connection to the Chicago Conspiracy Trial—as when Tom Hayden began running for office as a conventional politician or when Julius Hoffman drew a 78 percent

disapproval rating from Chicago lawyers in 1976 and was involuntar-
ily retired six years later. As the trial participants died—Julius Hoffman (1983); Edward Gignoux (1988); Abbie Hoffman (1989); Jerry
Rubin (1994); and then William Kunstler (1995)—obituaries invariably mentioned their experience in the Chicago trial.

The trial obviously impacted on all its participants, but it particularly affected Kunstler, who learned a great deal from his clients. From
their wit and theatrics, especially of Abbie Hoffman and Jerry Rubin,
Kunstler acknowledged that he "learned, for the first time, how wit
could be used by a trial lawyer to benefit his clients." According to
Abbie Hoffman, the high jinks and playacting had the purpose, among
others, "to allay the fear that we, personally, were a threat to the people
of Chicago." Abbie thought it worked well, that the defendants "were
accepted as local celebrities. People recognized us in restaurants and
bought us dinner, cabbies would turn the meter off and wish us well."
Kunstler noticed that at Berghoff's, a German restaurant near the courthouse, fellow diners often sent over free beer, and he trenchantly observed that "celebrity in America seems to override everything, even
disapproval."

Even if portraits of Che Guevara on the defense table, Vietnamese
flags, and insults and taunts to the judge made the defendants local
celebrities, these antics failed to impress the jury favorably. The jury,
and of course the public beyond, may well have been "exposed to
wholly new ways of life [and] to sense that there was a wider world
than they had ever conceived of before," as Kunstler gleefully reported
to *Playboy* in his October 1970 interview. However, at least the trial jury
did not like what it saw. After the trial, Edward Kratzke, the jury foreman, said, "I was a streetcar conductor. I've seen guys, real bums with
no soul, just a body, but when they went in front of a judge, they had
their hats off. These defendants wouldn't even stand up when the judge
walked in. When there is no more respect we might as well give up the
United States." Another juror, Ruth Petersen, told a reporter that the defendants "needed a good bath and a hairwash. They should have respected their elders. They should have respected the judge who is so
much older and wiser than them or us." Still another juror argued to her
fellow jurors that the defendants should be convicted "because of their
appearance, their language and, their life-style." In 1987, seventeen
years after the trial, Tom Hayden sought out Jean Fritz, yet another
juror. She informed him that her impression at the trial, and that of her

fellow jurors, was that the defendants were a "bunch of jerks. No one was sympathetic to the defendants."

This illustrates a fundamental dilemma of radical lawyering. One obvious political goal of the defendants was to show the country as a whole the beliefs and aspirations of the younger generation and the sincerity of their opposition to Vietnam. Pranks and courtroom taunts, whether they were spontaneous or planned, had the desired result of capturing media attention, and thereby spreading the political message to the country; they also alienated the jury. Often in a political defense of this nature, a tension builds between defending the cause and defending the client.

Regardless of how much the media attention helped the cause, or how much the pranks necessary to garner that attention hurt the clients, the defendants clearly were masters at media manipulation. Kunstler learned a great deal in Chicago about how to attract media exposure, how to cultivate interviews, and how to turn phrases that would become quotable. "Through the Chicago trial," as he put it years later in 1991, in reference to media exposure, "I learned the power of words."

Chicago also taught Kunstler how to conduct a *political* defense. Kunstler made an opening statement that emphasized the defendants' First Amendment rights, and they were furious with him. They wanted him to talk about Vietnam, not the Constitution. As Dellinger put it later, "We wanted to put the government on trial, not win our freedom on a technicality." Not only that, Kunstler realized that the defendants

> wanted to decide for themselves what happened during their trial. They wanted our legal strategies to reflect their political philosophies. After a time, I began to understand their point of view and act on it. . . . Len and I followed the defendants' lead. Every action we took, every statement we made, was an attempt to educate the jury, the audience, and the rest of the world about the politics of the antiwar movement and the counterculture.

The defendants and the attorneys made collective decisions. The lawyers had their say, disagreements were ironed out, but in any event the majority ruled.

Not only did Kunstler willingly become, as he put it, "the political agent of his client in the courtroom," he became attracted to those politics. On Moratorium Day, October 15, 1969, David Dellinger began reading the names of those killed in Vietnam in open court and asked for a moment of silence. Judge Hoffman ordered the jury to leave; Kunstler objected. The United States attorney jumped up and argued, "This is outrageous. This man [Kunstler] is the mouthpiece for these defendants. The Government protests this man's attitude and I'd like to note that he is wearing a black arm band [for Moratorium Day] like the defendants." A month later, Kunstler joined the March Against Death in Washington, D.C. When the trial resumed after the weekend, Judge Hoffman asked him what he had done in Washington. Kunstler replied, "I sang once and I listened to the speeches. I sat on top of a tractor trailer, and I was thrilled by what I saw as I looked out at what seemed to me half a million people who had one thought in mind, and that was to end the war in Vietnam." A few days later Hoffman observed to Kunstler, "you get awfully chummy with your clients." When the verdict was handed down, Kunstler called for mass street demonstrations and spoke at protest rallies.

The defendants rented a small suite of rooms in an old office building in the heart of Chicago's Loop. Volunteers worked in the office building, typing letters, answering the telephone, and scheduling speeches. Yippies Hoffman and Rubin had their own apartment on the South Side. Weinglass and the remaining defendants lived nearby in a large communal apartment, although the arrangements were very floating. The defendants held collective meetings and formulated strategy in the communal apartment. Hayden recalled that the pressures were incredible: "It was an eighteen-hour day: worrying about the next stage of testimony, settling disputes with other defendants, calling and readying witnesses, worry about their travel difficulties, getting our trial lawyers prepared to take the witnesses through their questioning, fighting with the mass media to obtain cameramen and films."

Weinglass and Kunstler each received only movement wages, $100 per week. Additionally, Kunstler received a small, separate, inexpensive apartment on the North Side. He said he needed privacy to study the daily court transcripts and also felt it appropriate to have his own place because he was more than twenty years older than the rest of the defense team. Although Kunstler often spent evenings planning tactics and working with the rest of the defense team, he frequently spent his lunch hours quite differently. He often lay down on the conference room floor in agony because of his migraine headaches. When untroubled by these, Kunstler often visited the Chicago Art Institute during the lunch hours.

Kunstler may not have spent as much time in work sessions as some of the defendants might have wished. According to Hayden, "it quickly became known that Kunstler was better at giving seat-of-the-pants speeches and partying at night than at the drudgery of preparing the legal defense." This was not just Hayden's observation. Dellinger also recalled that Kunstler "was so busy exploring the lifestyle of the youth at the time, very often he didn't do his homework." Criticism of work habits and lack of concentrated effort dogged Kunstler, not only in Chicago but in other cases as well.

Of all the defendants, Kunstler identified most readily with the Yippies, fellow New Yorkers who liked to party. During the Chicago trial, Kunstler grew his hair long, smoked dope with the defendants, and partied with them. Many of these parties were fund-raising events. A reporter recalled one party in an elegant townhouse on the Near North Side. It started sedately with a buffet downstairs, and then the party moved upstairs. There, the defendants, the guests, the lawyers, perhaps the reporters, all danced to rock and roll with increasing frenzy. The reporter noted that "before the night was over, Bill Kunstler had stripped off his shirt and Abbie Hoffman was down to his shorts." At several parties throughout the trial, when high on marijuana, Kunstler stripped down to his shorts. Actually, this was a reversion to an old tradition.

This identification with the defendants reflected Kunstler's old need for a sense of belonging, and paradoxically a desire to belong to a group in which he could never fully fit. He was, he realized when he took a separate apartment, twenty years older than his clients. Yet he craved the feeling of belonging with them. He told a reporter in 1990 that when he smoked marijuana with the defendants in Chicago, "I was part of it. I liked that." In some telling sentences in his 1994 autobiography, Kunstler recalled about Chicago that "I drew great strength from my closeness to the defendants; I belonged and felt cared about, even loved. We were in a great struggle, but we were together." Here, Kunstler drops the facade and reveals his inner insecurity.

Hayden, much more straitlaced personally than Jerry Rubin or Abbie Hoffman, correctly observed that whereas Weinglass "would work all night," Kunstler "had a much more colorful and free-floating life when trial would break." One aspect of this "colorful and free-floating life," much in evidence in Chicago, was Kunstler's enormous capacity for womanizing, an important topic separately considered in the next chapter. Suffice it to mention here that one evening during the trial, a defense attorney looked for Kunstler and could not find him. The next day the colleague learned that Kunstler had spent the night in a women's dormitory at the University of Chicago.

The defendants financed their food, lodging, trial transcripts, and expenses, not just through parties and rallies, but most importantly through speeches, usually at colleges. During the trial they were constantly in motion, especially on weekends. Even on the weekdays, after the trial recessed some of the defendants, with Hoffman and Rubin the most popular, would fly to California or elsewhere, speak on a campus, and take the late-night, red-eye flight back to Chicago. Kunstler took his turn with these speeches, during the trial and especially afterward.

Kunstler learned other lessons from Chicago. Becoming reacquainted with his roots in the theatre, he found that the courtroom itself "is like a stage." He learned how to use his deep and dramatic voice, his gestures and body language, to maximum effect. Kunstler's political changes were even more important, although he may have held radical views even before. Nevertheless, Kunstler claimed that Chicago was his "personal Rubicon," his moment of radicalization. Prior to Chicago, he explained in 1994, "I had faith in the courts—that all wrongs were righted. After the trial, I realized all that was horse manure." Or, as he put it in 1989, "Up to that time I guess I was a traditional civil rights attorney. I believed in the system. . . . After Chicago, it totally changed. I now see the legal system as an enemy."

David Dellinger recalled Kunstler speaking of the impact of Chicago at countless events where they both spoke. He remembered that Kunstler always claimed that Chicago radicalized him, and that

> step by step, through the examples of the defendants and the opposing examples of the prosecution, the judge, and the media, I came to understand that the justice system in this country is loaded against the defendants, both political defendants such as the Chicago Seven and other victims of society who are not called political defendants but ultimately are.

Abbie Hoffman put it the most simply. He wrote that "the trial made a radical of Kunstler. How the events registered on him and how he responded made up one of the trial's greatest dramas." Kunstler learned of the need to fight back at the prosecution and unjust judges. Proper courtroom decorum became "responding in kind to oppression from the bench or the prosecutor." In retrospect, toward the end of his life, he told a radio talk show host that he regarded the Chicago defendants as

> a heroic group. They taught me a lot about myself and about how to be a lawyer in the future. . . . I came away with an understanding of how dirty government could be when it wanted to get rid of certain people, and yet those people, if they stood up and fought and made their presence known, that they could overcome the system, not because of the law, but because of their own courage and righteousness during the trial.

In the process of fighting back, Kunstler learned from the Chicago experience that the government, its motives, personnel, and activities should be made the targets. To put the government on trial became a theme of the Chicago trial, and one that Kunstler would use over and over again. He made a classic statement of that technique shortly after the Chicago trial began:

> Our position has been from the beginning that the wrong defendants are in the dock. And the real defendants would be the mayor of Chicago, certain federal officials, certain high-placed people in the Democratic Party and certain state officials in Illinois who conspired together to absolutely ensure that there would be no protest demonstrations around that convention. And when all else failed, they resorted to the brutality of just clubbing the demonstrators senseless and frightening off or by force preventing the demonstrators from doing what they came to Chicago to do—namely, a peaceful demonstration around the convention to protest the war, racism and poverty in the United States.

Many of these lessons were certainly started before Chicago. Kunstler already was far left of center politically, already admired defendants, such as Rap Brown, who fought back, and already had begun his counterattacks on government. However, in all these areas the techniques became clearer and more pronounced after Chicago. Kunstler already had the capacity to identify with his clients, politically and personally.

Here again, this accelerated during Chicago. It was shortly after the trial ended that he made the controversial statement that he would only defend those he loved and whose goals he shared.

One of the most important consequences of the Chicago trial is that it gave Kunstler a national reputation. Accounts of the trial's progress and high jinks, often with Kunstler's comments, appeared on national television almost every night during its twenty-week duration. Hardly a week passed without a Kunstler quotation or interview in the *New York Times*, and its magazine section featured an in-depth study of Kunstler in April 1970. Kunstler already had a massive ego; now his sudden and pervasive fame raised new issues. How would he respond personally to celebrity? How would Kunstler use his fame for his clients and for his practice?

7

Directions outside the Courtroom

KUNSTLER HAD A full range of other leftist causes in the 1960s. He defended northern (as well as southern) civil rights groups, attacked the exclusion of blacks and Puerto Ricans from northern juries on behalf of minority criminal defendants, litigated security clearances for former communists, defended black officials of various antipoverty agencies against criminal charges, championed fired professors against university administrations, and persuaded a court to invalidate an archaic Kentucky state sedition statute on behalf of labor organizers. Kunstler, like all progressive or even liberal lawyers, became increasingly involved in the anti-Vietnam struggle. However, since so much of that activity overlapped into the 1970s, it can more conveniently be considered later.

Kunstler also represented famous clients involved in controversial incidents. Almost all of these were team representations, but teams in which Kunstler played a leading role. He and six other lawyers represented Abbie Hoffman and Jerry Rubin in a riotous session before the House Un-American Activities Committee in 1966, long before the Chicago trial. He participated in a team that represented Congressman Adam Clayton Powell in 1967 litigation where the U.S. Supreme Court ultimately countermanded the refusal of Congress to seat him. The team selected Arthur Kinoy to make the argument before the Supreme Court, which miffed Kunstler slightly, although he later realized that while "I wanted to make the argument, Arthur was clearly the better man."

In the mid-1960s Kunstler and Arthur Kinoy, along with other lawyers, unsuccessfully drafted motions for a new trial and handled other appellate work for Morton Sobell, convicted and imprisoned on atomic spy charges in 1953 along with Julius and Ethel Rosenberg, who were subsequently executed. However, the most interesting representation Kunstler undertook in the mid-1960s was his work on behalf on

Jack Ruby, the murderer of Lee Harvey Oswald, assassin of President John F. Kennedy.

It is a curious story. Kunstler claimed that the American Civil Liberties Union asked him to represent Oswald after Oswald's first choice had turned him down and he had turned to the ACLU. Kunstler grabbed the opportunity, influenced, he admitted, by the fact that it would be a "highly publicized trial," to understate matters. He raced to the airport to fly to Dallas, called his wife to say goodbye, and only then learned that Jack Ruby had shot Oswald. Perhaps it happened just this way, but it seems unlikely that a defense that would be under the world's spotlight would be offered to Kunstler, who in November 1963 was just beginning to make a name for himself. What seems more likely is that Kunstler was asked to check on Oswald's conditions of confinement on behalf of the ACLU, rather than to take on the defense.

Melvin Belli defended Ruby at his murder trial. The Ruby family floundered around afterward but eventually assembled a team of lawyers for the appeal. Kunstler was an active and important member of that team. That itself is curious. Although Oswald had been a leftist, Ruby was apolitical. About the only political aspect to the Ruby appeal was the death sentence imposed at trial. Since millions of television viewers had watched Ruby shoot Oswald, the only real issue in the case was whether Ruby had acted with malice. After a great struggle, including many side proceedings in both the federal and Texas state courts, Ruby's appellate team persuaded the Texas Court of Criminal Appeals to reverse the conviction of murder with malice. Jack Ruby was technically an innocent man awaiting retrial when he died of cancer.

The legal team brought Kunstler into the appeal as "chief counsel," as he described it. Prior to the final arguments in the Texas appellate court, Kunstler's actual involvement was primarily handling the side-issue *federal* appellate matters. However, he also acted as the anchor man, the rebuttal speaker, in the final arguments on appeal. According to Elmer Gertz, one of his cocounsel, Kunstler had a warming, "rhetorical grandeur . . . and on this occasion he was at his finest." Kunstler recalled that when he arrived in Dallas he was met by hundreds of protesting pickets, with signs calling him a communist and demanding he return to New York. That may also be stretched a bit, but there is no mistaking the genuineness of Elmer Gertz's warm description of Kunstler as a colleague in the years 1965–66:

Kunstler was highly articulate. . . . He was always coming from or going to some out-of-the-way spot and seemed to live out of suitcases and duffle bags. He was constantly making speeches before boards, committees, live audiences of every kind, and he was heard frequently on television and radio. He could easily have become an actor—he was a performer. He would tell indiscreet stories at his own expense and that of others. . . . Everything filled Kunstler with zeal and zest. . . . He could do sweet and thoughtful things.

Our review of Kunstler's high-profile cases is somewhat misleading. Even after he began his civil rights career in 1961, for the balance of the decade Kunstler always spent some of his time in a mundane civil practice. Although he did receive some fees from his civil rights and other movement cases, it was not enough on which to live. He remained dependent economically on Michael, his brother and partner, who kept up the firm's business back in New York.

Regardless of consequences, Kunstler felt compelled to continue his movement work, which held him, he wrote, "as strongly as any passionate love affair." He only hoped that Michael would continue to allow him his partner's draw. Michael was generous and allowed Bill the same draw as he took himself, even though his brother was hardly contributing his proportionate share to the firm's revenues. From time to time, Michael would complain, and then for a while Kunstler would spend more time in the New York office working on routine cases.

When he chained himself to the office practice, Kunstler did matrimonial work, routine criminal defense, even commercial litigation. He did an occasional incorporation and probate. Steven Hyman, who worked in the Kunstler firm from 1965 to 1977, first as an associate and later as a partner, recalls that Kunstler loved the clients, even in such routine cases. Since he also used the New York office as a staging platform for his movement work, Hyman observed Kunstler at work in both types of cases. Although Kunstler became engaged in his nonmovement work and did it with "élan and fervor," he never became as enthusiastic as with his causes. As Kunstler's fame and publicity grew, the numbers of crazy clients who dropped in on Kunstler, Kunstler, and Kinoy increased. They often claimed they had read about one of Kunstler's cases, and their problem was just like it. Hyman remembers that Kunstler had an art for getting rid of such people. However, he was never overbearing. Arthur Kinoy recalls that his attitude toward interns, subordinates, and secretaries, as well as colleagues, was always collegial.

Over time the frustrations mounted. The firm had financial crises, but while there would be fights and criticisms, Michael continued to support Bill. Even so, the frustrations took their toll. During one crisis, Hyman, then a partner, was importuning Bill Kunstler that they needed to do something to bring in some money, when Kunstler suddenly shouted, "I can't take it anymore!" flung the papers he was holding across the office, and stormed out.

When the Chicago Seven case came up, Kunstler began working primarily out of the Chicago defense office. There was no bad blood between the two brothers, but he seldom used his Fifth Avenue office thereafter. He told a reporter in April 1970 that he had not been to his office for six months (although his name was still on the door), and he made a complete break later that year. For a time Kunstler supported himself and his family from speaking engagements, some old cases, and a few new paying cases. Although there may have been no ill feelings between the brothers, there were unresolved issues.

When Michael was fifty-five his son Billy committed suicide. Although Michael knew that romantic and psychological problems caused Billy's suicide, he blamed himself, and withdrew from life where before he had been outgoing. Kunstler had told Michael frequently that he was not responsible for his son's suicide, but made no headway. Then William Kunstler began avoiding his brother. Kunstler had moved from Westchester into New York City, had a new family with Margie, and certainly was busy with his own practice.

There was more to it, however. Kunstler acknowledged, "I'm too impatient with people to be a really good listener. I'm not very sympathetic, and I get bored with people who complain or agonize over their problems, as Michael was doing . . . I'm sorry I wasn't of more help to Michael. He needed someone to listen to him, and I just couldn't do it." In 1984, when he was sixty-three, Michael effectively killed himself by putting off a needed open-heart operation and engaging in strenuous exercise that he should have avoided. To the end of his life, William Kunstler felt remorse for his brother's death.

In 1966 four attorneys formed the Center for Constitutional Rights. It sprang out of the warmth and mutual respect engendered from the in-

Kunstler as a soldier in World War II, standing with his parents, Monroe and Frances Kunstler. Courtesy, Karin Kunstler Goldman Collection.

(left): William and Lotte Kunstler, 1943. Courtesy, Mary Kunstler Horn Collection.

William and Lotte Kunstler with daughter Jane and Edith, a summer visitor under the Fresh Air program, 1954. The Kunstlers suffered hostility from their Port Chester neighbors because of Edith's visit. Courtesy, Karin Kunstler Goldman Collection.

Kunstler working, with Margie Ratner, in their Greenwich Village apartment, 1974.
Courtesy, Bruce Jackson.

Kunstler battling with a baby bottle, with Margie Ratner and daughter Sarah, 1977.
Courtesy, Bruce Jackson.

Kunstler exposing Sarah to art, late 1970s. Courtesy, Emily Kunstler Collection.

With Sarah and Emily at an Indian festival, early 1980s. Courtesy, Emily Kunstler Collection.

With Sarah and Emily on Halloween, mid 1980s. Courtesy, Emily Kunstler Collection.

Working at West Shokan summer house, early 1980s. Courtesy, Bruce Jackson.

Working in the kitchen, Gay Street, 1980s. Courtesy, Bruce Jackson.

Hailing a cab with Ronald Kuby, late 1980s. Courtesy, Bruce Jackson.

Performing at the West Shokan summer house, early 1980s. Courtesy, Bruce Jackson.

Kunstler surrounded by his daughters in the garden of his Gay Street home, 1985. To the left are Karin and Sarah, on his lap, and to the right are Jane and behind her, Emily. Courtesy, Emily Kunstler Collection.

Jewish Defense Organization team demonstrating in front of Gay Street residence, early 1990s. Courtesy, Bruce Jackson.

Kunstler in his Gay Street office, 1980s. Courtesy, Ronald Kuby.

Kunstler in his office, 1990s. Courtesy, Ronald Kuby.

An exuberant Kunstler dancing with his sister, Mary Kunstler Horn, at her fiftieth wedding anniversary party, 1993. Courtesy, Mary Kunstler Horn Collection and Shlomo Photography, Baltimore.

tense civil rights team practice of its founders, Arthur Kinoy, William Kunstler, Ben Smith, and Morty Stavis. They felt a need for a permanent organization of mutual support, legal and emotional. Kunstler added the insight that a tax-exempt organization facilitated donations.

The center broadened its coverage beyond civil rights to human rights more generally and became involved in a wide range of litigation involving governmental misconduct, racial injustice, international law, and criminal defense involving constitutional issues. It often filed affirmative litigation, seeking to stop or force government action, as an alternative to passively defending individuals charged with crime. With a small number of staff lawyers and a much larger pool of volunteer attorneys, it has operated on a small budget financed by donations from individuals and foundations. Because of the cases it takes, its often fierce antigovernmental stance, and its leftist orientation, the center has always attracted controversy.

Kunstler played a large role in the center, and served both as vice president and for many years as a member of the board of directors. His largest role was as a volunteer or cooperating attorney, and in that capacity Kunstler handled hundreds of cases through the center's auspices. The center itself rarely brought in any of these cases. Rather, a client would interest Kunstler in a case for which there was no money, not merely no money for fees but no money for expenses such as travel, depositions, investigators, and so forth. If it were a conventional criminal case, it might be possible to secure a court appointment and be assured of minimal fees plus expenses. However, the government will not pay expenses for a client affirmatively suing it to force its hand, and outside appointed counsel are not offered in all criminal cases.

If an interesting case without funding came into his office, Kunstler might ask the center whether it was willing to take it on. The center then considered whether the case fit within its purview and whether it might be able to raise funds around it. If it decided the case was appropriate, the center agreed to reimburse expenses. It never paid fees. The center financed the expenses, in whole or in part, of many of Kunstler's movement cases, including the Chicago Seven trial and the flag burning cases.

The major ways of raising funds for radical cases are private and foundation donations, often channeled through a defense committee; fund-raising parties or events; and speaking fees for talks, often before student groups. The many speeches Kunstler gave in connection with the Chicago Seven trial illustrate this method of financing litigation and making a living.

Kunstler already had given his share of speeches at colleges and rallies during the Chicago Seven trial, but his output soared following the trial's conclusion in early 1970. Between February and June 1970, Kunstler spoke at more than 150 colleges and universities. As late as October 1971, Kunstler spoke somewhere in the country three or four times a week. His speaking tour covered major private and state institutions in every part of the country.

Kunstler also spoke at meetings outside academe, as at an arts council–sponsored meeting at the Philadelphia YMCA, and, of course, at public rallies and protests, regarding the Black Panthers or the appeal of the Chicago Seven. He debated conservative opponents such as Russell Kirk, participated in the "levitation" of the Pentagon, and put his name on various denunciations of "incipient American fascism." By October 1970, the House Internal Security Committee (formerly Un-American Activities Committee) listed Kunstler among sixty-five "radical" campus speakers. Kunstler collected speaking fees of $1,000 per appearance; at least that was his fee at both Wisconsin and Notre Dame. He left the impression that most of his fee was going back into the movement, while at the same time he told a reporter that much of his own income came from lecture fees (and book royalties). Probably some of his fees went into the movement and some into Kunstler's pocket to pay for his and his family's livelihood.

Campus authorities feared riots following Kunstler's speeches, and tried vigorously to prevent his appearances. The University of Illinois trustees initially voted to ban his appearance, and then reversed themselves. A federal judge ordered officials in Jacksonville, Florida, to make an auditorium available for Kunstler. In California the chancellor of the state college system banned Kunstler from a scheduled talk at San Jose State, charging that "disorders involving personal injuries and property damage have occurred following certain of Mr. Kunstler's appearances." A federal judge voided the ban.

Actually, considering the temper of the times and the vehemence of the protest against the Vietnam War, very little violence followed Kunstler's appearances, and almost none honestly can be attributed to Kunstler. At Columbia University, 350 students battled guards after a Kunstler talk on April 8, 1970. However, Kunstler had told the much larger 1,500-student audience that violent acts were "not the right tactics at this time," and that "breaking windows does no good." Bombings and other violent acts "don't do anything except lose us our people." Much of the violence that did occur was actually aimed at the universities for their responses to Kunstler. At the University of Illinois the National Guard entered the campus to disperse a crowd of five thousand students, a hundred of whom had gone on a rampage through the Champaign business district smashing windows. What triggered the violence, however, was not Kunstler's talk but the news that the board of trustees had banned his appearance.

Kunstler's speech at the University of California at Santa Barbara on February 25, 1970, was related to the largest single incident of violence of his speaking tour. He had been invited by the student government and was paid handsomely: $2,000 of student funds, plus a percentage of the gate, plus a passing of the hat. Shortly after his remarks, more than a thousand students rioted in the nearby campus community of Isla Vista, torched a police car and a real estate office, and burned a Bank of America building to the ground. The National Guard was called and order was restored, but thirty-four policemen were injured in the disturbances. Superficially, it seems as though there was a causal connection between Kunstler's remarks and the riot. California's governor, Ronald Reagan, suggested that Kunstler be investigated for violation of the federal Rap Brown statute, crossing a state line with intent to cause riot—the very charge Kunstler had defended in Chicago. The actor Tom Selleck, then a frightened National Guardsman stationed in front of the hulk of the burned-out bank, charged years later that Kunstler had gotten the students riled up, "but when a riot broke out he wasn't so courageous leaving right afterward."

However, those closest to the scene did not feel that Kunstler had caused the rioting. There had been several other issues on the campus, most significantly the denial of tenure to a popular professor. Students had first attacked the bank the night *before* Kunstler arrived, although its total destruction followed Kunstler's talk. An investigative reporter for the *New York Times* concluded that although tensions were high when students gathered for a rally following Kunstler's speech, it was "the arrest of another student who was beaten and dragged off in full view of a large crowd" that actually touched off the riot that led to the injuries and most significant destruction. He also found that, although students and faculty of the school were divided on many issues, "they agree that the appearance here Wednesday of William M. Kunstler . . .

had little to do with igniting the trouble." Twenty years after the rioting, former student activists held a reunion in Santa Barbara. Kunstler was there.

Kunstler was personally involved in violence once on the tour. That was in Toronto, and the incident was more amusing than serious. When he began his June 22, 1970, talk before an audience of a thousand, a small group of right-wing pickets drowned him out. Kunstler asked the group to send a representative to the stage to speak, and their leader, F. Paul Fromm, took the stage. Kunstler offered Fromm a glass of water, which Fromm dumped into a pitcher of water, splashing Kunstler. Piqued by this behavior, Kunstler turned the entire pitcher on Fromm's head. Thirty of Fromm's supporters rushed the stage, beat Kunstler, and knocked him down. Members of the audience chased the attackers from the stage, and Kunstler continued his remarks, "rumpled, bleeding slightly, and with tears in his eyes."

Fromm and a confederate pressed charges, and Canadian police booked Kunstler for two charges of common assault in August 1970. Ultimately in December, the prosecutor asked for an acquittal on the basis of insufficient evidence that Kunstler struck the two complainants. Prior to the acquittal, two eyewitnesses, a Toronto lawyer and a member of the Canadian Parliament, had both testified that Kunstler neither struck nor tried to strike anyone. Kunstler quipped that the acquittal might "ruin my image as a battler, but the truth had to come out."

Numerous critics attacked Kunstler's speaking tour. The right-wing radio commentator Dan Smoot denounced him, as did various columnists in the *National Review*. David Duke, later to be a prominent Louisiana politician, donned a Nazi uniform to protest Kunstler's appearance at Tulane in July 1970. One report had Duke holding a sign reading "Kunstler is a Communist Jew," while in another version the sign read "Gas the Chicago Seven."

Regardless of the critics, the large student audiences (San Jose State, 1,500; Albany, 5,100; Virginia, 8,000) reacted enthusiastically. Kunstler usually spoke about the Chicago trial, but often analogized injustices in Chicago with others in the nation. He often spoke of the clenched fist, as at Illinois:

> We've gone into the age of that clenched fist, and that clenched fist is
> not so easily talked about by those of us up there in the 50–year range.

> . . . Raising the clenched fist is not easy for me, it's not natural for me. It's a gesture I didn't use until I became an attorney in the Chicago trial. It's a gesture of resistance.

He then would frequently explain that the clenched fist of the movement could open into a handshake of brotherhood or it could open gripping the trigger of a gun. He frequently spoke about a need to do more than merely protest if government refused to listen. At Notre Dame he prophesied, "People are no longer going to content themselves with a picket line around a building. People are going to occupy the building. People are going to take over the building. And I rather imagine unless Government listens, people are going to burn down the building." Kunstler moved from a low-keyed tone to a raised voice filled with indignation. He played the audience as might a performer in a drama. Kunstler's style struck a reporter who followed him through several college speeches as an

> odd combination of emotional excess (he's a laugher and a crier) and ostensible common sense. His platform manner is more lecturer than orator, yet the whole time I was with him there was not a woman whose hand he shook whose lips he did not also kiss. As a matter of fact, on two occasions he hugged and kissed me (much in the spirit with which another man might slap one on the back). . . . At the same time, in a very subdued way, Kunstler is part put-on.

Kunstler's performances went over extremely well with his youthful audiences. A reporter noted that after his University of Illinois talk the audience "is on its feet, fists in the air. Ten minutes of sustained shouting taper off only when Kunstler flees the stage," and at Notre Dame, "the audience is on its feet in a thunderous ovation." Another reporter recalled her own collegiate experience: "The crowd filled the hallway, the stage, another lecture hall opened up for overflow, and they loved him. Kunstler spoke of revolution, and we loved him; he clenched his fists, and we cheered; we believed for a moment that there was hope. . . . Everybody cheered, and Kunstler had to leave." In fact, Kunstler developed a near-cult following. The reporter who had tagged along his speaking tour wrote that "on the basis of a week and a half's attempt to keep up with Kunstler's frantic schedule, I can attest to the existence of an enthusiastic, admiring and committed Kunstler cult among the young, who see him as a courageous vagabond lawyer of folk-hero proportions."

Critics were quick to charge a cult nature to Kunstler's following. One wrote that Kunstler was a cult hero comparable to Che Guevara or Malcolm X. "He is probably the only member of the New York bar whose mere arrival on a campus can set off rejoicing and tumult. . . . He must be the only alumnus of the Columbia Law School capable of sending adolescents into Dionysiac ecstasy." Another critic found "something embarrassingly sexual about his relationship with the kids and the way he responds to their screams of approval." Even the august American Bar Association accused Kunstler of having a cult following.

Kunstler's ego obviously received massive massaging from the adulation of the youthful crowds. Kunstler wrote only briefly about these early 1970s speeches in his autobiography. He did mention the large and enthusiastic crowds of young people and that the "speeches were so exhilarating that I was never tired. After I walked on the stage, the audience would stand up and cheer as if I were a super-star."

We have seen before that Kunstler smoked marijuana with the Chicago Seven defendants and witnesses. Many of his other colleagues also smoked marijuana with Kunstler. Lotte recalls that during this pe-riod, he was a heavy user. Actually, however, his first acquaintance with pot came as late as the summer of 1966. Thereafter, marijuana use be-came a regular feature, and for the rest of his life he often used it to relax in the evenings. Kunstler became less approving of other drugs.

In December 1965 Kunstler was one of the comedian Lenny Bruce's lawyers. On Christmas Eve Bruce talked Kunstler into shooting up with heroin so he could "understand" the effect of drugs. Shortly thereafter, Kunstler passed out and had to be carried to a couch; his wife was summoned. He concluded that the incident foreclosed the possibility that he could ever have become addicted to heavy drugs. Indeed, when Bruce died from an overdose eight months later, Kunstler "saw at once the utter recklessness of what I had done." The following year he tried LSD but was frightened by "the absolute loss of boundaries within my consciousness."

Kunstler had a somewhat ambivalent attitude toward hard drugs. In the 1980s and 1990s he argued in letters to the editor and in talks that America's "unworkable drug-control policy" had caused much of the violent crime associated with drugs, and that there ought to be a national debate on decriminalization. Ultimately he concluded for himself that he "would not legalize some of the hallucinogens and amphetamines, which can have very serious effects on the body and mind," but would decriminalize marijuana, cocaine, and heroin and treat addiction as a social and medical problem, not a crime.

Kunstler's position on drugs reflects an interesting aspect of his character. In the late 1960s and early 1970s, when he had that near-cult following among the young, it would have been easy for him to adapt his own lifestyle to theirs. Yet he did not. Kunstler continued to wear suits to court and press conferences, not the clothing of the counterculture. He wrote in 1971,

> I've tried to maintain my own life style, and not simply adopt that of my clients. I know there are lots of clients who wear dungarees, boots and sombreros in court. I happen to find that not to my liking, and I question whether it's good for the client. . . . the close physical identification of the lawyer with the client may jeopardize the lawyer's effectiveness.

Likewise, Kunstler criticized the use of LSD, at a time when it was very popular among his youthful followers. He kept his taste in opera, while his clients were consumed with rock. Abbie Hoffman invited Kunstler to the upstate New York Woodstock Festival in August 1969. Kunstler smoked a little pot, listened to the music, and refused the LSD. An interesting self-revelation came to Kunstler:

> At some point during the festival, I became extremely aware of my age: I was a lover of opera and Rodgers and Hammerstein–style musicals, not rock and roll. Although I listened to the music along with the rest of that vast audience, I wasn't completely with it and realized that no matter how I tried, I simply could not identify fully with these young people. But I enjoyed the experience—at least until the thunderstorm came. As the earth turned into mud, I decided that it was time for me to go home.

Marijuana was the one lifestyle element of the counterculture that Kunstler enthusiastically adopted. So much so, that when he heard the news that arch-conservative Clarence Thomas had admitted during his confirmation process that he had sampled marijuana in college, Kunstler was moved to remark, "That's the only good thing I've heard about this man."

As Kunstler accelerated his legal practice after his initial involvement with the civil rights movement in 1961, he necessarily lacked the time for all the intellectual activities that he had used in the late 1950s and early 1960s to relieve boredom. His radio shows ceased within a couple of years, although he increasingly became the *subject* of radio interviews. He wrote an occasional political-legal article, publishing a piece on amnesty for those convicted during the McCarthy era and another on bail reform for the *Nation* in 1961 and 1963. Kunstler still wrote a rare book review, for the *New York Times* in 1964 and *Life* in 1965, and throughout the 1960s he occasionally read poetry, usually Dylan Thomas, at Greenwich Village coffeehouses.

Kunstler's major intellectual effort in these years, aside from the practice of law, was the publication of books. From 1963 to 1966 he published three books, a remarkable accomplishment in light of the frenetic pace of his practice. The first of these, ... *And Justice for All,* appeared in 1963, and stood in the same line as his earlier *First Degree* (1960) and *The Case for Courage* (1962). It compiled ten cases organized around the theme of unpopular (but mostly well-known) defendants who were victims of racial, religious, or political intolerance.

Kunstler published *Deep in My Heart,* a memoir of his civil rights struggles in the South, in 1966. Favorable reviews greeted the work, including one in the *Saturday Review* that hailed it as "a thoroughly readable narrative unfreighted with heavy legalistic explanations. . . . It is refreshing to find a lawyer who can write interestingly and comprehensively."

The middle book, sandwiched between the unpopular defendants compendium and the civil rights memoir, came in 1964. *The Minister and the Choir Singer: The Hall-Mills Murder Case* proved to be Kunstler's single most popular book and his only bestseller. A true-crime thriller, it told the story of a spectacular 1922 murder in New Jersey that involved double adultery, wealth, and social position. The trial of four defendants, which included a pastor's wealthy wife, drew a wide following and ended in an acquittal. Kunstler not only authored a well-written book about a fascinating and apparently unsolved case, but he made the provocative and well-argued suggestion that the Ku Klux Klan committed the murders.

Rex Stout, the noted detective writer, wrote a glowing review of the book for the *New York Times* that appeared on the first page of its book review section. *The Minister and the Choir Singer* soon became a best-seller, and Kunstler was able to sell the movie rights for $25,000, although the film never appeared. With that money, a large amount for 1964, Kunstler bought a spacious older house in Mamaroneck, where he would live until he separated from his wife Lotte in the early 1970s. Since the money to buy the house came from the Hall-Mills book, Lotte reversed the names and dubbed the house Mill's Hall. The house was at the end of a long driveway, and she had a signmaker create a sign for the end of the drive in the shape of a book with their address and name on the spine. Rutgers University Press reissued the book in 1980 under a slightly different title. The reissue drew favorable notices, and the murder case continues to draw the attention of feature writers, who always mention Kunstler's book favorably.

We have previously alluded to an element of Kunstler's character that is less than sterling, yet essential to understand the man's insecurities and desperate need for approval. Throughout his first marriage Kunstler was a truly large-scale womanizer, with a tremendous capacity and appetite for a large variety and quantity of women. Many men have occasional affairs. If this were all there were to Kunstler's flings we could pass over them. However, they were far more in quantity and quality, and their story is a telling element of his life. We are speaking here of literally many dozens of affairs, in addition to many hundreds of one-night stands. On top of that, Kunstler had long-term relationships with perhaps half a dozen women in cities scattered throughout the United States who were available to him whenever he tried a case in that town.

An element of innocent flirting was a standard feature of Kunstler's persona at cocktail parties and dinners. At times that went beyond innocence, and he became involved in several affairs even before his participation in the civil rights movement. However, the civil rights movement and the numerous groupies available to the militants working in the South were the aperitifs that induced Kunstler's large-scale appetite. The civil rights movement occasioned "exhaustion, strain, and tension. The demands were inordinate and there was very little in the way of extended release." Sex became the perfect mode of relaxation in such an atmosphere.

Then too, the macho ideology of the civil rights movement rele-gated women to a subordinate and sexual role. As Stokely Carmichael put it, "The proper position for women in the movement is prone." Kunstler recalled these days in his autobiography: "I began to see these other women as a natural part of life. I viewed myself as a glamorous movement figure, part of the counterculture. People in the movement encouraged women to sleep with me. . . . It was certainly not the right way to treat women, but we all did it."

Kunstler's opportunities increased with the Chicago trial. The de-fendant whose company he most enjoyed, Abbie Hoffman, changed "crash-pads" almost nightly during the trial, largely because he was sleeping with an assortment of women. Kunstler had an abundance of sexual energy and was eager to explore this lifestyle of the young peo-ple. With his high-profile trial celebrity, Kunstler attracted trial groupies. A female worker in the Chicago defense office explained, "you were either sleeping with a lawyer or a defendant, or you were nothing on this case." Kunstler "found these women hard to resist. Many times they would actually bang on my door and say, 'I'm here to spend the night with you.' It was the era of free love, and I participated enthusiastically."

When Kunstler traveled to different cities for trials or pretrial mo-tions, he acquired lovers in those cities for more extended liaisons. He explained later to a reporter, "I was away from home an awful lot. Es-pecially during a long trial, your mind and your body and your psy-che need more than just going home alone every night." His mind, body, and psyche found especial comfort with a young woman in Cincinnati.

The college speaking tour gave Kunstler vast opportunities. He still boasted of those days to reporters in the 1990s. To one, he explained that those were the days of free sex. "I spoke on many, many college cam-puses, and there were many beautiful young women who would make themselves available to me. I was a star. It happened all the time. What was I to do?" To another, his exploits were equated with simple cour-tesy: "You're away from home, and you're lonely, and a young woman knocks on your motel door. She starts to undress. How the hell can you resist? Almost seems impolite to throw her out."

Soon, Kunstler began acquiring girlfriends closer to home in New York, including some well-known actresses and lawyers. He acquired a reputation for sexual exploits and flaunted them in a way that angered some female colleagues. Sometimes it embarrassed him, as when a witness in a criminal case in New Haven testified that he and other defendants had hidden out in "one of Kunstler's lady friends' houses" that was "near Chinatown." Other times Kunstler embarrassed himself with hypocrisy, as when he criticized another lawyer for offering a compliment that Kunstler had "balls." Kunstler chided, "'Balls' is a male chauvinist expression. Say 'guts.'" Or when he ripped into *Playboy*, in an interview published in that magazine, because "it demeans and degrades women in a manner as inequitable as it is gross."

One thing must be said. Apparently Kunstler's exploits were all with willing women. There is no hint of pressure or harassment coming from Kunstler himself. In fact, evidence runs to the contrary. Mary King in 1963 was an attractive white woman, a recent college graduate, and active in the civil rights movement in the South. She seems like a prime candidate for Kunstler's attentions, yet she wrote that "Bill Kunstler treated me like a daughter."

Kunstler explained this womanizing somewhat disingenuously in his autobiography. He said he had been lonely and it was hard to resist, but also went beyond that to claim that "my first marriage had been falling apart for a long time." He said he had lost much intimacy with Lotte and that he had come to see her only as mother and housekeeper. He wrote that in the dangerous middle age for men, "where you have to prove to yourself that you've still got it, that you can still get it up," his affairs made him feel "youthful and wanted and wonderful," but that it really had been "childish behavior." All this may be true in part, but Kunstler probably aimed these remarks at his second wife and may have been unable to see the larger issue of insecurity, aside from middle-aged sexuality, that led to these affairs.

Kunstler's boastful tone offers a more helpful clue. By the end of the 1960s, as Todd Gitlin has explained, the movement's male stars became known as "heavies."

> By the late Sixties there were a few dozen men who stood out as incarnations of The Revolution, so that to sleep with them was the equivalent of taking political communion; and they cut a considerable swath. . . . In the rush toward the phantasmagorical revolution, women became not simply a medium of exchange, consolidating the male bond, but rewards for male prowess and balm for male insecurity.

The extent of Kunstler's affairs was proof, therefore, in Kunstler's own eyes and as offered to the eyes of others, that he was a true heavy in the movement. However, that is ego and not necessarily insecurity. We have seen that Kunstler had insecurities and craved admiration and adulation. What better way could Kunstler obtain the sense that other human beings truly admired him than for hundreds of willing women to offer him their bodies? Not only would the sexual act reassure him, it would give him something he could brag about with his male friends.

Kunstler did brag with his friends about his conquests, even those of groupies, although he was more proud of the longer-lasting relationships with women in various cities around the country. To those closest to him, Kunstler's womanizing seemed compulsive and they themselves related it to some feeling of insecurity. One male friend thought his stories wore thin after a while and that Kunstler told of his conquests in a style of "look at me I'm some kind of special guy." This compulsive and excessive male sexuality, called satyriasis in the psychological literature, is usually related to insecurity.

Lotte knew of her husband's infidelities. At least occasionally, he bragged of his women in her presence. Beyond whatever Lotte knew directly, Kunstler thought she suspected more. He was not unhappy in the marriage, and Lotte neither mentioned his affairs nor asked for a divorce. Although their marriage was obviously severely damaged by Kunstler's philandering, nevertheless it continued intact throughout the 1960s and until the early 1970s.

Kunstler's family life diminished after he became involved in the civil rights movement. There was no more opportunity for the picnics by the reservoir or playing Pepitone in the sandlot baseball games. There was still some time to read Dylan Thomas poetry to Jane (Karin left for college in the fall of 1961), help with homework, and go to the beach. Even so, he was out of town a great deal; Kunstler estimated that by 1969 he averaged over six out-of-town trips a month. His day-to-day relationship with wife and daughter suffered. He even missed Jane's high school graduation.

Both Jane and Lotte were philosophical about his absences. Jane knew as a child that "most kids' fathers were home more than mine, but I thought that what my father did was more important than what they were doing, and was excited by what he did." Now she concludes that "he loved us a lot, but work was always first." Lotte thought likewise, feeling "really and truly that what he was doing was so important that my giving certain things up was my contribution to that. And I still believe that and did. Now in retrospect, I think that was a little grandiose. Other people could have done for him what I did." Lotte may underestimate her importance, as the evidence suggests that she played a very important role in Kunstler's success.

From his beginning in the civil rights work and then increasing with his prominence, Kunstler received threats: postcards, letters, telephone calls. Kunstler's absences made the threats seem worse. In 1969 Kunstler told a reporter that he worried very little about threats to his life. "Mostly, these things are on the hysterical side. You get inured to them." However, his family did not. Jane recalls many telephone threats. One call she answered when she was twelve or thirteen particularly frightened her. A calm voice ordered her to "tell your father that all nigger lovers must die." Because it was so matter-of-fact, she believed her father was going to die. Equally daunting to a teenage girl must have been the thought that her telephone line was tapped, as it was by the FBI in the late 1960s.

Although frequently absent, when Kunstler was home he found time for dinner parties and cocktail parties, where he talked excitedly about his civil rights work. Bill and Lotte also held smaller gatherings with close friends. The Kunstlers formed an intimate circle with Milton Berner (with whom he once almost drowned in a sailboat), Fred Marks, their wives, Joan and Barbara, and two other couples, the Gorens and the Martins. Although Kunstler left his brother behind in Port Chester when he moved to Mamaroneck in 1965, he still socialized informally in backyard parties with these older friends.

Even in the company of intimate friends whom he had known for years, Kunstler was always on stage, always entertaining, always seeking praise. Fred Marks recalls that Kunstler always sought approval. "Sometimes he got on my nerves . . . his ego constantly had to be fed." He was a chronic name dropper. Fred and his wife used to talk about Kunstler's craving for attention and that it had an element of insecurity. A national figure, Kunstler still felt he needed to explain his practice to Lotte and seek her assurance and approval.

Kunstler's need for a fix of adulation extended even to youngsters. He was always kind to teenagers. One high school student who regularly took a shortcut through Kunstler's wooded acres in Westchester wrote much later of an occasion when he unexpectedly came face to face with Kunstler even as he was trespassing on his property. He expected to be chastised, lectured on the sanctity of private property. But no. Kunstler paused, pushed his glasses even higher on his forehead, "grinned at me, conspiratorially," and drove off in his green Volkswagen Beetle.

In the late 1960s Graham Marks, son of Fred, frequently attended the intimate-circle parties given by Kunstler or his friends. Graham was then sixteen or seventeen and he and the other teenaged children of the Kunstlers, Marks, Berners, Gorens, and Martins interacted considerably with Kunstler. Graham now recalls that Kunstler was "our hero and also our playmate at the same time." For example, he would come home from Chicago during the trial and drop names like Abbie Hoffman to impress the kids.

> In a funny way he would sort of look to us. . . . he would like show up with some pot or one time he showed up with this Corvette. And I remember getting in and it was really like going for a joy ride. It was like how fast can we get this thing up on this little suburban street. . . . there was sort of a sense of him wanting to impress us.

Kunstler became both the hero and the kid for these teenagers. Graham recalls Kunstler "holding court," wanting to be the center of the kids' attention as well as the adults'. "There was almost that sense like he was looking for a certain kind of approval from us as the kids." At the time, when a teenager, Graham simply thought, "Oh, wow, Bill is so great!" In retrospect, he is not cynical about Kunstler, but believes Kunstler played up things that he knew the teenagers esteemed, like marijuana, to show the kids he fit in, "definitely in a way that, let's say, he wasn't with my folks or the Berners. . . . a 'playing to' sort of aspect."

Lotte was a great help to Kunstler in his practice during the 1960s. She accompanied him a great deal, to the Southern Christian Leadership Conference meeting in 1961 when he first met Martin Luther King, several of the southern civil rights campaigns, the 1963 March on Washington, many of the Chicago Seven trial sessions, some of the campus speeches, and the Attica uprising. Lotte organized movement fundraisers, ranging from small gatherings to a large-scale event, with Peter Lawford and Sammy Davis, Jr., held at the Westchester County Auditorium. In the early 1970s Kunstler's schedule had become so hectic that Lotte turned her organizational talent to keeping his master schedule of appointments and trips. In 1970, perhaps not completely accurately,

Kunstler told a reporter that he consulted with Lotte on all his major decisions.

Because Kunstler was so often in the position of "holding court" with his listeners and in the posture of being the entertainer, his theatricality often generated half-truths, Mark Twain–style "stretchers," and sometimes outright lies. Kunstler never meant his embellishments on the truth maliciously and they never hurt anybody. He could sense the reaction of his audience, and as the audience reacted, he adapted and changed a story until perfected. Kunstler was such a good lawyer that he came to believe in most of his "stretchers," as he completely internalized them.

They could be simple things, like telling his daughter Jane he wrote a particular poem when he had not, or extending the age of his father's death as he himself approached the same age. Some other fibs count as more important. For example, he told many people, even reporters in interviews, that he was in Memphis at the Loraine Motel when Martin Luther King was shot in 1968. He stayed just a few rooms away, the story went, and had an appointment to meet with King the next morning to discuss a labor issue then current in Memphis. He even convinced the coauthor of his autobiography of the story, until she checked with Lotte Kunstler. Lotte told her that her former husband was with her in New York that night, and the book carried that version.

Another example is the image of the *David* statue we saw in the introductory chapter. Kunstler often used that image in public talks and in private conversation as a metaphor for courage in the face of danger, for going forward when it would be easy and unnoticed to retreat. In earlier versions of the story, the noted art critic Bernard Berenson was present with Kunstler at the Accademia in Florence, and it was he who told Kunstler that Michelangelo sculpted the only statue that shows David prior to killing Goliath and in a moment of hesitation. In some later versions, Berenson is dropped, although he comes back in the autobiography, albeit not necessarily immediately there in the museum.

Others who were with Kunstler on his 1968 trip to Italy, Lotte, his daughter Karin and son-in-law Neal, all insist that Bernard Berenson was not present and do not recall any sudden revelation. The moral to the story, however, was the point for Kunstler, not the reality of the story. Just before he took that trip to Italy, he spoke to the national convention of Unitarians on June 24, 1968. He used a poem of Robert Browning, "The Ring and the Book," involving the moral dilemma of a priest asked to violate his vows in order to prevent a murder. From the story, Kunstler extrapolated a moral lesson.

> Every man fights an inner battle within himself as to whether he will do an act so dangerous to himself that it may destroy him. And yet it is an act that only he will know he was asked to perform. . . . It is easy to be courageous when you are on the bank of the stream and someone is drowning and thirty people are watching you. Even the most fearsome will jump in the river rather than stand the utter, utter embarrassment and worse of having people know that at a crucial moment he did not respond. But how much more courage it takes when no one knows, when you're alone on the bank and no one will know whether you jump in or don't jump in. And if the person drowns, no one will know whether you were there on time or you weren't or could have helped or could not. Those are the hardest fights. The inner battles take place in the minds of men as to whether they will take a stand that is dangerous and significant when not to take the stand will not subject you to any censor at all, because no one will know . . . without anyone being the wiser.

This is precisely the David story without the *David*. In other words, Kunstler did not develop this moral lesson from Bernard Berenson, nor did he develop it himself after looking at Michelangelo's *David*. It was a moral point he wanted to make anyway, probably because he thought it was a high and stirring moral ground that might inspire people to take radical positions. With the *David* statue he found a new and better tool with which to make the same point that he had been making before with a different tool, the Browning poem. That is not to say that Kunstler did not believe passionately in the *David* story. He referred to it often. It was so much a piece of his life that his second wife, Margie, gave him a replica of *David* that he kept on his desk. He frequently mentioned the unreal though believed history of his contact with *David* and its meaning for him to reporters, and urged its lessons upon colleagues, law clerks, and anyone who would listen.

By the late 1960s and early 1970s Kunstler had developed enough notoriety that he was a public figure. In contrast to his near-cult following among teenagers, he had developed foes among other population segments. Some of these foes were high-placed. One was the chief right-wing guru, William F. Buckley, Jr., who editorialized in the *National Re-*

view that Kunstler ought to be disbarred and resolved not again to share a public platform with him. Kunstler, he wrote, "should experience the isolation which he has earned from the civilized community."

One notable source of foes was the Jewish community. At this relatively early time Kunstler did not experience nearly the hatred from New York Jews that he would years later when he regularly represented unpopular Arabs. Indeed, a large percentage of the Jewish community applauded his early work. However, antipathy was already beginning. The Law and Social Action Commission of the American Jewish Congress dropped Kunstler from membership in early 1969, apparently without informing him beforehand. One Auschwitz survivor, then a New York landlord, was quoted shortly after the fall 1971 Attica uprising as saying about Kunstler, "I hate him. He's a Jew and I'm a Jew. I know what it is like to live without law. He does not, but he talks all the time like he does. If I didn't have a wife and kids I would kill him."

Kunstler also took fire from less harsh critics, neither friends nor truly foes. Throughout his career, Kunstler received criticism that he was at times ill-prepared, at other times lazy, almost always too interested in self-glory and publicity. Some of this flack came from those who were jealous of Kunstler's high-profile practice. Other critics included those made uncomfortable by Kunstler's emotionally flamboyant style of constant hugging and kissing. But the quantity and credibility of his critics do not permit an easy dismissal. Charges of unpreparedness began in the 1960s, and as often as not came from liberals and other left-wing lawyers.

As early as December 1968, *Time* magazine reported that Kunstler's critics "say that his briefs can be careless," and by April 1970 a *New York Times* feature story noted "endless stories of meetings he has missed, deadlines he has overlooked, details he has ignored, committees he has failed, client bonds that have been forfeited, papers he hasn't filed." Many of the critics are, understandably, quoted anonymously. A prosecutor who defeated Kunstler in a major trial in the early 1970s contended that Kunstler "was winging it in court. He didn't look at the documents, the details, the papers that were necessary for cross-examination." A lawyer who knew Kunstler for years concluded in 1980 that "ill-prepared, Bill is still better than many lawyers prepared. But you can't always get away with his kind of sloppiness and carelessness." Another attorney who followed Kunstler's career said in 1969, "Bill's weakness is lack of preparation. He has fire and passion, and he's impressive in cases where eloquence is important. But his arguments can be more facile than profound. Judges are annoyed by that."

Some critics can be identified. Harriet Rabb, who worked with Kunstler at the Center for Constitutional Rights from 1966 to 1969, said of him that "he was certainly not the best researcher or writer, or the most well-prepared advocate. But it was a time when the issues were clear and dramatic." As to the civil rights work, chasing around the South trying to beat back segregation, Kunstler admitted that "sometimes the research was hasty, from the back seat of a car. But I think we lost very few of the ones I was associated with that came out of the movement work." Steven Hyman, in the 1960s an associate and partner with Kunstler, Kunstler, and Kinoy, remembered in 1996,

> Preparation was not necessarily Bill's strong suit. He would walk into court and often he would shoot from the hip, which was his reputation, and probably deservedly so. It wasn't that he was totally unprepared, but that he did not spend the time that other lawyers would spend putting everything together. I handled a couple of criminal cases with Bill and I still remember him cross-examining completely ad libbing. . . . he did a good job but often would walk into thickets that I wasn't sure that he intended.

In the Chicago trial, for example, Kunstler himself admitted he felt unprepared before trial because he had been rushing from trial to trial and "had never found the time to study the Chicago case." That Thomas Foran, the chief prosecutor in Chicago, thought Kunstler was "totally irresponsible, poorly prepared and more interested in fulfilling his own political agenda than representing his clients" hardly comes as a surprise. Yet the reporter for the *New York Times* who spent every day at the trial reached somewhat the same conclusion: "Thriving on the drama and excitement of courtroom confrontation, he was bored by long hours over books and briefs. Too often he was ill-prepared for an argument or a cross-examination. Nobody could 'wing it' like Kunstler, but even in a case like this one winging it wasn't enough." Even David Dellinger, aside from the Yippies the most sympathetic of the Chicago defendants to Kunstler's efforts, damned him with faint praise. Acknowledging that Kunstler "had an amazing ability to think on his feet, immediately getting to the heart of an unfamiliar situation," he still believed that sometimes during the trial Kunstler "spent so much time outside the court exploring the youth culture . . . that he didn't do the solid kind of preparatory work" that his cocounsel Weinglass did.

The criticism of unpreparedness and sloppy work appeared in other ways. A murder defendant grounded an appeal in 1979 on a poor defense by Kunstler. A federal judge permitted a defendant to remove Kunstler as his defense lawyer in 1983, commenting that the defendant "may profit from Mr. Kunstler's removal [since he] seems to have expended only a minimal effort." On the other hand, federal judge Jack B. Weinstein in Brooklyn, before whom Kunstler often appeared, thought Kunstler competent and prepared. A Florida lawyer recalled that Kunstler once arrived in Florida "completely unprepared, the night before he had to argue an appeal on a death-penalty sentence." In 1993 a mother of a young defendant complained that Kunstler's argument to an appellate court was top-heavy with generalities about racism and too light on the fact of her son's case.

Interestingly, Morton Sobell, the man convicted on spy charges along with the Rosenbergs, was quite bitter in his prison correspondence concerning delays occasioned by Kunstler's (and Arthur Kinoy's) representation. In mid-1965 he wrote to another attorney complaining of "the casual approach manifested by Bill and Arthur . . . . There is no reason to believe that they will find any more time for this case in the future than they have in the past." After he met Kunstler in person, Sobell wrote that his conference "verified my earlier impression. He is not what I'd call a technician."

In May 1965 Sobell wrote to Kunstler and Kinoy that although half a year had passed since they began representing him, he had seen no evidence "that you've become at all serious. . . . I am a plain person and would rather know that I don't have an attorney than live under the present illusion." A year later, in May 1966, Sobell sardonically wrote to Kunstler that he had noticed "from the Times, that you are quite popular as a lawyer these days. Congratulations! But I'm wondering if you will ever get around to filing this Petition and Brief. You wasted almost a year of my time fiddling around."

To this criticism it must be said that Kunstler was an extremely quick study. Often reporters noted that Kunstler appeared unprepared at the opening of a trial, yet by the second day engaged in brilliant cross-examination. His friend Milton Berner believes Kunstler had a photographic memory; for the short term, he had total recall of what he had read. Steven Hyman, his partner from the 1960s, recalls how Kunstler could sit down and dictate briefs effortlessly. Ronald Kuby, his partner in the 1990s, told of Kunstler's "amazing ability to process information." He saw Kunstler read through a foot-high stack of documents at breakfast, then use them in cross-examination as though he had studied them for weeks. Kunstler needed "less time to prepare than anyone else," according to Kuby.

In the 1960s Kunstler was a legal nymphomaniac; he just could not say no to prospective clients. At the end of 1968 he wrote in a private letter that "life has been very hectic for me and I am probably as over-extended as I've ever been." Obviously, this affected his preparation. Leonard Weinglass, his junior colleague in Chicago, maintained that what distinguished Kunstler from other movement lawyers was his willingness to take on so many difficult cases for no fee. As a consequence, Weinglass maintained that "I won't listen to criticism from any lawyer unless he does at least one-tenth of the pro bono work [public interest work at no compensation] Bill does."

To an extent, the criticism of unpreparedness assumes that Kunstler was trying his cases in a conventional manner. If Kunstler's role, as he defined it, were different—for example, if his primary goal were to politicize a case and to dramatize its political issues before the jury, media, and public—then the critique would be largely beside the point. For example, the Chicago Seven defendants and many observers praised Leonard Weinglass for his hard work and solid preparation in Chicago. So did Kunstler himself. In an October 1970 interview, Kunstler said that Weinglass "prepared the case and he knew the facts of what happened in Chicago more thoroughly than any other man in the courtroom." Kunstler added immediately, "My role was different."

This raises the issue, then, of what it means to be a radical lawyer. What are the goals and ideologies of such lawyers, and where does Kunstler fit within their belief systems? Finally, by what standards, adopted by radical lawyers and adhered to by Kunstler, can his practice be fairly judged? What, indeed, was Kunstler's role?

8

Radical Lawyers in Modern America

AMERICA HAS ALWAYS had activist lawyers dedicated to causes, and there is a rich literature that describes their political role. This broad category of activist lawyers includes radical attorneys whose sympathies tend toward basic, structural change in society and whose clients advocate its accomplishment through violent struggle. However, before the New Left of the 1960s, radical lawyers looked and acted much like all other lawyers. America also has always had political trials: criminal cases whose purpose is to stifle opposition to existing authority. Classic examples of political trials include the prosecution of the Wobblies in 1918, the Oklahoma anarcho-syndicalist trials of the late 1930s, and the prosecution of the Communist Party leadership under the Smith Act in the 1950s. But before the New Left of the 1960s, political trials looked much like all other criminal trials.

This was because, until the late 1960s, dissenters, even revolutionaries, in the words of one sociologist of radical lawyers, "accepted the traditional structure and process of the criminal procedure without challenging its fundamental political legitimacy." They behaved themselves in a courtroom. This would dramatically change with the New Left's rejection of the legitimacy of the judicial machinery itself, its associated desire to "put the system on trial" as a defense, and its willingness to engage in disruptive behavior as a tactic. Whereas the Old Left lawyers usually adopted at least the facade of professionalism in separating themselves from their clients and preserved the traditional correctness of their trial mannerisms, the New Left lawyers did not. New Left attorneys identified with their radical clients more completely, approved the strategy of placing the system on trial, and sometimes even participated in the tactics of disruption.

A major ideological difference split the old and new leftists. The traditional Left had been Marxist and its interest was centered in the working class. Although sympathetic to the plight of blacks, other minorities, and women, the Old Left saw their oppression as coming from membership in the working class rather than racism or sexism. The New Left was less Marxist and held a more diffused notion of oppression that definitely included racism and sexism. For both Old and New Left lawyers, it was a point of honor to represent clients who held a sympathetic and "correct" political viewpoint. However, the clients of choice for the Old Left were narrowly defined by its Marxist ideology. As one scholar put it,

> The majority of old left lawyers basically located their political professional work in terms of clients who were labor organizers, unions, or radical political parties. . . . In contrast, the new—and most typically non-Marxist—left espoused a much more elastic notion of the "good guys" which encompassed civil rights workers, black and ethnic militants, feminists, members of the anti-war movement, and ultimately anyone who expressed a sense of opposition to the "system."

In many ways Kunstler matches the profile of the New Left lawyer, but in some ways he does not. He came to his earliest political trials only after over a dozen years of a very conventional bourgeois practice. That made him older than most of his New Left contemporaries, and some generational differences set him apart. As we have seen, Kunstler tried to identify with his clients, and during the time of the Chicago trial he flirted with the lifestyle of the youth. However, he never abandoned his love for opera or for literature. Some New Left lawyers adopted the "street dress" style of their clients for court appearances. Kunstler always dressed in suit and tie, even if sometimes nearly threadbare. He once explained that he found wearing street clothes to court was "not to my liking" and not a service to his clients because it diminished the lawyer's effectiveness with the media. "I'm not sure that the lawyer who adopts the dress and clothes styles of his client isn't simply trying to prove that he's part of the movement by adopting its outer paraphernalia," he added.

A study of the values and ethical norms of the New Left lawyers with whom Kunstler identified is distinctly helpful in understanding some of Kunstler's actions and attitudes. For example, when we see the New Left's use of media as a deliberate tool to politicize trials, it becomes easier to reject a superficial analysis of Kunstler's own media manipulation as mere ego. Not that his own desire for personal public-ity was not a factor, but there was more to it than just egoism. We will examine these characteristics of the New Left lawyer by looking at first, their attitude and philosophy about law and the legal system itself; sec-ond, their approach toward selecting clients; and third, their tactics at trial.

Radical lawyers of the late 1960s and early 1970s were personally committed to profound social change of a socialist and egalitarian sort. They sought a revolution in American society, peaceable if possible, but most did not eschew violence if that were necessary. Traditionally, lawyers have viewed themselves as professional agents for their clients, and therefore at a cool remove from their clients' passions and interests. In contrast, these New Left lawyers saw themselves as participants in their clients' revolutionary struggles. A student of radical lawyers wrote, "Professionalism is an ideology concerned with detailing the unique contribution and status of professional work. In contrast, a rad-ical political ideology . . . addresses the issue of fundamental social change in terms of class, sex and race relations. This implies partisan-ship rather than neutrality on the part of professional actors."

This implies that the radical lawyer should be a political being him-self, not a technician hired to advance his client's aims. The radical lawyer ought himself to have a personal passion for revolutionary change. In her 1973 book, *The People's Lawyers*, Marlise James quotes from several radical lawyers from across the country. Here is a sam-pling:

—Kenneth Vern Cockrel [Detroit]: "A revolutionary lawyer is a person who is a member of a revolutionary organization who happens to be a lawyer."

—Charles Garry [Berkeley]: "What you have to change is the system. . . . I consider myself a person who believes in revolutionary change, a person who believes that when the law is tyranny, revolution is in order."

In his 1971 book *Radical Lawyers: Their Role in the Movement and in the Courts*, the radical attorney Jonathan Black also assembles the thoughts of dozens of radical lawyers:

Henry di Suvero [New York]: "The legal system can be radically altered only in the same manner that any other part of the superstructure can be radically altered, and that is by revolutionary change. . . . [Movement lawyers] are at the beck and call of the movement and service every legal need it has. They are lawyers who speak the language of the movement, share its objectives and work assiduously in its behalf."

Beverly Axelrod [San Francisco Bay area]: "Those of us who are committed to the idea of revolution recognize that reform cannot bring about the necessary changes. Therefore, as a radical lawyer, I am not concerned with getting better laws enacted, or improving the legal system."

Gerald Lefcourt [New York]: "Radical lawyers essentially believe that the system must be abruptly and fundamentally changed in a very short period of time with the economic system as a major target. . . . radical lawyers believe that the court system operates to oppress, and operates as an arm of the government to maintain the status quo and the class interests of society. . . . There's no question that lawyers have politics and that they do not play only a technician-supportive role. It's important that they think politically if they're involved in political cases, that they make suggestions to political clients."

Kunstler fits into this pattern of revolutionary commitment and rhetoric, but somewhat imperfectly. William Kunstler was a doer, a man of action, and not a systematic thinker. He spoke frequently of oppressed people, and that clearly included racial minorities and the poor. However, he was weak in an agenda for a replacement of the system, particularly the economic system. In the summer of 1970 Kunstler told a reporter that he had "come to the conclusion that capitalism as a system is destructive of human beings and must be replaced, but by what, I don't know." Later that year he told an interviewer that something was "terribly wrong with the existence of private property." While "a complete re-evaluation of our economic system" was needed, he could not "get into specifics yet, because I haven't thought it through; but I do know that to translate this conviction into my own life is very difficult, because I'm a completely middle-class person. I have a house in Westchester; I have a lot of the good things in life."

Kunstler never did think it through, but that is not really a criticism because, as we will see later in this chapter, his personal vision did not require a systematic political or economic viewpoint. Kunstler often linked his hesitancy in considering a fundamentally different economic system to his own middle-class lifestyle. That link was even clearer when he spoke with regrets of a perceived lack of his own personal engagement in revolutionary movements. In 1992, for example, he reflected that "I wouldn't say 'Do it' or encourage it [acts of revolutionary violence]. But that's because I'm still too much a middle-class white man. . . . you always get the feeling that you would like to be more of a revolutionary. . . . And yet maybe the times aren't right or you lack the guts."

Kunstler was too hard on himself. Certainly in the earlier days of the movement, Kunstler was himself a player. He participated fully in the collective decisions made in the Chicago trial and in other political trials. He attended conferences of radical lawyers held with nonlawyer political activists, for example, a major one in December 1968 in Texas. He served the conference as keynote speaker, and the conference served him by becoming the venue for a substantial number of sexual liaisons, enhanced by the easy availability of marijuana. Even though Kunstler never adopted the garments or lifestyles of the youthful revolutionaries, on matters of substance he always identified with them. He told Nat Hentoff in his *Playboy* interview that a lawyer "should, first of all, be part of a movement and then employ his skills in relationship to that movement. He should not be separated by professionalism, by educational or economic barriers nor by status from the people with whom he works." However, Kunstler was always wistful that perhaps he had not participated enough. Just a few months before he died he told two reporters, "I'm not sure lawyers who are still within the system have the right to call themselves radical. But many of the people I've represented have radical views, have crossed the line into violence when they figured that nonviolence would not do the trick."

Kunstler's own attitude toward violence in the revolutionary movement was ambivalent. One of the great sources of Kunstler's notoriety was statements he made concerning the killings of people he disapproved of politically. For example, after the Kennedy brothers were assassinated, Kunstler remarked that he "thought that the world was a better place without the Kennedys, that they were two of the most dangerous men America ever produced." It was widely quoted, but his explanation usually did not follow. Pointing to the Kennedys' involvement in the beginnings of Vietnam, their wiretapping of Martin Luther King, the encouragement of COINTELPRO, the FBI's internal spy program, the effort to assassinate Fidel Castro, Jack Kennedy's relationship with a Mafia moll, and his appointment of racist judges in the South, Kunstler concluded that bullets that stopped such an abuse of power had probably been beneficial.

Interviewers grilled Kunstler about this sort of statement, pointing out that the assassins of Martin Luther King, for example, probably thought the world would be a better place without him. But Kunstler stood his ground, stating that "I don't want to sound like some mealy-mouthed liberal who says, 'Everybody has got a right to live.'" Pointing out that many people thought the world would be far better off without a Hitler or a Saddam Hussein, Kunstler agreed that he was inconsistent on the principle of political killing but contended, "you make political choices . . . King's assassin was *wrong*." As Kunstler put it in his autobiography, "political assassination of the *right person* is not something that I would always describe as wrong" (emphasis added).

Justifications of black violence, especially when directed against whites, gained Kunstler considerable notoriety as well. After Larry Davis wounded six New York policemen, Kunstler's remark that "any black guy that shoots six cops and puts the fear of God in police officers, I think is great" garnered wide publicity. Less widely quoted was his explanation that police, fearful that blacks might fire back, would be less trigger-happy and less prone to shoot blacks in a ghetto confrontation. Kunstler reasoned that the only political weapon the black community had was the white community's fear of violence. Even the ghetto uprisings were beneficial as they drew attention to the problems of black neighborhoods and sometimes brought needed government services.

In 1967 a Plainfield, New Jersey, policeman had a confrontation with a young black man in the ghetto. The officer shot the youth twice in the stomach. A black crowd that witnessed the affray became frenzied and chased the policeman, caught him, and stomped him to death. Kunstler's reaction was that the cop "deserved that death. . . . The crowd justifiably, without the necessity of a trial and in the most dramatic way possible, stomped him to death." The justification came from the historic mistreatment of black communities by white policemen. This is one of Kunstler's more extreme statements justifying violence, again widely publicized. It was originally made before a Black Panther rally shortly after the incident. Kunstler acknowledged in 1994 that the "words were harsh," that he had been angry, and that he would not presently use the same language.

Actually, Kunstler held a relatively nuanced view of violence. He was far from being a pacifist, and at times viewed violence as necessary. For example, in regard to prisons, "only the threat or actuality of inmate rebellions offers any hope of humanizing penal institutions and release programs and procedures." Kunstler believed that violence had brought about many good things in American history, including the emancipation of the slaves. He believed that the American citizenry could alter the system by whatever means they saw fit, which certainly included revolution. However, in 1971 he felt that

> It is a bad tactic to employ violence. . . . [Violence] normally occurs at a time of the transfer of power, not at a time when that transfer appears so distant. Because the result of isolated acts of terrorism is to disunite the movement and to bring on a whirlwind of repression at a time when we're not prepared for it. It only alienates our friends and unites our enemies. . . . So my feeling is that as a tactic—and I talk only in tactical terms—I don't have moral scruples against violence—violence at the moment is bad for the movement.

Kunstler made it clear that he did not believe in isolating the Weathermen and others who did engage in violence. The principle was not violence, but political choice. As of 1971 he felt that the movement should not condemn those who caused violence. "In fact, we should do everything possible to protect them if their objectives are the same as ours. . . . I'm not one for disowning the Weathermen or any other group or individual whose goal is generally the same as mine." Although Kunstler preached the probability of revolution, more often than not he prophesied a peaceful one.

The probable distance of actual revolution did not preclude local violence directed at property. Kunstler often told his college audiences in the late 1960s,

> We have clenched the fist with mass resistance, and we can only open it in two ways: We can open it in brotherhood, if the system has the capability of responding to immediate human ends, or we can open it to

curl the index finger around a trigger. These are the choices. In time, the system will have to make its choice. And when it makes its choice, it makes ours.

Essentially, however, Kunstler thought of violence as justified only on a local level. For example, in August 1970 he argued,

> It may be right to burn a building in one area, and not in another. On a campus, if everything else failed to get a grievance recognized, I think broken windows would be perfectly proper, and if the broken windows didn't work, then burning a building would be perfectly proper, and if that didn't work, maybe getting rifles would be proper.

At other times he emphasized that buildings should be burned only when no one was in them, at a safe time. Movement violence, he contended, was nothing compared with the violence of the government itself, in its B-52 raids in Vietnam, Kent State, lynchings in the South, and so forth. The violence of the movement is "related primarily to property damage, which I can't hold in any capacity as sacred to human life." For understandable reasons, Kunstler's talk about revolution ceased after the collapse of the movement in the 1970s, and even the justification of violence became significantly diminished. However, another feature of radical lawyerism, a contempt for the judicial system, continued in full force.

It should hardly be surprising that the radical lawyers of the New Left regarded the legal system with contempt. Various radical lawyers mocked the courts and the judicial system as "simply the functional appendage of a larger system of racism, capitalism, and imperialism," "instruments of the status quo, extensions of the cop's club," and "only another arm of the oppressor, like the police." To Carol Goodman the law was "an illegitimate law designed to protect the interests of fascists, capitalists and imperialists" and the judge an "old, dyspeptic, impotent, racist, honky pig dressed in a black nightgown that should be a sheet."

Because of these views, radical lawyers scoff at efforts to improve or reform the legal system; their interest lies only in basic systemic change. However, as revolutionaries have always done, they are willing to adapt bourgeois institutions for their own purposes. They believe that the legal system, like all capitalist institutions, has contradictions that may be manipulated instrumentally to serve the radical movement's interests. A radical lawyer may make an elaborate argument based, say, on First Amendment grounds. However, he would have no abstract interest in civil rights, but would simply regard his argument as exploiting this loophole in the capitalist oppression to advance a political agenda that is entirely outside the realm of law or even civil liberties.

What then might radical lawyers hope to accomplish through the legal system? In a political criminal trial, one objective is to obtain the release of the activist defendants so that they might continue their organizing and revolutionary activities freed from authority's interference. An equal and sometimes overriding objective of any political trial, whether it involves criminal defense, management-union conflicts, or landlord-tenant disputes, is to engage in what radical lawyers call demystification.

"Demystification" is a very confusing term, yet it is an essential defining feature of the radical lawyer. It means that legal forums ought to be used to expose the legal system itself, to demonstrate to the clients, the jury, and if possible the wider public the true political realities underlying the litigation. In a political criminal defense, this would mean a demonstration of the oppressive nature of the prosecution. In civil cases, as the sociologist Nancy Anderson wrote,

> through demystification tenants should come to see tenant-landlord law as fundamentally skewed toward the landlord, while unions should learn that labor law is a tool for managing the capitalist system. Once the class nature of the law is understood, radicals hope that tenants and labor groups will neither pin all their expectations on court decisions nor entirely despair over unfavorable judicial outcomes. Thus, radical lawyers might try to encourage such clients and their allies to develop extra-legal modes of effective action.

The ultimate objective of demystification is to generate a loss of public confidence in the judicial system and, by extension, the entire government apparatus. This will speed the coming of revolutionary change, or perhaps the revolution itself. This purpose is evident in the rhetoric of several radical lawyers.

> Kenneth Cloke: "[Law] can secure limited reforms [but] . . . the major objective of work in law, however, ought to be to . . . show that

bourgeois law is not only hypocritical, but based on inequality and therefore, in our eyes, illegal."

Kenneth Vern Cockrel: "When we go into a court, we never defend. We're always attacking the American legal system, and we're also trying to get the client out."

Charles Garry: "The role of the lawyer is to see that the client gets out on the streets, but, while you're doing that, you have to expose the system that brought him there."

Henry di Suvero: "The counter objectives of the movement are to expose the hypocrisy of legal machinations and thus rob the verdict of its legitimacy."

The Bust Book: "One purpose of a political-legal defense is to use the courtroom as a classroom and teach about the role of law and courts in the United States. The defense can be conducted so as to reveal what, in fact, is on trial."

William Kunstler fits quite well into this pattern. Reporters widely quoted his statement after the Chicago trial that he realized that law was "all a living lie." His views did not seem to change over the years. In 1974 he told an interviewer that he regarded "law in the United States [as] just a terroristic device." In 1975 he wrote for publication that "the real purpose of law, and particularly criminal law, is the protection of the haves and their possessions from the have-nots." In 1982 he advised a crowd of Harvard law students that law was just the state's control mechanism. The students hissed. In the 1990s Kunstler published a book review in which he noted that "what passes for justice on these shores is the result not only of class control but of racial politics as well." It is fair to conclude that Kunstler had little respect for the law as such.

Nor did Kunstler have much respect for most judges. Barry Slotnick once asked Kunstler who were the top ten judges that he knew. He responded by asking whether he could name people who judged the Miss America contest. In 1993 he spoke at a conference sponsored by the New York Supreme Court Justices' Association. He told the assembled judges that "Judges are creatures of the Establishment. They do what's politically correct for them. The worst of them are mean-spirited, racist bastards. As for defending the Constitution, they probably violate it more than any other branch of government." This does not suggest that

Kunstler was always confrontational with judges in court, as he was with Julius Hoffman in Chicago. We are looking here merely at Kunstler's belief systems, not his conduct. Judge Jack Weinstein, a federal judge in Brooklyn before whom Kunstler tried many cases, remarked that Kunstler was always prepared and polite in his courtroom, and saved his "stump speeches" for the corridor. Several judges have noted that Kunstler in the courtroom was not the fire-breathing radical they had expected. Kunstler even complimented some judges, and a very few, as a matter of personality or mutual interests, he seemed to like.

Like other radical lawyers, Kunstler believed that the legal system had exploitable contradictions, and that he could "use the system's contradictions to manipulate it." In addition to attempting to free political defendants, Kunstler was anxious to use the courtroom for demystification. "The courts have many purposes besides trying cases," he remarked in 1969, and "the statement of radical politics is one of these." At the time of the Chicago trial, he said that "in a political trial such as this one, the court becomes not just a place to grind out a decision but also a place to educate the public and dramatize the contradictions between what the law preaches and what it practices."

He explained many times that radicals had one of their best forums in the courthouse. Radicals had no influence in the executive branch, and no congressman would present a radical viewpoint on the floor of Congress. However, a radical viewpoint could be presented as a defense in a criminal trial. The radicals could educate the jury and spectators, and, if they were lucky, the media might become interested and spread their message to the entire world. If a radical defense gained an acquittal, that presented yet another opportunity to attack the system by taking the line that the charges should never have been brought. Because of the disruption of the defendants' lives and their organizing activities, not to speak of the expense of a successful defense, the only fair trial would have been no trial at all.

Where did Kunstler's radical views come from, after a dozen years of a ho-hum bourgeois legal practice and a somewhat conventionally liberal civil rights campaign? Radical lawyers have a curious way of referring to a specific event or experience that "radicalized" them. It is much the same way conservative Christians can recall and discuss the occasion on which they were "reborn." Kunstler almost always referred to the Chicago trial as his radical Rubicon. Many times and in different variations he maintained that "up to that time I guess I was a traditional civil rights attorney. I believed in the system. I recognized that it didn't always work out the right way, but that in the main it would. After Chicago, it totally changed."

That seems to be too abrupt. Kunstler took many extreme and radical positions while defending the Black Power advocates prior to Chicago. In the spring of 1969, six months before the Chicago trial began, Kunstler was a member of a group of radicals who issued a call for opposition to preventive detention proposals. Many people of all political stripes opposed those laws, but what is significant is that Kunstler opposed them on the basis that they were "the first step to legalized fascism in this country. . . . The slogan for fascism in the United States will be 'law and order.'" Well before the Chicago trial, Kunstler had adopted a standard radical line.

It is speculative, but reasonable, to think that much of Kunstler's radicalization came from his association with Arthur Kinoy in the civil rights days of the 1960s. At that time, Kinoy was much more developed politically than Kunstler. Several of Kunstler's personal friends remarked on how much he admired Kinoy. In a 1996 interview Kinoy was modest but acknowledged that he had been more politically conscious than Kunstler in the 1960s, that he had "a little bit" of influence on Kunstler's politics before Chicago, and that it "could be" that this influence was a reason for Kunstler's growth in political consciousness.

Much of the intermediate agenda of radicals in the 1960s, aside from ultimate revolution, was reflected in a pale way by official government programs sponsored by Lyndon Johnson. The War on Poverty, elimination of racism, the giving of power to the poor to take charge of their own lives, projects, and programs are miniature versions of some of the things the radicals advocated. The point is that the 1960s radicals came out of a context of support. Even the American middle class was discovering that America had a racist society; the radicals simply went further with the implications of that fact. For an attorney to become radicalized in the much more conservative 1990s would require an incredibly strong and independent person. David Dellinger believes that Kunstler became even more radical in the last decade of his life, but a more reasonable inference is that he just did not change and seemed to be more radical because American society became more conservative.

There is the viewpoint among some radical lawyers that Kunstler never really left the system, that at heart he remained a constitutionalist, a believer in law as an abstract ideal. One holding that view is

Michael Ratner, a friend and sometime collaborator. The friendship was curious in that Michael Ratner was the second husband of Margie, who divorced him to marry Kunstler. They all remained close. Michael Ratner pointed out that in Kunstler's last two weeks of life, while he lived at his summer house across the road from Ratner, Kunstler had worked on a paper advocating the theory that the first five amendments to the Constitution were fundamental and could not themselves be amended. Ratner believes that Kunstler embraced the Constitution as worthy of serious study, something more than an instrument to obtain political goals. Ronald Kuby, Kunstler's longtime partner and such at the time of his death, pointed out that for Kunstler to practice as an advocate every day of his life required a personal belief that the persons he addressed, judges and juries, could be persuaded, and therefore he never completely rejected the legal system. However, both of those viewpoints are consistent with a primarily instrumentalist view of law.

Kunstler's rhetoric certainly reflects a purely manipulative view of the law. The best argument that Kunstler's rhetoric might have overstated his true feelings is derived from his strong need to be accepted, to be included, and to belong. Most of his professional colleagues and virtually all his politically minded acquaintances, including his wife Margie, had far more systematically developed radical views than did he. Put simply, he may have sometimes overstated his views to be part of the radical club. However, the preponderance of the evidence, including the frequency of his expressions, suggests that Kunstler was a true radical who had adopted a completely utilitarian, instrumentalist view of law. After Kunstler's death, Kuby himself made a statement that suggested Kunstler's practice was instrumental and not principled: "Bill always took cases that he should have lost. But when you lose, the idea is always to make the *system* pay. You erode the public perception of fairness in the case, so people say, 'Okay, the government won, but they won in a loathsome way.' You make people *ashamed* of their government."

Two of Kunstler's statements at the end of his life seem especially convincing. One is his response to a radio interview in October 1994 from Santa Monica, California. The interviewer asked whether Kunstler believed that "essential justice can be obtained through the courts." Kunstler answered, "No. I believe essential justice can be obtained by pressure of people in the streets, outside courthouses . . . power yields only to power." The interviewer then asked whether Kunstler saw the justice system "as just one method of bringing about social change." Kunstler responded that the "ruling class . . . uses the justice system, creates it and uses it for its own perpetuation. So, it's there. You can exploit it. It has certain exploitable factors and I try to do that. But I don't really believe in it. . . . I use the law politically. I use courtrooms politically. I think they are very good for that purpose."

In an interview with a print journalist earlier in 1994, Kunstler described his criminal defense practice as "fighting the system all the time. We fight for an individual on a case. But there's a secondary purpose—to use the individual fight to, in some way, hurt or cripple, inhibit or deter the system." Then the interviewer began a discussion of Kunstler's First Amendment work. A series of questions about anti-abortion groups dramatically demonstrates the primacy of political goal over abstract civil rights in Kunstler's belief.

The interviewer inquired whether Kunstler would represent Operation Rescue if it came to him for a First Amendment defense. Kunstler answered, "no, because I believe they are a vicious organization, trying to impress their religious beliefs on everyone else, and [they] have resorted to murder and violence at clinics. *I would just as soon love to see their free speech tampered with*" (emphasis added). "Is this inconsistent with your civil libertarian views?" asked the interviewer. "Totally inconsistent," Kunstler agreed with a smile, "but not inconsistent with my political views."

What has been discussed thus far is only that Kunstler operated his law practice to further political goals, and that he regarded the law, not as itself something worthy or that could be reformed so as to be worthy, but as an instrument for the advancement of political objectives. Kunstler's own political goals, where he stood in the stream of radical ideology, are a more complex issue than for most radical lawyers. Kunstler held a more nuanced political ideology than most, and we will return to this issue at the end of this chapter, after we have analyzed the radical lawyer's clientele and conduct of trials.

A signal factor of a radical lawyer's client selection is the refusal to accept any representation where the client's political viewpoint or conduct is inconsistent with the lawyer's own political judgment. This veto over clients is one of the most significant characteristics of radical lawyers, whereby "left lawyers validate their enterprise largely in terms of politically justified and changeable strategies of rejection. . . . the radical 'sector' is seen to be most clearly characterized by what it does *not* do—hiring itself out for a price."

What cases do radical lawyers reject? For crimes such as murder or robbery, the choice would be made politically. Murderers who were members of the Ku Klux Klan would be rejected; Weathermen or other radicals who blew up a building and in doing so killed someone would be accepted. A bank robbery committed to fund a militant organization (an "expropriation") would be acceptable. Kunstler was once asked how he felt about radical bank robbers, and he forthrightly responded that "from a political point of view I have no problem with expropriation for good causes. As a lawyer I have to recognize it's illegal. But Robin Hood has a strong hold on all people. I'm not cold-blooded, but I do recognize that we have an ongoing civil war."

Radical lawyers commonly reject the alleged perpetrators of certain other, politically undesirable crimes: rapists, wife beaters, non-addicted heroin dealers, for example. They dismiss the usual lawyerly argument that "everyone is entitled to a good defense" as naive. Equally naive in the radical lawyer's judgment is the position of the civil libertarian lawyer that behind a vile client may lie a pure and abstract right, such as the First Amendment. This judgment is a direct consequence of the radical's rejection of any abstract meaning to law itself. It follows that the underlying political reality is the *only* reality to be weighed and judged; the concept of abstract rights is merely doctrine to be manipulated. Therefore, the radical lawyer's true obligation is not to abstract rights or the law (a civil libertarian position), nor is it to the individual client (the mainstream legal position); rather, the radical lawyer's primary obligation is to "the values and political ideologies that stand behind the individual represented," in short, to the client's politics.

The American Civil Liberties Union regards the First Amendment as its true client. Consequently, it has represented notorious clients whose civil liberties were violated, including the Nazis who wanted to march in Skokie, Illinois, in front of the homes of thousands of Holocaust survivors. The ACLU reasoned that there was more danger from government censorship than from the rantings of a small fringe group. Kunstler felt there was no question that the Nazis were entitled to freedom of speech, but the ACLU should not have represented them. It was "an act of such perilous self-deception that it is hardly compensated for by abstractional pipedreams."

Kunstler's most famous expression of his philosophy of client selection followed a question in 1970 of whether he would defend the Minutemen (a right-wing militia) on the same grounds he defended the Black Panthers. Kunstler responded that he would not defend the Minutemen on any grounds. "I only defend those whose goals I share," he said. "I'm not a lawyer for hire. I only defend those I love." The American Bar Association promptly criticized Kunstler for his "cult of admirers rivaling—in behavior and, one suspects, intelligence—the teenage mobs who used to swarm around Elvis Presley and the Beatles." This stolid body of bourgeois respectability also criticized the statement as "antiprofessional":

> our ideal is to provide competent counsel for any person with a legitimate cause. . . . with respect to representing unpopular persons, not just poor ones, to be a "lawyer for hire" is a badge of honor. . . . A lawyer for hire is available to the bad and the ugly, the scorned and the outcast. We know from long collective experience that many will go without legal defense or representation if they must depend upon finding a lawyer who "loves" them.

This statement must be near the nadir of a century of ABA hypocrisy. The professional elite, those that largely control the American Bar Association, have always identified with their corporate clients, seeking out only those clients who would be financially and socially beneficial and rejecting those messy sorts of clients that they did not want their corporate presidents to inquire about. The elite corporate bar sends its children to the same private schools as the corporate presidents; they belong to the same country clubs; they identify themselves as members of a common culture with executives in exactly the same way as do radical lawyers with their activist clients. It has been pointed out that Kunstler was "the radical counterpart of the downtown Wall Street lawyers who represent Ford, General Motors and other big corporations. They identify emotionally with their clients."

In 1970, in the midst of great social upheaval, it was easy for Kunstler to say he would only represent those he loved. However, as the movement stalled in the mid-1970s and 1980s, there were far fewer activists around to share that love. Kunstler had to compromise, and the formula had to change. By 1988 he claimed to represent two types of people, "those who are politically active and whose politics I share, and those who come from an oppressed class." The last statement permitted him to accept so-called "objectively political" cases, in addition to the activists. By those years, he did not have to share the clients' politics: "I only represent those people in the clutches of powerful government, who are activists *from the left or center or those who are being persecuted* . . . I choose very politically" (emphasis added).

That criterion permitted him to represent mobsters in the 1980s, although he was careful not to take any compensation for representing John Gotti. He even had a political justification for his mobster representation, a topic we will examine in the chapter that concerns his 1980s practice. Kunstler sometimes represented neighbors and friends simply because they were such. Like all lawyers in private practice, Kunstler also took cases for no more exalted reason than to earn a fee. Political selectivity continued, although a more realistic statement of Kunstler's later position was that given to a reporter in 1994: "Today, I would say I only defend those who are being oppressed by society and whose beliefs are not anathema to me. That means I don't have to love them but I certainly can't hate them." Still beyond the pale were "wife beating cases, rape cases, child abuse cases. . . . it isn't a question of prejudging. Just politically, I make a choice." He would not have taken on O. J. Simpson "because it's a wife killing case." Nor would he have represented the hotel mogul Leona Helmsley, who, "although she has the same civil rights as anyone, is a rather detestable character with few redeeming qualities." Of course, the Oklahoma City bombers were far off limits: Kunstler declared: "I don't give a damn whether Timothy McVeigh gets a fair trial! . . . I don't take extreme right-wingers."

Although this client selectivity is the norm for all radical lawyers, there was an especially strong personal component to Kunstler's process of selection. We have discussed Kunstler's strong need to belong and be accepted. He was happy to live as part of a neighborhood and feel a member of it. A nationally famous lawyer, he was pleased to do such neighborly things as represent the local dry cleaner and the butcher near his summer house, and even to negotiate a territorial compromise between competing Greenwich Village panhandlers. A need for belonging required that Kunstler like his clients. A need to identify, to belong, even in less neighborly cases, affected who he accepted. He once said of his clients, "Every time I have a different case, I want to be the color or race. I want to be Indians. Sikhs I want to be. Blacks I want to be. I'd like to experience it all. I'd like to speak all the languages."

An additional defining characteristic of New Left radical lawyers is their desire to engage in political trials. This is not quite as simple as it appears because there are two major types of political trials. Usually political trials arise in the context of criminal prosecutions. The first type of political case is the "classical" political trial, where the defendants acted out of conscious political motives. Examples include the Chicago Seven trial, where the defendants led Vietnam protest marches in Chicago, and the trial of the Catonsville Nine, where the defendants seized five hundred draft files and burned them with napalm, the same inflammatory material the federal government was then using to bomb Vietnamese civilians. In these two cases, all the defendants had conscious political goals and motives.

A second type of political trial appears on the surface to be quite an ordinary crime, but either the defendant is a member of an oppressed class or there is something about the nature of the incident that can be used to "expose" elements of oppression in American society. The client is not "harassed because of the immediate political activity or identity [but rather] because of the client's 'objective' class and legal status" that is of the sort subjected to officialdom's repression. In this sort of case, as a sociologist of radical lawyers has noted, "the task of the revolutionary in the courtroom is to link the specific act in controversy to the exposure of oppressive underlying conditions in society."

Even though a prosecution may appear to be an ordinary robbery, murder, or shootout with police, and the defendant had no idea whatsoever of its political implications, a radical lawyer might be able to use the defense of the incident to expose capitalism, racism, imperialism, male sexism, economic exploitation, militarism, police brutality, or other political grievances. Once the case is demystified and stripped of the prosecutor's legalisms, the client, jurors, and hopefully the public generally can recognize the case's political context and the oppression it exemplifies. The radical lawyer does not see a court case as a "specific event or set of events, but as a mirror or representation of more fundamental underlying conditions." Therefore, the conscious motivation of the defendant is irrelevant; a bank robbery or murder could be political or not, depending entirely on the class of the perpetrator.

Kunstler believed that blacks had been subjected to so much oppression that any trial with a black defendant was political. He said this in many different ways over the years. In the 1980s he noted that "my representation of black defendants has been motivated by one of my strongest beliefs: that our society is always racist. Black people rarely get justice in our courts; so for me, cases in which defendants are black are political." As early as 1970 he told the *Playboy* interviewer that he found it "hard to conceive of most routine criminal cases not also being political cases. I say that because so often the person accused of a crime is poor or black and poor. He has been subjected to an oppressive system, and the very crime of which he is accused is probably a reaction to that oppressive system." In 1992 a reporter asked Kunstler the flat question of whether he believed that *all* black defendants are victims. Kunstler responded, "I guess I do."

His friends say that Kunstler did not use the term "objectively political," but that many people around him did. According to his daughter Karin, Kunstler always justified his cases in political terms. Kunstler extended the political nature of representation far beyond blacks. It eventually included American Indians, Muslims, and even mobsters such as John Gotti. Michael Ratner believes that Kunstler was more "flexible" than most New Left lawyers in finding political significance in certain facts and in certain clients, a matter that caused some disagreement with his wife Margie. Nowhere was that flexibility more apparent than in Kunstler's explanation of why his representation of mob figures had political significance:

> organized-crime figures . . . are no different from any of my other cases, because mob figures often serve as scapegoats for the government and quickly become everyone's favorite bad guys. This country has a long tradition of bias against Italian-Americans, and we love making villains out of individuals who are linked to organized crime. Defendants accused of such ties are almost always discriminated against, almost always assumed to be guilty. In America, if your last name ends in a vowel, you're immediately suspect.

When pressed on the violence committed by some mobsters, Kunstler shifted ground and asked whether corporate crime was any better: "the corporate executives who marketed thalidomide, the car manufacturers who made infernos out of their cars, . . . They don't get prosecuted. . . . these people don't go to jail."

There was never a large number of "classical" political trials, and they became fewer and fewer with the collapse of the movement in the 1970s. A 1980 study of radical lawyers reported that many of them had never had an opportunity to engage in a classical political trial. The notion of "objectively political" cases enables radical lawyers to justify their practices as political and provides an identity and validation for their work. This would explain Kunstler's increased expansion of oppressed classes, from blacks in the 1960s, and then the inclusion of American Indians in the 1970s, Muslims in the 1980s, and ultimately mobsters. Undoubtedly this was not a conscious decision, and certainly he would have denied doing this, but the expansion of oppressed groups helped him continue to validate his practice as essentially political.

Radical lawyers use somewhat different techniques in trying their cases than conventional attorneys. One difference is a much greater willingness, even eagerness, to participate in rallies, defense committees, and fund-raising events. While this participation is not strictly unethical, the bar traditionally has felt that the attorney ought to be removed and distant from such activities because they were not really "professional," still a favorite code word of the organized bar.

Radical lawyers, on the other hand, jumped into demonstrations, spoke at rallies, and helped organize defense committees to raise funds and pack the courtroom with supporters of the defendants. In addition to raising needed funds and providing emotional support for the defendants, speaking at rallies provided another opportunity for demystification. In fact, some radical lawyers looked to the ability to organize demonstrations in deciding whether to take a case. In 1971 Gerald Lefcourt explained his law commune's criteria: "For free, political cases, we usually use the criterion of a struggle going around the case and whether it has the possibility of organizing other people through demonstrations, support, education, etc. We'll take any case where there is a possibility of getting more people involved."

Kunstler did these things. He spoke enthusiastically at hundreds of rallies. He urged supporters of defendants to organize defense committees. Kunstler's traditional clientele—blacks, American Indians, Muslims—did not limit him. Jimmy Breslin recalled spotting Kunstler holding an Irish flag, picketing the British Information Office in New York with Irish militants, and speaking at Irish American rallies to raise bail money for IRA gun runners.

Radical lawyers also had distinct methods of trying cases in which their clients acted out of conscious political motives. In those "classical" political cases, most radical lawyers resisted the tendency of conventional attorneys to take control over strategy. Instead, they deferred to the political line of their clients, believing that the most important point of the trial was to give their clients an opportunity to present their political viewpoints to the public. At a minimum, radical lawyers resist what they regard as the elitism of their professional status and share all major strategic decisions with their clients.

Kunstler did not always have this attitude. In his civil rights days, he still felt himself the professional-in-charge and would make pronouncements and decide on strategy without consultation with his clients. In 1968 he tried to dominate the Catonsville Nine defense, and in 1969, as we have seen, he angered the Chicago Seven defendants with his First Amendment opening speech. But he came to believe that the legal system was "something to be used or changed, in order to gain the political objectives of the clients in a particular case." For the politically conscious defendant, the lawyer is simply a technician, a political agent for the client. Accordingly, "it's very important," Kunstler said in 1971, "that the lawyer recognize it's his role to accomplish what the client wants, and not vice versa. The client calls the shots, not the attorney."

That attitude had several consequences. For example, the defendants in the Chicago trial were determined that their political message not be thwarted and their movement tied up by a prosecution they thought designed to do just that. Their tactics were designed to put the system itself, represented by Judge Julius Hoffman, on trial, and to engage in enough courtroom antics and disruptions that the media would notice and report widely on what were essentially demonstrations continued in the courtroom.

Most attorneys believe that they should dissuade their clients from unruly behavior, not as an ethical obligation but as a duty arising from their position as officers of the court. Kunstler rejected that absolutely, assuming that the disruptions were a part of the political strategy his clients wanted to pursue. Years later, in 1994, Kunstler described this very lucidly. The defendants, he said, saw the trial

> as a chance to demonstrate in the courtroom what they had tried to demonstrate on the streets in Chicago sometime earlier, a year earlier. And they used the theatre and the burlesque and the satire that Abbie [Hoffman] and Jerry [Rubin] were so famous for. They used that to very good advantage. . . . They used it as theatre, very good theatre I thought. The judge couldn't take it. The prosecution couldn't take it.

. . . [the defendants] would fight in the courtroom, didn't respect the federal court and were determined to show . . . what happened in the streets of Chicago . . . how people were brutalized by a police riot. And so, [the trial] didn't degenerate. I thought it sort of raised up as a choice defense to a political trial to be rambunctious, clever, satiric in a courtroom.

This was a political choice of very political defendants. Kunstler was very clear on what he regarded as the limitations of his obligations:

The obligation of a lawyer for a defendant in a political trial is merely to explain to the client what the law is and what penalties he may suffer for certain political actions he may take in the courtroom. Once that's explained and the defendant decides on a political defense, the lawyer's responsibility is to help him do just that. In sentencing me for contempt, Judge Hoffman pointed out that I had never publicly admonished the defendants nor in any way called them to task for what they were doing in the courtroom. He was right. I hadn't. . . . I don't think it is my responsibility in a political trial to do that.

Open defiance could also be a political tactic, "fighting back, showing that you're not afraid, that the court is no sacrosanct place," as Kunstler once put it. At times Kunstler did shout at judges and engage in personally disrespectful conduct. Usually, however, Kunstler conducted himself in trial as a model of civility.

This discussion of trial tactics obscures the fact that Kunstler's most important courtroom tactic was simply to be a good lawyer, theatrical sometimes, but also witty, knowledgeable in the law, skillful in cross-examination, and organized. Most of Kunstler's maneuverings were straightforward legal tactics. For example, most of the political trials had a team of lawyers. If there were six defendants, usually one or two would be represented by one lawyer, another two by a second lawyer, and the remaining defendants by a third. The three lawyers were politically sympathetic and would fully cooperate, and the defendants and their counsel would operate as a team.

There was no political significance to a team approach. Although emotional support and trial preparation would be facilitated by a team of lawyers, even those were not the primary purposes. The most significant reasons for a team approach were far more legalistic. In the example of three lawyers, the defense could have up to three opening and closing arguments, three different cross-examinations of prosecution witnesses, and more peremptory challenges of prospective jurors. In the 1970s and 1980s Kunstler often spoke at law schools. Students frequently asked him what they had to do to become a radical lawyer. Invariably, Kunstler would tell them that the first thing they had to do was to learn to be an excellent lawyer.

In trial, Kunstler drew on his old love of acting, sometimes displaying anger, sometimes pathos. At times he cried. Inwardly, however, he claimed he was

> scared all the time. I always have the willies in my stomach when I stand up in court. But you have to look as though you're not scared. It's all acting, I guess. . . . Trials are theatrical events. . . . You're playing to a small audience of 12 people, but it's a crucial one to you. . . . You try to make sure that whatever you do in that courtroom has a theatrical effect wherever you can do it.

One of the uses of theatrics, for Kunstler and all other radical lawyers, was to politicize his trials and engage in that core function of the radical lawyer, demystification. Although it could occur in many forums, for example, rallies, press conferences, or newspaper columns, demystification developed most dramatically at trial. In 1994 he told a radio interviewer that

> it seems to me that the courtroom is an ideal forum in which to radicalize people, to expose the government and so on. . . . It's a battlefield. And it's a good battlefield. And it's one in which we have a forum. My people can't get on the floor of Congress. They can't get on the Supreme Court. They can't get in the oval office. But, by God, they have a spokesperson in that courtroom.

Kunstler was clever in bringing in political themes. He told a black jury in the Bronx that a police shootout with a black youth was really about "how the police treat young third world people in the depressed communities of our city." In 1968 he argued that the prosecution of five young blacks charged with plotting to steal weapons from an armory and blow up various bridges was merely "part of a plan to arouse the public so that it would be willing to tolerate police brutality during the racial rebellions expected that summer." In both cases the defendants were acquitted. In 1973, when American Indian militants were charged with illegally seizing federal land, Kunstler argued that "corporate America . . . stands to lose enormously if the Indians ever regain a fraction of their homelands."

Sometimes Kunstler's injection of politics into a case could come very suddenly and unexpectedly. The following vignette comes from a prosecutor and therefore may be colored by bias. In the Bronx in October 1974, jury selection was under way in an unpolitical trial of James Richardson, a young black man, for the murder of a white police officer. Ten jurors had been sworn, five of whom were blacks, and seven of whom could be appropriately characterized as young. Kunstler had just run out of peremptory challenges and moved to dismiss the entire panel as too old and biased against his client. The judge denied his motion, and the prosecutor began to question the next prospective juror.

The potential next juror was a young black man. After he stated that he was a longtime admirer of Kunstler, the prosecutor exercised one of his remaining peremptory challenges, whereupon "Kunstler leaped from his seat, his face contorted with rage, and yelled to the jury, 'See what a racist prosecution we are dealing with! He challenges every damn black and young person!'" The judge ordered both attorneys into his chambers, admonished Kunstler, and thereafter instructed the jury to ignore the outburst. Nevertheless, the prosecutor was worried because "there was simply no way for the jurors to erase from their minds what Kunstler had shouted, and, of course, he was well aware of this."

Although Kunstler certainly did demystify before the jury, his effectiveness was primarily in the boring business of being an effective lawyer: mastering documents, cross-examining witnesses, impeachment, developing direct testimony, and so forth. His greatest grandstanding, his greatest flamboyance, was not so much inside the courtroom as outside in the corridor, where he was a master at manipulating the media.

Legalistic defenses to ordinary crimes, such as murder, robbery, or conspiracy to riot, are boring and not newsworthy. If a lawyer can draw a political issue into the trial, convincingly raise the specter of class or racial oppression, for example, then the media will flock to the courthouse. It is a very common pattern for radical lawyers to attempt to gain widespread media coverage for their cases. Media exposure helps humanize the clients, paints a more favorable picture for the potential jury pool, and might even be helpful in raising funds for the heavy expenses of the defense. Most important for the radical lawyer, it promotes demystification by exposing the true issues and oppression that undergird the prosecution. The search for media coverage is therefore a commonplace for radical lawyers, and Kunstler must be seen not as an aberration, but merely as someone who was better than most radical lawyers at this task.

Kunstler regularly stopped by courthouse pressrooms, usually, according to reporters, with "a hard sell on his current case." He frequently called press conferences, and almost always made himself available for interviews. No matter how busy, he hardly ever spurned a telephone call from a reporter. He appeared frequently on radio and television interviews. A skeptical observer made a count of articles that appeared in the *New York Times* featuring Kunstler or referring to him sufficiently to merit him a place in the annual index. Between July 19, 1959 and September 1990, the *Times* carried 541 articles about Kunstler. Many more came later, about his controversial cases of the 1990s. Critics have often called Kunstler an egomaniac, concerned only with self-publicity. He acknowledged he had a big ego and that he had to watch his tendency to seek publicity "because it's almost like a narcotic." On the other hand, he justified the extensive publicity he drew because the status of being a celebrity "can give you an edge."

Kunstler thoroughly believed that the publicity he personally drew to a case redounded to his client's benefit. When indictments are handed down by a grand jury, prosecutors usually call press conferences and demonize defendants charged with high-profile crimes. At that point it is necessary to put a human face on the defendant, so the public, and especially the public from which the jury pool is drawn, sees that the defendant is a human being like everyone else. The media are co-operative because "it has to use up news all the time. ... if you have something that you can work that's newsworthy about your people, you can get it bruited about. And it sometimes offsets the mammoth barrage that accompanies the indictments and the arraignments, all coming from the prosecution." Then, too, in trial itself, "it's a very powerful thing," Kunstler noted, "to have jurors know who you are."

Kunstler referred to public relations as "one of my most important tools." One use was for demystification, and, particularly in objectively political cases, Kunstler always fed the media wonderfully quotable copy about the elements of oppression involved in his cases.

In his classical political cases, Kunstler deferred to the politics of the defendants and used his personal celebrity to gain the activists a wider audience. An incident following the Supreme Court arguments in *Texas v. Johnson*, the 1989 flag burning case that Kunstler argued, illustrates this. Kunstler had suggested to the activists that they prepare a statement for the reporters waiting outside the Supreme Court building, to be delivered before he answered any media questions. The activists selected Edward Hasbrouck to make their collective statement:

> As we came down the steps from the Supreme Court, Bill pushed me in front of him as reporters and photographers kept trying to shove me out of the picture. When I finally made it down to where the reporters had encamped, they kept shouting questions over me to Bill even as I began to read the statement. I will never forget hearing Bill shouting back from behind me, "Shut up and listen to him" when the reporters ignored me. Only when they realized that he wasn't going to say anything until the defendants, and me as their collectively-chosen spokesperson, had had our say, did they quiet down, reluctantly, for a moment. . . . This is the sort of "publicity hound" Bill Kunstler was. The flag-burners sought out Bill Kunstler to represent them in significant part because they trusted him to allow them to speak for themselves and not to distort their politics to maximize the chances of legal "victory."

Kunstler used publicity not only to promote a case's political aspects and to humanize the defendant, but also to develop a theme for the defense of particular defendants, around which the entire case could be built. Kuby provides a vivid description of these themes and the role of Kunstler's publicity efforts in creating them.

> Larry Davis, this was a case of a black man defending himself against white crooked killer cops. That was the theme. Colin Ferguson, black rage. Those two words. It didn't always work. Sometimes it misfired. But it was always very calculated in terms of the way he put it out. . . . So, all of these kinds of so-called grandstanding, it was all directed toward the theme that we were trying to create, inside and outside the courtroom. You spend a year talking about Larry Davis to the press. He becomes a folk hero. You speak at rallies. Jurors don't remember

much of what they hear, most of us don't. But what happens is they come into court thinking, "Oh yeah, Larry Davis. He was the one who was defending himself against a bunch of killer cops." Wonderful stuff! And that's what Bill did and he did it shamelessly, he did it passionately, he did it purposely.

As we have seen, the primary objective of radical lawyers in engaging in political trials is educational, to make their political points known as widely as possible. Radicalization of the public by means of using the trial to expose underlying oppression is generally more important than obtaining an acquittal for the defendant. The public generally thinks of lawyers as interested only in getting their clients out of the jam they are in. Indeed, most lawyers see their obligations as highly individualistic and owed primarily to their client. The radical lawyer's thought is so aberrant from both the public's viewpoint and most lawyers' that it must be emphasized again: in a political trial demystification is more important than acquittal. Henry di Suvero put this succinctly.

> The great trap in a political trial is the hope of getting the defendant off. To lawyers this means playing down the politics, and showing that you submit to the system, so as to persuade the system to let you free. When this happens, lawyers disassociate their clients from the movement, disavow political support as "uninvited." . . . Such actions have no place in a political trial. . . . The system has won by holding out the carrot of acquittal. In a political trial, the defendant must stoically recognize that a charade of legalities is all that will transpire; he must recognize further that his salvation lies not inside, but outside the courtroom, and can only be achieved by emphasizing, rather than de-emphasizing, the politics of his case.

The mainstream bar has raised serious questions about the ethical implications of radical lawyers' profound emphasis on the politics of a case. One problem is the use of "affirmative litigation" in contexts where it is hopeless to expect victory. A second problem is that on occasion the tactics of a defense lawyer, guided by politics, may actually work to the client's harm.

An "affirmative lawsuit" is in the nature of a legal counteroffensive, brought against a prosecutor or other public official. Their purposes are various: to relieve pressure on defendants by shifting the label of subversive or criminal from the defendants to the prosecutor, to bolster morale of a movement group, and to educate the public and demystify. For example, when Kunstler entered the Fountain Valley defense in the Virgin Islands in 1972, he immediately filed an action for damages against local police and FBI agents, alleging brutality in treatment of the defendants. In the mid-1980s the organization Kunstler helped found, the Center for Constitutional Rights, filed a lawsuit against the federal government seeking to stop its support for the Nicaraguan "contras." The purpose of the lawsuit, according to the center's own literature, was to "serve as an educational and organizing tool." During the civil rights movement in the 1960s, Kunstler sued J. Edgar Hoover and Robert Kennedy to force them to prosecute Mississippi sheriffs.

A common characteristic of these affirmative lawsuits is that while they may have short-term effects of bolstering morale among the radical troops and even long-term effects in educating the public about oppressive elements in society, they tend to lose. Judges usually dismiss them quickly. The ethical problem is this. It is entirely proper for an attorney to file litigation to test innovative theories of liability, even if he believes a trial court will turn him down and he will have to appeal to a higher court to achieve success. It is a vague and thin line between that and a lawsuit that the attorney himself believes is hopeless when commenced. Traditionally, however, a lawyer acts unethically when he crosses that line and has no bona fide belief in the possibility of eventual success of a lawsuit he has filed.

This ethical constraint does not bother radical lawyers, as the test for winning or losing is not the legal result, ruling, or verdict, but the political impact—whether the lawsuit improves morale, exposes oppression, facilitates organizing, and so forth. Arthur Kinoy put this well in his autobiography, reflecting on some of his early litigation on behalf of a militant union.

> The ultimate test of the appropriateness of a given legal strategy could not be solely the likelihood of success within the court structure. . . . The crucial question was what role it would play at that moment in protecting or advancing the people's struggle. If it helped the fight, then it was done, even if the chances of immediate legal success were virtually nonexistent. . . . [Early in my career] I felt a lurking uneasi-

ness, stemming from the notion of "professional responsibility" implanted so thoroughly in every law student. Since we knew there was little likelihood of success in the courts, was this really an honest, responsible use of legal techniques? . . . the answer gradually took shape. At certain moments, bringing a lawsuit can be a form of political expression for people in struggle. The court system, like all other branches of government, is an arena in which the rights of people can be asserted.

Without question, Kunstler held similar views. In the late 1970s he filed a lawsuit on behalf of a group of South Bronx residents to halt the filming of a movie that, Kunstler thought, "depicts the South Bronx as the home of pimps and prostitutes and pushers." Kunstler insisted that he knew the lawsuit would be thrown out of court, which it was. When asked whether that was not a frivolous lawsuit, Kunstler responded, "it may be frivolous in the *legal* sense, but since when do we judge everything by the law? Since I regard the law as an enemy anyway, I thought this was a good, imaginative use of it."

Before leaving the topic of untenable legal positions and frivolous lawsuits, it must be pointed out that this is conduct in which almost all public prosecutors—state and federal—engage on a daily basis. Since plea bargains resolve almost all criminal cases, prosecutors routinely overcharge. In their initial charges they add crimes they know they cannot prove to a jury's satisfaction, on top of those they think realistic for conviction. That gives them leverage, with something to bargain away in the negotiations. This is essentially the same as the conduct of the radical lawyers in their affirmative litigation. They both involve the court filing of a theory they regard as hopeless to gain a tactical advantage.

The other danger of placing politics at the head of the litigation agenda is that this sometimes conflicts with the best interests of the client. For some radical lawyers, as a critic put things, "the client may simply stand in for the community in order to make possible a mass assault on the dominant system of social relations. In these situations the individual client could be seen . . . as little more than a puppet, little more than a device allowing the lawyer to get his or her feet into court to assert political goals." Kunstler never went so far as to treat his clients as puppets, but his thinking sometimes tended in the direction of the critic's caustic remark.

In the late 1980s New York was galvanized by the story of Tawana Brawley, a young black girl who claimed she was raped and sodomized by six white men. As the investigation unfolded, it seemed increasingly clear that her story was a hoax. Although Kunstler did not represent the young woman, he applauded the efforts of the two attorneys who did. "It makes no difference anymore whether the attack on Tawana Brawley really happened." Hoax or no, he said, "a lot of young black women are treated the way she said she was treated. They [the attorneys] now have an issue with which they can grab the headlines and launch a vigorous attack on the criminal justice system." That is close to making the woman in question merely a pawn for the political exploitation her apparent lies made possible. In the 1990s New Yorkers were greatly agitated by Colin Ferguson, a young Jamaican who emptied his semiautomatic pistol on commuters of the Long Island Railroad, killing six. Kunstler's reaction to Ferguson's call for his assistance: "Black rage. It's a marvelous chance to pursue my agenda, which is to help people understand black rage."

Even if it does not go so far as rendering the client a mere pawn, pursuing political defenses and theories at trial may lead a radical attorney to ignore a more legalistic, technical defense that might lead to the client's acquittal. A consciously political client, anxious to spread his message, might appropriately waive that omission. However, in an objectively political case, where the client is not interested in any political line, the subordination of client to politics clearly violates legal ethics. Ronald Kuby insists that Kunstler never made that subordination, and that whenever Kunstler's politics "somehow clashed with the best interest of the client, it was always the best interest of the client that came first. Bill never, never used his cases as a means of putting out a political philosophy that redounded to the detriment of the client."

That may be true, but it certainly can be questioned. The defense of John Hill, an Attica prisoner tried for murder whom we will meet in the next chapter, became politicized in a way that arguably hurt Hill. The same could be said of Clayton Lonetree's court-martial in the 1980s. Over the years, at least three prosecutors who have opposed Kunstler in trial and obtained convictions have publicly stated that Kunstler's politicization of their trials hurt his client.

Far worse than the injection of political themes into the trial was the occasional situation where Kunstler refused to press a nonpolitical client's tactical advantage or a rule of evidence because of his own,

Kunstler's, political objection to the tactic or rule of evidence. Sometimes these were technical matters that a nonpolitical, nonlawyer client could never knowingly waive, and therefore defense counsel was duty-bound to assert on the client's behalf.

A telling example of this occurred in the 1974 murder trial of James Richardson. It speaks very poorly of Kunstler, but in fairness, it must be emphasized that it is the only such incident for which a written record has surfaced. First, the reader must understand that an attorney may ask an opposing witness whether he has ever been convicted of a grave, prison-level crime: a felony. The purpose of this is to try to show the jury that the witness is unreliable and his testimony should be distrusted. Second, the reader must understand that the district attorney is ethically bound to reveal to the defendant anything the prosecutor knows about a prior felony conviction of a witness called by the prosecution.

During the trial the prosecutor called a witness whom he had just learned had been convicted of a felony. After asking his questions on direct examination, the prosecutor asked for a conference with Kunstler and the trial judge, during which he advised that he had just learned of the felony conviction. This was to permit Kunstler to cross-examine appropriately on behalf of the defendant by asking about the felony conviction of the witness. Kunstler made a nearly unbelievable response.

> My policy is never to use convictions unless they go to the question of perjury . . . I'm against the use of these [criminal records] even though I know I have a right to do it. *I . . . prefer for my own political background* not to go into [this]. I'm going to ask my client, because I think I have an obligation to . . . but I think he will follow my dictates. (Emphasis added)

Kunstler's client was on trial for murder and faced life imprisonment. The witness had given damaging testimony and Kunstler held a tool with which to discredit the witness in the eyes of the jurors. They might well have disbelieved him had they heard of the felony conviction. Yet Kunstler refused to press this advantage on behalf of his client because of a political belief held, not by his client, but by himself. Kunstler did talk briefly with his client and Richardson, undoubtedly not understanding exactly what was at stake, blindly followed Kunstler's lead.

We have seen that Kunstler acted politically, but we have not yet examined what those personal politics were that fueled his immense

energy. Obviously, a hatred for racism and concepts of socialist egali-
tarianism are involved, but what more specific ideology can be attributed to Kunstler? In terms of articulated and conscious ideology, the answer is that Kunstler entertained few if any systematic theories. Kunstler was not a systematic thinker or theorist. Michael Smith, a fellow
lawyer of the Left, described Kunstler as "not so much a radical thinker
as a man of action." His close personal friends Bruce and Diane Jackson
recalled that he did not like ideology and never spoke in those terms, although others around him, including Margie, were much more political. Kuby remembers that "Bill was not a theorist. Bill didn't get bogged
down in this stuff. Bill's role was different. He acted when there was a
need to act and he really left the theorizing to other people." Kunstler
himself wrote, "for me, action is all."

Kunstler contributed almost nothing to the raging debates on the
legal Left between critical legal studies, radical race theory, critical feminist studies, or any other ideology. Nevertheless, some idea of Kunstler's underlying ideological beliefs can be teased out of his writings
and remarks, however unsystematic those expressions might be. Several factors combined to form Kunstler's ideological beliefs.

Opposition to antiblack racism was at the core of Kunstler's belief
system. His colleagues are united in that assessment. Although his
heart and soul were in fighting racism directed against blacks, Kunstler's opposition to racism was a moving line. In the 1980s his concern
for racism expanded to include American Indians. Still later, in the late
1980s and 1990s, racial antagonism directed against Arabs became an
object of Kunstler's struggle. He wrote in his 1994 autobiography that
"today Muslims are the most hated group in the country; the moment a
Muslim is accused of a crime, the specter of terrorism is raised, and
everyone panics."

There was also an antigovernment streak, a libertarian bent. "At
heart I'm a philosophical anarchist," he told a reporter in 1988, and in
1993 he commented that he saw the theme of fighting the government
as running through all his cases. He freely acknowledged that his cases
in the 1990s weren't "Martin Luther King, but they're still interesting."
Why? Because "it is a chance to beat the government. That's the key:
The government is always the main enemy. I believe that government is
evil, that Lord Acton's theory of power is correct: It corrupts, it moves
to maximize itself. My role is always to fight it, always to be the burr
under the saddle. That's all."

There is a paradox in Kunstler's brand of libertarianism. He and his fellow civil rights activists had used liberal lawyering to build up the federal government's powers in the 1960s to cure racism; that same government's tools could now be used for other purposes, to control the lives of private citizens in a manner that radicals thought oppressive. Both Michael Ratner and Ronald Kuby believe it unlikely that Kunstler ever thought about that; as far as they know, it certainly never bothered him. The anarchistic and libertarian streaks in Kunstler did, however, play a major role in the kind of socialist he became.

Kunstler was never a conventional Marxist, nor did he make the sort of "scientific" class analyses that Marxists so enjoy. He once joked that he was a registered Democrat and the "Communists are to the right of my own position." Many highly political people were critical and condescending, even contemptuous, toward Kunstler. Kunstler never believed, as communists do, that once the state controlled everything, we would be settled into paradise. Quite the contrary: Kunstler believed that "all governments are bad; some are just worse than others." His own was not necessarily the worst. "I'd have the same problems everywhere," he explained in 1993, "and here I have maybe a little more leeway than in some other countries."

"Not that I'd want a new system," Kunstler mentioned in 1994, "because I think I'd be an opponent of any system. Because all systems tend to corrupt." These thoughts were new. We have seen him quoted, in 1970, saying that capitalism must be replaced. Then in 1979 Kunstler refused to sign an open letter circulated among liberals that criticized North Vietnam for the imprisonment and torture of political prisoners. At the time he said, "I do not believe in public attacks on socialist countries, even where violations of human rights may occur." However, in 1995 Kunstler served as a cochairman of a gathering that packed Carnegie Hall for the benefit of Tibet House, a Buddhist cultural center founded by the Dalai Lama. Support for the Dalai Lama may be socially trendy, but it is also implicitly a criticism of communist China.

Many people who knew Kunstler very well feel that the biggest single drive in his ideology was simply instinctive. Kunstler had an instinctive sense of and opposition to many forms of oppression and injustice. He may have justified his actions politically, but it was more truly Kunstler's instincts that moved him to action. His daughter, his partner, colleagues, and friends all favor this theory of gut reaction and instinct as Kunstler's chief motivator.

Kunstler often put his legal struggles into what he regarded as Melvillian terms: "Good and evil are always at war. . . . the role of good men is to always fight against evil, hoping they can hold the line and not go under." The struggle against evil and oppression is endless, but only the daily fight prevents evil from overtaking us. Kunstler frequently spoke in these terms, but these high ideals obscure another important factor in Kunstler's motivation. He took on some of his most challenging cases because they were fun. Kunstler enjoyed cases that no one else wanted. If he won, that was splendid. If he lost, then at least he had prevented the government from running roughshod over the defendant. Either way, he had opposed the government, tweaked its beard, and made it struggle.

Kunstler was at his best in courtroom battles. Advancing the interests of the oppressed proved to be more difficult and elusive in other settings. No context showed that difficulty more clearly than Kunstler's representation of the Attica prisoners.

9

Representing the Attica Prisoners

IN SEPTEMBER 1971 Attica, a grim, gothic-style prison in upstate New York, witnessed a massive uprising. Over 1,200 inmates seized control of much of the institution, took dozens of guard and civilian hostages, organized themselves into a makeshift community, and for four days negotiated the fates of themselves and their hostages. It ·ended in the bloodiest denouement in American penal history. Kunstler served on a citizens' committee called in by both prisoners and the state of New York to observe the crisis and attempt to negotiate a solution. The entire Attica story is complex, but there is a wonderful literature on the uprising, with published accounts from all sides of the event's twists and turns.

Kunstler's own role in the Attica affair was complex. At times, he displayed only sincere empathy for the plight of the prisoners and their families and an honest effort to negotiate a settlement that would avoid bloodshed. At other times, however, Kunstler appeared to play the role of radical lawyer to an audience beyond the prison yard. Perhaps he thought that Attica might become an issue that could be used to radicalize people, but it turned out that the public was quite uninterested in the prisoners' fate. Kunstler has sometimes been wrongly accused of an attempt to inflame the inmates with his rhetoric inside the prison yard. Readers will have to decide whether or not to convict Kunstler of what would be a better-laid charge—an attempt to inflame public opinion *beyond* the prison yard.

Attica in 1971 was a large maximum security prison, overcrowded with over 2,200 inmates. Divided into four yards and cellblocks, the prisoners moved from their cells to the mess hall through interior passageways that met in the center of the four yards at a control point called Times Square. Typical of maximum-security prisons, Attica offered a minimum of rehabilitation programs and a maximum of warehousing and annoyance through unjustified restrictions and daily degradations.

The late 1960s saw a demographic shift in inmate population and orientation that significantly aggravated these conditions and polarized the relations between the kept and the keepers. Before the late 1960s the inmate population was predominantly white, but by 1971 it had shifted to 54 percent black and 9 percent Latino. More than 80 percent of the inmates came from urban ghettos. In addition, the inmate population had become politicized by the increasing representation of Black Muslims, Black Panthers, Weathermen, and militants. Less than a week before Attica erupted, Paul D. McGinnis, a retired state correction commissioner, warned of "a new breed of inmates." While the state might consider convicts as rapists, murderers, or thieves, many of the new breed felt they were "political prisoners jailed by a repressive society."

In contrast, the approximately 450 guards and supervisors were entirely white (excepting a single Latino guard) and rural. The official report of the Attica Commission concluded that racism, oppression, and injustice were the chief factors underlying the uprising. As another neutral source put it,

> Racism between the officers and the inmates was mutual. Rural white officers were suspicious of prisoners from the ghettos, and minority inmates did not trust the staff, who were viewed as hicks, cowboys, or good ol' boys. Each of their perspectives, or worldviews, was shaped ideologically. The white rural officers held traditional, conservative, and status quo views of law and order. By contrast, minority inmates were influenced by the radical social and religious manifestos promoted by the Black Panther party and the Black Muslims.

The uprising was touched off by a quotidian concern over an allegedly unjust disciplining of an inmate. Following breakfast on Thursday, September 9, 1971, inmates on their way back to their cells struck a guard in a hallway leading from the Times Square control point. Very few prisoners were involved in the initial conflict, but they managed to obtain the keys to open many of the cells in one of the four blocks. Still, the uprising could very easily have been isolated there. However, the inmates were able to break through the gates in the Times Square control point due to a defective metal welding. In their initial enthusiasm, the prisoners severely beat William Quinn, a guard stationed in Times

Square. From the central control, the inmates were able to obtain keys allowing them to roam at will throughout most of the prison.

Soon approximately 1,200 inmates controlled several cellblocks and yards and some ancillary buildings as well. Blacks constituted an overwhelming majority of the rebellious inmates, a higher majority than among the prisoner population generally, although Puerto Ricans and a few whites were also represented. Within a few hours authorities were able to recapture portions of the prison, but inmates had seized over fifty hostages, civilian workers and guards, and controlled two cellblocks and D Yard. In addition, there was a neutral yard as well as neutral passageways. An inmate government of sorts emerged, and internal prisoner security guards took over policing functions. The inmates seized food, as well as clothing, tents, fuel for campfires, and tools that could be fashioned into weapons. Although spontaneous in its origins, the leadership that emerged was ideologically oriented, and this affected subsequent negotiations. The leadership, a secretariat of prisoners armed with typewriters and paper, the guarded ring of hostages, and the majority of the prisoners in revolt all assembled in D Yard.

The inmates released the seriously injured hostages but kept thirty-nine guards and civilian workers for the duration of the uprising. In the early hours of the uprising, these men suffered beatings and were stripped and made to wear blindfolds. However, after internal order was established, inmate leadership appointed a cadre of Black Muslims to guard the hostages. These men were dedicated and disciplined and performed an excellent job of safeguarding the hostages and denying angry and hostile prisoners access to them. The inmates issued prison clothing to the hostages and removed their blindfolds. Although the death of the hostages was the primary negotiating card the prisoners held with the authorities and was constantly threatened, the prisoners actually treated their hostages well, given the circumstances. A doctor who was admitted to D Yard to treat the injured later wrote that the hostages' guards, that is, the Black Muslims, "appeared very solicitous, helping the men in their charge sit up to take their medications and, in general, trying to make them as comfortable as possible." A guard who had been held hostage told a reporter after he had been freed that "the inmates right around us [i.e., their Black Muslim guards] were there to protect our lives till just about the end. They did what they could. I really believe that. We got to eat what they got to eat."

No serious negotiations began until the 2:00 P.M. arrival of Russell G. Oswald, commissioner of the Department of Correctional Services for the state of New York. At 3:00 P.M. Herman Schwartz, an attorney who had represented several inmates, and Arthur Eve, a black state assemblyman from nearby Buffalo, entered D Yard and were presented with a typed document with five demands. It had an ideological portion, for example,

> WE are MEN! We are not beasts and do not intend to be beaten or driven as such. The entire prison populace has set forth to change forever the ruthless brutalization and disregard for the lives of the prisoners here and throughout the United States. What has happened here is but the sound before the fury of those who are oppressed.

The document also made five specific demands.

1. We want complete amnesty, meaning freedom from any physical, mental and legal reprisals.
2. We want now, speedy and safe transportation out of confinement, to a non-imperialistic country.
3. We demand that the FEDERAL GOVERNMENT intervene, so that we will be under direct FEDERAL JURISDICTION.
4. We demand the reconstruction of ATTICA PRISON to be done by inmates and/or inmate supervision.
5. We urgently demand immediate negotiation thru Wm. M. Kunstler, Attorney-at-Law [and then listing several other individuals and organizations, including Arthur O. Eve and the *New York Times* columnist Tom Wicker].

The demands for federal government intervention and supervisory powers over reconstruction were never seriously pressed, although the amnesty and transportation demands always floated alongside the more practical demands the prisoners subsequently made. Later in the afternoon, Oswald twice entered D Yard. He promised to invite citizen observers and to supply food and water to the inmates, and he was handed a document of more practical demands called "Fifteen Practical Proposals." Later in the afternoon and early evening, Herman Schwartz developed the idea of a stipulated federal injunction against administrative and physical reprisals. Oswald agreed to this, they drafted such an order, and Schwartz left to obtain a judge's signature.

He brought back a signed order the following morning, Friday, September 10. When he and Oswald entered D Yard to present it, the inmates promptly rejected it, on the formal (and erroneous) ground that it lacked a seal and for the more serious reservation that it would not protect them from criminal charges. The inmates were angry and there was talk of seizing Oswald as an additional hostage, but the leadership successfully argued that they should honor their promise of safe passage. Oswald returned to his command post and decided he would no longer negotiate directly with the prisoners. The role of the citizens' committee was never clear, but Oswald's resolution not to negotiate himself transformed the committee into more of a negotiating body than had been originally intended. Because the observers' group comprised almost the entire ideological spectrum, internal mistrust hampered its negotiating abilities. Although Arthur Eve came close to being the group's leader or chairman, there was never any organization, procedure, or rules.

Meanwhile, on Thursday evening and Friday morning, Arthur Eve summoned several of the observers the inmates had requested, including Kunstler. A telegram requesting his services reached Kunstler in West Palm Beach, where he was arguing a case. The judge there immediately released him after he learned that hostages had been taken. Kunstler asked Lotte to accompany him on the trip because, as he candidly acknowledged years later, "I felt better with her along; I'd never been involved in anything as potentially dangerous as this, and her presence gave me a sense of comfort." Kunstler was equally frank about why he became involved. He thought he could be useful, yes, but also the uprising "appealed to my sense of the dramatic. My reasons for becoming involved in any case or situation were all here: Attica was high stakes, in lives and in political importance, and it was high profile." The prisoners' motivation for requesting Kunstler, as related by one of the leaders, was also straightforward: "We wanted Kunstler for his legal mind. We felt that an involved lawyer like him would be the last person to allow a whitewash. . . . We felt that if he saw the conditions himself, he would definitely commit himself."

Kunstler arrived early Friday evening and told reporters, assembled in almost as many numbers as the state police, "I want to talk with the prisoners. I'll play it by ear and see what they want." By this time the observers' group had expanded to over thirty men. Some had been requested; others simply showed up and demanded a role. Kunstler was briefed on the situation, and almost immediately identified amnesty as the central issue. However, Kunstler surprised Oswald by his belief that there might be a realistic reform program mixed in with the Fifteen Practical Proposals, and he and Oswald went over them point by point. The observers then concluded that they needed to return to the yard to obtain a complete list of demands, their relative importance, and clarification from the inmates, never obtained, of how they wanted the committee to function.

The observers went into D Yard at 11:30 P.M. Friday and stayed until 4:30 A.M. on Saturday, September 11. Campfires lit up inmates and tents scattered throughout the yard, as did the brighter lights of the television cameras filming the proceedings. Because the meeting was filmed for television, everyone present understood that the rhetoric was addressed to a much wider audience than just the participants. The observers were introduced. The inmates made speeches, using an improvised amplification system, and the observers made speeches, in no clearly defined order. One inmate, Brother Flip, made a ringing declaration that "if we cannot live as people, then we will at least try to die like men!" When the roar died away, he turned to Kunstler and cried out, "Brother Kunstler! What did they do with you in court?" referring to Kunstler's contempt sentences from the Chicago trial. Kunstler rose from his chair, leaned across the table, threw his arms around Brother Flip, and shouted, "The same thing they did with you, Brother!"

Tom Wicker noted a huge ovation when Kunstler was introduced for his speech. Wearing his glasses customarily pushed high atop his forehead, Kunstler waited for the cheering to settle, and shouted, "Palante! All power to the people!" He assured the inmates that either Huey Newton or Bobby Seale would come to the negotiations. He did not know yet exactly what the issues were, but he could see that "you have power," clearly a reference to the hostages, "which means you can reach ears." Someone shouted a question about the injunction, to which he candidly replied that "the injunction is nothing. It's not worth the paper it's written on," a statement apparently resented by Schwartz.

"Many of us love you," Kunstler continued, "and many of us understand what a shitty decrepit system we have here in New York and elsewhere. We are your brothers, we hope." He emphasized that the inmates themselves had to articulate their demands. The observers could present their demands to the state, but the observers could not make an agreement on behalf of the prisoners. "You are the political people," he said as he finished. Then the chairman, Brother Herb, asked over the microphone, "Brother Bill, will you be our lawyer? Will you represent the brothers as only you can?"

Brother Kunstler went back to the microphone and accepted his new clients to another round of applause. Kunstler felt "thrilled and honored and from that moment on served as the inmates' counsel . . . these men, society's outcasts, were my people, my constituents. I felt close to them . . . I wanted to demonstrate that I was with them completely and that I recognized the significance of this moment." The observers and inmates then proceeded to go over their demands. Eve served as chair, and as demands were proposed, they were put to a voice vote. The Fifteen Practical Proposals served as a nucleus, but additions were made. Kunstler took notes and clarified positions, including the brothers' insistence on an amnesty from criminal prosecution for the uprising.

There was no support for the earlier demands for federal intervention or inmate supervision of reconstruction. Nor was there significant support for the earlier demand for transportation to a nonimperialist country, a point that becomes important for criticism sometimes made of one of Kunstler's later remarks. An inmate leader later wrote that "no one seriously thought we could get free passage out of the prison to North Vietnam or anywhere else." The observer Herman Badillo believed that when the demand for transportation came to a vote it received support from fewer than 20 of the 1,200 prisoners, and Kunstler reported to Oswald that the inmates were not serious about that issue. However, as Badillo also noted, "the vote demanding amnesty was practically unanimous."

Kunstler announced that he had a count of thirty demands, and the observers trooped out of the yard and back to the room they had been assigned in the administration building. In the discussion that followed, some observers accused Kunstler of playing with the hostages' lives by emphasizing to the inmates their power of negotiation; others defended him because he had won the prisoners' confidence. Some accused Kunstler of creating a conflict of interest between his representation of the inmates and his neutral role on the observers' committee. At some point near this time, Wyatt Walker, Kunstler's old ally from the civil rights struggles, quit the group, criticizing Kunstler for agitating the prisoners. Nonetheless, there was enough support for Kunstler that the observers' group elected him to an ill-defined, six-man executive committee.

Certainly the hostages were fearful that Kunstler's presence could embolden the prisoners and harden their resolve, and, indeed, a legal scholar years later opined that Kunstler had acted unethically in his first appearance in D Yard "when he made an unmistakeable reference to the bargaining leverage the prisoners had through their hostages . . . [that] came very close to encouragement of their criminal activity." Although perhaps not the best source, a prisoner released in the ordinary course just after the uprising told reporters that Kunstler's remarks had not inflamed them nor had he impeded the negotiations. In the days after the ultimate assault on D Yard, two of the observers charged that Kunstler had "heightened the expectations about getting amnesty." Kunstler denied this.

Three observers set out to confer with the local district attorney to explore the possibilities of an amnesty. In the early afternoon they returned with a vaguely worded statement promising only that he would not undertake any vindictive or indiscriminate prosecution. When this was presented to the observers as a whole, the lawyers among the group immediately opposed it. Kunstler pointed out that the prosecutor's letter did no more than restate the law and prosecutorial ethics. Furthermore, it might compromise criminal defenses to any charges arising from the uprising. The lawyers argued that the letter should not even be presented to the prisoners for fear it would discredit the observers, but the majority decided to disclose it without endorsement.

That Saturday during the afternoon the executive committee plus a few other observers sat down with Commissioner Oswald to negotiate over the Fifteen Practical Proposals plus the additional demands Kunstler had recorded the evening before. Kunstler was the chief negotiator and wrote out in his own hand the 28 Points that Oswald agreed to implement. Both Oswald and observer Badillo agreed that Kunstler was very effective in the negotiations, that all sides acted professionally, and that the spirit of that session was optimistic. Oswald rejected out of hand any possibility of amnesty, transportation to a third world country, or the firing of the warden. Some proposals that he agreed to in principle were subject to approval by the legislature, and he agreed to attempt to obtain that approval where needed.

Oswald agreed to provide better food, freedom of communication, better rehabilitation programs, and true religious freedom; to improve the library; to end censorship of publications; and to implement many similar items of reform. Oswald categorized the 28 Points as "the most a modern prison administration had ever offered rebellious prisoners," and *Newsweek* stated that "put into effect, it would have made Attica one of the most liberal prisons in America. To the astonishment of veteran penologists and the outrage of guards at Attica, Oswald agreed Saturday afternoon to put [them] into effect."

More cynically, the *New York Times* editorialized that the prisoner demands and the resulting 28 Points were "no more radical than decent food, good medical care, adequate recreational opportunities, better rehabilitation programs. These are things that ought to have been provided long ago." The truth is somewhere in between. Almost all the 28 Points concerned details of prison reform. Some of the more significant promises depended on legislative action, which might have been withheld, or administrative good will, which might have been denied. However, there were significant specific agreements that the prison administration could itself have authorized, for example, the establishment of an inmate grievance commission to confer with the administration and the appointment of an ombudsman. These and other provisions might have had significant long-term effects. The observers group as a whole reached the consensus that, as Wicker put it, "the package should be laid before the inmates as the best they could hope for, but without a recommendation that they should accept it."

Kunstler also spoke with the press that Saturday afternoon and informed the waiting reporters that "the prisoners were adamant in their demand for amnesty." He said that "agreement seemed assured on most issues," although there were some few that Oswald could not (paying the minimum wage and changes in conditional releases were legislative matters) or would not (breaking the four yards into one very large yard) accede to. Nonetheless, Kunstler was optimistic. There was, he maintained, "a good chance this could end [if] all bargain in good faith. We have assurances that there are no present plans to use force—I hope it continues. I hope the authorities don't precipitate tragedy because there might be a two or three-day negotiating span."

In the early evening on Saturday Bobby Seale, the Black Panther leader Kunstler had summoned, arrived at the Attica gates. At first, Commissioner Oswald refused to permit Seale's entry into the yard.

However, the observers persuaded Oswald, contrary to the advice of Governor Rockefeller's advisers, to allow Seale to meet with the inmates, pointing out that the prisoners had requested a Panther representative. Kunstler argued that perhaps Seale was the only one who could win acceptance of the negotiated 28 Points and assured Oswald that Seale would not be inflammatory. Meanwhile, Seale became irritated at the slow process, left, and had to be brought back. After this delay, Seale was ushered into the gathering of the observers, and made ready to go into the yard. Kunstler told Seale that he hoped he would be able to support the 28 Points.

Seale's remarks to the prisoners were extremely low-key. He spoke for only five minutes and said he had to consult with Huey Newton before giving an opinion on the 28 Points; he would do so and return. The prisoners booed him after he spoke, and Kunstler was bitterly disappointed that Seale had not followed his recommendation and endorsed the 28 Points. Seale left, accompanied by Kunstler, who returned to the yard after seeing Seale off.

While Kunstler was away, Clarence Jones, another observer and the black publisher of the *Amsterdam News*, read the district attorney's letter to the inmates and went over the 28 Points. He also emphasized the increasing hostility of the state troopers, specifically that they were "young, tense, and infected with racism, and would like nothing better than an excuse to blow the inmates' brains out." The inmates were angry, perhaps in part over the perfunctory performance of Bobby Seale, perhaps because it had been so long since the observers had met with them, perhaps in part because they resented the observers' apparent assumption of authority to negotiate for them. Jones told them that while it was ultimately for the inmates to decide, he thought the 28 Points were the best they could get. Tom Wicker later reported that "the inmates laughed and jeered bitterly after each new point was read. Their anger became palpable. . . . But Jones went courageously on, despite catcalls, angry shouts, and the heavy tension in the yard." When he was finished, an inmate leader jumped on top of the table, charged that the proposals were "trickery," and ripped up the paper on which the 28 Points were written.

At that point Kunstler reentered the yard. It was a moment of extreme tension. One of the inmates in charge of security told Kunstler, "there's going to be real trouble here. The men are in terrible shape. They're angry, bitter, frustrated." Someone shouted, "and what do you think, counselor?" As he made his way to the microphone, Kunstler's mood was "so deep and intense and all of my white, middle-class fears and images about prisoners had come to the fore and I guess I was going to say that they were right in tearing them up." However, Kunstler decided not to simply tell the prisoners what they wanted to hear, that they were right, but instead to tell them the truth.

"I'm speaking to you now as a lawyer," Kunstler said, "and that may destroy my credibility with you, but as a lawyer I can tell you this is the best we can do for you at this time." He added, "we don't want people to die. You can turn it down, though. You have an absolute right to do that, but I wouldn't be fair to you if I didn't tell you what the consequences might be. . . . I recommend that you accept it. I'm your lawyer, and I recommend that you accept the state's response and let the hostages go." By the time Kunstler was finished speaking the inmates' anger had largely dissipated. The atmosphere was significantly calmer. Tom Wicker leaned over and told Kunstler, "Bill, you've saved all our lives." Three observers later told Wicker that "they had no doubt that at that frightening moment in D-yard Kunstler had saved all their lives with his statement that backed them and the 28 points. Kunstler had put all his prestige on the line at the one moment when it really mattered."

During his speech, Kunstler mentioned another matter that had occurred just hours before: Officer William Quinn, the guard severely injured in the melee at the Times Square control post at the beginning of the uprising, had died. Kunstler mentioned it almost offhandedly, saying that this meant "a new ball game" and that "the amnesty section [i.e., the lack of a full, general amnesty in the 28 Points] is not acceptable to you now that a guard has died." Although there were some radios among the inmates, the guard's death was not yet generally known to them, and the news caused a loud gasp.

It *was* a new ball game, and the gasps were quite appropriate. New York had abolished the death penalty generally, but had retained it for narrow exceptions, including the murder of a prison guard. A great many of the inmates risked a charge of conspiracy to commit Quinn's murder. The stakes became higher immediately and the issue of amnesty, critical. Wicker mildly criticized Kunstler for mentioning the death, but Kunstler was straightforward in his own defense: if he had not told them, the prisoners "might have accepted a deal under false circumstances, and I could not have lived with such a deception. They deserved to know the truth before making their decisions."

Kunstler urged the inmates to talk it over and find some method to reach a consensus. Of course, the prisoners had no method to reach a consensus except a voice vote, and there is evidence that the more moderate inmates felt intimidated by the more radical leadership. The inmates rejected the 28 Points, and a very discouraged body of observers left D Yard shortly before midnight on Saturday, believing that a deadly assault, with probable killings on both sides, would commence shortly.

By Sunday morning, almost all the observers thought that the tension was palpable. The hundreds of state troopers and guards at and surrounding the prison bristled with firearms, and were obviously itching to use them. Prison tradition called for immediate and massive response to the taking of hostages, regardless of consequences. The approach of waiting out terrorists or other hostage takers was just beginning to come into vogue. When Seale returned early that morning and entered the prison with Kunstler, both were jeered by troopers and guards as "no-good commies." The troopers' hostility focused on both Oswald and the observers, the only two forces standing in the way of their desire to storm the prison, slaughter a lot of blacks, and heroically rescue the hostages. That morning, a woman at a local diner told three of the observers who were quietly trying to get some breakfast, "they ought to kill all of you people. Everyone of you!"

The racism of these small-town guards and troopers, always close to the surface, had became blatant and public. Several people reported these lawmen asking aloud that Sunday, "when are we going to go coon hunting?" and boasting that if they had an opportunity to shoot, they would not miss the inmates they had seen on the television reports. Residents of Attica, families and friends of the hostages, abused the relatives of the prisoners who had also gathered at the front gate, both groups awaiting word of their loved ones. One older woman, the mother of a prisoner, approached a guard to ask if there were any news. He turned away and said, "Get outta here, Nigger." As she walked back toward the cluster of prisoners' relatives, the townspeople of Attica shouted to her, "Go home, whore! Go back to New York City, bitch!"

Seale returned that Sunday morning, but apparently he refused to support the 28 Points or was unwilling to commit in advance to what he would tell the inmates. Kunstler later testified to an investigating commission that all Seale had indicated to him concerning the substance of his intended remarks was that the Black Panthers supported the prisoners' demand for transportation to a nonimperialist country. Kunstler then told Seale that he would not be admitted to D Yard on that basis, after which Seale left without meeting with Oswald. In any event, Seale did not reenter the direct negotiations.

As the observers discussed the situation, they felt that an assault on the prison was imminent. Kunstler argued that Oswald's position on the nonnegotiability of amnesty would make it difficult for the observers to reenter the yard. He did not wish "to go in there and die." He ascribed the impending "cosmic tragedy" of massive slaughter to racism, "the end product of my society." He said that all the observers could do was "work for time," and that he was "utterly sick at heart that these men will die and they'll die because of me [and others like him, who] had scrambled over their backs" in society. To at least one of the observers, these remarks did not seem unduly melodramatic, since he was feeling much the same emotions. Kunstler was in tears as he finished his talk, and acknowledged that "tears don't move monsters but they relieve the spirit."

The observers' principal activity of Sunday morning and early afternoon was an effort to persuade Governor Nelson Rockefeller to come to Attica, *not* to enter the yard or negotiate with the inmates, as has sometimes been stated, but to meet with the observers. The purpose was to gain time and to allow the governor to personally observe the immense tension and the probable slaughter that would result from an assault. Several of the observers telephoned Rockefeller to urge him to come, as did even Oswald. The observers talked with Robert Douglass, the governor's personal representative who had come to Attica. Kunstler told Douglass bluntly that Rockefeller's presence would be "at least buying time and not lives" and that if he did not appear, "he's condoning a massacre."

Rockefeller obstinately refused to leave his palatial estate of Pocantico Hills, where he had ensconced himself for the weekend, canceling all other appearances in order to better keep in touch with the Attica situation. The observers tried one other strategy: they issued a public statement to the media, urging the public to demand Rockefeller's presence. Drafted by Clarence Jones and Kunstler, the statement declared in part,

The committee of observers in Attica Prison is now convinced a massacre of prisoners and guards may take place in this institution. For the
sake of our common humanity, we call on every person who hears
these words to implore the Governor of this state to come to Attica to
consult with the observer committee, so we can spend time and not
lives in an attempt to resolve the issues before us.

In midafternoon on Sunday, Oswald took two significant actions.
He ordered the yard closed to further visits by the observers. He also
sent the inmates a statement at 2:10 P.M., demanding a response within
an hour. The long statement angered almost all the observers because of
the following portion: "I urgently request you to release the hostages
unharmed, now, and to accept the recommendations of the committee
of outside observers which recommendations were approved by me."
The observers were angry because the 28 Points were a result of negotiations and not "the recommendations of the committee" and because
the statement implied that the observers were a party to the ultimatum.
Oswald obviously had no appreciation for the nuanced position the observers had taken with the inmates: that the decision for acceptance or
rejection was theirs alone but that the 28 Points were the best deal that
could be obtained. Further, the observers had promised the inmates
that they would return at 3:00 P.M. with media representatives, who had
been promised an opportunity by the prisoners to interview the
hostages. While this promise should be kept, the observers argued, Oswald had put their credibility and therefore their lives at risk by the
statement.

Against the urging of all his advisers and the advice of Governor
Rockefeller, Commissioner Oswald permitted a small group of seven
observers, including Tom Wicker and Kunstler, to once again enter D
Yard, accompanied by media representatives who were to interview the
hostages. The inmates had received Oswald's earlier message and, as
predicted, felt betrayed by the observers. As soon as they crossed into
the prisoner-controlled portion of the prison, Brother Richard, the inmate leader who escorted them, turned to the observers and said,
"None of you can look us in the eye, why?" He then asked, "Why did
you betray us? You've jiving with our lives. Don't you realize there are
men inside there who want to kill you for what you did?"

The observers quickly explained that they had nothing to do with
the Oswald statement, that they had not betrayed the prisoners at all.

Still, the observers were a very frightened group of men. Kunstler was standing right behind Wicker and "watched the back of his neck turn, very slowly, a deep beet red." Kunstler himself was "as scared as I had ever been." That Sunday afternoon, for the first time, the authorities had demanded that the observers sign liability waivers before entering the inmate-controlled area. From that fact, plus the Oswald statement linking the observers to his own demand for the release of the hostages, Kunstler concluded that Oswald wanted the prisoners to kill the observers. That would give the authorities a perfect excuse for assaulting D Yard with guns blazing. There is no real evidence for such a plot, and it ascribes a greater capacity for calculated thought to Oswald than he probably at that moment possessed. Oswald was under just as much pressure as were the prisoners, and he was just as deprived of sleep as any of the inmates or observers.

In the event, the tension passed and the observers and television crew entered D Yard for their last visit, to interview the hostages and make a few final speeches. Almost all the observers by this time thought that a massacre would soon follow. Following an impassioned speech by Arthur Eve, an inmate shouted out to Kunstler, "What's this I hear about foreign countries?" At that point Kunstler made his final speech to the inmates, the single most controversial act of his time as observer. The remarks were captured by media tape. Kunstler began, "There are four Third World and African country people across the street from this prison, prepared to provide asylum for everyone who wants to leave this country for this purpose." Shouts and pandemonium then broke out from the inmates. Kunstler went on to give a misleading explanation as to why Seale had not reentered the yard that morning:

> Mr. Oswald said to him [Seale] that he wanted him to come in here and persuade you to accept conditions that are not acceptable to you. Bobby Seale would not enter this compound today because he would not compromise you. He . . . could not bring himself, as a black man, to come in here and tell you what the Man wanted you to do. So Bobby Seale left, but he wanted you to know that in every city with a black or Puerto Rican community, there are people who are watching Attica prison.

Kunstler concluded with catchwords that clearly anticipated not only an impending slaughter, but the possibility that the mass killings might become a rallying cry around which those outside the walls might be organized and radicalized. "The gringoes talk about 'Remember the Alamo!' Remember Attica!"

The governments of North Vietnam, North Korea, Algeria, and Congo Brazzaville had apparently indicated to the Black Panther Party that they would be willing to accept Attica prisoners who wished to leave, and that fact had been communicated to Kunstler early that Sunday morning. However, the notion that anyone was waiting across the street for them was blatantly untrue. Indeed, Kunstler testified before the official inquiry that after his remarks he explained to a group of inmates, but off the microphone, that really no third world representatives waited across the street and that the offer was available only to prisoners already released from prison. Kunstler made no retraction on the microphone.

Kunstler took a lot of criticism from different directions for his third world country remarks. The hostages thought that this was Kunstler at his most inflammatory. A legal scholar concluded,

> This untrue statement could only have been calculated to discourage a settlement [28 Points] that even Kunstler apparently believed was the best the prisoners could get. At that point it was clear to outside observers that it was either that settlement or deadly force. That is not only what they *should* have been told at that point, but what a competent lawyer less affected by his own political ideology and radical image must necessarily have told his clients. (emphasis in original)

More important, some of his fellow observers criticized Kunstler for these statements. Tom Wicker said he felt very uncomfortable about the remarks. Two other observers charged that Kunstler had tried to undermine the negotiations by misleading the inmates both as to the issue of amnesty and as to the third world countries. On the other hand, days after the massacre, the great majority of the observers issued a statement that included the observation that "no individual on the observer committee adopted any position which prevented or hindered a peaceful resolution of the crisis." In the official inquiry Wicker testified that he was "not aware of any speech that was made that in my judgment ever gave the prisoners any reason whatever to think that they were going to win their struggle. . . . I know certainly of no speech of any kind that made the suggestion that they were indeed likely to be flown off to any third-world country."

Indeed, the entire issue of third world asylum was a minor matter. Although included in the initial demands at the outset of the uprising, it had faded away as the matter of amnesty grew in importance. One leader of the inmates later told a reporter that "some of the radical young Blacks really believed what Kunstler said about political asylum, but it didn't matter to the great majority." Kunstler's third world remarks, while obviously untrue and lacking in judgment, did not really matter: they did not inflame or raise false hopes among most inmates, and did not cause them to hold out. Nonetheless, Kunstler's later reasoning as to why he said what he did seems particularly lame. A few days later he told a reporter that he thought the prisoners were as good as dead and the third world message "would make them feel better." In his 1994 autobiography he wrote that "although I knew the state would never let them go, I thought it was good to give the men hope . . . I thought at the time that gaining confidence for the observers was the most important thing."

Back inside the administration building, the observers pleaded with Oswald to give them more time and to postpone the assault. Kunstler suggested that the authorities consider a commutation plan, a promise by the governor to commute any sentences arising out of the Attica uprising to five, ten, or fifteen years, as a substitute for outright amnesty. Oswald refused, stating that this was "too slick a maneuver. . . . Either it's amnesty or it isn't amnesty." Kunstler again pleaded for more time, arguing, "everyone dies if the troopers go in." Oswald responded, "I'm going through the tortures of hell trying to make up my mind . . . all of us choose life" but that the pressures on him were enormous. Oswald told the observers, "I can give you no assurances that there will not be action," and the last meeting of the observers and Oswald concluded. Then Kunstler did something that no other observer is reported to have done or mentioned in their own accounts. He made telephone calls to the families of inmates who had requested that favor.

Several of the observers left the prison later that evening, Kunstler remarking wearily that there was still "no solution." That afternoon had been the first opportunity given the observers to meet with the hostages. Tom Wicker, the distinguished columnist for the *New York Times,* mounted an automobile with a black reporter for the *Amsterdam*

News to hold a press conference on the condition of the captive guards and civilian employees. As Wicker mentioned that there was an "absolute solidarity" among the inmates of all races, the crowd of white townspeople shouted, "Nigger-lover! You must live with niggers. Sonofabitch. What kind of white man are you? Standing on a platform with a nigger and help a nigger talking against your own. Why don't you talk about the unity of the guards? The police? You dirty double-crossing bastard. We ought to string you up."

The authorities permitted the troopers to go "coon hunting," as they so desperately wished, on Monday morning, September 13, 1971. There was a final exchange of ultimatum and rejection, and then, before the troopers went over the walls, there was one final display of defiance by the inmates. At 9:00 A.M., a few inmates led eight blindfolded hostages, of the thirty-nine, out on the catwalks that separated the four yards, in plain view of the air above and the adjacent portions of the prison controlled by the troopers. Each hostage had a knife held to his throat, and some were pulled back as though ready to be executed. The prisoners certainly knew an attack was imminent, and apparently this maneuver was designed to ward off an attack from the air, their most vulnerable side.

The assault did begin from the air, with a tear gas drop, followed by dozens of state troopers streaming down the catwalk, through the tunnels, and then into D Yard. Some ordinary guards conducted a turkey shoot into D Yard from a high perch. At the same time, state trooper sharpshooters killed many of the inmate-executioners on the catwalks instantly, as they had themselves become exposed to fire from the sides of the prison. Some of the inmate-executioners who were not killed immediately pushed their victim-hostages down, fell on top of them, and probably saved those guards' lives. At least two of these hostages with knives to their throats thought that when the crisis came, "their appointed executioners saved their lives." In any event, this threatening posture toward eight of the hostages did not set off the attack, which was set to begin in any event, although it may have hastened its beginning by a minute or two.

The lawmen's guns blazed murderous fire, and all resistance ended within ten minutes. Most of the troopers used shotguns loaded with multiple lethal projectiles, weapons that are quite inaccurate, a dangerous situation exacerbated by the poor visibility caused by the tear gas and the tear gas masks worn by the troopers. Several inmates reported that the assaulting forces shouted, "niggers, we're going to get you" as they attacked; Kunstler overheard the sheriff's deputies, not part of the assault but held in reserve, yell to the frontline troops, "Save me a nigger!"; a reporter heard a released hostage yell, "white power!" triumphantly as he emerged from captivity; and another released hostage, incensed that Commissioner Oswald and his deputy Walter Dunbar had not ordered an immediate assault, quit his job on the spot, and with tears in his eyes explained that "I don't want to work there so long as this state is run by the Oswalds, the Dunbars and the niggers."

Nine hostages and twenty-six inmates died in the assault; three hostages, eighty-five inmates, and one trooper were injured. Walter Dunbar, Oswald's deputy, informed reporters that it had been an "efficient, affirmative police action." That evening in Attica, some of the police involved in this efficient action "talked with pride about shooting 'niggers' that morning." They bantered back and forth, "Did you get one?" and "Oh, I got one." The report of the official inquiry commission noted that with the exception of Indian massacres in the late nineteenth century, the state police assault was the "bloodiest one-day encounter between Americans since the Civil War."

After the firing ceased, the authorities ordered the prisoners to crawl on their bellies from D Yard into another yard, where they were stripped of all clothing and personal effects, including watches, which were destroyed in front of their eyes. Then the authorities ordered the inmates to run through a gauntlet of prison guards, who beat them with the hard batons the guards called their "nigger sticks." The lawmen severely beat the leaders of the uprising, or those thought to be, as well as those showing the slightest resistance or remonstrance. Medical evidence and the testimony of one trooper with a conscience supported an overwhelming amount of inmate testimony as to the guards' barbarous reprisals. A few months later, a U.S. court of appeals, in ordering an injunction against such conduct, found that detailed evidence had been furnished that on the day of the assault and for the following few days,

> State Troopers and correctional personnel had engaged in cruel and inhuman abuse of numerous inmates. Injured prisoners, some on stretchers, were struck, prodded or beaten with sticks, belts, bats or other weapons. Others were forced to strip and run naked through gauntlets of guards armed with clubs which they used to strike the bodies of the inmates as they passed. Some were dragged on the

ground . . . some spat upon or burned with matches, and others poked in the genitals or arms with sticks. . . . Correctional officers, addressing inmates as "niggers" or "coons," threatened to . . . shoot or kill them. . . . a guard pointed a gun at an inmate's head, telling him that he was going to die, and started clicking the trigger, following which the inmate was kicked and beaten.

The guards forced Frank Smith, a black inmate, "to lie naked on a table for three to five hours holding a football with his chin. If he allowed the ball to roll away . . . he was told, he would be killed or castrated. As he lay on the table . . . guards struck his testicles with batons and dropped lighted cigarettes and shell casings on his body." Later in the day, a National Guardsman saw Smith naked on the floor while five or six guards beat him with clubs.

Oswald regarded the officers' proddings as "more in the manner of an old fraternity hazing than a beating." He said he did not condone but understood the more violent beatings. As the stories of these atrocities by the authorities became known, volunteer doctors and lawyers converged on Attica to help the prisoners. Authorities turned them away, even though one group had obtained a court order permitting their entry.

A reason for the fury of the guards toward Frank Smith is the account that Walter Dunbar gave to the press, the guards, and other state officials concerning the fate of the hostages. He told the press that the dead hostages were killed by stabbings and that one of the hostages had been castrated. Shortly after the retaking, Dunbar took Arthur Eve and Herman Badillo, two observers who were also state legislators, on a tour of the prison. He told them both that the hostages had been stabbed to death. Badillo recalled that Dunbar "showed us a big inmate [i.e., Frank Smith], stretched prone on a table in the yard, forced to balance a football between his chin and chest. This man, Dunbar said, had been seen castrating a guard named Michael Smith, and stuffing the guard's sexual organs into his mouth—'Mau Mau style.'"

Kunstler had not been inside the prison during the assault. He spent the night at his motel and was denied access in the morning when he returned. During the shootings he looked toward a guard and called the lawmen "murdering bastards. They're shooting them. They're murdering them." More calmly he told a reporter that "this will go down in history as a bloody mistake."

Kunstler went off to Buffalo for a rally held that very afternoon, just hours after the assault. He urged the small crowd of about four hundred to make an effort to see that the reforms embodied in the 28 Points were effected. He roused the crowd when he told them that "in the negotiations I came to realize for the first time in my life that there are many more decent persons in prison than on the outside." After a few more remarks the crowd began to chant, "Remember Attica! Remember Attica!" the catchphrase Kunstler had coined in his speech to the inmates only the day before. This talk was Kunstler's first of many efforts to exploit public sympathy and to organize around the issue of Attica. After Kunstler had finished, and without first giving an order to disburse, the Buffalo police waded into the crowd swinging nightsticks. The demonstrators had no permit for their loudspeaker.

The smugness of the official accounts of the Attica assault suffered a severe setback the next day, September 14, when autopsies revealed that all nine of the hostages killed in the assault had died from bullet wounds, none from stabbing, although some had nonlethal knife wounds. No guards had been mutilated. Michael Smith, for the sake of whose testicles the guards had brutally tortured inmate Frank Smith, in fact had been knocked unconscious during the assault but was fully intact and quite all right. Since the inmates had no guns, the implication was clear: the killings of the hostages had been accomplished only by the lawmen themselves. The autopsies shocked the town of Attica and the guards' families. Skeptical authorities ordered two additional doctors to examine the corpses, and the later doctors confirmed the original findings.

One dead hostage's relative crisply bespoke the political reality: "We feel that Carl was killed not by the prisoners but by a bullet that had the name Rockefeller written on it." Under political fire, Rockefeller appointed several commissions of inquiry, one to investigate the constitutional rights of prisoners against reprisals, headed by Judge Harry D. Goldman, and another to investigate the uprising as a whole, headed by Robert B. McKay, dean of the New York University School of Law. State prosecutors also began investigations, and even Congress established investigative teams. Attica had turned into a war of words.

Kunstler quickly termed Rockefeller a "murderer" and demanded that he resign. He spoke at the State University of New York at Buffalo the day after the assault, and argued that the authorities did not have to shoot but could have immobilized the prisoners through gas. He told the students that "the real murderers wore uniforms, the real murderers had state-issued weapons and ammunition, the real murderers had names, not numbers." A few days later Kunstler addressed a "Remember Attica" rally in Harlem. Two thousand blacks and Puerto Ricans shouted, "Give us Kunstler! We want Kunstler!" as a black politician droned on. After Kunstler spoke to the crowd, he confided to a reporter, "They didn't really think of me as a lawyer. They thought of me as one of them," yet another time when Kunstler briefly dropped his mask and revealed his consuming need for belonging.

On September 17 he was invited by students to speak at a "counterdedication" for the new law school center at Georgetown. Chief Justice Warren E. Burger was the speaker at the official dedication, and Kunstler was relegated to speaking from the bed of a pickup truck. Kunstler told the throng of law students that Burger was defending "a vile system" and that "he is not fit to dedicate that center." With his voice cracking with emotion, he went on, "'Remember Attica' has to be the watchword. Remember Attica and the heroes, the heroes in the finest sense of the word, the heroes who died there. [The inmates] were the finest men I have ever known. They were prepared to die for what they believed in. They knew they were going to die." Kunstler rejected the hope of liberal amelioration of wretched prison conditions. The reason the Attica prisoners' sacrifice was heroic was that, as he wrote a few years later, "only the threat or actuality of inmate rebellions offers any hope of humanizing penal institutions and release programs and procedures. If Attica means anything, it signifies the recognition of that fact of life—and death."

Others also bitterly accused Rockefeller and the state authorities of an atrocity. Assemblyman Arthur Eve thought "the Governor ought to be indicted." Bobby Seale likewise charged that the state officials "are guilty of murder. The best thing to do would be to charge Oswald and the others with first-degree, outright mass murder." Even the *New York Times* cautiously suggested that it was "far from clear that state officials were right in storming the compound when they did." Rallies and protests were held in Los Angeles, Manhattan, and Albany, featuring Angela Davis, David Dellinger, Kunstler, and others as speakers. Some of the rallies were organized by the People's Coalition for Peace and Justice, which the year before had sponsored a huge antiwar demonstration in Washington.

However, the Attica rallies went nowhere. The numbers in attendance were usually in the hundreds, not thousands. As a radical cause it failed to stir up sufficient emotion in sufficient numbers of people. That is not to say there was no criticism of the storming of the prison; there was considerable investigation and criticism. However, the angst was felt for the slain guards, not the slain inmates. Fear of crime was and is so embedded in the American consciousness that the dead inmates of Attica proved to be a poor issue around which to organize or mobilize public dissatisfaction. As a letter to the *New York Times* asked, "With the Kunstlers and Tom Wickers trying to make political prisoners out of hard-core criminals, what is next?"

Kunstler received criticism over Attica beyond letters to the editor. Rebuke came from so far to the right, however, that he probably took it as an honor. Russell Kirk critiqued a campus talk by Kunstler shortly after the uprising, in which Kunstler, according to Kirk's vivid but inaccurate phrases, "writhing snakelike as he gripped the podium, praised the criminals who had taken hostage guards and other prisoners and had hideously tortured to death some of their captives." William F. Buckley, in a fit of self-righteousness, announced in the *National Review* that in protest of Kunstler's "slander" of Rockefeller he, Buckley, had resolved never to share a public platform with Kunstler until he showed "contrition." He urged Kunstler's disbarment, but magnanimously allowed that he did not wish Kunstler jailed. It was in this specific context that Buckley made the wish, seen before, that Kunstler only "should experience the isolation which he has earned from the civilized community."

A few days after the assault, Kunstler told reporters at a news conference that he would shortly file a lawsuit in the federal district court charging the New York authorities with a violation of the inmates' civil rights. In fact, it was not until 1974 that a class action began the quest for damages on behalf of the inmates for the reprisals after the assault. Kunstler stayed on the sidelines in the civil proceedings, which for over two decades have been the major career case of a Brooklyn attorney, Elizabeth Fink. The litigation has run an extraordinarily complicated and slow-moving course.

Ultimately, in 1992 a jury found Karl Pfeil, a deputy warden, liable for injuries arising from the reprisal stage of the uprising, following the assault. The jury could not agree on the liability of Oswald for the reprisals. The case could not be settled for the entire class of 1,281 plaintiffs, so a separate trial on damages began to be tried for each individual plaintiff. These will continue past the millennium unless settlement is reached. Although not a separate defendant, New York state will ultimately pay for the damage awards because it is required to indemnify individuals for liability arising out of the performance of their duties.

The first plaintiff to be heard on damages was Frank Smith, or "Big Black," the inmate tortured by guards with lighted cigarettes, struck on his testicles, and beaten with clubs. A federal jury in Buffalo awarded him four million dollars in June 1997. Defense counsel immediately announced an appeal and told the press that the award "was plainly excessive. We had a runaway jury here. They obviously based their decision not on evidence, but on emotion or sympathy or punishment." Perhaps sympathy for the inmates and a desire to punish brutal officials are appropriate emotions.

A grand jury for Wyoming County, in which Attica is located, began to assess possible indictments on November 1, 1971. It sat for over three years, becoming, according to Anthony G. Simonetti, the special Attica prosecutor, the "longest-sitting Grand Jury in history." Ultimately it indicted sixty-two inmates for more than 1,400 counts; the charges ran from murder and kidnapping to sodomy and possession of contraband. The prosecution's investigation was extensive and cost an enormous sum. However, this first grand jury (there would be a second, later) issued no indictments against any guards or troopers, although there was an indication that the prosecutor had attempted to charge a trooper in connection with the death of one of the hostages but that the grand jury refused to return an indictment.

The venue for trials was changed to Buffalo, although the defendants requested New York City. Even in relatively conservative Buffalo, the early prosecutions did not go well for the state of New York. Trial prosecutors dropped and trial judges dismissed many cases for insufficient evidence; juries acquitted in others. Where prosecutors obtained a few convictions, the sentences handed out ran concurrently with prison time already in progress. Ultimately only John Hill, a young man of Italian and American Indian ancestry, whom Kunstler represented, and his codefendant Charles Pernasilice, represented by the former attorney general Ramsey Clark, received additional time for alleged crimes committed during the Attica uprising.

The state charged Hill and Pernasilice with the murder of William Quinn, the guard beaten on the face with a board in the Times Square control point. This occurred in the junction of the cellblock tunnels at the beginning of the uprising, when the metal security bolt gave way and allowed the prisoners to pass freely into the other yards and cellblocks. An Attica Brothers Legal Defense Committee, headed by Haywood Burns, attempted to coordinate the defenses of the separately represented sixty-two defendants. The committee's greatest challenge was to keep individualistic tactics within the fold of a common political strategy, a matter that arguably became quite important in Hill's trial. Another difficulty became clear when a young woman working with the defense committee disclosed that she had transmitted confidential tactical information to the FBI. Eventually the FBI and some state prosecutors admitted that the defense team had been spied on, just as they had been in Chicago.

Several inmates and prison officials identified John Hill, Kunstler's client, as one who struck Officer Quinn on the head with a piece of lumber. Some identifications were stronger than others, and Kunstler vigorously attacked the credibility of the witnesses. In addition, he charged that the inmate witnesses gave perjured testimony, bought by the prosecution through early paroles. Kunstler made an emotional, seven-hour closing argument, capping the five-week 1975 trial. His voice broke with emotion as he told the jury, "My Brother Dacajeweih [Hill's Indian name] is in your hands. Do well by him. He is an innocent man. Do well by him." Kunstler sobbed and then embraced his client. Unimpressed, the jury convicted Hill of murder; he received a sentence of twenty years to life.

Kunstler regarded the trial as political; he claimed that "basically, Johnny and Charlie Joe were indicted to represent all the inmates who had taken a whack at the guards. The state needed some scapegoats, and who better than two Native Americans?" However, he had a difficult time politicizing the trial because the trial judge would not admit social or political evidence, or testimony concerning matters either before or after the date on which Quinn was struck. Even the acerbic exchanges between Kunstler and the judge were short, and reconciliations followed. About the angriest remark of trial judge Gilbert H. King to Kunstler was the complaint "I'm fed up with your telling me I have no conscience." The temper of America was more conservative in 1975 than during the Chicago trial in 1970, and the Attica trial attracted much less interest from both the press and the American public generally.

Perhaps because he had so recently been successful in the leadership trial of the Wounded Knee Indian defendants, Kunstler tried his best to politicize the Hill/Pernasilice trial along American Indian lines. Although thwarted from introducing social evidence by Judge King's strict rulings, he played up the Indian angle at every possible turn. He called John Hill by his Indian name, Dacajeweih, even though Hill had not himself used that name at the time of the uprising. Kunstler wore Indian jewelry to trial, including an Indian-fashioned watchband, belt, and buckle. Apparently, he beat a tom-tom outside the courtroom for the press.

Hill himself made a spectacular appearance in the courtroom with a ribbon in his long hair. He was accompanied by fellow Mohawk tribesmen, who occupied over half of the forty-two spectator seats. One of the Indian spectators was Mad Bear, a spiritual leader, who wore a feather headdress in court. Early in the trial, Judge King had barred the Indian spectators from the courtroom because they refused to rise when he made his entrances and exits to and from the bench. Later King reversed course and allowed all Indians, including the defendants, to remain seated while everyone else in the courtroom rose for this customary rendering of respect. While in itself this all meant very little, still it was a means to bring home to the jury Kunstler's theory of the "Indianness" involved in the trial.

Some professional colleagues criticized Kunstler's conduct of this trial. The trial prosecutor ridiculed the Indian touches, thought the jury saw through those tactics, and concluded that "the idea that the prosecution of these men had anything to do with their being native Americans was ludicrous. But he'd [Kunstler] just come off of Wounded Knee, maybe he thought that was the thing to do." Kunstler himself thought he had made a mistake by heavy reliance on background investigations of potential jurors. One prospective juror, during the time of preliminary questioning, told the judge in the presence of the entire jury panel that he had resented being investigated. Kunstler concluded, "it turned the rest of the jurors against me."

Kunstler's biggest single error in the Hill trial was probably that articulated in 1980 by an unidentified "defense attorney" who, according to an investigative reporter, was "close to the case," who insisted that Kunstler had put on a very minor defense:

> The state tried to show that only two people hit the guard—but off the top of my head right now I can give you about 20 people who hit him. Lots of people should have been put on the stand to tell different stories of what they saw, and convey the total chaos. But Bill is a very sloppy lawyer, and he hadn't fully analyzed what his case was, so he made a decision that he was afraid of using inmate witnesses, and he rested his case.

There may be considerable insight in these remarks, but the failure to put on more inmate witnesses (Kunstler did put on inmate alibi testimony) was less a matter of laziness or incorrect analysis than a blindness caused by the political posture of the case. Although these were individual prosecutions, the Attica Brothers Legal Defense Committee coordinated defenses. Defense attorneys, Kunstler included, knew there were many inmate witnesses who could identify all sorts of people who struck Quinn, and that this evidence might well be persuasively argued before a jury to the effect that the state either did not really know who did the killing or had chosen not to prosecute the truly guilty parties. Kunstler, and Ramsey Clark as well, did not call these witnesses for political reasons, not out of laziness.

As the *New York Times* explained at the beginning of the trial, in a most revealing comment on a back page:

> Margaret Ratner, a civil liberties lawyer who is working with Mr. Kunstler in the defense of Mr. Hill, indicated yesterday that there were "political problems" raised by the calling of such witnesses, who might implicate other current or former Attica inmates. By "political problems" she explained, she meant that such a strategy might run counter to the philosophy of the entire Attica Brothers Legal Defense group, which takes the view that the Attica trials are political trials and that no one inmate's defense should be carried out at the expense of another inmate.

Therefore solidarity to the group put Hill's individual defense at risk. This is the classic problem of political defenses involving groups and is fully recognized by prosecutors when they prosecute defendants one or two at a time. Prosecutors often encourage defendants to speak out against others, to divide and conquer them. Group cohesion, even at the expense of harm to individual defendants in Hill's position, is the only way to combat this prosecutorial tactic. Kunstler would have grasped this point with no difficulty. To the extent he might have been reluctant to follow the group strategy, it was significant that the viewpoint was articulated by Margaret Ratner. At the time of the Hill trial, Kunstler had separated from Lotte, was living with Margaret Ratner, and was deeply in love with his new *inamorata*. Margie, as she is universally called, was even more political than Kunstler. He probably needed no direction, but had he, Kunstler, then at least, would have followed Margie's advice.

Kunstler wrote that the aftermath of the trial "was one of the few times in my career that I felt truly dejected." The feeling did not last long. Kunstler was always optimistic and looking forward to the next battle. By the time he was in the cab going to the airport, all he could talk about was how he was going to win the case on appeal.

The appeal was not needed to free Hill. A second grand jury was called by the special prosecutor to consider indictments against the guards and troopers for excessive force in the assault. Some time thereafter, the prosecutor in charge of presenting the evidence to this second grand jury resigned, alleging a cover-up by his chief. Simonetti allegedly obstructed the flow of evidence to this new grand jury to protect law enforcement officials. Two other prosecutors also quit. On December 31, 1976, Governor Hugh Carey halted all prosecutions, issued a pardon for some Attica inmates, and commuted the sentence of John Hill. That made him eligible for a parole, which he received after being passed over once. The civil suits were unaffected, and later the state made a healthy settlement with the heirs of the slain hostages. Carey concluded that there had indeed been a double standard in the indictment of law enforcement officers and that he should close the book on Attica.

Kunstler often wrote that Attica was seared into his memory. On significant anniversaries of the Attica uprising, Kunstler generally wrote a commemorative article or was interviewed by a reporter. Kunstler's rhetorical use of Attica changed over time. In the immediate aftermath, he took the position that not much changed after Attica. While participating in the memorial events one year after the uprising, Kunstler charged "that the prison authorities had failed to correct the health, educational, work, recreational and dietary shortcomings that . . . had caused the rebellion."

In the early 1980s, before a later serious prison overcrowding, Kunstler took a different tack. He acknowledged that by then Attica had brought about a considerable number of improvements, but he deplored the meliorations, since that lessened the radicalization and militancy of the inmates. The tenth anniversary of Attica in 1981 fell at a time when radicals felt frustrated, some even depressed, because of the sharp turn the American public had taken toward conservatism. Kunstler revealingly commented to a reporter on that tenth anniversary, "There were certainly a great many creature comforts that came out of the rebellion. On the other hand, of course, the creature comforts tend to co-opt the inmates. They [i.e., creature comforts] reduce resistance. Constant resistance is the only way to make anything tolerable."

In the 1990s Kunstler suggested that the deaths at Attica had prevented other violent reactions to inmate uprisings, but insisted that conditions themselves were not much better, some even worse, and all improvements were threatened due to renewed overcrowding. He made an amusing effort to link Attica not only to miserable prison conditions, but to capitalism generally. The insurrection arose out of a minor altercation when the inmates were able to break through the defective gate in Times Square, the central control post. According to Kunstler, "the reason a supposedly tough prison gate would give way so easily has to do with the shoddy way the institution was constructed and maintained. And with capitalism's eternal quest to make a few bucks on the side."

However, Kunstler did have a deep commitment to prison reform work, which he served in many capacities, for no publicity and little applause. Kunstler was an adviser and consultant in prison litigation where he was not counsel of record; he was a member of the advisory board to the *Penal Digest International,* a national and international inmate newspaper; and he wrote scholarly articles for lawyers about prisoners' rights. Kunstler's concern for the plight of prisoners went beyond the high-profile case.

10

Private Life and Practice in the 1970s

BY THE 1970s, Kunstler's persona and image had impressed themselves on the American consciousness: the glasses high on his forehead, the worried and concerned look, the bitter accusations of government malfeasance, the rumpled hair and clothing, and the deep, resonant voice. Kissing and hugging were the traits that caught the most attention of those who knew Kunstler beyond his picture in the newspaper or on the television screen, those who had come into contact with him personally. When Kunstler arrived for his 1970 *Playboy* interview at Nat Hentoff's apartment,

> He came out of the elevator looking gaunt, weary, his suit rumpled, as usual. We hadn't seen each other for some time, but he immediately placed an arm around my shoulders as we entered the apartment and then disengaged himself to kiss my wife, whom he had never met before. . . . He sank heavily into an armchair . . . but as soon as we began talking . . . he spoke well into the evening with unflagging energy and passion.

Kunstler's proclivity for hugging and kissing at times became a joke. Kunstler arrived late to a Harvard Law School forum in 1970. Opening the program without him, the civil liberties attorney Leonard Boudin predicted that "sometime in the next half hour, Bill will burst through the door and, with his long hair streaming behind him, he'll jump onto the platform, throw his arms around me, and kiss me—a wet kiss—on the forehead." Shortly thereafter the doors opened, Kunstler dashed in, hugged and kissed Boudin exactly as predicted, and kissed Alan Dershowitz, another panelist, as well. Usually Kunstler entered a room to applause, and he was puzzled by the audience's laughter.

That Kunstler hugged even his enemies, including federal prosecutors, amazed his supporters. On an airplane one day in 1984, Kunstler spotted Evan Hultman, a lead federal prosecutor against whom he had successfully defended two Indian activists charged with the murder of FBI agents in a bitter 1976 trial. Although they were both on their way to a contested hearing for a third defendant charged with those murders, Kunstler greeted Hultman warmly and hugged him. An Indian activist traveling with Kunstler questioned him about this affection. Kunstler shrugged his shoulders. "It's not affection, really, it's more like enemy soldiers who have shared so many of the same battles that a bond develops. In the beginning I wouldn't speak to those people, but I couldn't keep it up; we're human beings, after all."

Kunstler was famous in the 1970s, and fame brought him new friends and acquaintances. Bertrand Russell telephoned Kunstler to ask for representation against Honeywell, a war contractor that had used his image and name in advertising without permission. Kunstler negotiated a settlement, and Russell invited Kunstler to come to one of his peace tribunals, mock trials of the Vietnam War and other political actions. Russell died shortly thereafter and they never had an opportunity to meet. After Kunstler moved to Greenwich Village he developed a fleeting acquaintance with John Lennon and Yoko Ono when they lived on Bank Street, occasionally sharing a pizza and talking about Lennon's legal difficulties.

His acquaintances in high places included Harry A. Blackmun, a justice of the U.S. Supreme Court. They first met when they sat in adjacent seats on an airplane flight in 1976. After small talk about common acquaintances, Kunstler congratulated him on a recent liberal vote. He advised Blackmun to get out from under the shadow of his fellow Minnesotan, conservative Chief Justice Warren E. Burger, with whom Blackmun voted so consistently that he and Burger became known as the "Minnesota Twins." Blackmun replied that he hoped to join the liberal wing of the court more often in the future. When the plane landed, Kunstler gave Blackmun an enormous bear hug. Blackmun told the story to his law clerks, and they were impressed that Blackmun was so delighted by the radical Kunstler's praise.

Blackmun and Kunstler had some small correspondence thereafter, and embraced again at a chance encounter many years later in 1992, after Blackmun had become the Court's most liberal member. Kunstler insists that once when he appeared before the Supreme Court in argument, Blackmun saw him in the cafeteria and waved at him to sit down with him for lunch. For propriety's sake, Kunstler declined. His conclusion about Blackmun was mixed: "He is not a flaming liberal, though, and sometimes goes along with some bad decisions. But he's the very best we've got."

Fame in the 1970s also meant labeling. Reporters called Kunstler "the country's most controversial and, perhaps, its best-known lawyer" and one of the "high priests" of America's "radical intelligentsia"; his admirers were called the "Kunstler constituency." Awards came as well. Kunstler received the Senior Fellow Award of the University of Notre Dame, chosen by the senior class, in 1971, and became the first recipient of the Sacco-Vanzetti Memorial Award for Contributions to Social Justice in 1976.

Kunstler made friends with many of his clients. He babysat Abbie Hoffman's son in the 1970s, and we have seen his friendship with H. Rap Brown. Kunstler made a favorable impression on almost everyone he met personally. In the mid-1970s Renee Cohen was flying from New York to Memphis with her son when she thought she recognized Kunstler. "I went to talk to him, and said, 'Are you William Kunstler? I'm just Renee Cohen.' He verified that he was William Kunstler, but also said that no person is 'just.' . . . I've remembered his response all these years."

After 1974, when Kunstler moved out of the suburbs into New York City, it became harder for him to stay in touch with his friends from the 1950s and 1960s. He tried. For example, he had dinner with Milton Berner, a friend from Port Chester days, a couple of times after moving to New York; Berner joined Kunstler at some meetings and they had lunch occasionally. Kunstler went out to Berner's house to help him celebrate his seventieth birthday. However, at least one of his older friends, Fred Marks, felt that when Kunstler divorced Lotte, he also divorced and cut himself off from his old friends. Marks thought it was because his longer-term friends were simply a reminder to Kunstler of how old he was.

Marks's reaction may be simply idiosyncratic, since Kunstler did keep in contact with several of his longer-term friends, albeit their relationship was never as close as when he lived in the suburbs. However, Kunstler was beginning to sense his years, and sensitivity to age was becoming real. In September 1974, in between Wounded Knee and the Attica murder trial, Kunstler tried a murder case in the Bronx, rescued from obscurity only because the prosecutor wrote a book-length account of it. As they questioned prospective jurors, the prosecutor came to realize that Kunstler was "vulnerable to attacks on his self-esteem" and, in particular, "that he was sensitive about his age."

> I could not resist the temptation to exploit this weakness. Over and over, I stressed to the panel the fact that Kunstler was an old-timer, while I was a youngster. He was a "world-famous lawyer" with a well-deserved reputation for eloquence, whereas I was just a kid who didn't even belong in the same courtroom with this great man. . . . I asked prospective jurors whether they would vote to acquit merely because the old-timer could easily get the better of me. . . .
>
> The point of such questions was not only to get under Kunstler's skin but to cast myself as an underdog. . . . Since it was one of his own favorite postures, Kunstler was not insensitive to the virtues of the underdog's role, and he was irritated by my characterization. He assured the jury that he was not that old and that I was not that young.

Along with his fans and friends, Kunstler continued to draw critics and outright enemies during the 1970s. The district attorney who tried that 1974 murder case thought that Kunstler was unprepared at least at one point in the trial. However, a federal prosecutor in the same period thought that Kunstler was "well-prepared." Occasionally a client was dissatisfied and thought that Kunstler had not put much effort into his matter. There were other critics. Carroll O'Connor, the actor who played Archie Bunker, thought that "Kunstler . . . shouldn't be practicing law," and Ishmael Reed, a black intellectual, referred to whites who were "patronizing, promoting only their type of black . . . who thought they knew what was best for us" by a label: "the William Kunstler kind of guy." Rabbi Meir Kahane called Kunstler a "Jew hater" in 1972 because "he aligns himself with the anti-Semitic section of the black-nationalist movement." The actor John Wayne put his opinion of Kunstler simply when he asked in 1971, "Why is that dirty, no-good son of a bitch allowed to practice law?"

Others with more power were asking John Wayne's same question. Following the Chicago trial, a firestorm was directed at radical and progressive lawyers under the rubric of courtroom disruption, a talisman of conservative criticism in the early 1970s. A second storm aimed at Kunstler individually with the object of stripping him of his license.

Chief Justice Warren E. Burger kicked off the first campaign by complaining about a decline in courtroom manners and decorum in speeches and interviews five times between August 1970 and August 1971. In August 1970 he told the American Bar Association's annual meeting that "unseemly, outrageous episodes" in courtrooms plus overextended trials—a clear reference to the Chicago Seven—were "undermining some of the public confidence in the entire system." Simon H. Rifkind, a leading member of the bar, denounced Kunstler by name at this meeting and termed disruptive tactics "treason" against the legal system. Kunstler replied that traditional lawyers, such as Rifkind, were mere "eunuchs" for those who could pay and that they had failed to serve America's underdogs.

Burger returned to his theme in a May 18, 1971, speech before the American Law Institute. He acknowledged that only "a tiny fragment of reckless, irresponsible lawyers" were guilty, and a reporter noted that it was "widely assumed in the legal fraternity that he was alluding chiefly to William M. Kunstler." He urged bar associations to discipline "adrenalin-fueled" lawyers who disrupt proceedings, shout, and insult all whom they encounter. Kunstler responded to reporters that this focus on disruption was "a witch hunt of left lawyers," and that the disruption issue was a "myth he [Burger] is deliberately creating to control the bar. They are afraid of this new breed of lawyer."

Others joined in the attack. Many newspapers editorialized against courtroom disruption and the *American Bar Association Journal* accused Kunstler of being the spokesman for those who were "frantically impatient, defiantly nonobjective and intolerant, and eager for violence." The federal judge Milton Pollack demanded that lawyers who showed blatant disrespect for courts be "dealt with" by their colleagues, that is, disbarred. The reporter who covered his remarks concluded that Pollack "made it clear that he was alluding to William M. Kunstler."

This frenzy was an outgrowth of a sharp swing to the right, which was a part of the return to "law and order" successfully emphasized by Nixon in his 1968 campaign. The late 1960s, as Kunstler suggested, did produce a new breed of lawyers, although only a small percentage of the whole, who saw the courts as a means to effect social change for the benefit of the disenfranchised and the lower classes. The crackdown on liberal lawyering involved more than radical lawyers, who were merely the most obvious targets. Officials also weakened legal aid offices by underfunding them and curtailed the use of class action litigation to effect significant social and economic reforms.

As the political winds shifted toward the right in the late 1960s and early 1970s, the fundamentally conservative nature of the legal profession reasserted itself. One commentator noted that "the lawyer who served as the scapegoat for professional hostility was William Kunstler. As Kunstler began to identify with the flamboyant protest of his clients, and as his clientele became more radical, he emerged as the prime target of professional opprobrium. Kunstler became the lawyer who personified the counter-culture values that jeopardized the authority of the legal system."

From 1970 to 1972 the elite Association of the Bar of the City of New York conducted a detailed study of courtroom disruption, including a nationwide survey of over 1,600 judges and interviews with dozens of lawyers, including Kunstler. Its report appeared in book form in 1973 and concluded that there really was very little courtroom disruption. It was a nonissue that had been overblown. A secondary implication of the study was that the disruption in the Chicago trial had been largely caused by the provocations of Judge Hoffman. The federal circuit court of appeals that initially considered the contempt citations concurred in that conclusion, as did Kunstler himself. The 1973 bar report specifically attacked the frenzy that had been fed by Burger's ill-considered remarks:

> The bar as a whole misconstrued, both publicly and in its private councils, the dimensions and causes of courtroom disorders. . . . [the bar] acted at that time as if the courts of this country had suddenly been taken over by an organized group of radical lawyers interested only in destroying the system that was protecting their clients. This panic did great and lasting damage to the public perception of the processes of the laws, for it exaggerated far out of proportion the problems that had occurred in a few courtrooms, particularly Judge Hoffman's in Chicago. Further, it confused zeal in the defense of clients with revolution, and thus moved in the direction, with threats of disbarment, of intimidating defense counsel.

The bar's feeding frenzy on disruption continued even after the preliminary report of the national study became available in August 1971. Even after the final report was published, the Department of Justice attacked the National Lawyers Guild and the Center for Constitutional Rights for causing courtroom disruption, which it believed was one reason it lost many political trials. Kunstler and Margaret Ratner denounced the renewed appeal for disbarment based on disruption in an article appearing in the *Nation*, "The Myth of Disruption." Other lawyers associated with the Center for Constitutional Rights also assailed the government's position in the press. By the end of 1973, however, accusations of courtroom disruption had almost entirely ceased to be used to attack radical lawyers. The late 1970s and 1980s would see significantly more powerful weapons brought to bear by the federal government against radical lawyers; threats of disbarment for courtroom disruption would not be among them.

However, in the years after the Chicago trial, Kunstler's license to practice law was definitely in jeopardy. William F. Buckley demanded his disbarment in the *National Review* in November 1971. Generally, licensing agencies will not consider discipline while an attorney's alleged misconduct is still before the courts. Kunstler appealed the twenty-four contempt citations that Judge Hoffman gave him, the appellate court reversed them, and retrial of the contempt was not held until December 1973.

This delay angered Senator James L. Buckley of New York, who introduced a bill in Congress in 1971 to permit federal courts to disbar lawyers from federal practice for "unbecoming conduct" or incitement to riot. This would circumvent the traditional methods of bar discipline by state agencies and allow the federal system to intervene directly. Kunstler attacked the proposed bill as part of "the growing attacks on the independence of the American Bar." The bill went nowhere.

In December 1973 Judge Edward Gignoux retried the contempt charges, found Kunstler guilty of two of the original twenty-four, but imposed no sentence. Immediately thereafter, the Association of the Bar of the City of New York initiated disciplinary proceedings for eventual reference to the judicial appellate division for action. In doing so, its disciplinary committee invoked a special rule, adopted in March 1971, requiring such action upon initial conviction of contempt. The rule was never used against anyone except Kunstler. However, the association ignored its longer-standing rule not to take any action while court proceedings are still pending, and Kunstler had appealed Gignoux's finding. This required that the disciplinary charges be withdrawn.

In the fall of 1974 Gignoux's order was upheld by the circuit court of appeals, and an appeal to the U.S. Supreme Court failed. Nevertheless, the disciplinary proceedings were not reinstated. In 1976 Kunstler made his much-celebrated remark that he was "not entirely upset" by the assassinations of President John Kennedy and his brother Robert since they were "two of the most dangerous men in the country." Senator James L. Buckley again demanded that Kunstler be disbarred, declaring that Kunstler's sentiments were "so repugnant to the concept of law, so outrageous, that there can be no longer any excuse but to declare him unfit to practice law." The *New York Times* editorially joined in the call for the bar to discipline Kunstler. However, the demand had no effect. Kunstler's license to practice law remained secure until the 1990s, when there was another attack.

During the late 1960s and early 1970s the most protracted struggle of the left side of the political scale, from moderately liberal to extreme radical, was opposition to the federal government's war in Vietnam. Kunstler fully participated in that effort and gave antiwar speeches in high schools, such as Westchester County High School, and at colleges. For example, he gave a formal address at Notre Dame and spoke at a demonstration at Hofstra, where a nervous administrator recalls Kunstler's speech as "a real stem-winder, mount the barricades, etc. etc." Kunstler spoke against the war to large crowds—more than a thousand Quakers from the west steps of the national Capitol—and to smaller crowds, such as 350 persons gathered at the Jan Hus Presbyterian Church in New York.

Kunstler even participated, if in a minor way, in negotiations with the North Vietnamese. In October 1969 David Dellinger and Rennie Davis received a letter from Xuan Oanh, a spokesman for the North Vietnamese delegation to the Paris peace talks. The letter said Oanh had important information to give them regarding American prisoners of war. Dellinger and Davis were then on trial in Chicago and applied to Judge Hoffman for permission to leave the country for the weekend. When their request was denied, Kunstler flew to Paris in their place, met with Xuan Oanh for two hours, and brought back promises from the North Vietnamese of forthcoming information concerning American prisoners of war.

One of the climactic moments of the anti–Vietnam War struggle came on May 4, 1970, when the Ohio National Guard shot and killed four Kent State students, two of whom had been demonstrating against the war and two of whom had merely been walking by, and wounded nine others. Kunstler was invited to speak at a rally shortly after the killings. Because the university administration would not allow him to talk at the school, the event took place off campus. Among other things Kunstler said, he promised that if students or faculty were charged with any crime arising from the incident, he would organize a team of lawyers to defend them.

In the following years memorials of the massacre were held at Kent State, and Kunstler spoke at most of them. In 1977, when the university administration decided to build a gymnasium on the site of the killings, Kunstler was a lead attorney in the fight—ultimately lost—to preserve the site as a historical monument. Kunstler had to make good on that promise to defend the Kent State demonstrators. In an apparent attempt to better position themselves from civil suits brought against the state, the authorities indicted twenty-four students and one faculty member. Kunstler helped to organize the defense team without charge. After the first defendant was acquitted, the remaining indictments were dropped.

This was neither the first nor the last of Kunstler's legal cases connected to antiwar militants. For example, he helped defend a soldier facing court-martial in Vietnam in 1966, and a priest dismissed from his parish for having preached against the war in Vietnam in 1969. He also vindicated students from university disciplinary charges for antiwar disruptions at the University of Wisconsin in 1967 and Ohio State University in 1970. Kunstler's two most interesting and significant antiwar movement cases were those of the Catonsville Nine in 1968 and Karl Armstrong in 1973. They offer considerable contrast.

On May 17, 1968, nine persons, led by two Roman Catholic priests, Daniel Berrigan and his brother Philip, entered the draft board in Catonsville, Maryland, removed 378 draft files marked A-1, and burned them with napalm in an adjacent parking lot. The fire was filmed because they had alerted the media in advance. The nine demonstrators then prayed and quietly awaited their arrests. The Catonsville Nine, as they came to be called, were a part of a wider Roman Catholic "ultra-resistance," and inspired many similar raids on draft boards in the years following.

Authorities promptly indicted the Nine for various federal felonies, destroying federal property, impeding the work of the draft board, and so forth. Dissatisfied with their first attorney, they called Kunstler. "He told us right away," one defendant recalled, "that there was no hope of our being acquitted. He understood that acquittal would rob our action of meaning. We knew that he was the man we wanted." Their leader,

Daniel Berrigan, told Kunstler that they did not want a jury, since their participation in jury selection would make it appear that they thought the legal system was legitimate. Kunstler insisted on a jury, since without an audience it would be difficult to use the trial to educate America about the war. The two men reached a compromise whereby the Catonsville Nine would accept jury trial, but would play no role in selection, ask no questions of prospective jurors, make no challenges, but simply accept the first twelve to walk into the jury box. Kunstler later insisted that had this trial occurred after Chicago instead of before, he would have deferred to the political view of the defendants and there would have been no jury. Considering the defense that Kunstler mounted, a careful screening of the jury would have greatly improved the defendants' chances of acquittal.

The defense raised two issues. First, they denied the *intent* to violate the law, since the purpose of the burning was to protest the Vietnam War and not to destroy government property or hinder the draft board. Properly speaking, this was really not a defense at all, since the required intent under the statutes with which they were charged, after the prosecution dropped a conspiracy count, was simply whether they intended to do the very acts. The defendants acknowledged that they knew that what they burned were draft files and belonged to the government. The second defense asked the jury to nullify the law by acquitting against the evidence, a process usually known as jury nullification.

Since the end of the seventeenth century, Anglo-American judges have lost all power to punish jurors for their verdicts, even if a judge believes the jury's verdict to be bullheaded or contrary to the evidence, or that the jurors have deliberately refused to follow the court's instructions on the law. Since the jury has the power to acquit any defendant contrary to the clear evidence in a case, it possesses the power in effect to nullify an unpopular law. With the knowledge that they cannot be punished for their actions, the jurors can put their own consciences above the law; they can refuse to convict a defendant because of their belief that a particular law is unconscionable.

This power of juries to nullify the law has been heralded as providing a safety valve for conscience, a method of allowing the community to send quick messages of disapproval to authority (as in the many acquittals notwithstanding the evidence in prohibition cases), and a way society can extricate itself from a wretched policy over the heads of officials who are themselves implicated in that policy. Much material has appeared concerning jury nullification (some written by Kunstler him-self), and the concept is an old and honorable one. Colonial American juries frequently acquitted defendants in the face of clear evidence of guilt to express their disapproval of British regulations. In the 1850s northern juries frequently acquitted defendants who aided runaway slaves, against clear evidence that they had violated federal statutes, to express their moral horror of slavery. On the other hand, after the war and up until recent times, southern juries frequently acquitted Klans-men or other bigots, notwithstanding clear evidence of lynching or tor-ture of blacks.

The American judiciary traditionally has taken the position that juries have the *power* but not the *right* to acquit contrary to the evi-dence. Courts have recognized that juries can do this, and they have no power to stop them. However, judges reason that to legitimize the practice would tend toward lawless anarchy, and therefore juries should not be told about that power they in fact possess. In fact, judges instruct juries that they must follow the law as the court gives it to them in its charge. That is a standard part of the juror's oath, but one that he can violate with impunity. In the Catonsville Nine case, Kunstler proposed to *tell* the jury it could follow its conscience, notwithstanding the law.

The judge refused to permit this. In his opening argument, Kunstler told the jury that the defendants would not dispute the facts as the prosecutor outlined them, and, indeed, "they think it [the crimes al-leged] is one of the shining moments in their personal lives." However, this jury had "an historic moment: a moment when a jury may, as the law empowers it, decide the case on the principal issues involved." The trial judge immediately interrupted Kunstler and told both the defense and the jury that he would instruct the jury to decide the case "on the facts as they appear from the evidence and upon the law as it may be given to them by the Court."

Again in closing argument, Kunstler quoted from a classic argu-ment from the colonial American case of John Peter Zenger, urging ju-rors to "make use of their consciences and understanding," a clear ex-hortation for the jurors to judge the war itself. Again the judge inter-vened, an almost unheard-of interruption of closing argument, to emphatically tell the jury that its duty was "to follow the instructions of the court as to the law, as we do, and should do in each and every case if our system is to survive."

However, this exchange is misleading. The short, four-day trial was not acrimonious. Under the intent side of the defense, the judge gave extremely wide latitude for each defendant to describe in emotional and moving terms why he had come to oppose the war. Leading theologians and liberals testified about the war and as character witnesses. It was a brilliant move by the judge to expedite the trial and the conviction. It allowed the defendants to fully vent their moral anger. Indeed, it did permit them to broadcast their message condemning the war to the whole world, as the media covered the trial intensively.

After the evidence was presented, however, the judge proceeded to instruct the jury that "the only bad purpose the government is required to prove in this case is the intent and purpose to disobey, to do something that the statute forbids. . . . it is no defense that he or she also had one or more other intentions, such as to make an outcry or a protest against the Vietnam war." Kunstler appealed the resulting conviction, first to the circuit court of appeals and then to the Supreme Court. Predictably, he lost the appeals.

This brief account of the trial, and also what appear to have been heavy-handed rulings by Roszel C. Thomsen, the trial judge, is, in a sense, misleading. The nine defendants, six of whom were Roman Catholic priests or lay brothers, exuded sincerity. They dressed neatly, often in clerical garb, and testified quietly, articulately, and with sincere determination. They were poets, authors, teachers, nurses—anything but wild-eyed radicals. When the jury was in deliberation, Thomsen told Daniel Berrigan from the bench,

> You speak to me as a man and to me as a judge. To me as a man, I would be a very funny sort of man if I had not been moved by your sincerity on the stand and by your views. . . . I have not attempted to cut off any of these reasons so that you can spread it to the people as a whole. I have done that as a judge. I think many people will be inspired.

When the jury had left to deliberate, the defendants asked if they could engage in dialogue with the judge. Thomsen agreed, and a remarkably poignant discussion ensued that expressed the limitations felt by both judge and peace militants on their freedom of action. Thomsen and the defendants struggled for nearly half an hour in a dialogue that disclosed the moral compulsions and viewpoints to which they were, respectively, committed, in dialogue hauntingly reminiscent of Sophocles's and Anouilh's *Antigone*. It encapsulated an America wrenched out of shape by the government's policies in Vietnam. Finally, one of the defendants asked the judge if they could recite the Lord's Prayer. A quick check with the prosecutor revealed that the government had no objection, "in fact, it rather welcomes the idea." Judge, defense counsel, prosecutors, and spectators stood while the principal defendant, a Roman Catholic priest, led them in reciting the Lord's Prayer.

The Karl Armstrong case is more somber because there was a fatality. On August 24, 1970, Karl Armstrong, along with helpers acting under his direction, bombed the University of Wisconsin's Army Mathematics Research Center, causing many millions of dollars' worth of damage. That much was intended in an effort to block what they regarded as the federal government's killing machine. What was not intended was that the blast, coming at about 3:40 A.M., would kill a brilliant young physicist and wound others. Armstrong fled to Canada, was extradited, and was charged with first-degree murder by the state and numerous other charges by the federal government.

Kunstler joined the defense team. It made a plea bargain with the prosecutors: a plea to second-degree murder, a maximum of twenty-five years imprisonment, federal and state time to run concurrently, and a two-week sentencing hearing in which they would be free to bring out all the horrors of the government's war in Vietnam in mitigation. After a massive parade of witnesses, Kunstler gave a brilliant summation, stressing how it had been the children of the 1960s who had led the opposition to the war, and only later had their parents joined. He argued that for their leadership, the youth had been beaten, gassed, imprisoned, and spied upon by the government. The judge was moved but sentenced Armstrong to the maximum twenty-five years. He left prison on parole in 1980.

While defending Armstrong, Kunstler slept on a couch in an old rowhouse apartment on Frances Court in Madison (while the Catonsville Nine were tried in Baltimore, Kunstler stayed with his sister, Mary; she says he was a slob). While he was in Frances Court the FBI spied on him from a nearby warehouse. That actually turned to Kunstler's advantage one night. When a drunk tried to siphon gas out of his car, a squad of agents seized the miscreant and whisked him away; the FBI had saved Kunstler's gas.

Kunstler participated as one of the lawyers for many figures whose legal entanglements began in the 1970s and extended for decades: Murray R. Gold, the New York stockbroker who was tried four times for the murder of his in-laws; Joan Little, the black woman who was acquitted of the killing of her North Carolina jailer while defending herself against his sexual advances; Joanne Chesimard, now Assata Shakur, a member of the Black Liberation Army accused of killing a New Jersey state trooper; and William R. Phillips, the rogue cop who served as a star witness on New York City police corruption and was then accused of murdering a pimp and prostitute.

Kunstler continued to defend many blacks, activists and not, charged with heavy felonies. However, in the 1970s Kunstler was expanding his practice to help other minority groups as well as blacks. In this period he began significant representation of Indian militants. He also began representing Puerto Rican militants seeking independence, and Chicano activists, charged with murder and other serious felonies.

Kunstler also had some lighter cases. He represented an illegal climber of the Statue of Liberty; a Michigan convict elected to the Rhode Island House of Representatives while awaiting extradition; and Marvin Barnes, an erratic professional basketball player. Barnes told the press following an arrest for hitting his wife, "Bill called and cussed me out. He told me he'd come down and give me a whipping. I took it as constructive criticism and said it would never happen again. It's his job to keep me in line. That's gonna be a hard job."

Bizarre things seemed to happen regularly with Kunstler and his practice. In 1975 the FBI's chief informant in the Patty Hearst case alleged that the agency had offered him $10,000 "to entrap" Kunstler into a crime. When the press asked the FBI about the allegation, its spokesman "withheld comment." Also in the mid-1970s a woman reported two startling allegations to the Department of Justice: that Kunstler had paid a $10,000 bribe to kill a client's indictment and also that Kunstler was a sort of double agent and secretly worked for the FBI. The bureau investigated and took the charges absolutely seriously until it concluded that the woman was crazy. The investigating agents ribbed Kunstler that they might release the report that he was their secret employee anyway, for fun. Kunstler became hysterical and said it would ruin his practice if potential clients thought he might work for the FBI. The false rumor was never released.

After the violent, bomb-prone Weathermen had gone underground, they occasionally contacted Kunstler for information about the political situation, various clients, and legal developments. The cloak-and-dagger aspects of their meetings appealed to Kunstler; he would be directed to report to a remote location, a diner perhaps, and there await escorts who would take him to a safe house. These meetings also appealed to Kunstler's need for belonging: "Meeting with the Weather Underground gave me a chance to demonstrate that I was ready, willing, and able to take some chances; it increased the camaraderie we felt with each other."

During the Chesimard trial, Kunstler unsuccessfully moved for a mistrial on the basis that a juror, whom he named, had violated a sequestration order by sneaking out of the jurors' motel to buy a bottle of whiskey. The judge denied Kunstler's motion and concluded that his information was "a collection of double and triple hearsay." After the case was over and the jury released, the named juror read the newspapers, learned of the accusation, and sued Kunstler for defamation. A reluctant Kunstler settled the suit just before its trial date, publicly apologized, admitted that the statement was untrue, and paid a small monetary settlement. The *National Law Journal* titled its article "Kunstler Eats Crow."

Kunstler participated in at least one case in the 1970s that had monumental importance. It started out as a White Panther radical bombing case in Detroit. Led by Kunstler, the defense team made standard motions for the government to reveal wiretap evidence. In response, the Nixon administration made the extraordinary claim that the president had inherent powers to wiretap for national security, and if national security were the purpose, he need not obtain a judicial warrant. Kunstler argued that the government was asking for "carte blanche to violate the Fourth Amendment." The district court agreed, and ruled that there was no "national security" exception to the Constitution; the government had to obtain warrants. The federal government appealed to the circuit court of appeals, and Kunstler personally argued the case. The appellate court also held that the federal government had no authority to wiretap without court approval under a national security exemption.

The federal government appealed again, to the U.S. Supreme Court. Kunstler had been lead counsel throughout the district court and circuit court proceedings, but the defense team as a whole believed that Arthur Kinoy, who had considerable experience before the Supreme

Court, ought to make the argument before the high court. "This decision," Kunstler wrote, "wounded my ego substantially, and I walked around for days with a burning sensation in the pit of my stomach. Eventually, however, I came to realize that we would do best with Arthur."

Kunstler, Kinoy, and the team won the case by a vote of eight to zero. Justice Rehnquist did not participate since before his appointment to the Supreme Court, as a deputy attorney general, he had been a primary advocate of the national security exemption. This was one of the most important cases that Kunstler worked on in his entire career. Even though he did not make the victorious argument before the Supreme Court, his advocacy before the district court and circuit court was of critical importance in framing the constitutional issues involved. This placed the case in the best procedural posture for an ultimate victory condemning the high-handed attempt by the government to abrogate the Fourth Amendment whenever it claimed that national security was involved.

In the early 1970s Kunstler had both familial satisfactions and dissatisfactions. His daughter Karin had married and was a lawyer. His second daughter, Jane, graduated from the University of Wisconsin in 1970 and was on her way toward becoming a doctor. Then too, Kunstler's first grandchildren, Karin's twins, Daniel and Jessica, arrived in the early 1970s. Kunstler was so overjoyed with his grandchildren that he put their pictures on his personal checks.

Kunstler was not as happy with his marriage, which, through his own actions, had lost much of its luster. Kunstler began to see his wife as a glamourless housewife, without the allure of the many women with whom he had established liaisons or one-night stands. Still, the marriage tottered on, and the lack of intimacy Kunstler mentions in his autobiography is probably overdrawn. Then too, Kunstler was bored with suburban life in Westchester. During the high points of Chicago, "people [were] poised with microphones and pens at my every word. And then suddenly I was back in Westchester, going to the drugstore, taking out the laundry."

In the fall of 1972 Kunstler took on the defense of five blacks accused of a mass murder at the Fountain Valley Gold Club in St. Croix, Virgin Islands. He asked two acquaintances, Michael Ratner and his wife, Margie, both progressive lawyers, whether either wanted to work on the case with him. Margie Ratner was interested and accompanied him to the Virgin Islands for the pretrial motions and trial in the late spring and fall of 1973. Margie was a very attractive woman, twenty-six years his junior. Kunstler began an affair with her, and then something quite unexpected happened: he fell in love with Margie.

Kunstler moved out of his Mamaroneck home in late 1973, just before the leadership trial for the Wounded Knee siege. He commuted back and forth from St. Paul for the trial, spending weekends with Margie in her Greenwich Village apartment. Within a short time they shared an apartment, and within a couple of years thereafter, Bill and Margie divorced their respective spouses and married each other.

In 1976, while they were still living in a tiny apartment in the Village, they saw an advertisement for a Greenwich Village triplex for rent. Kunstler called the number, and the owner of the building asked if he were the same Kunstler who had been a major in the Philippines in 1944. It turned out that Kunstler had helped to get Leo Calarco, the owner of the unit, to a hospital after he had been wounded. Kunstler had not thought twice of it, but Calarco believed Kunstler had saved his life and was only too happy to rent his triplex to Kunstler for a low sum. In 1979 Kunstler bought the house, a narrow, Federalist-period row house, from Calarco's estate. Kunstler lived in this house, at 13 Gay Street, a short street near Sixth Avenue, until his death. He located his office in the semi-submerged ground-level floor.

Kunstler dearly enjoyed being back in New York City, and especially felt good about being a part of his neighborhood. He enjoyed knowing his neighbors, gladly represented local merchants and patronized local restaurants, especially Waverly Coffee Shop on Sixth Avenue, where he always pointed out his picture up on the wall. Mary recalls walking with her brother in Greenwich Village:

> People would come to him, and he'd stop and hug 'em and talk to 'em and he loved being recognized wherever he went. . . . He loved being recognized. . . . some people don't want people butting into their lives but Bill loved it. And he always had time for people. He was never in a hurry and he was always willing to give his time. He was a very patient man. Even if it held him up from some appointment, he gave his time. He never was in a rush.

With Margie came her dog, a cockapoo named Sam. Kunstler's earlier love of animals revived, and he came to celebrate Sam. For the rest of his life Kunstler surrounded himself with cats and dogs, in the house as well as in his office. Also with Margie came a summer home in West Shokan, a village in the Catskill Mountains, that she and Michael Ratner had owned together. Kunstler spent several weeks each year in West Shokan and thereby acquired a second neighborhood in which he could act as a good neighbor and satisfy his strong need for belonging. In West Shokan Kunstler again represented locals with enthusiasm. Here, this world-famous attorney defended a butcher put upon by the local power authorities in a trial in the tiny Ulster County Courthouse. Here, this notorious, radical lawyer served without charge as counsel for the modest Olive Free Library, his local summer library.

Life at home for Kunstler in the 1970s meant constant harassment from the FBI. In 1989 the FBI finally admitted that during the 1970s it had searched the garbage of National Lawyers Guild members' homes, which would include Kunstler, and placed taps on their telephones without court warrants. In 1978 someone broke into his office and stole only his file of telephone numbers. Kunstler suspected the FBI because in 1970, when he had lost another address book on an airplane, it was turned over to the FBI, which photocopied its contents and sent copies to its field offices. The Internal Revenue Service audited Kunstler almost every year.

More daughters quickly arrived: Sarah on November 5, 1976, and Emily on June 24, 1978. Kunstler reveled in his new fatherhood, admiring his new daughters and lavishing his attention on them. He talked constantly with the babies, as he did with everyone, just as though they were adults. In 1986 he told a reporter, "there's no way a man of my age can get old being around two smart kids like them," and in his 1994 autobiography he wrote that "with Sarah and Emily around, although I am ancient, I can't act decrepit. I have to show off for them."

Kunstler became far more involved in the raising of Sarah and Emily than he had been with Karin and Jane. He shared the chores and bottles and diapers when they were babies and the picking-them-up and dropping-them-off when they were girls. There were a number of reasons for this change, none of which suggest he loved Karin and Jane any less at all. The times were different, and men had discovered the "new fatherhood's" joy and insistence on paternal child care. Then too, Margie was a more demanding woman, and she insisted on his help. This greater paternal involvement is also a familiar pattern with men who have second families. Their greater hands-on experience with their second family comes from a combination of guilt over the first family and a sense of a Lord Jim–like second chance suddenly handed to them. Bruce Jackson once asked Kunstler point-blank whether he thought he was a better father with Sarah and Emily. He answered, "Yeah. I talk to these. I play with them."

Remarkably, Michael Ratner, the man Margie divorced to marry Kunstler, remained a good friend of both Bill and Margie. He admired Kunstler's work, highly esteemed Margie even after the divorce, and was very helpful to Bill and Margie. He babysat their children, and even cared for Sarah when she was a baby while Margie argued in court.

When Kunstler left Lotte, she told him, "before you get out of here, I want to know whether I was right or wrong about these things," and enumerated the names of the dozens of women she knew about. He admitted them all. Then Lotte asked him, "have you learned anything from this?" Cruelly (later in his autobiography he apologized for saying it), Kunstler responded, "I learned I don't want to do this same thing to Margie." Apparently he meant it. In the 1970s he still enjoyed young women running after him, and throughout his life he enjoyed talking with friends and reporters about his past exploits. However, there is no evidence he engaged in any further womanizing, and many indications to the contrary.

Although Kunstler published no books during the 1970s, he kept intellectually busy by publishing half a dozen political and legal journal articles, including several in the *Nation,* a dozen letters to the editor or opinion columns for the *New York Times,* and even a totally nonpolitical piece on a ballet version of the Lizzie Borden murder case. Kunstler continued to make speeches throughout the 1970s, although at a less hectic pace than immediately following the Chicago trial. He spoke at unusual places, such as a Roman Catholic mass, but his primary locale remained colleges. Beginning at the end of the 1960s and then continuing throughout his life, he stressed in his talks what he regarded as a Melvillian theme. Men must combat evil daily, even though they will never actually prevail. A stalemate is the best to be hoped, but we must struggle as we dare not lose the fight totally. He often quoted from G. K. Chesterton, "I tell you naught for your comfort, / Yea, naught for your desire / Save that the sky grows darker yet / And the sea rises ever higher," and from Goethe, "Of freedom and of life he only is deserving / Who every day must conquer them anew."

Sometimes Kunstler's speeches were impromptu, as at the 1970 convention of the National Lawyers Guild. Some fifty of the attendees, younger graduates and students, could not afford tickets for the traditional banquet and gathered outside the Washington, D.C., hotel ballroom, waiting for the program to begin after the other three hundred delegates finished their meal. After the young members had made several raids to purloin some of the dinner rolls, the guild posted members to guard the doors, so the organization would not get into trouble with the hotel management. Kunstler saw an economic injustice in this and a chance to make a stump speech. He went outside the hall to the students and, a witness recalls, "made a rabble-rousing speech and publicly burned his [dinner] ticket." According to another observer, the students carried Kunstler on their shoulders into the hall.

After leaving his brother's firm, and for most of the 1970s, Kunstler practiced by himself, assisted by a secretary, a paralegal worker, and student interns. Briefly he practiced in partnership with a black lawyer, C. Vernon Mason, who became notorious for his representation of Tawana Brawley. Kunstler told reporters and other lawyers that "he earned a handsome income from speeches, television shows and other public appearances. His courtroom work, in effect, was voluntary. He did not need it to put bread on his table." Ronald Kuby, Kunstler's associate and partner in the 1980s and 1990s, notes that "Bill created a sort of myth that he lived on speaker's fees. And that's just not true." It was probably not true for the 1970s either. Occasionally Kunstler admitted that he could not support himself from lectures and writing, and that he needed an income from his practice. Still, the speaking fees were undoubtedly substantial enough that they enabled Kunstler to handle far more no-fee defenses than would have otherwise been possible without that income.

Nevertheless, Kunstler did take far more than his share of pro bono trials, cases in which he passionately believed and took on without charge. Even in fee cases, Kunstler seldom received what his talent was worth. In the 1970s Kunstler sometimes wistfully fantasized about practicing in a law commune, but he always recognized that he loved the comforts of his middle-class life too much to live communally.

In 1970 Kunstler, like many radicals, was optimistic about the decade's prospects for the movement and for the leftist agenda. In June 1970 he prophesied to a group of business executives that "unless there is some shift in economic policies, some reconsideration of the concept of private property and some unequivocal act that would hasten the end of the Vietnam war, Armageddon is at hand. . . . there are elements in our society that are preparing for guerrilla warfare." That fall he returned to the same theme in his *Playboy* interview:

> I think there is a large reservoir of people, particularly among the young, who will turn the Seventies into a decade of movement from protest to resistance. . . . even though there are no formal alliances among the political dissidents in the United States, there is a growing feeling of comradeship and of working together. So, on the one hand, you have massive repression, but on the other, you have the beginnings of massive resistance.

Kunstler's prognostication for the future of the movement in the 1970s turned out to be poor. In fact, the left wing splintered into separate groups promoting rights and power for male homosexuals, lesbians, Chicanos, blacks, Indians, and militant feminists. The FBI's COINTELPRO caused some of the fragmentation, and the traditional tendency of the Left to splinter contributed the rest. Not only did the Left split up in the 1970s, but its component parts actively attacked each other as homosexuals were pitted against straights, feminists against traditional males, and Jews against blacks. Overriding all of this was the fact that the Vietnam War was clearly winding down from late 1970 onward, as Nixon accelerated his policy of withdrawing American troops. The mass basis of the movement, as distinct from the dozens of special interests, by the early 1970s had achieved its goal: the young had forced Johnson to forgo a run for reelection and then forced Nixon to begin to wind down the war.

By 1972 even the optimistic William Kunstler admitted, "there is a feeling that the movement is dead. There just isn't the same furor. I think it's the national mood. Nationally, the pace of and interest in the Left has certainly dropped way down." In 1973 the students at the Daley College campus of the City Colleges of Chicago became aggrieved over a curricular shift from liberal arts to more technical courses, and a variety of community issues. The students took over the administration building, and the president of the "alternative" student government invited Kunstler to attend, never thinking that he would.

However, Kunstler did show up for this modest protest at a modest community college. Pamela Capraro, the student president, recalls that

Kunstler was "unbelievably interested in what we were doing." Nancy LaPaglia, at the time a teacher there, remembers that Kunstler praised the student activists and said he was "heartened to see what was happening on our campus. It made him sad, he said, to see activism die elsewhere. What a pleasure to see it enduring on this two-year college campus." The faculty did not have the heart to tell Kunstler that the students at the community college, perhaps more traditional and restrained than the earlier college activists, were just beginning to be politically daring; it was not a matter of protest surviving from the 1960s.

Two years later, in 1975, Kunstler told a student crowd at Vanderbilt University that college students lacked revolutionary spirit. "American students have no spirit left," he told the audience. Within minutes, a young man with the wrong kind of spirit stepped onto the stage and splattered Kunstler with a chocolate cream pie.

Kunstler became somewhat depressed in the late 1970s. There was a lull in his career in the sense that there were no high-profile media cases. On the other hand, "there are still a lot of unknown ghetto kids who need a good lawyer, and who will get only a court appointed lawyer if I'm not around." While this was satisfying, because Kunstler had deep and sincere compassion for the underclass caught in the maws of the police and courts, still these cases did not feed his ego and need for attention and admiration as had the causes and the high-profile cases of the 1960s and early 1970s. His daughter Karin believes that those earlier years were such a high point that "it was hard for him not to continue that momentum. . . . [later, in the late 1970s and early 1980s] he was always charged up, but didn't "get the same results. . . . I don't think it was as exciting to him."

In 1979 Kunstler reflected on the decade to an acquaintance. In retrospect, he thought that too much of the movement had been attached to opposition to the Vietnam War and not larger social problems. It was, he thought, a mistake not to build the antiwar movement around bigger principles than just the war. He told his friend he was depressed. The next year, a young lawyer rode on a courthouse elevator with Kunstler and reminded him of when they had first met, in the early seventies. Kunstler said that that seemed ages ago, and then said suddenly, "I meet people all the time. They say things like, 'You defended my father in the Freedom Riders in Mississippi.' You feel like such an anachronism—like you should've died. And behind their eyes, I often see what's unspoken: 'I thought you were dead.'"

That is Kunstler at his most depressed, and uncharacteristic of the man. The movement never revived, certainly not its massive quality. Indeed, the nation's sentiment after the ending of Vietnam seemed to move only, and increasingly, to the right. However, the lull in the public character of Kunstler's career, of the late 1970s and early 1980s, dissipated by the mid-1980s. Once again, and to his great satisfaction, Kunstler would become a public figure in his advocacy.

11

Indian Defenses

THE 1960s AND early 1970s saw a rising political consciousness and series of demands from Native Americans that paralleled those of the Black Power movement. They complained about the misery and poverty of American Indians, both on the reservations and in urban areas, discrimination, alcoholism, and neglect of government promises of education and medical care. American Indians also attacked the larger historical record of the government's treachery in dealing with Indian tribes: blatant violations of treaties, willful destruction of Indian culture and language, and interference with tribal forms of governance.

The more moderate American Indians demanded merely that the government keep its promises, reform the Bureau of Indian Affairs (BIA), and compensate the various tribes for stolen lands and violated treaties. The more militant questioned the legitimacy of the government's role in Indian affairs altogether, and demanded the strict enforcement of nineteenth-century treaties, including the return to Indian control of vast tracts of land guaranteed to tribal groups under those treaties. The most prominent actions of the militant American Indians during these years were the 1969 seizure of Alcatraz Island in San Francisco Bay, the 1972 Trail of Broken Treaties March to Washington that resulted in the brief occupation of the BIA building, and the seventy-one–day occupation in 1973 of Wounded Knee, a tiny hamlet on the Pine Ridge Reservation in South Dakota.

The American Indian Movement (AIM) sponsored the Trail of Broken Treaties and the Wounded Knee occupancy. The movement was born in the late 1960s in the Upper Midwest. By 1973 two individuals dominated AIM's leadership: Dennis Banks, an Anishinabi (Chippewa) from Leech Lake, Minnesota, and Russell Means, an Oglala Lakota from the Pine Ridge Reservation. Both men were given to inflammatory statements denouncing government treaty violations and praising traditional Indian life, although both had spent the majority of their own lives in urban settings. This touches on an interesting distinction between Indian militancy and other social movements of the time. Young people were the natural constituency of both the anti–Vietnam War and Black Power movements. However, AIM, because of its insistence on enforcement of treaty rights and the return of vast tracts of land to direct Indian control, garnered the support of many older, full-blooded, traditional Indians. Its Indian enemies often were half-blooded, less traditional Indians living in reservation villages rather than in the countryside, and who had significant ties to the BIA.

In few places was this split between traditional, full-blooded Indians and half-blooded, village-living Indians clearer than on the Pine Ridge Reservation. In the early 1970s controversy roiled this windswept, poverty-stricken reservation. Many residents, especially the full-blooded, traditional Indians who lived in the countryside, loathed the tribal chairman, Dick Wilson, a half-blood plumber who lived in a reservation village. They accused Wilson of corruption and theft. In a gesture of in-your-face defiance, Wilson surrounded himself with a private militia he openly called his Goons (Guardians of the Oglala Nation). The Goons terrorized many of the residents; significant numbers of beatings and murders on the reservation went unresolved. Beyond a hatred for Wilson individually, many of the traditional Indians opposed the very form of tribal government favored by the federal government—elected council and tribal chairman usually drawn from the more assimilated half-bloods—and longed for the more traditional governance by full-blooded tribal chiefs.

Undergirding these concerns were localized complaints of poverty, unemployment, weak schools, poor health facilities, and especially a strong sense of having been cheated out of the sacred Black Hills and other lands specifically guaranteed the Oglala in the treaty of 1868. A feeling of hopelessness pervaded Pine Ridge. Many reservation residents blamed the BIA for not taking a firmer hand with Dick Wilson. Ironically, the BIA was then moving away from its earlier course of close control of tribal activities toward what it thought a more liberal policy of assistance and even deference toward the elected tribal leadership. However, in the eyes of the traditional Indians of Pine Ridge, that liberal policy made the BIA and its local representatives coconspirators in the thuggery and corruption of Dick Wilson. BIA Superintendent Stanley Lyman kept a daily diary during the Wounded Knee siege, and his account amply documents both the depth of the natives' hostility toward their elected government and Lyman's genuine surprise in discovering this.

Traditional chiefs and a reservation organization allied with traditional elements within the Oglala invited AIM to come onto Pine Ridge Reservation to dramatize their grievances with the government and with Dick Wilson. The FBI began to monitor AIM at least as early as the BIA occupation in 1972, planted informers within the organization, and by early February 1973 was aware that AIM planned to enter Pine Ridge. The authorities believed that the BIA building in Pine Ridge would be a takeover target, and accordingly, that small town swarmed with U.S. marshals, FBI, BIA police, tribal police, and even U.S. military representatives. Instead, AIM held rallies in smaller locations and on the evening of February 27, 1973, seized the hamlet of Wounded Knee, threw up roadblocks, and fired their guns at approaching traffic.

Heavy symbolism freighted the selection of Wounded Knee as the village seized. It was here in 1890 that the federal government conducted its last great Indian slaughter. More than two hundred men, women, and children were mowed down by Hotchkiss machine guns as they attempted to surrender to the Seventh Cavalry; for such bravery a grateful government awarded Congressional Medals of Honor to its soldiers.

The AIM militants seized food and equipment from the trading post and dug bunkers. The federal government quickly threw up its own roadblocks and bunkers, manned primarily by the FBI. After a few days, both AIM and the government permitted those who wished to leave the village to pass their barricades, but most residents remained. At times, Wilson's Goons maintained additional roadblocks. The ensuing seventy-one days saw many days of tranquility with no gunfire, but there were many days of intense firefights; the positions of both sides took an estimated 100,000 rounds. The gunshots killed two Indians and injured two federal officials, one severely. Approximately two hundred members of AIM and their supporters occupied the village, although this number fluctuated considerably. Notwithstanding the roadblocks, the security was porous, and nightly traffic of supplies and personnel, including reporters, ran up and down the hills and gullies leading to the village. On the federal side, approximately 250 FBI, marshals, BIA police, and a couple of military officers participated.

The militants demanded that three separate congressional committees conduct hearings on Indian treaties, investigate the BIA, and specifically investigate the Sioux reservations in South Dakota. The government responded that it would only negotiate the manner of AIM's surrender. An Iroquois chief for whom Kunstler had done some legal work the year before, and Pedro Bissonnette, a leader of the Pine Ridge traditional Indians, both asked Kunstler to become involved. He did so, and first arrived at Wounded Knee in early March, probably Saturday, March 3, 1973. The next day the government offered to allow the protesters to stack their weapons and leave peacefully; no arrests would be made, although some might follow later as a grand jury, already assembled, handed down indictments.

Many of the AIM Indians thought they ought to accept the offer; AIM had occupied Wounded Knee almost a week and it had already made a political point that had been widely publicized. Kunstler counseled against ending the siege early. "Of course, it's more dangerous to stay and not take this easy way out," he argued. "But on the other hand, what the hell did you do this for, anyway? Walking out, the time is lost. You've only been here a week." Had the government known that Kunstler actively encouraged the continued occupation of Wounded Knee, it likely would have indicted Kunstler as well. Means burned the government's offer before the television cameras.

Kunstler left Wounded Knee, returned on March 9 to participate in what appeared to be a fruitful turn in negotiations, then left permanently a few days later. Negotiations resulted in many abortive efforts at settlement until May 8, 1973, when the insurgents finally ended their occupation. Eventually, AIM supporters received a total of 185 indictments for crimes arising out of the occupation. Even while the occupation was continuing, sympathetic lawyers, headed by National Lawyers Guild members, organized a legal defense group, Wounded Knee Legal Defense/Offense Committee (WKLDOC, or "wickledock"). Almost all were outsiders to the region, sympathetic to AIM. Most South Dakota lawyers, beholden to local interests and bias, refused to represent these unpopular defendants.

A 1973 Memorial Day conference of fifty-four lawyers and legal workers from more than eleven states established the defense tactics and strategies. Many of the original attorneys withdrew after the group decided to coordinate defenses through a committee and to apply funds raised toward bail and material expenses of the defense, such as transportation and investigation, rather than attorney fees.

The government elected to try the leaders of the occupation, Russell Means and Dennis Banks, in a separate trial before the other defendants. Their trial would set the standard. The government did not charge them with insurrection or treason, which would have expressly opened their political stance. Instead, it charged Means and Banks with burglary of goods from the trading post, theft of a car, assault on two federal officers, obstructing federal agents in the performance of their lawful duties, and conspiracy.

Ken Tilsen, a St. Paul attorney experienced in representing activists, served as the overall coordinator of the defense effort. He and Kunstler represented Russell Means; Mark Lane (of Kennedy assassination *Rush to Judgment* fame) together with two other attorneys represented Dennis Banks. Kunstler and Lane led the public attack, but Tilsen really directed the defense effort. Federal judge Fred Nichol, chief judge of the South Dakota district and a Johnson appointee, moved the trial from South Dakota to St. Paul, Minnesota, where it was thought that anti-Indian prejudice would be less. Nichol traveled with the case to try it himself.

Jury selection began on January 8, 1974, in the St. Paul federal courthouse, and by February 5 a jury had been selected. That jury heard ninety-four witnesses, whose testimony comprised a transcript of 21,765 pages. The government called its first witness on February 12 and rested on July 24. Of that six and a half months, however, the taking of testimony took less than sixty days. In contrast, the defense called only five witnesses and put on its case in three days. Following a prosecution rebuttal case and closing arguments, the jury began deliberations on September 12.

The trial consumed over eight months, far longer than the actual occupation, and far longer than the Chicago Seven trial. Several factors account for its length, notwithstanding the brevity of the defense case. A case within the case, concerning prosecutorial misconduct, ran for approximately one month between mid-March and mid-April. Furthermore, Judge Nichol was liberal in granting delays to Kunstler, the other attorneys, and even the defendants, to allow them to attend to other pressing legal matters. Last, while the defense's own case was short, its cross-examination of prosecution witnesses often extended over days. In addition to the standard search for inconsistencies and contradictions, the defense sought openings to develop its issues of government violation of treaties, mistreatment of Indians, and specifically the corrupt and horrific conditions on Pine Ridge. In this manner, the political issue was depersonalized. Although the jury heard Banks and Means conduct opening arguments and some cross-examination (they were granted cocounsel status midway in the trial), they never took the stand.

The Wounded Knee leadership trial presented a classic political defense. Even before the jury was selected, Kunstler charged that the defendants were "on trial for what they believe and not what they did," and the media reported that the defense strategy "will be to put the Federal Government on trial—to accuse it of seizing Indian lands in the 19th century through trickery, and subjugating a once-powerful nation of Indians with false treaties and broken promises." Strategic decisions were made collectively, and the defense attorneys deferred to the politics of the defendants. Affirmative lawsuits brought by the defendants or sympathizers of the defendants against Dick Wilson, the FBI, and other federal and state officials swelled the dockets.

Defense attorneys, including Kunstler, participated in fund-raising rallies. By midtrial, Kunstler had made six or seven speeches a week that brought in $5,000 toward the $30,000 per month it took to keep the defense going. He himself drew only $35 per week and was housed and fed by friends. The court's ruling that Means and Banks were indigents opened up government funds. The defense received $30,000 through May, apparently used for investigation, bail, and other expenses, rather than attorney fees.

Kunstler did not throw himself into the St. Paul social scene with the same abandon as he had done in Chicago. He commuted back and forth to New York on weekends. In part, that reflects the greater allure of Chicago's Near North Side, but a more fundamental reason was that by 1974 Kunstler was in love and living with Margie Ratner in her Greenwich Village walk-up on Perry Street. He was not yet ready to reveal that publicly. When a reporter asked in 1974 about his roaming throughout the country and its effect on his marriage, Kunstler did not mention that he was separated and living with a paramour, but responded disingenuously that "My wife has a job. She has her friends and she has her own life."

Kunstler's style in this political trial was dramatic; he made accusations of excessive security and protested judicial efforts at courtroom control. Judge Nichol expelled him once, and the trial was briefly interrupted as marshals carried Kunstler out of the courtroom. A serious episode occurred in late August, when Judge Nichol threw Kunstler and Lane in jail overnight for contemptuous conduct. Margie came out from New York, retrieved the two men with a writ, and the judge and attorneys issued a joint statement of regret. There were disagreements within the defense committee over how far to push Nichol. As a matter of principle, Kunstler wanted to keep up the pressure, arguing, "it demystifies the court . . . you have to show the jury he's not a God." Nichol for his part thought that Kunstler was trying to treat him as he did Julius Hoffman, to "get my goat" so that he would "overreact." He refused to fall into that trap. Tilsen believed that Kunstler and Nichol had a love-hate relationship, and Nichol himself years later remembered that Kunstler "was a good lawyer."

Kunstler made great use of the trial to demystify and educate, a classic element of the political trial. At the opening of trial Kunstler hoped that much of the case might be tried beyond the courtroom "through the media and the people," sentiments echoed by Dennis Banks at an opening night rally of two thousand at the University of Minnesota campus. Kunstler and the other defense attorneys provided a regular flow of news releases and interviews. They gave reporters a preview every morning and summaries of the day's highlights at the close of each day. Tilsen praised Kunstler's feel for what news angles the press would use. Kunstler said the defense committee read the daily papers "religiously" because, in the classic sentiment of a radical lawyer, "it's our obligation to help the defendants reach the community." The media obliged; at the trial's opening, representatives appeared from the three television networks, all major domestic newspapers, and the German and Soviet media. It also helped the cause of publicity that Marlon Brando came twice to the trial to show his support for the defendants.

In late January 1974 Kunstler made appearances before the St. Paul Press Club and a local Jaycees dinner. The *Minneapolis Tribune* covered the Jaycees dinner and reported that several of the "clean, trim middle-class audience" had been deeply impressed by Kunstler. The reporter noted such comments as "When you hear the wild man talk he doesn't seem as wild as he does in the press" and "I think the government has built him up to look like a radical." Judge Fred Nichol attended that Jaycees dinner and allowed to the reporter that he had a growing respect for Kunstler.

Kunstler gave a large number of speeches, but one more should be singled out. In late March, in the middle of the hearing on government misconduct in the trial, Kunstler spoke to the St. Paul Rotary Club. He vigorously attacked government wrongdoing, and particularly its covert operations, and charged that "this once great country has been reduced to a nation of cheats and liars and burglars." Once again, Nichol attended. When asked by a reporter what he had thought of the remarks, Nichol said that he agreed with "a great deal" of what Kunstler had said.

What was happening was that, in a small way, both the jurors and the trial judge were becoming radicalized. Certainly Judge Nichol moved through the trial from a position of sympathy with the government at the outset to sympathy with the defendants at the close. Two important reasons explain this shift. First, the trial took place against the backdrop of the denouement of Watergate and the Nixon impeachment. Government misconduct and illegality appeared on every evening's news broadcast. Second, in a massive record of prosecutorial misconduct, the judge and jury could see before their very eyes the same sort of government prevarication, espionage, and duplicity that was involved in Watergate. By the time the trial ended, the original theme of the government's trickery toward American Indians and the Oglalas had largely become a theme of the government's trickery toward Dennis Banks and Russell Means.

At an early stage in the prosecution, Judge Nichol issued standard discovery orders, requiring the prosecution to turn over to the defense copies of statements given by prospective witnesses, documents that would be useful to the defense, names of all informants, and so forth. The prosecution made representations that there were no wiretaps or informants. As the trial went on, it increasingly appeared that the documentation turned over by the FBI was incomplete. Worse, some copies had been altered. After the alteration was discovered, Judge Nichol permitted the defense to go through the FBI files for themselves. Defense attorneys then discovered a total of 131 documents that should have been turned over pursuant to the earlier orders but had been retained. The judge's ire at the FBI seemed to mount daily, with increasing prosecutorial revelations and retractions, and he began making statements about the FBI not being what it once was, and using words such as "negligence" and "irresponsibility" to describe the behavior of the prosecutors.

In March 1974 the defense discovered that the government had installed a wiretap on a telephone in Wounded Knee, and had used that tap not only to monitor the defendants' ordinary telephone conversations but also to intercept calls between AIM and its attorneys, ordinarily protected by the attorney-client privilege. The defense filed a motion to dismiss, and a month-long hearing was held on the wiretaps and other prosecutorial misconduct. Judge Nichol found the wiretap illegal and excluded any evidence obtained from it.

Nichol blistered the prosecution. He called the government's response to his discovery orders "dilatory" and scored the false testimony given by the FBI's special agent in charge. However, he found this misconduct based on negligence and not intentional wrongdoing. On that basis he refused to dismiss the case. The judge reminded the government that a prosecutor (and also an FBI agent) "is the representative not of an ordinary party to a controversy, but of a sovereignty whose obligation [is] to govern impartially . . . and whose interest, therefore, in a criminal prosecution is not that it shall win a case, but that justice shall be done."

Nichol sternly warned the prosecution that the actions of the FBI

> have brought this court to the brink of dismissing this case. . . . the government should be forewarned that this court will continue to be acutely aware of its compliance, or lack thereof, with this court's discovery order and with the rules of law. . . . If further misconduct occurs on the part of the government, I would certainly consider a renewed motion by the defendants. It is my deepest hope and expectation that such a renewal shall not occur.

The judge heard the dismissal motion by himself. Once it was resolved, the jury returned to hear testimony. Shortly after the jury's return, the prosecutor again put on a witness whose statement had not been previously provided to the defense; he handed it to defense counsel only at the very last moment and claimed that the FBI had just given it to him. Judge Nichol exploded before the jury. "Someone better tell them [FBI] to get off their high pedestal." He called the FBI's actions "complete disrespect" for the court, said he could do something about their "arrogance" and that "one of the things I can do about it is dismiss this case entirely on the ground of government misconduct, which apparently appears to be deliberate."

The following day the prosecutor argued that Nichol's openly "hostile attitude" might prevent the government from receiving a fair trial. He cited news accounts of Nichol's agreement with Kunstler's criticism of the FBI campaign against the Black Panthers. Nichol retorted, "I don't give a damn. I agree with much of what he says." Somehow the prosecution recovered and staggered on until it rested and the defense put on its brief three-day case. Then once again the prosecution shot itself in the foot when it called Louis Moves Camp, a former AIM member, as a rebuttal witness.

At first, Moves Camp appeared to be a perfect prosecution witness. The government had no problem establishing that the trading post at Wounded Knee had been broken into and items taken, or that federal agents had been assaulted, or that a vehicle had been stolen. The difficulty was tying Banks and Means to these acts, establishing whether they participated in or encouraged them. Moves Camp supplied all the missing links, claiming that he had been in Wounded Knee during most of the occupation and had observed activities of the defendants that clearly linked them to the charged crimes. Kunstler grilled him thoroughly on cross, to pin him down specifically about times and dates and also to bring out pending felony charges against Moves Camp, with the suggestion that his testimony was manufactured to obtain lenient treatment. At one point during Kunstler's examination, the witness accused the attorney of "trying to put words in my mouth." Immediately, Kunstler shot back, "that's already been done by others."

Next, the defense brought in unimpeachable evidence in the form of television station logs, newspaper photographs, and handbills advertising speeches, as well as live witnesses, that established beyond real doubt that Moves Camp had been in California during much of the time he testified he was in Wounded Knee. That was not all. The defense learned that FBI agents had been entertaining Moves Camp at a Wisconsin resort prior to his court appearance. While under FBI protection, Moves Camp engaged in some drunken sexual conduct with a young woman he and the FBI agents met in a bar. The local police jailed him for rape, and the FBI (arguably) persuaded the local district attorney not to prosecute because of his important testimony needed at the St. Paul trial of Banks and Means. When the FBI's efforts to protect Moves Camp from local prosecution first came to the federal judge's attention, the federal prosecutor misrepresented the incident, falsely calling it a public intoxication charge and nothing more substantial.

All these revelations came during the closing weeks of the trial. The absolute nadir occurred late in the trial while Kunstler was cross-examining a witness. Much earlier the court had issued an exclusion order prohibiting prospective witnesses from staying in the courtroom. Kunstler noticed that a side door to the courtroom was slightly ajar. Slowly he made his way over to the door and yanked it open. Two clumsy FBI eavesdroppers tumbled out into the courtroom. Still, the prosecution tottered on. Then came the summations, "as good a closing," Kunstler thought, "as I have ever done. I was so emotionally involved that I gave it everything I had." The case was submitted to the jury on September 12, 1974.

The jury did not receive all the original charges, as many were dismissed for lack of evidence tying the defendants to the crimes. Nichol dismissed the charge of obstructing a "law enforcement officer lawfully engaged in the lawful performance of his official duties incident to and during the commission of a civil disorder" for the interesting reason that the FBI and marshal activities were not "lawful" within the meaning of that statute. Federal law specifically prohibits the use of military personnel and equipment, both present at Wounded Knee, to quell a civil disorder without a presidential proclamation.

When the jury began deliberations, Nichol dismissed the alternate jurors. Then, on the second day of the jury's work, one of the jurors became ill and was hospitalized with partial paralysis and high blood pressure. At that point, it was later learned, the jury had voted unanimously to acquit the defendants of the conspiracy charges but was divided in favor of acquittal on the remaining charges. When it became clear that the juror could not return, Judge Nichol called the attorneys to a conference and noted that there were four alternatives: the judge could have the deliberations continue with eleven jurors, which was his personal choice; he could declare a mistrial; he could dismiss the case; or he could enter an acquittal. The defense accepted the offer to proceed with eleven jurors; the prosecutor said he must wait for instructions from Washington. Pending receipt of the instructions, the defense filed a motion for acquittal, citing its earlier motion and the continued course of prosecutorial misconduct.

R. D. Hurd, the lead prosecutor, then publicly complained that "I don't think we've gotten a fair shake in this trial," and speculated on where a new trial might be held, doubtlessly believing he would make fewer mistakes in a new trial, that he would draw a more prosecutorially minded judge, and that the defendants would lack the energy and resources to remount such a vigorous defense. Acting on the recommendations of the trial prosecutor, the Department of Justice refused, as was its legal right, almost never exercised, to accept the verdict of an eleven-person jury.

Judge Nichol was livid, both that the government would prefer tactical advantage over justice and also at the prospective waste of eight months of many people's time. He called his court into session, treated the defense motion for acquittal as a motion for dismissal, granted the motion, and dismissed the prosecution forever. He based the dismissal on the continued prosecutorial misconduct, on the misleading information provided about the military's involvement, and above all, on the government's refusal to accept the verdict of the remaining jurors. "The misconduct by the government in this case," he noted, "is so aggravated that a dismissal must be entered in the interests of justice." "Because of the series of incidents of government misconduct, which, I feel, form a pattern throughout the trial, I am forced to conclude that the prosecution acted in bad faith at various times throughout the course of the trial and was seeking convictions at the expense of justice." The judge explained that he believed the government had not made an honest effort to comply with his discovery orders, that with Moves Camp the prosecutor had offered and then failed to correct obviously false testimony, and with another witness, that the prosecutor's use of "testimony that was directly contradicted by a document in his possession was inexcusable." He saved his chief wrath for the decision not to accept a verdict of the remaining eleven jurors. Nichol noted that although the government had a statutory right to reject the smaller jury, the prosecutor's reasoning violated his duty "to insure that justice is done, and not simply to seek convictions."

> the chief prosecutor [R. D. Hurd] made several statements to the media to the effect that he would not agree to accept the verdict of eleven jurors because he felt that the chances of obtaining a conviction from the remaining jurors were "slim." This blatant attempt to obtain a retrial and thus correct the many errors of the past eight months is a violation of the duty of the prosecutor. . . . Although it hurts me deeply, I am forced to the conclusion that the prosecution in this trial had something other than attaining justice foremost in its mind. . . . The fact that incidents of misconduct formed a pattern throughout the course

of the trial leads me to the belief that this case was not prosecuted in good faith or in the spirit of justice.

Never shamed by its own actions, two days later the Department of Justice announced that an award would be given to the Banks and Means prosecutors, citing their "superior performance" in the case that had just been dismissed for misconduct. This paralleled precisely the Congressional Medals of Honor given to the Seventh Cavalry for their murderous actions at Wounded Knee. The defense had always charged that the government's purpose was not a conviction but rather "to break the spirit of the American Indian Movement by tying up its leaders and supporters in court and forcing us to spend huge amounts of money, time and talent to keep our people out of jail, instead of building an organization that can work effectively for the Indian people." The probable truth of that analysis is shown by the government's appeal from Nichol's decision, an appeal so lacking in merit that it was dismissed by the Eighth Circuit Court of Appeals, and also a revealing admission made years afterward by the assistant prosecutor to an interviewer:

> I think to some extent the prosecutions accomplished as much by getting dismissed or an acquittal as they would have had there been a conviction. Because I think Russell Means and Dennis Banks realized even if you get off, sitting nine months in a courtroom isn't what they want to do, and that's what potentially would happen if they did this again.

Ten of the sixteen jurors and alternates in the Banks/Means leadership trial wrote a letter to the United States attorney general, urging him to dismiss the remaining charges pending against the dozens of other defendants. The government refused, yet again suggesting that the purpose of the trials was not to secure convictions. Indeed, the conviction rate of all of the original indictments arising out of Wounded Knee was only 7.7 percent, compared to an average in federal courts located in the Eighth Circuit of 78.2 percent, a comparison that the defense would argue amply proves the harassment purpose of the prosecutions to begin with.

One last indignity befell the Wounded Knee prosecutors in the spring of 1975. Douglas Durham, a security guard for Dennis Banks, confessed that he had acted as an informant for the FBI. In his capacity as security guard, Durham attended defense strategy meetings with the defendants and their attorneys. The FBI then admitted that Durham contacted them fifty times during the course of the St. Paul leadership trial, and that the FBI had notified Hurd and the other prosecutors of this informant. True to form, the prosecutors had earlier represented to the court and defendants during the trial that the FBI files "contained no material which could arguably be considered as evidence of an invasion of the defense legal camp."

Kunstler ultimately saw the Wounded Knee trial in a bittersweet light. "It was a wonderful victory," he realized, but he "mistakenly thought [it] meant that we were on the brink of a real turnaround in America. I felt that if a federal judge could be convinced, after some months of listening to all the facts about AIM and the FBI, that injustice had been done, the cleansing process in America had begun. Of course, I was wrong. What happened in that courtroom in St. Paul was an aberration."

While working with the Wounded Knee defendants, Kunstler immersed himself in the Indian culture. The Oglala invited him to their lodges, and he participated in many of their ceremonies, smoking the sacred pipe, and engaging in dances and songs. The Oglala gave him an Indian name, Wambli Wicasa, variously translated as "Soaring Eagle" or "The Eagle That Watches over Us." They gave Kunstler his own pipe and, significantly, an eagle feather he had earned as a warrior. Indeed, Kunstler would retain his tribal status as a warrior. In the years ahead he became engaged in the defense of many Native American causes.

The ending of the occupation of Wounded Knee did not halt violence on the Pine Ridge Indian Reservation. From 1973 to 1975 there were sixty-three documented murders on the thinly populated reservation, which many residents related to Wilson's Goon squad. The FBI apparently did not investigate these Indian deaths, but did maintain a presence on the reservation to enforce federal law and keep pressure on AIM supporters.

On June 26, 1975, two FBI agents drove separate unmarked cars into an area of the reservation known to be inhabited by AIM supporters. They were following another vehicle, ostensibly to serve an arrest warrant for a minor theft. A gunfight broke out between the agents and a dozen or more AIM supporters who occupied the hills surrounding the point where the FBI vehicles halted. No one knows exactly how the fight started. Although wounded by shots coming from a distance, the officers were murdered by shots fired at close range. A grand jury eventually indicted four men: Darelle Dean Butler, Jimmy Eagle, Leonard Peltier, and Robert E. Robideau. Peltier fled to Canada, and the government dismissed the charges against Jimmy Eagle. Because of anti-Indian prejudice in South Dakota and a large amount of adverse pretrial publicity, the trial of Butler and Robideau was moved to Cedar Rapids, Iowa. Kunstler became the lead attorney in a team of five lawyers that included Margie Ratner.

The defense contended that after the shootout the FBI engaged in a massive disinformation program, systematically portraying the engagement as a deliberate ambush. The trial began on June 7, 1976, and at that time the FBI issued a nationwide alert describing in great detail projected violence by AIM over the July 4 weekend. The alert claimed that a group of AIM members known as "Dog Soldiers" would be armed with M-16 rifles, blow up buildings, shoot policemen and tourists, and assassinate the South Dakota governor. The defense maintained that this and other warnings were deliberate efforts to roil the waters at the Butler/Robideau trial. When potential jurors arrived for examination of their qualifications to serve, they saw twenty United States marshals in the courtroom, visible SWAT teams on the roof, and a police helicopter constantly flying around the courthouse. This, the defense charged, was designed to create hostility and show the jury that these defendants were truly dangerous men.

Even though this would be a "hinterlands jury," as Kunstler later described the Cedar Rapids jury, he did his best to educate it and the Cedar Rapids community. As usual, Kunstler made himself available to the media and gave speeches before local groups. He gently but thoroughly questioned the prospective jury panel about what they had heard about the shooting and what they thought about Indians, constantly challenging them to think and talk about their beliefs. He even broke the ice about what they might think about him. One question, humorous on its face, yet searching in its implications, was "What do you think of an aging lawyer with long hair?" Celebrities, such as Marlon Brando and Dick Gregory, came to the trial to show their support for the defense. Kunstler felt that Marlon Brando's presence especially impressed the Cedar Rapids townspeople.

The prosecution had plenty of evidence that Butler and Robideau were among the Indian shooters from on top of the hills, but the case that these two defendants were those who actually shot the agents at close range was largely circumstantial, except for two discredited witnesses who claimed to have heard incriminating statements of the defendants. The defense pressed on with two related theories: first, that the FBI precipitated the violence by the disinformation it had spread about AIM and its implicit condonation of the Goon violence, and second, that the AIM members acted in self-defense. The Indian group had women and children with them in camp and claimed that, in the context of so many reservation murders, they had reasonable grounds to fear these two strangers who came racing up in unmarked cars with blazing guns.

In aid of these theories Kunstler had considerable freedom to present information that was damaging to the government. The COINTELPRO program had been directed not only against the Black Panthers but also against the American Indian Movement. Kunstler called Senator Frank Church, who testified about his congressional committee's investigation of COINTELPRO and how that FBI program had resulted in great damage, fear, and paranoia among the targeted organizations. He also subpoenaed Clarence M. Kelley, the director of the FBI. Kunstler went over with Kelley the wires and alerts that had been sent out in his name warning of the Dog Soldiers and the threats of AIM disruption and violence. When asked by Kunstler whether there was a "shred of proof" to support those allegations and warnings, Kelley responded, "I know of none."

Kelley handed Kunstler yet another triumph by becoming angry. Kunstler baited Kelley with a series of questions designed to show how the FBI acted more as a military organization on the Pine Ridge Reservation than it did in Cedar Rapids, armed with automatic weapons, army jackets, and bulletproof vests. Kunstler suggested that this was because Pine Ridge was more dangerous, and Kelley replied that it was more dangerous to the FBI agents, two of whom were slain. Kunstler then asked whether it were not true that hundreds of Native Americans had also been killed, alluding, of course, to the Goon activity. At this point Kelley lost his composure, raised his voice, and stated that the FBI agents had reason to be concerned about their own lives.

At that juncture Kunstler cleverly phrased a question that summed up both of the defense theories: FBI causation of the violence and self-defense. Kelley fell squarely into the trap with his voice raised and clearly out of control:

Q [KUNSTLER]: One of the reasons for equipping them this way is that there is a fear that strangers who come into isolated areas on the Pine Ridge Indian Reservation who are not known to the people there, might themselves come under attack out of fear. Isn't that correct?

A [KELLEY]: I don't care who it is that comes in! If they are threatened they have the right to protect themselves!

Kunstler then commented, "Exactly. Exactly. No more questions, your honor." Kunstler stressed to the jury his theory that this was precisely what the defendants were doing, in an isolated area of the reservation, protecting themselves and their families from unknown strangers. After five days of deliberation and once reporting itself deadlocked, the jury acquitted both defendants of all counts.

Leonard Peltier was extradited from Alberta, Canada, and tried in 1977. A jury convicted him of both murders, and he is currently serving a double life sentence. Kunstler did not act as his trial attorney, as he was then trying another murder case. However, after Peltier's conviction Kunstler served as lead counsel for numerous appeals, writs, and motions to attempt to obtain a retrial. After numerous failed appeals in the circuit courts and U.S. Supreme Court, Kunstler felt that "it was time for a new voice," and former U.S. attorney Ramsey Clark took over the lead role.

The Peltier case became and still is a cause célèbre among liberal and leftist groups. Peltier's supporters, urging a new trial or executive clemency, have included Don Edwards, U.S. representative and former FBI agent; Senator Daniel Inouye; the Reverend Jesse Jackson; Robert Runcie, Archbishop of Canterbury; Bishop Desmond Tutu; Robert Redford; and Amnesty International. Aside from the general issue of federal oppression of American Indians, two legal issues linger over the Peltier case. First, the FBI obtained Peltier's extradition from Canada in large part by the use of very damaging affidavits from an Indian woman whom the FBI should have realized was incompetent. She was so mentally deranged that the prosecutor did not call her as a witness at the trial.

Second, the defense obtained crucial FBI documents, in 1981 and long after the trial, under the Freedom of Information Act. These documents include ballistic testing that suggested that the casings found near the bodies of the slain agents did not match Peltier's gun. The prosecution was legally required to provide this potentially exculpatory evidence to the defense before trial, but did not do so. The appellate courts that considered Peltier's numerous petitions criticized the government's conduct of the case, but found that it did not rise to the level of prejudice necessary to reverse.

Kunstler spent an enormous amount of time and energy handling Peltier's appeals. In addition, he made speeches, wrote letters to the editor, and authored two magazine articles about the case. Although Clark became lead counsel in 1992, Kunstler remained very much involved with the Peltier matter for the remainder of his life.

Yet another matter continued over the years that related to the Wounded Knee experience. Dennis Banks and Russell Means had participated in a protest at the Custer, South Dakota, courthouse on February 6, 1973, just before the Wounded Knee occupation. At issue was the undercharging of a defendant who had killed an Indian with only second-degree manslaughter. A fight broke out between the activists and the police, and the courthouse burned. In 1975 Banks was convicted of assault and riot charges that arose out of that incident.

Banks heard reports that he would be murdered in a South Dakota prison. There was bad blood between Banks and William Janklow, the state attorney general, whom Banks had previously caused to be disbarred from the Pine Ridge tribal courts. Although the state attorney general had his office in the capital, Janklow personally supervised Banks's prosecution in Custer. Thinking his life was in danger, Banks jumped bail and fled to Oregon, then California, in advance of his sentencing.

At that point Kunstler began representing Banks, and with Marlon Brando and Jane Fonda collected 1.4 million signatures on a petition urging California to refuse South Dakota's request for extradition. California governor Jerry Brown offered to permit Banks to serve any prison sentence in a California prison. Banks accepted the offer; Janklow refused. Brown refused the extradition on the basis that Banks's safety would be in danger in South Dakota. Janklow sued Brown, but the California Supreme Court upheld Brown's decision. Banks stayed on in California for seven years, teaching at Stanford and in the University of California system, and became the chancellor of a community college. In 1982 the successful California gubernatorial candidate George Deukmejian campaigned on a promise to send Banks back to South Dakota.

In December 1982, days before Deukmejian's inauguration, Banks and his family fled to the Onondaga Indian Reservation just south of Syracuse, New York. Kunstler worked to persuade New York governor Mario Cuomo to grant Banks sanctuary of the same sort as had Brown. Cuomo refused, but indicated that his law enforcement personnel would not enter the Onondaga lands because of its sovereign status. However, Janklow, now South Dakota governor, did not request extradition from New York but instead asked the federal government to issue a federal interstate flight warrant and arrest Banks. The warrant was issued, but a standoff ensued as the FBI also declined to enter the Onondaga Reservation.

Banks, however, felt confined in the tiny 7,300-acre Onondaga Reservation and could not adequately support his family. Against Kunstler's advice, he decided to surrender to South Dakota authorities. In this circumstance, Kunstler did all he could to prevent the fear of harm from being realized. Kunstler widely publicized Banks's fear of Janklow's revenge in numerous interviews that led up to the surrender. Although Janklow's actions in regard to Banks could be characterized as petty, even malicious, it would be difficult to persuade hardnosed reporters that a governor of a state would actually encourage the murder of a state prisoner. Kunstler took a different tack. In arguing that the South Dakota authorities ought to grant Banks probation, he pointed out to reporters that "everybody knows the Governor's attitude toward him [Banks]." He suggested the likelihood that some prisoner serving a long term might "get the feeling that if he did harm to Dennis, maybe then the Governor would pardon him."

Kunstler beat the news drum so loudly that thirty reporters assembled at the Rapid City, South Dakota, airport where Banks surrendered to state authorities. An angry law enforcement official criticized the reporters for giving Banks so much publicity. However, Banks, in his own mind, had a well-founded fear of serious injury in South Dakota. Kunstler, accommodating to that fear, did all he could. Turning the spotlight of the media onto the surrender, Banks's fear of injury, and the reasons for that fear made it less likely that South Dakota could permit it to happen.

Things turned out well. Banks surrendered on September 13, 1984, received a three-year sentence, and left prison on parole in December 1985. Notwithstanding Banks's release, Kunstler pressed on with an appeal, ultimately lost, since he "felt as a lawyer and a friend of Dennis that it was my duty to at least point out the things that we thought were wrong with the trial." That pro bono appeal, uncompensated, dogged work when his client already had been released on parole, is an example of an endearing Kunstler character trait: enduring loyalty to his friends.

Throughout the remainder of his career, William Kunstler represented many Indian defendants and their causes. Some were simply ordinary criminal charges of murder, theft, or weapons violations, not overtly political, although Kunstler tried to politicize as many as possible. Other Indian cases did have express political overtones as, for example, his representation of two Tuscarora Indian activists who seized hostages in a North Carolina newspaper office in 1988 in order to draw attention to various grievances and his mid-1970s representation of a Blackfoot Indian mother charged with child neglect for withdrawing her daughter from school following the child's receipt of racial slurs.

Kunstler helped the Golden Hill Paugussetts, a Connecticut Indian tribe with a mini-reservation, in a long-running battle with the state authorities over taxes on cigarette sales from their tribal stand. Throughout a long legal battle from 1993 to 1995, Kunstler defended the tribe's sovereignty and its chief's refusal to collect state taxes. He also aided a traditionalist faction on the St. Regis Mohawk reservation in 1979–80, when more than one hundred Mohawks barricaded themselves in a dispute with New York authorities. A serious dispute arose in the Canadian town of Oka, Quebec, also involving a band of Mohawks. Oka planned to build a golf course on what the Mohawks claimed was ancestral land. In July 1990 this led to an armed standoff between more than two thousand Mohawks and the Quebec police. One officer was killed in a brief gunfight, although it was uncertain whose bullet felled him. The Canadian Mohawks invited Kunstler to Canada to advise the barricaded Indian activists, and he was briefly involved in those efforts.

In addition to expressing his concern with the Peltier case, Kunstler wrote letters to the editor correcting what he thought were inaccurate or insensitive articles about other Indian matters. The Native Americans remembered and respected Kunstler's loyalty to their causes. Representatives of many Indian nations attended the memorial service for Kunstler, held at the Cathedral of St. John the Divine in November 1995. The ceremonies opened with Indian drums and chants and closed with a pipe ceremony. During the memorial, Clyde Bellecourt, a cofounder of AIM, praised Kunstler and warmly called him "a true warrior."

12

The 1980s and a More Diverse Practice

KUNSTLER'S LAW PRACTICE was very diversified in the 1980s, and the variety of his cases even greater than in the 1970s. Kunstler continued to feel the radical lawyer's need to justify the cases he took on a political basis, and that became increasingly difficult. The standby rationale often employed was that the status of the defendant as a member of an oppressed group made the case political. However, the 1980s also saw some subjectively political cases, where the defendants acted with conscious political motives. The Macheteros prosecution became a major one.

In 1983 a Wells Fargo security guard overwhelmed two fellow guards in West Hartford, Connecticut, and absconded with $7 million. It was the second largest holdup in American history. The robbery was the work of an armed underground group, Los Macheteros, working for Puerto Rican independence, who used the proceeds to finance their revolutionary activities. The FBI made mass arrests of thirteen persons in 1985, and over the next few years made additional arrests so that a total of nineteen suspects were charged. Most of those charged were claimed to be coconspirators, involved with Los Macheteros but not directly with the robbery, and who had never left Puerto Rico. Nevertheless, they faced trial in Hartford.

The case presented the usual opportunities for Kunstler to complain about the lack of bail and the government's overkill with security, with hundreds of machine gunners on the streets and roofs of buildings ("This excess of security and paranoia is an attempt to color this case, to make the people of Connecticut think they are a bunch of dangerous animals"). He also complained about the open bail hearings ("The danger is that the press picks up on the uncorroborated evidence of the FBI. The effect is to poison the minds of prospective jurors by referring to these people as terrorists"). Kunstler and other defense counsel took every opportunity to portray the case as a political prosecution, and yet another example of the federal government's oppression of the Puerto Rican patriots who wanted independence. True to their typecasts, the prosecutor accused Kunstler "of using the hearing as a soap box," and the judge indignantly said, "I find no political overtones to this case."

Following the classic model of the 1960s and 1970s political trial, the defense filed an affirmative lawsuit ($1 million demanded of a jail guard who beat a defendant for displaying a Puerto Rican flag) and alleged that the prosecution was merely an effort to impede the defendants' political efforts ("They've [federal officials] accomplished their purpose, even if they lost the case, it is hard to keep up your activities while trying to defend yourself in such a momentous prosecution").

If it was the same tune as in the earlier political trials, it now sounded off-key. Things were different, and mostly because there was no mass movement behind the defense efforts. True, there were some rallies and fund-raisers held in Puerto Rico. In the United States, however, there was very little support. The most massive demonstration, held on the eve of the first arrests, drew only one thousand people. They paraded down Park Street in Hartford, Kunstler marching alongside the mother of the former robber-guard. There were issues in the case, especially illegal surveillance on the defendants' personal lives, that in other circumstances might have aroused anger and outcry. The sharp American swing toward conservatism in the 1970s and beyond was part of the reason for the lack of enthusiasm. Another reason was that, while the directly illegal activity—the robbery—was here, the political purpose—independence for Puerto Rico—was "over there," and concerned very few Americans. The defendants were ultimately convicted.

Kunstler's representation of several Sikh defendants also demonstrated the public's indifference to foreigners' political activity. In 1986 he represented Gurpartap Singh Birk, accused of conspiring to assassinate the Indian prime minister when he was visiting the United States and of attempting to foment revolution in India through weapons purchases. Kunstler tried to politicize the case, contending that Birk was being prosecuted in an attempt to win favor with India and Indian efforts to stop the Sikh people from creating an independent state. Kunstler did win an acquittal on the assassination portion of the charge, but failed to rouse much public attention. Likewise, there was general lack of interest in the fate of two other Sikhs that the Indian government sought to extradite for various murders and other terroristic activities.

The press showed intense interest in only one of the many bizarre twists and turns of the extradition case. The federal prosecutor, Judy Russell, prepared and then mailed death threats to the judge and to herself, with the result that there was an intense security alert for the extradition hearing and the defendants were forced to appear at the hearing in chains and shackles. When Russell was later prosecuted, a federal judge acquitted her of obstructing justice by reason of insanity, a "total whitewash" in Kunstler's view.

None of Kunstler's other consciously political defendants in the 1980s garnered much public sympathy or support. Kunstler represented Yu Kikumura, discovered in April 1988 on the New Jersey Turnpike with three large, pellet-packed bombs. Kikumura was probably a member of the Japanese Red Army, an international terrorist organization, and probably on his way to bomb a navy recruiting station in Manhattan.

Nor did Thomas Manning generate much excitement. Manning had an extended saga during the 1980s that almost matched the saga of H. Rap Brown, although Manning was considerably more violent. Kunstler represented Manning in three matters. Manning was a member of the Sam Melville-Jonathon Jackson Unit, later renamed the United Freedom Front, a white radical group mostly from New England. The group advocated violent change in the American political and economic structure, and opposed what it regarded as American imperialism. Manning was underground with his wife, a fellow revolutionary, and their three children for the ten years preceding his arrest in April 1985. Manning described himself to reporters as "a member of the armed, clandestine underground. . . . Weapons are a part of my life." That he might have to spend the rest of his life in prison was simply "a price you have to pay for fighting against the United States government."

He was charged, along with other members of the group, with crimes in three locales. Federal authorities in New York charged them with nineteen bombings and attempted bombings from 1982 to 1984 of federal military installations and the facilities of large corporations that did business with South Africa. New Jersey state officials wanted Manning and a single confederate for the murder of a state highway trooper. Additionally, federal prosecutors in Massachusetts alleged a conspiracy to overthrow the United States government, racketeering charges arising from the activities in New York and New Jersey, and also a series of ten bank robberies perpetrated to fund the group's operations. Some additional bombings were involved in the Massachusetts charges, including that of the Suffolk County Courthouse in Boston that injured twenty-two people.

The New York matter came up for trial first, in October 1985, and continued for several months. Kunstler's argument was that, while the defendants were "sympathetic" to the reasons that led to the bombings, the government offered no direct evidence of the defendants' participation. Instead, Kunstler urged, the government had "out of desperation" relied on "white lies" and "fabrication" to build a circumstantial case. Regarding the defendants' safe houses and paramilitary training in heavy armaments, he urged the jury, "Don't let that world—even your dislike of it and your feelings about it—influence you. The only issue before you is whether they are guilty of the charges."

During the thirteen days of deliberations, the lawyers occasionally played Trivial Pursuit, which prompted Kunstler to quip to a reporter that he hoped to draw the question, part of the game by then, that asked for the name of the defense lawyer in the Chicago Seven case. The jury returned guilty verdicts on more than two dozen counts but could not agree on forty-five other charges, which the judge set for retrial. Kunstler commented: "What the judge did was cruel and heartless. The Government got convictions on enough counts to give each defendant a long sentence and to seek more is asking for a pound of flesh." Manning received a sentence of fifty-three years in prison and thus became, as Kunstler saw it, "another victim of a political trial."

In the New Jersey case, tried in 1986–87 but involving a 1981 shooting, Kunstler took the tack that the trooper pulled Manning over for a traffic violation, "recognized him [as a fugitive] and tried to execute him without a trial." Manning shot the trooper, Kunstler conceded, but only in self-defense. Kunstler categorized Manning to the jury as "a proud and dedicated revolutionary who believes one must fight with more than meaningless platitudes the evils in our national and international society." He described Manning more pointedly to reporters as "a North American anti-imperialist freedom fighter dedicated to the overthrow of this government." Kunstler made his usual pitches for mistrial, including an exclusion of blacks from the jury and the usual heavy security of political-revolutionary trials ("I think that any potential jurors who saw that would say, 'My God, what do we have here—wild animals?' I think that's the impression they [the prosecution] are trying to convey").

Kunstler, doing this case without compensation, was clearly following Manning's line. He used descriptions of Manning that were dictated by Manning's own self-image. The defenses in both the New York and New Jersey cases were crafted so as to not offend Manning's revolutionary principles or deny that he was a revolutionary. Similarly, when the defendants refused to rise when the judge entered the courtroom, neither would their attorneys. Kunstler explained that "the defendants have no respect for the system. They see the court as an enemy. They won't show false respect. The attorneys remain seated to show unanimity with their clients." On the other hand, the entire defense table rose when the jury came in. "The jurors," according to Kunstler, "are not part of the system. The defendants rise to show their faith in the people." Not to be shown as faithless, the prosecutors began to rise for jury as well as judge. Notwithstanding the defendants' faith, the jury, in a confusing compromise verdict, found Manning guilty of a killing committed during a felony but could not reach agreement on his codefendant. Manning received a life sentence, with parole only after thirty years, to be served following the completion of the fifty-three-year federal sentence for the New York bombings.

Kunstler's participation in Manning's federal prosecution in Massachusetts was most remarkable for his being thrown off the case by the court. The Boston federal judge initially granted the defendants' request that Kunstler be appointed as one of their court-appointed attorneys. That would mean Kunstler would be paid at the minimal statutory rate for federal defenders. The U.S. attorney then objected that because Kunstler was from out of state, there would be additional expenses to the government, and that furthermore he was not licensed to practice law in Massachusetts. Throughout his career, Kunstler was licensed only in New York. However, it is a common courtesy to allow an out-of-state lawyer to represent a client who wants his representation in a specific case, notwithstanding the lack of a local license. The situation in the Manning case was different, however, since Kunstler was seeking a court appointment, which would carry some small compensation, and not merely the right to represent Manning on a private basis.

Notably, the judge rescinded Kunstler's appointment only after the prosecutor complained. In a contentious hearing, Kunstler loudly protested, but the judge insisted that the defendants would have to either accept court-appointed counsel from an official list or represent themselves. Thomas Manning insisted, "we are all political prisoners here. We demand political lawyers." As the judge prepared to leave, Kunstler shouted at him, "Why don't you reconsider before it's too late?" Then, in a manner reminiscent of the 1960s, federal marshals removed Kunstler and his cocounsel from the courtroom, Kunstler shouting, "take your hands off of me."

Outside, Kunstler told reporters, "it's an outrage." Later, he charged that "they are participating in a lynching of these defendants solely because they want to teach the American public that revolutionaries are going to be treated differently and more harshly than anybody else in the country. This is an orchestrated conspiracy between magistrates, a judge and U.S. attorney." More moderately, the head of the Massachusetts Civil Liberties Union observed that the judge changed his mind about Kunstler's representation only after the U.S. attorney complained. "The magistrate, without a hearing, revoked the appointments, giving the impression that this is not an independent judiciary but essentially a tool of the U.S. Attorney's office."

Kunstler pointed out that most of the attorneys on the court-appointment list were former prosecutors, and asked, "who would take a lawyer that came out of the same office that is prosecuting you. Anyone in his or her right mind would reject such a lawyer." That is a revealing statement, both superficially appealing and fundamentally flawed. First, Kunstler's argument would apply not just to public defenders but to the majority of the private criminal bar. A great number of criminal defense lawyers, if not the clear majority, have had experience in a prosecutor's office at some early point in their careers.

More fundamentally, the statement assumes that criminal defense lawyers, and especially those who accept court appointments, are as ideologically driven as Kunstler himself was. Most attorneys think of themselves as quite independent, which is to say, if anything, that they are driven by money but not ideology. Most attorneys, at least at a conscious level, would have no difficulty working for a prosecutor one year, giving their best efforts to convict, and the next year, in private practice, giving their best efforts to acquit. Indeed, it is the essential amorality of lawyers, not any ideological drive, for which they are often criticized. There *may be* some problem in that attorneys on the appointment list, or in public defender's offices, might not be as vigorous in their defense as Kunstler thought proper. This would arise from fear that judges would no longer appoint them or that they would be removed from a public defender's office, usually judicially supervised. However, a pecuniary fear of loss of position or appointment is not the politically ideological stance that Kunstler rather bluntly assumed every former prosecutor carries away from that job.

Thereafter, the judge transferred the trial to Springfield, which meant that a different judge would decide the thorny issue of representation. Kunstler claimed that the judge "could never admit that he made a mistake. The judge found a way to get out of it." The new judge permitted Kunstler to serve as an unpaid legal adviser for one of the defendants, but Kunstler growled that the defendants already had such long sentences in the other matters, another trial was simply "wasting the taxpayers money. . . . [The overkill] exhibits the fear of the government of these small revolutionary groups. They can't tolerate them." Then in the fifth month of jury selection, the government abruptly dismissed Thomas Manning from the case, and for Kunstler the matter was over.

However, consciously political clients were the exception during the 1980s. Kunstler often had to politically justify his participation in specific cases on the basis that the client was a member of an oppressed group. A good example was black politicians, and Kunstler represented many of them on a large variety of charges. Kunstler believed that the FBI and the Department of Justice systematically targeted black leaders in an effort to set them up, convict them of crimes for which whites were not targeted, and thereby disgrace blacks generally. "The pure number of black officials being investigated tells me there's a conspiracy and a belief at [the Justice Department] that blacks are not qualified to be in positions of leadership." This contention cannot be dismissed out of hand, since the indictment rate of black officials is far higher than that of white officials.

An example is Alcee Hastings, a black federal district court judge in Florida, charged with a bribery conspiracy in 1983, although not accused of taking money himself. He was acquitted of a criminal charge in 1983, but a special five-judge panel was convened to consider his fitness to remain on the bench. After taking evidence, later shown to have been in part falsified by the FBI, the panel recommended impeachment. Hastings was impeached, and the Senate empowered a committee to try the case and make a recommendation to the full Senate.

Kunstler became involved at this point. He attempted to enjoin the Senate consideration, alleging double jeopardy and also that the

Constitution required the full Senate to try the case. Kunstler asked the question, "Why this total vendetta against him?" and found the answer "grounded in racism." The federal district court rebuffed his effort for a stay, and the committee recommended impeachment, which a divided Senate accepted. Kunstler persisted with the litigation, and in 1992 a district court set aside the Senate's conviction on the grounds that the Constitution required the full Senate to try impeachments. The government appealed that determination, but the appellate court affirmed the need for a trial before the full Senate. Meanwhile, Hastings had won a House seat and was sitting in Congress.

What probably sustained the government's drive against Hastings was that as a judge he criticized President Reagan's policies frequently, especially the policies regarding Haitian refugees, some of which he held illegal. Kunstler denounced the proceedings against Hastings in letters to the editor and received a reply from Representative Don Edwards, who opined that the evidence against Hastings, "much of it developed after his criminal trial, is overwhelming." This evidence would be that obtained by the judicial panel in its hearings. In 1997 the Department of Justice revealed that the FBI "may have provided misleading testimony about the results of forensic tests used in [the] impeachment proceedings." A memo written by one agent indicated that another agent's testimony before the panel contained false statements and distortions "intended to strengthen the case against Judge Hastings."

Another objectively political civil case arose out of the notorious Bernhard Goetz subway shooting incident. On December 22, 1984, Goetz, a white man, and four black youths were riding a subway car together in Manhattan. One of the young men asked Goetz for money. Goetz thought he was about to be mugged and shot the four blacks. The incident, set amidst a public panic about street crime, became a cause célèbre. After a twisted course leading to trial, including one grand jury that refused to indict, and much national publicity, a criminal jury acquitted Goetz of attempted murder but convicted him of illegal gun possession. He received a sentence of six months.

Kunstler brought civil suit against Goetz on behalf of Darrell Cabey, who was paralyzed from the waist down and suffered brain damage. Kunstler managed to keep venue for the lawsuit in the Bronx, where minority juries are decidedly sympathetic with plaintiffs. Little love was lost between Goetz and Kunstler. Goetz sued Kunstler for libel twice for statements Kunstler made to the effect that Goetz was a racist, but in both cases his suit was dismissed. When informed that Goetz had testicular cancer, Kunstler replied, "It possibly makes me believe in God," echoing the response he made when he was informed that Roy Cohn had AIDS.

The civil suit dragged on interminably and did not come to trial until after Kunstler's death. Ronald Kuby, his former partner, told a reporter when he was preparing for trial that "the poignancy of this case is going through the files, seeing Bill's notes, suggestions and writings. The only sad thing about this case taking so long is that Bill isn't here as lead counsel." The Bronx jury of four blacks and two Hispanics awarded Cabey $43 million, a largely symbolic award since Goetz had few assets. "Bill's shoes will never be filled, but this is the sweetest, happiest, best victory of them all," Kuby rejoiced.

More typically, however, Kunstler's representation of clients he thought oppressed involved criminal defendants, not civil suits. A few examples from the 1980s include Wayne Williams, Lemuel Smith, and James York.

Wayne Williams was a young black man convicted in 1983 of the murder of two other black men, but implicated in a series of more than two dozen murders of Atlanta children during the years 1979–81. Kunstler visited Williams in prison after he read a book and saw a video concerning Williams that strongly suggested his innocence. In 1985 he became part of a team of attorneys who sought a new trial, although he was not the lead counsel. The team sought to reopen the case on several theories, the most significant of which was prosecutorial misconduct in failing to disclose to trial counsel that the police had information linking the Ku Klux Klan to the slayings. Kunstler and the team claimed that the authorities feared a race riot if the Klan's involvement became known; hence Williams became a scapegoat. As Kunstler put it, "They needed a fall guy who wouldn't create a civil war. From the beginning to the end it [the trial] was a horror show. Wayne never had a chance."

In 1981 Lemuel Smith was serving a life sentence in New York's Green Haven prison when he was accused of murdering Donna Payant, a female guard. New York had undone all its capital punishment laws, except for precisely these circumstances. Where a lifer was convicted of murder, the death penalty was automatic. Kunstler took the case at the request of Smith's mother, primarily because it involved the death sanction. Kunstler was, as he said, "so strongly opposed to the death penalty that I feel committed to taking on any client who, no matter the under-lying circumstances, could be sentenced to death if convicted."

At trial, Kunstler tried to make a case that a prison guard killed Payant to prevent her from exposing a drug ring that several guards op-erated inside the prison. The rogue guards then set Smith up as a scape-goat. The jury did not buy the story, but Kunstler, with Kuby writing the brief, did convince the New York Court of Appeals to invalidate the sen-tence by finding this last provision of the state's death penalty legisla-tion unconstitutional. New York appealed to the U.S. Supreme Court, which declined to hear the case.

The York case began on the evening of April 16, 1981, when police officers John Scarangella and Richard Rainey pulled over a white van because it fit a description of one involved in a burglary. Two men jumped out of the van and fired twenty-five shots into the police car. Scarangella died and Rainey was forced to retire because of his injuries. Anthony LaBorde and James York, former Black Panthers, were charged. Kunstler represented York, and went through three complete trials with him, plus appeals and motions.

The defense essentially was that the defendants were being perse-cuted because they were former Black Panthers. In the first trial the jury found the two defendants guilty of attempted murder in the wounding of Rainey but could not agree on the murder charge. The second jury deadlocked. The third jury convicted, in a trial held five years after the shooting. The defense filed motions challenging the prosecution's exer-cise of peremptory challenges to exclude black jurors, but the convic-tions held up after several hearings, including a remand to the trial court to take evidence about the prosecution's use of its challenges.

The majority of Kunstler's cases in the 1980s were quite eclectic, ei-ther straining the objectively political definition to the breaking point or not political at all. He took some cases because they involved neighbors or friends, others because they were interesting challenges or were fun. Every now and then when Authur Kinoy asked Kunstler why he took a particular case, Kunstler responded "I had to make some money. I had to get a fee." Even when he charged, considering Kunstler's reputation and skills, his fees were low. Ronald Kuby remembers that from 1982 to 1995 there were only two matters in which Kunstler received a fee larger than $100,000. Lillian Goldman paid him $200,000 for four months' work in late 1989. Kunstler helped her sue her children to over-turn the will of her deceased husband, real estate tycoon Sol Goldman, and recover part of his $2 billion estate. That fee computerized the Kunstler and Kuby office. Kunstler justified this classically greed-motivated estate litigation by disingenuously observing that Lillian Goldman was "someone who wants to do more with her life than just be Sol Goldman's widow and seems genuinely interested in doing something for the civil rights movement."

The other large fee was a flat fee of $100,000 paid to defend a Hell's Angel group for state murder and federal weapons charges in Cleveland, Ohio. One club member promised Kunstler he would put a tattoo of Lenin on his left shoulder to match Hitler's on his right. The Sikhs contributed cumulative fees of $100,000, but that was for several clients over an extended period of time. Most of Kunstler's criminal fees were in the area of $3,000 to $5,000, and half of his office time was spent on uncompensated cases or cases that paid the next-to-nothing court-appointment rates. Kunstler made some money from speaking fees, but it was not a large amount, primarily because he spoke so often for free to law student groups, the National Lawyers Guild, or tiny meetings sponsored by organizations such as WBAI, the leftish New York radio station. Kunstler told a reporter in 1989 that the gross income generated by himself and Kuby the previous year, including his speaking fees, was between $150,000 and $175,000.

One very strange case involved Ray O'Prey, a white detective who led a small troupe of cops who jazz-danced in their uniforms. Kunstler met O'Prey after his group performed at Sarah's school. O'Prey told Kunstler that the police bosses were ridiculing him for his extracurricular dancing. They had piled on meritless disciplinary citations and assigned him to menial positions. Kunstler brought a civil rights action in federal court, and the judge persuaded the parties to settle. O'Prey received a good amount of money and retired at full pension. Then O'Prey mounted his former detective shield on a plaque, which he had engraved "To William Moses Kunstler, honor to a good man." Kunstler was so touched that he hung the plaque on his office wall, as a reminder that "injustice can be directed at anyone, that I must remember not to make assumptions about people, even cops."

Another eclectic matter concerned rock 'n' roll. Local New York musicians for years had organized a concert in Central Park's Naumberg Bandshell called Rock Against Racism. Concerned about resident complaints of noise, the city enacted an ordinance in 1986 that required groups performing at the bandshell to use a city-supplied system and sound technician. The musicians believed that this violated their First Amendment right to free expression by forcing them, in effect, to submit to the city's controls. Kunstler took the case through several layers of tribunals up to the U.S. Supreme Court. After Kunstler made a folksy, almost familiar, presentation at oral argument, the justices, by a six-to-three vote, upheld the city's ordinance.

In still another unusual mid-1980s case, Kunstler represented an American Legion Post in Greenwich Village with predominantly elderly Italian American members. It was a client, as Kunstler acknowledged, "totally different than we normally represent." A combined gang of plainclothed police and FBI agents with drawn guns raided the club without a warrant, looking for a suspect in a cop shooting. They forced all the club's patrons present, the youngest of whom was sixty-six, to line up against the wall, pushing and shoving those too feeble to move quickly. Then the cops turned over tables, scrawled the words "No killing cops" on the post's display case, and searched the elderly World War II veterans while calling them "scum" and "bastards." The post called on Kunstler, who explained to a reporter why he took the case. "I can't say that I'm as conservative as the American Legion, but we're all united that such unlawful break-ins should not happen in a country with civil rights. Besides, this is my community here—I live here in the village. These are neighbors of mine."

The federal judges on the Second Circuit Court of Appeals apparently approved of this sort of police activity. They reversed the lower judge's denial of a motion for summary judgment in the post's suit for damages. Relying on the circumstance that the front door was unlocked, the federal appellate judges held that as a matter of law there was no civil liability for such police conduct even if these facts were correct. One of the elderly veterans told a reporter, "I was brought up to respect the police. . . . Now my opinion is changed."

A sampling of other Kunstler cases in the 1980s includes a state senator caught in an FBI sting involving money laundering; customers of Citibank who had their account erroneously credited with $97,000 and then were accused of theft; a prostitute and a man who claimed he could not have normal sexual relations in a suit to declare the New York prostitution statute unconstitutional; a group of Syracuse cabdrivers in a beef with their city over access to the airport; a Bronx elementary school principal charged with crack possession; a man charged in a plot to illegally sell arms to Iran; a female entertainer who attacked a passport clerk; a fiery black Baptist minister jailed in contempt for refusing to give up the membership list to church dissidents; a homeless black man who murdered a Rockette; a black marine who became a Muslim and refused to go to Lebanon because he feared the wrath of Allah; and two graffiti artists who alleged that New York City had failed in its duty to provide a space for public art.

Kunstler represented more policemen than just the jazz-dancers. He defended a former New York City officer charged with murdering a pimp and prostitute, an officer facing departmental charges of wrecking a numbers shop, and a policeman forced into more hazardous duties following his cooperation with a police corruption investigation. He brought a federal civil rights action on behalf of a Ridgefield policeman who claimed he was forced to work the graveyard shift and assigned to protect an empty park because he had criticized a miserly pay increase.

Kunstler took on an eviction defense after two tenants about to be thrown out walked up to him in the Bronx County Courthouse and begged his help. His friend Bruce Jackson recalls the incident: "They had no money, his calendar was totally overloaded and his staff told him not to take the case. But he took it and saved their home for them." One day Kunstler was dropping off his shirts at his local cleaners "and saw this man crying—my heart went out." The owners of the cleaners, Jewish immigrants from the Soviet Union, had invested their life savings into the cleaners, and the city buildings department had suddenly withdrawn its approval to operate. Kunstler took on their case, beat the publicity drum for them, organized a petition of three hundred neighbors in favor of the cleaners, and accepted his fee in cleaning and tailoring services. Kunstler even represented at least one real capitalist, Jeno Paulucci, a real estate dealer in Florida. Paulucci was accused of wrongdoing and contacted Kunstler for help. "He told me to buy an ad or write a letter to the editor to make my case, not to sue. Bill kept me out of a lot of lawsuits with his advice. My other lawyers would be saying to sue, and he often said, 'Let's try another way.'" A very odd couple, Kunstler and Paulucci kept in touch and even developed a friendship of sorts.

Probably the most controversial of Kunstler's representations, which most seriously challenge his claim to screen his clientele for rectitude of political position, were his mobster clients. It began in the mid-1970s when the New England Mafia boss Raymond Patriarca asked

Kunstler to represent him in a civil rights case. A Providence, Rhode Island, newspaper sued the FBI to obtain transcripts of illegal FBI wiretaps. Patriarca had not been the target, but his voice was on several of the tapes. An unusual team of the Justice Department and Kunstler, representing Patriarca, sought to block release of the documents. The trial judge ordered their release, but was reversed on appeal to both the U.S. Court of Appeals and the U.S. Supreme Court. At the appellate hearing, Kunstler asked for a separate counsel table so he did not have to sit with the Justice Department lawyers, with whom he was nominally allied. "I think they're the enemy," he explained.

Shortly thereafter Kunstler and his wife Margie were invited to a party in New York's Little Italy to celebrate the victory. Margie was the only woman at the table; the hosts' wives all ate at a different table. The waiters fretted over whom to serve first: the don or the woman. After the wine arrived, someone suggested that Kunstler propose a toast. Having no idea what to say, Kunstler raised his glass and said "Here's to crime." Absolute silence ensued, and Margie whispered to Kunstler that his toast had been a faux pas and a grave insult. John Gotti had been a young mobster present at that dinner. Years later he told Kunstler that after Kunstler and his wife had left the dinner, the assembled mobsters roared with laughter.

Several years later, in 1981, he represented Patriarca again. A federal judge had given the FBI permission to bug the office of an attorney in Providence who represented Gotti. The case had obvious Sixth Amendment right-to-counsel implications, and the American Civil Liberties Union sent observers. Kunstler declared, "If this stands up, then no law office is safe." He was successful in obtaining an order declaring the wiretap illegal.

Charles Garry, the lawyer originally scheduled to try the Chicago Seven case, asked Kunstler in 1985 to represent Joe Bonanno in resisting a subpoena to testify in a Mafia case that did not involve him personally. There was conflicting testimony about Bonanno's health. Four doctors submitted affidavits that the eighty-year-old former Mafia boss was senile, that he had phlebitis and cerebral and cardiovascular diseases, and that the stress of testifying could result in a heart attack and "possible death." The government's doctor, quite naturally given his position, testified that Bonanno could give a deposition in a hospital. After holding a hearing in Bonanno's hospital, the federal judge, quite naturally given his position as collaborator with the prosecutor—as at least Kunstler would believe—ordered Bonanno to testify. Reporters watching the proceeding on closed-circuit television described Bonanno as "frail." He told the U.S. district judge Richard Owens, "My doctor told me I could die so I'm not in a position to testify. I obey my doctor," and asked for his medication. Owens found this an "absolutely arrogant" refusal to testify, and threw the eighty-year old man out of the hospital and into a federal prison.

The mobster representation that garnered Kunstler the most publicity was that of John Gotti, the "dapper don" of New York, and allegedly a major Mafia boss. Juries had acquitted Gotti at a whole series of trials, but the government kept prosecuting in the hopes it would get him eventually. What the government did get was a federal judge, I. Leo Glasser, who, in Kunstler's view and that of many civil libertarians, became the prosecutor's colleague in putting Gotti away. Glasser denied Gotti the right to choose his own attorney. This was not a matter of court appointment; Gotti had plenty of money to pay. The federal judge just wouldn't let Gotti have the benefit of the attorney who had won the previous acquittals. Nor would Glasser allow Gotti's codefendant to have the attorney of his choice either. Ultimately the federal judge forced four defense attorneys off the case. During the trial it was revealed that one alternate juror had failed to disclose that she was married to a former FBI agent. The judge let her stay on, although apparently another juror was dismissed when it was learned she had once worked for a defense attorney.

Kunstler was not on Gotti's trial team, nor was he among the appellate attorneys. Kunstler advised Gotti at various stages, but only represented him on motions, mostly posttrial efforts to obtain a new hearing. Although the judge and prosecutor advanced grounds for excluding the first choice lawyers, they were probably a pretext for their desire to easily put Gotti away for life. There were additional allegations that while most of the jury was sequestered, a favored few jurors occasionally were allowed to go home. Two of the jurors submitted posttrial affidavits alleging irregularities. However, Glasser refused even to hold a hearing. Jimmy Breslin, the New York columnist, sensed that the judge had determined that "nobody was going to ruin a perfect game in his courtroom." Kunstler quoted Glasser himself in explanation: "I have an incredible amount of power as a federal judge . . . more powerful than perhaps the president of the United States in many respects." Undeniably, the evidence against Gotti was stronger in this trial than in his previous trials. However, it also seems that Gotti as a criminal defendant was tried by special rules, administered by a despotic judge, and designed to grease the skids for conviction to put him in prison for life.

The major biographical question is why Kunstler took on these Mafia cases, so far removed from his radical clientele or even his clients who were objectively political. Kunstler offered all sorts of dubious explanations, their very multiplicity suggesting that Kunstler was trying to convince himself. In no particular order, one explanation was that the mobsters were not really that bad, they just killed each other (he suggested once that they were more efficient than the FBI at that and should be given an award), and that the Mafia certainly was "more honest than the major American corporations [he often added the government here], which do just as much killing—even more." He often had little arguments with his partner Ronald Kuby concerning John Gotti. Kunstler asked Kuby, "How was John Gotti worse than General Motors?" Kuby responded, "He's not. We don't represent GM either."

Another explanation was that "this country has a long tradition of bias against Italian-Americans, and we love making villains out of individuals who are linked to organized crime. Defendants accused of such ties are almost always discriminated against, almost always assumed to be guilty." Furthermore, the government was overzealous and for sinister reasons. Dismissing Gotti's lawyers was "part of a pattern of conduct by the government to get rid of lawyers that they fear," he declared. He once told a reporter, "The government uses the mobster cases to get bad law to use against everybody else. I take those cases because they have important principles in them."

In an alternate explanation, Kunstler cited his attraction to their paternalism and power and a romantic attraction to a folk hero quality. As renegades and bandits, "they also rip off the system." A gleeful, naive quality pervades much of Kunstler's mobster work. In the 1970s someone somehow arranged for a lavish mob banquet, with wine, steaks, and the prisoners' wives, held inside the maximum-security unit of Rhode Island's Adult Correctional Institution. A remarkable photograph depicts Kunstler sitting at a table with five mobsters, obviously enjoying his personal participation in their camaraderie and power. In the 1980s Barry Slotnick, a fellow Manhattan attorney, bumped into Kunstler and mentioned Kunstler's work for Joe Bonanno. "That's not your speed," he said. Kunstler responded, "Yes. He's oppressed." In a later incident, John Gotti publicly kissed Kunstler on the cheek one day in the federal courthouse. Kunstler loved that public recognition, and proudly shared it with his wife Margie at home that night. Margie, none too happy with the Gotti matter, asked her husband, "And why do you think he did that?" Without irony, Kunstler suggested, "He admires my work."

Kunstler sometimes protested that he represented mobsters only as a matter of civil rights and that he never received compensation. "I never made a nickel on an OC [organized crime] case," he told a reporter in 1988. He told another reporter the year before that he defended mobsters because they were victims of government persecution, and he did not accept a fee. Like his similar comments about not accepting fees in civil rights cases, where we have seen earlier that in fact he did, these remarks also appear to be stretchers.

There is no smoking gun here, as the Mafia does not have its correspondence and payment records neatly archived as does CORE and SCLC. However, Kunstler represented several other Mafia figures, beyond Patriarca, Bonanno, and Gotti, and who seem to have no conceivable connection with a civil rights claim. In 1981 he defended Charles Flynn, charged with, and acquitted of, a gangland slaying of a bookmaker. Then he represented Lawrence Dentico and Dominick D'Agostino, convicted of racketeering in 1982. The next year Kunstler represented the reputed mobster Frank "Bobo" Marrapese against charges of arranging false testimony. Then, over the years, there were John and Gerard Ouimette and Dante Sciarra in a wiretapping matter, Ilario "Larry" Zannino in a loansharking and gambling trial, Louis Ferrante in a credit card fraud trial, and Anthony Viola, charged with conspiracy to distribute narcotics. All these matters involved individuals represented by Kunstler and believed to be associated with organized crime. Did all ten mobsters have compelling enough civil rights claims for representation without fee?

By the time of his 1994 autobiography, Kunstler limited his claim to that of representing John Gotti without fee. For Gotti, Kunstler was asked only for consultation and motions, not for the extensive time involved in a full trial or appeal. That claim was probably correct, but the earlier claims that he never accepted a fee from any alleged mobster were probably stretching the truth.

The actual William Kunstler trying a case was usually quite different from the flamboyant William Kunstler of popular image. Except in those few cases where he tried to provoke the judge into error, or political cases in which the defendants had severely disrespectful attitudes toward courts, Kunstler was quite civil in jury trial. Standing tall, with his eyeglasses on the top of his head and his flyaway grey hair, by the 1980s Kunstler bounded through courtrooms as though he were a lion prowling his domain. At the same time, he was a study in civility, laughing and joking in his deep bass voice with prosecutors and court clerks, smiling at the jury, hugging and slapping backs, and always speaking kindly with the elderly spectators hanging around the courtrooms. "I've learned a few tricks from them," he once acknowledged.

Kunstler won more trials through lawyerly skills of impeachment, skillful analysis, persuasion, and rules of evidence than through flamboyance. Whenever law students asked him, as they often did, how they could become radical lawyers, he always advised them to concentrate on becoming good lawyers first. That said, Kunstler also loved the action, the sheer challenge of taking on an impossible case and then winning an acquittal. This motivated him as much as ideology. It was outside the courtroom, in his remarks with reporters and the defendants' supporters, that Kunstler became most flamboyant.

Some judges became upset by the political attacks outside the courtroom, while Kunstler was doing his "demystification" work. Others, such as Jack B. Weinstein, a federal judge in Brooklyn before whom Kunstler tried many cases, let it pass by him. In fact, he found Kunstler "prepared. I would put him in the category of a good professional. Probably in the top 25 percent of lawyers that I see. . . . I always could depend on him telling me the truth. He never misled me . . . and always acted as a fine professional man. . . . Outside the court, in the corridors, he became crass. . . . It was a different story."

In the same vein, Sol Wachtler, the highest judge in the New York state judicial system, considered him in the 1980s

> one of the best [oral advocates] that ever came before the New York Court of Appeals. We found him to be well prepared . . . he knew the court very well and members of the court [and] addressed their concerns very appropriately, and was very impressive. [He] seemed so conscientious . . . and always pled his case with . . . great ability and very persuasively.

At eight o'clock on a January 1982 morning, Ronald Kuby, a Cornell law student in his mid-twenties, knocked on Kunstler's door at 13 Gay Street to interview for a summer internship. Kunstler appeared at the door, half dressed in shirt and boxer shorts, pulled Kuby in and offered him coffee and a summer job. Kuby proved to be politically compatible and tolerant of Kunstler's occasional irascibility. Kuby was also such a good and quick lawyer-in-the-making that Kunstler asked him to transfer from Cornell to New York University so he could continue to work for him.

Cornell would not permit that late a transfer, but after Kuby finished law school the following year he began to work for Kunstler. Kuby, like his mentor, was and is friendly and personable. Once described by a reporter as a "yuppie radical," he sports a long ponytail and buys his suits at Barneys. He brought considerable sartorial improvement to the office. As Kunstler described it in his autobiography, Kuby worked for him as an associate for ten years and then became his partner. They were more than mere partners or colleagues. They became friends, and Kunstler described Kuby as his "partner and alter ego." After Kuby's arrival, Kunstler continued to collaborate on specific cases with younger attorneys, such as he did with Lynne Stewart on the Davis matter. However, after he had that relationship, in-house, with a thoroughly trusted colleague, those ad hoc collaborations became less necessary.

Student interns were still helpful even after Kuby's arrival, both for menial running of paperwork and also research. As the clouds of the 1980s conservatism closed in on the radical world, it became more difficult to attract top clerks. "We used to get the cream of the law school crop," Kunstler complained in 1985. "Now they're in the Yuppie stream, trying to make big bucks or work as prosecutors." However, Kunstler continued to search for talented and diverse law clerks.

How diverse? Well, one, Elison Elliott, became a Republican and a government bond dealer, and ran for the Brooklyn city council. Another, Daniella Korotzer, is now doing criminal defense work in the Kunstler tradition. She was one of Kunstler's last student clerks and recalls her interview with him in 1993:

> Bill assumed that your legal skills were up to par and he had no interest in looking at my writing sample. He simply asked if I had the heart

and courage to take the types of cases he takes. I said yes. And that's all he needed to know. And then he yelled out to Ron [Kuby], "Do you think she's of high enough moral character to work in this office?"

As the country grew increasingly conservative throughout the 1970s, 1980s, and into the 1990s, governments took many steps to make the vigorous defense of unpopular clients more difficult. In the 1960s and 1970s defense attorneys lost the right in federal courts to question prospective criminal jurors directly, and the Supreme Court found constitutional the practice of a few states that permitted conviction by less than a unanimous jury.

In the 1980s the federal government streamlined its process of sending defendants to prison. In part, the new techniques aimed at defendants were simply tougher substantive laws with stiffer penalties. For example, traditional crimes were repackaged as "racketeering" under the RICO statutes in an effort to impress juries with the wickedness of defendants' activities. Additionally, the federal government created specific devices to deprive defendants of effective counsel. Under the Comprehensive Forfeiture Act of 1984, assets from criminal activity could be forfeited, and the government could seek forfeiture even of assets already transferred to a third party. This meant that a retainer paid to an attorney could be snatched away by the prosecutors, an obvious disincentive to defense attorneys to take cases where the fee was paid by the defendant. The lawyer might later lose his entire fee.

Even where the fee was paid by a third party, the courts permitted prosecutors to subpoena defense attorneys before a grand jury and force them to disclose the source of the fee. Those paying the fees frequently might not wish to be themselves the subject of a grand jury investigation, and the fact that they might become that by paying a fee discouraged third party payments. That in turn hampered the ability of defendants to obtain representation, which was, perhaps, the intended result of the demand for disclosure. The more that talented lawyers can be discouraged from representing certain defendants, the easier it is for the government to imprison them. Also in the 1980s and 1990s, federal prosecutors increasingly used the grand jury as an improper discovery tool, post-indictment, by claiming that there was a "continuing investigation." This gave the government subpoena power to force reluctant witnesses to testify—not at trial where both parties would be stuck with their answers—but before the grand jury. If the testimony was favorable, the prosecutors could then compel them to testify at trial. If unfavorable, the prosecutors could forget about them as witnesses.

Increasingly in the 1980s and continuing into the 1990s, judges granted prosecutors' requests for anonymous juries, in which the jurors' very names were forbidden to defense counsel. The federal courts compelled John Gotti to be tried before a secret panel, and the practice, although never common, was used with increasing frequency. It is impossible for defense counsel to ferret out possible biases that a prospective juror might not disclose if counsel does not even know the juror's name. Defense attorneys argue that this practice moves our society away from the ideal of a public trial toward the secrecy characteristic of a police state. These new obstacles placed in the paths of defense lawyers had a counterpart on the civil side of the court. Although many federal statutes provide for attorney fees in successful public interest and civil rights suits, in the early 1990s the amounts of those fees were sharply curtailed. That discouraged civil rights litigation.

However, these "crackdowns" on defense counsel did not affect Kunstler severely. Although he did suffer somewhat from declining fees for public interest and civil rights cases, most of his work was criminal defense. Much of that was uncompensated or by court appointment, and even the fee-generating cases were not the type, such as drug trafficking, where it was likely that the fee was derived from criminal activity. Nevertheless, three governmental crackdowns on defense lawyers in the 1980s and 1990s did have a great impact on Kunstler and his practice. These included blocks erected for out-of-state lawyers appearing *pro hac vice* (for this case only) in a state where the attorney was not regularly licensed, the increasing issuance by judges of gag orders directed at the parties' attorneys, and federal sanctions directed against attorneys for filing allegedly frivolous lawsuits.

The romantic image of the itinerant lawyer appealed to Kunstler, but there was sound theory behind the practice. Out-of-area counsel in a notorious criminal case are free from local pressures and the community's passions and prejudices. As Kunstler himself observed, the traveling lawyers "often can be bolder and more aggressive in their advocacy than attorneys who depend upon their communities for their living, their status and their well-being." If an individual lawyer is unlicensed in a state, neither the state courts nor federal courts located in that state are required to permit him to practice, even if a criminal defendant wants his services. However, it is a common courtesy to permit out-of-state attorneys to appear *pro hac vice*.

Generally, Kunstler had few problems obtaining permission to appear, although there were some. West Germany refused to permit Kunstler to appear in its courts to defend some radicals in 1975, and a federal judge in Topeka, Kansas, rejected Kunstler's application to appear before him in 1972, scoring Kunstler for having constantly shown "disdain and contempt" for the judicial process by his argument that "courts are not the place to get justice."

An Indiana case in 1973 gathered the most publicity of all Kunstler's disputes involving a temporary appearance. The criticism of the federal district judge went to the heart of the radical lawyer's demystification program. Judge Cale J. Holder refused Kunstler the right to appear because Kunstler had "engaged in a pattern of pretrial publicity—i.e., public statements, interviews and press conferences," and these activities had reduced "the prospect of obtaining a fair and impartial jury," or put otherwise, had inconvenienced the prosecution. Kunstler appealed this determination to the appellate court, which reversed the trial judge and permitted Kunstler to appear. In turn, the government appealed that decision to the U.S. Supreme Court, and the American Bar Association filed a brief in support of the judge's discretion. The Supreme Court first agreed to hear the case, but ultimately declined to review the appellate court's decision that Kunstler could practice before the Indiana federal court.

We have seen that as late as March 1987, a federal judge in Boston refused to appoint Kunstler to represent Thomas Manning, essentially because he was from out of town. Kunstler always felt that the opposition to *pro hac vice* appearances was fueled by the government's fear of dedicated lawyers willing to travel around the country to defend unpopular clients. After the 1987 incident, he returned to that theme and said that the episode was an example of government efforts to "break up the itinerant lawyer . . . to attack lawyers who are taking the cases of anybody who is really disliked by the government. They're going after the 'have writ, will travel' types." Although obtaining the right to appear in courts outside New York was never a significant problem for Kunstler, the issue was a thorn that could never be completely removed.

Whenever an indictment for a serious crime appears, especially in a political prosecution, the prosecutors make a big public display in the media. One of the standard techniques of radical lawyers is to attempt to counteract the prosecutorial propaganda with their own—criticizing the politics of the case, attacking the operations of the police, and affirmatively putting a human face on the defendants after their demonization by the prosecutors. This is done in an attempt to favorably impress the prospective jury pool. Defense attorneys did such a good job at this that prosecutors, judges, and state bars developed tools in the 1970s and thereafter to gag the defense bar. In some states, courts simply ordered attorneys not to speak out on their current cases, the classic gag order. In other states, blanket court rules accomplished the same job without the need for a specific court order.

The problem with these court rules and gag orders, from Kunstler's viewpoint, was that they prevented defense counsel from responding to prosecutors' "deliberate poisoning of the pool of prospective jurors" by "inflammatory comments," since the gag order comes only "after the prosecutor has enjoyed a field day with the televised release of the charges." Kunstler also pointed out that gag orders prevented the defendants from appealing for financial support through their attorneys and prevented the discovery of important defense witnesses that can come about through publicity.

Kunstler had always run afoul of arrogant state judges on the issue of their gag orders. In 1976 Judge Theodore Appleby of New Jersey ordered Kunstler to show cause why he should not be thrown off a case, depriving the defendant of her counsel, and thereafter held in contempt because he had "declared that he hoped to conduct rallies and seminars and explain the legal proceedings to the people in lay terms" and "stated an opinion relative to the guilt or innocence of his client." Heinous acts, indeed!

However, it was only after the U.S. Supreme Court held in a 1991 case that attorneys do not enjoy the same First Amendment rights as the rest of the population, that the viciousness of some federal judges and prosecutors exploded. Bruce Cutler, the lawyer John Gotti was deprived of by order of Judge I. Leo Glasser, told reporters that the prosecutors "threw the Constitution out the window" in their treatment of his client. For those remarks, a federal judge found Cutler in contempt of court and sentenced him to ninety days' home confinement and suspended his right to practice his profession for six months. Kunstler faced similar contempt citations brought by state prosecutors in the Colin Ferguson case in 1994, and federal prosecutors in the World Trade Center conspiracy case in 1993. Kunstler generally ignored prior restraints on his free speech, and had a knack of skating perilously close to danger yet avoiding it. Gag orders and state bar rules gagging defense counsel were a significant threat to Kunstler, and continue to be so for all defense attorneys.

Underlying this contentiousness is a fundamental difference in philosophy. In conventional, orthodox legal theory, a criminal trial is to be a mechanism for the ascertainment of truth. Some judges even believe that idea, but to most defense lawyers, radical or not, the notion is hypocritical cant. Defense lawyers are uninterested in any ethereal "truth"; they want to get their client off, to secure an acquittal. They know that their opponents, the prosecutors, are not interested in any truth ascertainment either. The prosecutors want to convict. That is what is at stake. The radical defense lawyer would add that the criminal trial is largely a political struggle; one ideology is confronting another. The political lawyer understands that no one really wants an unbiased jury. The expression of that thought is likewise hollow cant. The prosecution wants a jury that is biased toward it; the defense, vice versa. Publicity is merely a tool in the struggle. To worry that it might contaminate a jury pool is beside the point. Both sides want to reach the jury.

The difference between orthodox legal theory and the radical perspective becomes even clearer when we view collateral lawsuits, such as a defendant's civil rights suit against a jailer, a defense suit to enjoin certain police or prosecutorial practices, and the like. To the radical lawyer, these are affirmative lawsuits, a form of taking the initiative, of fighting back against the entrenched powers. To the orthodox viewpoint, these kinds of affirmative lawsuits are generally without merit and frivolous. They are frivolous to the orthodox precisely because they do not aid the primary purpose of truth ascertainment: what did the defendant in fact do regarding the specific charges against him. They are not frivolous to the radical lawyer, because the entire process of a criminal trial is a political struggle. Affirmative lawsuits, accusing power of abuse, are merely weapons in that struggle.

An amendment in 1983 to Rule 11 of the Federal Rules of Civil Procedure required attorneys filing a lawsuit in a federal court to determine that their case is well-founded in fact, not frivolous, and not designed to harass their opponent. Federal courts can impose sanctions for violation of the rule directly on the offending lawyers. The federal courts have levied truly monstrous fines for violation, often in the $50,000–$100,000 range. Steady criticism has charged that these fines have a chilling effect on civil rights claims and public interest litigation that affects the poor, and especially that they inhibit innovative efforts to modify existing law, although there is some indication that in recent years the courts have ameliorated the rule's harshest interpretation.

A scholar noted in 1992 that "a number of lawyers in civil rights and other areas have been driven from the practice because of this rule." Kunstler put the same thought more vigorously in 1986: "Courage is courage. But if it means going bankrupt, who's going to do it? If you sock it to civil rights lawyers every time, what attorney's going to do it?" In 1991 Kunstler spoke of Rule 11's "enormous chilling effect on all civil rights attorneys. It's such dirty business on the part of the courts, to do this type of work for 50 years and then see that they can put you out of business with these monstrous fines." Rule 11 had a particular impact on *radical* civil rights lawyers, as it made it much more difficult to use affirmative lawsuits, counterlitigation, as a technique of defending against cases they regarded as political repression through criminal prosecution.

Rule 11 sanctions eventually ensnared Kunstler. His problem arose out of a North Carolina case. For years Robeson County, North Carolina, had a reputation for bigotry, discrimination, and even murder directed against its Indian population, coupled with corruption of local public officials. On February 1, 1988, two armed Tuscarora Indians seized a small newspaper office in Robeson County to protest and to demand the appointment of an investigating commission. No one was injured, and the gunmen surrendered after twelve hours. The federal courts tried them for various federal violations. Kunstler represented one of the two defendants, but was in the middle of the Davis trials in New York. The North Carolina federal judge refused to continue the trial, and Kunstler's client was forced to represent himself. Many of the supposed hostages from the newspaper office were highly sympathetic to the defendants' grievances, and the jury acquitted the two men.

Then North Carolina announced plans to go forward with state charges arising out of the same incident. In January 1989 Kunstler and local counsel filed a federal civil rights action against various county and state officials, alleging corruption and various civil rights deprivations, and seeking an injunction against the state criminal charges. Thereafter, the state criminal charges were settled, and in April 1989 Kunstler dismissed the federal lawsuit. Shortly thereafter,

North Carolina officials brought a Rule 11 motion, seeking sanctions against Kunstler for filing a frivolous federal lawsuit.

The federal district court refused to hold a hearing, but nevertheless determined that Kunstler's "primary motives in filing the complaint were to gain publicity, to embarrass state and county officials, to gain leverage in criminal proceedings, to obtain discovery for use in criminal proceedings, and to intimidate those involved in the [state] prosecution." This summary is almost a perfect description of the radical lawyer's conception of affirmative litigation. The federal judge fined Kunstler and his local counsel $122,384. The circuit court of appeals affirmed the sanction, although clearly stating that these motives alone would not justify a Rule 11 sanction if the lawsuit itself had merit. It sent the case back to the district court to hold a hearing and reduce the amount of the fine.

The principal actors in the drama reacted to the huge fine in the character of their roles. North Carolina's attorney general, Lacy Thornburg, sang the old southern song of outside agitators: "I hope that this decision will send a loud, clear message to those who would exploit the problems of Robeson County. By disciplining these lawyers who would agitate problems in Robeson County, and even create problems, the court has removed a major obstacle to change." Kunstler, in turn, remained true to his tradition of defiance: "I'll tell you this," he told one reporter. "I'm not going to pay any fine. I'm going to rot in jail if that's what I have to do to dramatize this thing. I think I could do no better thing for my country."

The U.S. Supreme Court refused to review the sanction, but the trial court reduced the fine to $43,325, which the circuit court then approved. A committee, composed of show business personalities Spike Lee, Oliver Stone, Ruby Dee, Ossie Davis, and Robert De Niro, and abstract painter Brice Marden, solicited funds. Their fund-raising, together with money from the Center for Constitutional Rights, paid off the fine.

Rule 11 became a real threat to Kunstler's practice. In 1993 he brought an action in state court to block the New York Saint Patrick's Day Parade because of the city's refusal to allow homosexuals to march with their own banner. The defendants transferred the case to a federal court, where the federal judge found it frivolous and wanted to fine Kunstler. He could not do so since the lawsuit had not originally been filed in federal court, but in his memorandum opinion the judge stated he would have fined Kunstler had the lawsuit been started in the federal system. Kunstler's reaction was that "rule 11 scares me more than anything else, because it could put me out of business."

Suddenly Kunstler received a reprieve of sorts. At the end of 1993 Rule 11 was again amended to eliminate sanctions if allegedly frivolous claims are withdrawn promptly after challenge to their accuracy, and if the factual statements in a pleading have "evidentiary support" rather than the harsher 1983 standard of "well grounded in fact." Kunstler figured personally in the first significant appellate case to clarify the new amendment. A federal judge in New York dismissed a lawsuit Kunstler filed and found certain factual allegations false and the lawsuit frivolous. He imposed a fine on the client and censured Kunstler, writing of Kunstler that he "is apparently one of those attorneys who believes that his sole obligation is to his client and that he has no obligations to the court or to the processes of justice." Kunstler responded with a letter to the judge questioning whether his ruling reflected an "animus toward activist practitioners," to which the judge replied with a diatribe against both Kuby and Kunstler, concluding that no particular consideration was owed to "an attorney who places himself and his causes above the interests of justice."

The appellate court reversed the sanctions in March 1995, just months before Kunstler's death, finding that the manner in which the trial judge imposed them suggested both "a personal attack" against Kunstler and "perhaps, more broadly, against activist attorneys who represent unpopular clients or causes." Kunstler commented that it was "refreshing to have a significant federal appellate court recognize that lawyers are sometimes attacked by judges, federal or state, simply because they represent persons who are not favored by the Establishment."

Although Kunstler may have had a very diverse practice in the 1980s, as we have seen, two cases stand out from all the rest, measured by notoriety and publicity. They were the defense of Private Clayton Lonetree for espionage, and the defense of Larry Davis for murder and attempted murder. They are so different, one from the other, that they deserve closer study. Considered side by side, they neatly illustrate the sorts of cases in which Kunstler was able to work his rhetorical charms and the sorts of cases in which he could not.

13

The Scapegoat and the Killer Cops

TWO CASES OF the late 1980s illustrate the limits of Kunstler's ability to manipulate the media and politicize a case. In the Clayton Lonetree case Kunstler failed, but in the Larry Davis prosecution he achieved a stunning success. By looking at these two cases, we can see the limits to Kunstler's artistry and the milieu in which it worked best.

In the fall of 1985, while serving as a marine guard assigned to the American embassy in Moscow, Sergeant Clayton J. Lonetree fell in love and had an affair with Violetta Seina, a young Russian woman who worked in the embassy. She introduced him to her "Uncle Sasha," whom Lonetree realized was a KGB agent. Lonetree provided Uncle Sasha with the identification of CIA agents who worked out of the American embassy, floor plans that Lonetree annotated as to the location and control of secret offices and security devices, and information about the vulnerabilities of American employees on account of homosexuality, drugs, or alcohol. In turn, the KGB gave Lonetree $3,500 and access to his "honey trap."

At first, Lonetree fantasized that he could play a double agent role with the KGB, but by December 1986 realized that he was in over his head, and confessed to the CIA. The CIA debriefed him, promising him "confidentiality" for his statements. His confession was, however, later used against him at trial and was also the basis for a second series of confessions taken by the Naval Investigative Service (NIS) after Lonetree had been given a proper warning of his right to remain silent. When Lonetree appeared to falter in his confession, the investigator urged him to "make something up. Tell me a lie." Lonetree did just that, and his confessions have truthful elements and completely fabricated portions as well. The military investigators justified the tactic as a method to encourage Lonetree to keep talking.

The marines held Lonetree in solitary confinement in Quantico awaiting trial. The NIS told the media it had caught "the first master spy in the Marine Corps," and secretary of defense Caspar Weinberger urged that Lonetree be hanged or shot. In March 1987 a second marine, Arnold Bracy, confessed that he had conspired with Lonetree to shut off the alarm system at night and had allowed KGB agents to wander through the embassy, presumably purloining documents and planting secret cameras and microphones. With this revelation, together with the arrests of several more marines on charges of involvement with Soviet women, additional charges were pressed on Lonetree.

A public hysteria ensued. The marine scandal made the front cover of *Time* magazine; some labeled it one of the worst espionage cases of the century. All twenty-eight of the Moscow marine guards were recalled, the embassy was presumed completely compromised, and the staff, including the ambassador, were required to handwrite any secret messages for Washington and to transmit them by physical carriers. Almost immediately, Bracy recanted and alleged that his confession had been coerced. The military offered him immunity if he would testify against Lonetree, but Bracy refused. The marines dropped the new charges levied against Lonetree, of allowing the Soviets access to the embassy, and the scandal began to unravel. However, considerable public interest and concern remained by the time Lonetree was brought to trial in the summer of 1987.

Under the rules of military courts-martial, defendants are entitled to civilian representation in addition to the military lawyer assigned them. Major David Henderson became Lonetree's military lawyer. Lonetree's mother, a Navajo Indian named Sally Tsosie, arranged for Michael Stuhff, a civilian attorney in Las Vegas, to represent her son. Stuhff had considerable experience representing Navajos and had once represented her. Lonetree's father was a Winnebago Indian, and it was he who interested Kunstler in the case. Although Lonetree ultimately designated Stuhff his lead attorney, Stuhff, himself a progressive advocate of civil rights and an admirer of the older Kunstler, generally deferred to Kunstler's tactics. Henderson knew of Kunstler's reputation as a vigorous, outspoken advocate and as a radical lawyer and believed that Kunstler's tactics would not be successful before a military court-martial. He tried to persuade Lonetree not to accept Kunstler's services. At first Henderson succeeded, but after Kunstler and Stuhff had talked with Lonetree, they became his chief attorneys. Much later, at a time when it was in his interest to denigrate his civilian lawyers, Lonetree filed an affidavit claiming that the two attorneys clearly wanted to politicize the case.

> Mr. Kunstler and Mr. Stuhff told me that I was legally innocent. . . . They kept assuring me that "we'll beat this" . . . Kunstler and Stuhff told me that the military, the State Department, and the Government had things to hide and were trying to make me a scapegoat. They also said the only way I could avoid this was by going public and going to trial. They told me that the Government was trying to "get me" because of my American Indian background, and told me we needed to show the public how the white man treated American Indians. I told them that I did not think racial prejudice had anything to do with the case, but they told me I was wrong and that I should listen to them because they knew the facts and were more experienced than I was. . . . They told me that . . . [his military counsel] did not have my interests at heart, and that I should remember that they "wore the same uniform as the people who were trying to get me and put me in jail."

At an early stage in the proceeding, before the preliminary hearing and before the civilian attorneys were deeply involved in the case, there was informal discussion of a possible plea bargain. Henderson understood that a five-year sentence might settle the case at any early time when Lonetree might still be useful to investigators. When Kunstler entered the case, and after the hysteria over the Bracy confession settled down, Henderson advised Kunstler that a plea agreement would be the best approach. However, according to Lonetree's later recollection, Kunstler and Stuhff insisted that he "should not listen to Major Henderson and should not plea bargain." Henderson later believed that the case could have been settled before trial with a ten-year sentence.

In the weeks before the August 1987 trial, the defense presented many detailed motions. A major motion was for an open trial. The government wanted to close the trial to spectators and allow the press to view the proceedings through a closed-circuit television hookup, so that the camera could be stopped as soon as anything involving national security was mentioned. Kunstler urged that the trial be opened, that a closed trial was not only illegal but an effort by the government to camouflage "the criminal negligence of the State Department, the intemperate prejudgment of the Pentagon, the lies of the CIA, and the

brutal excesses of the Naval Investigative Service." The motion was denied, and the press excluded from coverage of approximately 25 percent of the trial.

The judge denied motions to dismiss for undue command influence
based on the statements expressing belief in Lonetree's guilt made by
those having command over the officers-jurors. The judge likewise rejected motions to suppress the confessions based on failure of warnings.
The military prosecution moved for permission to present a secret witness, a man who would testify without identification and who could
not be cross-examined as to his background or name. The presiding
judge, a military officer himself, granted the motion, showing dramatically how the American military justice system regards the Sixth
Amendment right to confront one's accusers.

It was only at this point, when the pretrial motions had all been lost,
that Stuhff and Kunstler became interested in considering a plea bargain. However, Kunstler expressed a disdain for such negotiations and
offered only a plea to lesser charges with a sentence limitation of two
years. The marines insisted on greater punishment. Henderson and
Lonetree both later testified that Lonetree had expressed interest in a
plea bargain, but backed away after discussions with civilian counsel,
who had urged him not to plea bargain and assured him that he would
not be convicted. Henderson submitted an affidavit on Lonetree's appeal that he had been discussing a sentence "in the realm of 5 to 10
years."

The court-martial began on August 11, 1987. The prosecution took
seven days to develop its case. Kunstler and Stuhff engaged in a running dispute with the judge and frequently complained that the military judge was favoring his fellow officers of the prosecution by narrowly limiting the scope of cross-examination. Nevertheless, some defense themes were developed—perhaps too many. There did not seem
to be any specific theme, but rather a confusing array of possible
themes.

The American intelligence community had a working relationship with "Uncle Sasha," and this gave rise to a defense charge that
Lonetree was set up by the State Department to give Sasha credibility
with the KGB by providing him with low-grade American security
information. In fact, many scandals had recently engaged the
marines, security in Moscow was a disgrace, and the NIS had a miserable reputation for the quality of investigations. That led Kunstler to

argue in trial that Lonetree was "the scapegoat for the State Department, the CIA, the Naval Investigative Services and the Marines."

Then too, Kunstler portrayed Lonetree as a foolish young man who had done no more than make a "mistaken" attempt to "become a double agent." Not only were the investigators who took Lonetree's confessions overbearing, but, Kunstler charged, they "encouraged him to feed his fantasy world," and even encouraged him to "just say something. Tell us a lie." The NIS "indulged Lonetree's fantasies." In addition, Kunstler developed the notion that what Lonetree actually supplied Uncle Sasha was merely "junk," a phone book "dug out of the trash." As for identifying the CIA agents, that information was already available to the KGB. What Lonetree did, Kunstler told a reporter, "was so inconsequential that I don't think it rises to the level of what you call espionage."

These total six separate themes: Lonetree was set up to give credibility to Uncle Sasha; Lonetree became a scapegoat for American government agencies; Lonetree made a foolish effort to become a double agent; the investigators were overbearing; the government encouraged Lonetree to lie in his confession; and the information Lonetree provided to the Soviets was mere junk. Kunstler's arguments were too many and too varied to have had coherence.

After the prosecution closed its case, the defense did not call Lonetree as a witness for fear he would collapse on cross-examination. The defense wanted to call two marines who would testify of Lonetree's pro-American sentiments, two experts who would testify about the NIS's interrogative abuses and how they led to false confessions, and a former CIA agent who would testify that the Soviets probably already had all the information Lonetree provided. The military officer-judge allowed only the two marine witnesses and ruled the other testimony irrelevant, even though the prosecution had called an expert in its case on the operations of the KGB and how the data supplied by Lonetree fit into its pattern of obtaining information. Allowed to call only two of its witnesses, the defense refused to put on a case and rested.

Kunstler alleged that the military judge had foreclosed their opportunity to present a defense. The judge even prevented the defense from presenting and arguing the undisputed fact that the NIS investigators had urged Lonetree to lie in his confession. At the beginning of the trial, Kunstler was asked whether he thought Lonetree would get a fair trial. He replied, "I have no hope whatsoever, absolutely none." Even before the preliminary hearings, before the suppression motions had been heard, Kunstler predicted, "I'm afraid they just want to execute some-body—get one good conviction to show that the Marine Corps is still tough. . . . To ask Marine officers to sit in judgment on this man is like asking the officers of a company to be the jury in a case affecting their own company."

During the trial, Kunstler held news conferences in which he usu-ally lambasted the judge. At the end of the trial, Kunstler told one re-porter that "this judge violated his oath of office. He is a disgrace." To another he said that "the judge was an animal as far as we're concerned. He refused to let in anything that would benefit" Lonetree.

Perhaps from Kunstler's viewpoint all that was true. It does seem as though the military judge was a military martinet, whose function was primarily to smooth the way to the defendant's conviction. A larger point is that this sort of criticism made absolutely no impact on a jury composed of military officers. Kunstler was obviously playing to an au-dience beyond the courtroom, to the public. He was trying to expose the corruption of the justice system. The public, however, was more inter-ested in what happened to an alleged spy, who after all had confessed, than in the alleged rottenness of the military tribunal. Fighting for a cause, rather than the client, made no sense here; it was a wasted effort on Kunstler's part.

If one of Kunstler's political purposes for the Lonetree trial was to mock the military justice system, then another was surely to remind the American public of how badly the government treated American Indi-ans. In the period when Arnold Bracy, a black man, had confessed and when the government offered him immunity to testify against Lonetree, Kunstler claimed that the Marine Corps was attempting to "turn a black man against a red man so they can execute the red man." At the time of the pretrial motions to suppress, Kunstler claimed to detect "an anti-In-dian bias here." Lonetree, he contended, made an ideal scapegoat. "Being an Indian made him a good target. . . . They zeroed in on Lone-tree because he was vulnerable, could be manipulated and would get little support."

During the trial itself, Kunstler made references to Lonetree's status as an American Indian, and suggested that this was one of the reasons he was scapegoated for such a minor security breach. In an op-ed piece for the *Los Angeles Times,* he bitterly contrasted the "superstar status" given to Lieutenant Colonel Oliver North, who had recently confessed to several crimes in connection with the Iran-Contra scandal, with the solitary confinement given Clayton Lonetree, and suggested that the Indian racial background of Lonetree was the key to an explanation. Kunstler distributed a terrible poem to reporters in July that made the same point:

> Lt. Col. North gets on the stand,
> Confessing to a mass of federal crimes,
> . . . .
> The colonel's called a hero by his boss,
> And does not spend a moment in a jail
> Or lose the right to get his point across.
> The sergeant [Lonetree] undergoes a converse fate,
> An Indian maligned by Reagan's men,
> And forced these many months to sit and wait,
> So isolated in a Naval pen.
> The difference rubs the Constitution raw—
> There is no equal justice under law.

It was not just Kunstler's rhetoric that brought an Indian consciousness to Lonetree's trial. Lonetree's seventy-two-year-old grandfather, an Indian elder and medicine man, appeared in court one day in a full Indian headdress. During a recess he held up a peace pipe, blew on a flute-like instrument, chanted, and tapped Lonetree on the back repeatedly with feathers. In addition, Kunstler invited two Indian groups to Quantico to demonstrate. A group of traditional Sioux beat on a drum and chanted a spiritual song by the flagpole while two dozen AIM members from different tribes demonstrated at the entrance to the base.

Kunstler's efforts to infuse an Indian theme into the trial failed for more reasons than simply public apathy. Native Americans themselves did not respond well to the appeal. In particular, American Indian military veterans were unsympathetic, among many of whom the valor of the World War II Navajo Code Talkers was still an active tradition. Efforts to raise funds through defense rallies flopped; a rally in Denver yielded only $612 and another in St. Paul netted a mere $220. Furthermore, the Indian theme did not play well inside the courtroom, either. Lonetree's original confession included the statement "I guess some of my actions were based on my hatred for the prejudices expressed in the

United States against Indians. What I did was nothing compared to what the white man and the United States government did to the American Indian one hundred years ago."

The *prosecutor* argued the Indian theme as a motive for Lonetree's actions. That in itself significantly diminished the impact of Kunstler's point.

The jury convicted Lonetree after only a few hours of deliberation. The prosecution then urged a life sentence, and the military defense lawyer requested a ten-year sentence. The jury, which has the sentencing function under the military system, gave Lonetree thirty years. Kunstler immediately denounced the sentence as "a kick in the teeth. [The jury] knew they were doing a bad thing. To make it palatable, they gave less than the prosecution asked for." The government offered a five-year reduction in exchange for debriefing under immunity. Kunstler urged Lonetree to refuse the offer, arguing that it would weaken his appellate position and that it was a "dirty, dirty business" that would be used to force Lonetree to testify "about a false spy ring."

At that point, Lonetree and his father fired Stuhff and Kunstler, citing their failure to consult with the family on tactics, their inexperience in military trials, and their failure to call any defense witnesses. New civilian counsel accepted the five-year reduction, criticized Kunstler as "more interested in trying the system than in trying to help his client," and prepared an appeal. The appeal raised the issues of the secret trial, the secret witness, the admissibility of the confessions, other trial errors, and the inappropriateness of the sentence. Appellate counsel also alleged an ineffectiveness of trial counsel's assistance, so severe as to amount to a violation of the Sixth Amendment right to counsel. The ineffectiveness of counsel argument was based on Lonetree's claim that Stuhff and Kunstler urged him not to engage in plea bargaining.

When a reporter questioned Kunstler about Lonetree's appellate allegations, Kunstler refused to dispute the charge as a matter of principle. "Whenever a client claims I did something wrong I would never publicly deny it. If they can win their case by proving any dereliction on my part, it would be all for the good and I cheer him on because it would end an unjust conviction and a savage sentence." Stuhff was not so charitable, denouncing the appeal's allegations as "completely dishonest" and demanding a retraction. However, Kunstler stuck to his guns. "If they want to hang it on me and it gets him off—fine."

The U.S. Navy-Marine Corps Court of Military Review affirmed the conviction and sentence in all respects in 1990. However, on further review, the U.S. Court of Military Appeals in 1992 affirmed the conviction, but held that "Lonetree offers us colorable claims consistent with the existing record that civilian counsel [i.e., Stuhff and Kunstler] offered him bizarre and untenable advice" that "left the young Marine with so heavy a sentence." It ordered a rehearing as to the sentence. On rehearing in October 1993, the sentence, now at twenty-five years, was further reduced to twenty years.

That made Lonetree eligible for parole, as he had served one-third of his sentence. However, Lonetree refused parole out of fear that if he said or did something the government disliked, his parole could be revoked and he would be sent back to prison. A much greater spy scandal then erupted when the CIA agent Aldrich Ames admitted to massive counterintelligence for the Soviet Union. Ames alleged that he had asked the KGB to set up a diversion to draw attention away from him, and that the Lonetree affair had served that purpose. The Lonetree family rehired Stuhff and Kunstler, the original prosecutor suggested that the case be reopened, and the marines further reduced the sentence to fifteen years.

On February 27, 1996, the government released Lonetree from prison. He had served nearly nine years and, with six years off for good behavior as a model prisoner, he was set free, not on parole but without restriction. Neither he nor his Soviet swallow, Violetta, had married, and both still expressed affection for each other. Henderson had believed he could have obtained a ten-year plea-bargained sentence for Lonetree. If he had, and if Lonetree had earned good-time credit at the same rate, Lonetree would have been released after serving six years. Thus it ended up that Lonetree spent three additional years in prison for the satisfaction of never having admitted guilt before a kangaroo military court. Whether that was worth it to Lonetree's dignity, only he can say.

■

In November 1986 more than two dozen New York City policemen raided an apartment to arrest Larry Davis, a young black resident of the Bronx. In an extensive firestorm, Davis wounded six policemen and escaped unscathed. Defending Davis at his subsequent trial, Kunstler developed an incredibly bold theory: the police had come not to arrest Davis, but to kill him for reneging on a mutual drug deal. Davis simply fired back in self-defense against the "killer cops." The defense played out in a series of trials.

Between 1987 and 1991 Davis faced a criminal jury on four separate occasions. In his first trial, which began on December 21, 1987, and lasted until March 1988, authorities charged him with the murder of four drug dealers in the Bronx. The second trial, which started on July 26, 1988, and lasted over seventeen weeks, charged Davis with the attempted murder of nine police officers together with six counts of aggravated assault on police officers and several counts of illegal possession and use of firearms. Kunstler represented Davis in these two trials and secured a stunning victory: acquittal of all counts in both trials excepting the illegal possession of firearms.

The prosecutors kept after Davis and tried him for the murder of a Manhattan drug dealer in November 1989, which also resulted in an acquittal. It was not until the fourth trial, in the spring of 1991, that the police were able to make a charge stick, when a jury finally convicted Davis of second-degree murder and robbery of two additional drug dealers.

The timing of events played a role in the defense theory. On October 9, 1986, another person's confession implicated Davis in the murder of the Manhattan drug dealer, the murder for which Davis was tried and acquitted in his third trial. Then on October 30, police took gunfire from several robbery suspects, who fled into a Bronx park. A witness identified Davis as one of the suspects. That same day, police discovered the bodies of four murder victims, two of whom were drug dealers, in a Bronx apartment. An informant disclosed that Davis participated in that shooting.

The following day, October 31, 1986, several detectives went looking for Davis at the home of his mother, Mary Davis. After they left, Mary Davis telephoned the Civilian Complaint Review Board to complain that one of the detectives told her, "You raised a dirty bastard, a dirty bastard. You tell your son that he is going to get a fucking bullet right in front of his fucking forehead." Allegedly, the detective then pointed a finger at Mary Davis's forehead.

On November 19, 1986, more than two dozen police (some versions have twenty-four and others twenty-seven) raided the apartment of Larry Davis's sister, having information that he was there. There is a predictable dispute as to which side fired first, but unquestionably a shoot-out ensued, and Davis got the best of it. A stray bullet from an officer's gun unlocked a neighboring apartment, and Davis was able to make his escape, but not without having first injured six policemen, three of them seriously. Neither Davis nor any member of his family was hurt.

The raid generated a great deal of confusion, most of which cannot be resolved. At first, the police said that their motive in going to the apartment was to question Davis; later, they claimed that they intended to arrest him. It is clear and undisputed that there was no arrest warrant for Davis until after the raid. It was the defense theory, based on officer testimony, that some detectives and one in particular rushed forward into the apartment ahead of the others. That may well be true, since several of the wounded officers filed claims with the city of New York alleging that the raid was negligently planned and executed. One claim specifically alleged that a detective prematurely charged ahead. Following an intense seventeen-day manhunt, police surrounded a Bronx apartment house in which Davis held a woman and two children hostage. After six hours of negotiations and without gunfire, Davis released the hostages and surrendered. For his success in the shoot-out and his skill in evading an intense dragnet, Davis had already become somewhat of a cult hero in the black community of the Bronx. He had a cheering section that chanted, "Lar-ry! Lar-ry!" as he was led to the police car, and later a new dance in the South Bronx was named after him. This was before Kunstler even entered the picture.

At first, Stanley Cohen of the Bronx Legal Aid Society represented Davis. But a conflict of interest developed with a codefendant in the four-murders case, and the court designated Kunstler and Lynne Stewart as counsel. The two had already joined forces for several previous trials, and the alliance was typical of those forged by Kunstler in the 1980s. A younger attorney, ideologically sympathetic, contributed legal grunt work in the preparation of the case, and Kunstler brought in his skill as a strategist and his abilities to publicize the case. In the trials of Davis, however, Stewart contributed far more than grunt work. She participated in witness examination and gave the closing summation. Kunstler praised her "eloquence, instant recall and her shrewd analysis of the evidence."

Kunstler developed an audacious theory of the case. Larry Davis had been dealing in drugs for rogue cops during a five-year period that began when he was just fifteen years old. In the fall of 1986 Davis refused further dealings, and failed to pay a considerable amount of money, one million dollars, for the street proceeds of drugs the drug-dealing cops had delivered to him. The crooked police were angered to the point of homicide because of the withheld money and also their fear that Davis would expose them. The admonition of the detective to Davis's mother that he would end up with a bullet in his forehead was a warning. The warrantless raid on his sister's apartment was not intended to talk with him or to arrest him. Instead, the leaders of that raid, the detectives who rushed in, intended to murder Davis.

As always, Kunstler justified his representation ideologically. At first, he saw Davis only as an objectively political case. Davis was himself nonpolitical and his representation was justified only because he was a member of "one of the groups in society which is perennially oppressed." Later, Kunstler ascribed more political significance to Davis's actions. He saw the case as an affirmation that black people could stand up to police brutality. Kunstler declared in 1990 that "Larry Davis became a symbol of resistance to police violence."

Stanley Cohen later claimed that he was the one who devised the strategy that Davis was involved with drug-dealing cops who were intent on killing him. However, the approach has such a Kunstlerian stamp to it, the turning of the tables and putting the authorities on trial, that at least the execution of the concept at trial seems authentically Kunstler. Who knows? Perhaps the basic idea of Davis as a renegade toady for crooked cops came from Davis himself, although that seems somewhat unlikely, because the concept changed slightly over time. In April 1987 Kunstler was saying that "it's our theory they [the police] went there to kill him because he was a drug *informant* and knew too much" (emphasis added). Kunstler was still talking about Davis having been a police informant as late as May and August 1987. However, closer to and during the first two Davis trials, the theory became that Davis was a *dealer* for the cops, who refused to deal further and reneged on the payment of proceeds. If the client were himself the source of the defense theory, it does not seem as likely that it would change over time.

Kunstler spread widely the theme of the "killer cops" and Davis's involvement with drug-dealing police. He made these points repeatedly in media interviews in the twelve months between Davis's arrest and the first of his trials. Lynne Stewart and Ronald Kuby both made similar allegations. More important, Kunstler and his colleagues spoke before church groups, defense committee rallies, and at other occasions before black audiences in the Bronx, trying to familiarize the potential jury pool with their theme. On the eve of the first trial, a reporter for the *New York Times* found that the defense account that Davis had merely shot at the police in simple self-defense had "found some acceptance among some people in the city's black community, where mistrust of the police runs high. Many black religious and political figures express a willingness to hear out the defense at least."

There was good reason for doubting the police. Very recently, thirteen officers from Brooklyn's Seventy-seventh Precinct had been indicted for taking narcotics from arrested dealers and then selling the proceeds for their own profit. In 1987 and 1988 there were numerous incidents in which New York policemen beat and shot civilians. A poll conducted by *Newsday* in 1988 found that almost 50 percent of city residents felt that the police used too much force. This belief was even higher among blacks. Stephen Ralston of the NAACP Legal Defense Fund wryly noted in 1988 that "the experience of blacks in the criminal-justice system may make them less prone to accept the word of a police officer." Much more bluntly, Kunstler said that black residents of the Bronx "see police as an occupying army there to terrorize the ghetto."

Long before trial, Kunstler implanted his theme in the minds of the Bronx jury pool, preparing them for his play of the race card at trial. He succeeded. Two months before the first Davis trial, the Reverend Calvin O. Butts, executive pastor of the Abyssinian Baptist Church in Harlem, told a reporter he believed that "many police officers are involved in the drug trade—selling it, busting drug dealers and taking it for their own use, or providing drugs to the dealers." As for Davis, he thought "there may be more of a connection than people think."

Davis was continuously incarcerated from his arrest in November 1986. During the period before the first trial in December 1987, Kunstler loudly denounced what he categorized as attempts by the jailers to kill Davis. This was a clever effort to build his case that the police were out to murder Davis for his refusal to participate in the police drug trade, and hence the shoot-out was in self-defense. Well-publicized incidents of injuries to Davis in the jail could convince the potential jury pool that the jailers had attempted to kill Davis. In turn, that would validate the suggestion that the police had made the same attempt earlier.

On March 18, 1987, Kunstler reported to the media that Davis told him a guard at Rikers Island jail had closed an electronically run door on Davis's arm and fractured it. "He claims he screamed and the guard was laughing," Kunstler said. The official response to the allegation typified all those that followed: acknowledge the injury, minimize the extent, and deny knowledge of how it happened. For those who wanted to believe the police, there was no smoking gun; for those who were disposed to disbelieve the police, there was still ample smoke.

On March 25, 1987, the New York newspaper *Newsday* published an article quoting unidentified police sources who described Davis as a former police informer. Apparently, Davis had a quick temper and was not well-liked by his fellow inmates. In May 1987 eight inmates staged a hunger strike to protest Davis's unruliness. Kunstler turned that around and charged that the police were trying to set a death trap for Davis by describing him as a prison informant. "There is a lot of heat on Larry," Kunstler said. "Corrections is setting in motion what has to be set in motion to kill Larry. They have broken his arm already [a reference to the earlier incident in which according to the jail spokesman no bones were broken] and are attempting to destroy him before he can get to trial."

Then, on August 12, 1987, another prisoner slashed Davis with a razor. Davis was taken to the hospital and fourteen stitches were needed to close the wounds. Kunstler filed a motion to transfer Davis from Rikers Island to another jail. On August 20 the New York City Department of Corrections transferred Davis to the Bronx House of Correction. A spokesman claimed that it was "standard procedure," but Kuby pointed out that defense had requested the transfer to protect Davis from "repeated harassment by inmates and guards." By September 1987 Davis used a crutch to hobble into his court appearances.

Next, on November 25, Davis claimed that guards had beaten him so severely that he had welts on his back. Again a typical jail spokesman response: Davis had to be forced back to his cell after a telephone call, limited force was employed, and a prison doctor said the wounds were superficial. Kunstler had the better lines. He alleged that because of Davis's

> charges of attempted murder by police officers and of a corrupt police ring, we feel that he is going to be killed in prison. He's on crutches now. He's been stabbed and his hand was broken by a guard who closed a gate on his arm. I guess they're saying the welts are self-inflicted and that's totally crazy. . . . It wouldn't surprise me if he died in prison. If he does, boy, the blood is on this city's hands.

The judge halted jury selection that was under way for the first trial, examined the welts, and sent Davis for treatment.

An even more significant incident erupted on December 1. Davis arrived at his trial bruised and bandaged and alleged that another inmate had cut his throat with a razor and that guards stood by watching the attack and had done nothing. The jail spokeswoman said, "it's a very minor incident." The judge again halted jury selection and held a hearing. Davis identified the assailant as Jeffrey Bolden, the same inmate who had attacked him before in Rikers Island. Authorities had placed Bolden in a cell near Davis, and while Davis was standing near the door of his own cell, a guard used a remote-control mechanism to open the lock on Bolden's cell. Bolden dashed down a thirty-foot catwalk, "grabbed me from behind and started cutting" with a single-edge razor. "He was trying to get my jugular. [The guards] didn't do anything." Kunstler claimed that to place an inmate who had previously attacked Davis in a nearby cell "was obviously a setup. They were trying to kill him again."

By the second day of the special hearing, the Department of Corrections would acknowledge only that a fistfight had occurred between Davis and Bolden. As for the rest, according to the department's assistant general counsel, "of course he's making it up." However, a new sensation delayed the start of the second day. The guards assigned to escort Davis to court had themselves attacked him, and his injuries required further treatment. According to a reporter, there "appeared to be a severe welt on his right wrist, which he said had been inflicted by the officers during an argument over whether he would be allowed to use the bathroom. He added that the same officers slammed him backward against a wall, raising a large bruise on the back of his head." The prosecutors and corrections counsel argued, somewhat incredibly, that all these incidents were manufactured to improve Davis's chances of release or transfer to a different prison. Kunstler was now talking about a conspiracy of both police and corrections officials to murder his client, and his argument was gathering more and more publicity and credence in the minds of many.

On the third day of the special hearing Lowell Holmes, the captain in charge of the guards watching Davis, testified about the nonexistence of any conspiracy to murder Davis. Kunstler took him on blistering cross-examination. Holmes conceded that he had no explanation of how an inmate who had once before attacked Davis had managed to get out of his cell ("a mechanical failure," he speculated). The senior guard testified that he was baffled as to how, in another incident, someone was able to enter Davis's cell and slash the suits Davis needed to wear to court. He had no explanation for how Bolden, moments after the attack on Davis had been halted, managed to obtain a "Dixie cup full of hot water" to throw at Davis. The guard conceded that he had sent Bolden to the prison hospital before Davis, notwithstanding that Davis was injured and Bolden was not, and acknowledged that Davis was not given medical treatment until three hours after he had been slashed.

As the hearings continued, the defense introduced an affidavit from an inmate that he had been offered money to cut up Davis and that he had overheard guards make a similar offer to another inmate. Within a few days, the prosecutor acquiesced to the suggestion that Davis be transferred to federal custody. His stated reason, and also that of the judge, was that the hearings into Davis's jailhouse treatment were delaying the murder trial. The prosecutor probably was concerned also over the adverse publicity and how that would affect the jury pool. At first, the New York City commissioner of correction would not go along with the plan. He called a news conference in which he showed videos of Davis threatening correction officers and acting violently in his cell. However, the commissioner quickly fell into line and agreed. At minimal damage to his client, Kunstler had succeeded in generating an enormous amount of publicity on how badly Davis was treated in jail. Not only did that generate sympathy for Davis, but more important, it tended to validate the basic theme of his case: that the corrections officers, and by extension the police, were trying to murder Davis because he backed out of his drug dealing and because he knew too much.

The trial for the murder of the drug dealers opened on December 21, 1987. Kunstler immediately linked these murders to the later shoot-out, telling the jury that "all of the charges that you're trying him on today were all originated after the shoot-out of November nineteenth, not before . . . because now that raid had to be justified." He suggested that the present charges were fabricated to give plausible cover to the raid intended to kill Davis. He told the jury that Davis had been "recruited at age 15 by a corrupt policeman into a corrupt drug ring. He worked for the police four or five years. For one reason or another, he decided to leave the ring, and at that moment he became a deadly liability."

Kunstler referred to the numerous business cards of various policemen, including narcotics officers, found in Davis's possession. He said the police tried to explain the cards by circulating a rumor that Davis was an informer, a position Kunstler himself had taken only a few months previously. However, he shifted ground and said that the rumor "wasn't true, but the purpose was to have him killed in prison." Then Kunstler reviewed all the altercations and woundings Davis had experienced in jail. These had all occurred "because if he couldn't be killed on November nineteenth [the date of the botched raid], then perhaps it could be done later when he was in custody." He concluded his opening by urging the jury to judge with an unbiased mind. "If you do not do it that way, then someday, somewhere, somehow, in the early hours of the morning, you will wake up screaming." Kunstler made that same plea about waking up screaming to the officer-jury in the Lonetree case, only to have it backfire in that case by the prosecutor, who suggested that the screams in the night would be from the tortured cries of Soviet citizens working for the United States whose identities had been compromised by Lonetree's indiscretions.

The prosecution's direct case was fairly strong. It had bullets from the murder scene that matched a gun in Davis's possession when he surrendered and another gun taken from the scene of the shoot-out. Kunstler attacked the chain of custody and suggested that the failure of the officer who found the casings to scratch his initials on them indicated they might be later plants. The prosecution had a Davis fingerprint from the murder scene. Kunstler suggested that the fingerprints had been "lifted" and placed there to frame Davis. The prosecution also had two witnesses who testified that Davis had admitted the killings to them, but their questionable credibility was vigorously attacked.

The prosecutors were too ardent, too heavy-handed, and became themselves exhibits for the defense in its theory of official wrongdoing. Both Kunstler and Stewart picked away meticulously at an abundance of minor errors and inconsistencies in the prosecution's case. In its own case, the defense concentrated on its theory of why the police were out to murder Davis. It highlighted the numerous police business cards and officers' home telephone numbers in Davis's possession, the testimony of his mother that many policemen used to call on Davis over the years, the threat to Davis made through his mother, and the police negligence suits that alleged that the raid was not made according to regulations, suggesting a murderous intent of the angry detectives who charged ahead. A shotgun slug was recovered from a dresser drawer in the back bedroom of the sister's apartment, into which Davis retreated at the start of the raid. The dresser faced the hallway through which the officers approached Davis. The defense argued that this showed an officer had fired first. If Davis had fired first, the cops would not have gone down that corridor and the slug could not have gotten into that dresser.

Stewart gave an excellent summation. She emphasized the difficulty of proving a police conspiracy, that no cop would be willing to come forward, and that they were not all in on the plot. The jury of seven blacks, three Hispanics, one white, and one Asian deliberated for nine days before acquitting Davis. Both Davis and Kunstler cried. Of course, Kunstler had a lot to say to the media. He said, "I don't think Larry ever believed it could happen to him, that he could be acquitted in this society. The jury remains the only bulwark we have." Anticipating the future trial that Davis faced for the shoot-out itself, Kunstler told a reporter that the acquittal was a crucial affirmation of the defense view that the murder trial just concluded was a "fake trial in order to give a legitimate face to the shoot-out." He also told the press that this acquittal had led to his first courtroom tears since the Chicago trial. At the very least, that last statement was arrant nonsense.

Prosecutors and defense counsel agreed that obtaining the right jury would be the key to success in the shoot-out trial. The acquittal in the drug dealer murder case stunned the district attorney's office, and it was determined to win the shoot-out case. The lineup of prosecutors and defense counsel was exactly the same, and Davis even faced the same judge. However, the prosecution had added a jury consultant to its roster, the first time the Bronx district attorney used an expert to evaluate potential jurors.

The Bronx itself was a difficult place for prosecutors. By 1988 the Bronx was two-thirds black and Hispanic. It had an acquittal rate in criminal cases of 42 percent, compared with a citywide average of 29 percent and a rate of 25 percent in Westchester County. A homicide prosecutor acknowledged, "it's bizarre. Everything here [the Bronx] is truly stood on its head. The jurors are overwhelmingly suspicious of cops. If you have a case involving cops, you are almost certain to lose." Kunstler bluntly tied this to race.

> There's no question it's because of their race. A white Westchester jury
> would be composed of people whose relationship with the police was

always a cordial and friendly one, helping, getting their kids across the street. In the Bronx, they do not necessarily look at them as a friendly force. They may be a dangerous presence. They are not going to automatically believe a police officer. They will look on him with suspicion.

Obviously the key to the case for the defense was to pack the jury with black and Hispanic jurors, and for the prosecution to pack the jury with whites. Kunstler at his most candid would have said that America is racist, American whites have played the race card for centuries, and there is nothing wrong with blacks doing the same. For public consumption he put his preference for minority jurors on a more race-neutral basis:

> their own life experience has been such that they will watch more carefully the nature of the accusation and the type of evidence that is brought to sustain it. They're wary of the police, they're not over-awed by the judge and the courtroom atmosphere and they're more understanding of the defendants themselves and the circumstances that bring them into court.

The prosecutors never were as candid about their preference for white jurors.

Traditionally, the law allowed both defense and prosecution several peremptory challenges, a right to exclude specific jurors arbitrarily without disclosing any reason. For practical purposes that right has now disappeared, since counsel must disclose a reason for the exclusion so a judge may examine it and determine whether it is free of any racial basis. The right to peremptory challenges began to crumble with the 1986 case of *Batson v. Kentucky,* in which the U.S. Supreme Court ruled that prosecutors could not use their arbitrary challenges to exclude jurors on the basis of race. At the time of the jury selection in the Larry Davis shoot-out case, the *Batson* ruling was being slowly extended to include peremptory challenges exercised by defense attorneys, although there had not yet been a conclusive Supreme Court ruling.

After two weeks of jury selection, five black men and one Hispanic woman had been selected for service. However, Kunstler had exercised peremptory challenges against all of the eight white prospective jurors who had appeared. The prosecution then brought a *Batson* motion and alleged that Kunstler and Davis were "racists who are systematically attempting to exclude all whites and most of the Hispanics from jury service and pick as black a jury as possible for this black defendant." Kunstler responded that all the prosecution was concerned about was a conviction and they would like to "force on this jury as large a number of white people as they can, because they know white people will be more apt to convict, given the fact that all the victims are white police officers and the defendant is black."

The judge ruled with the prosecution, dismissed the six jurors who had been selected, and began jury selection all over again. Kunstler said, rather extravagantly, but perhaps with an eye to the Bronx audience, that "the result is going to be the same as when blacks were excluded from juries in the Deep South." Two months later a jury of eleven minorities and one white were empaneled. Before hearing any testimony, the sole white juror asked to be excused because his wife feared *police* harassment if he voted to acquit. At the mutual request of prosecution and defense, the judge declared a mistrial, and, having already been at it for two and a half months, they began jury selection again. Eventually, after three months, the final panel consisted of nine blacks and three Hispanics (a black alternate replaced one of the Hispanics during the trial). Both the prosecutor's efforts to obtain white jurors and Kunstler's fear of them went for naught; simple Bronx demographics determined the jury's composition.

Kunstler went directly to the race issue in his opening statement. He told the all-minority jury that the case was about "how the police treat young third world people in the depressed communities of our city." He spun the story of Davis's recruitment at age fifteen to be the cops' drug dealer. After Davis backed out, this "gang of corrupt police officers . . . became worried about him. One that he might tell on them, and two, that he took their money." Accordingly, they planned a raid to kill him, and the first detective, the one whom other police testified had rushed ahead, "went into that apartment with one thing in mind, to kill Larry Davis." It was then a simple matter of self-defense. "Larry wasn't going to be Eleanor Bumpurs [a black woman allegedly recently murdered by the police] and just die there on the floor."

Kunstler acknowledged that the "police will never admit that they were ever in league with Larry Davis or that they fired the first bullet." However, he pointed out that the police had no warrants and asked why they would assemble an entire task force of over two dozen cops with bulletproof vests and sawed-off shotguns unless they were bent on killing Davis. He reminded the jury that there was not a single black cop on that task force. Immediately, the prosecutor objected and the remark was stricken from the record, but the jury got the point.

Kunstler had to overcome the distraction caused by Steven McDonald, a former New York City policeman shot in the line of duty and paralyzed from the neck down in 1986. He sometimes appeared in courtrooms, his crippled body strapped in a wheelchair, in cases involving cop shootings in order to generate sympathy for the police or to prejudice the jury, however one wishes to describe it. It seems fair to say that judges were far more upset about his presence in cases where the effect would be to prejudice the prosecution, as where a cop on trial for killing a civilian claims self-defense and McDonald's presence was to remind the jury of the consequences to a policeman of not shooting first.

In the Davis case, McDonald remained quiet through the prosecutor's opening statement, but when it came time for Kunstler to speak, he began to wheeze and groan through a respiratory tube. Although many jurors looked at McDonald, Kunstler remained coolly indifferent. Outside court Kunstler denounced the police tactics of bringing McDonald as "indecent" and "police histrionics." Privately to a friend, Kunstler acknowledged that "there's no way I'm gonna say this crippled policeman is not entitled to stay here," and that the cost of making any fuss would do him more damage than good. Many uniformed detectives attended the trial, all wearing their badges. The only visual aid the defense had was a cane, with which Davis now walked, a sign and symbol of jailers' beatings. However, with Davis now elevated to a folk hero in the Bronx, himself a symbol of resistance, the cane was a daily reminder to the jury.

As far as the defense was concerned, the shoot-out trial proceeded in much the same manner as the drug dealers murder case had. The same allegations were made, with little real evidence. Kunstler and Stewart made heavy use of innuendo and ridicule to attack police witnesses. After a seventeen-week trial, on the fifth day of deliberations, the jury acquitted Davis of all charges except illegal gun possession. One of the jurors said, "I've lived in the South Bronx a great part of my life, and I happen to know police officers who use cocaine, smoke reefer, and do a lot of the things the criminals do." Some representative comments from Bronx residents: Gloria Thomas, forty-one, "People at my job [Department of Social Services] jumped up in elation when they heard he was acquitted"; Willie Daly, sixty-three, "I'm glad he got acquitted, because if it had been the other way around, the police would have been acquitted"; Jothern Smith, eighteen, "He's a hero to me. He stood up for himself."

The police asserted that the verdict was racist, but Kunstler was ecstatic. He told reporters that Davis was "a symbol of fighting back that probably makes people feel that there is some retribution for all those others shot down. He is kind of a folk hero. He won't be a hero to middle-class white people or the police, but heroes come in strange circumstances. He's a hero in almost the classic sense." Kunstler compared Davis to Nat Turner, the famous leader of a slave revolt. More specifically, Kunstler remarked that the verdict "sends out a message that white officers are not going to be able to shoot down black youths without a proper response" and speculated that "maybe there will be no more black Sambos, only black Rambos. Maybe this means there will be fewer shootings of blacks and young Latinos in this city." His most incendiary comment was to the *Village Voice*: "any black guy that shoots six cops and puts the fear of God in police officers, I think is great."

The district attorney demanded the maximum sentence of ten years minimum to twenty years. Kunstler argued for no sentence at all, but if there were to be a sentence, he suggested the same six months that the white man Bernhard H. Goetz had received for illegal gun possession after acquittal of charges of attempted murder of four black youths in a subway shooting in 1987. A thousand off-duty officers blocked traffic and demonstrated outside the courthouse during the sentencing hearing. The judge handed down a five-to-fifteen-year sentence, which Kunstler denounced as "racist" and Phil Caruso, president of the Patrolman's Benevolent Association, disparaged as "a slap on the wrist."

Following the shoot-out trial, Kunstler and Stewart had a falling out, either over Kunstler's hogging of most of the publicity or over disagreements concerning several black activists' hopes for commercialization of the Davis story. Kunstler did garner most of the publicity, even though Davis himself once said that "everyone thinks Kunstler beat the case. Lynne Stewart beat the case." The cops were angry over the result, but by their own macho code they could not attack Stewart. However, Kunstler not only received more of the publicity, he was also a man and could be bruised. Therefore, when the inevitable cop assault came, it fell on Kunstler. It happened following a 1989 Brooklyn hearing involving the activist lawyer C. Vernon Mason. Kunstler and several other lawyers attended to show solidarity with Mason.

After the hearing, the court officers attempted to clear the court-room. People apparently did not move fast enough, there was a com-motion in the back of the courtroom, and then, according to Kunstler, "the white court officers went berserk, pushing and shoving everyone. . . . They threw me on my back with my arms behind me, bending my knees up so violently that the left one eventually required surgery. One officer kicked me in the chest, hard, breaking one of my ribs and shouted, 'This one's for Larry Davis!'" The police threw Kunstler and most of the lawyers with him in jail, told them they were charged with riot, but then released them the next day. Kunstler filed a claim with the city of New York, but eventually decided not to sue because he "wasn't going to ask the system to undo what the system had done." A stinging pain in his left knee bothered Kunstler for the rest of his life.

■

A comparison of the Lonetree and Davis cases suggests that the seeds of Kunstler's magical rhetoric and publicity would bear fruit only when not tossed onto totally barren ground. It is not simply that Kunstler could weave his spell only before a "third-world" jury of blacks and Hispanics. We must recall that he secured an acquittal of the Indians Butler and Robideau by a white jury in Cedar Rapids, where major themes of the case were perjury by government witnesses and persist-ent mistreatment of American Indians by the federal government. Nonetheless, it was a genuine jury before which Kunstler operated in Cedar Rapids.

In the Lonetree trial, in contrast, the jury was composed of military officers who rigidly held a fixed ideology within a caste profession. They were immune to influence from what they read in the newspapers or heard on the radio. Therefore, Kunstler's efforts to manipulate the media in that case, while it might have had an impact on the public gen-erally, had absolutely no effect on the jury members. A sizable number of the jury pool for Davis, residents of the Bronx, followed with interest Kunstler's efforts in the media to portray Davis as a victim of white po-lice corruption and as a symbol of fighting back. In contrast, there was no jury pool, in the ordinary sense, for Lonetree. To the extent that the marine officers saw any symbolism in Lonetree, he appeared as a trai-tor, not only to his country but, just as importantly to these denizens of a closed society, to the rigid code of marine honor. That was a nut that even Kunstler's magic could not crack.

14

A Return to the Limelight

KUNSTLER'S PRACTICE AGAIN became highly publicized in the early 1990s. In these years he defended flag burners before the Supreme Court; Yusef Salaam, one of the Central Park rapist gang; and Colin Ferguson, the multiple murderer on the Long Island Railroad. He also represented Qubilah Shabazz, daughter of Malcolm X, who allegedly plotted to murder the rival black leader Louis Farrakhan; El Sayyid Nosair, the purported assassin of the radical rabbi Meir Kahane; and Sheik Omar Abdel-Rahman, the Muslim cleric who, along with other Arabs, was accused of plotting the destruction of many New York landmarks, including the bombing of the World Trade Center. These front-page cases made Kunstler a national figure to a degree he had not been since the Chicago Seven trial. However, these cases, especially his representation of Arab clients, also caused Kunstler considerable personal difficulty.

The first of these notorious cases, involving the flag burners, had roots in the 1980s. In 1984 Gregory Lee Johnson burned an American flag during a demonstration outside the Republican National Convention in Dallas, Texas. A local Texas court convicted Johnson, a member of the Revolutionary Communist Youth Brigade, and sentenced him to a year in jail and a $2,000 fine. The American Civil Liberties Union appealed to the Texas Criminal Appeals Court, which reversed the conviction. The local district attorney then appealed to the U.S. Supreme Court, which accepted the case for hearing to be held March 21, 1989.

Johnson was well pleased with his Texas lawyers but decided to retain Kunstler to represent him before the U.S. Supreme Court. A scholar who interviewed everyone concerned concluded that the motivation for the change was that "Kunstler's high public profile, his obvious fondness for publicity, and the media's reciprocal attraction to him made him more likely to conduct the type of public, political defense that Johnson wanted." David Cole, a bright lawyer working for the

Center for Constitutional Rights, researched and wrote the brief, and Kunstler made the oral argument.

Kunstler argued the case on straight First Amendment grounds: the destruction of the American flag was a symbolic statement of hostility toward the country, and Johnson was convicted because of the content of his speech. He told a reporter that "to insulate the American flag from such treatment is not only to eliminate one form of direct protest against the government, but to continue the veneration of a piece of cloth and the false patriotism it so often cloaks." His manner before the Court was bantering. At one point in the argument Justice Anthony Kennedy queried Kunstler whether the armed forces might compel a soldier's respect for the flag. Kunstler responded, "You might have a case there." At another point, Kunstler and Chief Justice William H. Rehnquist were discussing an earlier precedent when Kunstler remarked, "I don't know if I've convinced you, but . . ." Rehnquist interjected, "Well, you may have convinced others." Later Rehnquist good-naturedly remarked, "I don't think we're going to reach eye to eye on this." Laughter followed, but when it subsided Kunstler replied comfortably, "I have that distinct feeling."

The Supreme Court, by a vote of five to four, held the Texas flag desecration law unconstitutional. Effectively, this invalidated similar statutes passed in almost all states. A political firestorm ensued. The Senate passed a resolution, ninety-seven to three, deploring the decision. President Bush proposed a constitutional amendment prohibiting the burning or similar destruction of the flag. Kunstler called the proposed amendment the work of "pandering politicians who want to jump on the flag-waving bandwagon and get the public to give up some of its rights." Kunstler realized that the flag stirred emotions and was a potent force, but "that is why it [flag burning] is such an effective protest mechanism. It criticizes policy in the harshest and most powerful way."

Eventually Congress passed a federal law punishing flag desecration, but did not propose a constitutional amendment. Protesters immediately tested the law and drew two prosecutions, one in Seattle and the other in Washington, D.C. They hired Kunstler and Cole to represent them at the trial level. A colleague of the defendants later explained that, once again, they sought out Kunstler "because they trusted him . . . not to distort their politics to maximize the chances of legal 'victory.'" After the hearing in Seattle, Kunstler rendered a poetic criticism of the new federal Flag Protection Act for the benefit of reporters. It was a sonnet with the concluding couplet: "The Founding Fathers' ghosts have sadly learned / It was the First Amendment that was burned." Federal judges in both Seattle and Washington threw out the new federal act as unconstitutional, setting the stage for a new Supreme Court hearing. The Supreme Court gave the cases expedited review and heard them on May 14, 1990.

Before the hearing there was a good-natured tussle between Cole and Kunstler as to who should argue the case before the High Court. Cole, who wrote the second set of briefs, thought it was his turn to argue as well, and Kunstler resisted. In good radical form, they left the decision up to their seven clients, who voted four to three in favor of Kunstler. Kunstler felt a little guilty over the issue, and in his autobiography referred to the incident as "a clear example of my good angel fighting my bad one. The bad angel won out." On May 14, 1990, Kunstler had a more tender duty before the Court than arguing about flag desecration. A long tradition requires that attorneys desiring to practice before the Supreme Court must first be vouched for by an existing member of the Supreme Court bar. Minutes before the contested hearing, Kunstler, a veteran of five previous appearances before the High Court, made the necessary motion for the admission of his daughter Karin to practice before the Supreme Court. To thank her father, Karin presented him with a pen.

The argument was lackluster. Kunstler himself commented afterwards that "it seemed like we were all beating a dead horse. It wasn't a stimulating argument." Nevertheless, Kunstler made two telling remarks. The first was the observation that "one of the most foolhardy things is an overabundance of patriotism goaded on by politicians." The second was his strong conclusion, contending that the government was attempting to turn the flag into a "golden image" that must be worshipped. Respect for the flag must be voluntary, he argued, because "once people are compelled to respect a political symbol, then they are no longer free and their respect for the flag is quite meaningless. To criminalize flag burning is to deny what the First Amendment stands for." The Court quickly invalidated the federal Flag Protection Act by a vote of five to four.

An interesting First Amendment sequel came with a case out of St. Paul, Minnesota, where Kunstler was not involved. A teenager was convicted of placing a burning cross on the lawn of a black couple who had just moved into a white middle-class neighborhood. The authorities charged him under a local ordinance that had nothing to do with burning crosses or other actions. Instead, it prohibited any expression, anywhere, that the speaker had reason to know would arouse "anger, alarm, or resentment" on the basis of "race, color, creed, religion or gender." The case was appealed to the U.S. Supreme Court, which in 1992 struck down the ordinance as violating the First Amendment.

Burning crosses on a black family's lawn? One would expect Kunstler, always critical of American racism, to strongly support the law. Indeed, most liberal and black groups did urge the Supreme Court to uphold the hate speech ordinance. The youth was not prosecuted for an act of placing a burning cross on the blacks' lawn. He was prosecuted for the thought he expressed when he knew it would alarm others. The problem of the blacks and white liberals concerned with the case, as Kunstler explained it, was that "all they could see was the burning cross." Instead, Kunstler took a very principled position, not held by many liberals or blacks. Kunstler said he was "opposed to any ordinance like this. . . . I'm a strict First Amendment supporter. If this ordinance stands up, the First Amendment will be in shambles."

A more violent case began when New York was shocked by a vicious assault in the early morning hours of April 20, 1989. A gang of about thirty Latino and black youths went on a rampage in Central Park, a "wilding" as they called it, attacking several joggers and homeless men. Near the 102d Street crossover drive, about a dozen of them came upon a white twenty-eight-year-old female investment banker out for an early morning run. The young men, fifteen to eighteen years old, cruelly beat the woman, gang raped her, and left her for dead. The woman lost 80 percent of her blood and was in a coma for two weeks.

The next day the police rounded up several suspects for interrogation, including Yusef Salaam, a fifteen-year-old black youth. Salaam falsely told the police that he was sixteen, and the police interrogated him, obtaining an oral confession of his involvement in the crime. New York state law requires that a parent or guardian be present for the questioning of any suspect under sixteen. In order to induce Salaam's confession, his questioners used typical—but not illegal or coercive—misrepresentations. During his interrogation, the police refused to allow his aunt and his "Big Brother," (ironically an assistant U.S. attorney) permission to see Salaam. After about ninety minutes of questioning,

Salaam's mother arrived at the precinct station, informed the police that her son was only fifteen, and the questioning stopped.

Salaam was tried with two codefendants. He had a publicly paid attorney who everyone agreed made disastrous mistakes. Two of the jurors specifically criticized the effectiveness of Salaam's attorney. The codefendants had videotaped confessions, but as Salaam had not signed or videotaped a confession, a detective testified as to what Salaam had told him. No physical evidence linked Salaam or the other defendants to the beating and rape. The jogger could not identify them, and the DNA tests of their semen did not match that taken from her body. Indeed, a semen stain on her clothing was traced to her boyfriend. It is fair to say that the only thing that convicted Salaam was his own confession, taken in violation of New York law, although Salaam misrepresented his age.

The case, with its potent mixture of race, interracial sex, and the seemingly inexplicable motives of these young men from working-class families, played out to intense media coverage. After the conviction, Salaam's family fired his publicly funded attorney and obtained Kunstler's representation. Salaam maintained his innocence at sentencing, and Kunstler commented, "I'm convinced that what occurred here was a legal lynching." As Kunstler prepared his appeal, the jury foreman appeared on a WBGO-FM radio program and mentioned that one of the jurors had routinely read newspaper articles about the case during the trial, and shared their contents with his fellow jurors, contrary to the court's instructions. Kunstler moved the trial judge to set aside the conviction for jury misconduct, but in a December 20, 1990, hearing the judge refused, citing a lack of affidavits and no evidence that the jury relied on the newspaper reports.

Kunstler appealed the conviction to the Appellate Division and then the Court of Appeals, New York's highest court. He charged error in not setting aside the conviction for the jury misconduct, but relied primarily on the police questioning. Kunstler argued that the police ought to have checked school records to find Salaam's true age, waited until his mother arrived, or permitted other family members and his "Big Brother" to have access.

At the oral argument on the appeal, Salaam's mother was disappointed in Kunstler's performance. She thought that Kunstler spoke too much about the mistreatment of black suspects in general, and not enough about the facts of her son's case. The appellate court rejected

Kunstler's arguments, although one of the justices on the Court of Appeals vigorously dissented. Upon the final affirmation of the conviction, Kunstler remarked that "Had Yusef Salaam been born with white skin to a middle-class family, his interrogation by the police would have been halted by a knowledgeable parent or available attorney. Today's ruling reaffirms . . . that there are two systems of justice in existence in this state—one for whites and the other for minorities."

Kunstler acknowledged that his representation of Salaam caused many of his female colleagues at the Center for Constitutional Rights to look on him with contempt and disdain. He felt he had to take the case "because Yusef was another in a long line of those who are hated by society; with the odds against him, he needed a good lawyer to stand by him." Actually, however, Kunstler's principal difficulties in the case came not from female acquaintances, but from the very real possibility that he might be suspended from practice in consequence of the contempt citation he received from the trial judge while arguing the motion to set aside Salaam's conviction. After the judge had refused to hold a hearing, denied his motion, and was moving to the next matter on his calendar, Kunstler commented, "You have exhibited what your partisanship is. You shouldn't be sitting in court. You are a disgrace to the bench."

The judge held Kunstler in contempt of court and summarily fined him $250 or thirty days in jail. Kunstler told a reporter afterward, "I'm not going to pay a nickel. I'll do the 30 days." Actually, represented by Morton Stavis, president of the Center for Constitutional Rights, Kunstler appealed the contempt, first to the Appellate Division, where he lost four to one, the court calling Kunstler's remarks "disorderly, contemptuous and insolent." Then, in December 1991, the Court of Appeals unanimously affirmed the contempt conviction. Kunstler continued to insist he would take the jail alternative, reasoning that "I do not think white middle-class lawyers should be able to buy their way out of jail time when so many Third World people are rotting in pretrial detention." A police journal in Orange County, New York, hoped Kunstler would choose jail because "if there is any justice in life, he'll drop his soap in the shower and learn first-hand what it's like to be a victim!" Ultimately, however, an anonymous benefactor paid the $250 fine over Kunstler's objections.

However, this was not the end of Kunstler's vexations over the incident. The Appellate Division hauled Kunstler up for discipline, which

could have resulted in suspension or revocation of his license to practice law. The first stop was a hearing before a two-lawyer, one-layper-
son committee charged with making a recommendation to the Appellate Division. Kunstler waived confidentiality, and the committee's
hearing was packed with more than a hundred of his supporters. Four
judges appeared as character witnesses for Kunstler, and he himself testified that he "regretted" the words he had used in the December 1990
hearing, but "not the feelings that evoked them." Kunstler allowed that
his anger "took away my judgment." The committee divided, one
member recommending public censure and two proposing a more lenient penalty, not authorized by statute, of public reprimand.

The hearing panel, or at least its majority, noted that Kunstler had
served long and hard for many years, often without compensation, in a
"commendable attempt to insure justice to the needy" and "to preserve
the personal liberties of oppressed and threatened members of our society. At least in part, his strenuous efforts have resulted in significant
improvements in our social and political order." Kunstler allowed that
the statement "made me feel terrific." He was less pleased in late December 1993, when a five-judge panel of the Appellate Division rejected
the advice of the committee and imposed a harsher public censure, although still without real penalty. Kunstler immediately referred to the
judges' decision as "the establishment speaking. They're going to put
the screws to me as much as they can." Two weeks later he referred to
his censure as a "badge of honor" and said that "it will not curb my
vigor in defending clients who, I believe, are being oppressed by the
legal system." Pointing to the commendation of the hearing committee,
he pointedly noted, "I doubt anybody on the appellate division can end
their career with that kind of an accolade."

If New Yorkers had been shocked by the Central Park jogger rape, they
were enraged by the December 7, 1993, shooting spree on the Long Island Railroad that left six dead and nineteen wounded. A passenger
calmly pulled out a gun and walked up the aisle of the moving train,
shooting fellow passengers, mostly white. The shooter, Colin Ferguson,
was a Jamaican immigrant from an affluent family. Initially represented
by a different court-appointed attorney, Ferguson later decided he
wanted Kunstler as his lawyer. Kunstler found it hard to resist, and for
the usual reasons. In Ferguson, as with most blacks charged with crime,
Kunstler saw a man "whom I knew was going to get the shaft here as

hard and as fast as it could be thrown." Kunstler and his partner Kuby represented Ferguson without payment since the Nassau County Court would not authorize public payment to lawyers who did not live in the county.

Kunstler proposed a defense of insanity based on "black rage," caused by "years of exposure to white racism," as Kuby put it. Always poorly understood, as Kunstler expounded it, this defense required an already insane person, whom white racism merely pushed over the edge into violence. That Ferguson came from a privileged Jamaican background added to his psychosis, according to Kunstler, since he had "never developed the defense mechanisms to white racism that American-born blacks are forced to learn." Once he arrived in the United States, so the theory went, Ferguson was confronted by a racist society and forced to accept menial jobs and endure racial discrimination; eventually he snapped. Some evidence supported this defense, such as notes filled with racial hatred found in Ferguson's pockets after the shooting. Several experts opined knowledgeably to reporters about black rage in the United States. Kunstler had given great publicity to a novel approach to an insanity defense, only rarely invoked before, and soon several law review articles appeared in which legal scholars debated the merits of the defense. A book-length study argued in 1997 that although black rage may be a legitimate defense, the Colin Ferguson case presented the wrong context in which to invoke it.

Innovative as the defense was, one of Kunstler's motives for offering it was not just to defend Ferguson but to serve his own radical purpose to demystify. "There is an educative factor," he acknowledged. "We want this to be an instructive case so people can learn about black rage and racism." Kunstler thought it presented a great opportunity. "I've never been able to put experts on the stand to talk about the effect of white racism in America on black people. . . . This case gives us that vehicle." Ronald Kuby waxed even more enthusiastic; he claimed that the Ferguson case offered an opportunity "to get people to think about racism as a mental-health issue, as a disease that has deformed our national character."

Kunstler was never able to put those experts on the stand. Ferguson was so crazy that he believed he never actually shot his victims, notwithstanding the dozens of eyewitnesses, and that he could represent himself. He fired Kunstler and Kuby before trial and conducted his own defense, asserting that someone took his gun and shot all the victims. Predictably, the jury convicted Ferguson, and the court sentenced him to life in prison.

Kunstler received massive criticism for his black rage theory of insanity. Some columnists reacted quite emotionally. Jack Walker called black rage "another stellar example of [Kunstler's] ludicrous views," and Don Feder wrote that Kunstler was "near the bottom of the food chain." James Lileks had "the sense he applauds his client's intention; he's like a parent caught between disciplining a child for drawing on the wall and applauding the creative spirit. I'm amazed that Kunstler has not shot up a train himself. Surely he's tired of second-hand thrills by now." Numerous letters to the editor joined in the attack.

Most of his more coherent critics made the point that if black rage were recognized, then why not Hispanic rage, American Indian rage, Jewish rage, or Christian fundamentalist rage? Indeed, in a time when many white males felt aggrieved by poorer employment opportunities because of affirmative action for blacks, why not white rage?

Although a poll conducted by the *National Law Journal* indicated that 68 percent of blacks and 45 percent of whites found the black rage theory at least "somewhat compelling," many black intellectuals and columnists were in the forefront of its critics. Clarence Page spoke for many blacks in finding it demeaning. "At best, I think it says we black people can't control ourselves." Another black journalist felt "a danger that legitimate black anger, which many whites already find difficult to accept, will end up further discredited by this line of so-called reasoning." Even the Reverend Al Sharpton, seldom a moderate, told a reporter that what Kunstler "is really suggesting is that, based on black rage, we all have the right to go out and shoot people on the subway or on the LIRR, and I don't agree with that."

Colin Ferguson was clearly not Kunstler's most successful case. First, he was not able to try the case. Second, his coined insanity syndrome, black rage, was consistently criticized and, worse, misunderstood. Kunstler clearly stated that the defense applied only as a factor that generated violence in an already insane person. In an April 1994 interview a reporter asked why there was not more black rage violence, given the resentments of the black community. Kunstler's answer was that "most people, black or white, are not insane," and the violence of black rage occurs "only if the person involved is sick to begin with." In a September 1994 radio interview he repeated the point that "you've got to start with an insane man and then the defense carries on as only a generative factor. Black rage is not a defense. Otherwise any black person could say 'I'm raged . . . therefore, I can go out and kill and do anything I want.' That's not the issue. You've got to be crazy first." Few of his many critics heard this nuanced explanation.

Kunstler's defense of Qubilah Shabazz on murder-for-hire charges proved much more successful. It became Kunstler's last major case before his death. Shabazz is the daughter of the controversial Black Muslim leader Malcolm X, who broke from the mainstream Nation of Islam and was gunned down in 1965 in Harlem's Audubon Ballroom, in the presence of four-year-old Qubilah Shabazz. Three Nation of Islam members were convicted of the assassination, but there were serious suspicions that someone higher in the organization ordered the killing. Louis Farrakhan, a present-day notorious black leader, was then a rising lieutenant, and over the years made extreme statements implying that Malcolm X's death was a matter of internal discipline. In March 1994 Betty Shabazz, the widow of Malcolm X and mother of Qubilah, stated publicly that she believed Farrakhan had a role in the murder.

According to the January 1995 indictment handed down in Minneapolis federal court, Qubilah contacted Michael Fitzpatrick, an old high school chum, to arrange for the murder of Farrakhan, and then moved to Minneapolis, where Fitzpatrick lived, to further the arrangement. The six-lawyer defense team, headed by Kunstler, argued that Fitzpatrick, acting as an undercover operator for the government, took advantage of an emotionally disturbed woman who thought her old friend was going to marry her, fostered the idea of a murder in her mind, and entrapped her. Kunstler was brilliant in his manipulation of the media.

The defense was able to destroy Fitzpatrick's credibility long before the date of trial. He turned out to be a cocaine addict and a professional stool pigeon and agent provocateur, whose past snitches, government rewards, and efforts to foment trouble in leftist groups Kunstler showed to an eager media. The year before, Fitzpatrick had filed for bankruptcy; now he was being paid $45,000 plus living expenses for digging up dirt by talking with Shabazz. The tapes themselves demonstrated that the FBI stool pigeon was the one who repeatedly brought up the subject of a killing. Moreover, the FBI allowed Fitzpatrick to make the tapes on his own, without supervision and without assurance they were not edited. If bankruptcy and the $45,000 payment were not enough motive to lie,

Fitzpatrick was also facing state cocaine charges and had been implicated in a federal fraud investigation prior to being put on the protected
witness program for gathering evidence against Shabazz. Kunstler
charged that "a clearer case of attempted entrapment by a vile and evil
seducer could not possibly be imagined," and told reporters that Fitzpatrick's calls were "the constant urging of a vulnerable woman to plot
to kill Louis Farrakhan. She's a very passive woman who said virtually
nothing." The FBI's stool pigeon "saw the gravy train before him. It's a
life without working where he's supported by the government . . .
doing the things he does best . . . informing, entrapping."

The other rhetorical device Kunstler used was to immediately compare the prosecution with the much-discredited COINTELPRO program. In all his radio and television appearances he analogized the indictment with the FBI's effort in the 1960s to sow the distrust between
Malcolm X and the Nation of Islam that led to the assassination. Kunstler charged that the FBI was using the Shabazz prosecution to attempt
to divide the black community, "a continuation of an old scheme of divide and conquer, force dissention and get people killed." Specifically,
the government was encouraging "some crazy out there to assassinate
Louis Farrakhan" because Farrakhan had the capacity to become a
black messiah who could "galvanize the black community, organize
them into a solid mass—and it scares the bejesus out of the system."
Farrakhan himself came out strongly against the prosecution, saying he
did not believe that Qubilah Shabazz had tried to kill him and that the
prosecution was a "diabolical scheme" of the government.

If this were the government's purpose, not totally out of sight but
still difficult to envisage, then it failed utterly. Betty Shabazz and Louis
Farrakhan, before estranged, now appeared together in a major rally to
denounce the prosecution. Every major black leader came out against it;
on black radio stations all over the country voices were heard decrying
the case; and petitions were signed urging Shabazz's innocence, including one circulated by Kunstler's daughter Emily, a student at the
same United Nations International School where Shabazz and Fitzpatrick once attended together.

The defense team, all of whom worked without fee, hammered
out an extremely favorable settlement the night before trial, in early
May 1995. Shabazz signed a statement in which she accepted responsibility for the plot, agreed that the statement she had given the FBI under
questioning was not coerced, although inaccurate in some details, and

conceded that the government had acted in good faith. Her not guilty plea was maintained, and trial was put on hold for two years. If she completed a two-year psychiatric and chemical dependency program and got a job or attended school, the case was slated for dismissal at the end of the two years. To one reporter Kunstler crowed, "It's an enormous defeat for the government. When you have a weak case, this is how you get rid of it and save face if you're the government." To another reporter he scolded, "In my opinion, the case was designed to do what the government did more than 30 years ago, that is to split the black community into warring camps. Fortunately, it did not succeed."

Kunstler had lesser roles in several other very public cases during the last years of his life. In 1990 he briefly represented Marlon Brando's son Christian, charged with killing his half-sister's boyfriend. Marlon Brando replaced Kunstler with Robert Shapiro, apparently after Brando became upset over Kunstler's comparison of the judge to a toad after she had refused bail. However, Kunstler was unrepentant of his remarks: "It's good for these judges. I don't think you get anywhere by bending a knee to them. I believe in attacking." In 1991 Kunstler became one of the attorneys who represented Washington, D.C., mayor Marion Barry in the appeal of his drug conviction, and in 1993 he successfully argued the appeal of Margaret Kelly Michaels, convicted of 115 counts of child abuse at a Maplewood, New Jersey, nursery school. Kunstler became cocounsel on the case in substitution for his old colleague Morton Stavis, who died shortly before the arguments. In 1995 Kunstler represented Glenn Harris, a New York City gym teacher who ran off with a fifteen-year-old student for two months, allegedly to protect her from parental abuse.

Kunstler represented a highly variegated cast of characters in less publicized matters, usually for no fee or a low fee: military dissenters during the 1991 Gulf War; black officials accused of wrongdoing of all sorts; tenant-rights squatters; and gay activists regarding their participation in the New York St. Patrick's Day Parade. He defended a theatre company that produced a play, *The Cardinal Detoxes*, in an eviction sought for offensiveness by its landlord, a Roman Catholic church. The church, Kunstler said, brought the case "in the wrong country and in the wrong century."

He issued an open offer to represent without charge any windshield-wiping squeegee man arrested under Mayor Giuliani's "quality of life" program. The squeegee men attacked windshields of cars stopped at red lights, ostensibly cleaned them, and then demanded money. New Yorkers found them annoying to the extreme, but Kunstler lectured that "this is New York, and there's no law against being annoying." According to Ronald Kuby, their office received far more antagonistic phone calls from the public concerning their proposed representation of the squeegee men than for any other of Kunstler's seemingly more controversial cases. During the last five years of his life, as he had for many years previously, Kunstler took cases that he found fun and amusing, or that presented opportunities to barb the government, to develop larger issues in the public consciousness, or to defend clients viewed by the public as pariahs by virtue of their race or ethnicity and to insure they would receive fair play. Occasionally he took a case simply for the fee, provided it did not clearly offend his political views.

With the beginning of the Nosair case in the fall of 1990, Kunstler began a different phase in his practice: the representation of Arabs. These new clients would have the greatest impact, by far, on Kunstler personally, on his family and their security, and on Kunstler's public esteem. Because Kunstler was a Jew, many people in the Jewish community, even those who had previously esteemed his work, became affronted that he represented Arabs and especially Nosair, an Arab who allegedly had killed a rabbi. Similarly, although many members of the general public had never held Kunstler in high regard, the greatest intensity of public hatred and his acquisition of a truly pariah status came with his Arab representation. Kunstler saw in Arabs, especially Arab Muslims, newer victims of American racism. Whereas blacks had once been the most despised group in America, by the 1990s "Muslims are the most hated group in the country; the moment a Muslim is accused of a crime, the specter of terrorism is raised, and everyone panics."

On November 5, 1990, someone shot and killed Rabbi Meir Kahane in a crowded room in the East Side Marriott Hotel, shortly after he finished a speech. Kahane was a zealot Jewish leader who founded the Kach Party in Israel and the Jewish Defense League in the United States, and favored the harsh repression of Arabs and their forcible removal from occupied Palestine. There was a single Arab listening to his speech that day. Several witnesses saw him in the crowd that surrounded Kahane after his talk, and one saw him shoot Kahane. After the shooting, the single Arab fled, wounding an old man as he made his escape. Outside, he commandeered a cab that was pursued by angry Kahane supporters. Once midtown traffic ground the cab to a stop, the suspect fled, traded shots with a postal police officer, and fell to the ground wounded. Police found a .357 Ruger near his hand, the type of gun that apparently killed Kahane. The captured suspect was El Sayyid Nosair. It seemed like an open-and-shut case, so much so that the authorities were incredibly sloppy in their gathering of evidence, a fact that Kunstler brilliantly exploited at trial.

Kahane had a considerable number of admirers as well as critics. He also had bitter enemies in the Arab community. Kahane was a strenuous and effective activist for causes he believed in and was also a complex man. Probably, Nosair did kill Kahane, as both the evidence in the state case and his subsequent federal conviction suggest. (This discussion is limited to the state trial, Kunstler's attitudes toward Nosair, and especially Kunstler's advocacy. It is not designed to show that Nosair should have been acquitted.)

Kunstler believed that Nosair and defendants like him would simply be railroaded into prison or the electric chair, unless experienced attorneys stepped forward. Nosair would do better with an attorney like Kunstler than the young and inexperienced public defender he would otherwise be forced to accept. However, Kunstler strained a little in his autobiography to justify the case. Rather than maintain Nosair's innocence in retrospect, he took the tack that he really did not know, but that Nosair was entitled to a defense regardless. Even if he had believed Nosair guilty, "it's ethically correct to defend someone who I believe is guilty. Otherwise, only the innocent would have lawyers." Beyond all that, he saw a potential for good in Nosair's act:

> If Nosair did kill Kahane, it was a political assassination. And political assassination of the right person is not something that I would always describe as wrong. Defending an individual accused of killing a man such as Kahane can be viewed as a positive act because Kahane's racism and fundamentalism had the potential for interfering with peace negotiations between Arabs and Jews.

When Kunstler first began representing Nosair, he began to develop the themes of temporary insanity or, alternatively, emotional disturbance to reduce what would otherwise be murder to the lesser crime of manslaughter. The political Left is sharply opposed to Israel's treatment of the Palestinians, and a mental defense might have allowed Kunstler the maximum amount of demystification. Kunstler told a reporter that under a plea of mental disturbance, he would try to bring in the misery of the Palestinians. "You can get in the whole political framework: human rights violations on the West Bank, why a Muslim would feel strongly enough to shoot and kill a proponent of anti-Arab feelings." It was a foreshadowing of the black rage defense Kunstler wanted to mount for Colin Ferguson four years later.

Unfortunately for Kunstler's desire to mount a straightforward political symposium on Arab rage, Nosair, like Ferguson later, refused to go along. Nosair adamantly denied he had done the act. This forced Kunstler to switch theories of the case several months after the proposed mental defense was already out before the public, very much contrary to generally accepted defense strategy. His new theory was that there had been an internal feud within Kahane's organization over finances. The dissident faction killed Kahane, and then tried to pin the blame on Nosair, the only Arab at the scene. As for the postal policeman, it was Kahane supporters pursuing Nosair that had shot him. The gun by Nosair's hand was a plant by one of the conspirators who actually murdered Kahane.

Simultaneously, Kunstler set organizing teams to work to raise funds for investigators and assure that the courtroom would be packed with supporters. "We had people in the courtroom every day," Kunstler recalled. "We had people raising funds. We had people talking to outside media. We had people organizing in their homes and in auditoriums." Nosair's cousin Ibrahim El-Gabrowny, later to become a defendant in the bombing conspiracy, headed the support committee. "A one-man whirlwind," Kunstler recalled, "he worked like a dog for us. He did everything from rushing down to buy transcripts, organizing supporters to come to the trial, organizing demonstrations and doing the legwork we required." The fund-raising went spectacularly well and raised over $163,000.

Public relations was always among Kunstler's most important defensive tools. He made the most of press conferences and court filings in which he disclosed startling facts and interpretations of the case. For example, when the emergency medical personnel arrived, a Jewish doctor acting in a crazed manner interfered with the emergency medical personnel and prevented their intubating Kahane. Kunstler's interpretation: "The doctor might have been someone from his own party who went in there to make sure Rabbi Kahane was surely dead." At a news conference in the Hilton Hotel, Kunstler's accusations of a conspiracy so enraged three Kahane supporters that they rushed at Kunstler. A bodyguard hired by the defense brandished a licensed pistol to hold the would-be assailants at bay. The police were summoned to restore order.

The trial was tense. The Jews sat on one side of the courtroom, and the Arabs on the other. On one occasion the Jewish Defense Organization (JDO) members charged the well of the courtroom. The bailiffs then required both groups to sit toward the back, with empty rows between them and the front of the courtroom as security. Slogans such as "Jewish justice" and "Death to Nosair" appeared in spraypaint and shouts in the washrooms and hallways.

The police work in the Kahane case had been extremely sloppy. Police had failed to test the bullet remaining in the gun for fingerprints; police moved the gun itself and smudged the fingerprints; police failed to test Nosair's hand with paraffin to determine whether he had recently fired a weapon. Police waited for two weeks before canvassing the mid-town neighborhood for witnesses. The medical examiner did not perform an autopsy of Kahane's body out of deference to his Orthodox views; this meant that there was no way to trace the trajectory of the bullet to determine the exact location from which it had been shot. A proper chain of custody had not been maintained on certain inflammatory materials the authorities found in Nosair's apartment, with the result that they could not be introduced for motive. Kunstler skillfully played on these and other blunders, indignantly magnifying their significance and suggesting that the conspiracy to murder Kahane might run even deeper than the JDO dissidents.

Some writers have suggested that Alvin Schlesinger, the trial judge, was friendly to Kunstler and much more critical of the prosecutor. However, that certainly was not true of his evidentiary rulings, which sharply favored the prosecutor. Although Kunstler did discuss facts in his opening statement that tended to support his theory of dissidents within the Kahane organization being responsible for the killing, the prosecutor brought a motion midway through trial to prevent Kunstler from presenting that evidence to the jury unless there was direct evidence of the dissidents' involvement in the killing. Because of this ruling Kunstler was unable to present evidence of skimming of money from the JDO's bank account, previous threats made to Kahane by some of his faction, the history of infighting within the organization, and testimony that the hotel was called the day of the killing by a man with a "Brooklyn Jewish accent" asking about security arrangements for Kahane.

It does not sound like the work of a friendly judge to prevent the defense counsel from presenting evidence that others than the defendant had motives to kill the decedent, especially in a case where the prosecution failed to offer its own motive evidence. That others had plenty of motive to kill Kahane was the heart of the defense. Kunstler managed to insinuate most of these matters through questions that were abruptly stricken, and actually the jury may have sensed that the judge was trying to suppress the defense. In any event, after long deliberations, the jury acquitted Nosair of the most important charges: Kahane's murder and the attempted murder of the postal policeman. It convicted him of several assault and weapon charges.

Shouts of "Revenge" and "Death to Nosair" greeted the verdict and the police dragged several Kahane supporters from the room. Kunstler went off to Puerto Rico for a vacation, but his critics remained behind. Right-wing Jewish groups threatened to march on jurors' homes, and the judge denounced the verdict as "against the overwhelming weight of the evidence" and "devoid of logic and common sense." Alan Dershowitz, one of Kunstler's biggest critics, called the defense "laughably amateurish," and remarked in connection with the Nosair case that "Kunstler knows better than anybody in America how to manipulate the ethnic prejudices and biases of a jury."

Critics persisted in that accusation over time. A 1995 account on race relations in American juries characterized the Nosair trial as a "largely black jury in New York [that] refused to convict an Arab who had shot a Jewish extremist" after Kunstler "played the race card." That is just wrong. Kunstler may well have played the "race card" on occasion; indeed, for modern times, he practically invented it. However, that was not the defense theme in Nosair. Rather, it was "somebody else did it, and here was their motive," coupled with the suggestion that perhaps some of the authorities were in on it. The jury that voted unanimously for acquittal was only half black; it also had five whites and a Hispanic. No race card was involved.

The Nosair case was only a prelude to several others that Kunstler handled for Arab defendants. The most spectacular cases, and ones that garnered international attention, were the World Trade Center bombing and the related conspiracy to blow up several New York buildings and assassinate several public figures. In the conspiracy case especially, Kunstler played a major role at the beginning but was forced from the case by the supervising judge.

During the lunch hour of February 26, 1993, a one-thousand-pound bomb ripped through the parking garage of the World Trade Center, causing six deaths, injuries to more than a thousand people, and the closure of the 110–story twin towers for weeks. To that date, it was the worst terrorist attack committed on United States soil. The FBI almost immediately found the vehicle identification number of the rented van used to bring the bomb into the garage. This stroke of good luck, coupled with the incredible stupidity of one of the principal bombers in returning to the car rental agency to recover his security deposit, enabled the authorities to quickly swoop down on the principal defendants.

Margie pressured her husband not to become involved with the case, and Kunstler took as a client the defendant least tied to the bombing and the one he thought Margie would find most acceptable. That was Ibrahim El-Gabrowny, Nosair's cousin, and the man who had been so helpful to Kunstler during Nosair's case. The defendant who had rented the truck for the bomb had used El-Gabrowny's address on his driver's license. During a search of that apartment El-Gabrowny punched the FBI agents and was arrested for obstruction of justice and possession of fraudulent passports in the name of his cousin Nosair.

Later, in June 1993, the government indicted ten Muslims for a New York plot to blow up the Lincoln and Holland Tunnels and the United Nations and Javits federal buildings, and to assassinate several public officials. It linked this master plot to the World Trade Center bombing. In this new case Kunstler and Kuby represented Siddig Ibrahim Siddig Ali, a Sudanese Muslim and security expert. Still later, the government widened the net of this alleged conspiracy, which Kunstler and Kuby derisively labeled the "plot to bomb everything and kill everybody," to bring in new defendants. El-Gabrowny was brought into these new charges, and his earlier charges consolidated with them. Significantly, the government added Sheik Omar Abdel-Rahman, the fiery blind Muslim cleric thought to be the driving force behind the terrorists. After he had a falling out with his first lawyer, Abdel-Rahman turned to Kunstler and Kuby.

At first, Kunstler and Kuby dominated the media coverage of this highly publicized case, trading charge and countercharge with the prosecutors over the credibility of witnesses and leaked transcripts of secret recordings. The tone became increasingly bitter. Kunstler and Kuby demanded that Michael B. Mukasey disqualify himself as judge, charging that his Orthodox Jewish beliefs and ties to Israel made him biased against their clients. Mukasey refused, and moreover made sure that Kunstler and Kuby would be unpaid for their work in the case by refusing to designate them as court-appointed attorneys. Ostensibly, he refused because these two highly qualified defense counsel were not members of the Criminal Justice Act panel. However, when Kunstler and Kuby applied for membership on that panel, a committee of federal judges rejected them. The radical bar views this as a catch-22: since the federal judges control and supervise those who are appointed for government payment, only obsequious, less effective lawyers need apply; vigorous and aggressive attorneys are not wanted.

In November 1993, on the petition of the prosecutors, Judge Mukasey found that there was a conflict of interest in Kunstler's representation of the three defendants. Abdel-Rahman waived any potential conflict of interest, but the judge ruled that he did not understand the potential for a conflict, and ordered Kunstler and Kuby to make an election of which clients they would represent. When Kunstler and Kuby refused, insisting on their clients' Sixth Amendment right to retain counsel of their own choice, not that of the federal judiciary, the judge ordered that Kunstler and Kuby would represent Siddig Ali and El-Gabrowny only.

Thereafter, the federal prosecutors brought another motion to disqualify Kunstler and Kuby from representing any defendant because of alleged conflicts of interest. Kunstler snorted that "the Government is going absolutely berserk here. They've given 50,000 reasons why we should be disqualified. They don't like us because they are afraid we may be good, aggressive lawyers." However, Judge Mukasey did the United States attorneys' will and in August 1994 barred both Kunstler and Kuby from the case, notwithstanding client choice or the Sixth Amendment's right to counsel. Kunstler commented, "Increasingly, the government has attacked attorneys who are perceived as being too zealous in defense of their clients or too critical of the government's practices." Kunstler also stated that "for his part, Judge Mukasey has refused to appoint counsel of choice for defendants, insuring that they receive only those lawyers approved and paid by the court."

The Arab turmoil caused significant security concerns for Kunstler. In addition, the Muslim representation exacerbated, although it did not cause, two other personal controversies for Kunstler: conflicts between himself and his wife, Margie, and conflicts between Kunstler and the civil rights attorney Alan Dershowitz.

Kunstler was already accustomed to public hatred of his person because of his work. He had received threats as early as his civil rights work. There was a major difference in the 1990s. Earlier, before his marriage to Margie, Kunstler's work had carried him far afield: into the South for civil rights, to Chicago for the Chicago Seven trial, to Minnesota and Iowa for the Wounded Knee and Pine Ridge shoot-out cases. Although he continued to travel after his second marriage, his love for Margie and desire to have an active hand in raising his youngest children precluded the long, out-of-town trials he had once relished. That was fine, so far as it went, but it also meant that hate engendered by New York and New Jersey cases would be right in his backyard.

During the Nosair case, members of the Jewish Defense Organization, an offshoot of the Jewish Defense League founded by Rabbi Meir Kahane, physically besieged Nosair's defense lawyers. Police and guards of the Nation of Islam escorted Kunstler in and out of the courthouse. The Jewish Defense Organization also demonstrated in front of Kunstler's house at 13 Gay Street in Greenwich Village. Gay Street is a short, narrow street, with Federalist row houses separated from the street itself only by a very narrow sidewalk. The Kunstlers' living room was in the front, separated from the street by only a few feet. A fanatic would find it an easy task to throw a bomb or fire a gun into the living room.

The Kunstlers had experienced demonstrations at home once before. When Kunstler had represented a black teenager shot by Bernhard Goetz on the subway, ten members of the Guardian Angels, a self-appointed public security force, wrapped bandages around themselves and smeared themselves with ketchup to represent blood. Masquerading as crime victims, they then lay in the street in front of Kunstler's home. Eventually the police arrested Curtis Sliwa, the group's founder, and the protest dispersed. It had all been in good humor, however. Sliwa rang the doorbell and presented Kunstler personally with his group's Hall of Shame Award, Kunstler accepted it, and returned a "snide laugh" to Sliwa. There is nothing at all humorous about the machinations of the Jewish Defense Organization.

During the Nosair case, the JDO demonstrated outside Kunstler's house almost continuously, sometimes late at night. From the street side of a police barrier, six to twelve angry radical Jews waved placards and screamed, "self-hating Jew, self-hating Jew," and at night, "Not one night of sleep until William Kunstler is off the street!" Kunstler slipped notes under his neighbors' doors: "I hope you will bear the inconvenience with the fortitude that the Framers expected all of us to exhibit when strident voices were raised against anyone or any cause. So please forgive me and remember that, just like a trip to the dentist, it will feel so good when the JDO is finished." They were very supportive. Kunstler occasionally sent coffee and doughnuts out to the demonstrators. The JDO returned to picket during the World Trade bombing case, but not quite with the same fervor.

It was not just picketing. The JDO also shattered Kunstler's windows with paint pellets, threw paint on the stoop, jammed his answering machine with hate, and telephoned his daughters on his home number with vile messages. Death threats against Kunstler and his family and obscenities frequently arrived by mail and phone, even late at night. One man called repeatedly, burped, and then said, "that's for your Arab clients." The police regarded the death threats seriously enough that they assigned a security detail. It is curious that with all the crazies Kunstler represented in his lifetime, and with all the southern white hatred directed at him for his civil rights work, radical Jews were the first to harass and threaten his family.

Their activities did not stop with Kunstler's death. Emily Kunstler, the youngest daughter, recalls that just after her father died, a call came in on the home telephone. She recognized the voice as belonging to the Jewish Defense Organization, and the one who had called with hate five times each week. He asked whether Kunstler had really died. When Emily said yes, the zealot said, "Thank God." The JDO would not let go even then. Two months later, it picketed Kunstler's memorial service at the Cathedral of St. John the Divine. Mordechai Levy, a JDO leader, shouted across a police barrier at the mourners filing into the church, "William Kunstler is where he belongs!"

Kunstler also experienced vigorous criticisms that were not threats. During the World Trade Center case he was at Carnegie Hall with his then sixteen-year-old daughter, when a man walked by and shouted, "traitor." A cab driver got out of his cab and bellowed, "fuck you, Kunstler," got back into his cab, came out again and delivered a second blast, then drove away. Kunstler told the reporter seated with him, "some people like me, some people don't." Liberal attorneys, even

National Lawyers Guild members, criticized his World Trade Center representation. Kunstler was philosophical. He asked Jimmy Breslin, "can you imagine a life where everything you do gets immediate approval? That is just another way of dying."

All of this led to the Kunstlers taking some precautions. Kunstler locked his office, kept people around him, and watched where he walked. Margie was often critical of Kunstler's somewhat more relaxed attitude toward the outside world and the girls. Over the years she criticized the lack of a sharp dividing line between the office and the home: his press conferences in the living room, the overflow of the office into the kitchen, the constant ring of the six office and home telephone lines in every area of the house, and, with the Muslim cases, the need for heightened security. Kunstler heeded Margie's security concerns, but they originated with her. For example, she would not permit the girls' photographs to be run in the media, especially at angles that showed their faces. She insisted they be walked to school, a task for which Kunstler took his full share of toil. However, there was never any elaborate security system or guards.

In his 1994 autobiography Kunstler wrote that he was "still very much in love with Margie," and that his feelings for her "if anything, increased fivefold" over the years they were married. There is every reason to believe that. However, as he also wrote, "Nothing is placid with two people like us. She's enormously bright and can fly off the handle the same way I do, and we both have low boiling points." At times these arguments were loud. Some arguments centered over the fact that his law practice was William Kunstler's consuming passion, and from the viewpoint of his spouse, he did not spend enough time with her and his family. Everyone close to him, including Margie, indicates that Kunstler worked virtually all the time. However, the couple also argued about the cases Kunstler took and whether they were politically appropriate. She found political fault with several of his cases. Kunstler's tactic in these contretemps was usually to placate Margie, and then do exactly what he wanted to do.

Essentially a New Leftist, Margie herself is a very political person, more so than Kunstler was. She is also a feminist. A little thing perhaps, but whereas Kunstler always wore his wedding band, Margie wore no ring, although Kunstler had given her one. In any event, Margie criticized Kunstler's handling of the Central Park rapist case from a feminist perspective. She asked Kunstler to not take the Nosair and the

World Trade Center bombing cases. She did not like the Muslims' attitudes toward women, and was alarmed about the security problems the
cases would represent for the family. Undoubtedly, she foresaw those
long before Kunstler did. By the same token, and largely for safety reasons, both his older daughters, Karin Kunstler Goldman, a lawyer living in Brooklyn, and Jane Kunstler Drazek, a physician living in Kansas,
asked or strongly suggested he not take these cases. However, Kunstler
went ahead, as he almost always did when he saw himself as the only
barrier between a pariah client and the awesome powers of the state. He
"couldn't say no to Nosair and live up to my own moral code, so I
didn't follow her [Margie's] advice."

Another tension that the Muslim representations exacerbated was
that between Alan Dershowitz and Kunstler. Dershowitz is a law professor, a civil rights attorney, and as much a publicity hound as Kunstler. Dershowitz has often represented, as appellate counsel more than
at trial, very high-profile and high-paying clients, such as Leona Helmsley, Michael Milken, O. J. Simpson, and Mike Tyson. He has represented Kunstler himself, and was a part of the team that appealed the
contempt convictions arising from the Chicago Seven trial.

At some point in the late 1970s Dershowitz attacked the National
Lawyers Guild. That stirred Kunstler's ire, and a running, very public
feud developed between them. Dershowitz labeled Kunstler a player of
the "race card" and a lawyer who defended on the basis of "abuse-ex-
cuses." Kunstler accused Dershowitz of exploiting his students to do
his work, labeled him a phony civil libertarian, concerned with the civil
liberties of only the wealthy, and joked privately that "as long as the
color was green you could get Dershowitz on board." Even in print, the
dispute was sharp. Dershowitz charged that Kunstler was a hypocrite
because "he can contort everything and present the argument that he is
right and everyone else is wrong. There's a moral hypocrisy that runs
through his choice of clients. . . . He is a race-baiter." Not to be outdone,
Kunstler called Dershowitz a hypocrite in print and charged that Dershowitz was "a big-money lawyer who has a pretense of being a civil
libertarian but whose services are usually bought by very monied people. He is also extremely vindictive to anyone who doesn't share his beliefs on everything."

Then came the Muslim cases, which heightened the stakes since
Dershowitz is an ardent Zionist. Dershowitz called Kunstler "virulently
anti-Israel" and "the David Duke of the legal profession [who] defends

people who want to murder Jews randomly on 47th Street." Kunstler responded that Dershowitz was "a pretty horrible person on almost every level." Somewhat later, their positions softened. They appeared together at a public forum in October 1994 at the 92d Street Y, and Dershowitz publicly supported Kunstler when the court deprived Sheik Abdel-Rahman of Kunstler's services. Kunstler wrote Dershowitz a gracious private note thanking him. By the time of Kunstler's death, the two men, while hardly friends, had shed much of their acrimony. The dispute had been grist for many newspaper columns and became one thing, among so many things, that added to Kunstler's growing fame, a topic considered next.

15

Kunstler in His Final Years

IN THE FINAL ten years of his life, Kunstler was undoubtedly America's most famous lawyer. After years of holding news conferences, calling reporters, always being available to their calls, supplying quotable snippets, and representing notorious clients, that fame was just as it should be. As for those who called him a showboat and publicity seeker, he admitted freely that their criticisms had "the ring of truth. I enjoy the spotlight," while insisting that his purpose, broader than ego, was "to keep the state from becoming all-domineering, all powerful." Jack B. Weinstein, a federal judge before whom Kunstler often appeared, agreed that "the long-standing publicity helped with some of the minority jurors. They knew him. They had some confidence in him."

With fame came very public recognition and very public criticism. Brice Marden, a close friend, remembers that on the street with Kunstler, or in an airport, people often came up to him who admired his work or who had benefited from his help in the past. Of course, as we have seen, people also criticized in direct confrontation. He took it in stride. One day he was walking through the Village when a man yelled at him, "you fag loving son-of-a-bitch!" Kunstler turned to his companion and asked, "do you think he knows my work?" Others chose to criticize Kunstler from the safety of letters to the editor, although an occasional letter of praise also made its way into print. Several politicians criticized Kunstler as well, but none as bitterly as Senator Al D'Amato. He called Kunstler a "sanctimonious creep" and a "wacko."

Kunstler was very highly regarded among many in the black community, a group that he especially wanted to help. Black prisoners regarded him with fondness, as one who was really trying to uphold the presumption of innocence by providing a vigorous defense. Kunstler attained the status of near folk hero in America's prisons. As Kunstler aged, he was often approached by lawyers and judges who had followed his civil rights career as youths. In 1992 a recently appointed black federal judge in Pennsylvania called Kunstler to the bench and told him, "I knew of you when I was a boy in Lynchburg [site of the Wansley case]. I followed what you did, and it helped influence me to become an attorney." Kunstler felt great gratification when told this, as he often was.

The blacks in Harlem and the Bronx knew him best. Bruce Jackson tells a story of a subway ride to the Bronx that captures their admiration and Kunstler's response. They were riding together up to the Bronx where Kunstler was to make some preliminary legal maneuvers. Kunstler started to do the crossword puzzle. He was an inveterate fan of crossword puzzles and did the *New York Times* puzzle on a daily basis. Jackson looked up and with apprehension saw three black men approaching, somberly looking down at them. He thought they were going to be mugged. One of them stared at Kunstler and asked, "You remember me?" Kunstler was never afraid. Unperturbed, he looked up from his puzzle and said, "no." The young man said, "You defended me." Kunstler asked, "How did I do?" "You got me off." "Good," Kunstler replied, followed by handshakes all around.

The subway continued uptown, and the white folks disappeared until Kunstler and Jackson were the only whites left. From the end of the car an elderly black man had been staring at them. He got up to leave and went by Kunstler. "You're him, ain't you?" Kunstler replied, "yeah." "I want to thank you for what you do," the man said, shook his hand, and left at 125th Street. An older black woman had been watching the whole thing unfold. She got up to leave at the next stop, came over to Kunstler, and said simply, "Me too." Kunstler asked, "Can I give you a kiss?" She said yes, Kunstler bussed her cheek, and she got off the train. Bruce Jackson calls it a "quintessential 'Bill in New York' story."

Kunstler enjoyed fame and status as the leading elder of the legal Left, and he received many honors and prizes. He did not mellow and refused to be co-opted into the legal establishment he despised. Invited to speak to a 1993 conference of New York state trial judges, he attacked them and charged that the worst of them were "mean-spirited, racist bastards" who violated the Constitution.

The New York State Association of Criminal Defense Lawyers awarded him the Thurgood Marshall Award for lifetime achievement in 1994. Kunstler noted the irony that a white man should be given this award, went on to attack the courts for their alleged refusal to protect defendants' rights, and in summary charged that the law "is nothing

other than a method of control created by a socioeconomic system determined, at all costs, to perpetuate itself by all and any means necessary, for as long as possible."

In January 1996 the New York state bar posthumously honored
Kunstler with the Michaels Memorial Award for "courageous efforts in
promoting integrity in the criminal justice system," a subject matter that
no doubt would have evoked a pithy comment. Probably the honor that
most pleased Kunstler was the National Lawyers Guild's banquet in his
honor in 1985. Kunstler was pleased that his old friends H. Rap Brown
and Harry Belafonte both attended. Belafonte recalled that Kunstler
had persuaded him to bring a plane into the siege at Wounded Knee,
that almost everything Kunstler had ever talked him into was illegal,
but that they were some of the best moments of his life. At a high point
in the evening, the speaker asked, "Will the mothers stand?" Approximately forty black women stood up, all mothers of sons whom Kunstler
had represented. Of these forty cases, only one or two had ever appeared in the media, despite the criticism sometimes heard that Kunstler accepted cases only for their publicity value.

Kunstler's image and mannerisms had such a hold on the public
that the media often used him as an object of analogy or comparison,
even in articles that were unconcerned with him. A columnist referred
to a photograph of herself as an "old, frowzy, Kunstler-esque photo," a
writer described the American revolutionary Samuel Adams as being
"as badly dressed as William Kunstler," and a movie reviewer mentioned that an actor had adopted "the eyeglasses and hair of William
Kunstler." A lawyer became "a William M. Kunstler type of counselor
to the radical-left," and even Clarence Darrow was called, only partly
tongue-in-cheek, "the William Kunstler of his day."

Kunstler is sometimes compared to Darrow. They shared a reputation for rumpled suits, a gadfly nature, and great oratory, but actually
they were quite different. Although Darrow was a friend of the poor
and defended radicals, he himself was not a radical. Indeed, Darrow
was skeptical of all ideologies. Darrow was more traditional in his practice and in the range of his clients, often representing the wealthy as
well as the poor, and carried no particular torch for racial minorities. Finally, although Darrow authored several books, Kunstler was a much
better writer.

Another indication of Kunstler's fame and notoriety is the sheer
volume of public criticism by columnists. A sampling of how colum-

nists described Kunstler as it appeared around the country during his last ten years includes: "tiresome lawyer," *Chicago Tribune*; one of the "professional practitioners of the racism racket," *Washington Times*; "lawyer-disrupter," *Dallas Morning News*; "gassy, unavoidable radical," *Minneapolis Star Tribune*; "world-class excuse-maker," *Los Angeles Times*; "'60s detritus," *Boston Globe*; "a disease America contracted in the '60s from which we suffer periodic recurrences," *Boston Herald*; "the lawyer for causes of which none is more unpopular than he," *Washington Post*; "a schlemiel with an edge," *New York Times.* Kunstler answered that last criticism, about the only one to which he directly responded. He denied he was a schlemiel (unlucky bungler or chump) and suggested that a more accurate description of him might be chachem or momser (clever fellow or learned man). Talk show hosts on the radio and television lambasted Kunstler as well, none so frequently as Rush Limbaugh.

However, Kunstler's relationship with the media was symbiotic. They fed off each other. Kunstler was a constant guest on radio and television shows. He appeared, in most cases several times, on *Face the Nation*, the *Today Show, Good Morning, America, Sixty Minutes, Larry King, Primetime Live* (where in keeping with its tradition, in 1993 he was one of the celebrities forced to sing "Winter Wonderland"), the *Donahue Show, Geraldo,* local television, and countless radio shows. In June 1990, backstage for the *CBS This Morning* show, Kunstler learned that Richard Nixon, his old ideological enemy, was being prepped for another talk show. After his interview, Kunstler raced about crying, "Where is he? I've got to find him," and finally found Nixon in a makeup room. The two ideological foes from a past era shook hands and chatted a bit about the aging process and also the Chicago Cubs.

Reporters solicited his opinions on a wide variety of topics, including the nomination of U.S. Supreme Court Justice Clarence Thomas, the American invasion of Panama to arrest Manuel Noriega and Noriega's subsequent trial, the William Kennedy Smith rape trial, and, inevitably, O. J. Simpson. Kunstler was one of the earliest to declare O. J. Simpson unconvictable, and although he appeared over a dozen times on CNN to discuss the case, he also said, "the number of talking attorneys disgusts me." He said he talked for free. In 1993 the *National Law Journal* conducted a survey that revealed Kunstler was among the seven American lawyers most frequently appearing in the media.

Gossip columnists referred to Kunstler's doings, such as his seventy-fifth birthday party at Gus' Place or his patronage at Balducci's market on Sixth Avenue. In 1990 *Time* magazine consulted him for advice on the hundred most important Americans; the year before, the cat Felix, or rather his handlers, engaged Kunstler to represent cats on a television "trial" to determine America's favorite pet; *New York* magazine in 1994 featured Kunstler as one of several celebrities on the subject of summer beach reading, and a year later, in 1995, ran Kunstler dressed to the nines, along with the vice president's wife, Tipper Gore, and the political commentator Cokie Roberts, in a rotogravure feature on "The Politics of Dressing."

More permanent media mentioned Kunstler. In his 1992 book *Parliament of Whores,* the humorist P. J. O'Rourke wrote that Kunstler had "eyebrows the size of squirrels" and wore "a hobo literature-professor-type suit no doubt carefully pre-rumpled at the special Pinko Dry Cleaner and Valet." In the 1990s reviewers noted several books with major characters based on Kunstler. Critics also spotted three movies with central characters modeled after Kunstler: *True Believer* (1989), *Class Action* (1991), and *Night Falls on Manhattan* (1996). The last was close enough to Kunstler that he was asked to, and did, approve of the characterization.

In the 1990s not only was the Kunstler character being portrayed on the screen, Kunstler himself was doing some portraying. In the last few years of his life, Kunstler acquired a new, albeit minor, field of endeavor in the entertainment industry. His critics might have said that he was merely extending the acting career he already had in the courtroom. To an extent that is true, and Kunstler himself always acknowledged, as he put it in 1987, that "there's something about the courtroom that's theater itself." Then too, over the years Kunstler appeared on panels in films and several videos that focused on the practice of law, the movement, or cases in which he had been involved. However, he also became an actor as such.

He first played himself, in a 1971 play written by Daniel Berrigan and based on the Catonsville Nine trial. Originally opened as a benefit performance, it was revived in 1987 in Washington, D.C. (without Kunstler) and enjoyed a modest run. However, Kunstler's greatest success in his acting career came in the movies. Filmmakers' attention may have been drawn to Kunstler because he represented Miramax Films in a 1990 lawsuit against the Motion Picture Association of America. Kunstler sued the MPAA to compel it to withdraw its X rating of Miramax's film *Tie Me Up! Tie Me Down!* and rate it R. Kunstler and Miramax lost the lawsuit, but Kunstler's argument, echoing others, that there ought to be a rating between X and R, lead to the MPAA's abandonment of the X rating and the creation of the NC-17 rating. In 1994 Kunstler represented Miramax regarding another of its films, *The Advocate.*

Oliver Stone sought out Kunstler as a consultant for a film Stone was contemplating about Wounded Knee, but then in 1990 hired him as an actor to play a cameo part in *The Doors.* Kunstler played Jim Morrison's lawyer in his obscenity trial. The lines for the jury summation sounded wrong to Kunstler, and he persuaded Stone to let him substitute parts of a summation speech he had previously used when he defended Lenny Bruce. "Coming up with my own material gave me a bigger part, too," Kunstler admitted. Most reviews noted Kunstler's bit part when the movie was released in 1991. One reviewer even commented on his performance: "He plays himself. As usual, he's unbelievable."

Next he consulted with the director Spike Lee for the *Malcolm X* film and was hired on to play, in an ironic twist, the racist judge who sentenced Malcolm to prison. Reviewers appreciated the irony. Kunstler could not change the script on this film. He felt mean giving Malcolm X his eight to ten years in prison and told Lee he was going to give Malcolm a suspended sentence. Lee replied, "you do that and you're out of the film." Although he only worked for the union pay scale, Kunstler enjoyed making the film. He told a reporter for *People* magazine, "I love it. I'm a method actor, you see, though I don't know what method."

Kunstler's next film was *Carlito's Way.* Kunstler played an old lecher who takes his girlfriend to a strip bar. His daughter Sarah Kunstler, then sixteen years old, played his girlfriend. Kunstler did not have a speaking role, but did get to stuff dollar bills into the strippers' G-strings. "I never thought I'd get tired of looking at bare asses, but after eighteen takes, my God!" he recalled. Kunstler was quick to add that he did not endorse any message the film might have had. "I mean, politically, I didn't think it was so great, but I need to do one movie a year to keep my Screen Actors Guild card." He thought enough of his role that he sent out a press release to the media after he and Sarah filmed their scene.

Kunstler's final film appeared in 1994. Ron Howard's movie *The Paper* was about journalism in New York City and had Kunstler in a cameo part. Gus' Place, in real life Kunstler's favorite restaurant and located just around the corner from his house, was one locale for the film.

The film showed Kunstler, as one reviewer put it, "blathering at a party."

In a rare moment of modesty, Kunstler acknowledged, "I don't think I'm any more talented than those cameo roles." Nevertheless, he received much satisfaction from his films. He listed all his movie credits and his membership in the Screen Actors Guild in his résumés and joked about being "a little distressed to watch the Academy Awards and not see a category for cameo actors."

Although most of Kunstler's appearances on television were in talk shows or panel shows discussing serious issues, he also entertained in that medium as well as in the movies. Halfway between serious talk and pure entertainment, he appeared several times on cable's Comedy Central show *Politically Incorrect*, in which guests engaged in quite undignified talk, much as though they were at a cocktail party. Another time Kunstler appeared on *Comedy Central News*, where he read the Paula Jones complaint against Bill Clinton verbatim, whatever humor there may have been in that.

His largest television role came in October 1994 when he played himself under his own name as the defense lawyer on a segment of NBC's *Law & Order* show. A reviewer wrote that "the veteran, colorful barrister delivers a credible performance." Sam Waterston, who played one of the show's main prosecutors, praised Kunstler's appearance because it "reflects his sense of fun and humor. It mirrors Kunstler's attitude toward the establishment. He does not do what one might expect a lawyer to do. It was very sophisticated." Actually, while himself a viewer of television, especially if the New York Mets were playing, Kunstler was hostile to the medium. He acknowledged his hypocrisy, but believed "this country is mad, filled with idiots," as he once told a reporter. "Not that they're unintelligent—they're diverted, totally. At night, half the country is glued to this flickering screen."

Kunstler's last role as an entertainer was as a stand-up comic. On August 9, 1995, two days after a pacemaker was implanted, and less than a month before he died, Kunstler made his debut as a stand-up comic at Caroline's, the New York comedy club. He read some of his satiric poetry, especially newer O. J. Simpson sonnets, told lawyer-bashing jokes, especially about the Simpson trial attorneys, and reminisced over the Chicago Seven trial. He dedicated the performance to the Grateful Dead guitarist Jerry Garcia, with whom he first dropped acid, at the Woodstock Festival. "Is the statute of limitations expired?" Kunstler asked the crowd.

Kunstler was good at short anti-lawyer jokes. One of his best, although from the year before: "What is the difference between a lawyer and a spermatozoan? Very simple. The spermatozoan has one chance in six million to become a human being." A review of his performance noted that Kunstler was "warmly applauded by a full house that seemed largely to share his liberal outlook, including many representatives of the media."

Another index of Kunstler's status as a senior statesman of the American Left was his growing participation in various reunions and commemorations. We have already seen that he was enthusiastic about such events, and have noted his part in the reunions of the Chicago Seven, the Abbie Hoffman memorial parties, and Kunstler's speeches on the anniversaries of the Ohio National Guard's slaughter of the Kent State students. This commemorative spirit grew in the 1990s. In March 1990 Kunstler joined several hundred former student activists in Santa Barbara, California, to commemorate the twentieth anniversary of the student burning of the Bank of America office. That event had followed one of his more heated talks. Later that year, he traveled to Jackson, Mississippi, to celebrate along with other lawyers the twenty-fifth anniversary of the Mississippi Challenge to its congressional delegation, discussed before. The year 1991 saw the dedication of the National Civil Rights Museum in Memphis, where he and H. Rap Brown were on the program. In 1993 he returned to Wounded Knee, taking Margie along with their daughters, for an emotional reunion with Russell Means and his own former legal colleagues for the twentieth anniversary of the Wounded Knee seige.

Kunstler celebrated much more intimate rituals and commemorative occasions as well. For the last eight years of his life, on virtually every Friday morning, Kunstler breakfasted with his daughter Karin at Waverly Coffee Shop on Sixth Avenue, one of his favorite haunts. In his last two years, she met her father at his home on Friday mornings. In another long-running tradition, Karin had dinner on her birthdays with both her father and her mother, Lotte Kunstler. Karin lived across the river in Brooklyn and these things were feasible; Jane lived in far-off Kansas and similar traditions were impossible. Throughout his life, Kunstler spoke with his sister, Mary, almost every week, generally on

Sundays. He enthusiastically participated in the celebration of her fifti-eth wedding anniversary in 1993.

As he aged, Kunstler had the melancholy duty to eulogize departed client-friends and colleagues. In 1991 and 1993 he spoke and read poetic tributes at memorial services for Charles Garry, the West Coast radical lawyer, and Morton Stavis, a longtime colleague and cofounder of the Center for Constitutional Rights. In 1989 he attended the funeral serv-ices of friends and clients Abbie Hoffman and Huey Newton, one of the Black Panther founders, and eulogized Bruce Bailey at the funeral serv-ice for the murdered tenant organizer. Kunstler wrote obituaries of Charles Garry, Huey Newton, Abbie Hoffman, and Jerry Rubin (who died in 1994) for the English newspaper the *Independent*, and of Abbie Hoffman for the *Los Angeles Times*.

Kunstler was gracious to the dead, even to those with whom he had disagreed. Many had criticized Jerry Rubin's conversion from Yippie to stockbroker. Kunstler more tolerantly pointed out that he had a family to support and argued that "Jerry fully paid his dues in the 1960s and early 1970s and the fact that his life had later changed should not be al-lowed to detract one whit from [his] enormous contributions." He was even tolerant to living ex-radicals. Kunstler remarked of Bernardine Dohrn, once a very militant Weatherman, when she had become a lawyer in a conservative firm, "People get older. They're saddled with more responsibility. . . . Maybe she can convert that law firm." Kunstler was forgiving of his once arch-opponent, Judge Julius Hoffman of Chicago Seven notoriety, when he died in 1983. Although he voiced some criticism, Kunstler allowed that Hoffman had been a "worthy op-ponent," that he was "well read and literate," with an ability to "re-spond with a witticism and some of them were funny." Kunstler said that he had "come to realize that [Judge Hoffman] was only doing what the government told him to do and . . . making him into the very char-acterization of the corrupt judge." He became "as much a victim of gov-ernmental misconduct as my clients had been."

The passing of so many of his colleagues and friends bothered Kun-stler. His oldest daughter, Karin, noted that the 1960s and early 1970s were the high point of her father's life, and it was hard and certainly less exciting for him not to continue that momentum. At the end of his life, Kunstler worried that he might not be taken seriously, that he was becoming an anachronism. He wrote that he sensed a "growing sense of isolation, a feeling that my friends and comrades of that marvellous era were dying around me and that perhaps I had lived too long."

Kunstler worried especially about the young people, their materialism and lack of social activism. Much of what he wrote in his *Los Angeles Times* obituary of Abbie Hoffman spoke to his own concerns, anxieties, and hopes. He mentioned that shortly before he died, Hoffman had expressed regret that young people were no longer willing to play an active role in resolving social issues. Hoffman "was giving grudging recognition to the hard fact that the yuppie road taken by Rubin . . . had proved far more alluring to today's young people than the one . . . on which he [Hoffman] was eventually to find himself quite alone." Yet Kunstler refused to "dismiss him as an anachronism" or "just another aging hippie who refused to cut his hair and trim his sails." What Hoffman did affected our society. Moreover, the memory of Hoffman, his books and actions "will, I so fervently hope, outlive his corporeal presence and well may convince those latter-day college students . . . that Rubin indeed took the wrong road and that the one that truly leads to the Emerald City is the hardy avenue he [Hoffman] traveled." William Kunstler clearly was speaking for himself as well.

To a certain extent, Kunstler mellowed in his final years. Having once said he would never criticize civil rights violations in socialist countries, he sharply criticized the Chinese slaughter of the students in the 1989 Tiananmen Square massacre and attended a benefit for the Tibet House in 1995. He was less doctrinaire in other ways too, as when he confessed that he was "leery" of a "very arbitrary" black trial judge in New York whose "reasonableness and rationality" he questioned.

Kunstler continued on the lecture circuit during the late 1980s and the 1990s, speaking at such widely diverse schools as DePaul, New York University, Stanford, and Wake Forest, among many others. He also spoke before countless county and state bar associations, criminal defense organizations, and civil liberties groups, a whirlwind of speaking engagements. Two years before he died, Kunstler estimated his annual income at $100,000, and said most of it was derived from fees for talks and royalties on his books. While he had frequently claimed over his career that most of his income came from other than the practice of law, in the last few years of his life the claim may have become true. Kunstler had a speakers' bureau agency to book his engagements, and the advance on royalties from his 1994 autobiography was substantial.

Among his academic engagements, Kunstler had three unusual experiences. He lectured to groups of police in 1984 after he was invited to a training session to "raise their consciousness" and from whom he received a "chilly reception" and no applause. More agreeably, Kunstler returned to New York Law School in the fall of 1992, where he had taught thirty years previously, offering a seminar on constitutional litigation with Arthur Kinoy. When the noted trial lawyer Gerry Spence organized a seminar on his Wyoming ranch for the top American plaintiff and criminal defense trial lawyers, he included Kunstler on the faculty.

Right until the end of his career, Kunstler continued to speak at fund-raising and other rallies on behalf of clients, such as Nosair, the World Trade bombing defendants, and Qubilah Shabazz. He continued to address and participate in demonstrations for many liberal and left-wing causes of the late 1980s and early 1990s: opposition to American involvement in Central America, the Middle East, and the Gulf War; tenant squatters; student concerns; and black causes. Kunstler not only participated in protesting the continued United States blockade of Cuba, but also escorted $70,000 worth of medicine for sick children to that island.

Kunstler testified in opposition to William H. Rehnquist's nomination for Chief Justice in 1986, and voiced opposition to the Clarence Thomas nomination to the Court in 1991 ("he's a black snake"). He spoke at a "Free Pee-Wee" rally on behalf of Paul Reubens, the actor who played Pee-Wee Herman, following his indecent exposure arrest in Florida. Inspired by his younger daughters Kunstler became interested in animal rights late in life. He spoke at a session on "Animal Rights: The Issue of the 1990s" at an American Bar Association meeting in 1992, and wrote a vigorous foreword to a book on animal rights published in 1995. He equated ill treatment of animals with racism: "'speciesism,'" Kunstler wrote, "or the use of species to determine membership in the moral community, is no more morally justifiable than using race, sex, or age to determine who has rights and who does not. . . . Like us, animals are individuals with [legally protectable] interests."

Kunstler's last political speech was on July 27, 1995, about six weeks before his death. He spoke at Verso Books on Eighth Street in Manhattan on behalf of Mumia Abu-Jamal, a journalist convicted of murder who had become a cause célèbre on the Left. His ending remarks were in classic Kunstler form:

There is a time to act. There is a time to break the law—wasn't that how
we were formed in the first place? Don't we celebrate that, every July?
. . . There is only one thing that moves government, on any level—it's
utter, stark fear. . . . [Being] scared shitless . . . is the only thing that
moves them. . . . Electo [*sic*] politics doesn't really bother them that
much. They always think that there are enough lunatics out there to
vote them back in.

Kunstler continued to write until the end. In fact, Kunstler's literary output for the last fifteen years of his life, 1980–95, rivaled that of the
late 1950s and early 1960s and far exceeded that of the 1970s. In the early
productive period, Kunstler primarily wrote books and book reviews,
but from 1980 to 1995 he primarily wrote shorter legal and political material, although he did publish three books and was planning more
when he died. He wrote most of the legal and political works by himself, although some were coauthored by others, especially his partner,
Ronald Kuby.

The bulk is impressive. Between 1980 and 1995 Kunstler contributed thirty-five published letters to editors, twenty-five of those to
the *New York Times.* They concerned cases in which he was involved,
commentary on current political and legal topics, and corrections of
what he saw as errors in news accounts and op-ed pieces. In addition,
he authored twenty-three relatively short editorial-page articles for
more evenly distributed publications, including the *National Law Journal* (seven), the *New York Times* (three), the *Los Angeles Daily Journal*
(three), and the *Los Angeles Times* (two). Articles published from 1980 to
1995 included four in the *Nation* and eight articles of legal scholarship,
four of these coauthored, that appeared in legal journals. Kunstler reviewed a handful of books during these years as well, including the autobiography of his colleague Arthur Kinoy. He also wrote a chapter and
forewords for five books.

Kunstler also wrote poetry. He had published his first book of poetry as an undergraduate and returned to the genre in the 1980s, jotting
down lines on a legal pad during quiet times at trial or at free moments
of the day. Reporters commented on this practice, and occasionally in
the early 1980s a few of his poems saw the light of publication in newspapers and legal journals. In 1985 Kunstler published a slim volume of
poetry with Grove Press under the title *Trials and Tribulations.* The

poems primarily concerned specific trials, demonstrations, persons, mostly political personalities, with whom Kunstler had been involved, and also nonspecific aspects of the trial process, such as poems entitled "Jury Selection" or "Character Witnesses." With each poem Kunstler wrote a prose description of the subject to help the reader whose recollection of the events may have dimmed.

Thereafter, Kunstler's poetry appeared with more regularity in newspapers and magazines, and he contributed a weekly poem to the *Amsterdam News*, taking pride in being the poet of the Bronx. In 1994 a second collection of poetry, *Hints & Allegations*, appeared as a book with the same format. In the year of his death Kunstler was planning a new collection of poems about O. J. Simpson and his trial, to be called *The Simpson Sonnets*. The book never appeared, but Kunstler did readings with pieces of his Simpson project and some of the poems appeared in print.

Few people regarded Kunstler's rhyming doggerel as fine poetry. *Trials and Tribulations* sold fewer than two thousand copies, and published commentary about *Hints & Allegations* was gently critical. The famous poet Allen Ginsberg wrote a foreword to *Hints & Allegations*, praising its political revelations yet saying he would "bear false witness" if he praised the work as "elegant poesy." The poetry was all in classic sonnet form, three four-line rhymed stanzas followed by a couplet. Kunstler liked the sonnet form "because, like the law, it has a rather rigid and well-defined structure" that "is long enough to get the message across and short enough to prevent boredom." The couplet at the end gave an opportunity to summarize, "to drive your message home."

Kunstler insisted that his poetic form, the sonnet, was "an ideal vehicle to treat political subjects and make them palatable to many people," and that he seriously intended them as a teaching device. To his agent, Kunstler explained that writing sonnets was "a perfect activity for filling dead time on bus rides or in courtrooms." Kunstler liked to use poetry in his talks. Occasionally he would recall a poem, want to use it in a speech, and could not find it. He would call his friend Diane Jackson, an English professor, announce that "this is an emergency poetry call," and she would find the poem for him. Kunstler enjoyed writing poetry, but he also used what he wrote in his speaking. There were only so many ways he could criticize a political situation, judge, or politician without appearing preachy or tendentious. Reading a poem, employing ridicule or humor, made his political points more palatable to his audience.

In late 1991 Kunstler began an autobiography, written in his voice by Sheila Isenberg. It was a difficult process for her to interview Kunstler because he was always in motion and their sessions were constantly interrupted. She taped the interviews and told the story often through his verbatim language. His first publisher, even after payment of a substantial advance, rejected the manuscript because it sounded like it was dictated. There was consideration of substantial rewriting, but by that time Kunstler was beginning to fail physically and he wanted the book out quickly.

Isenberg had problems because of Kunstler's tendency to embellish on the truth. Originally, Kunstler's claim that he was present when Martin Luther King was shot was to be in the book; Lotte Kunstler set Isenberg straight. Isenberg noted in her preface that Kunstler was "the principal embellisher of his own myth," that "he sometimes adheres to a truth that is deeper than a factual one, so if it serves a political purpose to gloss over or fudge a little, Bill does, no doubt about it," and that her job often was to select a version of his story "that strays the least from the truth." Several reviews of the book, which were mixed in any event, spotlighted this remarkable disclaimer.

Another difficulty for Isenberg was Kunstler's inability to be self-analytical, or, as she put it, he "didn't look back." Kunstler wrote that "for me, action is all." His associate and friend Michael Ratner agreed that "Bill always looked forward, never backward." While that emotional orientation made possible Kunstler's amazing ability to spring into action while others merely dithered, it also meant, as his partner Ronald Kuby noted, that Kunstler was "one of the least introspective people in the world . . . [and] didn't spend a lot of time analyzing his inner life." Because of this, his autobiography suffers from a lack of reflection, and this too was noted in several of the reviews.

Birch Lane Press published the autobiography in 1994. That autumn it sent Kunstler on a cross-country book tour to many major cities, for book signings, talks on college campuses, and appearances on talk shows. Already he was feeling ill and required help with the logistics. He continued to promote his book in eastern cities during the spring of 1995, and sold an option for the movie rights for a substantial sum. Since the late 1980s he had considered writing a book, tentatively titled

Rebels at the Bar, about lawyers who became revolutionaries: Ho Chi Minh, Castro, Lenin, Robespierre, and so forth. Although St. Martin's Press expressed serious interest in it, the project was never completed.

Of course, Kunstler had a home life as well, and it was unusual in some ways and normal in others. The phones rang incessantly on six lines in every part of the house. In between calls or when the ringer was turned off, and pleas for help were piling up, he read mysteries, poetry, and history, watched the Mets on television, and listened to opera. He fed the many household and office animals (three cats and two dogs at his death), walked the dogs, and took out the garbage. He once advised a junior leftist lawyer, "Never believe your press. When you go home, put out the garbage. You can't exist 24 hours a day as this famous lawyer type." However, repair work was beyond him as he was immensely inept at mechanical matters. He had difficulty with mechanical games, destroyed household furniture through attempted repairs with glue, and had difficulty recognizing that his stereo would not work with wires pulled out of the speakers. However, mostly what he did at home, as in the office, was work.

When the phones were turned off, or there was a break, the "family gathering place" was the parental bed, "the place where our kids spend an awful lot of their time, snuggling with their parents, doing their homework or watching TV." The family animals joined them and it became "the warmest place in this house." From that bed he would talk with the kids or read for hours. He often told reporters that Sarah and Emily kept him young. He took them on Sunday outings, going to the zoo, the planetarium, or a museum. If Kunstler left town for a trial, he often took Sarah or Emily with him. Kunstler was proud of their growing independence. He was pleased that they demonstrated (and were arrested) over the exclusion of homosexual groups from the New York St. Patrick's Day parade in 1993, and that Sarah held her own press conference in 1994 to publicize one of her causes. "The apple doesn't fall far from the tree," he said of her media endeavors. As of 1993, however, neither daughter wanted to become a lawyer.

When younger, the girls often played with Karin's children, and sometimes Kunstler took daughters and grandchildren to a baseball game. It was the frustration of seeing her father often but amidst the confusion and noise of so many children that prompted Karin to suggest the plan of Friday breakfasts that they carried out quite religiously for the last seven or eight years of his life. Kunstler did not have as much opportunity to see Jane's children in Kansas, but Jane and her family traveled to New York once or twice a year. The day before he died, Kunstler talked with his preteen grandson, Chris Drazek, on the telephone and asked, "how are the girls treating you?"

Kunstler had simple personal tastes. At home he preferred steak, mashed potatoes, sometimes tomato soup to eat. Always wide awake and fully energized in the mornings, he made breakfasts, German pancakes for guests, and coffee for Margie. Kunstler did not drink, play cards, or go out with the boys, although he smoked a little marijuana in the evenings to relax. He paid no attention to his clothing and replaced nothing until Margie told him that a particular suit or shirt was too worn for further use. Most of his time, upstairs in the home as well as downstairs in his office, was spent working, even in a room crowded with people and conversation. Although the Kunstler family never lived lavishly, they did have hired hands to help with the domestic chores. The family home was just above the office. The Kunstlers did not lock their front door during the day until the JDO protests. Before then, one family domestic chore was to sometimes direct apparently crazy people wandering into the house to the office below.

For years he hosted Memorial Day and Labor Day barbecues, held in a small patio, with a charming fountain and small pond, behind his house. Kunstler remained on stage, always talking, entertaining his guests. Margie was the moderating influence. Sometimes when Kunstler went too far and claimed he had done something he had not, she would simply say, "No, you didn't" and he would respond, "Oh, maybe I didn't." When the girls were younger, the family spent a month or more at its summer home in the Catskills, sometimes returning for the holidays at year end; they used it somewhat less in later years.

Kunstler did not have a large number of close friends. He did have a close personal relationship with H. Rap Brown, but did not see him often. Kunstler became close friends with Bruce and Diane Jackson, faculty at the University of Buffalo, in the mid-1970s when they met in Buffalo while Kunstler worked on one of the Attica trials. The two couples visited back and forth in each other's homes, and traveled together on several vacations, to Bermuda in 1989 and Oaxaca, Mexico, in 1990.

He met the painter Brice Marden in the early 1980s when their daughters went to the Little Red Schoolhouse together in Greenwich Village. Kunstler liked Brice Marden more than he liked his abstract paintings, but as the friendship developed he talked more and more about seeing Marden's studio. One day Kunstler showed up at the studio and quickly looked over Marden's paintings. Marden could tell that Kunstler was not really very interested in them, but took it as a gesture of friendship. The Kunstlers visited Brice and Helen Marden at their summer place on the Greek island of Hydra in 1994, where, characteristically, Kunstler did some work, reading the galleys of his autobiography. He was already seriously ill, and that trip was a strain. Toward the very end of his life, the political comic Randy Credico became a good friend, and accompanied him on the book tour for his autobiography.

Although Kunstler had only a limited number of close personal friends, he would have claimed friendship with thousands. This was a part of the phenomenon noticed by so many friends and family members of his great need for admiration, love, and a sense of belonging. It also suggests a key contradiction in his life: how could a man who so craved admiration and love make such outrageous statements, for example, that the Kennedy assassinations were good things, and take on such notorious, publicly hated clients? Kunstler's actions would seem almost calculated to bring about public disapprobation and opprobrium, rather than love and admiration. How can that be reconciled with a craving for admiration?

The key is that Kunstler cared very little for public opinion in the abstract, and cared very much for the love and admiration of those persons around him, those he could see and touch. One way to measure this is how he treated the many people who came up to him in public. He was empathetic and put himself in the position of everyone he met. His statement to a reporter that we have seen earlier, that when he was with a Sikh he wanted to be a Sikh, when he was with a black person, he wanted to be black, he repeated to friends. He talked with cab drivers and beggars just as seriously as with reporters. Even were a person he met a reactionary, Kunstler took him as a human being and would try to persuade him from his position.

The Chicago Seven trial was a great aberration. In trial, Kunstler was usually a study in civility. A reporter who had covered many of Kunstler's trials wrote after his death that "while some criticized Kunstler for craving attention, the most important source of his persuasive power was, ironically, the attention he paid to others. He couldn't walk into a room without a hello for everyone. He made every juror, bailiff, and clerk in a courtroom feel special." The result was just what Kunstler wanted: "Even when you disagreed with him, Bill was hard not to like, and as a result, you often found yourself agreeing with him."

Long after he had given up his womanizing, he remembered the art of flattery to women. More often than not, Kunstler found something about a female reporter's clothing he could praise: a hat, a scarf, once even the buttons on her blouse. To a female district attorney who had opposed him in court, he sent flowers to congratulate her on the birth of her first child. As a result of this personal attention, many of those most likely, by reason of their professions, to dislike Kunstler actually were fond of him, provided they knew Kunstler personally. Prosecutors, opposing attorneys in civil cases, and, yes, even some policemen actually liked Kunstler.

After his death, a New York City police lieutenant wrote to the *New York Times* that

> Bill Kunstler was the guy we cops loved to hate. . . . However, *those of us who got to know him* realized that he was a bundle of contradictions, and *he actually wanted the cops he met to like and respect him*. . . . He was also entertaining and funny, and made those around him feel as if they were making history with him. He will be missed, even by some of us cops. (Emphasis added)

Personal contact was the key. At a postmortem program sponsored by the Association of the Bar of the City of New York in June 1996, near shouting broke out between those who loved and those who hated Kunstler. An unidentified man commented that

> it seems as if there were two Bill Kunstlers, given the rage on the one side and the adoration on the other. I think that those of you who only knew him from what you read really didn't know the man at all. And that's why there's so much anger about it. Those of us who knew him up close and personal have a deep abiding affection for him.

While abstractions such as admiration, love, and respect meant little to Kunstler, he craved the admiration, love, and respect of those who surrounded him in the flesh. Two of the obituaries caught it precisely. One reporter wrote that the "little boy in Kunstler was at once his danger and his protection. He was so immensely engaging in the flesh that the dislike that spread rather wide was critically dependent upon reducing him to an abstract idea. To see him was somehow to be conquered by the little boy." Another reporter put the same thought more simply: "By reputation, Kunstler was an easy man to dislike. By experience, he was a hard man to resist."

In June 1994 Kunstler wrote to a friend in an off handed manner that "as you know, I plan never to retire and never to die." He made these claims to his daughters, friends, and associates. His partner Ronald Kuby believes that Kunstler never accepted, even intellectually, that he was going to sometime die until his last two weeks. At some cerebral level, of course, he must have known. In 1992 he recorded a living testament for KBDI Channel 12, Denver, for a program called *The 11th Hour*, addressing the issue "In facing your own mortality, what final message would you leave for future generations?" Perhaps he did not think his departure was imminent, since his talk concerned criticisms of very current judicial actions he regarded as inroads into the Bill of Rights. It was not at all a searching survey of his career or thought. In 1993 he told a reporter that retirement was "a dirty word—dirty word. I'd be bored. And part of what I do here [the interview was in his crowded, chaotic office] is I don't want to be bored. I want to do exciting things."

However, by the mid-1990s the practice was becoming less exciting. He remarked in 1994 that he believed the civil rights laws had not ended white racism and that "minorities, and blacks in particular, get almost nothing from civil rights legislation. At best it's a sop; at worst it's hypocrisy. The only way they will get anything is by going into the streets." However, very few protesters were going into the streets anymore. Kunstler felt that "we're in an aimless society that's going nowhere, has no real goals. Just being angry at it, constantly angry, is not the best weapon. . . . It's not a time for screamers." It was discouraging.

Over the years Kunstler had never been concerned with money. In 1970 he advised students at the University of Cincinnati that they should "just get enough to live on. Animals that overeat die." He had always stuck to his principles and had refused many well-paying cases where the politics were wrong. At the end of his career he was still making only $100,000 a year, more or less, from his earnings in practice and from speaking engagements. He had doubts about the financial security of his family, and had hopes for the success of his autobiography.

Margie threw a gala party for his seventy-fifth birthday, July 7, 1994, at Gus' Place, his favorite restaurant. People got up and made remarks, there was a hired comic, and over 125 friends and family members attended, including the Jacksons and the Mardens, and everyone enjoyed themselves. Kunstler was especially pleased that H. Rap Brown had come up from Atlanta. Margie had prepared a huge birthday cake that looked like a newspaper page with articles that celebrated her husband's major trials and struggles. However, by the time of this party, Kunstler clearly looked gaunt and seriously ill.

Kunstler had been in good general health over the years. He had been diagnosed with gall bladder cancer, but that was in remission and not life threatening. In 1994 he began to cough, lose weight, and appear gaunt. He returned home from his fall 1994 book tour exhausted, and promised his family and friends to take it a little easier on himself. In spring 1995 he told a reporter in Minneapolis that the Shabazz case, just settled, would be his last outside New York. In February 1995 progressive heart failure was diagnosed, and excess fluid began filling his lungs. However, he still practiced actively in New York through May and June 1995.

In June 1995 he spent a week in St. Vincent's Hospital, listened to opera, and again promised to slow down. He called David Dellinger, his client from the Chicago Seven days and with whom he had kept in close touch. Dellinger was hospitalized himself, and they joked about who was going to give whose eulogy. Kunstler had a pacemaker implanted on August 7, and two days later performed as a stand-up comic at Caroline's Comedy Club. The next day he went to the summer home in the Catskills, but within two days, he was unable to breathe, and an ambulance brought him back to St. Vincent's.

During the last week of August he transferred to Columbia-Presbyterian Hospital. Kunstler listened nearly constantly to the music of Charlie Parker and Lester Young, reminded Ron Kuby to mail a birthday card to his grandson Andrew, visited with his family, and enjoyed Raisinettes and malted milk balls that Lotte brought him. Karin recalls that her father joked in one visit, so characteristically and so sincerely, "I can't die before Labor Day because all the first-line stringers will be on vacation and I won't get good press." There, in a sunny, sixth-floor room overlooking the Hudson River, William Moses Kunstler died of heart failure on September 4, 1995, Labor Day.

Kunstler did receive a good press as he wished: dozens of obituaries, and more dozens of editorials and letters to the editor. In keeping with the controversy that always surrounded Kunstler, they were mixed, but the vast majority was favorable. His cremated ashes were placed in a rock outcropping in the Catskill Mountains. The Cathedral of St. John the Divine hosted a memorial service that drew over three thousand well-wishers. Chicago held a much smaller memorial.

Although Kunstler may have been famous, he was not wealthy. His estate was valued at less than $400,000, represented almost entirely by the Greenwich Village brownstone that housed his home and office. He had unfortunately left one matter very much unresolved at his death, and that was the status of his practice. There was obvious affection between Kunstler and Kuby, and Kunstler told at least one reporter that he regarded Kuby as a surrogate son. In his interviews, in his résumé, and on his letterhead, Kunstler referred to Kuby as his partner. In the autobiography, he called Kuby not only his partner but his alter ego. However, there was no partnership. Not only was there no written agreement, but Kunstler paid Kuby a salary.

Moreover, Margie Ratner, Kunstler's widow, and Kuby never had a cordial relationship. Even before Kunstler's death, Margie would not allow Kuby to come upstairs into the home. One observer close to them reports that Margie regarded Kuby as sexist. Kuby, in turn, charged that Margie shouted at and abused all the office staff, including himself, and treated them all as her personal servants. Without William Kunstler around to moderate, these conflicting passions rapidly came to a head. Soon after Kunstler's death, Kuby announced he was continuing the practice under their former name of Kunstler and Kuby. By February 1996 Margie and Kuby no longer spoke together and Kuby moved out of the townhouse into another office but still used Kunstler's name in the practice. By the end of the year, Margie Ratner sued and obtained an injunction barring Kuby from referring to himself as Kunstler's partner or otherwise using Kunstler's name in his work. It was a squalid end to a splendid practice.

It had been a splendid practice, indeed. Kunstler brought a first-rate intellect to the courtroom and could match wits with the best of litigators. He was a master of the sound bite in the years before that expression was invented. He sought out the media and they sought out him. He used his newsworthiness, in part out of personal vanity, but even more to advance the case and the cause of his client. His idea was to take the offensive, to question the motives or techniques of the government, and to humanize his clients. Kunstler participated in more than 200 federal district court cases, more than 150 federal appeals, including six appearances before the U.S. Supreme Court, and hundreds of New York state trials.

The key to Kunstler's lawyering is that nothing inhibited his zealous representation of his clients, their causes, or the social causes they could be made to stand for. Kunstler cared nothing for money, so whether a particular client's representation would advance his career in the public eye was meaningless. He was gutsy and willingly to take risks because he cared little for the approval of fellow attorneys and even less for the approval of judges, for whom he had no particular respect except what some few individually earned. Thought and reflection make cowards of us all, to paraphrase Shakespeare. However, Kunstler acted instinctively, without calculating risk, filing affirmative lawsuits or holding press conferences while others equivocated.

Kunstler took on cases that no other lawyer would touch. He was occasionally accused of lack of preparation and sloppy work, but such infrequent lapses were due to an overextended caseload, not laziness. Indeed, Kunstler worked feverishly, as Ronald Kuby once put it, "like a man who was about to run out of time." A more substantial criticism is that occasionally the politics of his cases interfered with the best interests of individual clients. Notwithstanding that these conflicts were rare, Kunstler seemed insensitive to them.

Always looking forward, he saw life as an endless struggle against authoritarianism, against racism, against all manner of oppression. The only consolation Kunstler saw was that the world would be far more grim if we failed to make our daily struggle. He made the courtroom a tool for advancing a cause, as much as defending a client, and demanded that his trials turn on broad issues of social justice. However, it was also in this breadth of vision that the particularities of individual clients were sometimes overlooked, to their occasional detriment.

Kunstler fought for his own personal vision of equal justice for all, even the poor, racial minorities, and those whom the state considered its enemies. Doubtless, it was easier psychologically to fight these battles in the 1960s, when millions were on his side. However, Kunstler held onto his political compass and fought the good fight throughout his life, even in the absence of a mass movement.

Kunstler had a very healthy ego, and what seemed an insatiable and self-centered craving for the limelight caused some to dislike him. However, the publicity he generated actually did help his practice and his clients. Then too, there was more than mere ego involved, as Kunstler's strong needs for approval, admiration, and belonging must certainly have masked some deep insecurities. Most people who actually met the man enjoyed his company, regardless of how they stood on Kunstler's politics or public posturings.

Kunstler's choice of clientele caused most of the public dislike for the man. Kunstler deliberately aligned himself with the despised, the enemies of the government, the pariahs. Because the public hated his clients, the public hated Kunstler. However, minorities trusted him, and people without power hailed him as a savior because so very often they had no one else toward whom to turn.

Race has always been a prominent feature in American courtrooms. However, Kunstler was the first to turn American racism on its head and use it affirmatively to gain the acquittal of minority clients. He was the precursor of the O. J. Simpson trial, and showed the way. While much criticized for this, Kunstler saw the use of racial identification of the jury with the defendant as merely an opportunity for minorities to have justice. Kunstler certainly did not create the police culture that rewards "testilying" and planting evidence, nor did he create slavery, segregation, or racism. To Kunstler, the race card was simply a tool he could use to bring the lesson of racism home to the public and to free his clients, in much the same way other lawyers might use the legal rules of evidence as a tool. This may be a stretch in logic, but it is an easy extension if one, like Kunstler, cares nothing for judges or for the approbation of the bar establishment.

Kunstler's significance ultimately depends on the politics brought to the evaluation. For conservatives, Kunstler at best was a pest, for some perhaps, a threat. He promoted reverse racism and perverted trials into media circuses. For radicals, Kunstler was one of their own, and in his final years a sort of senior statesman of the Left. Liberals admired Kunstler's sincerity in a cynical world. They pointed to the importance of a Kunstler as a counterbalance to power, as an important gadfly in a democratic society, and as a symbol of the need to provide even pariahs with a full defense. This was the tack taken by many liberals following his death. The columnist Murray Kempton wrote that Kunstler "did the state . . . the signal service of providing its enemies with a fair fight." A surprising number of judges praised Kunstler after he died. "We need more Bill Kunstlers to stand up to the arrogance of power and the cynicism of wealth," said one federal judge, while a Wisconsin state judge declared that "it is extremely important that there are attorneys willing to take the positions he took and represent the people he represented. It protects all of our liberties."

For libertarians, Kunstler's importance is even more urgent. Libertarians would argue that the federal judiciary, especially the Supreme Court, recently has become much more interested in aggrandizing the power of the organization for which it works, the federal government, than the integrity of the Constitution. For many libertarians these recent steps, some of which are mentioned in the preface, measure the extent of the despotism under which we already live, and to combat which literally thousands of Kunstlers are needed.

For whatever significance, merits or demerits the public might attribute to him, Kunstler the man was pleased with his life. Both Ronald Kuby and Margie Ratner, who join together on very little, agree that Kunstler lived his life with a tremendous amount of joy, and held no hidden angst or regret. In an interview for a 1988 documentary, *Growing Up in America*, Kunstler commented,

> Despite all my dire forebodings about the future of this country, I feel that I on the personal level have had a good and fruitful life. I've done what I wanted to do, I've gotten as much independence as you can get in this world, I feel that I've lived the way I've wanted to live. . . . If some miracle worker came along and said, "Bill, go back now, you're 21, now start all over again," I would probably walk the same road that I've walked now and I was damned lucky to be able to walk it.

Kunstler usually closed his talks with poetry, and so must this biography be closed. The injunction of Walt Whitman on how to live, from the preface to the 1855 edition of *Leaves of Grass*, was not something that Kunstler himself quoted. However, its lines perfectly describe Kunstler's loves and hatreds and how he lived his life. They are inscribed onto the smoothed surface of the rock outcropping that contains his ashes.

This is what you shall do: Love the earth and sun and the animals, despise riches, give alms to every one that asks, stand up for the stupid and crazy, devote your income and labor to others, hate tyrants, argue not concerning God, have patience and indulgence toward the people, take off your hat to nothing known or unknown . . .

Notes

Page

1 "The Pariah's Farewell": *Nation,* October 2, 1995, p. 341.

1 a second reminded: *Los Angeles Daily Journal,* September 14, 1995, p. 6.

1 recalled that the *New York Times*: *Toward Freedom,* November 1995, p. 18.

1 "the most celebrated and detested": *London Times,* October 8, 1993, p. 16.

1 "critics came in all colours": *Economist,* September 16, 1995, p. 121.

1 over three thousand: *New York Times,* November 22, 1995, p. 2.

1 "William Kunstler is where he belongs!": *New York Times,* November 20, 1995, p. B11.

2 "Bill was a radical": *Charlie Rose Show,* WNET, September 5, 1995, transcript (Westlaw).

2 "I have great compassion": *USA Today,* September 5, 1995, p. A3.

2 "identified with those": speech by Nancy Kurshan at Kunstler Celebration, November 5, 1995, on Internet.

2 "friend of the people": *Refuse & Resist,* undated computer posting, fall 1995.

3 "disliked, even despised": William M. Kunstler (with Sheila Isenberg), *My Life as a Radical Lawyer* (New York: Birch Lane Press, 1994), p. 313.

3 "No longer satisfied": Kunstler, *My Life,* p. xiv.

3 violence "is as American": *Guardian,* April 29, 1993, p. 4.

3 "the only way these honkies": quoted in Kunstler, *My Life,* p. 176.

5 "In Chicago": Kunstler, *My Life,* p. 43.

5 "a battler rather": Kunstler, *My Life,* p. 44.

6 "our society" through "an acquittal": Kunstler, *My Life,* pp. 211, 285–86.

6 "law in the United States": *The Law Report,* Australian Broadcasting Corporation, September 12, 1995.

6 "law is a control mechanism": *ABA Journal,* May 15, 1987, p. 32.

7 law "is nothing other than": quoted by Margaret Ratner, "Afterwords," in Kunstler, 2d ed. (1996), *My Life,* p. 403.

7 "an enemy": Kunstler, *My Life,* p. 394.

7   "an abiding faith": interview with Ronald L. Kuby, July 17, 1996.

7   "lawyers must take chances": Kunstler, *My Life*, p. 191.

7   "I pay a steep price": Kunstler, *My Life*, p. 317.

8   "*I'm* the one": Kuby interview.

8   "Where? where?": Kuby interview.

8   "I yelled, 'William Kunstler'": "In the Mail," *New Yorker*, October 23, 1995, p. 10.

8   "Bill lived his life": Kuby interview.

8   he dragged his partner: interview with Arthur Kinoy, July 15, 1996.

8   singing Puccini duets with Mario: Ratner, "Afterwords," p. 405.

8   home for coffee: Kuby interview.

9   "I so loved the chance": Andria Fiegel, Internet posting.

9   "impenetrable warren of books": *New Yorker*, September 18, 1995, p. 39.

9   typical day, irritations, "after a day with Bill": Kuby interview.

10   "Hey, it's great!": Kunstler, *My Life*, p. 396.

10   two secretaries: interview with Susan Bailey and Rosa Maria de la Torre, July 17, 1996.

10   230 jury trials: interview with Michael Ratner, July 18, 1996.

11   "dumbfuck" and "hilarious": Stew Albert, Internet posting.

11   "best kosher dills": Kunstler, *My Life*, p. 182.

11   "just enough": Kunstler, 1970 talk at University of Cincinnati, *New York Times*, September 10, 1995, sec. 4, p. 7

11   half of his legal work: Kuby interview.

12   Bourke-White photograph and quotation: Marvin Heiferman and Carole Kismaric, *talking pictures: people speak about the photographs that speak to them* (San Francisco: Chronicle Books, 1994), p. 45.

12   "an instinctive understanding": Kuby interview.

13   "It was the first time": *New Jersey Law Journal*, September 7, 1989, p. 5.

13   "a white-coated doctor": Kunstler, *My Life*, p. 51.

14   "I only defend": quoted in Connie Bruck, "William Kunstler: Actor without a Stage," *American Lawyer*, August 1980, p. 24.

14   "even though I don't share": *Los Angeles Times*, April 5, 1987, p. 34.

14   "those were people": *State Journal-Register* (AP release), August 29, 1993, p. 15.

14   "Today, I would say": *National Jurist*, January 1994, p. 13.

14   "To some extent": *New York Times*, September 5, 1995, p. B6.

14   lawyers who worked with Bill: Kuby interview.

14   theory advanced by Margie: Kunstler, *My Life*, pp. xi, 318.

15   "Why am I doing this?" and theme development: Kuby interview.

15   David as analogy: *Nation*, September 25, 1995, p. 299.

15   "David is standing there": Kunstler, *My Life*, pp. 314–15.

NOTES TO CHAPTER 2

Page

18   "solid, middle-class Jewish family": quoted in Connie Bruck, "William Kunstler: Actor without a Stage," *American Lawyer,* August 1980, p. 25.

18   Kunstler pronounced his name in two ways: interviews with David Dellinger, June 15, 1996, and Ronald L. Kuby, July 17, 1996.

18   "but I'm no magician": *Esquire,* July 1969, p. 108.

18   tightly defined area: interview with Mary Kunstler Horn, October 17, 1996.

18   primary education: *New York Times,* September 7, 1968, p. 38.

18   mischievous at school: Mary Kunstler Horn interview.

18   hitting other kids: interview with Fred Marks, February 25, 1997.

19   interracial gang: William M. Kunstler (with Sheila Isenberg) *My Life as a Radical Lawyer* (New York: Birch Lane Press, 1994), pp. 58, 64; Ron Rosenbaum, "The Most Hated Lawyer in America," *Vanity Fair,* March 1992, p. 92.

19   pranks and sledding accident: Mary Kunstler Horn interview; Kunstler, *My Life,* pp. 54, 57.

19   baseball: Mary Kunstler Horn interview; Kunstler, *My Life,* pp. 57–58; later allegiance to Mets: interview with Bruce and Diane Jackson, October 12, 1996; Kuby interview.

20   contrast between Michael's calmness and Kunstler's loquaciousness: Bruce and Diane Jackson interview; interview with Lotte Kunstler, October 14, 1996; Mary Kunstler Horn interview; Kunstler, *My Life,* p. 59.

20   disregard for money: Mary Kunstler Horn, Bruce and Diane Jackson, and Kuby interviews.

20   migraine headaches: interview with Jane Kunstler Drazek, October 8, 1996; Kunstler, *My Life,* pp. 34, 53–54, 96–97.

21   books as closest friends: Kunstler, *My Life,* pp. 60–61; *GQ,* June 1994, p. 194.

21   "was snobbish" and "called out": Kunstler, *My Life,* pp. 55–56.

21   "But then I told my father": Rosenbaum, "The Most Hated Lawyer in America," p. 92.

21   staying power of story: Lotte Kunstler interview; *Esquire,* July 1969, p. 108; Rosenbaum, "The Most Hated Lawyer in America," p. 92.

22   "You can hear it in his voice": Rosenbaum, "The Most Hated Lawyer in America," p. 92.

22   "All white men": *Esquire,* July 1969, p. 108.

22   "I would like to be black": ibid.

23   "Oh, yes, I belong": Nat Hentoff, "Playboy Interview with William Kunstler," *Playboy,* October 1970.

23   "I guess I haven't got the nerve": ibid.

24   ambivalent relationship with father: Kunstler, *My Life*, pp. 52, 264–65.

24   Pa Moe accomplishments and character: Kunstler, *My Life*, p. 50; Lotte Kunstler interview; interview with Karin Kunstler Goldman, October 15, 1996; Mary Kunstler Horn interview.

25   not in obituary: *New York Times*, May 10, 1956, p. 31.

25   official greeter: *GQ*, June 1994, p. 195.

25   "always wanted to be": Kunstler, *My Life*, p. 49.

25   "liked the limelight": Mary Kunstler Horn interview.

25   high school and swimming team: Kunstler, *My Life*, pp. 61–62; Mary Kunstler Horn interview.

26   leader of swim team: telephone conversation with Milton Kamen, December 1, 1997.

26   "my parents": Kunstler, *My Life*, p. 62; Karin Kunstler Goldman and Lotte Kunstler interviews.

26   "It's too bad my parents": interview with Margie Ratner, June 9, 1998.

26   "throughout my career" and "when my mother and father": Kunstler, *My Life*, pp. 112, 62.

26   drive for approval and recognition: Lotte Kunstler, Karin Kunstler Goldman, Mary Kunstler Horn, and Kuby interviews.

27   "far away": Diane Jackson interview.

27   Margie's thoughts on Kunstler's craving for limelight: Kunstler, *My Life*, p. 318.

27   "too conservative, too ordinary": Karin Kunstler Goldman interview.

27   breakfast for wives: Kunstler, *My Life*, p. 55; Kuby interview.

28   mother and religion: Kunstler, *My Life*, pp. 56, 192–93; interview with Manny Horn, October 17, 1996.

28   religious views and practices: *Springfield (Illinois) State Journal-Register*, August 29, 1993, p. 15; *New York Times*, July 6, 1993, p. B1; Ronald Kuby, "Afterwords," in Kunstler, *My Life*, (2d ed., 1996), p. 410.

28   St. Jude medallion: Victor S. Navasky, "Right On! With Lawyer William Kunstler," *New York Times Magazine*, April 21, 1970, p. 92.

29   early sexual experiences and trip to Spain: Kunstler, *My Life*, pp. 62–64, 69–70.

30   meeting Lotte: Lotte Kunstler interview; *Esquire*, July 1969, p. 108; Kunstler, *My Life*, p. 74.

30   spawning ground": quoted in Bruck, "William Kunstler: Actor without a Stage," p. 25.

30   experiences at Yale: Kunstler, *My Life*, pp. 65–69, 244.

30   Kunstler as squeamish: Jane Kunstler Drazek interview.

31   "for the thrill": William Kunstler to Marianne Brock, April 1, 1941,

Mount Holyoke College Archives and Special Collection, Kathryn Irene Glascock Poetry Prize Records. I am grateful to Patricia J. Albright for advising me of Kunstler's participation in this contest.

31 "I come to you": William Kunstler and William Stone, *Our Pleasant Vices* (n.p.: 1941), poem XIX.

32 interview in French: Kuby interview.

32 interest in music: Mary Kunstler Horn and Kuby interviews.

32 "I heard so much anti-Semitism": *New York Law Journal,* September 18, 1995, p. 2.

32 "The message given" and acknowledgment of Christian themes: Kunstler, *My Life,* p. 67.

32 "If I forget thee": Kunstler and Stone, *Our Pleasant Vices,* poem XXXVII.

33 traits of personality developed in college years: Mary Kunstler Horn interview.

33 left-wing politics: Kai Bird, *The Color of Truth: McGeorge Bundy and William Bundy: Brothers in Arms, a Biography* (New York: Simon and Schuster, 1998), p. 63. I am indebted to Bryn Roberts of Indian Springs School for this reference.

33 "We had a group of fellows": Manny Horn interview.

34 "I no longer had anyone": Kunstler, *My Life,* p. 62.

35 moped incident in Bermuda: Bruce and Diane Jackson interview.

NOTES TO CHAPTER 3

Page

36 "once in uniform" and attempt to enlist in navy, etc.: William M. Kunstler (with Sheila Isenberg), *My Life as a Radical Lawyer* (New York: Birch Lane Press, 1994), p. 72.

37 enjoyed service in army: interviews with Mary Kunstler Horn, October 17, 1996, and Neal Goldman, October 15, 1996.

37 "We had a full house": *New York Times,* September 7, 1968, p. 38.

37 "Everyone in the cast": Kunstler, *My Life,* pp. 72–73.

37 "He was an actor": interview with Jane Kunstler Drazek, October 8, 1996.

38 Kunstler as friendly and businesslike: interview with Bill Hurst, February 4, 1997.

38 "It's good to have the Nigras": Kunstler, *My Life,* p. 74.

38 description of Lebanon apartment: interview with Lotte Kunstler, October 14, 1996.

38 "It was thirty miles": ibid.

39 It all ended well: ibid. and Kunstler, *My Life,* p. 75.

39 "Take good care of your father": interview with Karin Kunstler Goldman, October 15, 1996.

39 "From my berth": Kunstler, *My Life,* pp. 75–76.

39 "he used to talk": Karin Kunstler Goldman interview.

40 service record: A fire destroyed the actual service record, but the National Personnel Records Center furnished the information from alternate sources on May 15, 1997, pursuant to a request under the Freedom of Information Act.

40 "he got the Purple Heart": Lotte Kunstler interview.

40 "I leaped under the jeep": Kunstler, *My Life,* p. 76.

40 "crawled out": Kunstler, *My Life,* p. 76; other versions, Karin Kunstler Goldman interview; interview with Diane Jackson, October 12, 1996.

40 "said he knew": Neal Goldman interview.

40 "Then it ended": Kunstler, *My Life,* p. 78.

41 bayonetting claim: Kunstler, "The Harsh Government Prosecution of Military Resisters," in *War Crimes: A Report on United States War Crimes against Iraq* (Washington, D.C.: Maisonneuve Press, 1992), p. 201; "he said that the only time": Neal Goldman interview.

41 "not only because": Kunstler, *My Life,* p. 79.

41 guilt for years: Karin Kunstler Goldman and Neal Goldman interview.

42 "Karin was standing there": Kunstler, *My Life,* p. 80; details confirmed in Mary Kunstler Horn interview.

42 "not go to law school": Kunstler quoted in *New York Times,* September 7, 1968, p. 38.

42 "he was going to be a writer": Mary Kunstler Horn interview.

42 decision to become a journalist: Kunstler, *My Life,* p. 81.

42 "for no other reason": ibid., p. 82.

42 "for all the wrong reasons": *Independent,* September 6, 1995, p. 14.

43 not a serious student and bridge in the lounge: interview with Jack B. Weinstein, July 16, 1996.

43 "a joiner, not an active member": interview with Arthur Kinoy, July 15, 1996.

44 Macy's: Kunstler, *My Life,* p. 85.

44 *Christ v. Paradise: New York Law Journal,* September 18, 1995, p. 2.

44 "I was bored": *People,* September 18, 1995, p. 225.

44 Mrs. Wightman's estate: Kunstler, *My Life,* pp. 87–88.

45 Dylan Thomas as client: *Esquire,* July 1969, p. 135; Kunstler, *My Life,* p. 69.

45 dates of teaching: résumé of William M. Kunstler, 1995, latest résumé prior to his death, provided by Ronald Kuby.

45 teaching writing in Columbia's School of General Studies: *New York Times,* September 7, 1968, p. 38.

46   teaching at New York Law School: interview with Milton Berner, March 24, 1997; interview with Professor Joseph Koffler, New York Law School, October 29, 1996 ("Broadway Bill"); Edwin S. Clare to David J. Langum, December 24, 1997.

46   "when I heard he died of AIDS": Kunstler, *My Life*, p. 89.

46   "Bill would go in there": Lotte Kunstler interview.

46   literary activities in law school: Kunstler, *My Life*, p. 83.

47   proud of book reviews: interview with Fred Marks, February 25, 1997.

47   incident at Anglers & Writers: interview with Brice Marden, October 15, 1996.

48   WJZ *World Security Workshop*: sample program, "What Is Best Solution for Palestine?" November 30, 1947, on deposit with Museum of Television and Radio, New York; *New York Times*, July 19, 1959, sec. 2, p. 11.

48   WMCA productions: *National Jurist*, January 1994, p. 11; *Argumentation and Advocacy*, winter 1995, p. 142; Kunstler, *My Life*, pp. 94–95; David Gallen, *Malcolm X as They Knew Him* (New York: Carroll and Graf, 1992), p. 16; a transcript of the March 3, 1960, radio show with Malcolm X is in Clayborne Carson, *Malcolm X: The FBI File* (New York: Carroll and Graf, 1991), pp. 180–90.

49   WNEW *Counterpoint*: transcript of interviews with Cohn and Sharp, together with publicity concerning the show, in Records of the Committee to Secure Justice for Morton Sobell, box 26, folder 3, Radio and Television, 1952–1953, 1958–1962 (microfilm edition 1976, reel 13), State Historical Society of Wisconsin.

49   WEVD *Famous Trials* and Kunstler quotation: *New York Times*, July 19, 1959, sec. 2, p. 11.

49   Barry Gray show: William M. Kunstler, *Deep in My Heart* (New York: Morrow, 1966); William M. Kunstler to Martin Luther King, Jr., September 7, 1962, King Papers, King Library and Archives, Atlanta.

49   "It was talking": Lotte Kunstler interview.

50   "every night I'd hang out": *National Jurist*, January 1994, p. 11.

50   two hundred houses and closings: Berner interview.

50   personal life of Bill Kunstler and his family in the 1950s based on Karin Kunstler Goldman, Manny and Mary Kunstler Horn, Lotte Kunstler, Jane Kunstler Drazek, and Berner interviews; interview with Fred Marks, February 25, 1997; Kunstler, *My Life*, p. 87.

52   nonprescription glasses: interview with Ronald L. Kuby, July 17, 1996; James Barron, "The Auction Aftermath," *New York Times*, April 28, 1996, p. 35.

53   NAACP and Urban League: Kunstler, *My Life*, p. 95; Committee on Social Action: *Judaism: A Quarterly Journal of Jewish Life and Thought*, fall 1994, p. 350.

54   summer space to black youth: Fred Marks interview.
54   Paul Redd case and antidiscrimination work: Karin Kunstler Goldman and Fred Marks interviews; Kunstler, *My Life,* p. 95.
54   excitement with antidiscrimination work and local reputation: Lotte Kunstler and Karin Kunstler Goldman interviews.
54   first Worthy suit: Kunstler, *My Life,* pp. 95–96; "taste for a certain kind of law": *Los Angeles Times,* April 5, 1987, p. 34.
55   "This was my first experience": Kunstler, *My Life,* p. 97.

NOTES TO CHAPTER 4

Page
56   "You don't have to do anything": William M. Kunstler, *Deep in My Heart,* (New York: Morrow, 1966), p. 4.
57   "under circumstances such that": Mississippi Session Laws, 1960, ch. 250.
57   "Fuck the ACLU": Kunstler's recollection in Ron Rosenbaum, "The Most Hated Lawyer in America," *Vanity Fair,* March 1992, p. 86.
58   "it is an indecency" and "Why don't you shut": Kunstler, *Deep in My Heart,* p. 38.
59   "Just why are you" through "I'm available": Kunstler, *Deep in My Heart,* pp. 42, 44.
59   "gulped, backed away" and Ross Barnett, Jr., incident: John R. Salter, Jr. (now John Hunter Gray), *Jackson, Mississippi: An American Chronicle of Struggle and Schism* (Malabar, FL: Robert E. Krieger, 1987), p. 97.
59   other extraordinary remedies: *New York Times,* July 22, 1961, p. 46 (apparently the first article in the *Times* dealing with Kunstler's practice of law).
60   "lay practically dormant": quoted in Victor S. Navasky, "Right On! With Lawyer William Kunstler," *New York Times Magazine,* April 21, 1970, p. 92.
60   "counterfeit citizens": William M. Kunstler to William Harold Cox, September 5, 1961, and September 13, 1961, Congress of Racial Equality, Records, 1941–1967 (microfilm edition).
62   "it was a grievous error": William M. Kunstler to Wyatt T. Walker, September 5, 1961, Papers of the Southern Christian Leadership Conference, subgroup 2, series 3, Records of Wyatt T. Walker, King Library and Archives, Atlanta.
62   "the right to self-defense": quoted in Navasky, "Right On!" p. 31.
62   "a purpose behind": William M. Kunstler (with Sheila Isenberg), *My Life as a Radical Lawyer* (New York: Birch Lane Press, 1994), p. 108.

62   "I don't remember": Kunstler, *Deep in My Heart,* p. 76.

63   "I am not counsel": William M. Kunstler to Peter Kihss, November 30, 1964, King Papers, King Library and Archives.

63   "over the years": Kunstler, *My Life,* p. 111.

63   "We had to secure": Martin Luther King, Jr., to "Doctor," February 6, 1962, in Taylor Branch, *Parting the Waters: America in the King Years, 1954–63* (New York: Simon and Schuster, 1988), p. 571.

63   "Thank you for sending me": Martin Luther King, Jr., to William M. Kunstler, December 30, 1963, King Papers.

64   his services were available: see, e.g., Kunstler to Walker, October 19, 1961, and January 8, 1962, SCLC Papers, Walker Records.

64   King entertained Kunstler: see, e.g., William M. Kunstler to Martin Luther King, Jr., August 13, 1962, and March 26, 1965, King Papers.

64   Wyatt Walker also entertained Kunstlers: see, e.g., Walker to Kunstler, January 26, 1962, June 25, 1962, July 3, 1963, SCLC Papers, Walker Records.

64   different legal groups: Some materials on these differing legal groups, told from different perspectives, can be seen in Steven E. Barkan, *Protesters on Trial: Criminal Justice in the Southern Civil Rights and Vietnam Antiwar Movements* (New Brunswick: Rutgers University Press, 1985), pp. 41–46; Nadine Cohodas, "The Trials of Mississippi Freedom Summer," *Legal Times,* June 13, 1994, p. 1; Jack Greenberg, *Crusaders in the Courts* (New York: Basic Books, 1994), pp. 347–53; and Len Holt, *The Summer That Didn't End* (New York: Da Capo Press, 1965, reprint, 1992), pp. 88–94.

65   Greenberg and Motley: James Frank, "Still Crazy after All These Years," *Spy,* September 1990, pp. 66, 70; interview with Constance Baker Motley, October 17, 1996.

65   "started living": Fred Marks interview.

65   *New York Times* letters: see, e.g., July 8, 1963, p. 28; May 17, 1965, p. 34; local newspaper: *Port Chester Item,* December 29, 1962, copy in SCLC Papers, Walker Records.

65   *Nation* articles: November 4, 1961, pp. 351–52, 354; June 8, 1964, pp. 576–80 (with Arthur Kinoy); December 28, 1964, pp. 507–9.

66   ten thousand pages of depositions: Lynne Duke, "At Civil Rights Reunion, Fresh Concern," *Washington Post,* October 15, 1990, p. A5.

67   "was a very jovial type": interview with Fred Shuttlesworth, November 18, 1996.

67   "among the best known": Len Holt, *An Act of Conscience* (Boston: Beacon Press, 1965), p. 19.

67   "one of the legal mainstays": Howard Zinn, *SNCC: The New Abolitionists* (Boston: Beacon Press, 1965), pp. 246, 272.

67 "I have never taken fees": "Untiring Civil Rights Defender: William Moses Kunstler," *New York Times,* September 7, 1968, p. 38.

67 "from the time Kunstler": Connie Bruck, "William Kunstler: Actor without a Stage," *American Lawyer,* August 1980, p. 26.

67 1994 autobiography: Kunstler, *My Life,* p. 110.

67 monthly retainer from CORE: William M. Kunstler to James Farmer, January 18, 1962, CORE Papers (microfilm edition).

68 ACLU and travel money: see, e.g., Kunstler to Walker, September 5, 1961, and January 26, 1962; and Walker to Kunstler, April 26, 1962, SCLC Papers, Wyatt Records.

68 correspondence between Kunstler and Walker concerning $500 fee: at letters indicated in SCLC Papers, Walker Records.

68 Shuttlesworth and Wansley fees: correspondence indicated in SCLC Papers, Walker Records; Lowry fees: Kunstler to Walker, September 12, 1961, October 12, 1961, and February 28, 1964, SCLC Papers, Walker Records.

68 waiver of fee: see, e.g., William M. Kunstler to Clarence B. Jones, December 17, 1965, SCLC Papers, Walker Records.

69 "came forward with arms outstretched": Pat Watters, *Down to Now: Reflections on the Southern Civil Rights Movement* (New York: Pantheon, 1971), p. 288.

69 "When Lotte and I": Kunstler, *Deep in My Heart,* pp. 250–51.

70 joint book project: Branch, *Parting the Waters,* p. 804.

70 Kunstler foreword written for King: Kunstler, *My Life,* p. 111.

71 "we're going to have that kid": Charles McCarry, "A Few Soft Words for the Rabble-Rousers," *Esquire,* July 1969, p. 133.

71 "he managed to keep up": Kim Isaac Eisler, "William Kunstler in Lynchburg: The Real Measure of the Man," *Legal Times,* September 11, 1995, p. 42.

72 "Kunstler statute" and "playing with the courts": Holt, *An Act of Conscience,* pp. 137–38.

72 "We were constantly receiving": Arthur Kinoy, *Rights on Trial: The Odyssey of a People's Lawyer* (Cambridge: Harvard University Press, 1983; reprint, Larchmont, NY: Bernel Books, 1994), pp. 210–11.

73 "when Bill and I were together," "Bill always used to," and "would always try": interview with Arthur Kinoy, July 15, 1996.

73 "the brains and strategist": quoted in Bruck, "William Kunstler, Actor without a Stage," p. 25; "Bill was the able": quoted in Elliot Pinsley, "At 70, the Cause Is Still Supreme for Kunstler," *New Jersey Law Journal,* September 7, 1989, p. 5.

73 "they worked very well together": interview with Steven Hyman, July 17, 1996.

73   "There was a difference": Kinoy interview.

74   "I wanted to practice meaningful": Kunstler, *My Life*, p. 112.

74   "Such open trust": Kunstler, *Deep in My Heart*, p. 83.

74   His heart and soul: interviews with Ronald L. Kuby, July 17, 1996; Michael Ratner, July 18, 1996; and Karin Kunstler Goldman, October 15, 1996; comments of Alan Dershowitz and Gerald Lefcourt on *Charlie Rose Show*, WNET, September 5, 1995, transcript (Westlaw).

74   "minorities, and blacks": David B. Oppenheimer, "Martin's March," *ABA Journal*, June 1994, p. 56.

75   Kinoy's views: see Kinoy, *Rights on Trial*; and Arthur Kinoy, "The Making of a People's Lawyer," *Science & Society*, vol. 45 (1981), pp. 324–34.

75   Kunstler admired Kinoy: Hyman interview; interview with Lotte Kunstler, October 14, 1996.

75   "The . . . case was the beginning": Kunstler, *My Life*, p. 105.

75   "Lawyers should be guided": Kunstler, *My Life*, p. 189.

76   "a lawyer is just another worker": Kunstler, *Deep in My Heart*, p. 50; "surrogate to the movement": William M. Kunstler, "Journey to Understanding: Four Witnesses to a Mississippi Summer," *Nation*, December 28, 1964, pp. 508–9.

NOTES TO CHAPTER 5

Page

77   rise and decline of black insurgency: see generally Doug McAdam, *Political Process and the Development of Black Insurgency, 1930–1970* (Chicago: University of Chicago Press, 1982).

78   COINTELPRO: see generally Nelson Blackstock, *Cointelpro: The FBI's Secret War on Political Freedom* (New York: Anchor Foundation, 1975); Ward Churchill and Jim Vander Wall, *Agents of Repression: The FBI's Secret Wars against the Black Panther Party and the American Indian Movement* (Boston: South End Press, 1988); James Kirkpatrick Davis, *Spying on America: The FBI's Domestic Counterintelligence Program* (Westport, CT: Praeger, 1992).

79   "the government's strategy": Anthony Oberschall, "The Decline of the 1960's Social Movements," in Louis Kriesberg, ed., *Research in Social Movements, Conflicts, and Change* (Greenwich, CT: JAI Press, 1978), pp. 277–78.

79   wounding of Black Power movement: Earl Caldwell, "Panthers' Meeting Shifts Aims from Racial Confrontation to Class Struggle," *New York Times*, July 22, 1969, p. 21.

80   "Off the Pigs!": Todd Gitlin, *The Sixties: Years of Hope, Days of Rage* (New York: Bantam, 1987), p. 348.

80 Civilian Complaint Review Board: *New York Times,* September 7, 1968, p. 1, and April 28, 1970, p. 44; assisting out-of-town counsel: *New York Times,* September 2, 1970, p. 28.

80 bail for carrying weapons on airplane: *New York Times,* January 25, 1969, p. 60.

81 Brooklyn Criminal Court bail hearing: *New York Times,* August 24, 1968, p. 30.

81 hearings on bail reduction: *New York Times,* August 24, 1968, p. 30, and August 28, 1968, p. 23.

82 Turco trial and plea: *New York Times,* June 17, 1971, p. 32; July 1, 1971, p. 43; July 2, 1971, p. 20; February 15, 1972, p. 29.

82 Kunstler during trial in Baltimore: interview with Mary Kunstler Horn and Manny Horn, October 17, 1996.

82 Panther 21 arrests and pretrial motions: *New York Times,* April 3, 1969, p. 1; May 14, 1969, p. 48; June 12, 1969, p. 35; August 6, 1969, p. 32; March 7, 1970, p. 19.

84 *Life* article and quotation: "'The Blackest White Man I Know': Civil Rights Lawyer William Kunstler Is Soul Brother to Radicals of Many Colors," *Life,* July 25, 1969, pp. 50, 50B.

85 coin tossing with Lefcourt: William M. Kunstler(with Sheila Isenberg), *My Life as a Radical Lawyer* (New York: Birch Lane Press, 1994), p. 14.

85 immediate acquittal, etc.: *New York Times,* May 14, 1971, p. 1.

85 "deluged with state and federal charges": Kunstler, *My Life,* pp. 177, 180.

85 neutral sources: Clayborne Carson, *In Struggle: SNCC and the Black Awakening of the 1960s* (Cambridge: Harvard University Press, 1981), pp. 252–57, 289–90; Maceo Dalley, Jr., "H. Rap Brown," in David DeLeon, ed., *Leaders from the 1960s: A Biographical Sourcebook of American Activism* (Westport, CT: Greenwood, 1994), pp. 50–54; official judicial opinions in the cases involving Brown; and articles from the *New York Times* for August 20, p. 1; August 21, p. 29; August 22, p. 25; September 9, p. 20; October 6, p. 35 (1967); November 26, p. 23 (1968); August 17, p. 55 (1969); March 10, p. 34; March 11, p. 1; March 12, p. 1; March 17, p. 32; March 19, p. 38; March 31, p. 28; April 21, p. 26; April 22, p. 20; April 23, p. 27; April 28, p. 44 (1970); January 16, p. 1; January 20, p, 17; February 13, p. 15; March 20, p. 23; May 9, p. 24; October 17, p. 1; October 21, p. 40 (1971); May 9, p. 8; May 11, p. 32; June 1, p. 13; June 2, p. 23; June 3, p. 18; November 21, p. 47; November 23, p. 22; November 29, p. 49 (1972); January 14, p. 46; January 16, p. 48; January 30, p. 43; February 1, p. 69; February 2, p. 4; February 15, p. 32; February 16, p. 75; February 21, p. 48; February 22, p. 44; February 24, p. 18; March 2, p. 42; March 22, p. 36; March 30, p. 14; May 10, p. 12; No-

vember 7, p. 27; November 22, p. 35 (1973); July 3, 1974, p. 10; January 25, 1975, p. 25; September 25, p. 32; October 22, p. 18 (1976).

86   "We stand on the eve": H. Rap Brown, *Die Nigger Die!* (New York: Dial Press, 1969), pp. 106, 124, 144–45.

89   "I hope your children": Brown, *Die Nigger Die!* p. 113.

91   Rap Brown "says much the same": William M. Kunstler, "Lawyers Look at Civil Disturbances," *New York County Bar Bulletin,* 1967–68, p. 122.

91   "The people have the right": William M. Kunstler, speech before National Convention of Unitarians, June 24, 1968 tape in possession of State Historical Society of Wisconsin, Madison.

95   "he was taking very good care of it": *United States v. H. Rap Brown,* 539 F.2d 467, 468 (1976).

96   Brown as imam: *New York Times,* May 3, 1993, p. 1.

97   "the entire case": Kunstler, *My Life,* p. 175.

97   "The fact they had to plead": *New York Times*, April 8, 1973, sec. 4, p. 3.

98   "In my opinion he deserved that death": Victor S. Navasky, "Right On! With Lawyer William Kunstler," *New York Times Magazine,* April 21, 1970, pp. 30–31; for other information on case, see *New York Times,* March 29, 1970, p. 46; April 29, 1970, p. 32; April 30, 1970, p. 38.

98   "It is an unprovable truism": Kunstler, "Lawyers Look at Civil Disturbances," pp. 120–21.

99   "He's the blackest white man": "'The Blackest White Man I Know,'" p. 90A.

99   "legal lynching," "very much a part," and "Bill Kunstler doesn't know me": Roy Reed, "Judge in Panther Trial: Israel Myer Augustine, Jr.," *New York Times,* July 10, 1971, p. 18.

NOTES TO CHAPTER 6

Page

100   "probably the most important": J. Anthony Lukas, "8 Go on Trial Today," *New York Times,* September 24, 1969, p. 29.

100   "one of the most political and publicized": Jeffrey Needle, review of *My Life as a Radical Lawyer, Trial,* April 1995, p. 82.

100   journalists' books: the best that have been consulted include Jason Epstein, *The Great Conspiracy Trial* (New York: Vintage Books, 1970); M. L. Levine, G. C. McNamee, and Daniel Greenberg, *The Tales of Hoffman* (New York: Bantam Books, 1970); J. Anthony Lukas, *The Barnyard Epithet and Other Obscenities: Notes on the Chicago Conspiracy Trial* (New York: Harper and Row, 1970); and John Schultz, *Motion Will Be Denied: A New Report on the Chicago Conspiracy Trial* (New York: Morrow, 1972).

101   memoirs: Dave Dellinger, *More Power Than We Know: The People's Movement toward Democracy* (Garden City, NY: Anchor Press/Double-day, 1975); David Dellinger, *From Yale to Jail: The Life Story of a Moral Dissenter* (New York: Pantheon, 1993); Tom Hayden, *Trial* (New York: Holt, Rinehart and Winston, 1970); Tom Hayden, *Reunion: A Memoir* (New York: Random House, 1988); Abbie Hoffman, *Soon to Be a Major Motion Picture* (New York: G. P. Putnam's Sons, 1980); William M. Kunstler (with Sheila Isenberg), *My Life as a Radical Lawyer* (New York: Birch Lane Press, 1994); Jerry Rubin, *Do It! Scenarios of the Revolution* (New York: Simon and Schuster, 1970); Jerry Rubin, *Growing (Up) at Thirty-Seven* (New York: M. Evans, 1976); Bobby Seale, *Seize the Time: The Story of the Black Panther Party and Huey P. Newton* (New York: Random House, 1970).

101   scholarly accounts: It is surprising how little there is. The best two are merely articles: David J. Danelski, "The Chicago Conspiracy Trial," in Theodore L. Becker, ed., *Political Trials* (Indianapolis: Bobbs-Merrill, 1971) and James W. Ely, Jr., "The Chicago Conspiracy Case," in Michal R. Belknap, ed., *American Political Trials* (Westport, CT: Praeger, 1994). A specialized scholarly study is Juliet Dee, "Constraints on Persuasion in the Chicago Seven Trial," in Robert Hariman, ed., *Popular Trials: Rhetoric, Mass Media, and the Law* (Tuscaloosa: University of Alabama Press, 1990).

101   BBC-TV: Hoffman, *Soon to Be a Major Motion Picture*, p. 187; *New York Times*, May 19, 1987, p. C18.

101   HBO version and positive reviews: see, e.g., *Chicago Tribune*, May 15, 1987, p. C5; *New York Times*, May 19, 1987, p. C18; and *Washington Post*, May 16, 1987, p. G1.

101   A&E documentary: *New York Times*, November 30, 1994, p. 5C; *Chicago Sun-Times*, August 27, 1996, p. 37.

101   radio: *Chicago Tribune*, June 8, 1993, p. C2.

101   stage play: *USA Today*, October 15, 1991, p. D4; *Chicago Tribune*, September 24, 1991, p. C18; *Los Angeles Times*, March 25, 1994, p. F25; *The Nation*, November 21, 1994, p. 625.

102   "During the week": Daniel Walker, *Rights in Conflict: A Report Submitted to the National Commission on the Causes and Prevention of Violence* (New York: Bantam Books, 1968), pp. 1–5, as quoted in Danelski, "The Chicago Conspiracy Trial," p. 144 (biographical information on Walker on p. 136 n. 8.

104   "to jail in one prosecution": *The Conspiracy* (New York: Dell, 1969), p. 27.

104   scholars and journalists observed: Danelski, "The Chicago Conspiracy Trial," p. 146; Lukas, "8 Go on Trial Today," p. 29.

104   "approximately twenty principal leaders": William M. Kunstler and Stewart E. Albert, "The Great Conspiracy Trial of '69," *Nation,* September 29, 1979, front cover and p. 273.

105   "We want to make sure": Tom Hayden, "Join the Conspiracy," *The Movement,* May 1969, in Clayborne Carson, ed., *The Movement, 1964–1970* (Westport, CT: Greenwood, 1993), p. 610.

105   "At the beginning": Dellinger, *More Power Than We Know,* p. 231.

105   Hoffman and Rubin: Kunstler, *My Life,* p. 13.

105   Dellinger's choice and "was a liberal": David Dellinger, "Search for the Truth: The Late William Kunstler, the Chicago Seven Trial, and the Never-Ending Struggle for Justice: A Reminiscence," *SF Bay Guardian,* September 13, 1995.

106   Hayden's personal choice: Hayden, *Reunion,* p. 347.

106   $375, bill: Hoffman, *Soon to Be a Major Motion Picture,* p. 192.

106   chief counsel and no disrespectful behavior: Hayden, *Reunion,* p. 347.

106   agreement with Garry: Dellinger, *From Yale to Jail,* p. 345.

106   Dellinger argued for Kunstler: ibid., p. 342.

106   "there's something inside him": interview with David Dellinger interview, June 15, 1996.

106   "Bill Kunstler swallowed": Hoffman, *Soon to Be a Major Motion Picture,* p. 193.

107   "the defense in any criminal case": Epstein, *The Great Conspiracy Trial,* p. 99; see also Lukas *The Barnyard Epithet,* p. 42.

107   "Tell me something": Lukas, *The Barnyard Epithet,* p. 1.

108   "Trial decorum often": *United States v. Dellinger,* 472 F.2d 340, 385–87 (7th Cir. 1972).

109   "fell below the standards": ibid., p. 389.

109   "our first big break": Kunstler quoted in Stephanie B. Goldberg, "Lessons of the '60s: 'We'd Do It Again,' Say the Chicago Seven's Lawyers," *ABA Journal,* May 15, 1987, p. 32.

109   "I think the trial": Nat Hentoff, "Playboy Interview with William Kunstler," *Playboy,* October 1970.

109   the "Black Panther" notes: Danelski, "The Chicago Conspiracy Trial," pp. 153–54; Epstein, *The Great Conspiracy Trial,* pp. 149, 183–85.

110   "Prior to and during the trial": Kunstler, *My Life,* p. 13.

110   later FBI documents and judicial review of same: *United States v. Dellinger,* 657 F.2d 140, 142–43, 146 n. 15 (7th Cir. 1981).

111   "we know what's illegal": *New York Times,* November 18, 1969, p. 26.

112   "Your Honor, are we going" and other portions of transcript: Judy Clavir and John Spitzer, *The Conspiracy Trial* (partial transcript), (Indianapolis: Bobbs-Merrill, 1970), pp. 166, 169.

114   "The defendants taught us": Kunstler, *My Life,* p. 22.

115   "the nonlinear route": Hoffman, *Soon to Be a Major Motion Picture*, p. 188.

115   "put the government on trial" through "offset his hostility": Kunstler, *My Life*, pp. 22, 32.

115   "You know it is not right": quoted in Lukas, *The Barnyard Epithet*, pp. 83–84.

116   "It is a criminal case": quoted in Danelski, "The Chicago Conspiracy Trial," p. 167.

116   marijuana motion: Kunstler, *My Life*, pp. 27–28.

116   "burnt that night": Scott Fornek, "That Wild Trial of Chicago 7," *Chicago Sun-Times*, September 25, 1994, p. 16.

117   "the principal cause of this disintegration" through "each reacted to provocation by the other": *In the Matter of David T. Dellinger*, 370 F. Supp. 1304, 1311, 1321 (N.D. Ill. 1973).

118   Hugh Hefner as potential witness: Kunstler, *My Life*, p. 23.

119   "I have tried with all of my heart": Clavir and Spitzer, *The Conspiracy Trial*, pp. 589–90.

119   reversal of contempts: *United States v. Seale*, 461 F.2d 345 (7th Cir. 1972); and *In the Matter of David T. Dellinger, et al.*, 461 F.2d 389 (7th Cir. 1972).

120   "cannot control the American jury system": *New York Times*, October 29, 1973.

120   Kunstler's character witness: Kunstler, *My Life*, p. 40.

120   retrial of contempts and refusal to impose sentence: *In the Matter of David T. Dellinger, et al.*, 370 F. Supp. 1304 (N.D. Ill. 1973); refusal of 1981 challenge: *United States v. David T. Dellinger, et al.*, 657 F.2d 140 (7th Cir. 1981).

120   "the demeanor of the judge and prosecutors": *United States v. David T. Dellinger, et al.*, 472 F.2d 340, 391 (7th Cir. 1972).

120   "Dubious charges opened": *New York Times*, May 15, 1972, p. 34.

120   "I don't think the Government": *New York Times*, November 22, 1972, p. 14.

120   government will not retry original charges: *New York Times*, January 5, 1973, p. 22.

121   October 16, 1971, reunion: J. Anthony Lukas, "Bobby Seale's Birthday Cake (Oh, Far Out!)," *New York Times Magazine*, October 31, 1971, p. 42.

121   Lotte Kunstler recalls: interview with Lotte Kunstler, October 14, 1996.

121   reunion with HBO cast: Kunstler, *My Life*, photo gallery.

121   screening of HBO: *Los Angeles Mirror*, May 18, 1987, pt. 5, p. 1.

121   Chicago reunion in 1988: Tricia Drevets, "Programs More Than Reunion to '68 Convention Veterans," *Chicago Tribune*, August 26, 1988, p. 10.

121   1993 panel at New York Law School: *New York Law Journal,* March 17, 1993, p. 2.

121   1994 panel, Learning Alliance: *New York Times,* October 27, 1994, p. B22; October 30, 1994, p. 43.

121   1996 reunion: *Chicago Sun-Times,* August 9, 1996, p. 4; *Dallas Morning News,* August 26, 1996, p. A9; *Los Angeles Times,* August 23, 1996, p. 1; *Washington Post,* August 26, 1996, p. D01.

121   Hoffman commemorations: *New York Times,* November 30, 1994, p. B8; *New York,* December 12, 1994, p. 22; *Washington Times,* December 2, 1994, p. A2; *New York Times,* December 3, 1995, p. 8.

121   feature stories: e.g., *Chicago Sun-Times,* August 7, 1994, p. 12; *St. Louis Post-Dispatch,* February 11, 1990, p. C1 (first of three parts).

121   Hayden: *Newsweek,* June 7, 1976, p. 22; Julius Hoffman: *Newsweek,* September 6, 1976, p. 8; *New York Times,* June 24, 1982, p. 16; *Washington Post,* July 2, 1982, p. A15.

122   obituaries: see, e.g., Julius Hoffman: *New York Times,* July 2, 1983, p. 8; *Washington Post,* July 2, 1983, p. D6; Gignoux: *New York Times,* November 6, 1988, p. 52; *Washington Post,* November 10, 1988, p. D15; Abbie Hoffman: *Los Angeles Times,* April 19, 1989, p. 4; *Newsday,* April 14, 1989, sec. 2, p. 2, and April 19, 1989, p. 04; *New York Times,* April 14, 1989, p. D17; Rubin: *Houston Chronicle,* November 30, 1994, p. 16; *New York Times,* November 30, 1994, p. B13; *People,* December 12, 1994, p. 53; *Washington Times,* November 30, 1994, p. A8; Kunstler: *New York Times,* September 5, 1995, p. XZX; *Jerusalem Post,* September 6, 1995, p. 4; *Times* (London), September 6, 1995, features; *Vancouver Sun,* September 6, 1995, p. A12; numerous American newspapers.

122   "learned, for the first time": Kunstler, *My Life,* p. 26.

122   "to allay the fear" through "wish us well": Hoffman, *Soon to Be a Major Motion Picture,* p. 196.

122   "celebrity in America": Kunstler, *My Life,* p. 34.

122   "I was a streetcar conductor": quoted in Lukas, *The Barnyard Epithet,* p. 26.

122   "needed a good bath": quoted in Epstein, *The Great Conspiracy Trial,* p. 42–43.

122   "because of their appearance": Kay S. Richards (one of the jurors), "Chicago 7 Verdict: Step by Step," *Boston Globe,* February 22, 1970, p. 1.

123   "bunch of jerks": Hayden, *Reunion,* p. 352.

123   "Through the Chicago trial": *Newsday,* January 6, 1991, p. 8.

123   "We wanted to put the government on trial": Dellinger, *From Yale to Jail,* p. 343.

123   "wanted to decide": Kunstler, *My Life,* pp. 19, 21.

123   "the political agent": Hentoff, "Interview with William Kunstler."

124 "This is outrageous": *New York Times,* October 16, 1969, p. 18.

124 "I sang once" and "you get awfully chummy": Lukas, *The Barnyard Epithet,* p. 90.

124 mass street demonstrations: *New York Times,* February 19, 1970, p. 17.

124 "It was an eighteen-hour day": Hayden, *Trial,* p. 108.

124 $100 per week: Hentoff, "Interview with William Kunstler"; Carol Ruth Sternhell, "A Brief Encounter with a Lawyer Named Kunstler," *McCall's,* January 1971, p. 102.

124 North Side apartment: Kunstler, *My Life,* p. 33.

125 "it quickly became known": Hayden, *Reunion,* p. 380.

125 "so busy exploring": Dellinger interview.

125 smoked dope with the defendants: Hoffman, *Soon to Be a Major Motion Picture,* p. 162; Nile Southern and Mark Amerika, "An Impolite Interview with Paul Krasser," *Write Stuff, Altx.Com* (website/magazine), January–February 1996.

125 stripped off his shirt: Lukas, *The Barnyard Epithet,* p. 65; Kunstler, *My Life,* p. 34.

125 at several parties stripped to shorts: Margo Howard to David J. Langum, October 1, 1997, and telephone conversation, November 25, 1997.

125 "I was part of it": Kunstler quoted in James Frank, "Still Crazy after All These Years," *Spy,* September 1990, p. 71; Kunstler, *My Life,* p. 44.

125 "would work all night": Tom Hayden, quoted in Stephanie Benson Goldberg, "A Fighting Chance," *Student Lawyer,* November 1987, p. 37.

126 women's dormitory: story related by Margo Howard in letter to David J. Langum, October 1, 1997.

126 defendants' speaking engagements: Marty Jezer, *Abbie Hoffman: American Rebel* (New Brunswick: Rutgers University Press, 1992), pp. 210–13; Hoffman, *Soon to Be a Major Motion Picture,* pp. 210–21.

126 "is like a stage" and "personal Rubicon": Kunstler, *My Life,* pp. 43, 42.

126 "I had faith in the courts": quoted in Fornek, "That Wild Trial of Chicago 7."

126 "Up to that time": quoted in Elliot Pinsley, "Kunstler Still Making the Left's Case," *Manhattan Lawyer,* August 1–7, 1989, p. 1.

126 "step by step": quoted in Dellinger, "Search for the Truth."

126 "the trial made a radical": Hoffman, *Soon to Be a Major Motion Picture,* p. 202.

127 "responding in kind": quoted in Goldberg, "Lessons of the '60s: 'We'd Do It Again.'"

127 "a heroic group": *Charlie Rose Show,* WNET October 28, 1994, as rebroadcast on September 5, 1995, transcript (Westlaw).

127   "Our position": quoted in Randy Furst, "Kunstler's Legacy Includes Famous Twin Cities Court Battles," *Minneapolis Star Tribune,* September 5, 1995, p. A7.

128   *Times* feature article in magazine section: Victor S. Navasky, "Right On! With Lawyer William Kunstler," *New York Times Magazine,* April 21, 1970, p. 30.

NOTES TO CHAPTER 7

Page

129   examples of miscellaneous representations include Kentucky sedition statute: *New York Times,* August 19, 1967, p. 12; and Anne Braden, "Fighting Jim Crow," in Griffin Fariello, ed., *Red Scare: Memories of the American Inquisition: An Oral History* (New York: Avon Books, 1995), pp. 480–82; civil rights groups: *New York Times,* August 27, 1964, p. 37, and September 24, 1968, p. 1; exclusion from juries: *New York Times,* November 5, 1967, p. 51; security clearance: *New York Times,* May 13, 1969, p. 10; black officials: *New York Times,* January 18, 1969, p. 1; fired professor: Milton Viorst, *Fire in the Streets: America in the 1960s* (New York: Simon and Schuster, 1979), p. 475.

129   House Un-American Activities Committee: *New York Times,* August 18, 1966, p. 1, and August 19, 1966, p. 16; William M. Kunstler (with Sheila Isenberg), *My Life as a Radical Lawyer,* (New York: Birch Lane Press, 1994), pp. 13, 170–72.

129   Adam Clayton Powell: Kunstler, *My Life,* pp. 184–87.

129   Morton Sobell: *New York Times,* August 1, 1965, p. 66; voluminous correspondence in Records of the Committee to Secure Justice for Morton Sobell (microfilm edition, 1976), State Historical Society of Wisconsin, especially microfilm reels 19 and 24.

130   Oswald representation: Kunstler, *My Life,* pp. 153–54.

130   chief counsel: Kunstler correspondence quoted in Elmer Gertz, *Moment of Madness: The People vs. Jack Ruby* (Chicago: Follett, 1968), p. 152.

130   "rhetorical grandeur": Gertz, *Moment of Madness,* p. 422.

130   pickets: Kunstler, *My Life,* p. 155.

131   "Kunstler was highly articulate": Gertz, *Moment of Madness,* pp. 149–50.

131   Michael Kunstler's generosity: Kunstler, *My Life,* pp. 110, 112, 115, 131; William M. Kunstler, *Trials and Tribulations* (New York: Grove Press, 1985), p. 127.

131   Kunstler's general practice: interview with Steven Hyman, July 17, 1996; for incorporation, see David Finkelstein Papers, State Historical Society of Wisconsin, box 1, folder 2; for probate litigation, see Mary

Mokarzel Papers, Immigration History Research Center, University of Minnesota, Correspondence, box 1.

132 collegiality: interview with Arthur Kinoy, July 15, 1996.

132 "I can't take it anymore!": Hyman interview.

132 Chicago Seven and not using office: ibid.

132 not been to office for six months: Victor S. Navasky, "Right On! With Lawyer William Kunstler," *New York Times Magazine,* April 21, 1970, p. 30.

132 break in 1970: Kunstler, *Trials and Tribulations,* p. 127.

132 supported himself: Navasky, "Right On! With Lawyer William Kunstler," p. 88; Nat Hentoff, "Playboy Interview with William Kunstler," *Playboy,* October 1970.

132 "I'm too impatient" and Michael Kunstler's death: Kunstler, *My Life,* p. 266.

132 foundation of Center for Constitutional Rights: Kinoy interview; Arthur Kinoy, *Rights on Trial: The Odyssey of a People's Lawyer* (Cambridge: Harvard University Press, 1983; reprint, Larchmont, NY: Bernel Books, 1994), pp. 243, 281; Kunstler, *My Life,* p. 176.

133 operation and controversy of Center for Constitutional Rights: "Labor Trouble on the Left," *The Progressive,* January 1995, p. 17; Edward A. Adams, "Constitutional Rights Center: 13 Years of Unpopular Causes," *New York Law Journal,* June 23, 1989, p. 1; Bruce Olson, "An Activist-in-Charge Departs after 12 Years," *National Law Journal,* December 12, 1988, p. 8; Fred Strasser, "The FBI: Playing By Its New Rules," *National Law Forum,* February 15, 1988, p. 3; E. R. Shipp, "Group Marks 20 Years of Fighting for Rights," *New York Times,* December 28, 1986, p. 37; Sarah Bottorff, "Legal Group Wins Kudos, Case Law, and Controversy," *Los Angeles Daily Journal,* November 14, 1986, p. 1; Kirk Johnson, "Manila Panel Seeking Marcos Assets Is Faulted by Some over Its Lawyers," *New York Times,* May 22, 1986, p. 10; Sidney E. Zion, "Untraditional Law Group Assisting Anti-Establishment Forces," *New York Times,* August 17, 1969.

133 operation of Center for Constitutional Rights: interview with Ronald Kuby, July 17, 1996; Kinoy interview.

134 150 colleges and universities: Carol Ruth Sternhell, "A Brief Encounter with a Lawyer Named Kunstler," *McCall's,* January 1971, p. 101.

134 three or four times a week: J. Anthony Lukas, "Bobby Seale's Birthday Cake (Oh, Far Out!)," *New York Times Magazine,* October 31, 1971, p. 46.

134 Philadelphia meeting: Navasky, "Right On!" p. 88; rallies and protests: *New York Times,* April 16, 1970, p. 44; September 9, 1970, p. 31; October 31, 1970, p. 26; debates with Russell Kirk: Russell Kirk, *The Sword of*

Imagination: Memoirs of a Half-Century of Literary Conflict (Grand Rapids, MI: Eerdmans, 1995), pp. 405–6; name on denunciations: Jason Epstein, *The Great Conspiracy Trial* (New York: Vintage Books, 1970), p. 119; and *New York Times*, March 7, 1969, p. 48; list of sixty-five radical speakers: *New York Times*, October 15, 1970, p. 23.

134   $1,000 fees and income from fees: Michael Steven Smith, "A Case for Courage," *Against the Current*, 1995, p. 41; Navasky, "Right On!" pp. 88, 92.

134   campus authorities feared riots: Illinois: *New York Times*, March 3, 1970, p. 26; March 4, 1970, p. 32, March 19, 1970, p. 50; Jacksonville: *New York Times*, June 6, 1970, p. 4; San Jose State: *New York Times*, May 25, 1970, p. 37; May 27, 1970, p. 18.

134   Columbia incident: *New York Times*, April 9, 1970, p. 49, April 10, 1970, p. 33; John R. Coyne, Jr., "The Kunstler Constituency," *National Review*, May 5, 1970, p. 467.

135   Illinois violence: *New York Times*, March 3, 1970, p. 26; March 4, 1970, p. 32; March 19, 1970, p. 50.

135   materials on Isla Vista/Santa Barbara riot: Steven V. Roberts, "Violence by Students Is Linked to 'Powerlessness,'" *New York Times*, March 1, 1970, p. 72; Alexander Bloom and Wini Breines, "'*Takin' It to the Streets': A Sixties Reader* (New York: Oxford University Press, 1995), pp. 401–3; David Sheff, "Tom Selleck: Playboy Interview," *Playboy*, December 1983, p. 79; Catherine Foster, "Activists Gather to Check Ideals," *Christian Science Monitor*, March 1, 1990, p. 8.

136   Toronto incident: *New York Times*, June 23, 1970, p. 18; August 10, 1970, p. 14; December 2, 1970, p. 13.

136   David Duke: *New York Times*, November 10, 1991, p. 1; *Houston Chronicle*, January 19, 1992, p. 1.

136   "We've gone into the age": Navasky, "Right On!" p. 92.

137   "People are no longer": ibid., p. 91.

137   "odd combination": ibid., p. 91.

137   Illinois and Notre Dame: ibid., pp. 92, 91.

137   "The crowd filled": Sternhell, "A Brief Encounter," p. 54.

137   "on the basis": Navasky, "Right On!" p. 88.

138   "He is probably the only": Joseph W. Bishop, Jr., "Will Mr. William Kunstler Please Step Down?" *Esquire*, April 1971, pp. 115–16.

138   cult following: "A Lawyer for Hire" (editorial), *American Bar Association Journal*, June 1970, p. 552.

138   "something embarrassingly sexual": Coyne, "The Kunstler Constituency," p. 467.

138   "speeches were so exhilarating": Kunstler, *My Life*, p. 35.

138   many colleagues recalled: e.g., Stew Albert, "Remembering Bill Kunstler," Internet posting; Michael Kennedy, "The Man Who Made America a Safer Place for Outlaws," *High Times,* January 1996, n.p.

138   Lotte recalls: interview with Lotte Kunstler, October 14, 1996.

138   first marijuana use: Kunstler, *My Life,* p. 176.

138   heroin and LSD use: Kunstler, *My Life,* pp. 168, 195.

138   "unworkable drug-control policy": William M. Kunstler, "The Charade Known as the War on Crime," *Connecticut Law Tribune,* May 9, 1994, p. 10 (keynote address before Hartford County Bar Association Law Day ceremony); William M. Kunstler, "Why Not Sell at the Local Pharmacy?" *Los Angeles Times,* December 15, 1989, p. B7 (op-ed); Kunstler's final conclusions: Kunstler, *My Life,* pp. 169–70.

139   "I've tried to maintain": "An Interview with William Kunstler," in Jonathan Black, ed., *Radical Lawyers: Their Role in the Movement and in the Courts* (New York: Avon Books, 1971), p. 302.

139   "At some point": Kunstler, *My Life,* p. 195.

140   "That's the only good thing": *USA Today,* July 12, 1991, p. A3.

140   *Nation* articles: December 30, 1961, pp. 526–28; July 27, 1963, pp. 52–3.

140   book reviews: *New York Times,* October 11, 1964, pp. 48–49; *Life,* December 3, 1965, p. 15.

140   reading poetry: Navasky, "Right On!" pp. 90–91.

140   . . . *And Justice for All* (Dobbs Ferry, NY: Oceana Publications, 1963); *Deep in My Heart* (New York: Morrow, 1966).

140   Jon R. Waltz, "Equality and the Court" (review of *Deep in My Heart*), *Saturday Review,* March 12, 1966, pp. 40–41.

140   *The Minister and the Choir Singer: The Hall-Mills Murder Case* (New York: Morrow, 1964).

141   Rex Stout, "Was the Murderer in the Jury Box?" (book review of *The Minister and the Choir Singer*), *New York Times Book Review,* February 2, 1964, pp. 1, 22.

141   movie rights and use of money: Lotte Kunstler interview.

141   reissue: *The Hall-Mills Murder Case: The Minister and the Choir Singer* (New Brunswick: Rutgers University Press, 1980).

141   notices of reissue: *New York Times,* December 14, 1980, sec. 11NJ, p. 6; *Wilson Library Bulletin,* March 1981, p. 532.

141   subsequent articles: *New York Times,* September 11, 1988, sec. 12NJ, p. 23; *Minneapolis Star Tribune,* September 6, 1995, p. A10.

141   womanizing: except as noted, this material is drawn from Kinoy interview and interviews with David Dellinger, June 15, 1996; Lotte Kunstler, September 30, 1996 and October 14, 1996; Fred Marks, February 25, 1997; Milton Berner, March 24, 1997; and Graham Marks, March 25, 1997.

141   "exhaustion, strain, and tension": Mary King, *Freedom Song: A Personal Story of the 1960s Civil Rights Movement* (New York: Morrow, 1987), p. 211.

142   "I began to see": Kunstler, *My Life,* p. 262.

142   Hoffman at trial: Jack Hoffman and Daniel Simon, *Run, Run, Run: The Lives of Abbie Hoffman* (New York: Putnam's Sons, 1994), p. 133.

142   "you were either sleeping": told to Helene E. Schwartz, *Lawyering* (New York: Farrar, 1975), p. 91.

142   "found these women": Kunstler, *My Life,* p. 34.

142   "I was away from home": James Frank, "Still Crazy after All These Years," *Spy,* September 1990, p. 70.

142   "I spoke on many, many": *Washington Post,* September 6, 1995, p. C01.

142   "You're away from home": Craig Wolff, "Not Guilty," *GQ,* June 1994, p. 197.

142   flaunting exploits and angered female colleagues: Connie Bruck, "William Kunstler: Actor without A Stage," *American Lawyer,* August 1980, p. 26.

143   "one of Kunstler's lady friends' houses": *New York Times,* August 7, 1970, p. 14; August 14, 1970, p. 22.

143   "'Balls' is a male chauvinist": Bruck, "William Kunstler: Actor without a Stage," p. 26.

143   "it demeans and degrades women": Hentoff, "Interview with William Kunstler."

143   "Bill Kunstler treated me": King, *Freedom Song,* p. 84.

143   "my first marriage": Kunstler, *My Life,* pp. 262–63.

143   "By the late Sixties": Todd Gitlin, *The Sixties: Years of Hope, Days of Rage* (New York: Bantam, 1987), p. 372.

144   six out-of-town trips: Charles McCarry, "A Few Soft Words for the Rabble-Rousers," *Esquire,* July 1969, p. 108.

144   "most kids' fathers": interview with Jane Kunstler Drazek, October 8, 1996.

144   "really and truly": Lotte Kunstler interview.

145   "Mostly, these things": quoted in McCarry, "A Few Soft Words for the Rabble-Rousers," p. 132.

145   "tell your father": Jane Kunstler Drazek interview.

145   FBI wiretap: M. Wesley Swearingen, *FBI Secrets: An Agent's Expose* (Boston: South End Press, 1995), p. 86.

145   "Sometimes he got": Fred Marks interview.

146   "grinned at me": Warren Strugatch, *Newsday,* September 7, 1995, p. A37.

146   "our hero and also our playmate" through "definitely in a way: Graham Marks interview.

146 Lotte's accompaniment: both *Deep in My Heart* and *My Life* have information; Lotte Kunstler interview; as to presence at campus speeches, see, e.g., *New York Times,* March 8, 1970, p. 49 (Albany).

146 Westchester County Auditorium event: Kunstler, *My Life,* p. 113.

147 consulting on major decisions: Navasky, "Right On!" p. 92.

147 stretchers in general and death of King: Jane Kunstler Drazek and Lotte Kunstler interviews; interview with Karin Kunstler Goldman, October 15, 1996; Kunstler, *My Life,* p. 151; Ron Rosenbaum, "The Most Hated Lawyer in America," *Vanity Fair,* March 1992, pp. 86, 88.

148 "Every man fights": William M. Kunstler, speech before National Convention of Unitarians, June 24, 1968, tape in possession of State Historical Society of Wisconsin, Madison.

149 "should experience the isolation": William F. Buckley, Jr., "Kunstler," *National Review,* November 5, 1971, p. 1258.

149 Law and Social Action Commission: McCarry, "A Few Soft Words for the Rabble-Rousers," p. 132.

149 "I hate him": quoted in "Parting Shots," *Life,* October 1, 1971.

149 "say that his briefs": *Time,* December 13, 1968, p. 60.

149 "endless stories of meetings": Navasky, "Right On!" p. 89.

149 "was winging it in court": quoted in Elliot Pinsley, "Kunstler Still Making the Left's Case," *Manhattan Lawyer,* August 1–7, 1989, p. 1.

149 "ill-prepared": quoted in Bruck, "William Kunstler: Actor without a Stage," p. 26.

149 "Bill's weakness": quoted in McCarry, "A Few Soft Words for the Rabble-Rousers," p. 132.

150 "he was certainly not": Bruck, "William Kunstler: Actor without a Stage," p. 25.

150 "sometimes the research was hasty": quoted in Pinsley, "Kunstler Still Making the Left's Case," p. 1.

150 "Preparation was not necessarily": Hyman interview.

150 "had never found the time": Kunstler, *My Life,* pp. 17–18.

150 "totally irresponsible": quoted in *Baltimore Sun,* May 10, 1995, p. D1.

150 "Thriving on the drama": J. Anthony Lukas, *The Barnyard Epithet and Other Obscenities: Notes on the Chicago Conspiracy Trial* (New York: Harper and Row, 1970), pp. 90–91.

150 "had an amazing ability": David Dellinger, *From Yale to Jail: The Life Story of a Moral Dissenter* (New York: Pantheon, 1993), p. 345.

151 1979 murder appeal: *New York Times,* February 22, 1979, p. B2.

151 "may profit from": United Press International, New York Metro, February 25, 1983.

151 competent and prepared: interview with Jack B. Weinstein, July 16, 1996.

151   "completely unprepared": Frank, "Still Crazy after All These Years,"
       p. 70.
151   a mother complained: Wolff, "Not Guilty," pp. 195–96.
151   "the casual approach": Morton Sobell to Marshall Perlin, August 1,
       1965; "verified my earlier impression": Sobell to Marshall Perlin, Au-
       gust 11, 1965; "that you've become": Morton Sobell to William Kun-
       stler and Arthur Kinoy, May 2, 1965; "from the Times": Sobell to Kun-
       stler, May 1966, all in Records of the Committee to Secure Justice for
       Morton Sobell, box 36, folder 5, Sobell, Morton, General Outgoing Cor-
       respondence 1951–1961, microfilm reel 19, State Historical Society of
       Wisconsin, Madison.
151   reporters noted: for example, the Arietta Venizelos trial, noted in
       Bruck, "William Kunstler: Actor without a Stage," p. 26.
151   photographic mind: Berner interview.
152   dictate briefs effortlessly: Hyman interview.
152   "amazing ability": quoted in *Newsday,* January 6, 1991, p. 8.
152   "life has been very hectic": Kunstler to Morton Sobell, December 17,
       1968, Records of the Committee to Secure Justice for Morton Sobell,
       microfilm reel 19.
152   "I won't listen": quoted in Pinsley, "Kunstler Still Making the Left's
       Case," p. 1.
152   "prepared the case": Hentoff, "Interview with William Kunstler."

NOTES TO CHAPTER 8

Page
153   rich literature: see, e.g., Austin Sarat and Stuart Scheingold, eds., *Cause
       Lawyering: Political Commitments and Professional Responsibilities* (New
       York: Oxford University Press, 1998); Gerald N. Rosenberg, *The Hollow
       Hope: Can Courts Bring About Social Change?* (Chicago: University of
       Chicago Press, 1991); Joel F. Handler, *Social Movements and the Legal
       System* (New York: Academic Press, 1978); Jerold S. Auerbach, *Unequal
       Justice: Lawyers and Social Change in Modern America* (New York: Oxford
       University Press, 1976); and Stuart A. Scheingold, *The Politics of Rights:
       Lawyers, Public Policy, and Political Change* (New Haven: Yale Univer-
       sity Press, 1974).
153   "accepted the traditional structure": David Sternberg, "The New Rad-
       ical-Criminal Trials: A Step towards a Class-for-Itself in the American
       Proletariat?" *Science & Society,* fall 1972, p. 276.
154   "The majority of old left lawyers": Nancy Ellen Anderson, "Radical
       Lawyers: An Examination of the Left-Wing 'Sector' of the Bar" (Ph.D.
       diss., New York University, 1980), pp. 239, 218.

154 "not to my liking": interview in Jonathan Black, ed., *Radical Lawyers: Their Role in the Movement and in the Courts* (New York: Avon Books, 1971), p. 302.

155 "Professionalism is an ideology": Anderson, "Radical Lawyers," p. 88.

155 Marlise James, *The People's Lawyers* (New York: Holt, Rinehart and Winston, 1973); Cockrel quotation, p. 151; Garry quotation, pp. 310–11.

156 Black, *Radical Lawyers*; di Suvero quotation, p. 57; Axelrod quotation, p. 70; Lefcourt quotation, pp. 311–12.

156 "come to the conclusion": "We Talk To . . . ," *Mlle*, August 1970, p. 297.

156 "terribly wrong with the existence": Nat Hentoff, "Playboy Interview with William Kunstler," *Playboy*, October 1970.

157 "I wouldn't say": quoted in Ron Rosenbaum, "The Most Hated Lawyer in America," *Vanity Fair*, March 1992, p. 90.

157 Texas conference: Clayborne Carson, ed., *The Movement, 1964–1970* (Westport, CT: Greenwood, 1993), p. 539 (original issue of February 1969).

157 keynote speaker, sexual liaisons: James M. Simons to David J. Langum, January 2, 1998.

157 "should, first of all": Hentoff, "Interview with William Kunstler."

157 "I'm not sure": quoted in "Politics," *SF Bay Guardian*, September 13, 1995.

157 "thought the world" and "I don't want to sound": quoted in Rosenbaum, "The Most Hated Lawyer in America," pp. 88, 90.

158 "political assassination of the right person": William M. Kunstler (with Sheila Isenberg), *My Life as a Radical Lawyer* (New York: Birch Lane Press, 1994), p. 324.

158 "any black guy": Rosenbaum, "The Most Hated Lawyer in America," p. 72.

158 only political weapon: William M. Kunstler speech before National Convention of Unitarians, June 24, 1968, tape in possession of State Historical of Wisconsin, Madison.

158 "deserved that death": quoted in Victor S. Navasky, "Right On! With Lawyer William Kunstler," *New York Times Magazine*, April 21, 1970, pp. 30–31.

159 "words were harsh": William Kunstler, radio interview with Gil Gross, CBS Radio, September 19, 1994.

159 "only the threat or actuality": Leonard Orland, "Can We Establish the Rule of Law in Prisons?" *Civil Liberties Review*, vol. 2, no. 2 (1975), p. 70.

159 "It is a bad tactic": Black, *Radical Lawyers*, p. 306.

159 "In fact, we should": quoted in Carol Ruth Sternhell, "A Brief Encounter with a Lawyer Named Kunstler," *McCall's*, January 1971, p. 101.

159   "We have clenched the fist": Hentoff, "Interview with William Kunstler."

160   "It may be right": "We Talk To . . . ," *Mademoiselle*, p. 297.

160   "related primarily to property damage": Black, *Radical Lawyers*, p. 306.

160   quotations from James, *The People's Lawyers*: "simply the functional": Kenneth Vern Cockrel, p. 150; "instruments of the status quo": Vincent Hallinan, p. 192; "only another arm of the oppressor": Charles Garry, p. 310.

160   Goodman quotation: Black, *Radical Lawyers*, pp. 249–50.

161   "through demystification": Anderson, "Radical Lawyers," p. 222. This dissertation has a very lucid discussion of demystification; see also Nathan Hakman, "Old and New Left Activity in the Legal Order: An Interpretation," *Journal of Social Issues*, no. 1, 1971, pp. 105–21.

161   Cloke, di Suvero, and *Bust Book* quotations: Black, *Radical Lawyers*, Cloke, p. 42; di Suvero, p. 61; *Bust Book*, p. 102.

162   Cockrel and Garry quotations: James, *The People's Lawyers*, Cockrel, pp. 150–51; Garry, p. 310–11.

162   "all a living lie": quoted in Connie Bruck, "William Kunstler: Actor without a Stage," *American Lawyer*, August 1980, p. 26.

162   "law in the United States": *The Law Report*, Australian Broadcasting Corporation, September 12, 1995.

162   "the real purpose": Orland, "Can We Establish the Rule of Law in Prisons?" p. 70.

162   "law just control mechanism": Stephanie B. Goldberg, "Lessons of the '60s: 'We'd Do It Again,' Say the Chicago Seven's Lawyers," *ABA Journal*, May 15, 1987, p. 37.

162   "what passes for justice": William M. Kunstler, book review, *Science & Society*, 1992–93, p. 476.

162   Miss America contest: Barry Slotnick at program, "William Kunstler: Champion or Charlatan?" Association of the Bar of the City of New York, June 19, 1996.

162   "Judges are creatures": Kunstler, *My Life*, p. 360.

163   "stump speeches": interview with Judge Jack B. Weinstein, July 16, 1996.

163   several judges: Leon Friedman, "A Provocative Lawyer Who Challenged Rules," *National Law Journal*, September 18, 1995, p. A22.

163   "use the system's contradictions": Kunstler, *My Life*, p. 319.

163   "The courts have many purposes": Charles McCarry, "A Few Soft Words for the Rabble-Rousers," *Esquire*, July 1969, pp. 133–34.

163   "in a political trial": quoted in Robert Monroe, "Outcasts', Underdogs' Attorney William Kunstler Dies in NYC," *Chattanooga Free Press*, September 5, 1995.

163   "up to that time": Elliot Pinsley, "Kunstler Still Making the Left's Case," *Manhattan Lawyer,* August 1–7, 1989, p. 1; see also, e.g., F. Peter Model, Sid Lerner, and Hal Drucker, "Chatting with Bill Kunstler over General Noriega's Cookies," *New York Law Journal,* September 18, 1995, p. 2; David Dellinger, "William Kunstler: Thunder and Justice," *Toward Freedom,* November 1995, p. 18.

164   "the first step": Sylvan Fox, "Radicals See Pretrial Detention as a Step to Fascism," *New York Times,* March 7, 1969, p. 48.

164   Kunstler's admiration for Arthur Kinoy: interviews with Fred Marks, February 25, 1997, and Bruce and Diane Jackson, October 12, 1996.

164   "a little bit" and "could be": interview with Arthur Kinoy, July 15, 1996.

164   Kunstler became more radical: interview with David Dellinger, June 15, 1996.

165   Kunstler as believer in legal system: interviews with Michael Ratner, July 18, 1996; and Ronald Kuby, July 17, 1996.

165   "Bill always took cases": Alex Williams, "The Rhetorical Brush Strokes of Bill Kunstler," *New York,* September 18, 1995, p. 21.

165   "essential justice can be obtained": radio interview with William Kunstler, Will Lewis, KCRW Radio, Santa Monica, CA, October 18, 1994.

166   "fighting the system" through "totally inconsistent": Steven T. Taylor, "They Love Him, They Hate Him," *National Jurist,* January 1994, p. 11.

166   "left lawyers validate": Anderson, "Radical Lawyers," pp. 124, 135, 136–37.

167   "from a political point of view": quoted in Jon Kalish, "The New York Newsday Interview with William Kunstler," *Newsday,* June 23, 1988, p. 81.

167   "the values and political ideologies": Madeleine C. Petrara, "Dangerous Identification: Confusing Lawyers with Their Clients," *Journal of the Legal Profession,* 1994, p. 199.

167   "an act of such": quoted in "A.C.L.U., at a Parley on Free Speech, Defends Its Aid to Nazis at Skokie," *New York Times,* June 14, 1978, p. 18.

168   "I only defend those": quoted in Navasky, "Right On!" p. 92.

168   "cult of admirers" and "our ideal": editorial, "A Lawyer for Hire," *American Bar Association Journal,* June 1970, p. 552.

168   "the radical counterpart": Navasky, "Right On!" p. 93.

168   "those who are politically active": quoted in Kalish, "Interview with William Kunstler," p. 78.

169   "I only represent those": Jerry Schwartz, "'Chicago 7' Attorney William Kunstler Still Champion of the Political Underdog," *Los Angeles Times,* April 5, 1987, p. 34.

169   "Today, I would say": Taylor, "They Love Him, They Hate Him," p. 13.

169   "wife beating cases": Kunstler, interview with Gross.

169   "because it's a wife killing": ibid.

169   "although she has the same": Kunstler, *My Life*, p. 315.

169   "I don't give a damn": Holly Selby, "He's 75, but the Fires of Justice Still Burn, Says Radical Attorney," *Baltimore Sun*, May 10, 1995, p. D1.

169   "Every time I have": Sam Howe Verhovek, "At 69, Kunstler Is Still Moved by Fervor," *New York Times*, July 28, 1988, p. B1.

170   "harassed because of": Anderson, "Radical Lawyers," p. 236.

170   "the task of the revolutionary": Hakman, "Old and New Left Activity," p. 108.

170   "specific event or set": ibid.

170   "my representation": quoted in Rekha Basu, "Curtain on a Class Act," *Des Moines Register*, September 10, 1995, Opinion, p. 1.

171   "hard to conceive": Hentoff, "Interview with William Kunstler."

171   "I guess I do": Rosenbaum, "The Most Hated Lawyer in America," p. 80.

171   did not use term "objectively political": Bruce and Diane Jackson interview.

171   daughter Karin noted his political justification: interview with Karin Kunstler Goldman, October 15, 1996.

171   Kunstler more "flexible": Michael Ratner interview.

171   "organized-crime figures": Kunstler, *My Life*, p. 340.

171   "the corporate executives": quoted in David Barton, "The Lion Roars," *Sacramento Bee*, October 13, 1994, p. E1.

172   many never engaged in classical political trial and justify practices as political: Anderson, "Radical Lawyers," pp. 107, 156, 215, 218–19, 236–37, 240–41, 266, 271; and Nancy E. Anderson, "Demystifying Demystification: A Study of the Radical Bar," *Contemporary Crises*, 1981, pp. 230, 240, 242–44.

172   radical lawyers and demonstrations, etc.: Hakman, "Old and New Left Activity," pp. 117–18; Steven E. Barkan, *Protesters on Trial: Criminal Justice in the Southern Civil Rights and Vietnam Antiwar Movements* (New Brunswick: Rutgers University Press, 1985), p. 20.

172   "For free, political cases": Black, *Radical Lawyers*, p. 311.

172   Kunstler urging organization of defense committees: for one example, involving defendants in World Trade Center bombing case, see, Kunstler *My Life*, p. 338.

172   Kunstler with Irish militants: Jimmy Breslin in program, "William Kunstler: Champion or Charlatan?"

173   deferred to political line of their clients: Hakman, "Old and New Left Activity," p. 116; Anderson, "Demystifying Demystification," pp. 234, 240; Malcolm Burnstein, "From Arrest to Verdict," pp. 49, 64–65, and

Ann Fagan Ginger, "The Relevant Lawyers, the Law, and the Practice," in Ann Fagan Ginger, ed., *The Relevant Lawyers* (New York: Simon and Schuster, 1972), pp. 31–32.

173 Catonsville Nine: Kunstler, *My Life,* p. 188–90.

173 "something to be used": Kunstler, *My Life,* p. 105.

173 "it's very important": quoted in Black, *Radical Lawyers,* p. 306.

173 courtroom antics: well-described for Chicago Seven and Panther 21 trials in Sternberg, "The New Radical-Criminal Trials," pp. 281, 283–90.

173 "as a chance to demonstrate": Kunstler interview with Lewis.

174 "The obligation of a lawyer": Hentoff "Interview with William Kunstler."

174 "fighting back": quoted in Barton, "The Lion Roars."

174 Kunstler shouting at judges: for example, in the 1973 Fountain Valley murder trial in Virgin Islands, as noted in *Ratner v. Young,* 465 F. Supp. 386, 391 (D.C. V.I. 1979).

175 learn to be an excellent lawyer: for example, at Washington University Law School, recollections of Professor Robert Goodwin, Cumberland School of Law.

175 "scared all the time": quoted in Barton, "The Lion Roars."

175 demystification developed most dramatically at trial: Sternberg, "The New Radical-Criminal Trials," pp. 290–91; Anderson, "Demystifying Demystification," pp. 229, 231, 234, 236, 240; Hakman, "Old and New Left Activity," pp. 108, 112, 115–18; Barkan, *Protesters on Trial,* pp. 19–20; Burnstein, "From Arrest to Verdict," pp. 52, 56; Mary Kaufman, "War Crimes and Cold-War 'Conspiracies,'" in Ginger, *The Relevant Lawyers,* pp. 212–13.

175 "it seems to me that the courtroom": Kunstler interview with Lewis.

175 "how the police treat": quoted in Verhovek, "At 69, Kunstler Is Still Moved by Fervor."

175 "part of a plan" and "corporate America": Williams, "The Rhetorical Brush Strokes of Bill Kunstler."

176 James Richardson trial and quotations: Steven Phillips, *No Heroes, No Villains: The Story of a Murder Trial* (New York: Vintage, 1978), pp. 135–36.

176 search for media coverage a commonplace: Anderson, "Demystifying Demystification," p. 233; Hakman, "Old and New Left Activity," p. 117; Barkan, *Protesters on Trial,* pp. 20–21.

177 "a hard sell": Bruck, "William Kunstler: Actor without a Stage," p. 24.

177 541 articles: James Frank, "Still Crazy after All These Years," *Spy,* September 1990, p. 70.

177   "because it's almost" and "can give you an edge": quoted in Rosen-
      baum, "The Most Hated Lawyer in America," p. 84.

177   "it has to use up news": Kunstler interview with Lewis.

177   "it's a very powerful thing": quoted in Michael T. Kaufman, "A High
      Court Fantasy: Kunstler Ponders a Fancy," *New York Times,* April 14,
      1993, p. B3.

177   "one of my most important tools": Kunstler, *My Life,* p. 319.

178   "As we came down": Edward Hasbrouck, "William M. Kunstler,
      1919–1995," "The Flag Burning Page" Web site, September 5, 1995.

178   "Larry Davis, this was a case": Kuby interview.

179   demystification more important than acquittal: Anderson, "Demysti-
      fying Demystification," p. 232.

179   "The great trap": quoted in Black, *Radical Lawyers,* p. 61.

179   legal counteroffensive: Black, *Radical Lawyers,* pp. 16, 283; Anderson,
      "Radical Lawyers," p. 220; Hakman, "Old and New Left Activity," p.
      117.

180   Fountain Valley and action for damages: *Ratner v. Young,* 465 F. Supp.
      386, 390 (D.C. V.I. 1979).

180   "serve as an educational": quoted in Joshua Muravchik, "Manipulat-
      ing the Miskitos: The Sandinista Propaganda War Comes to the Sen-
      ate," *New Republic,* August 6, 1984, p. 21.

180   suit against Hoover and Kennedy: Navasky, "Right On!" p. 92.

180   "The ultimate test": Arthur Kinoy, *Rights on Trial: The Odyssey of a Peo-
      ple's Lawyer* (Cambridge: Harvard University Press, 1983; reprint,
      Larchmont, NY: Bernel Books, 1994), p. 71.

181   "depicts the South Bronx" and "it may be frivolous": quoted in Bruck,
      "William Kunstler: Actor without a Stage," p. 24.

181   "the client may simply": Petrara, "Dangerous Identification," pp.
      190–91.

182   "It makes no difference": 1988 statement quoted in Jim Sleeper, "He
      Played a Role That Was No Model," *New York Daily News,* September
      7, 1995, p. 45.

182   "a lot of young black women": quoted in Jon Kalish, "From the
      Chicago 8 to Our Uncounted," *Newsday,* June 23, 1988, p. 81.

182   "Black rage": quoted in Craig Wolff, "Not Guilty," *GQ,* June 1994, p.
      194.

182   more legalistic defense: see also Barkan, *Protesters on Trial,* p. 21.

182   "somehow clashed": Kuby interview.

182   three prosecutors: Michael Zaleski (Armstrong bombing) quoted in
      Mike Miller, "Kunstler Joined Anti-War Case," *Madison (Wisconsin)
      Capital Times,* September 5, 1995, p. B6; Thomas Foran (Chicago Seven)

quoted in Selby, "He's 75, but the Fires of Justice Still Burn"; unspecified prosecutor ("who defeated him in a major trial more than 15 years ago") quoted in Pinsley, "Kunstler Still Making the Left's Case."

183   Richardson trial and Kunstler quotation ("My policy is never"); Phillips, *No Heroes, No Villains,* pp. 167–68.

184   like many radical attorneys, not systematic thinker: Anderson, "Radical Lawyers," p. 267.

184   "not so much a radical thinker": Michael Steven Smith, "William Moses Kunstler (1919–1995): A Case for Courage," *Against the Current,* 1995, p. 41.

184   did not like ideology and never spoke in those terms: Bruce and Diane Jackson interview.

184   "Bill was not a theorist": Kuby interview.

184   "for me, action is all": Kunstler, *My Life,* p. 314.

184   opposition to antiblack racism at core: Kuby and Michael Ratner interviews; Gerald Lefcourt and Alan Dershowitz in *Charlie Rose Show,* WNET, September 5, 1995, transcript (Westlaw).

184   "today Muslims": Kunstler, *My Life,* p. 317.

184   "At heart I'm a": Verhovek, "At 69, Kunstler Is Still Moved by Fervor."

184   "Martin Luther King" and "it is a chance": quoted in Scott Spencer, "William Kunstler: 1919–1995," *Rolling Stone,* October 19, 1995, p. 89.

185   unlikely that Kunstler thought about that: Michael Ratner and Kuby interviews.

185   Kunstler not a conventional Marxist; did not make "scientific" class analysis: Dellinger and Kinoy interviews.

185   "Communists are to the right": "Gus Hall Assails Kunstler as Baiter," *New York Times,* August 30, 1970, p. 52.

185   political people critical: Bruce and Diane Jackson interview.

185   never believed, as communists do: Kuby interview.

185   "all governments are bad": quoted in Michael Ratner interview.

185   "I'd have the same problems everywhere": quoted in Kaufman, "A High Court Fantasy."

185   "Not that I'd want a new system": quoted in "Books; Taking Hard Left on Rights; Kunstler Still Fights System at 75," *Boston Herald,* September 19, 1994, p. 031.

185   "I do not believe in": quoted in Colman McCarthy, "Amnesty International's Freedom Fighter," *Washington Post,* April 22, 1996, p. C01.

185   Kunstler as cochairman: Ian Katz, "Hey Buddhies, Can You Spare a Dime?" *Guardian,* March 2, 1995, p. T4.

185   instinctive theory favored: Karin Kunstler Goldman, Kuby, Dellinger, and Bruce and Diane Jackson interviews; Michael Standard, quoted in Bruck, "William Kunstler: Actor without a Stage," p. 25.

186   "Good and evil are always": quoted in Sternhell, "A Brief Encounter,"
       p. 54.

NOTES TO CHAPTER 9

Page
187   observers: Herman Badillo and Milton Haynes, *A Bill of No Rights: At-
       tica and the American Prison System* (New York: Outerbridge and
       Lazard, 1972); Tom Wicker, *A Time to Die* (New York:
       Quadrangle/New York Times Book Company, 1975); Julian Tepper
       and Terry Fitch, "Attica Chronicle," *Washington Post,* September 19,
       1971, p. A1.
187   prison commissioner: Russell G. Oswald, *Attica—My Story* (Garden
       City, NY: Doubleday, 1972).
187   hostages: Warren H. Hanson, "Attica: The Hostages' Story," *New York
       Times Magazine,* October 31, 1971, p. 82.
187   prisoners: Richard X [*sic*] Clark and Leonard Levitt, eds., *The Brothers
       of Attica* (New York: Links Books, 1973); Robert Harsh, "Inside Attica,"
       Christianity and Crisis, May 29, 1972, p. 127 (interview of inmate
       leader); Eric Pace, "Inmate Just Released from Attica Says Revolt Was
       Originally Scheduled for July 4," *New York Times,* September 23, 1971,
       p. 67.
187   Special Commission: *Attica: The Official Report of the New York State Spe-
       cial Commission on Attica* (New York: Praeger, 1972) (McKay Commis-
       sion).
188   "a new breed": *Buffalo Evening News,* September 9, 1971, p. 43.
188   "Racism between the officers": Michael Welch, *Corrections: A Critical
       Approach* (New York: McGraw-Hill, 1996), pp. 332–33.
189   "appeared very solicitous": Hanson, "Attica: The Hostages' Story,"
       pp. 78–79.
189   "the inmates right around us": *New York Times,* September 14, 1971,
       p. 29.
190   "WE are MEN" and five specific demands: Wicker, *A Time to Die,* pp.
       315–16.
191   "I felt better" and "appealed to my sense": William M. Kunstler (with
       Sheila Isenberg), *My Life as a Radical Lawyer* (New York: Birch Lane
       Press, 1994), p. 216.
191   "We wanted Kunstler": Clark and Levitt, *The Brothers of Attica,* p. 65.
191   "I want to talk": *New York Times,* September 11, 1971, p. 1.
192   Kunstler in first meeting with observers' group: *Attica: The Official Re-
       port,* pp. 243–44; Oswald, *Attica—My Story,* p. 112; Wicker, *A Time to
       Die,* p. 69.

192   "if we cannot live" through "the same thing": Wicker, *A Time to Die*, p. 97; *Attica: The Official Report*, p. 245; Kunstler, *My Life*, p. 218.

192   Kunstler's speech, "Palante" through Brother Herb's request that he be their lawyer: Wicker, *A Time to Die*, pp. 76–80, except for "the injunction is nothing," from Kunstler, *My Life*, p. 218, and Schwartz's resentment, from James Frank, "Still Crazy after All These Years," *Spy*, September 1990, p. 73.

193   "thrilled and honored": Kunstler, *My Life*, p. 218.

193   format of listing demands: *Attica: The Official Report*, p. 244; Wicker, *A Time to Die*, pp. 115–16.

193   support for various demands: Badillo and Haynes, *A Bill of No Rights*, pp. 59–60; Clark and Levitt, *The Brothers of Attica*, p. 112; Oswald, *Attica—My Story*, p. 114.

193   discussion about Kunstler among observers, early Saturday morning: *Attica: The Official Report*, pp. 247–48; Kunstler, *My Life*, p. 217; Wicker, *A Time to Die*, 118–19.

194   hostages fearful: *Attica: The Official Report*, p. 242.

194   legal scholar: F. Thomas Schornhorst, "The Lawyer and the Terrorist: Another Ethical Dilemma," *Indiana Law Journal*, summer 1978, p. 702.

194   released inmate: *New York Times*, September 23, 1971, p. 67.

194   two observers: *New York Times*, September 17, 1971, p. 30.

194   Kunstler denied: ibid., and Steve Bloom, "Welcome to the Terrordome," *High Times*, October 1991, p. 23.

194   prosecutor's letter: *Attica: The Official Report*, p. 250; Badillo and Haynes, *A Bill of No Rights*, p. 63; Wicker, *A Time to Die*, pp. 142–43.

194   negotiating the 28 Points: Badillo and Haynes, *A Bill of No Rights*, p. 71; Oswald, *Attica—My Story*, pp. 117–18, 222; Wicker, *A Time to Die*, pp. 150, 152.

195   "the most a modern": Oswald, *Attica—My Story*, p. 118.

195   "put into effect": *Newsweek*, September 27, 1971, p. 37.

195   "no more radical": *New York Times*, September 11, 1971, p. 26.

195   "the package should be laid": Wicker, *A Time to Die*, pp. 153–54.

195   "the prisoners were adamant": *New York Times*, September 12, 1971, pp. 1, 72.

195   Seale's arrival and admittance: *Attica: The Official Report*, pp. 259–60; Oswald, *Attica—My Story*, pp. 222–23; Wicker, *A Time to Die*, p. 155.

196   Seale's remarks: Kunstler, *My Life*, p. 219; *Newsweek*, September 27, 1971, p. 37.

196   "young, tense": *Attica: The Official Report*, p. 263; "the inmates laughed": Wicker, *A Time to Die*, p. 173.

196   "there's going to be": Kunstler, *My Life*, p. 220; "and what do you

think": Badillo and Haynes, *A Bill of No Rights,* p. 71; "so deep and intense": *Attica: The Official Report,* p. 263.

197   "I'm speaking to you": *Newsweek,* September 27, 1971, p. 37.

197   "we don't want" and "Bill, you've saved": Kunstler, *My Life,* pp. 220–21; "they had no doubt": Wicker, *A Time to Die,* p. 174.

197   "a new ball game": *Attica: The Official Report,* pp. 263–64; "the amnesty section": Wicker, *A Time to Die,* p. 174; Wicker critical: ibid.; "might have accepted": Kunstler, *My Life,* p. 221.

198   "no-good commies": *Attica: The Official Report,* p. 311; "they ought to kill": Wicker, *A Time to Die,* p. 189.

198   "when are we going": *Attica: The Official Report,* p. 311; "Get outta here": Joseph W. Grant, "Stop the Presses, I Want to Get Off: A Brief History of the *Penal Digest International,*" in Ken Wachsberger, ed., *Voices from the Underground,* vol. 1, *Insider Histories of the Vietnam Era Underground Press* (Tempe, AZ: Mica's Press, 1993), p. 538.

199   "to go in there" through "tears don't move": quoted in Wicker, *A Time to Die,* pp. 193, 197.

199   "at least buying time": Wicker, *A Time to Die,* p. 204.

200   "The committee of observers": *Attica: The Official Report,* p. 271.

200   "I urgently request": quoted in Wicker, *A Time to Die,* p. 223.

200   observers' anger at Oswald statement: *Attica: The Official Report,* pp. 277–78; Badillo and Haynes, *A Bill of No Rights,* pp. 83–84; Tepper and Fitch, "Attica Chronicle," p. A18; Wicker, *A Time to Die,* pp. 223, 226.

200   "None of you": *Attica: The Official Report,* p. 280; "why did you betray": Clark and Levitt, *The Brothers of Attica,* p. 117.

201   "watched the back": Kunstler, *My Life,* p. 223; Oswald wanted observers killed: ibid.

201   "There are four" through "Remember Attica!": quoted from tape in Clark Whelton, "Of Attica and the Alamo," *Village Voice,* September 23, 1971, p. 83.

202   governments willing to take inmates: Afeni Shakur, "Go Back Where You Came From," *New York Times,* September 23, 1971, p. 35; Wicker, *A Time to Die,* p. 185; offer limited: *Attica: The Official Report,* pp. 290–91.

202   Kunstler at his most inflammatory: Hanson, "Attica: The Hostages' Story," p. 82; and especially, exchange of letters in *New York Times Magazine,* November 28, 1971, p. 18.

202   "This untrue statement": Schornhorst, "The Lawyer and the Terrorist," p. 702.

202   Wicker uncomfortable: Wicker, *A Time to Die,* p. 241; two other observers: *New York Times,* September 17, 1971, p. 30; "no individual": *New York Times,* September 19, 1971, p. 60; "not aware of any": *Attica: The Official Report,* p. 291.

203   "some of the radical": Harsh, "Inside Attica," p. 135; "would make them": *Newsweek,* September 27, 1971, p. 37; "although I knew": Kunstler, *My Life,* p. 224.

203   commutation proposal: Wicker, *A Time to Die,* pp. 258–59; "everyone dies": *Attica: The Official Report,* p. 315; "I'm going through": Tepper and Fitch, "Attica Chronicle," *Washington Post,* p. A18; "I can give you": *Newsweek,* September 27, 1971, p. 37; Kunstler's telephone calls: Tepper and Fitch, "Attica Chronicle," p. A18.

203   "no solution": *New York Times,* September 13, 1971, p. 71; "Nigger-lover!": reported in Badillo and Haynes, *A Bill of No Rights,* p. 88, Nat Hentoff, "Rockefeller's Bullets and the Press," *Village Voice,* September 23, 1971, p. 32; Wicker, *A Time to Die,* pp. 251–54.

204   "their appointed executioners": *New York Times,* September 15, 1971, p. 34.

205   "niggers, we're going": *New York Times,* September 19, 1971, p. 60; "Save me a nigger": Kunstler, *My Life,* p. 225; "white power": *New York Times,* September 14, 1971, p. 28; "I don't want to work": *New York Times,* September 15, 1971, p. 34.

205   statistics: Wicker, *A Time to Die,* pp. 301, 314 (this does not include four additional deaths: Officer Quinn and three prisoners murdered by their fellow prisoners during the course of the uprising); "efficient, affirmative": *New York Times,* September 14, 1971, p. 1; "talked with pride": Malcolm Bell, *The Turkey Shoot: Tracking the Attica Cover-Up* (New York: Grove Press, 1985), p. 353; "bloodiest one-day": *Attica: The Official Report,* p. xi.

205   "State Troopers and correctional": *Inmates of the Attica Correctional Facility v. Rockefeller,* 453 F.2d 12, 18–19 (2d Cir. 1971).

206   "to lie naked": testimony of Frank Smith, reported in *New York Times,* June 6, 1997, p. A20; also in Wicker, *A Time to Die,* p. 291; and Badillo and Haynes, *A Bill of No Rights,* p. 114; "more in the manner": Oswald, *Attica—My Story,* pp. 289–91.

206   press report about stabbings: *New York Times,* September 14, 1971; Eve's account of Dunbar's remarks: *New York Times,* September 19, 1971, p. 60; "showed us a big inmate": Badillo and Haynes, *A Bill of No Rights,* p. 98.

206   "murdering bastards" and "this will go down": *New York Times,* September 14, 1971, pp. 28, 1.

207   "in the negotiations" and breakup of rally: *Buffalo Evening News,* September 14, 1971, p. 31; "Remember Attica!": Oswald, *Attica—My Story,* p. 301.

207   autopsies, shock, and disbelief; "We feel that Carl": *New York Times,* September 15, 1971, pp. 1, 32, September 16, 1971, p. 48.

207 appointment of commissions: *New York Times*, September 16, 1971, pp. 1, 48.

207 "murderer": *New York Times*, September 16, 1971, p. 48; September 17, 1971, p. 30; "the real murderers": Kunstler, *My Life*, p. 227.

208 "Give us Kunstler" and other remarks at Harlem rally: "Parting Shots," *Life*, October 1, 1971.

208 "a vile system" and other remarks at Georgetown: *New York Times*, September 18, 1971, p. 25.

208 "only the threat": comment by Kunstler in Leonard Orland, "Can We Establish the Rule of Law in Prisons?" *Civil Liberties Review* vol. 2, no. 4 (1975), p. 70.

208 "the Governor ought" and "far from clear": *New York Times*, September 15, 1971, pp. 32, editorials; "are guilty of murder": *New York Times*, September 14, 1971, p. 30.

208 Attica rallies: Oswald, *Attica—My Story*, pp. 302–304, *New York Times*, September 21, 1971, p. 46.

209 "With the Kunstlers": *New York Times*, September 19, 1971, sec. 4, p. 14.

209 "writhing snakelike": Russell Kirk, *The Sword of Imagination: Memoirs of a Half-Century of Literary Conflict* (Grand Rapids, MI: Eerdmans, 1995), p. 407; "slander," "contrition," and "should experience": William F. Buckley, Jr., "Kunstler," *National Review,* November 5, 1971, p. 1258.

209 Kunstler to file lawsuit: *New York Times*, September 17, 1971, p. 30.

209 complicated and slow-moving lawsuit: Daniel Wise, "Champion of Attica Inmates Set for Trial—20 Years Later," *New York Law Journal,* October 16, 1991, p. 1; William M. Kunstler, "Back to Attica," *Nation,* March 25, 1991, p. 364; *Al-Jundi v. Mancusi,* 926 F.2d 235 (2d Cir. 1991).

209 liability trial: *Al-Jundi v. Oswald,* 1993 WL 22829 (W.D.N.Y., January 16, 1993); *Al-Jundi v. Oswald,* 1993 WL 22818 (W.D.N.Y., January 19, 1993).

210 Frank Smith's damage trial: *New York Times*, June 6, 1997, p. A20.

210 first grand jury: Wicker, *A Time to Die*, pp. 309–10 (including "longest-sitting"); *New York Times*, June 10, 1974, p. 61; *Newsweek,* April 14, 1975, p. 81.

210 early prosecutions: *Economist,* April 12, 1975, p. 72; Bruce Jackson, *Disorderly Conduct* (Urbana: University of Illinois Press, 1992), p. 123.

211 difficulties facing defense committee: *New York Times*, June 10, 1974, p. 61; Jackson, *Disorderly Conduct*, p. 127; Michael Ratner and Eleanor Smith, "W. Haywood Burns: To Be of Use," *Yale Law Journal,* vol. 106 (1996), pp. 770–71; Steven Phillips, *No Heroes, No Villains: The Story of a Murder Trial* (New York: Vintage, 1978), p. 240 (state

prosecutor involved in a different murder trial with Kunstler acknowledges federal agent's admission of spying on Attica defense team).

211   "My Brother Dacajeweih": *New York Times,* April 3, 1975, p. 25; also for trial, *New York Times,* February 25, 1975, p. 42; February 27, 1975, p. 39; March 1, 1975, p. 29, March 6, 1975, p. 34; March 30, 1975, p. 35; April 2, 1975, p. 18.

211   "basically, Johnny and Charlie Joe": Kunstler, *My Life,* p. 229; trial evidence: *The Economist,* April 12, 1975, p. 72, Jackson, *Disorderly Conduct,* p. 125; few bitter exchanges: *New York Times,* March 30, 1975, p. 35; "I'm fed up": *Newsweek,* April 14, 1975, p. 81.

212   Indian jewelry: *New York Times,* December 2, 1974, p. 37; Connie Bruck, "William Kunstler: Actor without a Stage," *American Lawyer,* August 1980, p. 26.

212   "Indianness" of trial: *New York Times,* March 30, 1975, p. 35; December 2, 1974, p. 37.

212   "the idea that the prosecution": Bruck, "William Kunstler: Actor without a Stage," p. 26; "it turned the rest": *New York Times,* March 25, 1984, sec. 11NJ, p. 28.

213   "The state tried": quoted in Bruck, "William Kunstler: Actor without a Stage," p. 26.

213   "Margaret Ratner": *New York Times,* February 25, 1975, p. 42.

213   "was one of the": Kunstler, *My Life,* p. 230; cab ride to airport: interview with Michael Ratner, July 18, 1996.

214   Second grand jury, cover-up, scandal, and commutation: see generally Bell (prosecutor who resigned), *The Turkey Shoot: Tracking the Attica Cover-Up.*

214   "that the prison authorities": *New York Times,* September 6, 1972, p. 26.

215   "There were certainly": quoted in Joseph Mianowany, "Attica: A Decade Has Passed since the Nation's Bloodiest Prison Riot. Some Things Have Changed. Some Remain Ominously the Same," UPI, Regional News (dateline: Albany), September 6, 1981.

215   1990s: William M. Kunstler, "Twenty Years Later: Attica! Attica!" *High Times,* October 1991, p. 23; "Remembering Attica," *U.S. News & World Report,* September 16, 1991, p. 16; Kunstler, *My Life,* pp. 226–27.

215   "the reason a": Kunstler, *My Life,* p. 229.

215   advisory board: Grant, "Stop the Presses," pp. 504, 514, 537; scholarly articles: see, e.g., Ronald L. Kuby and William M. Kunstler, "Silencing the Oppressed: No Freedom of Speech for Those behind the Walls," *Creighton Law Review,* 1993, p. 1005.

NOTES TO CHAPTER 10

Page

216   "He came out of the elevator": Nat Hentoff, "Playboy Interview with William Kunstler," *Playboy*, October 1970.

216   "sometime in the next half hour": Victor Rabinowitz, *Unrepentant Leftist: A Lawyer's Memoir* (Urbana: University of Illinois Press, 1996), p. 192. The story is also told in Alan M. Dershowitz, *The Best Defense* (New York: Vintage Books, 1982), p. 408.

217   "It's not affection": Peter Matthiessen, *In the Spirit of Crazy Horse* (New York: Viking, 1983; 1991 ed.), p. 568.

217   Russell and Lennon acquaintance: William M. Kunstler (with Sheila Isenberg), *My Life as a Radical Lawyer* (New York: Birch Lane Press, 1994), p. 204.

217   Kunstler and Blackmun: Kunstler, *My Life*, pp. 361–62, 374; Bob Woodward and Scott Armstrong, *The Brethren: Inside the Supreme Court* (New York: Simon and Schuster, 1979), p. 417.

218   "The country's most controversial": Victor S. Navasky, "Right On! With Lawyer William Kunstler," *New York Times Magazine*, April 21, 1970, p. 88.

218   "high priests" and "radical intelligentsia": Thomas J. Osborne, "1776 and the New Radicalism," *Thought*, 1973, p. 23.

218   "Kunstler constituency": John R. Coyne, Jr., "The Kunstler Constituency," *National Review*, May 5, 1970, p. 467.

218   Senior Fellow Award: "Notre Dame Prize Goes to Kunstler," *New York Times*, April 4, 1971, p. 57.

218   Sacco-Vanzetti Award: UPI, April 26, 1981.

218   babysat Abbie Hoffman's son: Michael Cooper, "House of Yippies: Chicago Convention a Recurring Dream," *New York Times*, April 7, 1996, sec. 13, p. 6.

218   Renee Cohen: Renee Cohen to David J. Langum, September 29, 1997.

218   Berner friendship: interview with Milton Berner, March 24, 1997.

218   Marks friendship: interview with Fred Marks, February 25, 1997.

219   "vulnerable to attacks": Steven Phillips, *No Heroes, No Villains: The Story of a Murder Trial* (New York: Vintage Books, 1978), pp. 139–40.

219   Kunstler not prepared: Phillips, *No Heroes, No Villians*, p. 183.

219   "well-prepared": interview with David S. Gould, November 17, 1997.

219   dissatisfied client: John Stanley to David J. Langum, September 28, 1997 (regarding 1971 civil matter).

219   Carroll O'Connor: Richard Warren Lewis, "Playboy Interview with Carroll O'Connor," *Playboy*, January 1973.

219   Ishmael Reed: Arthur Cooper, "Call Him Ishmael," *Newsweek,* June 2, 1975, p. 70.

219   Meir Kahane: Walter Goodman, "Playboy Interview with Meir Kahane," *Playboy,* October 1972.

219   John Wayne: Richard Warren Lewis, "Playboy Interview with John Wayne," *Playboy,* May 1971.

220   1970 ABA meeting: Fred P. Graham, "Burger Finds Courts Imperiled by Breaches of Civility at Trials," *New York Times,* August 8, 1970, p. 1.

220   "a tiny fragment" and "a witch hunt": Robert Reinhold, "Bar Study Notes Little Court Disorder Despite Burger Views on Unruliness," *New York Times,* August 9, 1971, p. 1.

220   "adrenalin-fueled": Tom Goldstein, "Court Disorders Held Overblown," *New York Times,* January 13, 1974, p. 21.

220   newspaper editorials: e.g., "Order in Court," *New York Times,* December 8, 1973, p. 34.

220   "frantically impatient": "A Lawyer for Hire," *American Bar Association Journal,* June 1970, p. 552.

220   "dealt with" and "made it clear": Craig R. Whitney, "Unruly Lawyers Seen as Court Ill," *New York Times,* September 13, 1970, p. 39.

221   "the lawyer who served": Jerold S. Auerbach, *Unequal Justice: Lawyers and Social Change in Modern America* (New York: Oxford University Press, 1976), pp. 289–90.

221   Kunstler himself: Kunstler, *My Life,* p. 205.

221   "The bar as a whole": Norman Dorsen and Leon Friedman, *Disorder in the Court: Report of the Association of the Bar of the City of New York, Special Committee on Courtroom Conduct* (New York: Pantheon, 1973), pp. xiii-xiv.

222   William M. Kunstler and Margaret L. Ratner, "The Myth of Disruption," *Nation,* May 31, 1975, p. 656.

222   other lawyers: Doris Peterson and Morton Stavis, "Of Kunstler, Hoffman and Disorder in the Court," *New York Times,* December 20, 1973, p. 38.

222   William F. Buckley: William F. Buckley, Jr., "Kunstler," *National Review,* November 5, 1971, p. 1258.

222   James L. Buckley and Kunstler response: Fred P. Graham, "Buckley Seeking Curb on Lawyers," *New York Times,* June 10, 1971, p. 23.

222   Kunstler disciplinary proceedings: see articles by Tom Goldstein, *New York Times,* "Bar Unit Shifted in Kunstler Case," January 30, 1974, p. 52; "Bar Reassesses Kunstler Action," February 10, 1974, p. 50; "Bar Group Withdraws Charges against Kunstler," February 21, 1974, p. 34.

222   Gignoux upheld: "Kunstler Loses Bid on Contempt Ruling," *New York Times,* September 7, 1974, p. 56.

223   "so repugnant": "Buckley Asks Bar to Find Kunstler Unfit to Practice," *New York Times*, February 6, 1976, p. 59.

223   *New York Times* editorial suggesting discipline: "Condoning Murder," *New York Times*, February 1, 1976, sec. 4, p. 16.

223   Westchester County High School: Kunstler, *My Life*, p. 203.

223   Notre Dame: *New York Times*, April 4, 1971, p. 57.

223   Hofstra: John E. Ullmann to David J. Langum, October 3, 1997.

223   west steps of Capitol: *New York Times*, May 4, 1972, p. 21.

223   Jan Hus Presbyterian Church: *New York Times*, June 9, 1971, p. 44.

223   meeting with Xuan Oanh in Paris: John Kifner, "Two of 'Chicago 8' Are Denied Paris Trip to Discuss P.O.W.'s," *New York Times*, October 25, 1969, p. 16; *New York Times*, October 26, 1969, p. 2; October 27, 1969, p. 2; October 28, 1969, p. 15; October 29, 1969, p. 3; Ben A. Franklin, "Two Civilian Groups Release Purported POW Lists," *New York Times*, November 13, 1969, p. 4. On importance of Kunstler's trip, see Amy Swerdlow, *Women Strike for Peace: Traditional Motherhood and Radical Politics in the 1960s* (Chicago: University of Chicago Press, 1993), pp. 225–26.

223   rally at Kent State shortly after killings: Kunstler, *My Life*, pp. 201–2.

224   annual memorials: Kunstler, *My Life*, p. 203; for slight information on memorials in the 1990s, see Francis Wilkinson, "Trigger Happy: The Cult of Kent State," *New Republic*, May 13, 1991, p. 16; Lekan Oguntoyinbo, "1970 Kent Killings Recalled; Vigil, Speeches Mark Anniversary," *Plain Dealer*, May 5, 1994, p. B2; *Asheville Citizen-Times*, May 3, 1995, p. D6.

224   preservation of site: Michael Drexler, "Honing Double-Edged Career," *The Plain Dealer*, July 23, 1994, p. E1; Staughton Lynd, "William Kunstler: In His Own Defense," *Washington Post*, September 18, 1994, p. X3.

224   legal defense of Kent State demonstrators: Kunstler, *My Life*, p. 202; John Kifner, "Curbs Modified on Kent Report," *New York Times*, October 18, 1970, p. 95; John Kifner, "Student Head and Teacher Are Seized at Kent State," *New York Times*, October 20, 1970, p. 1; *New York Times*, October 25, 1970, p. 70.

224   court-martial in Vietnam: Edith Evans Asbury, "G.I. Refusing to Kill Gets Legal Aid," *New York Times*, May 22, 1966, p. 9.

224   priest dismissed: *New York Times*, June 30, 1969, p. 41.

224   University of Wisconsin: Jonnel Licari, "Kunstler Defended Armstrong in UW Bombing Case," *Wisconsin State Journal*, September 5, 1995, p. A2.

224   Ohio state disciplinary hearing: *New York Times*, October 31, 1970, p. 26; November 1, 1970, p. 26.

224 "He told us right away": quoted in Charles McCarry, "A Few Soft Words for the Rabble-Rousers," *Esquire,* July 1969, p. 133.

225 issue of jury trial: Kunstler, *My Life,* pp. 188–89.

225 account of Catonsville Nine trial: discussion drawn from John F. Bannan and Rosemary S. Bannan, *Law, Morality and Vietnam: The Peace Militants and the Courts* (Bloomington: Indiana University Press, 1974), pp. 124–50; Steven E. Barkan, *Protesters on Trial: Criminal Justice in the Southern Civil Rights and Vietnam Antiwar Movements* (New Brunswick: Rutgers University Press, 1985), pp. 87–93, 121–48; J. Justin Gustainis, "Crime as Rhetoric: The Trial of the Catonsville Nine," in Robert Hariman, ed., *Popular Trials: Rhetoric, Mass Media, and the Law* (Tuscaloosa: University of Alabama Press, 1990), pp. 164–78.

226 sampling of jury nullification articles by Kunstler: "The Crown v. John Peter Zenger," *New York Law Journal,* August 6, 1985; "Jury Nullification in Conscience Cases," *Virginia Journal of International Law,* 1969, pp. 71–84; by others: David Farnham, "Jury Nullification: History Proves It's Not a New Idea," *Criminal Justice,* winter 1997, pp. 5–14; Dan Siegel, "Juror Nullification," *Whole Earth Review,* fall 1991, p. 45; "Jury Nullification: When Jurors Leave the Law Behind," *Trial,* May 1996, pp. 12–14.

228 Armstrong case based on: Tom Bates, *Rads: The 1970 Bombing of the Army Math Research Center at the University of Wisconsin and Its Aftermath* (New York: HarperCollins, 1992); Mike Miller, "Kunstler Joined Anti-War Case," *Madison Capital Times,* September 5, 1995, p. B6; Susan Lampert Smith, "Apartments Sink in History; Frances Court Was Icon of '60s," *Wisconsin State Journal,* November 16, 1995, p. C1; *New York Times,* October 16, 1973, p. 12.

229 Murray R. Gold: see, e.g., articles in *New York Times*: September 29, 1977, sec. 3, p. 2; James Brooke, "Decade after Double Murder, Suspect May Face a 4th Trial," April 4, 1985, p. B1; "Connecticut Court Appeal for Man Tried Four Times," January 17, 1992, p. B16; Tracy Cochran, "In Short: Nonfiction," March 24, 1992, sec. 7, p. 14; Kirk Johnson, "Back to Court for Ex-Broker in '74 Killing of His In-Laws," p. B4; Jack Ewing, "Famed Case Back in Court after 4 Trials; Murder Case Drags on 17 Years after Killings," *Hartford Courant,* January 16, 1992, p. A1; Lynne Tuohy, "Supreme Court Voids Ruling in Murder Case," *Hartford Courant,* June 9, 1992, p. B1; Joseph Calve, "Fool's Gold: On Appeal, a Happy Ending Is Rewritten," *Connecticut Law Tribune,* June 15, 1992, p. 2.

229 Joan Little: see, e.g., Kunstler, *My Life,* pp. 274–75; articles in *New York Times*: May 20, 1978, p. 23; June 6, 1978, sec. 2, p. 4; Wolfgang Saxon, "Joan Little, Tried for Killing Jailer in 1974, Is Arrested in New Jersey,"

February 26, 1989, p. 34; Robert McG. Thomas, Jr., "Hamilton H. Hobgood, 87, North Carolina Judge," November 19, 1995, p. 51; Mark Mooney, UPI May 24, 1981.

229   Joanne Chesimard: Kunstler, *My Life,* pp. 275–77; Assata Shakur [Joanne Chesimard], *Assata: An Autobiography* (Westport, CT: Lawrence Hill, 1987), pp. 247–52; articles in *New York Times*: September 22, 1976, p. 87; Barbara Lynch, "Chesimard Case Recalls Hall-Mills," January 16, 1977, sec. 6, p. 12; Joseph F. Sullivan, "Joanne Chesimard Faces Trial Today," January 17, 1977, p. 55; Joseph F. Sullivan, "Chesimard Trial in Murder Case Halted by Filing," January 20, 1977, p. 79; Joseph F. Sullivan, "Chesimard Defense Loses on Shift," January 21, 1977, sec. 2, p. 18; Walter H. Waggoner, "Mrs. Chesimard's Defense Seeks to Change Site of Murder Trial," February 4, 1977, sec. 2, p. 15; Donald Janson, "Mrs. Chesimard Bids U.S. Court Bar Trial Sessions on Her Sabbath," February 19, 1977, p. 51.

229   William R. Phillips: Kunstler, *My Life,* p. 397; *New York Times,* September 27, 1980, sec. 2, p. 27; Gay Jervey, "Sympathy for the Devil," *American Lawyer,* April 1987, p. 128.

229   Puerto Rican nationalists: articles in *New York Times*: "Bomb Case Figure Found Guilty Here," September 19, 1973, p. 21; "300 Puerto Ricans Rally Here to Free Would-Be Assassin," November 2, 1975, p. 42; Arnold H. Lubasch, "3 Brothers Jailed for Contempt in Inquiry into Terrorist Bombings," August 23, 1977, p. 14; Lee A. Daniels, "A Murderer Is Set Free in Extradition Mix-Up," July 29, 1980, p. 1.

229   Chicanos: "'The Blackest White Man I Know': Civil Rights Lawyer William Kunstler Is Soul Brother to Radicals of Many Colors," *Life,* July 25, 1969, pp. 50A-50D; "Kunstler, Coleman, Cunningham: People's Lawyers Take Case," *El Mestizo* (El Paso), March 1976, p. 1.

229   statue climber: *New York Times,* May 13, 1980, sec. 2, p. 4.

229   Michigan convict: *New York Times,* June 22, 1977, sec. 3, p. 2.

229   "Bill called and cussed me": Jane Gross, "Barnes Is Kunstler's New Cause," *New York Times,* June 8, 1979, p. 22.

229   "to entrap": *New York Times,* August 18, 1975, p. 15.

229   false rumor of FBI employment: Gould interview (Gould was then a deputy U.S. attorney).

230   meeting with Weathermen: Kunstler, *My Life,* p. 200.

230   defamation suit against Kunstler: *New York Times,* May 10, 1977, p. 71; February 3, 1978, p. 16; Larry Bodine, "Kunstler Eats Crow," *National Law Journal,* June 2, 1980, p. 35.

230   discussion of White Panther case (national security exception to wiretap warrant) drawn from: Agis Salpukas, "Detroit Radicals Face Bomb Trial," *New York Times,* January 17, 1971, p. 49; Fred P. Graham, "White

House View of Wiretap Right Denied on Appeal," *New York Times,* April 9, 1971, p. 1; *United States v. United States District Court for the Eastern District of Michigan,* 407 U.S. 297 (1972), affirming, 444 F.2d 651 (6th Cir. 1971); Kunstler, *My Life,* pp. 205–9; Kenneth Shuster, "Stunting Big Brother's Growth: Reflections on *U.S. v. U.S. District Court,*" *Hamline Law Review,* fall 1994, p. 64.

231 grandchildren's pictures on checks: Eagle Harbor Book Company to David J. Langum, September 24, 1997.

231 glamourless housewife: Kunstler, *My Life,* p. 263.

231 "people poised with microphones": quoted in Connie Bruck, "William Kunstler: Actor without a Stage," *American Lawyer,* August 1980, p. 26.

232 Calarco rental: Kunstler, *My Life,* p. 77.

232 "People would come to him": interview with Mary Kunstler Horn, October 17, 1996.

233 butcher representation: Sheila Isenberg, preface to Kunstler, *My Life,* p. ix.

233 Olive Free Library: letter from Florie Scheintaub to David J. Langum, October 19, 1997.

233 government harassment: Kunstler, *My Life,* p. 273; *National Law Journal,* October 23, 1989, p. 6; Clyde Haberman and Albin Krebs: "Kunstler's Lost Address Book Got F.B.I. 'Protection,'" *New York Times,* March 27, 1979, sec. 3, p. 6; and "Kunstler Hit for Numbers," *New York Times,* December 18, 1978, sec. 3, p. 14.

233 only adult talk with babies: interview with Bruce and Diane Jackson, October 12, 1996.

233 "there's no way": Claude Lewis, "Reviled and Revered Lawyer Dies: The Law May Never Be Quite the Same," *Dayton Daily News,* September 10, 1995, p. B7.

233 "with Sarah and Emily around": Kunstler, *My Life,* p. 399.

233 greater involvement with Sarah and Emily: interviews with Arthur Kinoy, July 15, 1996; Karin Kunstler Goldman, October 15, 1996; Jane Kunstler Drazek, October 8, 1996; Margie Ratner and Emily Kunstler, June 9, 1998.

234 "Yeah. I talk to these": Bruce and Diane Jackson interview.

234 Michael Ratner cared for Sarah: interview with Constance Baker Motley, October 17, 1996.

234 "before you get" and "I learned": interview with Lotte Kunstler, October 14, 1996; see also Kunstler, *My Life,* pp. 263–64.

234 enjoyed young women running after him: Gould interview.

234 enjoyed talking about past exploits: James Frank, "Still Crazy after All These Years," *Spy,* September 1990, p. 70; Bruce and Diane Jackson interview.

234   political and legal articles: *Crawdaddy*: "Crackpots and the Kings," September 1978, p. 60; "Two-Faced World-Political Prisoners, East and West," October 1978, p. 65; *Nation*: "Political Trials: The Myth of Disruption" (with Margaret L. Ratner), May 31, 1975, p. 656; "Germany's Pariah Hunt: The Bundestag vs. the Terrorists," July 5, 1975, p. 7; "FBI Letters: Writers of the Purple Page," December 30, 1978, cover page; "Open Resistance: In Defense of the Movement," in Robert Lefcourt, ed., *Law against the People* (New York: Vintage Books, 1971), pp. 267–75; "Jury Nullification in Conscience Cases."

234   letters to the editor in *New York Times*: January 29, 1976, p. 28; February 10, 1976, p. 36; September 12, 1976, sec. 6 (Magazine), p. 90; October 16, 1977, sec 7 (Book Review), p. 51; November 13, 1977, sec. 6 (Magazine), p. 18; December 10, 1979, p. 26.

234   opinion columns in *New York Times*: "Juries in Jeopardy," June 24, 1972, p. 31; "The Traveling Lawyer," July 7, 1974, sec. 4, p. 15; "The Vanishing Jury," September 27, 1975, p. 29.

234   Lizzie Borden: "De Mille's Borden—How Important Is Truth? *New York Times*, May 13, 1979, sec. 2, p. 22.

234   Roman Catholic mass: Harvey F. Egan, "Dancing, Singing, Climbing toward a New Community; St. Joan of Arc Parish, Minneapolis, Minnesota," *National Catholic Reporter,* October 14, 1994, p. 2 (concerning mass held at unspecified earlier time, inferentially in the 1970s).

235   "made a rabble-rousing": Dan Lund, "The 1970 Convention in Washington," in Ann Fagan Ginger and Eugene M. Tobin, eds., *The National Lawyers Guild: From Roosevelt through Reagan* (Philadelphia: Temple University Press, 1988), pp. 300–301.

235   carried into the hall: Rabinowitz, *Unrepentant Leftist,* p. 192.

235   partnership with C. Vernon Mason: Nina Bernstein, "High, Dry—and Mad: Clients' Complaints Lead to Probe of Attorney Mason," *Newsday,* November 4, 1991, p. 5.

235   "he earned a handsome income": Phillips, *No Heroes, No Villains,* p. 120 (1974 conversation with deputy district attorney); to same tenor, see Carol Ruth Sternhell, "A Brief Encounter with a Lawyer Named Kunstler," *McCall's,* January 1971, p. 102.

235   "Bill created a sort of myth": interview with Ronald Kuby, July 17, 1996.

235   occasionally Kunstler admitted he needed fee cases: Jerry Schwartz, "'Chicago 7' Attorney William Kunstler Still Champion of the Political Underdog," *Los Angeles Times,* April 5, 1987, p. 34.

235   fees helped to subsidize no-fee cases: Ben A. Franklin, "Kunstler Agrees Left Is Less Militant," *New York Times,* February 21, 1972, p. 21.

235   commune fantasy: see, e.g., Navasky. "Right On!" pp. 89, 92.

235 "unless there is": Thomas W. Ennis, "Militancy on Rise, Businessmen Are Told," *New York Times,* June 18, 1970, p. 67.

236 "I think there": Hentoff, "Interview with William Kunstler."

236 splintering and collapse of movement: among many accounts, see the following contemporary sources: Jerry Rubin, *Growing (Up) at Thirty-Seven* (New York: M. Evans, 1976), pp. 88–91; J. Anthony Lukas, "Bobby Seale's Birthday Cake (Oh, Far Out!)," *New York Times Magazine,* October 31, 1971, p. 44; *New York Times,* August 29, 1973, p. 1.

236 "there is a feeling": Franklin, "Kunstler Agrees Left Is Less Militant," p. 21.

237 "unbelievably interested": Pamela M. Capraro to David J. Langum, December 3, 1997.

237 "heartened to see": Nancy LaPaglia to David J. Langum, October 2, 1997.

237 "American students have no spirit": *New York Times,* April 20, 1975, p. 44.

237 lull in Kunstler's career: interview with Michael Ratner, July 18, 1996.

237 "there are still": quoted in Franklin, "Kunstler Agrees Left Is Less Militant," p. 21.

237 "it was hard": Karin Kunstler Goldman interview.

237 mistake to tie movement to Vietnam: Gould interview.

237 "I meet people all the time": quoted in Bruck, "William Kunstler: Actor without a Stage," p. 24.

NOTES TO CHAPTER 11

Page

240 Stanley Lyman diary: Stanley David Lyman, *Wounded Knee, 1973: A Personal Account* (Lincoln: University of Nebraska Press, 1991).

241 100,000 rounds: Martin Waldron, "Wounded Knee Trial Opens with Revolt Warning," *New York Times,* February 13, 1974, p. 14.

241 three demands: John William Sayer, *Ghost Dancing the Law: The Wounded Knee Trials* (Cambridge: Harvard University Press, 1997), pp. 32–33.

242 Kunstler involvement: William M. Kunstler (with Sheila Isenberg), *My Life as a Radical Lawyer* (New York: Birch Lane Press, 1994), pp. 235, 237.

242 March 3 arrival: Lyman, *Wounded Knee, 1973,* p. xxv.

242 "Of course, it's more dangerous": Kunstler, *My Life,* pp. 238–39.

242 Kunstler return on March 9: Douglas E. Kneeland, "Accord Reported at Wounded Knee," *New York Times,* March 10, 1973, pp. 1, 13.

242 185 indictments and Memorial Day conference: Sayer, *Ghost Dancing the Law,* pp. 228, 45.

243   trial sequence drawn from: Ron Christenson, *Political Trials: Gordian Knots in the Law* (New Brunswick, NJ: Transaction, 1986), pp. 201, 205, 209–10; Sayer, *Ghost Dancing the Law,* pp. 69, 105–6, 143.

244   "on trial for what" and "will be to put": Martin Waldron, "Role of 2 Indians Element in Trial," *New York Times,* January 12, 1974, p. 30.

244   deferred to defendants' politics: Sayer, *Ghost Dancing the Law,* p. 43.

244   affirmative lawsuits: ibid., pp. 58, 79, 113.

244   fund-raising rallies: ibid., pp. 43, 54, 61, 69.

244   Kunstler's $5,000 per week speaking income and $35 weekly draw: Martin Waldron, "Kunstler Works Untiringly on Latest Cause," *New York Times,* March 3, 1974, p. 32.

244   finding of defendants' indigency and expenses paid: Martin Waldron, "U.S. to Pay Costs in Indians' Trial," *New York Times,* January 15, 1974, p. 13; Martin Waldron, "Judge Is Cautious on Wounded Knee," *New York Times,* June 18, 1974, p. 15.

244   living with Margie Ratner: Kunstler, *My Life,* p. 244.

244   "My wife has a job": Waldron, "Kunstler Works Untiringly," p. 32.

245   expulsion from courtroom and overnight jail: Waldron, "Wounded Knee Trial Opens," p. 14 (expulsion); "2 Lawyers Jailed at Indians' Trial," *New York Times,* August 24, 1974, p. 1; "Kunstler and Lane Freed after Night in Prison," *New York Times,* August 25, 1974, p. 20; "Wounded Knee Trial Resumes in Accord," *New York Times,* August 27, 1974, p. 24 (jailing).

245   disagreement among defense attorneys and recollections of Kunstler, Nichol, and Tilsen: Sayer, *Ghost Dancing the Law,* pp. 135–36, 273 nn. 61, 67.

245   "through the media" and other Kunstler comments, Tilsen praise: ibid., pp. 70, 301 n. 25, 264 n. 47.

245   Jaycee dinner and comments: ibid., pp. 79–80.

246   St. Paul Rotary Club: ibid., pp. 116–17.

246   prosecutorial misconduct hearing and order of Judge Nichol: *United States v. Banks,* 374 F. Supp. 321–36 (D.S.D. 1974).

247   "is the representative not of an ordinary party": quoted by Judge Nichol from *Berger v. United States,* 295 U.S. 78, 55 S.Ct. 629, 79 L.Ed. 1314 (1935).

247   "Someone better tell them" and other Nichol remarks: Sayer, *Ghost Dancing the Law,* p. 125.

248   "hostile attitude" and "I don't give a damn": ibid., p. 126.

248   "trying to put words" and "that's already been done": ibid., p. 162.

249   "as good a closing": Kunstler, *My Life,* p. 246.

249   vote to acquit: Sayer, *Ghost Dancing the Law,* p. 198.

249   "I don't think": ibid., p. 191.

250 Judge Nichol's dismissal order and comments quoted: *United States v. Banks,* 383 F. Supp. 389–97 (D.S.D. 1974).

251 "superior performance" award: Sayer, *Ghost Dancing the Law,* pp. 200–201.

251 "to break the spirit": ibid., p. 201.

251 appeal dismissed: *United States v. Means,* 513 F.2d 1329–36 (8th Cir. 1975).

251 "I think to some extent": Sayer, *Ghost Dancing the Law,* p. 228.

251 ten of the sixteen jurors and alternates: ibid., p. 201.

251 conviction rates: ibid., p. 228.

251 Durham affair and Hurd denial: ibid., pp. 207–8, 211; Ward Churchill and Jim Vander Wall, *Agents of Repression: The FBI's Secret Wars against the Black Panther Party and the American Indian Movement* (Boston: South End Press, 1988), pp. 220–27.

252 "It was a wonderful victory": Kunstler, *My Life,* p. 247.

252 Kunstler's immersion into Indian culture: remarks of Clyde Bellecourt at Kunstler's memorial service, November 19, 1995.

253 Cedar Rapids trial generally: the only two sources of general information concerning the shootout of June 26, 1975, are unfortunately biased in favor of the defendants. They are Peter Matthiessen, *In the Spirit of Crazy Horse* (New York: Viking, 1991), pp. 154–315 and *Incident at Oglala,* a 1992 Miramax documentary produced by Robert Redford.

253 disinformation and "Dog Soldiers" alert: Churchill and Vander Wall, *Agents of Repression,* pp. 261–85; and Paul Delaney, "F.B.I. Chief Admits Alert on Indians Lacked Proof," *New York Times,* July 8, 1976, p. 16.

253 marshals, SWAT teams, and helicopter: Bruce H. Ellison, "Remembrance: William Kunstler: A People's Lawyer," *South Dakota Law Review,* vol. 41 (1996), p. 231.

253 "hinterlands jury": Kunstler, in *Incident at Oglala.*

253 voir dire examination of jury: Ellison, "Remembrance: William Kunstler," pp. 231–32.

253 Marlon Brando and Dick Gregory: Kunstler, *My Life,* p. 249.

254 "I know of none": Delaney, "F.B.I. Chief Admits Alert on Indians Lacked Proof," p. 16.

254 Kunstler exchange with Kelley: Delaney, "F.B.I. Chief Admits Alert on Indians Lacked Proof," p. 16; Matthiessen, *In the Spirit of Crazy Horse,* pp. 307–8.

255 "Exactly": Delaney, "F.B.I. Chief Admits Alert on Indians Lacked Proof," p. 16.

255 Peltier trials and appeals: an abundance of tendentious material has appeared concerning Peltier, including *Incident at Oglala,* the Redford

film; Matthiessen, *In the Spirit of Crazy Horse*; and Jim Messerschmidt, *The Trial of Leonard Peltier* (Boston: South End Press, 1983). There are a number of short neutral articles, but three have some substance: Joan M. Cheever, "Conviction of Convenience?" *National Law Journal*, June 25, 1990, p. 28; Paul McEnroe, "Peltier Lawyers Return to Court," *National Law Journal*, November 30, 1992, p. 3; and John Elvin, "Indian Murders Still Beg the Question of Justice," *Washington Times*, July 1, 1996, p. 18.

255   "it was time for a new voice": quoted in McEnroe, "Peltier Lawyers Return to Court," p. 3.

256   speeches: for example, a 1995 speech on Capitol Hill marking the twentieth anniversary of the agents' death, *Chicago Tribune*, June 28, 1995, p. 10.

256   letters to the editor: *New York Times*, October 3, 1987, p. 26; March 10, 1993, p. A18; *Minneapolis Star Tribune*, December 28, 1992, p. A9.

256   magazine articles: William M. Kunstler, "The Ordeal of Leonard Peltier," *CovertAction*, summer 1985: 25–29; William M. Kunstler, "By Hook or by Crook," *Hamline Law Review*, October 1985, pp. 611–24.

257   "everybody knows": E. R. Shipp, "Indian Leader, 9 Years a Fugitive, Surrenders for Jail Term in Dakota," *New York Times*, September 14, 1984, p. B5.

257   thirty reporters and law enforcement criticism: Wayne Hejka, UPI release, September 13, 1984.

257   "felt as a lawyer," parole, and appeal: Janelle Krause Toman, "Indian Activist's Riot Conviction Upheld," UPI release, May 2, 1986.

257   Banks extradition generally: other useful information may be found in Michele Abruzzi, Reuters release, March 1, 1983; UPI releases of September 12, 13, October 5, 6, 8, 1984; Francis J. Flaherty, "When Can a State Refuse An Extradition Request?" *National Law Journal*, July 11, 1983, p. 3; Joseph B. Treaster, "Lawyers Say Dennis Banks is Set to Give Up," *New York Times*, February 27, 1983, p. 37; "Indian Leader Gets Jail Sentence," *New York Times*, October 9, 1984, p. B8; Connie Leslie, "Dennis Bank's [sic] Last Stand," *Newsweek*, February 21, 1983, p. 28; Mary Thornton, "Indian Movement Leader Surrenders After 9–Year Flight," *Washington Post*, September 14, 1984, p. A2.

258   Tuscarora Indians: *Los Angeles Times*, March 11, 1989, p. 29; *Washington Times*, October 2, 1989, p. A1.

258   Blackfoot Indian mother: *New York Times*, October 21, 1975, p. 41; October 18, 1977, p. 41; January 29, 1978, p. 33.

258   Golden Hill Paugussetts: numerous articles in the *Hartford Courant* throughout 1993, 1994, and 1995; *New York Times*, March 20, 1994, p. 13CN; March 19, 1995, p. 13CN; and May 23, 1996, p. D25.

258 Mohawk barricade in 1979–1980: *New York Times,* August 29, 1979, sec. 2, p. 4; June 2, 1980, p. B3.

258 Quebec standoff: AP and UPI accounts in *Bergen Record,* July 18, 1990, p. A12 (Four Star B and One Star editions, respectively); *Maclean's,* July 30, 1990, p. 12.

258 Kunstler corrected inaccurate or insensitive articles: e.g., *Washington Post,* June 11, 1988, p. A23; *New York Times,* March 10, 1993, p. A18.

258 "a true warrior": from audiotape of memorial service

NOTES TO CHAPTER 12

Page

259 "This excess of security": quoted in James Brooke, "11 Wells Fargo Robbery Suspects Appear in Hartford Court," *New York Times,* September 4, 1985, p. 25.

259 "The danger is that": quoted in UPI, September 1, 1985.

260 "of using the hearing" and "I find no political": quoted in Lyda Phillips, "Alleged Cuban Agent Labeled Terrorist Leader," UPI, October 4, 1985.

260 affirmative lawsuit: UPI, August 13, 1986.

260 "They've accomplished their purpose": quoted in Ken Brown, "Fourth Anniversary of Wells Fargo Robbery," UPI, September 11, 1987.

260 one-thousand-person demonstration: Lyda Phillips, "March Supports Wells Fargo Robbery Defendants," UPI, September 1, 1986.

260 attempt to seek favor with India: Leonard Buder, "Sikh Held in Gandhi Murder Plot Is to Go on Trial," *New York Times,* March 10, 1986, p. B4.

260 partial acquittal: "Sikh Found Innocent of Rajiv Gandhi Assassination Plot," Reuters, March 20, 1986.

261 for interest in Judy Russell, see, e.g.: Rita Henley Jensen, "A Career Careens Off Track," *National Law Journal,* April 11, 1988, p. 1; Rita Henley Jensen, "Probe Widens of an Ex-Prosecutor," *National Law Journal,* July 4, 1988, p. 29; Ethan Schwartz, "Ex-Prosecutor Found Insane in Case of Faked Threats," *Washington Post,* March 11, 1989, p. A4; Tracy Schroth, "Former Prosecutor Is Spared Disciplinary Action," *New Jersey Law Journal,* December 23, 1991, p. 5.

261 for several major articles on Kikumura: see articles by Robert Hanley in *New York Times*: "U.S. Links Man with 3 Bombs to a Terror Plot," February 4, 1989, p. 30; "Suspected Terrorist Convicted in Bomb Case," November 30, 1988, p. B1; "Defendant Gets 30 Years in Jail in Bombing Plot," February 8, 1989, p. B2.

261 "a member of the armed": quoted in "Accused Trooper Killers Defend Radical Violence," UPI, September 28, 1986.

262   "sympathetic": quoted in Jesus Rangel, "Government Lists Evidence in Suspected Bombers' Trial," *New York Times*, October 22, 1985, p. B3.

262   "out of desperation" through "Don't let that world": quoted in Leonard Buder, "Jury Deliberating in Radicals' Trial," *New York Times*, February 16, 1986, p. 43.

262   Trivial Pursuit quip: Leonard Buder, "Reporter's Notebook: 2 Bombing Defendants Wed," *New York Times*, February 27, 1986, p. B5.

262   "What the judge did": quoted in Leonard Buder, "In Partial Verdict, U.S. Jury Finds 6 Radicals Guilty of 2 Bombings," *New York Times*, March 5, 1986, p. B3.

262   "another victim": quoted in William M. Reilly, UPI, May 2, 1986.

262   "recognized him": quoted in Frances Ann Burns, "Manning to Take Stand in Trooper Killing Trial," UPI, November 10, 1986.

262   "a proud and dedicated": quoted in Donald Janson, "Trial of Two in the Slayings of Trooper Opens in Jersey," *New York Times*, November 11, 1986, Sect. B, p. 2.

262   "a North American anti-imperialist": quoted in Josh Meyer, "Radical to Fight Court-Ordered Blood Test," UPI, July 11, 1986.

262   exclusion of blacks: "Judge: No Mistrial for Radicals," UPI, November 20, 1986.

262   "I think that any potential": quoted in Frances Ann Burns, UPI, October 27, 1986.

263   "the defendants have no respect": quoted in Donald Janson, "Reporter's Notebook: A Custom Falls," *New York Times*, November 30, 1986, p. 50.

263   sentence: Paul A. Basken, UPI, February 18, 1987.

264   "we are all political" through "take your hands": quoted in "8 in Sedition Case Object to Court Naming Counsel," *New York Times*, March 10, 1987, p. 21.

264   "it's an outrage": quoted in Steven Bredice, UPI, March 9, 1987.

264   "they are participating" through "who would take": quoted in Ken Cafarell, "Kunstler blasts judge in radicals trial," UPI, March 11, 1987.

265   "could never admit": quoted in Steven Bredice, "Judges [*sic*] Orders Radical Trial Moved," UPI, March 12, 1987.

265   "wasting the taxpayers money": quoted in Kenneth R. Bazinet, "Attorney: Revolutionaries Trial Won't Start until Fall," UPI, May 13, 1987.

265   dismissal: "'Revolutionary' Begins Life Term in 1981 Killing of State Trooper," *New York Times*, September 4, 1988, p. 55.

265   "The pure number": quoted in Mark Curriden, "Are Black Officials Investigative Targets?" *ABA Journal*, February 1992, p. 54.

265   selective prosecution of blacks: see, e.g., ibid. and James Neff, "Is Justice Blind?" *George*, October 1996, p. 126.

266   "Why this total vendetta": quoted in "Kunstler Joins Hastings' Team," *Legal Times,* June 5, 1989, p. 3.

266   "much of it developed": Don Edwards, "Evidence against Hastings Overwhelming," *New York Times,* September 10, 1988, p. 26 (op-ed letter).

266   "may have provided" and "intended to strengthen": Neil A. Lewis, "F.B.I. Role in an Impeachment Is Reviewed," *New York Times,* February 26, 1997, p. 11.

267   "It possibly makes": quoted in James Brady, "Holiday Season Didn't Seem Kinder and Gentler to Some," *Crain's New York Business,* January 15, 1990, p. 9.

267   "the poignancy of this case": quoted in Larry McShane, "Same Questions to Arise in Lawsuit against Goetz," *Las Vegas Review-Journal,* April 8, 1996, no page indicated.

267   four blacks and two Hispanics: Larry McShane, "Jury Orders Goetz to Pay $43 Million," *Chattanooga Times,* April 24, 1996, p. A5.

267   "Bill's shoes": quoted in Corky Siemaszko, "A 43M Shot at Goetz by Jury," *New York Daily News,* April 24, 1996, p. 3.

267   "They needed a fall guy": quoted in UPI, November 11, 1985; more on this allegation is in Mark Curriden, "New Questions in Atlanta Murders: Did Prosecutors Withhold Evidence of Klan Involvement in Children's Deaths?" *ABA Journal,* May 1992, p. 36; Mary A. Fischer, "Was Wayne Williams Framed?" *GQ,* April 1991, p. 228; "Klan Link Is Cited in Child Killings," *New York Times,* October 10, 1991, p. 20.

267   "so strongly opposed": William M. Kunstler (with Sheila Isenberg), *My Life as a Radical Lawyer* (New York: Birch Lane Press, 1994), p. 288.

268   refused to review New York Court of Appeals: "High Court Refuses Death-Law Case," *New York Times,* February 20, 1985, p. B2.

268   York trials and ultimate disposition: Ronald Smothers, "Decision Is Mixed in Police Shooting," *New York Times,* August 10, 1982, p. 1; "Judge Reserves Decision on Third Trial for Two Former Black Panthers," UPI, October 7, 1983; Philip Newman, UPI, June 6, 1986; Gary Spencer, "No Special Procedures for Batson Hearings; Oaths, Cross-Examination Held Not Required," *New York Law Journal,* June 6, 1996, p. 1.

268   "I had to make some": interview with Arthur Kinoy, July 15, 1996; see also interview with Kunstler in Jerry Schwartz, "'Chicago 7' Attorney William Kunstler Still Champion of the Political Underdog," *Los Angeles Times,* April 5, 1987, p. 34.

268   fees and finances: interview with Ronald L. Kuby, July 17, 1996.

269   "someone who wants to do more": quoted in Timothy Clifford, "Kun-

stler on Goldman Family Fortune Case," *Newsday,* September 15, 1989, p. 22.

269   tattoo promise: Kunstler, *My Life,* p. 351.

269   Hell's Angels representation: Kunstler, *My Life,* pp. 350–51; Mark Rollenhagen, "Use of DNA Evidence in Criminal Trials Upheld," *Cleveland Plain Dealer,* December 16, 1993, p. B2.

269   between $150,000 and $175,000: Elliot Pinsley, "Kunstler Still Making the Left's Case," *Manhattan Lawyer,* August 1–7, 1989, p. 1.

269   jazz-dancing cops: Kunstler, *My Life,* pp. 349–50; UPI, March 16, 1987.

269   Rock Against Racism: see articles by Linda Greenhouse in *New York Times*: "Supreme Court Accord: Rock Music Is Loud," February 28, 1989, p. 1; "High Court Upholds Noise Rule for the Central Park Bandshell," June 23, 1989, p. B1; Jessie Mangaliman, "Top Court Upholds City Concert Rule," *Newsday,* June 23, 1989, p. 33.

270   "totally different": quoted in Dan Andrews, UPI, January 24, 1986.

270   "I can't say": quoted in Don Mullen, "Legionnaires File Lawsuit against Police, FBI," UPI, June 25, 1986.

270   "I was brought up": quoted in Jim Dwyer, "Wrenching the Life from the 4th of July," *Newsday,* July 4, 1990, p. 2.

270   American Legion Post incident: in addition to the above three articles, see Todd S. Purdum, "Veterans Post Raided in Slaying Case," *New York Times,* January 25, 1986, p. 31; Jacqueline M. Bukowski, "Washington Square Post #1212 v. Maduro," *New York Law Journal,* July 23, 1990, p. 5.

271   "They had no money": quoted in Dave Condren, "Longtime Friend Says Kunstler Had 'Immense Heart,'" *Buffalo News,* September 5, 1995, p. A5.

271   "and saw this man crying": quoted in Rhea Mandulo, "Jewish Couple Who Fled Russia Ordered Out of Cleaning Shop," UPI, April 18, 1986.

271   "He told me to buy": quoted in Jack Snyder, "Paulucci Fondly Remembers Kunstler; Entrepreneur Began Working with Famed Lawyer in 1985," *Orlando Sentinel,* September 18, 1995, p. 6.

272   "I think they're": quoted in Gay Jervey, *American Lawyer,* March 1994, p. 44; for information on transcripts litigation, see also, obituary of Raymond L.S. Patriarca, UPI, July 11, 1984.

272   "Here's to crime": this story has been told many places, including Jimmy Breslin, "It's Last of 9th in Gotti's Game," *Newsday,* June 23, 1992, p. 2; Mike Kelly, "Gangster Activism," *Bergen Record,* June 25, 1992, p. B01; Steven T. Taylor, "They Love Him, They Hate Him," *National Jurist,* January 1994, p. 12; Kunstler, *My Life,* p. 342.

272   "If this stands up": quoted in "FBI Bugging Followed by $100 million Lawsuit," UPI, June 6, 1981.

272   wiretap found illegal: "Federal Judge Rules against FBI Bugging,"
UPI, August 12, 1981.

272   Bonanno incident: William Reilly, UPI, August 28,1985; Edward B.
Havens, UPI, September 6, 1985; Arnold H. Lubasch, "Judge Requires
That Bonanno Gives Testimony," *New York Times,* September 5, 1985, p.
B3; UPI, September 5, 1985; Arnold H. Lubasch, "Bonanno Jailed after
Refusing to Be Witness," *New York Times,* September 6, 1985, p. 1.

273   "nobody was going to ruin": Breslin, "It's Last of 9th in Gotti's
Game".

273   "I have an incredible amount of power": quoted in Linda Stasi, "Gotti:
Was It Rigged?" *Newsday,* June 17, 1992, p. 2.

273   Gotti trial: "Gotti Convicted of Racketeering," *Facts on File World News
Digest,* April 9, 1992, p. 251 D2; Arnold H. Lubasch, "Judge Wraps Jury
in Secrecy and Bars a Lawyer as Gotti Trial Opens," *New York Times,*
January 22, 1992, p. B4; Arnold H. Lubasch, "Lawyers Seek a New Trial
In Gotti Case," *New York Times,* June 23, 1992, p. B1; Edward Frost,
"Gotti Gets Life Sentence; Motion for Retrial Denied," *New York Law
Journal,* June 24, 1992, p. 1; Jerry Capeci and Gene Mustain, "They Say
He Asks a Lot of His Lawyers," *National Law Journal,* February 3, 1992,
p. 8.

274   "more honest than the major": quoted in Alan M. Dershowitz, *The Best
Defense* (New York: Vintage Books, 1982), p. 410.

274   "How was John Gotti worse": Kuby interview.

274   "this country has a long tradition": Kunstler, *My Life,* p. 340.

274   "part of a pattern": quoted in "Gotti Won't Fight for His Lawyer's Return," *Legal Intelligencer,* January 27, 1992, p. 5.

274   "The government uses": quoted in Jon Kalish, "From the Chicago 8 to
Our Uncounted," *Newsday,* June 23, 1988, p. 78.

274   "they also rip off": Kunstler, *My Life,* p. 341.

274   prison banquet: W. Zachary Malinowski, "Three Strikes and He's In,"
Providence Journal-Bulletin, February 2, 1996, p. 1; interview with
Margie Ratner, June 9, 1998.

274   "That's not your speed": Barry Slotnick in program, "William Kunstler: Champion or Charlatan?" Association of the Bar of the City of
New York, June 19, 1996.

275   "And why do you think": interview with Bruce Jackson, October 12,
1996.

275   "I never made a nickel": quoted in Denis Hamill, "A Road Map to the
Trial," *Newsday,* July 27, 1988, p. 7.

275   mobsters were victims and he did not accept a fee: Schwartz,
"'Chicago 7' Attorney William Kunstler Still Champion of the Political
Underdog."

275   Flynn: Ken Franckling, "State Dropping Remaining Charges in Gang-land Slaying Case," UPI, July 16, 1981.

275   Dentico and D'Agostino: UPI, July 7, 1982.

275   Marrapese: UPI, November 24, 1983.

275   Ouimette brothers and Sciarra: UPI, January 8, 1982.

275   Zannino: Ralph Ranalli, "Former Mob Chief Seeks Conviction Reversal," *Boston Herald,* May 20, 1994, p. 026.

275   Ferrante: Michele Salcedo, "Gotti Rapper Guilty in Fraud," *Newsday,* June 24, 1994, p. A27.

275   Viola: Scott Ladd, "Feds Ready Drug Indictment," *Newsday,* September 19, 1991, p. 23.

276   "I've learned a few tricks": quoted in "Catching Matinee At the Courthouse; A Group of Regulars Keeps Watching," *New York Times,* July 9, 1993, p. B1.

276   "prepared. I would put him": interview with Jack B. Weinstein, July 16, 1996.

276   "one of the best": interview with Sol Wachtler, January 25, 1998.

277   meeting of Kuby and Kunstler: Larry McShane, "Kunstler and Kuby Law Firm Remains but Not Same without Fiery Mentor," *Los Angeles Times,* October 22, 1995, p. 22.

277   "yuppie radical": Julie Salamon, "At Lunch With: Ronald L. Kuby; Crispy Fries and Radical Causes," *New York Times,* June 7, 1995, p. C1.

277   associate and "partner," and "partner and alter ego": Kunstler, *My Life,* pp. 291 and photo section.

277   "We used to get the cream": quoted in Bruce Rosen, "A Law 'Collective' for Radical Clients," *National Law Journal,* December 9, 1985, p. 13.

277   Elison Elliott: "Council Districts," *Newsday,* November 3, 1991 p. 4.

277   "Bill assumed that your": quoted in Jan Hoffman, "For Next Generation, New Kunstlers," *New York Times,* September 18, 1995, p. B 1.

278   direct questioning of jurors and non-unanimous verdict: articles by William M. Kunstler in *New York Times*: "Juries in Jeopardy," June 24, 1972, p. 31; "The Vanishing Jury," September 27, 1975, p. 29; "It Takes a Lawyer, Not a Judge, to Quiz Prospective Jurors," March 11, 1983, p. 30.

278   fee forfeiture: see, e.g., discussion in Sam Adler, "Criminal Bar Discovers Sure Profits in Civil RICO," *Manhattan Lawyer,* August 22, 1989, p. 1; David Rudovsky, "The Right to Counsel under Attack," *University of Pennsylvania Law Review,* June 1988, p. 1965.

278   forced disclosure of source of fees: see, e.g., discussion in Jeffrey Kanige, "Silver Lining Seen In Subpoena Ruling," *Manhattan Lawyer,* August 8–14, 1989, p. 1; Elliot Pinsley, "Stewart Gets Support in Fight with Johnson," *Manhattan Lawyer,* August 1–7, 1989, p. 7.

278   use of grand jury for discovery: see, e.g., discussion in Elliot Pinsley, "Use of Marcos Grand Jury after Indictment Blasted," *Manhattan Lawyer*, November 15–21, 1988, p. 5.

279   anonymous juries: William Glaberson, "Courts under Challenge for Anonymity of Juries," *New York Times*, December 12, 1997, p. 20; William M. Kunstler, "The Threat of Anonymous Juries," *Nation*, October 22, 1983, p. 360.

279   civil rights and public interest litigation fees: see, e.g., discussion in "The Unquiet Death of Contingency Fees" (including Kunstler as one interviewee), *California Lawyer*, July 1993, p. 31; William M. Kunstler, "Suitable Fees for Rights Lawyers," *Wall Street Journal*, March 10, 1986, p. 17.

279   "often can be bolder": William M. Kunstler, "The Traveling Lawyer," *New York Times*, July 7, 1974, sec. 4, p. 15.

279   *pro hac vice*: Thomas C. Canfield, "The Criminal Defendant's Right to Retain Counsel Pro Hac Vice," *Fordham Law Review*, April 1989, p. 785; for a discussion of famous American cases tried by attorneys *pro hac vice*, see *Flynt v. Leis*, 574 F.2d 874, 878–79 (6th Cir. 1978), rev'd on other grounds, 439 U.S. 438 (1979)(per curiam).

280   Germany: Craig R. Whitney, "German Ruling Disturbs U.S. Lawyers," *New York Times*, April 15, 1975, p. 8.

280   "disdain and contempt": "Kunstler Incurs a Judge's Wrath," *New York Times*, January 28, 1972, p. 69.

280   "engaged in a pattern": quoted in John Kifner, "Kunstler Upheld by Appeals Court": *New York Times*, May 19, 1973, p. 34.

280   appellate process of Indiana case: Kifner, "Kunstler Unheld by Appeals Court"; William E. Farrell, "Court Is Urged to Bar Kunstler," *New York Times*, August 26, 1973, p. 19; "High Court Will Hear Free-Speech Case Involving Kunstler," *New York Times*, January 22, 1974, p. 19; *Holder v. Banks*, 417 U.S. 187 (1974)(dismissing petition for certiorari as improvidently granted).

280   "break up the itinerant lawyer": quoted in Schwartz, "'Chicago 7' Attorney William Kunstler Still Champion of the Political Underdog."

281   "deliberate poisoning" and "inflammatory comments": William M. Kunstler, "Lawyers Forced to 'Exploit Media Attention,'" *New York Times*, June 11, 1987, p. 26.

281   "after the prosecutor" and other criticisms: William M. Kunstler, "Gag Order's No Joke for Defendants," *Crawdaddy*, May 1978, p. 60.

281   1976 New Jersey contempt citation: Martin Waldron, "Kunstler and the Courts in a Battle on Right to Discuss Pending Trial," *New York Times*, December 3, 1976, sec. 2, p. 2.

281   1991 case: *Gentile v. State Bar of Nevada*, 111 S.Ct. 2720.

281   expansion of gag orders and state bar rules: Jan Hoffman, "May It Please the Public: Lawyers Exploit Media Attention as a Defense Tactic," *New York Times,* April 22, 1994, p. B1; Andrew Blum, "Court to Lawyers: 'Shut Up,'" *National Law Journal,* January 24, 1994, p. 10; Kelly Ann Hardy, "Order in the Courtroom, Silence on the Courthouse Steps: Attorneys Muzzled by Ethical Disciplinary Rules," *Seton Hall Law Review,* 1992, p. 1401; Michael E. Swartz, "Trial Participant Speech Restrictions: Gagging First Amendment Rights," *Columbia Law Review,* June 1990, p. 1411.

281   Bruce Cutler: John Sullivan, "Gotti's Top Lawyer Is Suspended 3 Months for Contempt," *New York Times,* December 14, 1996 (n.p.; from Internet).

281   Colin Ferguson gag order: Hoffman, "May It Please the Public."

281   World Trade Center contempt motion: Blum, "Court to Lawyers."

282   criticism of Rule 11 fines: see discussion in: John Rather, "A Suffolk Case Raises Major Rights Issues," *New York Times,* April 27, 1986, sec. 11LI, p. 1; Ruth Marcus, "Rule 11: Does It Curb Frivolous Lawsuits or Civil Rights Claims?" *Washington Post,* April 12, 1991, p. A17; Stephen Labaton, "Solution to Wasteful Lawsuits Becomes a Problem," *New York Times,* June 14, 1992, sec. 4, p. 2; Jeffrey Neal Cole, "Rule 11 Now," *Litigation,* spring 1991, p. 10; Carl Tobias, "Public Law Litigation and the Federal Rules of Procedure," *Cornell Law Review,* 1989, p. 270; Carl Tobias, "Rule 11 and Civil Rights Litigation," *Buffalo Law Review,* 1989, p. 485; Carl Tobias, "Rule 11 Recalibrated in Civil Rights Cases," *Villanova Law Review,* February 1991, p. 105; Carl Tobias, "Reconsidering Rule 11," *University of Miami Law Review,* March 1992, p. 855; Carl Tobias, "Civil Rights Conundrum," *Georgia Law Review,* summer 1992, p. 901; Carl Tobias, "Some Realism about Empiricism," *Connecticut Law Review,* spring 1994, p. 1093; Donna Marino, "Rule 11 and Public Interest Litigation: The Trend toward Limiting Access to the Federal Courts," *Rutgers Law Review,* summer 1992, p. 923.

283   "a number of lawyers": Professor Stephen B. Burbank, quoted in Labaton, "Solution to Wasteful Lawsuits Becomes a Problem."

283   "Courage is courage": quoted in UPI, April 27, 1986.

283   "enormous chilling effect": quoted in Tony Mauro, "USA's Lawyers the Losers in Supreme Court Session," *USA Today,* April 16, 1991, p. A8.

283   Robeson County background and federal acquittal: Montgomery Brower, "The Murder of Julian Pierce Provokes Grief and Grievances in Troubled Robeson County," *People,* April 18, 1988, p. 60; "Editor Tells of Siege at His Office," *Bergen Record*, October 2, 1988, p. A43; "2 Carolina Indians Acquitted in Hostage Taking," *New York*

Times, October 15, 1988, p. 9; "Indians Who Seized Office Acquitted in N. Carolina," *Washington Post,* October 15, 1988, p. A3.

284   "primary motives in filing" and remand to reset fine: *In re Kunstler,* 914 F.2d 505, 520 (4th Cir. 1990).

284   "I hope that this decision": quoted in Michael Hedges, "Christics, Lawyer Fined $100,000 in 'Frivolous' Suit," *Washington Times,* October 2, 1989, p. A1.

284   "I'll tell you this": quoted in Don J. DeBenedictis, "Rule 11 Snags Lawyers: Critics Charge Rulings Will Discourage Civil-Rights Cases," *ABA Journal,* January 1991, p. 16.

284   Supreme Court and further review of fine: Dawn Ceol, "Court Takes Mississippi Bias Case," *Washington Times,* April 16, 1991, p. A4; "Kunstler Assessed," *National Law Journal,* July 20, 1992, p. 6.

284   committee and payment of fine: Andrew Blum, "Kunstler's Rent Party," *National Law Journal,* October 19, 1992, p. 2; Kunstler, *My Life,* p. 390.

285   "rule 11 scares me": quoted in "The Unquiet Death of Contingency Fees," p. 34.

285   quotations concerning 1995 case clarifying 1993 amendments to Rule 11: Deborah Pines, "Bases for Sanctioning Lawyers Clarified in Ruling for Kunstler," *New York Law Journal,* March 3, 1995, p. 1.

NOTES TO CHAPTER 13

Page

286   "make something up": Rodney Barker, *Dancing with the Devil: Sex, Espionage, and the U.S. Marines: The Clayton Lonetree Story* (New York: Simon and Schuster, 1996), pp. 46, 179.

286   "the first master spy": Alex Shoumatoff, "The Silenced Love Song of Pvt. Clayton Lonetree; Espionage Case," *Esquire,* November 1993, p. 105.

287   Caspar Weinberger: Barker, *Dancing with the Devil,* p. 72.

287   Henderson attempts to dissuade Lonetree from Kunstler representation: Barker, *Dancing with the Devil,* p. 65; affidavit of Clayton J. Lonetree (hereinafter Lonetree affidavit), in *United States v. Lonetree,* 31 *Military Justice Reporter* 849, at 874 (1990).

288   "Mr. Kunstler and Mr. Stuhff told me": Lonetree affidavit, p. 873.

288   five-year sentence: Barker, *Dancing with the Devil,* p. 63.

288   plea bargain best approach: ibid., p. 82.

288   "should not listen": Lonetree affidavit, p. 873.

288   Henderson's belief: Barker, *Dancing with the Devil,* p. 214.

288   "the criminal negligence": quoted in Barker, *Dancing with the Devil,* p. 175; discussion of motions: ibid., pp. 174–82.

289   plea bargaining: ibid., pp. 102, 182–84.

289   "in the realm": affidavit of Major David Henderson, quoted in *United States v. Lonetree,* 31 *Military Justice Reporter* 849, at 875 (1990).

289   give Sasha credibility: Ben A. Franklin, "Espionage Trial of Marine Hears from C.I.A. Agents," *New York Times,* August 14, 1987, p. 2.

290   "the scapegoat for the State Department": quoted in Claire Robertson, "Marine Found Guilty in Espionage Trial; Lonetree Could Receive Life Sentence," *Washington Post,* August 22, 1987, p. A1.

290   "become a double agent": quoted in Ben A. Franklin, "Testimony Begins in Trial of Marine," *New York Times,* August 12, 1987, p. 10.

290   "encouraged him to feed . . . just say something": quoted in Greg Henderson, UPI, July 30, 1987.

290   "indulged Lonetree's fantasies": quoted in Nicholas C. McBride, "Marine Spy Trial Under Way," *Christian Science Monitor,* July 23, 1987, p. 3.

290   "junk . . . dug out of the trash": quoted in Nicholas C. McBride, "Sgt. Clayton Lonetree: Inheritor of Two Proud Traditions," *Christian Science Monitor,* July 30, 1987, p. 1.

290   "was so inconsequential": quoted in Greg Henderson, UPI, July 27, 1987.

290   judge prevented the defense: Ben A. Franklin, "Marine Convicted by Court-Martial of Embassy Spying," *New York Times,* August 22, 1987, p. 1.

290   "I have no hope": quoted in Franklin, "Testimony Begins in Trial of Marine," p. 10.

291   "I'm afraid they just": William C. Rempel, "Lonetree Seeks Civilian Trial, Doubts Military Fairness," *Los Angeles Times,* April 14, 1987, p. 17.

291   news conferences: George E. Curry, "Marine's Spy Trial Has Side Drama," *Chicago Tribune,* July 29, 1987, p. 4.

291   "this judge violated his oath": quoted in Greg Henderson, UPI, August 21, 1987.

291   "the judge was an animal": Sue Baker, "Lonetree Lawyers Vow to Fight Verdict to End," Reuters, August 22, 1987.

291   "turn a black man against": quoted in Nicholas C. McBride, "US Embassy Spy Case: Fantasy or Infamy?" *Christian Science Monitor,* April 30, 1987, p. 1.

291   "an anti-Indian bias": quoted in "Spy Trial Begins for Embassy Guard," *Chicago Tribune,* July 23, 1987, p. 4.

291   "Being an Indian": quoted in Sarah Helm, "Marines Begin Court-Martial of Sgt. Lonetree," *Washington Post,* July 23, 1987, p. A4.

291   op-ed piece: William M. Kunstler, "An Un-Uniform Code of Military Justice; For Sgt. Lonetree, North's 'Hero' Status Is a Double Standard at Best," *Los Angeles Times,* July 27, 1987, pt. 2, p. 5.

292   Kunstler's sonnet quoted in Richard McFarland, "Father Says Marine Sgt. Lonetree Is 'Upbeat' about Trial, Attorneys Optimistic, but the Father Isn't," UPI, July 17, 1987.

292   grandfather's ritual: Greg Henderson, "Defense Attorney Says State Department Could Clear Lonetree," UPI, July 24, 1987.

292   Indian demonstrators: Barker, *Dancing with the Devil,* p. 170; Richard Halloran, "Trial of a Marine in Spy Case Opens," *New York Times,* July 23, 1987, p. 5.

292   defense rallies: Barker, *Dancing with the Devil,* p. 151.

292   "I guess some": quoted in ibid., p. 41.

293   "a kick in the teeth": quoted in "U.S. Marine Sgt. Lonetree Sentenced as Soviet Spy; 30–Year Term in Moscow Embassy Case," *Facts on File World News Digest,* August 28, 1987, p. 624F2.

293   "dirty, dirty business": quoted in Julie Brienza, UPI, October 20, 1987.

293   Kunstler and Stuhff fired: "Lonetree's Father Says the Convicted Marine Will Fire Attorneys," UPI, October 22, 1987; "Convicted Marine Spy Could Get Reduction in Sentence," Reuters, October 22, 1987.

293   Kunstler was "more interested": Lee Calligaro quoted in "Lonetree Hires New Lawyer," UPI, December 31, 1987.

293   "Whenever a client claims": quoted in Neil A. Lewis, "Top Military Court Hears of a Marine Convicted of Spying," *New York Times,* May 13, 1991, p. 11.

293   "completely dishonest": quoted in Tom Hamburger, "Lonetree Guilt Affirmed, but Sentence Set Aside; Military Court to Consider Fairness Issues," *Star Tribune,* October 1, 1992, p. A7.

293   "If they want to hang": quoted in Shoumatoff, "The Silenced Love Song," p. 105.

294   *United States v. Lonetree,* U.S. Navy-Marine Corps Court of Military Review, 31 *Military Justice Reporter* 849 (1990).

294   "Lonetree offers us colorable claims": *United States v. Lonetree,* U.S. Court of Military Appeals, 35 *Military Justice Reporter* 396, at 413–14 (1992).

294   sentence reduced five additional years: "Marine in Espionage Case Now Eligible for Parole," *New York Times,* October 31, 1993, p. 21.

294   parole refused: Jim Parsons, "Marine Spy Lonetree Walks Out of Prison Today, a Free Man," *Star Tribune,* February 27, 1996, p. A5; Ann

Merrill, "A Contrite Lonetree Says He Is Ready to Start Life Anew," *Star Tribune,* June 22, 1996, p. A1.

294   diversion for Ames; Kunstler rehired: Greg Gordon, "Lawyer Says Lonetree Was a Cover for Ames," *Star Tribune,* September 30, 1994, p. A1; "Soviets May Have Persuaded Lonetree to Confess," *Star Tribune,* October 1, 1994, p. A7; Tony Mauro, "Ames' Statements May Help Convicted Embassy Guard," *USA Today,* September 28, 1994, p. A7.

294   Lonetree released: Karren Mills, "Freedom Won't Remove Stain on Lone Marine Spy Lonetree," *Memphis Commercial Appeal,* February 25, 1996, p. A9; "Intrigue Follows Embassy Spy," *Arizona Republic,* February 28, 1996, p. A2.

295   between 1987 and 1991: a good description of the first three trials is in Amy Singer, "Larry Davis Beats the Rap," *American Lawyer,* May 1990, p. 62; the fourth trial is described in the appeal, *People v. Adam Abdul Hakeem, a/k/a Larry Davis,* 619 N.Y.S. 2d 33 (1994).

295   "You raised a dirty bastard": quoted in Singer, "Larry Davis Beats the Rap.".

296   "Lar-ry!, Lar-ry!": Pamela Reynolds, "A Verdict Cheers South Bronx, and 'Us-against-Them' Rift Grows," *Boston Globe,* December 6, 1988, p. 3.

296   "eloquence, instant recall": quoted in Sheryl McCarthy, "Her Case for Larry Davis," *Newsday,* December 15, 1988, pt. 2, p. 3; on role of Lynne Stewart, see also Jeffrey D. Schwartz, "In Defense of Larry Davis: Leftist Lawyer with a Cause," *New York Law Journal,* November 21, 1988, p. 1.

297   "one of the groups": quoted in Sam Howe Verhovek, "At 69, Kunstler Is Still Moved by Fervor," *New York Times,* July 28, 1988, p. B1.

297   "Larry Davis became a symbol": quoted in James Frank, "Still Crazy after All These Years," *Spy,* September 1990, p. 74.

297   Stanley Cohen claim of authorship: Leonard Levitt, "Defending Larry Davis," *Newsday,* March 21, 1988, pt. 2, p. 3.

297   "it's our theory": quoted in Mark Perkiss, UPI, April 29, 1987.

297   May and August references: Rhea Mandulo, "Prisoners Plan to Kill Davis," UPI, May 5, 1987; Ellen Wulfhorst, "Davis Transferred from Rikers Island," UPI, August 20, 1987.

298   "found some acceptance": Howard W. French, "Davis Murder Trial, Opening This Week, May Test Police Motives," *New York Times,* October 12, 1987, p. B3.

298   police used too much force: Elaine Rivera, "Police Story: Blood, Tarnish on the Shield," *Newsday,* January 1, 1989, p. 5.

298   "the experience of blacks": quoted in Tamar Jacoby with Tony Emerson, "Are Juries Colorblind?" *Newsweek,* December 5, 1988, p. 94.

298   "see police as an occupying army": quoted in Elliot Pinsley, "Kunstler Still Making the Left's Case," *Manhattan Lawyer,* August 1–7, 1989, p. 1.

298   "many police officers": quoted in French, "Davis Murder Trial, Opening This Week, May Test Police Motives."

298   "He claims he screamed": quoted in William K. Rashbaum, UPI, March 18, 1987.

299   Davis as police informer: Leonard Levitt, "Cops Say Davis was an informer," *Newsday,* March 25, 1987, p. 4.

299   "There is a lot of heat": quoted in Mandulo, "Prisoners Plan to Kill Davis."

299   fourteen stitches, "standard procedure," and "repeated harassment": Wulfhorst, "Davis Transferred from Rikers Island."

299   using a crutch: Howard W. French, "Larry Davis Is Applauded as Judge Is Named," *New York Times,* September 11, 1987, p. B3.

299   "charges of attempted murder": Rhea Mandulo, "Kunstler: Davis Must Be Released from Prison," UPI, November 25, 1987.

300   "it's a very minor incident": UPI, December 1, 1987.

300   "grabbed me from behind": David E. Pitt, "Davis Accuses Guards of Role in His Slashing," *New York Times,* December 2, 1987, p. B1.

300   "of course he's making" and "appeared to be a severe welt": David E. Pitt, "Official Says Davis Lied about His Slashing," *New York Times,* December 3, 1987, p. B3.

300   cross-examination of Captain Holmes: David E. Pitt, "No One Allowed Davis Slashing, Official Testifies," *New York Times,* December 4, 1987, p. B5.

301   offer to inmate, prosecutor acquiescence, commissioner recalcitrance: Sam Howe Verhovek, "Correction Chief Opposes Transfer of Larry Davis to Federal Prison," *New York Times,* December 8, 1987, p. B3; Douglas Martin, "Jail Commissioner Criticizes Davis and Orders Isolation," *New York Times,* December 9, 1987, p. B3; "Davis to Be Held in Federal Custody," UPI, December 9, 1987.

301   opening statement quotations and summary of evidence: Singer, "Larry Davis Beats the Rap," except "recruited at age 15," which is quoted in "Larry Davis Case Goes to Jurors," *Bergen Record*, February 24, 1988, p. A05.

303   longest deliberations and acquittal: Sam Howe Verhovek, "Larry Davis Cleared in the 1986 Slayings of 4 Drug Suspects," *New York Times,* March 4, 1988, p. 1.

303   "I don't think Larry": quoted in Verhovek, "Larry Davis Cleared in the 1986 Slayings of 4 Drug Suspects."

303   "fake trial": quoted in Sam Howe Verhovek, "2 Sides Split on Impact of Davis Verdict," *New York Times,* March 5, 1988, p. 31.

303   first time tears since Chicago: "Suspect in Drug Slayings Acquitted," *Bergen Record*, March 4, 1988, p. A03.

303   acquittal statistics: Sam Roberts, "On Bronx Juries, Minority Groups Find Their Peers," *New York Times,* May 19, 1988, p. B1.

303   "it's bizarre" and "There's no question it's": quoted in John Kifner, "Bronx Juries: A Defense Dream, a Prosecution Nightmare," *New York Times,* December 5, 1988, p. B1.

304   "their own life experience": Roberts, "On Bronx Juries, Minority Groups Find Their Peers."

304   "racists who are": quoted in Leonard Levitt and Bob Drury, "Kunstler Accused of Biased Jury Picks," *Newsday,* May 3, 1988, p. 21.

305   "force on this jury": quoted in William G. Blair, "A Judge Orders New Jury Panel for Davis Trial," *New York Times,* May 17, 1988, p. B3.

305   "the result is going to be": quoted in Roger Parloff, "Davis's Counsel Prohibited from Excluding White Jurors," *Manhattan Lawyer,* May 17–23, 1988, p. 4.

305   mistrial because of juror's fear of police harassment: Leonard Levitt and T. J. Collins, "Mistrial Declared in Davis Case," *Newsday,* June 29, 1988, p. 5; William G. Blair, "Judge Declares 2d Mistrial in Larry Davis Case in Bronx," *New York Times,* June 29, 1988, p. B3.

305   "how the police treat": quoted in Verhovek, "At 69, Kunstler Is Still Moved by Fervor."

305   "gang of corrupt police" and "went into that apartment": quoted in Manuel Perez-Rivas, "1st Police Officer at Shootout Is Set to Testify at Davis Trial," *Newsday,* September 27, 1988, p. 19.

305   "Larry wasn't going": quoted in Manuel Perez-Rivas, "Opening Arguments in Davis Trial," *Newsday,* July 27, 1988, p. 7.

305   "police will never admit": quoted in William G. Blair, "Reasons for Shootout Are Disputed at Davis Trial," *New York Times,* July 27, 1988, p. B1.

306   judges more upset when McDonald aids defense: an example is described in Robert Hanley, "Officer's Trial in Teaneck Is Disrupted," *New York Times,* February 1, 1992, p. 23.

306   wheezing and groaning: Denis Hamill, "A Road Map to the Trial," *Newsday,* July 27, 1988, p. 7.

306   "indecent" and "police histrionics": quoted in Blair, "Reasons for Shootout Are Disputed at Davis Trial."

306   "there's no way": interview with Bruce and Diane Jackson, October 12, 1996.

306 cane: Murray Kempton, "It's Not Happening in the Bronx," *Newsday,* September 7, 1988, p. 6.

306 "I've lived in the South Bronx": quoted in Singer, "Larry Davis Beats the Rap."

306 representative comments: quoted in Reynolds, "A Verdict Cheers South Bronx, and 'Us-against-Them' Rift Grows."

307 Davis was "a symbol": quoted in ibid.

307 "sends out a message": quoted in Sheryl McCarthy, Chapin Wright, and Manuel Perez-Rivas, "Davis Acquitted in Shooting of Cops, Guilty of Gun Counts," *Newsday,* November 21, 1988, p. 5.

307 "maybe there will be no more": "Davis Acquitted in Police Shootout; Found Guilty on 6 Weapons Counts," *Bergen Record,* November 21, 1988, p. A01.

307 "any black guy": quoted in Ron Rosenbaum, "The Most Hated Lawyer in America," *Vanity Fair,* March 1992, p. 72.

307 sentencing and demonstration: William G. Blair, "Larry Davis Gets 5 to 15 Years for Conviction on Weapons," *New York Times,* December 16, 1988, p. 1.

307 "racist": quoted in "5–15 Years in N.Y. Shootout; 6 Cops Wounded in '86 Battle," *Bergen Record*, December 16, 1988, p. A07.

307 "a slap on the wrist": quoted in Leonard Levitt and Ellis Henican, "Davis Gets 5–15–Year Sentence; Cops Irked by 'Slap on the Wrist,'" *Newsday,* December 16, 1988, p. 4.

307 "everyone thinks Kunstler": quoted in McCarthy, "Her Case for Larry Davis."

308 clearing the courtroom: "Held in Scuffle at 'Outrage' Hearing," *New York Times,* October 29, 1988, p. 33; Howard W. French, "Sharpton and 15 Others Arrested in Court Scuffle," *New York Times,* October 30, 1988, p. 39.

308 "the white court officers" and "wasn't going to ask": William M. Kunstler (with Sheila Isenberg), *My Life as a Radical Lawyer* (New York: Birch Lane Press, 1994), pp. 299, 300; for report of melee, see Katherine Foran and Bob Liff, "Brawley Aunt, 16 Others in Court Melee," *Newsday,* October 30, 1988, p. 3.

308 stinging pain in left knee: Craig Wolff, "Not Guilty," *GQ,* June 1994, p. 192.

NOTES TO CHAPTER 14

Page

309 history of Johnson case: Martin Garbus, "Supreme Court Retreat? The 'Crime' of Flag Burning," *Nation,* March 20, 1989, p. 369; for a complete

history, see Robert Justin Goldstein, *Burning the Flag: The Great 1989–1990 American Flag Desecration Controversy* (Kent, OH: Kent State University Press, 1996).

309   "Kunstler's high public profile": Goldstein, *Burning the Flag,* p. 95.

309   David Cole wrote the brief: William M. Kunstler (with Sheila Isenberg), *My Life as a Radical Lawyer* (New York: Birch Lane Press, 1994), p. 368; Goldstein, *Burning the Flag,* p. 271.

310   "to insulate the American flag": quoted in Curtis J. Sitomer, "Symbolic Speech," *Christian Science Monitor,* March 2, 1989, p. 13.

310   "You might have a case": quoted in M. R. Montgomery, "Literary Life," *Boston Globe,* May 30, 1989, p. 60.

310   "I don't know if I've convinced": quoted in Peter Irons, ed., *May It Please the Court: The First Amendment: Transcripts of the Oral Arguments Made before the Supreme Court in Sixteen Key First Amendment Cases* (New York: New Press, 1997), p. 224.

310   "I don't think we're going to reach": quoted in Lyle Denniston, "Flag-Burning and Free Speech," *American Lawyer,* May 1989, p. 118.

310   "pandering politicians": quoted in John Dillin, "Bush's Call Sparks Ardent Debate," *Christian Science Monitor,* July 6, 1989, p. 8.

310   "that is why it is": quoted in Carlos Sadovi, "Unrepentant Flag-Burner Criticizes Bush," *Christian Science Monitor,* June 30, 1989, p. 7.

310   "because they trusted him": Edward Hasbrouck, "William M. Kunstler, 1919–1995," on "The Flag Burning Page," Web site, September 5, 1995.

311   "The Founding Fathers'": quoted in Jack Broom, "Flag Is Still a Burning Issue Here: Judge Hears Arguments in Case That's Expected to Go to High Court," *Seattle Times,* February 15, 1990, p. D1.

311   Cole wrote second brief: David Margolick, "Law: At the Bar; The Lawyer Who Helped Set the Flag Debate Aflame Calmly Prepares to Move On," *New York Times,* June 22, 1990, p. B5.

311   "a clear example": Kunstler, *My Life,* p. 370; the disagreement between Cole and Kunstler and its resolution are also discussed in James Frank, "Still Crazy after All These Years," *Spy,* September 1990, pp. 69–70.

311   admission of daughter to Supreme Court bar: Susan Heller Anderson, "Chronicle," *New York Times,* May 16, 1990, p. B5.

311   "it seemed like we were all": quoted in Tony Mauro, "Flag-Case Forecast: No Switch in Nine," *Legal Times,* May 28, 1990, p. 11.

311   "one of the most foolhardy things": quoted in "Quotelines," *USA Today,* May 15, 1990, p. A10.

311   "once people are compelled": Goldstein, *Burning the Flag,* p. 278.

312   "all they could see": quoted in Edward J. Cleary, *Beyond the Burning*

Cross: The First Amendment and the Landmark R.A.V.*Case* (New York: Random House, 1994), p. xiv (introduction by Nat Hentoff).

312 "opposed to any ordinance": quoted by Nat Hentoff, "This Is the Hour of Danger for the First Amendment," *Village Voice,* January 28, 1992, p. 21, as reprinted in Cleary, *Beyond the Burning Cross,* p. 239 n.94.

312 general background of Central Park jogger case: see Timothy Sullivan, *Unequal Verdicts: The Central Park Jogger Trials* (New York: Simon and Schuster, 1992).

313 ineptness of trial counsel mentioned in: Mary Billard, "Notorious Trial, Anonymous Counsel," *Manhattan Lawyer,* July–August 1990, p. 29; Emily Sachar, "Lawyers Fired in Jogger Case; Convicts Hire Mason, Kunstler," *Newsday,* September 11, 1990, p. 3; Timothy Sullivan, "Jogger Juror Threatened to Block Verdict," *Manhattan Lawyer,* October 1990, p. 1.

313 no physical evidence: Emily Sachar, "Videotape, Confessions Back Case," *Newsday,* July 27, 1990, p. 3; Carol Agus, "The Defense Is Offensive," *Newsday,* September 12, 1990, p. 3.

313 "I'm convinced that what occurred": quoted in Emily Sachar, "Judge Gives 'Marauders' 5-10 Years in Jogger Case," *Newsday,* September 12, 1990, p. 3.

313 motion to set aside conviction: Emily Sachar, "Jogger Verdict Overturn Sought," *Newsday,* November 9, 1990, p. 4; Cerisse Anderson, "Kunstler Loses 3d Mistrial Bid in Jogger Case; Judge Again Rejects Attempt to Vacate Salaam Conviction," *New York Law Journal,* August 20, 1991, p. 1.

313 Salaam's mother disappointed: Craig Wolff, "Not Guilty," *GQ,* June 1994, pp. 195-96.

314 "Had Yusef Salaam been born": quoted in Gary Spencer, "Court Upholds 'Jogger Case' Conviction; Confession Admitted Despite Defendant's Age," *New York Law Journal,* December 17, 1993, p. 1.

314 "because Yusef was another": Kunstler, *My Life,* p. 304.

314 "You have exhibited": language of contempt taken from transcript reproduced in *Matter of Kunstler, petitioner, v. Galligan, respondent,* decided June 18, 1991, decision reprinted in *New York Law Journal,* June 24, 1991, p. 21.

314 "I'm not going to pay": quoted in "Lawyer in Jogger Case Held in Contempt; Kunstler Calls Trial Judge a Disgrace," *Bergen Record,* December 21, 1990, p. A03.

314 Appellate Division decision: reprinted in full, with dissent, in *New York Law Journal,* June 24, 1991, p. 21; Court of Appeals decision discussed in *New York Law Journal,* December 19, 1991, p. 1.

314 "I do not think": quoted in "Across the Nation," *San Diego Union-Tri-*

bune, January 18, 1992, p. A2.

314 "if there is any justice": from *Orange County Shield,* quoted in Anthony Scaduto, Doug Vaughan, and Linda Stasi, "Inside New York," *Newsday,* January 17, 1992, p. 13.

314 fine paid by anonymous benefactor: "Today's News Update," *New York Law Journal,* January 21, 1992, p. 1.

315 disciplinary committee hearing: Daniel Wise, "Kunstler Disciplinary Hearing Takes on Conciliatory Tones," *New York Law Journal,* November 16, 1992, p. 1.

315 committee recommendation: "Today's News Update," *New York Law Journal,* May 26, 1993, p. 1.

315 "commendable attempt to insure": quoted in Frances A. McMorris, "Kunstler Censured," *National Law Journal,* January 10, 1994, p. 2.

315 "to preserve the personal liberties": quoted in William Murphy, "Kunstler Censured for Bark at Judge," *Newsday,* December 29, 1993, p. 7.

315 "made me feel terrific": Kunstler, *My Life,* p. 392.

315 Appellate Division opinion: text of opinion attached to Frances A. McMorris, "Kunstler Censured for Comments to Trial Judge," *New York Law Journal,* December 29, 1993, p. 1.

315 "the establishment speaking": Murphy, "Kunstler Censured for Bark at Judge."

315 "badge of honor" through "I doubt anybody": McMorris, "Kunstler Censured."

315 "whom I knew was going": William Kunstler, radio interview with Gil Gross, CBS Radio, September 19, 1994.

316 Kunstler representation of Ferguson: Michael Alexander, "Ferguson Lawyers Denied Funds," *Newsday,* April 22, 1994, p. A07.

316 "years of exposure": quoted in Sylvia Adcock, "'Black Rage' Strategy: New Insanity Defense in LIRR Massacre," *Newsday,* March 15, 1994, p. 7.

316 "never developed the defense": quoted in Acel Moore, "Justice for a True Villain," *Tampa Tribune,* March 25, 1995, p. 19.

316 experts: Michael Alexander, "Black Rage," *Newsday,* May 9, 1994, p. B04; Tracie Reddick, "Black Rage; Anger over Racism Is Blamed for a Rampage That Left Six Dead," *Tampa Tribune,* December 4, 1994, p. 1.

316 law review articles: see, e.g., Richard J. Bonnie, "Excusing and Punishing in Criminal Adjudication: A Reality Check," *Cornell Journal of Law and Public Policy,* fall 1995, p. 1; Kimberly M. Copp, "Black Rage: The Illegitimacy of a Criminal Defense," *John Marshall Law Review,* fall 1995, p. 205; Robert P. Mosteller, "Syndromes and Politics in Criminal Trials and Evidence Law," *Duke Law Journal,* December 1996, p. 461;

and Judd F. Sneirson, "Black Rage and the Criminal Law: A Principled Approach to a Polarized Debate," *University of Pennsylvania Law Review,* June 1995, p. 2251.

316 book-length study: Paul Harris, *Black Rage Confronts the Law* (New York: New York University Press, 1997), pp. 154–62.

316 "There is an educative factor": quoted in Alexander, "Black Rage."

316 "I've never been able": quoted in Robert I. Friedman, "The Color of Rage," *Vanity Fair,* January 1995, p. 30.

316 "to get people to think": quoted in Paul Vitello, "Ugly Scenes in America's House," *Newsday,* March 17, 1994, p. 8.

317 "another stellar example": Jack Walker, "'Black Rage' Defense Could Be Adapted to Any Group," *Buffalo News,* April 25, 1994, p. 2.

317 "near the bottom": Don Feder, "Victims' Blood All the Same Color," *Boston Herald,* June 9, 1994, p. 029.

317 "the sense he applauds": James Lileks, "Hate America? Just Call Kunstler," *Plain Dealer,* March 27, 1994, p. C6.

317 national poll: Rorie Sherman, "Crime's Toll on the U.S.: Fear, Despair and Guns," *National Law Journal,* April 18, 1994, p. A1.

317 "At best, I think": Clarence Page, "Black-Rage Defense Smacks of Old Stereotypes," *Bergen Record,* May 31, 1994, p. D07.

317 "a danger that legitimate": Joel Dreyfuss, "This Defense Plays into White Hands," *Newsday,* March 30, 1994, p. 34.

317 "is really suggesting is that": quoted in Jim Dwyer, "Al Sharpton, Ambassador?" *Newsday,* April 1, 1994, p. 2.

317 "most people, black or white": quoted in Ronald A. Taylor, "Jail Inmates Beat Shooting Suspect," *Washington Times,* April 4, 1994, p. A8.

317 "you've got to start": Kunstler, interview with Gross.

319 "a clearer case": quoted in Randy Furst, "Shabazz Defense and Prosecution Clash over Meaning of Statement," *Minneapolis Star Tribune,* February 28, 1995, p. A1.

319 "the constant urging": quoted in Margaret Zack, "Shabazz Attorney Alleges Government Misconduct; Kunstler Will Move to Have Case Dismissed," *Minneapolis Star Tribune,* February 14, 1995, p. B1.

319 "saw the gravy train": quoted in Carolyn Pesce, "Farrakhan Case Witness Says Feds Are Paying Him $45,000," *USA Today,* March 24, 1995, p. A7.

319 "a continuation of an old scheme": quoted in Carolyn Pesce, "'My Daughter Had Nothing to Do with This,'" *USA Today,* January 19, 1995, p. A2.

319 "some crazy out there": quoted in Joe Conason, "Farrakhan Is Right: Reopen the X Files," *San Francisco Examiner,* February 20, 1995, p. A19.

319 "galvanize the black community": quoted in Elaine Rivera, "'Terrible

Irony': Supporters of Malcolm X Rally for Daughter's Trial," *Newsday*, February 19, 1995, p. A29.

319 "diabolical scheme": quoted in Richard Jerome, "In the Name of Her Father; The FBI Claims Malcolm X's Daughter Qubilah Plotted to Kill Louis Farrakhan," *People*, January 30, 1995, p. 40.

319 black reaction to case: Geordie Greig, "Malcolm X Haunts His Daughter's Trial," *Sunday Times* (London), February 26, 1995, in "Overseas News."

319 petition circulated by daughter: Zack, "Shabazz Attorney Alleges Government Misconduct".

320 "It's an enormous defeat": quoted in Rogers Worthington, "U.S. Strikes a Deal in Farrakhan Plot; Malcolm X's Daughter Admits Role, Avoids Trial," *Chicago Tribune*, May 2, 1995, p. 1.

320 "In my opinion, the case": quoted in Malcolm Gladwell, "U.S., Shabazz Settle Farrakhan Murder Plot Case," *Washington Post*, May 2, 1995, p. A01.

320 "It's good for these judges": quoted in Louis Sahagun, "Brando Case Is a Natural for Kunstler," *Los Angeles Times*, May 29, 1990, p. B1.

320 "in the wrong country": quoted in "N.Y. Judge Turns Down Church Plea to Shut Play," *Bergen Record*, October 12, 1990, p. A08.

321 "this is New York": quoted in "Voices: 1994," *Life*, Annual 1994, p. 8.

321 "Muslims are the most": Kunstler, *My Life*, p. 317.

322 "it's ethically correct": ibid., p. 319.

322 "If Nosair did kill Kahane": ibid., p. 324.

323 "You can get in the whole": quoted in Sam Adler, "Centre Street's Tough Guy," *Manhattan Lawyer*, March 1991, p. 1.

323 "We had people in the courtroom": quoted in "Kunstler Urges Muslims to Back Bombing Suspects," *Bergen Record*, November 8, 1993, p. A04 (recalling earlier Nosair case).

323 "A one-man whirlwind": quoted in Bill Gertz, "Bombing Suspect Assisted Defense in Kahane Trial," *Washington Times*, March 10, 1993, p. A3.

323 "he worked like a dog for us": quoted in Patricia Cohen, "Judge Denies Bail to Second Suspect," *Newsday*, March 6, 1993, p. 5.

323 $163,000: Jim Dwyer, David Kocieniewski, Deidre Murphy, and Peg Tyre, *Two Seconds under the World: Terror Comes to America—The Conspiracy behind the World Trade Center Bombing* (New York: Crown, 1994), p. 129.

323 "The doctor might": quoted in "Indictment Stands in Kahane Killing; Judge Denies Dismissal Move," *Bergen Record*, October 17, 1991, p. A12.

324 press conference disturbance: Emily Sachar, "Kahane Charges Spark

Melee," *Newsday,* October 16, 1991, p. 20; "Clash Erupts at Hotel over the Kahane Case," *New York Times,* October 16, 1991, p. B2.

325   "Brooklyn Jewish accent": Emily Sachar and Wendell Jamieson, "A Not Guilty in Killing of Rabbi Kahane," *Newsday,* December 22, 1991, p. 4.

325   "Revenge" and "Death to Nosair": Jonathon Schachter, "Convicted of Four Lesser Charges Nosair Acquitted of Killing Meir Kahane," *Jerusalem Post,* December 23, 1991, "News" section.

325   proposed march on jurors' homes: "Jews Urge New Probe in Slaying; Acquittal in Death of Kahane Ripped," *San Diego Union-Tribune,* December 23, 1991, p. A3.

325   "against the overwhelming weight": quoted in "Judge Criticizes Acquittal in Kahane Death," *Chicago Tribune,* January 10, 1992, p. 3.

325   "laughably amateurish": quoted in "Prosecutors Blamed in Nosair's Acquittal," *Bergen Record,* December 24, 1991, p. A03.

325   "Kunstler knows better": quoted in Laurie Goodstein, "Kahane Jurors Explain Acquittal on Main Counts," *Washington Post,* December 23, 1991, p. A4.

325   "largely black jury": Patrick Brogan, "Race and a Running Back," Glasgow *Herald,* October 4, 1995, p. 8.

325   jury's racial composition: Goodstein, "Kahane Jurors Explain Acquittal on Main Counts."

326   Margie pressured: Kunstler, *My Life,* p. 329.

326   "plot to bomb everything": ibid., p. 332; interview with Ronald L. Kuby, July 17, 1996.

327   denial of court-appointed status: Andrew Blum, "Sharing Fees," *National Law Journal,* February 21, 1994, p. 2.

327   "the Government is going absolutely berserk": quoted in Richard Bernstein, "As Prelude to Terrorism Case, Prosecution and Defense Team Wrangle," *New York Times,* August 21, 1994, p. 47.

327   "Increasingly, the government": quoted in "2 Lawyers Ousted from Bomb Case," *Chicago Tribune,* August 26, 1994, p. 22.

327   "for his part, Judge Mukasey": quoted in Richard Bernstein, "Judge Disqualifies Kunstler Firm from Role in Bombing-Plot Trial," *New York Times,* August 26, 1994, p. 1.

328   JDO besieged Kunstler at courthouse: "Kahane Suspect's Lawyers Besieged," *Bergen Record,* February 26, 1991, p. A03; Sheila Isenberg, "Afterwords," in Kunstler, *My Life* (2d ed., 1996), pp. 418–19.

328   "snide laugh" and Sliwa demonstration: UPI, March 15, 1985.

329   "self-hating Jew": Larry McShane, "Bill Kunstler Leaves His Mark, Outrageously Fighting for the Underdog," *Los Angeles Times,* Decem-

ber 19, 1993, p. 44; interview with Bruce and Diane Jackson, October 12, 1996.

329   "Not one night of sleep": Steven T. Taylor, "They Love Him, They Hate Him," *National Jurist,* January 1994, p. 12; David Margolick, "Still Radical after All These Years," *New York Times,* July 6, 1993, p. B1.

329   "I hope you will bear": Taylor, "They Love Him, They Hate Him," p. 12; Margolick, "Still Radical."

329   neighbors supportive: Kunstler, *My Life,* p. 319.

329   coffee and doughnuts: Wolff, "Not Guilty," p. 196.

329   harassment and threats: Kunstler, *My Life,* p. 319; Ben Macintyre, "A Man Who Is Courting Hate," *Times* (London), October 8, 1993, n.p.; Laurie Goodstein, "Muslim Acquitted in Kahane Slaying, Found Guilty on Weapons Charge," *Washington Post,* December 22, 1991, p. A4; Taylor, "They Love Him, They Hate Him" p. 12; Wolff, "Not Guilty," p. 196.

329   "that's for your Arab clients": Margolick, "Still Radical."

329   "Thank God": Emily Kunstler, interview with Margie Ratner and Emily Kunstler, June 9, 1998.

329   "William Kunstler is where he belongs!": quoted in Richard Perez-Pena, "1,000 Honor Kunstler, Defender of Their Faith," *New York Times,* November 20, 1995, p. B11 (subsequently the attendance estimate was corrected upwards to three thousand).

329   "traitor": Michael T. Kaufman, "A High Court Fantasy: Kunstler Ponders a Fancy," *New York Times,* April 14, 1993, p. B3.

329   "fuck you, Kunstler!": Paul Moses, "At Age 71, Attorney William M. Kunstler Still Relishes a Tough Fight for Unpopular People and Causes," *Newsday Magazine,* January 6, 1991, p. 8.

330   liberal lawyers criticized: Kunstler, *My Life,* p. 329; Rekha Basu, "Curtain on a Class Act," *Des Moines Register,* September 10, 1995, Opinion, p. 1.

330   "can you imagine": quoted in Jimmy Breslin, "Never Popular, Always Fighting," *Newsday,* September 5, 1995, p. A02.

330   "still very much," "if anything, increased," and "Nothing is Placid": Kunstler, *My Life,* pp. 263–64.

330   arguments between Kunstler and Margie: this description is based on interviews with over six friends and associates. I am satisfied that the essentials are accurate. It would serve no useful purpose to specify the individuals, the names of some of whom I have promised not to reveal.

330   wearing of rings: Margaret Ratner, "Afterwords," in Kunstler, *My Life* (2d ed., 1996), pp. 406–7.

331   Karin Goldman and Jane Drazek requests: Kunstler, *My Life,* p. 329;

interviews with Jane Kunstler Drazek, October 8, 1996, and Karin Kunstler Goldman, October 15, 1996.

331   "couldn't say no": Kunstler, *My Life,* p. 314.

331   "as long as the color": Kuby interview.

331   "he can contort" and "a big-money lawyer": quoted in Taylor, "They Love Him, They Hate Him," p. 14.

331   "virulently anti-Israel": Alan M. Dershowitz, *Chutzpah* (Boston: Little, Brown, 1991), p. 81.

331   "the David Duke of the legal": quoted in F. Peter Model, Sid Lerner, and Hal Drucker, "Chatting with Bill Kunstler over General Noriega's Cookies," *New York Law Journal,* September 18, 1995, p. 2 (1993 interview).

332   "a pretty horrible person": quoted in ibid.

332   92d Street Y: Richard Perez-Pena, "At the Bar," *New York Times,* October 28, 1994, p. 29; Mary Voboril, "3 Lawyers with Egos Out of Order," *Newsday,* October 30, 1994, p. 32.

332   private note thanking Dershowitz: Kuby interview.

NOTES TO CHAPTER 15

Page

333   "the ring of truth": quoted in David Margolick, "Still Radical after All These Years," *New York Times,* July 6, 1993, p. B1.

333   "the long-standing publicity": interview with Jack B. Weinstein, July 16, 1996.

333   Brice Marden observation: interview with Brice Marden, October 15, 1996.

333   "you fag loving son-of-a-bitch": interview with Bruce and Diane Jackson, October 12, 1996.

333   critical letters: Fred Roth, "Lindbergh: A Traitor, but No Killer," *Bergen Record,* April 28, 1993, p. C06; Billups P. Percy, "Criminal Justice Concerns," *Times-Picayune,* March 1, 1995, p. B6; F. A. Pflugh, "A Lack of Moral Fiber?" *Bergen Record,* May 31, 1995, p. 002.

333   "sanctimonious creep": Al D'Amato, *Power, Pasta and Politics: The World According to Senator Al D'Amato* (New York: Hyperion, 1995), p. 301.

333   black prisoners: interview with Sol Wachtler, January 25, 1998.

334   "I knew of you": William M. Kunstler (with Sheila Isenberg) *My Life as a Radical Lawyer* (New York: Birch Lane Press, 1994), p. 129.

334   "you remember me?" and subway story: Bruce and Diane Jackson interview.

334   "mean-spirited, racist": Kunstler, *My Life,* p. 360.

334   "is nothing other than": quoted in Margaret Ratner, "Afterwords," in Kunstler, *My Life* (2d ed., 1996), p. 403.

335   "courageous efforts": Robert W. Vinal, "Panel Discusses Sentencing Reform," *New York Law Journal,* January 24, 1996, p. S7.

335   Harry Belafonte recollections: Bruce and Diane Jackson interview.

335   "will the mothers stand?" and forty mothers: Gerald Lefcourt recollections in Paul Moses, "At Age 71, Attorney William M. Kunstler Still Relishes a Tough Fight for Unpopular People and Causes," *Newsday Magazine,* January 6, 1991, p. 8.

335   "old, frowzy, Kunstler-esque": Jill Schensul, "Finding Myself," *Bergen Record,* March 31, 1996, p. T01.

335   "as badly dressed as William Kunstler": Lewis H. Lapham, "Jefferson on Toast; Mock Movie Concept; Column," *Harper's Magazine,* June 1995, p. 7.

335   "the eyeglasses and hair": Stuart Klawans, "Roger and Me," *Nation,* October 30, 1989, p. 505.

335   "a William M. Kunstler type of counselor": John Tagliabue, "Terrorist Lecture Spurs Debate," *New York Times,* December 5, 1980, p. D1.

335   "the William Kunstler of his day": Bill Tammues, "Words for the Wise, or Weary or Whoever Listens," *Kansas City Star,* April 23, 1995, p. I4.

336   "tiresome lawyer": *Chicago Tribune,* August 13, 1989, p. 5.

336   "professional practitioners": *Washington Times,* April 17, 1990, p. F2.

336   "lawyer-disrupter": *Dallas Morning News,* October 19, 1992, p. A17.

336   "gassy, unavoidable": *Minneapolis Star Tribune,* March 29, 1994, p. A17.

336   "world-class excuse-maker": *Los Angeles Times,* May 26, 1994, p. F10.

336   "'60s detritus": *Boston Globe,* December 11, 1994, p. 86.

336   "a disease America contracted": *Boston Herald,* December 29, 1994, p. 027.

336   "lawyer for causes of which none": *Washington Post,* May 16, 1995, p. A17.

336   "schlemiel with an edge": *New York Times,* June 2, 1995, p. B6.

336   Kunstler response suggesting "chachem" or "momser": *New York Times,* June 7, 1995, p. A26.

336   media appearances: résumé of William M. Kunstler, April 1995 (for most); *Larry King*: William F. Buckle, "The Simpson Trial—Up from Witchcraft," *Buffalo News,* July 13, 1994, p. 3; *Geraldo*: Andy Edelstein, "TV Spots," *Newsday,* August 2, 1994, p. B53.

336   "Winter Wonderland": Verne Gay, "TV Spots," *Newsday,* December 30, 1993, p. 85.

336   "Where is he?": "Names in the News; Nixon, Kunstler Meet at Studio," *Los Angeles Times,* June 14, 1990, p. P9; John Carmody, "The TV Column," *Washington Post,* June 15, 1990, p. C4.

336   "the number of talking attorneys": quoted in Kevin Johnson and Dennis Cauchon, "Simpson Prosecutors to Hit Core of Case," *USA Today*, February 14, 1995, p. A4.

336   *National Law Journal* survey: reported in Merrie Morris, "About Town; Merrie-Go-Round," *Washington Times*, November 2, 1993, p. C15.

336   seventy-fifth birthday: carried in many New York newspapers, but also in *Sacramento Bee* (California), July 7, 1994, p. A2.

336   shopping at Balducci's: Jim Holt, "Celeb City: New York's Frenzy of Renown; Manhattan Name-Dropping," *New Republic*, September 7, 1992, p. 11.

337   hundred most important Americans: *Time*, special issue, fall 1990, p. 101.

337   pet trial: Joseph L. Baldwin, *Courier-Journal*, May 18, 1989, p. A2; Karen Payne, "Are Cats Really the Top Dogs?" *National Law Journal*, May 22, 1989, p. 43.

337   beach reading: Matthew Flamm, "Page Turners," *New York*, June 27, 1994, p. 120.

337   fashion photo feature: Timothy Greenfield-Sanders, "The Politics of Dressing," *New York*, February 27, 1995, p. 58.

337   P. J. O'Rourke, quoted in Danny Goldberg, review of *Parliament of Whores, Nation*, June 22, 1992, p. 866.

337   books with major characters based on Kunstler: review of Peter Abrahams, *Revolution #9*, in *Kirkus Reviews*, June 1, 1992; review of Lawrence Block, *A Long Line of Dead Men*, in *Publishers Weekly*, July 18, 1994, p. 237; review of Robert Daley, *Tainted Evidence*, in *Kirkus Reviews*, January 1, 1993.

337   reviews of *True Believer*: Jay Carr, *Boston Globe*, February 17, 1989, p. 85; Jack Garner, *Courier-Journal*, February 18, 1989, p. S19; Dave Kehr, *Chicago Tribune*, February 17, 1989, "movie review," p. D.

337   review of *Class Action*: David Klinghoffer, *Washington Times*, March 15, 1991, p. E3.

337   reviews of *Night Falls on Manhattan*: James Ryan, "The Comeback Kid Tries Again," *New York Times*, January 14, 1996, sec. 2, p. 11; "Fall Movie Preview," *Entertainment Weekly*, August 23 and August 30, 1996 (double issue), p. 28.

337   approval of characterization: "Good Morning," *Daily Variety*, November 6, 1995, p. 2.

337   "there's something about": quoted in UPI, January 18, 1987.

337   films and several videos: for example, Reliance National and the American Bar Association's *Creative Defenses*; California Newsreel's *Doing Justice: The Life and Trials of Arthur Kinoy* (1993); Robert Redford's *Incident at Oglala* (1991), PBS's *Mississippi, America* (1995), HBO's *Con-*

spiracy: The Trial of the Chicago 8 (1987); Morley Markson's *Growing Up in America* (1989); and Jack Baxter and Jefri Aalmuhammed's documentary about the assassination of Malcolm X (1994) (not to be confused with Spike Lee's feature-length film).

337 The Trial of the Catonsville Nine (play): Joe Brown, "At Castle Arts, Antiwar and Remembrance," *Washington Post,* August 17, 1987, p. C2.

337 *Tie Me Up!* and NC-17 rating: Doris Toumarkine, "Dershowitz on 'Clerks' Case," *Hollywood Reporter,* August 10, 1994; Kirk Honeycutt, "'Advocate' Gets a Famous One: William Kunstler," *Hollywood Reporter,* August 9, 1994.

338 *The Advocate*: Greg Evans, "Miramax Films Taps Kunstler," *Daily Variety,* August 9, 1994, p. 6.

338 substituted Lenny Bruce argument: Debra Carr, "William Kunstler Is Shown the Doors," *National Law Journal,* March 18, 1991, p. 43.

338 "Coming up with my own": quoted in "Radical Interpretations," *New Yorker,* July 19, 1993, p. 27.

338 filmed in May 1990: *USA Today,* May 25, 1990, p. D2.

338 "He plays himself": Paul Baumann, "Sex, Drugs & Rock 'n' Roll: Oliver Stone's 'The Doors,'" *Commonweal,* May 3, 1991, p. 295.

338 "you do that": quoted by Kunstler in Karin Lipson, Steve Garbarino, and Joey Berlin, "Culture Vulture," *Newsday,* January 26, 1992, p. 3.

338 worked for scale: Anthony Scaduto, "Inside New York," *Newsday,* September 20, 1991, p. 13.

338 "I love it": Robin Micheli, "Here Come de Judge," *People,* September 2, 1991, p. 31.

338 "I never thought I'd": quoted in "Radical Interpretations."

338 press release: *New York Law Journal,* June 30, 1993, p. 1.

338 Gus' Place: "Party for the First Part," *Minneapolis Star Tribune,* July 7, 1994, p. B3.

339 "blathering at a party": Bart Jansen, "Little Depth in 'The Paper,'" *Capital,* April 1, 1994, p. T14.

339 I don't think I'm": quoted in Lipson et al., "Culture Vulture."

339 "a little distressed": quoted in Matthew Purdy, "Cameos Bloom, and Not Subtly Either," *New York Times,* April 10, 1994, sec. 2, p. 29.

339 *Politically Incorrect*: Paul Levy, "'Political Correctness' on the Stage," *Minneapolis Star Tribune,* July 25, 1993, p. E3; Lawrence Christon, "Television; In Too Deep?" *Los Angeles Times,* September 5, 1993, calendar sec., p. 5; Mick LaSalle, "Political Satire among the Ruins," *San Francisco Chronicle,* December 16, 1993, p. D1.

339 *Comedy Central News*: Ben Kubasik, "TV Spots," *Newsday,* June 1, 1994, pt. 2, p. 73.

339 "the veteran, colorful barrister": Adam Sandler, "Law and Order WHITE RABBIT," *Daily Variety*, October 19, 1994.

339 "reflects his sense of fun": quoted in Simi Horwitz, "'Law & Order' Gets Tough DA, Better Ratings," *Washington Post*, November 27, 1994, p. Y6.

339 "this country is mad": quoted in David Barton, "The Lion Roars," *Sacramento Bee*, October 13, 1994, p. E1.

339 timing of pacemaker to comedy show: James Barron, "Chronicle," *New York Times*, August 9, 1995, p. B4.

340 "Is the statute of limitations": quoted in Bruce Weber, "May It Please the Audience: Kunstler Does Comedy," *New York Times*, August 10, 1995, p. B3.

340 "What is the difference": quoted in "Eye Spy," *Austin American-Statesman*, November 13, 1994, p. G1.

340 "warmly applauded by a full": Weber, "May It Please the Audience."

340 Santa Barbara commemorative: Catherine Foster, "Activists Gather to Check Ideals," *Christian Science Monitor*, March 1, 1990, p. 8.

340 Mississippi Challenge: Moses, "At Age 71, Attorney William M. Kunstler Still Relishes a Tough Fight."

340 National Civil Rights Museum: "Tragic Motel Dedicated as New Museum," *Chicago Tribune*, July 5, 1991, p. 4; Wayne Risher, "Museum Speakers Received Payment," *Memphis Commercial Appeal*, July 10, 1991, p. B1.

340 Wounded Knee reunion: Kunstler, *My Life*, pp. 258–60; Bruce H. Ellison, "William Kunstler: A People's Lawyer," *South Dakota Law Review*, 1996, p. 229.

340 activities with Karin: interview with Karin Kunstler Goldman, October 15, 1996.

340 activities with Mary: interview with Mary Kunstler Horn and Manny Horn, October 17, 1996.

341 Charles Garry: William M. Kunstler, "Obituary: Charles Garry," *Independent*, August 22, 1991, p. 35; "Charles Garry," *San Francisco Chronicle*, September 21, 1991, p. C10.

341 Morton Stavis: "Memorial Service for Morton Stavis," *New York Law Journal*, February 5, 1993, p. 2.

341 Abbie Hoffman: "The Nation," *Los Angeles Times*, June 11, 1989, p. 2; Katherine Foran, "Friends Recall Man Who Stood Larger Than Life; Life with 'No Regrets,'" *Newsday*, June 18, 1989, p. 4.

341 Huey Newton: Steve Rushin, "Chapter Four: The Long, Hard Run," *Sports Illustrated*, August 16, 1994, p. 57.

341 Bruce Bailey: Mitch Gelman, "Tenant Organizer Eulogized: 'Bruce's

Work Will Not Die,'" *Newsday,* June 25, 1989, p. 38; D. D. Guttenplan, "Who Killed Bruce Bailey?" *Newsday,* July 16, 1989, p. 4.

341   Charles Garry obituary: Kunstler, "Obituary: Charles Garry."

341   Newton, Hoffman, and Rubin obituaries: Godfrey Hodgson, "Obituary: William Kunstler," *Independent,* September 6, 1995, p. 14.

341   *Los Angeles Times* obituary: William M. Kunstler, "'Ruckuses' Abbie Hoffman Raised Were Part of the Greening of America," *Los Angeles Times,* April 19, 1989, pt. 2, p. 7.

341   "Jerry fully paid": William M. Kunstler, "Obituary: Jerry Rubin," *Independent,* November 30, 1994, p. 03.

341   "People get older": quoted in Esther Pessin, UPI, August 26, 1985.

341   "worthy opponent" through "respond with": quoted in "Judge Julius Hoffman Dies; Presided over 'Chicago 7' Trial," *Washington Post,* July 2, 1983, p. D6.

341   "come to realize": quoted in Bruce Olson, "Whole World No Longer Watching," UPI, July 2, 1983.

341   "as much a victim": William M. Kunstler, *Trials and Tribulations* (New York: Grove Press, 1985), p. 30.

341   1960s Kunstler's high point: Karin Kunstler Goldman interview.

341   "growing sense of isolation": quoted in Hodgson, "Obituary: William Kunstler."

342   "was giving grudging recognition": Kunstler, "'Ruckuses' Abbie Hoffman Raised Were Part of the Greening of America."

342   Tiananmen Square: William M. Kunstler, "Criticism of Socialist Nations for Rights Violations by the Left," *Los Angeles Times,* June 24, 1989, pt. 2, p. 9.

342   Tibet House: Ian Katz, "Hey Buddhies, Can You Spare a Dime?" *Guardian,* March 2, 1995, p. T4.

342   "very arbitrary": quoted in Patricia Hurtado, "Furor Is Nothing New for Jurist; He Gets Mixed Reviews," *Newsday,* March 1, 1989, p. 4.

342   $100,000 income derived from talks and royalties: Larry McShane, "Bill Kunstler Leaves His Mark, Outrageously Fighting for the Underdog," *Los Angeles Times,* December 19, 1993, p. A44; John S. Curtiss, "Justice Was Served," *Cincinnati Enquirer,* September 23, 1995, p. A11.

343   "raise their consciousness": Daniel Seligman, "Only in America," *Fortune,* April 16, 1984, p. 147.

343   New York Law School seminar: "New York Law Adds Kunstler and Kinoy," *New York Law Journal,* July 8, 1992, p. 4.

343   Spence's seminar in Wyoming: Thomas Scheffey, "Happy Trails to You," *Connecticut Law Tribune,* July 3, 1995, p. 3; Michael Sneed, *Chicago Sun-Times,* June 10, 1994, p. 2.

343 Nosair: "Muslim Activist's Lawyer," *Pittsburgh Post-Gazette,* November 8, 1993, p. A4.

343 World Trade bombing defendants: Kevin McCoy, "Bomb Suspects Backed," *Newsday,* November 7, 1993, p. 3; "Kunstler Urges Muslims to Back Bombing Suspects," *Bergen Record,* November 8, 1993, p. A04.

343 Qubilah Shabazz: Brian Ballou, "Daughters Unite; Rights Leaders' Children Join to Aid Qubilah," *Newsday,* January 26, 1995, p. A15; Charisse Jones, "Crowds Fill Apollo to Witness Shabazz and Farrakhan Meet," *New York Times,* May 7, 1995, p. 45; Malcolm Gladwell, "Farrakhan Seeks End of Rift with Shabazz," *Washington Post,* May 8, 1995, p. A01.

343 Central America: Tito Davila, UPI, June 9, 1984; UPI, June 7, 1984; "Thousands in Midtown," *New York Times,* June 10, 1984, p. 44.

343 Middle East: Karen Freifeld, "Hundreds Protest Mideast Action," *Newsday,* September 14, 1990, p. 19; Joyce Price, "Leftist 'Network' Leaps into Action," *Washington Times,* September 25, 1990, p. A9; Anthony Scaduto, Doug Vaughan, and Linda Stasi, "Inside New York: No War, No Way," *Newsday,* January 11, 1991, p. 11.

343 tenant squatters: "Protest in Tompkins Square Park," *Newsday,* May 10, 1989, p. 19.

343 student concerns: Edward A. Adams, "Few Area Schools Participate in National Student Protest," *New York Law Journal,* April 6, 1990, p. 1; "C.C.N.Y. Students Protest Tuition Increases," *New York Times,* April 25, 1989, p. B3.

343 black causes: "Jury Ends 11th Day of Deliberations in Howard Beach Death Case," *Los Angeles Times,* December 21, 1987, p. 23; Steven Erlanger, "500 Mourn Man Killed in Queens," *New York Times,* December 21, 1987, p. B1; Laurie C. Merrill and Elizabeth Llorente, "Appeal for Calm; Outrage Erupts in N.Y.C.," *Bergen Record,* May 2, 1992, p. A01.

343 Cuba protest: Pamela Newkirk and Wendell Jamieson, "High Fidel-ity Rally; U.S. Urged to Lift Bars to Travel, Trade with Cuba," *Newsday,* January 26, 1992, p. 3.

343 medicines to Cuba: "Kunstler, Others Take Medicine to Cuba," *Washington Times,* July 16, 1992, p. A2.

343 Rehnquist testimony: Andrea Neal, UPI, August 1, 1986.

343 "He's a black snake": quoted in Wayne Risher, "Kunstler Tells Rights Symposium: Thomas No Ally of Minorities," *Memphis Commercial Appeal,* July 2, 1991, p. A1.

343 Pee-Wee Herman: Anthony Scaduto, Doug Vaughan, and Linda Stasi, "Inside New York: Fast Facts," *Newsday,* August 7, 1991, p. 13; James Steinberg, "Prisoner of Conscience," *San Diego Union-Tribune,* August 9, 1991, p. D-2.

343   Animal Rights session: Alice Kahn, "Outgoing Bar President Epito-
      mizes Today's Lawyer," *San Francisco Chronicle,* August 10, 1992, p.
      A13.

343   "'speciesism'": William M. Kunstler, foreword to Gary L. Francione,
      Animals, Property, and the Law (Philadelphia: Temple University Press,
      1995), p. x.

343   "There is a time to act": quoted in Alexander Cockburn, "The Pariah's
      Farewell: Attorney William M. Kunstler," *Nation,* October 2, 1995, p.
      341.

344   *Nation* articles, 1980–95: October 22, 1983, p. 360; June 30, 1984, p. 796;
      March 25, 1991, p. 364; January 23, 1995, p. 81.

344   law review articles: "Symposium on Federal and State Methods of Re-
      pressing Political Activism," *New York University Review of Law and So-
      cial Change,* June 1987, p. 429; "The Bill of Rights—Can It Survive?"
      New York University Review of Law and Social Change, 1990–91, p. 5; "A
      'Real World' Perspective on the New Property," *University of San Fran-
      cisco Law Review,* winter 1990, p. 291; "William O. Douglas Lecture: The
      Bill of Rights—Can It Survive?" *Gonzaga Law Review,* 1990–91, p. 1;
      "Enduring the Storm: Conscientious Objectors in the Persian Gulf
      War," *St. John's Law Review,* 1992, p. 655 (with Ronald L. Kuby); "Si-
      lencing the Oppressed: No Freedom of Speech for Those behind the
      Walls," *Creighton Law Review,* June 1993, p. 1005 (with Ronald L. Kuby);
      "Mugging the Fourth," *Covert Action,* Summer 1995, p. 53 (with Phillip
      Smith); "So Crazy He Thinks He Is Sane: The Colin Ferguson Trial and
      the Competency Standard," *Cornell Journal of Law and Public Policy,* fall
      1995, p. 19 (with Ronald L. Kuby).

344   Kunstler review of Arthur Kinoy's *Rights on Trial: The Odyssey of a Peo-
      ple's Lawyer*: *National Law Journal,* February 6, 1984, p. 33.

344   chapter: in Ramsey Clark, ed., *War Crimes: A Report on United States
      War Crimes against Iraq* (Washington, D.C.: Maisonneuve Press, 1992).

344   forewords: in Bruce Jackson, *Disorderly Conduct* (Urbana: University of
      Illinois Press, 1992); Ronald Fernandez, *The Disenchanted Island: Puerto
      Rico and the United States in the Twentieth Century* (New York: Praeger,
      1992); Ken Wachsberger, ed., *Voices from the Underground,* vol. 1, *Insider
      Histories of the Vietnam Era Underground Press* (Tempe, AZ: Mica's Press,
      1993); Francione, *Animals, Property, and the Law.*

344   reporters commented and early publications: UPI, April 21, 1983;
      "Legal Sonnets," *National Law Journal,* April 23, 1984, p. 13; David Bird
      and Eleanor Blau, "Advocate and Poet," *New York Times,* January 25,
      1986, p. 31.

344   *Trials and Tribulations* (New York: Grove Press, 1985).

345   *Hints & Allegations* (New York: Four Walls Eight Windows, 1994).

345   Simpson sonnets: "To an O. J.," *Esquire,* September 1994, p. 50; "When the Cheering Stopped; Poem," *Harper's Magazine,* February 1995, p. 28; Wilder Penfield III, "By the Numbers," *Toronto Sun,* May 18, 1995, p. 64; Dennis Cauchon, "Today in Court: Poet's Corner," *USA Today,* February 1, 1995, p. A8; "Shall I Compare Thee to a Bloody Glove?" *New York,* April 17, 1995, p. 36; Cathleen Schine, "Endpaper: The 13th Sign," *New York Times,* February 19, 1995, Sect. 6, p. 64.

345   sales less than two thousand: Max Gartenberg (Kunstler's agent for this book) to David J. Langum, November 20, 1997.

345   gentle criticism: "Some Season's Readings for Lawyers," *National Law Journal,* December 26, 1994–January 2, 1995, p. A22; "To an O. J."

345   "bear false witness": Allen Ginsberg, foreword to Kunstler, *Hints & Allegations,* p. 7.

345   "because, like the law": Kunstler, *Trials and Tribulations,* p. 11.

345   "is long enough": Kunstler, *Hints & Allegations,* p. 8.

345   "to drive your message": quoted in Matthew Flamm, "The Rhymes They Are A-Changin'" *Entertainment Weekly,* November 25, 1994, p. 68.

345   "an ideal vehicle": Kunstler, *Hints & Allegations,* p. 8.

345   teaching device: Flamm, "The Rhymes They Are A-Changin.'"

345   "a perfect activity": Gartenberg to Langum, November 20, 1997.

345   "emergency poetry call": Bruce and Diane Jackson interview.

345   enjoyed writing poetry and also used it politically: Bruce and Diane Jackson interview; interviews with Arthur Kinoy, July 15, 1996; and Ronald Kuby, July 17, 1996.

346   process of writing autobiography: Sheila Isenberg, Preface to Kunstler, *My Life,* p. xi: "Afterwords," in Kunstler, *My Life* (2d ed., 1996), p. 421; interview with Michael Ratner, July 18, 1996.

346   "the principal embellisher": Isenberg, preface, p. xi.

346   reviews and disclaimer: Jeffrey Rosen, "The Trials of William Kunstler," *New York Times,* September 18, 1994, sec. 7, p. 16; Judith Bolton-Fasman, "Kunstler's Name Born of Notorieties," *Baltimore Sun,* October 16, 1994, p. E6; Evan Gahr, "For the People, by the People, Stuff and Nonsense," *Washington Times,* October 24, 1994, p. 32.

346   "didn't look back": Isenberg, "Afterwords," p. 420.

346   "for me, action is all": Kunstler, *My Life,* p. 314.

346   "Bill always looked forward": Michael Ratner interview.

346   "one of the least introspective": Kuby interview.

346   reviews and lack of introspection: *Kirkus Reviews,* August 1, 1994; *Publishers Weekly,* August 22, 1994, p. 46; Paul Reidinger, "The Importance of Being Kunstler: The Radical Lawyer Is a Legend in His Own Mind, Yet Someone to Reckon With," *ABA Journal,* December 1994, p. 106 (the

single most insightful review); James M. Altman, *New York Law Journal,* January 24, 1995, p. 2.

346   book tour: Ronald Kuby, "Afterwords," in Kunstler, *My Life* (2d ed., 1996), p. 411.

346   movie option: Kuby interview.

347   revolutionary lawyers book: Eileen Swift, "Rebel Lawyer's Cases Never Rest," *Newsday,* February 14, 1993, p. 1; correspondence between St. Martin's Press, Max Gartenberg, and Kunstler furnished to the author. Courtesy of Max Gartenberg.

347   home life: unless otherwise indicated, this material is based on interviews with Margie Ratner and Emily Kunstler, June 9, 1998; and Kuby, Marden, Karin Kunstler Goldman, and Bruce and Diane Jackson interviews.

347   "Never believe your press": quoted in Jan Hoffman, "For Next Generation, New Kunstlers," *New York Times,* September 18, 1995, p. B1.

347   "family gathering place": quoted in Adolph Green, "Places of the Heart: Where Cupid Turns a Spark into a Glow," *New York Times,* February 14, 1992, p. C18.

347   daughters kept him young: Jon Kalish, "From the Chicago 8 to Our Uncounted," *Newsday,* June 23, 1988, p. 78; Claude Lewis, "Reviled and Revered Lawyer Dies: The Law May Never Be Quite the Same," *Dayton Daily News,* September 10, 1995 (quoting 1986 interview), p. B7.

347   "The apple doesn't fall": quoted in Liz Willen, "'Slip' Cited for False Report; TV Wrongly Says Kunstler Girl Has AIDS," *Newsday,* May 19, 1994, p. A04.

347   neither daughter to be lawyer: Lena Williams, "Revolution Redux?" *New York Times,* March 28, 1993, sec. 9, p. 1.

348   "how are the girls": author conversation with Chris Drazek, October 8, 1996.

349   need for love and admiration: many sources, but especially Karin Kunstler Goldman, Mary Kunstler Horn, Bruce and Diane Jackson, and Margie Ratner and Emily Kunstler interviews.

349   people came up to him on street: many sources but especially interviews with Mary Kunstler Horn, Marden, Bruce and Diane Jackson, and Emily Kunstler interviews.

349   talk with all with empathy and attempt to persuade: Bruce and Diane Jackson, Emily Kunstler, and Karin Kunstler Goldman interviews.

349   "while some criticized": David Cole, "William Moses Kunstler, 1919–1995," *Village Voice,* September 19, 1995, p. 12.

350   buttons on blouse and flowers: James Frank, "Still Crazy after All These Years," *Spy,* September 1990, pp. 68–69.

350   prosecutors: ibid.; Mike McAlary, "Consummate Showman at the Bar," *Daily News,* September 6, 1995, p. 8.

350   opposing attorneys: Michael Steven Smith, "A Case for Courage," *Guild Notes,* fall 1995, p. 33.

350   "Bill Kunstler was the guy": Michael J. Gorman, letter to the editor, *New York Times,* September 11, 1995, p. 14; Gorman also commented on Kunstler in other letters to the editor: *Newsday,* September 8, 1995, p. A49; *National Law Journal,* June 26, 1995, p. A20; *New York Law Journal,* March 21, 1994, p. 2.

350   "it seems as if": tape of program, "William Kunstler: Champion or Charlatan?" Association of the Bar of the City of New York, June 19, 1996.

350   "little boy in Kunstler": Murray Kempton, "Farewell, Little Boy," *Newsday,* September 5, 1995, p. A05.

351   "By reputation, Kunstler": Lewis, "Reviled and Revered Lawyer Dies."

351   "as you know": William M. Kunstler to Lauren Wachtler, June 15, 1994, copy in possession of author.

351   "In facing your own": transcript, *The 11th Hour,* KBDI Channel 12, of address delivered February 21, 1992, Trinity Church, Denver.

351   daughters: Emily Kunstler and Karin Kunstler Goldman interviews; interview with Jane Kunstler Drazek, October 8, 1996.

351   friends and associates: Smith, "A Case for Courage"; Kuby interview.

351   "a dirty word—dirty word": quoted in Larry McShane, "Attorney Bill Kunstler: For 30 Years He Has Taken on Causes, People That Were Unpopular with Many Americans," *Springfield (Illinois) State Journal-Register,* August 29, 1993, p. 15.

351   "minorities, and blacks in particular": quoted in David B. Oppenheimer, "More to Be Done," *ABA Journal,* June 1994, p. 56.

351   "we're in an aimless": quoted in Moses, "At Age 71, Attorney William M. Kunstler Still Relishes a Tough Fight."

351   "just get enough": quoted in David Stout, "Word for Word: William M. Kunstler," *New York Times,* September 10, 1995, sec. 4, p. 7.

351   $100,000: McShane, "Attorney Bill Kunstler."

351   hopes for monetary success of book: Wachtler interview.

352   details of seventy-fifth birthday party in: Nadine Brozan, "Chronicle," *New York Times,* July 6, 1994, p. B6; Kuby, "Afterwords," p. 409.

352   gall bladder: Margie Ratner interview.

352   course of fatal illness and hospitalization: Kuby, "Afterwords," pp. 411, 414–16.

352   no more cases outside New York: Randy Furst, "Kunstler's Legacy In-
      cludes Famous Twin Cities Court Battles," *Minneapolis Star Tribune,*
      September 5, 1995, p. A7.

352   joking with David Dellinger: interview with David Dellinger, June 15,
      1996.

352   "I can't die before Labor Day": quoted in Karin Kunstler Goldman in-
      terview.

353   New York City memorial: Richard Perez-Pena, "1,000 Honor Kunstler,
      Defender of Their Faith," *New York Times,* November 20, 1995 p. B11.
      This article was vigorously attacked, not only as to head count, but as
      to tone and content: Steffie Kinglake, "Young, Old, White and Black
      Came to Celebrate Kunstler's Life," *New York Times,* November 24,
      1995, p. 34; Alexander Cockburn, "Petty Putdown," *Nation,* December
      11, 1995, p. 737; John Trumpbour, "A Letter From the Memorial,"
      Refuse and Resist Web site, posted November 20, 1995. The *New York
      Times* corrected the attendance figure: "Corrections," *New York Times,*
      November 22, 1995.

353   $400,000: Surrogate's Court, County of New York, State of New York,
      File #4541–1995, Petition for Probate filed by Margaret Ratner, No-
      vember 8, 1995.

353   surrogate son: Mary Reinholz, "Ron Kuby Is a Zealous Advocate and
      Defender of Unpopular Clients," *Newsday,* November 17, 1993, p. 60.

353   Kuby will continue practice: Andrew Blum, "'Bill' Gone, but He'll
      Carry On; Kunstler and Kuby," *National Law Journal,* September 18,
      1995, p. A4.

353   litigation: Lynette Holloway, "Kunstler's Widow Sues over Use of
      Firm's Name," *New York Times,* December 5, 1996, p. 33; Jan Hoffman,
      "Kunstler's Partner in Life Battles His Partner in Law," *New York Times,*
      December 15, 1996, p. 49; Jan Hoffman, "Ruling Curbs Use of Name of
      Kunstler," *New York Times,* December 19, 1996, p. B10.

354   over two hundred federal district court cases: Leon Friedman, "A
      Provocative Lawyer Who Challenged Rules," *National Law Journal,*
      September 18, 1995, p. A21.

354   "like a man who": Kuby interview.

356   "did the state": Kempton, "Farewell, Little Boy." p.A05.

356   "we need more": Miles Lord, quoted in Furst, "Kunstler's legacy In-
      cludes Famous Twin Cities Court Battles."

356   "it is extremely important": Sarah O'Brien, quoted in Mike Miller,
      "Kunstler Joined Anti-War Case," *Madison Capital Times,* September 5,
      1995, p. B6; another judge, Mark Frankel is also quoted. See also ap-
      preciation written by New York state judge Gustin L. Reichbach, "Bill

Kunstler: An Appreciation," *New York Law Journal,* November 13, 1995, p. 2.

356 "Despite all my dire": quotation provided to author by Morley Markson, producer of *Growing Up in America.*

356 inscription on rock: Kuby, "Afterwords," p. 416

Index

443

About the Author

DAVID J. LANGUM is a professor of law at Samford University, Cumberland School of Law. Langum received his law degree from Stanford University and his doctorate from the University of Michigan. He is the author of several books and the recipient of the J. S. Holliday Award, the James Willard Hurst Prize, and the Caroline Bancroft Prize.